Stephen Cobb

Quattro Pro 4 Inside & Out

Osborne **McGraw-Hill**

Berkeley New York St. Louis San Francisco
Auckland Bogotá Hamburg London Madrid
Mexico City Milan Montreal New Delhi Panama City
Paris São Paulo Singapore Sydney
Tokyo Toronto

MW01236122

Osborne **McGraw-Hill**
2600 Tenth Street
Berkeley, California 94710
U.S.A.

For information on translations and book distributors outside of the U.S.A., please write to Osborne McGraw-Hill at the above address.

This book is printed on recycled paper.

Quattro Pro 4 Inside & Out

234567890 DOC 998765432

ISBN 0-07-881797-8

Quattro Pro 4
Inside & Out

Publisher
Kenna S. Wood

Acquisitions Editor
Elizabeth Fisher

Associate Editor
Scott Rogers

Technical Editor
Matthew Lafata

Project Editor
Erica Spaberg

Copy Editor
Lynn Brown

Proofreaders
Audrey Baer Johnson
Colleen Paretty

Indexer
Lynn Brown

Computer Designer
Helena Charm

Word Processor
Lynda Higham

Cover Designer
Mason Fong

Contents at a Glance

Contents

12 *Further Macros and Macro Commands* 629

Acknowledgments

My sincere thanks to the readers and reviewers who have supported this book through its previous incarnations and made suggestions for improvements, many of which were incorporated into this extensive revision. Several chapters were entirely reworked, not only to reflect changes in the software, but also to make the material more accessible.

Programs grow ever more powerful and books that do justice to them take more and more effort to produce. Many thanks are due to the team at Osborne: Liz, Hannah, Scott, Erica, and Helena. Hopefully this book we built is suitable reward and justification for the patience shown and the care taken.

Many thanks are due to the folks at CompuServe for making California just an upload away from a cottage in Scotland (they don't do it for free, but they do it right). Federal Express also deserves a round of applause for safe handling of those items you just can't squeeze into the phone. The book also benefited from the generous loan of a very reliable Tandon 486/33, courtesy of the good folks at Tandon plc.

As to the lasses in the front line, suffice it to say without Erin and Chey there would be no book. Thanks to you once more yet for everything.

Introduction

This book is a complete guide to Quattro Pro 4, the powerful presentation spreadsheet from Borland International. As a Quattro Pro 4 user you will enjoy numerous state-of-the-art features, such as multiple spreadsheets with dynamic linking between them and sophisticated graphing capabilities, including a complete drawing and slide show facility. There are also such helpful features as an undo key, complete mouse support, and direct access to database files from such programs as Paradox. By learning to use Quattro Pro 4, you will be mastering one of the best implementations of desktop computer power.

About This Book

If you are new to electronic spreadsheets, the best approach is to read this book chapter-by-chapter. Topics are presented in a natural order of progression, based on years of experience in conducting spreadsheet training seminars. By following the examples, learning Quattro Pro 4 is made easy. Users who are experienced with other spreadsheets can probably skim the first chapter and note the special features of Quattro Pro 4. If you just want to read about certain topics, you can turn straight to the chapters that interest you and examine the examples to see how Quattro Pro 4 is applied to typical spreadsheet tasks as well as more advanced applications like desktop presentations. The index allows you to use the book as a complete reference to Quattro Pro 4's commands and features.

Armed with this book and Quattro Pro 4 you can tackle such tasks as budget projection, financial recordkeeping, statistical analysis, and custom applications development, including slide shows and automated presentations. You will quickly learn a system of commands that is logical, accessible, and easily customized.

How This Book Is Organized

The first chapter introduces you to the basics of spreadsheets and points out important capabilities and features of Quattro Pro 4. You are also introduced to the basic concepts of the program's operation, such as entering data and using the menu system. Chapter 2 demonstrates the operation of the main spreadsheet commands, while Chapter 3 discusses more advanced spreadsheet operations, such as printing and formatting.

In Chapter 4 you will find a detailed examination of how to use the built-in functions that give Quattro Pro 4 its tremendous mathematical capabilities. In Chapter 5, you will learn how to use Quattro Pro 4 as a database manager. The chapter also explores techniques for developing presentation-quality spreadsheets with visual enhancements. Chapter 6 demonstrates many of the customizable aspects of the program, such as international currency, date formatting, and color display. Chapter 7 shows how Quattro Pro 4 File Manager simplifies hard disk management. The program's ability to read data from such programs as 1-2-3, Reflex, dBASE, and Paradox is also described.

Chapter 8 presents an in-depth discussion of Quattro Pro 4's extensive graphics capabilities with numerous tips for effective chart making. Chapter 9 explains advanced techniques. It also describes advanced techniques for regression analysis, backward solving of equations, matrix arithmetic, frequency distribution, and what-if tables, and demonstrates the use of XY graphs. Quattro Pro 4 commands for transforming text data into paragraphs and values are illustrated with numerous examples in Chapter 10, which covers the string functions and parse feature.

For users seeking to streamline their work, Chapter 11 provides tips on the use of Quattro Pro 4 Shortcuts. The simple technique of recording keystrokes in macros is described along with other methods of macro creation. Step-by-step examples lead you through each method. Chapter 12 shows you how to automate tasks with special macros. The command language of Quattro Pro 4 is discussed with examples of how it can be used to create worksheet-specific menus. You will also find tips on creating and modifying user interfaces and developing linked spreadsheet applications. In Chapter 13 you will find more examples of Quattro Pro 4's unique features, including the graph annotator, slide shows, and Paradox access, showing how these can be applied to typical office tasks.

Appendix A offers ideas for setting up Quattro Pro 4 on a hard disk system. Appendix B offers tips for networking with Quattro Pro 4. Appendix C describes the Print Manager, used for background printing with Quattro Pro 4.

The Look of Quattro Pro 4

Ever since the first version of Quattro was introduced, one of the hallmarks of the program has been its flexible interface. Whether it is simply a matter of changing the screen colors, or a complete reorganization of the menu system, the program can be customized so that commands are presented as effectively as possible for as many different types of users as possible. For example, mouse users get a mouse button bar, but those without a mouse do not.

With the release of Quattro Pro 4 this flexibility has been taken even further. The WYSIWYG display mode gives you accurate on-screen details of your work, such as typestyles, charts, and graphics. The WYSIWYG mode also gives you attractive command "buttons" with a three-dimensional sculpted look. Not every PC, however, can display this feature and Quattro Pro 4 was designed to run on a wide range of different systems to give as much computing power to as many users as possible. If you have a VGA or EGA display you will be able to use WYSIWYG, if not you can still use the Quattro Pro 4 spreadsheet in character mode and display full-screen graphs.

Since Quattro Pro 4 has many different faces, the pictures used in this book to illustrate how Quattro Pro 4 works were created on a variety of displays. In most cases, WYSIWYG screens are displayed, but in some screens the alternative character mode is used. There may be times when the style of display used in the book differs from what you have on your monitor but the important point is that the contents will essentially be the same.

A Final Note

If you are using an earlier version of Quattro Pro, such as Quattro Pro 3, the majority of the instructions in the book will be accurate. However, it is strongly recommended that you take advantage of Borland's very reasonable upgrade plan to get Quattro Pro 4. You will find that the added features and improved performance are well worth it.

Besides being a powerful business tool, Quattro Pro 4 is a lot of fun to work with, and to write about. Here's hoping that you enjoy learning Quattro Pro 4 inside and out.

CHAPTER

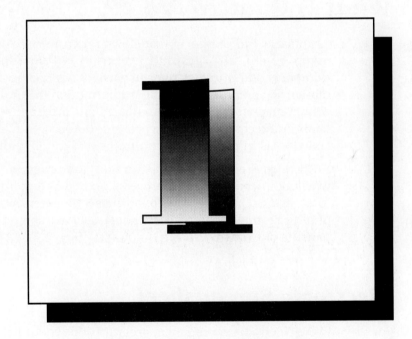

Getting Started

Chapter 1 tells you what Quattro Pro 4 is and how to start using it for a variety of tasks. It introduces the basic concepts of Quattro Pro 4, thereby helping you build a foundation for the many procedures you will learn in the rest of the book. By the end of this chapter you will have learned how to enter data, create formulas, and store your work. The chapter begins with a look at the main features and benefits of Quattro Pro 4.

What Is Quattro Pro 4?

Quattro Pro 4 is a spreadsheet program with integrated database management and graphic presentation capabilities. *Spreadsheet, database,* and *graphics* refer to ways of organizing and analyzing information. A spreadsheet arranges information in columns and rows like a columnar pad. A database management program stores information in fields and records. A graphic presentation program presents information visually, as in pie charts, bar graphs, diagrams, and slide shows.

Quattro Pro 4 is the latest version of a program for DOS-based PCs, which has been steadily improved since it was first introduced by Borland International in 1987. The following sections review the general features of a modern electronic spreadsheet, as well as summarize the specific benefits of Quattro Pro 4.

Electronic Spreadsheet

An electronic spreadsheet program adds computer power to the simple but effective method of arranging information used by accountants for centuries: the columnar pad. Instead of writing numbers on a paper pad, you enter them on a computer screen. Instead of calculating numbers on a calculator, you tell the spreadsheet program to calculate them for you. Instead of putting the columnar pad in a filing cabinet or desk drawer, you tell the program to store your work in a file, known as a worksheet, on a computer's disk. When you want a paper report, you tell the program which columns and rows you want to send to your computer's printer.

When you load a Quattro Pro 4 worksheet on your personal computer, you immediately see how the column and row arrangement is translated into a screen image. This is shown in Figure 1-1, where you can see a worksheet recording how many people taking Northern flights were in First, Business, and Coach class for each of four quarters. The capital letters across the top of the worksheet identify the columns; the numbers down the left side of the worksheet identify the rows. The collection of words and numbers you see in Figure 1-1 is referred to as a model, because it describes, or models, a particular set of circumstances, in this case, the passenger volume on certain airline routes.

Each junction of a spreadsheet column and row produces a box, or cell, into which you can enter a number or text. The column letters and row numbers are combined to give each cell a unique address. In Figure 1-1 you can see that the word Northern has been entered in column A, row 1, known as cell A1. The number 125 has been entered in cell B5.

The numbers in row 9 are the results of calculations that add up the three figures for each quarter. The numbers in column F are totals of each of the three classes of travel. Because these totals are calculations, changing the number in B5 will cause the totals to change.

FIGURE 1-1   Typical Quattro Pro 4 worksheet

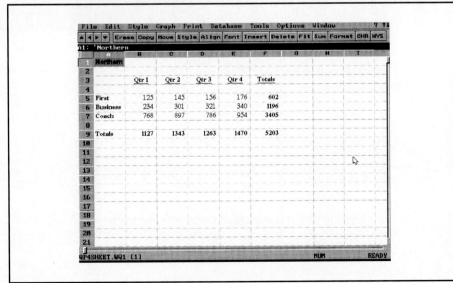

Worksheet in Figure 1-1 with different numbers

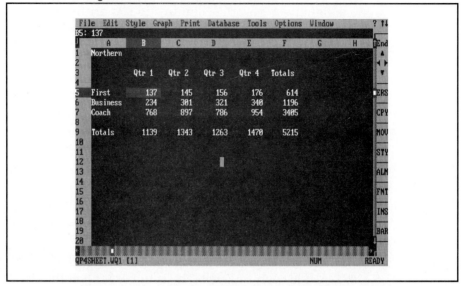

In Figure 1-2 you can see that 125 has been altered to 137. You can also see that three other numbers changed: the total for Qtr1, the total for First, and the grand total in cell F9. When you calculate with a spreadsheet, you do not have to use an eraser to make changes. In fact, Quattro Pro 4 has a key that can undo any change.

As a spreadsheet program, Quattro Pro 4 offers a full range of features, including the following:

❑ 256 columns and 8192 rows, that is, more than 2 million cells, per worksheet

❑ Several worksheets loaded and displayed at the same time

❑ Links between worksheets to enable you to build consolidated worksheets

❑ More than 100 built-in formulas, known as functions, to simplify calculations

❑ Background calculation to enable you to keep working while formulas are being calculated

❏   The ability to create large spreadsheets on modest computer hardware

❏   The ability to display spreadsheets on screen exactly as they will appear when printed out

❏   Direct exchange of files with other spreadsheet programs, such as Lotus 1-2-3 Releases 2.3 and 3.1, including Allways and WYSIWYG formatting

Is What You See What You Get?

You probably noticed that Figure 1-2 looks quite a bit different from Figure 1-1, even though both screens show the same worksheet. In Figure 1-2 you still have the column and row arrangement, but you cannot see the grid of lines identifying the columns and rows. This is because of the fact that Quattro Pro 4 draws the spreadsheet differently on different computers.

More powerful computers, with what are known as EGA and VGA displays, have the ability to display greater detail. When you load Quattro Pro 4 on one of these computers, the program can take advantage of this ability to provide extra detail. This ability is known as the WYSIWYG mode of display. WYSIWYG is an acronym for "what you see is what you get"; it refers to the ability to show on screen an exact image of what Quattro Pro 4 will print when the time comes to produce a report from the spreadsheet. In Figure 1-3 you can see a report printed from the worksheet in Figure 1-1. Note that the actual shape and style of the letters in the report match the screen displayed in WYSIWYG mode in Figure 1-1.

The display mode in Figure 1-2 is called character mode because the screen is composed from a fixed set of characters. Even lines drawn on the screen are made up of characters. There are 25 lines of characters in Figure 1-2, with 80 characters on each line. Even though some PCs cannot display Quattro Pro 4 in WYSIWYG mode, even the oldest PCs can display it in character mode. This allows Quattro Pro 4 to run on a wide range of equipment.

Later in this chapter, the section "Of Mice, Menus, and the SpeedBar" discusses the commands for switching between display modes. Users of

FIGURE
1-3
Printed report

Northern

	Qtr 1	Qtr 2	Qtr 3	Qtr 4	Totals
First	125	145	156	176	602
Business	234	301	321	340	1196
Coach	768	897	786	954	3405
Totals	1127	1343	1263	1470	5203

some PCs will have more than two choices for display mode. Special modes that allow more columns and rows to be placed on the screen are available. Users of color monitors can change the colors used by Quattro Pro 4 to display the various parts of the screen.

When you want to print your work, Quattro Pro 4 offers a variety of typefaces or fonts, plus underlining, line drawing, and shading. It even has a command that automatically shrinks large reports so they fit on a single page. In Figure 1-4 you can see a 12-month expense projection printed on a single page. In summary, the WYSIWYG features Borland has incorporated in Quattro Pro 4 are as follows:

❏ Adjustable display modes, including WYSIWYG for EGA and VGA users.

❏ Wide selection of screen and print fonts automatically generated by the program using Bitstream Font Scaling Technology. Quattro Pro 4 also supports LaserJet fonts, 35 PostScript printer fonts, and Bitstream Fontware.

❏ Choice of colors and shading for all parts of the screen and worksheet, plus conditional colors such as negative values in red.

❏ Options to display/hide spreadsheet gridlines, column and row headings, and zero values. In Figure 1-5 you see Quattro Pro 4 in

FIGURE 1-4

Results of the Print-to-Fit feature

Quattro Vadis Travel - Total Amount: $103,407

Expenses - Monthly Growth Factor of: 1.015

	JAN	FEB	MAR	APR	MAY	JUN	JUL	AUG	SEP	OCT	NOV	DEC	YEAR
POLK ST.													
Lease	350	355	361	366	371	377	383	388	394	400	406	412	4,564
Phones	230	233	237	241	244	248	251	255	259	263	267	271	2,999
Telex	110	112	113	115	117	119	120	122	124	126	128	130	1,435
Electric	120	122	124	125	127	129	131	133	135	137	139	141	1,565
Res. Rent	500	507	515	523	531	539	547	555	563	572	580	589	6,521
VAN NESS													
Lease	500	507	515	523	531	539	547	555	563	572	580	589	6,521
Phones	250	254	258	261	265	269	273	277	282	286	290	294	3,260
Telex	150	152	155	157	159	162	164	166	169	172	174	177	1,956
Electric	225	228	232	235	239	242	246	250	253	257	261	265	2,934
Res. Rent	835	848	860	873	886	900	913	927	941	955	969	984	10,889
UNION SQ.													
Lease	1,200	1,218	1,236	1,255	1,274	1,293	1,312	1,332	1,352	1,372	1,393	1,414	15,649
Phones	300	304	309	314	318	323	328	333	338	343	348	353	3,912
Telex	250	254	258	261	265	269	273	277	282	286	290	294	3,260
Electric	205	208	211	214	218	221	224	228	231	234	238	241	2,673
Res. Rent	890	903	917	931	945	959	973	988	1,003	1,018	1,033	1,048	11,607
EMBARCADERO													
Lease	900	913	927	941	955	970	984	999	1,014	1,029	1,044	1,060	11,737
Phones	275	279	283	288	292	296	301	305	310	314	319	324	3,586
Telex (AUG)	0	0	0	0	0	0	0	150	152	155	157	159	773
Electric (AUG)	0	0	0	0	0	0	0	0	0	0	0	0	0
Res. Rent	580	589	598	606	616	625	634	644	653	663	673	683	7,564
TOTALS	7,870	7,988	8,108	8,229	8,353	8,478	8,605	8,884	9,018	9,153	9,290	9,430	103,407

WYSIWYG mode with the column and row headings and gridlines
turned off.

❏ Print-To-Fit command, which scales down reports to fit on the page.

❏ Ability to place live charts and graphic images in spreadsheets, as
shown in Figure 1-5, as well as to print combined charts and graphs.

❏ Line drawing, boxes, shading, and bullet characters to dress up
spreadsheet reports.

❏ A screen preview mode that you can use to inspect each page of a
report before you send it to the printer.

❏ Named styles and style libraries to simplify spreadsheet formatting.

Hardware Factors

Quattro Pro 4 works with a wide range of PC displays and can be loaded
on just about any hardware configuration. The term "hardware
configuration" is a way of saying "collection of equipment," and Quattro
Pro 4 can run on any IBM-compatible PC that has a hard disk and at
least 512K of RAM. The expression "512K of RAM" refers to the size of

Customized Quattro Pro 4 display

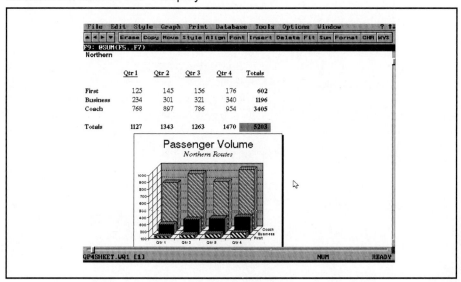

the memory area used by a PC to hold programs and data temporarily while they are being used.

Information and the space it takes up in a computer system is measured in bytes; one byte is roughly the amount required to hold one character. One kilobyte, or K, is 1,024 bytes, so 512K means 524,288 bytes. In fact, 512K is exactly one half of a megabyte, which is 1,024K.

You might wonder how Quattro Pro 4 is able to operate in a relatively small amount of RAM when it consists of several megabytes of program files. The answer is that it uses a clever piece of software technology developed by Borland and christened VROOMM, which stands for Virtual Runtime Object Oriented Memory Manager. In simple terms this mouthful of technospeak means that only those parts of Quattro Pro 4 needed for the task at hand are loaded into memory. Although Quattro Pro 4 can perform many different tasks, it only works on one or two at a time. The program code for only those one or two tasks is loaded into memory, leaving more room for spreadsheets. Moreover, whereas many programs are divided into several parts, called overlays, the code that makes up Quattro Pro 4 consists of hundreds of small program modules. The VROOMM technology swiftly shuffles these modules in and out of memory as needed so the impression you get is that the entire program is on hand as soon as you issue a command.

Memory Matters

When you are working with Quattro Pro 4, your computer's RAM contains one other thing besides your spreadsheet and the Quattro Pro 4 program modules: the disk operating system, or DOS. This is the piece of software that controls basic computer operations such as arranging files on disk. In fact, it is only after you have loaded DOS that a program like Quattro Pro 4 can communicate with your hardware. When you tell your computer to load Quattro Pro 4, it is actually DOS that carries out this command. When you tell Quattro Pro 4 to store a worksheet in a disk file, it is DOS that handles the nuts and bolts of the operation. Quattro Pro 4 and other programs, such as WordPerfect and Paradox, that work through the operating system to apply your hardware to practical tasks are referred to as applications.

Quattro Pro 4 works with all versions of PC-DOS and MS-DOS numbered 2.0 or higher and any other compatible operating system, such as DR-DOS. Quattro Pro 4 does not require you to use any software besides DOS. Some applications, such as Microsoft Excel, do require you to use additional software; that is, to load DOS, then to load what is called an operating environment, which provides the font, mouse, and printer control the application requires. For example, Excel requires the Windows operating environment. This imposes an additional burden on your hardware, requiring more RAM. Quattro Pro 4 provides its own font, mouse, and printer support; at the same time, however, it can be operated within the Windows environment if you desire.

Having said that Quattro Pro 4 works with 512K of RAM, it must be said that 640K is preferable, and you will get even better performance if you have expanded memory. This is extra memory beyond 640K that meets the requirements of the Expanded Memory Specification, or EMS. If you plan to make extensive use of the WYSIWYG mode, several megabytes of expanded memory will substantially improve performance, plus let you create much larger spreadsheets than are possible with only 640K. Quattro Pro 4 can use up to 8 megabytes of EMS memory. For more about EMS see Appendix A.

There is an important distinction to be made between disk storage and random access memory, or RAM. The RAM in your computer is the area that holds program files while you use them plus the data on which the program is working, such as the worksheet file you saw in Figure 1-1. The information in RAM constantly changes while you use your computer and is wiped out when you turn off the computer.

The disks you use—either the removable floppy disks or the fixed disks, known as hard disks, within the computer—store information permanently. This means that when you turn off the computer the information in disk files stays there, ready for the next time you need it. That is, unless there is a physical problem with the disk, the files should remain as you left them until the next time you need them. Quattro Pro 4 requires that you have six megabytes of free disk space on your hard disk before it can be installed.

When information is being stored on a disk it is said to be written into a file. When it is retrieved, the file is read from the disk. The process of reading and writing is known as disk access and is one of the few aspects of computing that requires moving parts. This means that accessing information on disk is much slower than working with it in RAM, which is electronic. Hard disks, which spin very fast, access data quicker than floppy disks.

The most important nonmoving part of your computer is the central processing unit, or CPU, the single chip that is at the heart of the PC's electronics. There are basically four levels of CPU, known by their Intel product codes, each one more powerful that its predecessor. Quattro Pro 4 works well with all four of them: 8088, 80286, 80386, 80486. Quattro Pro 4 will also take advantage of a math coprocessor if you have one installed in your computer. To summarize the hardware requirements of Quattro Pro 4, they are a PC with

❏   At least 512K RAM

❏   DOS 2.0 or later

❏   Six megabytes of available hard disk space

In Table 1-1 you can see the features available in Quattro Pro 4 according to the display system on your PC. As far as printing goes, Quattro Pro 4 supports a wide range of dot-matrix, laser, PostScript, and letter-quality printers. For graphics, it supports a range of plotters. Bitstream soft fonts are supported on laser, ink jet, and dot-matrix printers; a collection of soft fonts comes with Quattro Pro 4. Also included is a program called Borland Print Spooler, described in Appendix C, which enables you to manage print operations while you continue to work on a spreadsheet.

Beyond the Spreadsheet

Although the ability to enter, calculate, and print out figures quickly is the main appeal of an electronic spreadsheet and the principal reason this type of software enjoyed a rapid rise in popularity during the 1980s, modern spreadsheets go much further than that. As do competing products such as Lotus 1-2-3 and Microsoft Excel, Quattro Pro 4 offers database management and graphics.

Features According to Display System

Adapter	Monitor	Features
VGA Plus	High resolution color	WYSIWYG Character modes 132 column mode Adjustable colors Graph View/Annotate
Plain VGA	High resolution color	WYSIWYG Character modes Adjustable colors Graph View/Annotate
Plain VGA	Black/white/gray	WYSIWYG Character modes Adjustable gray scale Graph View/Annotate
EGA	Medium resolution color	WYSIWYG Character modes Adjustable colors Graph View/Annotate
EGA	Black and white	WYSIWYG Character modes Black/white palette
CGA	Color	Character mode Adjustable colors Graph View/Annotate
Hercules mono	Monochrome	Character mode Adjustable attributes Graph View/Annotate
IBM PC mono	Monochrome	Character mode Adjustable attributes

Database Management

A database is a collection of information organized in a meaningful way. Anything from a telephone directory to a filing cabinet of medical records can be considered a database. Database management is the electronic storage and organization of such information. A database involves grouping pieces of information as records and organizing them into fields. For example, in Figure 1-2 the figures for the three classes of travel could be sorted alphabetically by name or numerically by the largest total.

Another aspect of database management is the ability to locate specific information. For example, in Figure 1-6 you can see a list of employees. Using the database commands in Quattro Pro 4, you can find all the records for employees earning above a certain amount. You can even copy their names to a separate part of the worksheet, then sort them. The database features of Quattro Pro 4 are summarized as follows:

❑ Sorting using up to 256 keys or categories

❑ Querying on simple and complex criteria, with record extraction from separate worksheets and even foreign files, including dBASE and Paradox databases

❑ Direct reading and writing of foreign database files, including Reflex, Paradox, and dBASE

❑ Direct links with Paradox, including hot-key switching into Quattro Pro 4 from Paradox and use of Paradox SQL Link

Graphs

The value of pictures in conveying information has been appreciated for thousands of years, and computers make it easy to create graphs and charts that greatly speed up our assimilation of facts and figures, as well as help us understand their implications. In Quattro Pro 4 there are simple commands that draw a graph from numbers and words you entered into your spreadsheet. Whenever the numbers in the spreadsheet change, the graph is updated. Graphs can be pasted into the spreadsheet, as shown in Figure 1-5, or viewed full screen, as shown in Figure 1-7.

The limitations of black-and-white on paper do not do justice to the vibrant colors seen on a good computer monitor, but you can see that the use of an image is effective in conveying information, in this case the trend in passenger volume figures shown in earlier examples. The type of graph in Figure 1-7, a three-dimensional ribbon chart, is one of more than a dozen chart styles Quattro Pro 4 offers. Unlike some programs,

FIGURE 1-6

Employee database

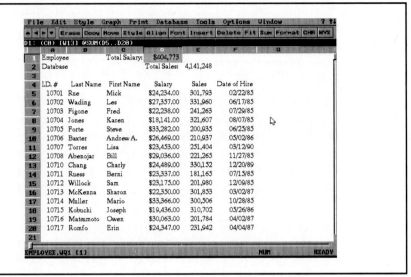

FIGURE 1-7

Full-screen graph

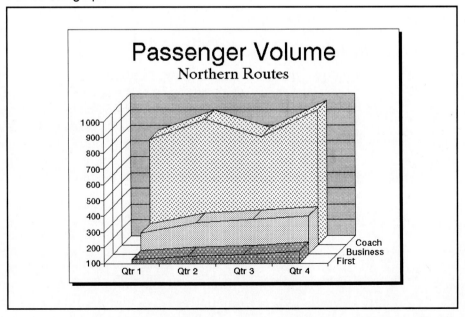

Quattro Pro 4 does not require you to load additional software to get this graph-making capability. Designing and printing of graphs are managed entirely within the Quattro Pro 4 program.

With Quattro Pro 4 Borland introduced several new graphing tools. You can create analytical graphs that calculate and chart moving averages or aggregates. For example, if you have charted one month's worth of daily sales figures you can ask Quattro Pro 4 to show weekly aggregates without entering any additional data. You can also generate linear and exponential lines to fit the data you are graphing. The results of analytical graphing are not confined to graphs. You can ask Quattro Pro 4 to create a table of results from an analytical graph in your worksheet.

The ability to analyze data by means of a graph may well encourage you to chart larger collections of data. This is why Quattro Pro 4 includes commands to help you view large graphs. For example, you can chart a full year's worth of daily sales figures and then zoom the graph so that you are viewing just a few week's worth of data. You can then pan through the zoomed graph a week at a time, from the beginning of the year to the end.

Sometimes, what you need to make a point is a text chart consisting of a bulleted list of points, as shown in Figure 1-8. Such lists can be created in Quattro Pro 4, even though they do not use numbers. The purpose of Quattro Pro 4 is to allow you to present information effectively, regardless of the type of information with which you work. Moreover, Quattro Pro 4 images can be saved in special files ready to be processed by slide bureaus.

Sometimes you want your presentations to have character and style; that is, you want them to use more than just words. For this reason, Quattro Pro 4 provides the Graph Annotator, a complete drawing package with which you can embellish charts or draw freehand illustrations. A variety of predrawn artwork, known as clip art, is included with Quattro Pro 4, ready to be pasted into your own designs. You can see the Graph Annotator at work in Figure 1-9.

These days computers are not only used to create paper illustrations and 35 mm slides, they are used to make presentations on a large screen or overhead display system. With Quattro Pro 4 you can put together a series of graphs that are then displayed one after another at your command or by simple user input. A variety of visual effects can be used to fade from one slide to another, and sound effects can be added to create

FIGURE 1-8

Text chart printed from Quattro Pro 4

Take Over Air Lines

Your airline for the roaring 90s

❑ *Aggressive*
  ☑ Acquired Sky High Shuttle, May 1989
  ☑ Reduced costs by 50% in 12 months
❑ *Efficient*
  ☑ Best "on-time" record in 89 and 90
  ☑ Lowest lost luggage claims
❑ *Committed to Profits*

FIGURE 1-9

Chart being enhanced in Graph Annotator

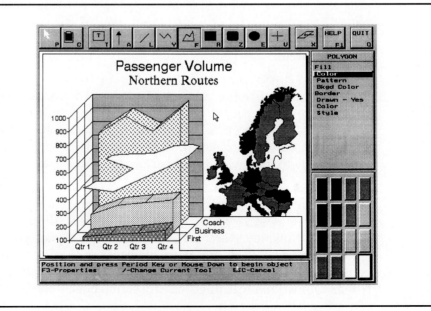

a full presentation environment. The graphic features in Quattro Pro 4 can be summarized as follows:

❑ Wide range of chart types, including three-dimensional charts

❑ Fast Graph command to draw graphs from spreadsheet data automatically

❑ Analytical graphs to plot moving averages, aggregates, and trends

❑ The Graph Annotator to embellish graphs with freehand drawings and clip art

❑ Comprehensive slide show facility, complete with graph buttons, a variety of fade in/fade out styles, and digitized sound effects

❑ Zoom and pan commands to handle large graphs

Of Mice, Menus, and the SpeedBar

Now that we have discussed what Quattro Pro 4 is and some of the things it can do, it is time to look at how you relate to the program, that is, how you tell Quattro Pro 4 what you want it to do. The way you issue instructions to a program is known as the program interface. In this, as in so many other areas, Quattro Pro 4 is extremely flexible.

You have already seen that Quattro Pro 4 provides different screen modes to match the abilities of different equipment. The program also offers different interfaces for different users. For example, if you have an EGA or VGA system and know how to load Quattro Pro 4 on your computer, you can try the following experiment, which switches Quattro Pro 4 between WYSIWYG and character modes. If you do not yet know how to load Quattro Pro 4, see the instructions given later in this chapter. If you do not have an EGA or VGA system, you can follow the text and illustrations. Note that even if you think you will always use WYSIWYG mode, it is helpful to know how to access character mode, because this mode is less work for the computer; therefore, Quattro Pro 4 runs faster in character mode.

Across the top of the Quattro Pro 4 screen is a list of items: File, Edit, Style, and so on. This top line of the screen is known as the menu bar and provides a simple but effective way of issuing commands to Quattro Pro 4. To use the menu, press the F3 key or the slash key (/), which is usually below the question mark. Either F3 or / activates the menu bar. When you press F3 or /, the first item on the bar, File, becomes highlighted. You can move this highlighting by pressing the RIGHT ARROW key on your keyboard. To select an item, highlight it, then press ENTER. To cancel a selection, press the ESC key. You can also select an item by pressing the F3 or / key, then typing the first letter of the menu item, for example, **O** for **O**ptions. Try this now; you will see the Options menu appear, as shown in Figure 1-10.

There are many items on the Options menu. To select one, you can type its key letter—usually the first letter of the item name, or you can move the highlighting to the item and press ENTER. Select Display Mode; you will see the menu shown in Figure 1-11 (unless your system can only use one mode). This is referred to as the Options Display Mode menu.

Now, if you are currently using WYSIWYG mode, select 80x25. If you are currently in character mode, choose WYSIWYG. When you make a choice from the Options Display Mode menu, the screen will be redrawn and the Options menu will reappear. You put the Options menu away by pressing ESC or typing Q for **Q**uit.

FIGURE
1-10

Options menu

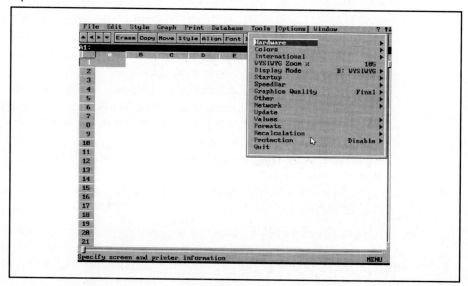

FIGURE
1-11

Options Display Mode menu

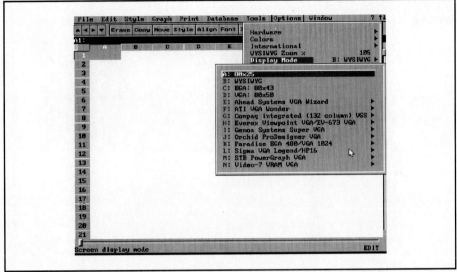

You can see that Quattro Pro 4 offers you several ways of interacting with the program. You have two keys you can press to activate the menu, F3 or /. You have two ways of selecting menu items, highlight and enter or type letter. You have two ways of leaving a menu, ESC or Quit.

You can also choose between two types of menu display in Quattro Pro 4, referred to as wide and narrow. Normally you will see wide versions of the menus. Figure 1-10 shows the wide version of the Options menu, and you can see that it lists several of the current settings, such as WYSIWYG Zoom % and Display Mode. In Figure 1-12 you can see a narrow version of the Options menu. This reveals less information about the current settings, but shows more of the underlying worksheet. To change a menu from wide to narrow display you press the minus key (–) on the numeric keypad. To switch from narrow to wide you press the plus key (+) on the numeric keypad.

As well as accepting commands from the keyboard, Quattro Pro 4 responds to instructions issued by a mouse. If you have a mouse installed on your computer, Quattro Pro 4 displays a mouse pointer on the screen

FIGURE 1-12 The narrow version of the Options menu

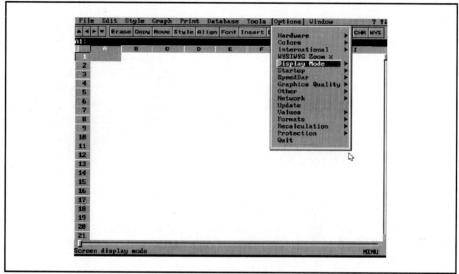

when you load the program. In WYSIWYG mode this looks like an arrow, as you can see from Figure 1-12. In character mode the mouse pointer is a small shaded rectangle, visible near the center of the screen in Figure 1-2 and again in Figure 1-13, which shows character mode using the 80x50 Display Mode setting available on VGA monitors.

As you move the mouse with your hand the computer moves the mouse pointer on the screen. You can select an object on the screen or an item on a menu simply by moving the mouse pointer over it then clicking the left-hand mouse button (*clicking* means quickly pressing and then releasing the button).

In WYSIWYG mode Quattro Pro 4 displays a series of boxes or buttons across the top of the screen, labeled Erase, Copy, Move, and so on. This area of the screen is referred to as the SpeedBar. It provides mouse users with quick access to frequently used commands. In character mode the SpeedBar, which was referred to as the mouse palette in earlier versions of Quattro Pro, is displayed at the right of the work area, with abbreviated

FIGURE
1-13

Mouse pointer and screen in 80x50 Display Mode

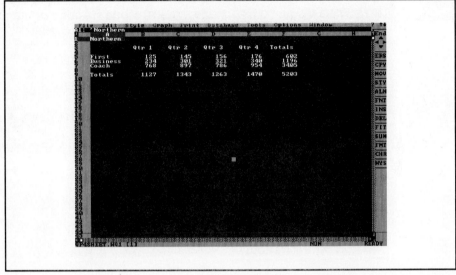

button names, as shown in Figures 1-2 and 1-13. (Note that because the 80x25 character mode option gives you limited space on the screen, the SpeedBar is split into two parts. You can switch between the two parts with the BAR button seen in Figure 1-2).

In Table 1-2 you can see a list of the SpeedBar buttons visible in different display modes. To use the SpeedBar to switch between character and WYSIWYG modes, you simply click on the button labeled WYS for WYSIWYG and click on the one that says CHR for character mode.

You can also use the mouse to pick the desired option from the menu system. You select an item from the menu by pointing to it and clicking the mouse button. At the end of this chapter you will find further tips on using a mouse with Quattro Pro 4. Chapter 6 tells you how to modify the SpeedBar to include your favorite commands. Chapter 12 shows how to use the Edit Menus command to customize the Quattro Pro 4 program menus as well as how to write and record macros that automate common tasks. Now, however, it is time to take a look at the main keystrokes that operate Quattro Pro 4 and to begin working with the program.

TABLE
1-2

The SpeedBar Buttons

WYSIWYG Mode	80x25 Mode	80x50 Mode	Action or Menu Equivalent
Erase	ERS	ERS	Edit/Erase
Copy	CPY	CPY	Edit/Copy
Move	MOV	MOV	Edit/Move
Style	STY	STY	Style/Use Style
Align	ALN	ALN	Style/Alignment
Font	FNT	FNT	Style/Font
Insert	INS	INS	Edit/Insert
—	BAR	—	Other half of SpeedBar
Delete	DEL	DEL	Edit/Delete
Fit	FIT	FIT	Style/Block Size/Auto Width
Sum	SUM	SUM	TurboSum (no menu equivalent)
Format	FMT	FMT	Style/Numeric Format
CHR	CHR	CHR	Options/Display/80x25
WYS	WYS	WYS	Options/Display Mode/WYSIWYG

Using the Keyboard

Nearly all of Quattro Pro 4's features can be controlled from the keyboard. There are several different PC keyboard layouts in use today.

As you can see in Figure 1-14, the basic differences are in the placement of the cursor and function keys. These differences should not be a problem when learning or using Quattro Pro 4. Although it might be annoying to adjust from one keyboard to another, you should realize that the keys work the same, even if their locations are different. For this reason, in this book the keys will be referred to by the names that are on them, rather than by their location.

For example, the key marked ESC or ESCAPE may be on the left or the right side of the keyboard. However, pressing ESC does the same thing whether the location is left or right. Quattro Pro 4 uses the ESC key the same way many other programs do, to let you change your mind. After you have selected an option from a menu, pressing ESC lets you deselect the option. Keys used extensively by Quattro Pro 4 are shown in Table 1-3.

Quattro Pro 4 uses the cursor-movement keys extensively for highlighting options and moving around the screen. These are the arrow keys: UP ARROW, DOWN ARROW, LEFT ARROW, and RIGHT ARROW. These keys may be found in a separate group or may share keys with the numeric keypad.

Alternative keyboard layouts

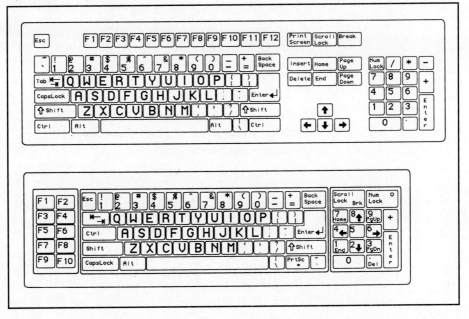

Keys Frequently Used in Quattro Pro 4

Key	Purpose
ENTER	Enter data into worksheets; select highlighted menu items; confirm block coordinates and other settings.
ESC	Cancel changes on the edit line; exit a menu; return you to READY mode; unlock block coordinates.
BACKSPACE	Remove characters to the left on the edit line; unlock block coordinates; return beginning coordinate to current cell.
DELETE	Delete cell contents; remove current character from edit line.
INSERT	Control OVERSTRIKE mode as you edit.
SHIFT	Access the character shown on upper half of any key, including capitals *A* through *Z*, symbols such as $, and numbers on the numeric keypad.
CAPS LOCK	Type *A* through *Z* as capital letters without shifting; does not affect any other keys.
NUM LOCK	Lock numeric pad into numbers; lock out cursor movement with those keys.
SCROLL LOCK	Switch betweeen Move and Size to adjust windows.
CTRL	Used with certain keys to execute commands, such as CTRL-BREAK, which stops macro execution, CTRL-D, which prepares cell for data entry, and CTRL-ENTER, which assigns shortcuts.
PRINT SCREEN	Print current screen; this key will not print graphs.
@	Precedes built-in formulas, the @functions.
/	In READY mode activates the menu; in formulas used for division.
\	Used as cell fill command to repeat characters; also used in naming instant macros.

TABLE
1-3
Cont.

Keys Frequently Used in Quattro Pro 4

Key	Purpose
	Both plus keys are used to begin formulas and perform addition. The plus key on the numeric keypad expands menus
*	Used for multiplication sign.
–	Used for subtration; the minus key on the numeric keypad contracts menus.

When you turn on your computer the arrow/number keys may be set to numbers, just as the alphabet keys are set to lowercase. Use the SHIFT key to produce arrows instead of numbers, or lock in arrows by pressing the NUM LOCK key. This process is the same as using either SHIFT for the capital letters *A* through *Z* or locking in capital letters with the CAPS LOCK key. Full use of the cursor-movement keys is discussed when you begin working the first example in this chapter.

Quattro Pro 4 makes effective use of the function keys, labeled F1, F2, and so on. These keys are either down the left side or across the top of the keyboard, depending on the layout. The function keys as used in Quattro Pro 4 are listed in Table 1-4, and they will be explained as they are used in the examples.

Starting Quattro Pro 4

A great deal of effort went into making Quattro Pro 4 an easy program to start on almost any computer. There are two steps: installing the program (something you only need to do once) and issuing the command that begins the program (something you do at the start of every Quattro Pro 4 session). Most hard disk drive systems have a hard disk drive that is called C and a floppy disk drive that is called A. To install Quattro Pro 4 you place disk 1 of the program into drive A and *log on* to that drive. This means that you make drive A the *active drive*, which is done by typing **A:** and pressing ENTER at the DOS prompt. The DOS prompt will

TABLE
1-4

Function Keys

Key	Regular	Alt	Shift
F1	Help		
F2	Edit	Macro Menu	Debug
F3	Menu/Choice	Function List	Macro List
F4	Absolute		
F5	Goto	Undo	Pick Window
F6	Pane	Zoom	Next Window
F7	Query	All Select	Select
F8	Table		Move (in File Manager)
F9	Calc		Copy (in File Manager)
F10	Graph		Paste (in File Manager)

Note also ALT-N, which selects window *N*, and CTRL-F10, used to switch from Paradox to Quattro Pro.

probably look like C> or C:\> and then change to A> or A:\> when you execute this command.

With drive A active, type **INSTALL** and press ENTER to initiate the installation process. When the program files are copied onto the hard disk, you will need to answer some questions about your system. Having answered these, Quattro Pro 4 will be installed and ready to use. To load Quattro Pro 4 from the DOS prompt, type **Q** and press ENTER when you are in the QPRO directory. You will either see a screen like the one shown in Figure 1-15 or, if your computer is using the character mode, a screen like the one in Figure 1-16. Both screens have been annotated to show the terms used by Quattro Pro 4 for the main part of the working area. You are now ready to start working with the program. Next time you use your system, type **CD\QPRO** followed by **Q** to run the program, where QPRO is the name of the directory in which Quattro Pro 4 has been installed. If Quattro Pro 4 is installed in a different directory, apply the correct name instead of QPRO.

Opening screen: WYSIWYG mode

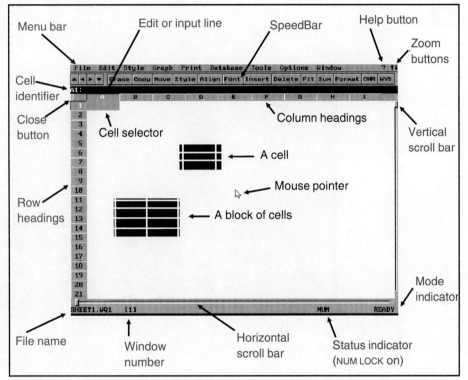

Startup Problems

If you do not know what the DOS prompt is or how to get to it, if you have difficulty following the installation process described here, or if you do not get a screen similar to the ones shown in Figure 1-15 or 1-16, you should consult Appendix A. If you want to customize such features as the way Quattro Pro 4 handles your screen or the menu structure, consult Chapter 6. If you have a black-and-white monitor, you should start the INSTALL program using a special command or "switch" that makes the screens easier to read. You should enter **INSTALL/B** instead of just **INSTALL**. Note that if you do not have a mouse driver installed on your computer, the SpeedBar will not appear.

FIGURE 1-16

Opening screen: Character mode

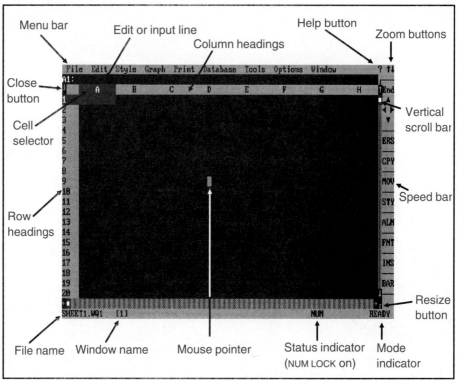

Menu bar

Edit or input line

Help button

Zoom buttons

Column headings

Close button

Cell selector

Vertical scroll bar

Row headings

Speed bar

Resize button

File name   Window name   Mouse pointer   Status indicator (NUM LOCK on)   Mode indicator

Starting and Leaving Quattro Pro 4

As you have seen, you can start Quattro Pro 4 by typing **Q** at the DOS prompt. This is the basic method of starting the program on a hard disk. The command can be incorporated into a hard disk menu system, or Quattro Pro 4 can be started automatically, as soon as your system is turned on or reset. The procedures for setting up these methods are explained in Appendix A. You can instruct Quattro Pro 4 to load a worksheet as soon as the program loads. Commands for doing so are explained in Chapter 6.

When you type **Q** and press ENTER, the program loads into memory. This takes a matter of seconds, depending on the type of hardware you are using. You are then presented with the opening screen (shown in

Figures 1-15 and 1-16). Leaving the program can be done in several ways and is discussed in the section "Saving and Ending" later in this chapter. Normally, you will want to store the work you have done in a file on disk. However, if you do not need to store any of your work, you can simply turn off the computer or restart it. If you want to go directly back to the DOS prompt, you can type **/** followed by **F** for **F**ile and then **x** for E**x**it. If you have done any work that has not been saved on disk, you will be prompted to confirm the Exit command.

Spreadsheet Concepts

This section introduces the basic concepts of spreadsheets and prepares you for the next chapter. Some brief examples demonstrate how to enter and calculate numbers with Quattro Pro 4 and familiarize you with the special keys and the menu system.

The Worksheet Area

When you first load Quattro Pro 4 you have an empty electronic work space called a *worksheet* in which to place numbers, words, and instructions (formulas and calculations). As you can see in Figures 1-15 and 1-16, there is a line of letters above the work area and a list of numbers down the left side. The letters represent a series of columns and the numbers a series of rows. The intersection of each column and row forms a rectangle, a box into which you put information. These boxes are called *cells*. One of them is highlighted when you start the program. This highlighted cell is called A1 because it is in column A on row 1. Every cell has a name based on its location, or *coordinates,* just like a map. You move from cell to cell to lay out information. When you first start Quattro Pro 4 you are in cell A1. If you were to enter information at this point, it would be placed in cell A1. The cell you are in is called the *current cell.*

The highlighting that marks the cell you are in is called the *cell selector.* It can be moved with the cursor keys or the arrow keys. When you move the cell selector, the horizontal and vertical borders indicate which column and row you are in, using reverse highlighting. Your exact location is recorded at the top left of the screen. A guide to your relative location within the worksheet is provided by the vertical and horizontal scroll bars on the right and bottom of the worksheet.

Worksheet Size

The worksheet is very large; the columns continue off the side of the screen through column Z. Additional columns are numbered AA through AZ, then BA through BZ, and so on. After repeating the alphabet nine and a half times, you get to the last column, IV, for a total of 256 columns. The rows go down to 8192. Multiplying the columns and rows together gives you a total of over 2 million cells. Obviously your monitor can show you only a small portion of this huge work area at a time. The screen acts like a window, showing you different parts of the worksheet as you move the cell selector around.

Quattro Pro 4 provides important information around the edge of the screen. The horizontal and vertical borders, the top menu bar, the edit line, and the bottom status area work like a dashboard or control panel. The *mode indicator* shows you a variety of messages about the current task. Near the top of the screen the *cell identifier* shows the contents of the current cell, its display format, and its width setting.

Movement Keys

To explore the work area, press the RIGHT ARROW key once. You will see the highlighting move to the next cell to the right, B1. You are now in cell B1. Press the DOWN ARROW key once and you will be in cell B2. Notice that the cell identifier shows your current location. This is very helpful, as eyeballing your location is notably prone to error, particularly after several hours of staring at the screen.

Your keyboard has the ability to repeat keystrokes and will do so if you push and hold down, rather than just press, a key. Throughout the rest of this book you should take the term *press* to mean lightly tap rather than push and hold down. To see the keyboard repeat feature in action, press the DOWN ARROW key and hold it for two seconds. You will see the cell indicator move quickly down the screen and the numbers at the left will scroll by rapidly. You can see that you are dragging the screen with you to view a different area of the spreadsheet. Now try pressing the HOME key. It takes you back to A1.

The UP ARROW, DOWN ARROW, LEFT ARROW, and RIGHT ARROW keys move you one cell in each of their respective directions. Used with the CTRL key, the RIGHT ARROW and LEFT ARROW keys move a screen at a time across the worksheet. You hold down the CTRL key, then press the arrow key. A similar effect can be achieved with the TAB and SHIFT-TAB keys, respectively. The PAGE UP and PAGE DOWN keys move you a screen at a time up and down the worksheet. The HOME key always places you in A1 (unless you are using locked titles, described in Chapter 3). The END key followed by the UP ARROW, DOWN ARROW, LEFT ARROW, or RIGHT ARROW key takes you to the last cell in that direction. The last cell means the last occupied cell in a row or column or the first occupied cell if the next cell is empty. Do not use the END key like the CTRL key; you press END, release it, and then press the arrow key. Note that if the cell selector is in a blank cell, and there are no more entries in the direction you point, your cell selector will reach the end of the spreadsheet. If this happens, just press HOME to return to the top of the spreadsheet.

The INSERT and DELETE keys are often grouped with the cursor keys. Pressing DELETE removes the contents of the current cell. Pressing INSERT changes the way that the EDIT mode works and enables you to add text to the middle of a value or label without typing over other characters. Note that the INSERT and DELETE keys are not the same as the Insert and Delete buttons on the SpeedBar, which are described later in this chapter.

Types of Information

Quattro Pro 4 categorizes all information into one of two types of data: values or labels. To oversimplify, values are numbers and calculations, and labels are words or text. Quattro Pro 4 treats the two categories of data differently. By looking at the first character of each new entry into the worksheet, Quattro Pro 4 determines the appropriate category for that data—value or label.

Values

To see how to enter information into Quattro Pro 4 and how the program recognizes values, try the following exercise. With the cell selector in cell A1, type **789** from the row of numbers at the top of the keyboard. Do not press ENTER or any other key; just observe what has happened. Notice that the number 789 has not yet been placed into the worksheet. Instead, it is on the edit or input line. The cursor is positioned after the number 9. At this point you can either continue to type or use the BACKSPACE key to erase what you have typed. Also notice that a change has taken place in the bottom status area. The mode indicator now says VALUE. This tells you that Quattro Pro 4 is reading what you have typed as a value. If you pressed the ENTER key prematurely or otherwise caused the number to leave the top line of the screen, just type **789** again and observe what happens before you press ENTER.

Mode Indicator

You can now place the number 789 into the worksheet. To do so, press the ENTER key and observe that the number disappears from the edit line and is placed into the worksheet in the cell you are highlighting, as shown in Figure 1-17. The cell identifier now lists the contents of the cell. Although the cell identifier might seem like a duplication of effort, you will see in a moment that what Quattro Pro 4 shows you in the cell identifier is sometimes different from what it displays in the worksheet.

FIGURE 1-17

The first value entered in A1

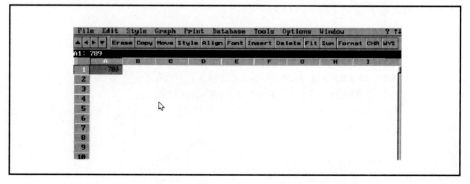

The cell identifier shows the exact content of the cell as Quattro Pro 4 reads it.

When you have pressed ENTER you will also see that the mode indicator returns to READY. Notice that the numbers you have entered are placed on the right-hand side of the cell. Quattro Pro 4 normally aligns numbers evenly with the right of the column. This is referred to as *flush-right alignment*.

Locking Capitals

Now that you are back in the READY mode, you can move to another cell. Press the RIGHT ARROW key once and you will be in cell B1. Here you will enter a label. Before you type, take a look at your keyboard and locate the CAPS LOCK key. This key enables you to type in capital letters without using the SHIFT key. Many people find it convenient to type labels all in capitals. Press the CAPS LOCK key once and notice the bottom status area reflects this change with the message CAP. When you use locked capitals, the letters *A* through *Z* are automatically typed as capitals. However, you must still use the SHIFT key to access symbols and commands that appear on the upper half of the keys.

Labels

In a moment you are going to type the word *BASE* because you will use Quattro Pro 4 to figure out the full price of a car from, among other things, the base price. When you type the letter **B**, notice that the mode indicator says LABEL. Also notice that the word is being typed on the edit line so you can change it with the BACKSPACE key if you make an error. Type **BASE**, press ENTER, and observe the cell identifier. In front of the word you typed is an apostrophe ('). The apostrophe was automatically placed there by Quattro Pro 4 as a reminder that this is a label. Although you are not likely to confuse this particular label with a number, later you will encounter instructions that look like labels but are in fact values.

The apostrophe not only tells you that this is a label but also signifies that this is a left-aligned label. Labels can either be left-aligned, right-aligned, or centered in the column. Right-aligned labels are preceded by a quotation mark ("). Centered labels begin with a caret (^), which is the shifted 6 on the keyboard. Rather than make you type one of the three label align characters (', ", or ^) before every label, Quattro Pro 4 assumes one of them. This is the *default label alignment* and, as you can see, it is left-aligned. You can change the default, as described later, or change the alignment of a block of labels. To enter a label aligned differently from the default, just type the desired alignment before the text of the label. If you want the label to begin with one of the alignment characters, use two of them. Thus, entering **""Right On"** will actually produce a right-aligned label that reads "Right On".

Entering with Arrows and the Mouse

You will now enter another label directly below BASE. This will be the word PREP, for dealer preparation costs, but you will use a slightly different method to enter it into the cell. First press DOWN ARROW to move to cell B2, and then type **PREP**. It will appear on the edit line like the numbers **789** and **BASE** did before. Now press the DOWN ARROW key again. Doing so enters the label and moves you down to the next row. This can be a very useful feature if you want to enter a series of labels or numbers. The direction keys will enter what you are typing and move you in a particular direction with one keystroke. For this reason it is important not to press the cursor keys when you are entering information into an empty cell. Practice this method of entering by typing **TAX** and then pressing the DOWN ARROW key, followed by **TOTAL** and the DOWN ARROW key. The results will look like Figure 1-18.

If you are using a mouse with Quattro Pro 4, you will see what you type on the Edit line is preceded by [Enter] [Esc]. These act as buttons that you can select by clicking the mouse. Click on [Enter] to confirm your entry. Click on [Esc] to cancel what you have typed.

Editing Cells

Changing worksheet entries and correcting mistakes is one of the most important procedures you will need to know. In this example, 789 is a

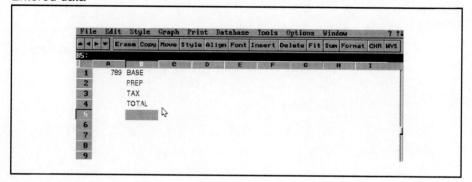

FIGURE
1-18

Entered data

ridiculously low price for a car, so you need to change it. Press HOME; you will be highlighting cell A1 and the number 789. To change a cell entry completely, just type a new entry. Type **8000** and press ENTER. Do *not* put commas in the thousands when entering numbers in Quattro Pro 4; they will be put in later. The new number completely replaces the old one.

What if you want to modify the contents of the cell, rather than completely replace them? For example, you might want to change 8000 to 8095 to reflect a price increase. When you do not need to completely change a cell, you can change part of it using the Edit key, F2. In this case, you press F2 while your cell selector is in A1. When you do so, the contents of the cell are returned to the edit line, as shown in Figure 1-19. Press BACKSPACE twice to back over the last two zeros, and type **95**. Now press ENTER to see the modified contents returned to the cell. Note that if you are using a mouse with Quattro Pro 4 you will see [Enter] [Esc] on the edit line when you are editing. You can click on [Enter] to confirm the contents as they exist on the edit line, or you can click on [Esc] to cancel the editing and restore the cell contents as they were before you began editing.

Suppose you now want to add a figure for dealer preparation costs to the worksheet. First press DOWN ARROW once. You will be in cell A2. Type the number **567**, and enter it into the cell by pressing the DOWN ARROW key. You are now in cell A3 and ready to do some math with Quattro Pro 4.

FIGURE
1-19

Editing a cell

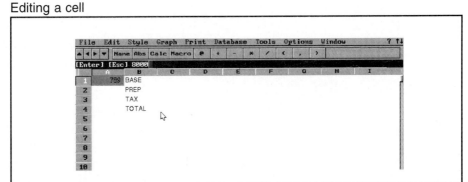

Instructions and Formulas

In cell A3 you want a figure for the tax that must be paid on the base price of the car. Assume that the tax rate is 10% or 0.1. The figure you want in cell A3 is 8095x0.1. You want Quattro Pro 4 to calculate this for you, so you are going to type an instruction into cell A3 that will tell the program to multiply the number in cell A1 by 0.1 and place the answer in cell A3. Note that you are not going to tell the program simply to multiply the number 8095 by 0.1. Quattro Pro 4 can do that, but that is not the true power of a spreadsheet. What you want to do is establish a relationship between the cells so that, even if the number in A1 changes, the relationship will remain and A3 will continue to give you 0.1 times the content of A1. The instruction will be entered as **.1*A1**. Quattro Pro 4 uses the asterisk for a multiplication sign. Although the instruction contains a letter as well as numbers, the program considers the decimal point to be a *value indicator* and so reads what follows it as a value. Type **.1*A1** and press ENTER. You will immediately see the tax figure calculated, as shown in Figure 1-20.

When you look at the cell identifier you can see that Quattro Pro 4 is not concerned about the actual number in cell A3. It simply records the relationship between the two cells. This will remain the same, whatever number is in cell A1.

Suppose that the base price goes up. Press HOME to move to 8095 in cell A1. Change it by typing **8900**, the new price, and pressing ENTER. Instantly, Quattro Pro 4 updates cell A3. If you move the cell selector

FIGURE 1-20   Calculation entered

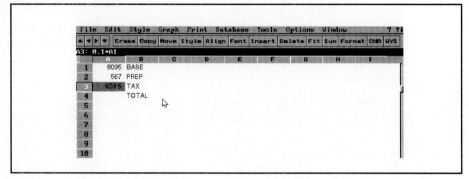

down to cell A3 and look at the cell identifier, you will see that the cell contents have not changed. They are still the same formula you entered before.

Now you want to calculate a total price for the car including the base price, preparation costs, and tax. You will need to add several cells together. To do this, first place the cell selector in the cell that is to contain the answer—in this case, cell A4. Now you will type an instruction that tells Quattro Pro 4 that this cell will contain the sum of cells A1, A2, and A3. You might think that you could type **A1+A2+A3**, and this is almost correct. However, instructions involving only cell references need special treatment because Quattro Pro 4 will read the letter *A* as a label. To get around this and to make sure that Quattro Pro 4 knows that what you are typing is a value, type a plus sign first and then the cell reference. Make sure the cell selector is in A4, and then type the formula **+A1+A2+A3** and press ENTER.

The Function Instruction

If you decided to take out a loan to finance the full price of this car, you might want to calculate how big a monthly payment you would have to make. A loan payment calculation involves three pieces of information. Labels for these three items will be typed into column D, starting in D1. Move the cell selector to D1. Then, using the DOWN ARROW key to enter them, type the three labels **AMOUNT**, **INTEREST**, and **TERM**. Also type one more label, **PAYMENT**, and then move back up to cell E1 where you will enter the principal amount. Your screen should look like Figure 1-21. The amount you want to finance is the total price from cell A4. Instead of typing the number again, simply type **+A4** and press ENTER. This establishes a relationship between these two cells so that whatever is in cell A4 is also in cell E1.

Now move the cell selector to E2. Here you want to enter the rate of interest you will pay. This needs to be expressed as a rate per period of the loan. Suppose you are going to make monthly payments. You need to enter the amount of interest you will pay in one month. If the bank is charging 12% per annum (A.P.R.), the rate is 0.01, or 1%, per month. Type **.01** in cell E2 and press DOWN ARROW to go to cell E3. In this cell type the term, the number of months for the loan, say **36**, and press DOWN ARROW.

A formula for the payment will be entered in cell E4. You do not need to know the actual formula. Quattro Pro 4 knows exactly how to calculate a loan payment if it is given the principal, interest, and term because it has a special built-in function. In fact there are dozens of built-in functions covering most common calculations. Press the Function Choices key, ALT-F3, and you will see a list of these pop up over the worksheet, as in Figure 1-22. Press PAGE DOWN and you will see more of these formulas. Press PAGE DOWN until you see the function you need, PMT. Highlight the PMT function and press ENTER. The function will be typed on the edit line for you and the menu of choices will disappear. Notice that the name of the function is preceded by the @ sign. This is a

FIGURE 1-21

More labels entered

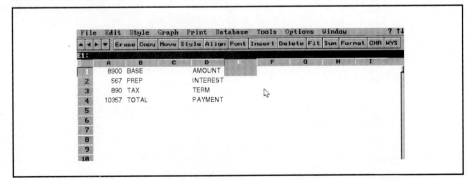

FIGURE
1-22

Functions list

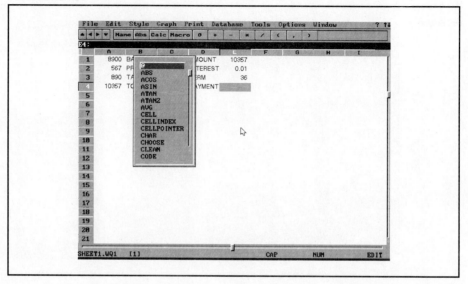

special code that helps Quattro Pro 4 distinguish functions from other entries. This gives rise to the term *@functions* for the built-in formulas that use this code.

The PMT function needs to know the amounts for principal, interest, and term of the loan. This information is presented to the function within parentheses; Quattro Pro 4 has already typed the open parenthesis, (. Now type **E1,E2,E3** followed by the closing parenthesis,), and press ENTER. These three items inside the parentheses are called *arguments*.

You do not have to use the Functions key to create this formula. You could simply type the entire formula **@PMT(E1,E2,E3)** and press ENTER to place it into the cell. Either method is acceptable and produces the monthly payment, as shown in Figure 1-23.

To give you an idea of how flexible a spreadsheet can be, you can now try some changes to the assumptions that produce the answer in E4. For example, if you were considering a more expensive model you could type the new price in A1 and immediately see the new payment in E4. To reduce the amount of the monthly payment, enter a longer term, such as 48 months, into E3.

FIGURE

1-23

The monthly payment

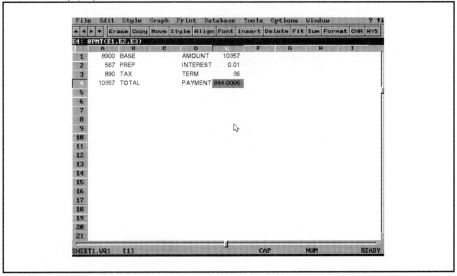

Using the Menu System

The manipulation of facts and figures in cells is only part of the power of Quattro Pro 4. A whole range of commands arranged in a series of menus and submenus can be accessed through the menu bar at the top of the screen. This is activated by pressing the Menu key, which is either F3 or the forward slash key. Type /, and you will see that the menu bar is activated, with the first option, File, highlighted. You can use the RIGHT ARROW key to highlight Edit, and continue across the bar to highlight each of the items in turn. Notice that the word MENU appears in the mode indicator at the lower right of the screen. An explanation of what each of the items does is given on the bottom row of the screen.

Now type **F** or press DOWN ARROW and the first menu, File, will be pulled down, as shown in Figure 1-24. The items you see listed in the box are the categories of file operation that Quattro Pro 4 offers. The words across the bottom of the screen tell you what the option on the menu does. For example, in Figure 1-24 the item "New" is highlighted. You can see that this opens a new spreadsheet window. You can pull down each of the menus in turn by pressing the RIGHT ARROW key with the File menu visible.

FIGURE
1-24
The File menu

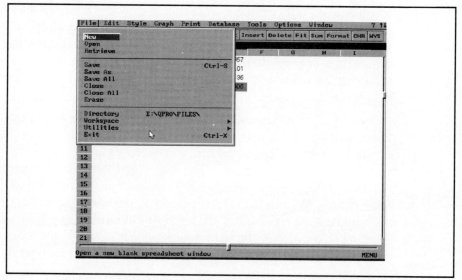

If you keep pressing RIGHT ARROW or LEFT ARROW you will return to the File menu.

You can select any item on a menu by typing the highlighted letter, which is usually the first letter. Alternatively, you can first press DOWN ARROW to put the menu bar on the desired option and then press ENTER. Try moving the highlight to the word Utilities and you will see the message "Access DOS, the file manager, or SQZ! settings." Notice that this menu item has a small triangle next to it. This means that a submenu will appear when this item is selected. Select the Utilities option and you will see DOS Shell, File Manager, and SQZ! Press ESC to go back one step in the menu system. You leave the menu completely by pressing ESC several times until you are back in the READY mode (you can also get from any menu to READY mode by pressing CTRL-BREAK).

Saving and Ending

Having completed this series of calculations, you may decide to take a break. You need to think about where the information you have created is located. So far, all of the work you have been doing is in the computer's memory. The only problem with this is that the memory is only as good as the power to your computer. If you accidentally pull the plug or your system suffers an electrical failure, the memory's contents are lost. You must transfer the data to permanent storage on disk. This has to be done on a regular basis and should always be done before you leave your PC unattended.

Type **/** to bring up the menu and then type **F** for File. Now type **S** for Save. You will see a prompt like the one in Figure 1-25. You can type in a name for the file into which you want Quattro Pro 4 to store this worksheet. The name can be any eight letters or numbers, like QLOAN101, but no spaces are allowed within the name (QLOAN_MY is acceptable). Although you can use some punctuation in file names, not all punctuation characters are valid in file names. For this reason, it is best to avoid punctuation when naming files. For complete details on file naming, see Chapter 3. When you have typed the name, press ENTER.

Note that the first time you save a spreadsheet the program will suggest storing it on the same drive and directory you started the program from, typically C:\QPRO or C:\QUATTRO. You may want to avoid storing data files among program files. To change this before saving the file, select

FIGURE 1-25

The File Save prompt

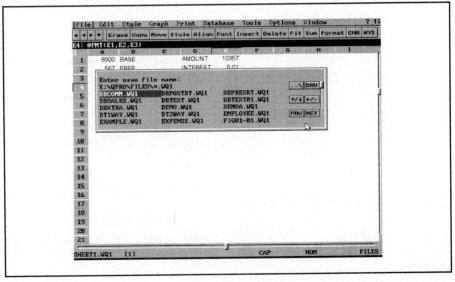

Directory from the File menu and type the name of a data file directory that you have already created on your hard disk. Then press ENTER. From now on until you restart the program, Quattro Pro 4 will save spreadsheets to this directory rather than to the directory occupied by the program files.

To make this change permanent, you can type / and select Options, Startup, and then Directory. Enter the desired drive and directory and press ENTER, and then press ESC to return to the Options menu. Now select Update, which will store your choice in a small file on the disk. Quattro Pro 4 refers to this configuration file every time you load the program. See Appendix A for more on configuration files and directories.

Now that you have saved your work, you can either turn off your system or return to DOS by typing / to activate the menu and selecting File followed by Exit. Quattro Pro 4 knows if you have not saved changes to your work and, if this is the case, prompts you to confirm the Exit command. If you do not want to stop working with Quattro Pro 4 but want to begin a fresh file after saving the last one, you can clear the worksheet area by typing /, selecting File, and then Erase. Again, Quattro Pro 4 will prompt for confirmation if you have not saved changes to the worksheet on the screen. For more information on file saving, see Chapter 3.

Navigating Your Worksheet

You have seen that Quattro Pro 4 provides several ways of moving the cell selector. You can use the arrow or cursor movement keys to move from cell to cell. The PAGE UP and PAGE DOWN keys move the cell selector up and down through the worksheet one screen at a time. You can move the cell selector one screen to the right or left using TAB/SHIFT-TAB or CTRL-RIGHT ARROW/CTRL-LEFT ARROW. The HOME key places the cell selector in A1.

One key that works a little differently is END. You can test the END key in the loan worksheet you have just made. First press HOME to move the cell selector to A1. Now press END. You will see the message END appear in the bottom status line. Now press the DOWN ARROW key. The cell selector moves down to the last consecutively occupied cell in the column, in this case A4. Now press END followed by the RIGHT ARROW key. The cell selector moves to the last consecutively occupied cell in the row—in other words,

B4. Now press END followed by the UP ARROW key and the cell selector moves to B1, the last occupied cell in the direction you pointed.

If you press END and then RIGHT ARROW while the cell selector is in B1, Quattro Pro 4 will move the cell selector to D1, the next occupied cell in the direction you pointed. If the current cell is C1, an empty cell, pressing END and then RIGHT ARROW will also select D1. However, if C1 is the current cell and you press END and then DOWN ARROW, Quattro Pro 4 moves the cell selector all the way down to C8192 (you can just press HOME to get back to A1).

The action of the END key followed by an arrow key can be summarized as moving the cell selector to either the last or the next occupied cell in the direction indicated by the arrow. The END key is particularly handy when you are navigating large worksheets. If you are using a mouse, you can simulate pressing END plus an arrow key by clicking on one of the four arrow buttons at the beginning of the SpeedBar.

Another handy key for navigating large worksheets is F5, the Goto key. When you press F5 a message appears on the edit line, asking you to type the address of the cell to which you want to move the cell selector. For example, to make E3 the current cell you would type **E3** (you can also type **e3**; the command is not case sensitive). After you type the cell address, press ENTER, and the cell selector is moved for you.

Working with a Mouse

With the excellent mouse interface built into Quattro Pro 4 and the increasing popularity of these devices you may well want to use a mouse to select cells, commands, and actions. The first step is to make sure that your mouse and mouse driver are installed correctly. If the mouse is installed, then Quattro Pro 4 will place a *mouse pointer* on the screen for you. This is a small rectangle if you are displaying Quattro Pro 4 in character mode, or a small arrow if you are using WYSIWYG mode. If you are having trouble seeing the mouse pointer, just move the mouse and you should see the pointer move on the screen. If a mouse pointer fails to move or even to appear, check the installation instructions that came with the mouse.

Mouse actions consist of pointing, clicking, and dragging. *Pointing* means placing the mouse pointer over a specific object on the screen.

Clicking means pressing and then quickly releasing the mouse button when you are pointing to an object. For most commands you use the button on the left. *Dragging* means pointing to an object and then holding down the mouse button while moving the mouse. For example, you can point to cell B2 and then drag the mouse pointer to cell D10 to highlight cells B2 through D10. When you release the mouse button, the cells remain selected.

Another technique for selecting a group of cells with the mouse makes use of the right mouse button. Suppose the current cell is B2 and you want to select cells B2 through F9. Place the mouse pointer over F9 but do not click it. Now press and hold down the right mouse button, then click the left button. The worksheet area between the current cell and F9 is selected. This technique, referred to as "right-hold/left-click," is handy when you want to select a large group of cells that extends across several screens. Instead of having to drag the highlighting across the screens you can select the top left cell, move through the worksheet until you can see the bottom right cell and perform right-hold/left-click.

The mouse can be very powerful when you are using Quattro Pro 4. For example, to delete the contents of a cell you can click on the cell, and then click on Erase or ERS in the SpeedBar. To erase a group of cells you can drag the highlight across the cells in question and then click on Erase. You can use the mouse to pick menu items by clicking on the item you want. Any command that requires a group of cells to be selected will accept cells highlighted by dragging with the mouse. To dismiss a pull-down menu you do not have to press ESC—you can just click anywhere on the worksheet, outside of the menu.

Quattro Pro 4 enables you to preselect cells for some commands. Thus you can highlight a block of cells using the mouse, then use the Style Numeric Format command to assign a format to all of the cells. The selected cells are automatically assumed to be the ones to which you want to apply the command. The cells remain selected after you issue the Numeric Format command. This enables you to issue further commands, such as Style Font, to the same set of cells, without selecting them over and over again.

Parts of Quattro Pro 4 consist of lists, which you can navigate with the mouse. You can see a list *scroll bar* on the right of the file list in Figure 1-25. Furthermore, each worksheet window has scroll bars so that you can use your mouse to move around the worksheet. The vertical scroll bars have an up arrow at the top and a down arrow at the bottom. Clicking on these moves the highlighting up or down one line at a time. The horizontal scroll bars on worksheet windows have left and right arrows that can be clicked to move one column at a time. To move around more quickly you can point to the elevator box within the scroll bar and drag it along the bar. This moves the highlighting relative to the list or worksheet area. For example, if you drag the elevator box to the middle of the vertical scroll bar, the highlighting will be moved to the middle of the list or halfway down the occupied area of the worksheet.

You select items from lists and menus by pointing at them and clicking. You can click outside of a menu or list to put it away. If you have selected a menu item that leads to a further menu you can move back one level in the menus by clicking on the top, left, or bottom border of the previous menu. This returns you to that menu.

When you are editing data on the edit line you can click on the [Enter] or [Esc] buttons that appear to either accept or cancel your editing. To edit a particular cell you first click the cell then click the edit line to switch to EDIT mode.

In Quattro Pro 4 mouse users have direct access to several commands by means of the SpeedBar, described earlier in this chapter. In WYSIWYG mode the SpeedBar is displayed above the work area, whereas it appears to the right of the work area in character mode. In both modes you see four arrows at beginning of the SpeedBar. These move the cell selector, simulating the "End plus arrow key" movement, described earlier in the chapter under "Navigating Your Worksheet." The action of these arrow buttons can be summarized as moving the cell selector to either the last or the next occupied cell in the direction of the arrow you click.

As you will see in the next chapter, Quattro Pro 4 enables you to open several worksheets at once. In fact, you can display as many as 32 worksheets on the screen at the same time. Each worksheet is displayed in a separate window, the size and location of which can be adjusted if you are operating in character mode (in WYSIWYG mode multiple windows are fixed in size and location). The keystrokes and mouse commands for adjusting windows are described in Chapter 3. They make use of the zoom buttons; the up and down arrows seen at the top right of the screen; as well as the resize button, a small rectangular button that appears at the bottom right of the worksheet in character mode.

CHAPTER

Building a Spreadsheet

*T*his chapter shows you how to build a basic spreadsheet model, from data entry to numeric formatting and absolute cell referencing. You will learn how to use the requisite menus, keystrokes, and mouse commands. Some of the fundamental concepts of spreadsheet work will be explained, including cell blocks and formula copying. A sample model is used to demonstrate many of the features and commands under discussion.

Entering and Editing Information

This section builds on what you learned in Chapter 1 about entering information into spreadsheet cells. You will learn more about data entry techniques, the editing of worksheet entries, and how Quattro Pro 4 handles labels.

The Sample Model

By following the numbered steps listed here you can test for yourself the techniques described in this section. Together with further steps given later in the chapter, the steps create a model used to illustrate spreadsheet commands in this and several other chapters. The model shows projected revenue for a regional office of a computer company. Begin by loading Quattro Pro 4. When the program has been loaded you will be presented with a fresh worksheet. The cell selector will be in cell A1. Check that CAPS LOCK is off (the message CAP should not appear in the bottom status line).

1. With the cell selector in A1 type **Revenue Projection** and press DOWN ARROW. This enters the label and moves the cell selector to A2.

2. Now enter four more labels in the same way, placing **Office:** in A2, **Period:** in A3, **Total:** in A4, and **Rate:** in A5.

3. Move the cell selector to B2, type **Chicago**, and press ENTER.

The results so far will look something like Figure 2-1. The model will be used to calculate the total projected revenue for the company's

Chicago office, based on a particular growth rate. Don't worry if you make a mistake carrying out these instructions. You can refer to the section on "Correcting and Undoing Mistakes" for help in correcting them. Note that Figure 2-1 shows Quattro Pro 4 in WYSIWYG mode. Furthermore, the screen has been "zoomed" to enlarge the cell entries. You can read how to do this at the end of the chapter, under "Zooms and Defaults."

Spreadsheet Defaults

In a program as flexible as Quattro Pro 4, you can change many aspects of the way the program works. For example, the columns can be 1 to 254 characters wide. However, the program gives a new worksheet some basic settings known as the *defaults*. In computer terms, a default is what the program does, or assumes, unless you tell it differently. In a new worksheet the labels are normally aligned on the left. The format for displaying values is the *General format*, which shows numbers with no commas in the thousands and no decimal places unless they are entered or calculated by a formula.

By default, the worksheet columns are wide enough to accommodate 9 characters. When you start working on a spreadsheet, you can change the default settings for that sheet. For example, you can make all columns 12 characters wide. The commands for controlling columns are discussed later in this chapter. Chapter 6 explains how to make permanent changes to the default settings in Quattro Pro 4, including such items as colors and worksheet storage.

Beginnings of the sample model

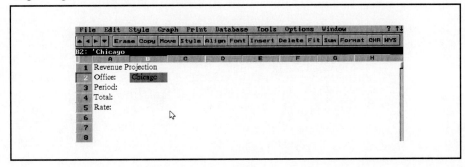

All About Labels

As you saw in Chapter 1, there are two types of data in a spreadsheet: values and labels. The information you have entered so far in the sample model consists of labels. These are automatically aligned on the left of the cell. Although spreadsheets are thought of as number-crunching tools, the role labels play is very important. Labels tell you and anyone else using the worksheets what the numbers mean. Avoid entering numbers and formulas without first placing appropriate labels to indicate what the numbers represent. Quattro Pro 4 creates a label whenever a new cell entry begins with one of the following *label indicators*:

A through Z ! % ^ & ^) _ { [\ < > : ; ! ~ ? }] _ | ' "

In addition to these characters, a space at the beginning of an entry also tells Quattro Pro 4 that you are typing a label.

Normally, Quattro Pro 4 aligns labels on the left and puts an apostrophe in front of the text to remind you that this is a label. You can tell Quattro Pro 4 to center a label in the column by starting the label with the caret sign (^). A label is placed flush right by preceding it with the double quotation mark ("), sometimes called a double prime. You can try this in the sample model. With the cell selector in B2 type **"Chicago** and press ENTER. The label moves to the right, as seen in Figure 2-2.

The label alignment characters can be activated in several ways. The Options Formats Align Labels command shown in Figure 2-2 can be used to tell Quattro Pro 4 to make all new labels in the current spreadsheet align left, right, or centered. This command affects the current worksheet, and the settings it creates are saved with the worksheet file. The command does not affect other worksheets or the labels you have already entered in the current worksheet. To explore this command and practice using the Quattro Pro 4 menu system follow these steps:

1. Type **/** to activate the menu.

2. Now type **O** to pick Options. This is probably quicker than the alternative method of selecting Options, which is to press the RIGHT ARROW key until Options is highlighted and then press ENTER or DOWN ARROW.

FIGURE
2-2

The Align Labels choices

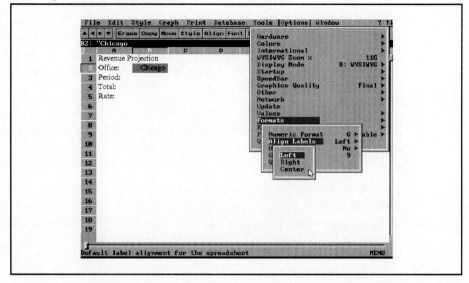

3. With the Options menu displayed type **F** to select Formats and then **A** to select Align Labels. You will now see the three options shown in Figure 2-2.

4. At this point you *could* type the first letter of the alignment you prefer or move the highlighting to the item and press ENTER (press the LEFT ARROW, RIGHT ARROW, UP ARROW, or DOWN ARROW key or the SPACEBAR to cycle through the menu options). However, you do not need to change the setting for the sample model, so press ESC.

5. Pressing ESC moves you one step back in the menus; however, in this case you want to leave the menu system entirely, so instead of repeatedly pressing the ESC key press CTRL-BREAK. This takes you directly back to READY mode.

Mouse users can try the following steps to navigate the Quattro Pro 4 menu system:

1. Move the mouse pointer over Options and click the left button to display the Options menu.

2. Click Formats to display the Formats menu.

3. Click Align Labels to see the three options shown in Figure 2-2.

4. At this point you could click on the alignment you prefer. However, because you do not need change the setting for the sample, move the pointer outside the menus and click to put them all away and return to the READY mode.

Mouse users should note that you move back to a previous level in the menus by clicking on the top, left, or bottom border of the underlying menu.

When you want to vary individual labels from the default label alignment setting, you can simply type the appropriate prefix ahead of the text of the label, as in "**Chicago**, which will align the word "Chicago" on the right of the cell. To change the alignment of a group of cells you use the Alignment command from the Style menu. This command also enables you to change the alignment of numbers, which can be positioned on the left or in the center of a column, as well as on the right where they normally appear. The Style Alignment command is described later in this chapter under "Style and Alignment."

Repeating Labels

There is one other label prefix, the backward slash (\), which is also known as the "cell fill" character. This is used when you want one or more characters to be repeated in order to fill up a cell. For example, if you enter *, Quattro Pro 4 fills the cells with as many asterisks as the cell can hold. If you widen the column, then Quattro Pro 4 automatically adds more asterisks. The number of asterisks are reduced if the column is narrowed.

The main reason for the cell fill feature is that early spreadsheet programs could not underline text within cells the way that Quattro Pro 4 can, nor could they draw lines for borders. As an alternative, an extra row was added and cells were filled with hyphens (-) or equal signs (=), creating the impression of a line beneath a label or across a spreadsheet as a visual divider. You may want to use this technique if your printer has limited graphics capabilities. Figure 2-3 shows equal signs used for a dividing line in cells A2 and B2 of the sample model, working in character mode. To do this a fresh row was inserted below the title (do not do this in your model). To create these lines the \ is followed by the character you want to repeat. Thus, \= produces =========, whereas \+= produces +=+=+=+=+, and so on.

The cell fill technique is a lot quicker than manually entering a series of symbols and has the added advantage that when columns are altered in width, the command keeps the correct number of characters in the cell. There are alternatives to repeating characters for underlining and dressing up your spreadsheet. These include the Font, Line Drawing, and Shading commands on the Style menu. They are described in Chapter 3.

Long Labels

Quattro Pro 4 labels can contain as many as 254 characters. You seldom require all these characters, but you should know how Quattro Pro 4 acts on labels wider than one column. In Chapter 10 you will see that Quattro Pro 4 can wrap long labels into a rectangular area on the spreadsheet to let you compose text for letters, memos, and notations on spreadsheet models. For now, consider the label in A1 of the sample model. This label is wider than column A. When a label like this is entered, Quattro Pro 4 gives no indication that it will exceed the current column width, and the label is still legible (it will print clearly when you print this worksheet). If you press HOME to highlight A1 and then look at the cell identifier, you will see that all of the title is considered as the contents of cell A1.

Using cell fill (\) to draw lines in character mode

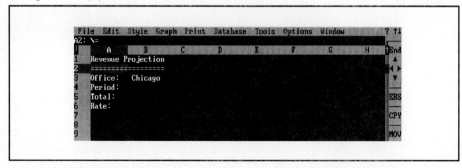

Long labels simply borrow space from adjacent cells to display their contents. If you place the cell selector in B1 and refer to the cell identifier, you will see that there is nothing in this cell. As you can see from Figure 2-4, cell B1 is empty. The contents of cell A1 simply flow over into that display area. Unfortunately, this presents a problem when you want to enter a long label to the left of an occupied cell. Figure 2-5 shows the effect of entering 1993 in cell B1. Quattro Pro 4 can no longer display the full label. However, the missing letters are not lost, as you can see from the cell identifier.

There are several solutions to this problem. You can abbreviate the long label, move the adjacent entry, or widen the column. Later in this chapter you will read how to move cells and widen columns. At this point, the entry in B1 can simply be deleted by highlighting it and pressing the DELETE key.

Entering with Arrows

Whether you are entering values or labels there are two methods of entering data into the spreadsheet. You can either type your entry and press ENTER, which puts the data into the cell and leaves you highlighting that cell, or you can type your entry and press a cursor movement key, which enters the data and moves the cursor in the direction of the key you pressed. In both cases, you put the cell selector on the cell you want to receive the data before you begin typing. At this point your cell selector should be in B3.

The label in A1 does not occupy B1

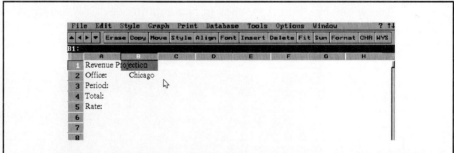

An entry in B1 limits display of the long label in A1

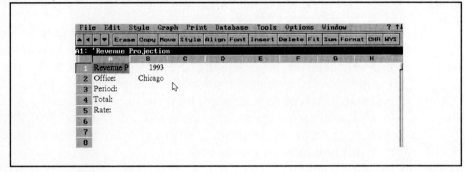

1. In B3 type **1993** and press DOWN ARROW twice (the Total figure will be supplied later).

2. In B5 you need to enter a value that represents a growth rate of ten percent. Type **10%** and then press ENTER.

The results can be seen in Figure 2-6. Note that both entries are values so they are aligned on the right of the column. Also note that the rate you entered in B5 is displayed as 0.1 or one tenth. Because you typed a % sign after 10, Quattro Pro 4 divided the figure by 100 for you. Later you will read how to change the appearance of cell B5 so that it looks like a percentage.

Entering a value as a percentage

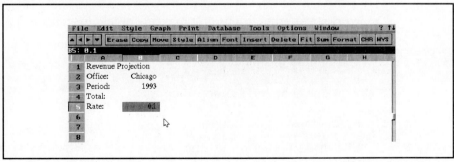

Correcting and Undoing Mistakes

Sometimes you will need to change or cancel an entry as you type it. This happens when you start typing a new piece of data and realize that your cell selector is occupying the wrong cell, as if, in the current example, you had started typing 1993 with the cell selector still in B2. Data that you type first appears on the edit or input line, just above the work area. If you start typing a new entry and then press ENTER or an arrow key or click on the [Enter] button, Quattro Pro 4 puts the data from the input line into the current cell.

If there is already data in the cell, the new data will replace the old. If you had entered **1993** in B2, then you would have to reenter **Chicago**, as well as **1993** in cell B3. If the cell was empty but nevertheless the wrong cell for the new data, for example, if you had entered **1993** in C3, then you would have to remove the incorrect entry.

Fortunately, Quattro Pro 4 lets you change your mind before you enter what is on the input line. If you press ESC or click the [Esc] button, whatever you had begun to type is removed from the input line, and you are back in READY mode. The READY mode enables you to move the cell selector to the correct location.

Quattro Pro 4 also has an Undo key, ALT-F5, which reverses the last action you performed. Press ALT-F5 after making an erroneous entry and the entry will be undone. For example, move the cell selector to B4, which is currently empty. Now type **50** and press ENTER. Now press ALT-F5. The entry is removed and the cell is empty again. The Undo key reverses the last "undoable" operation you performed. Undoable operations are

❑ Cell entries and cell edits, including cell delete and block erase

❑ Worksheet edits, including moves, copies, inserts, and deletions

❑ File retrievals, spreadsheet erasures, and deletion of named graphs and named blocks

Operations that you cannot undo are

❑ Format and style changes

❑ Changes to program settings such as Print Block, Sort Block, and Options

❏   File Manager operations such as file copying

Note that Undo will work to reverse the last undoable operation even after you have performed several operations that cannot be undone. Also note that there is a possibility that when you press ALT-F5 you will get this message:

```
Undo is disabled. Cannot undo it.
```

If this happens, you can enable the Undo feature after clearing the error message by typing / to activate the main menu and select Options. Now choose Other Undo Enable. Next, issue the Options Update command to make the change permanent (see Chapter 6 for details about the Options menu). If Undo did not remove the contents of B4, delete them by pressing the DELETE key.

If you start typing a new piece of data in the right place but make an error or a spelling mistake, you can use the BACKSPACE key to back the cursor over the data in the input line until you have erased the error, and then resume typing. Remember, you should not press the LEFT ARROW key to go back and correct mistakes while you are typing a new entry. Doing so will simply enter the data into the cell.

Cell Editing

As you can see from Figure 2-6, the data you have entered appears on the input line whenever the cell is selected. You can change the contents of a cell in several ways. The method you use will depend on the type of change you need to make. The following paragraphs explain the different ways of editing using Figure 2-6 as an example.

Reentry

When you reenter data into a cell, the contents of the cell are changed. The simplest method of reentry is to type the new data over the old, completely replacing it. For example, if you place the cell selector on B2, which contains the word "Chicago," type **Fargo**, and press ENTER, the entire word "Chicago" will disappear, not just the first five letters. Press ALT-F5 to change "Fargo" back to "Chicago."

The Edit Key

If you want to change "Chicago" to "Chicago South," you can avoid retyping the entire entry by using function key F2, the Edit key. When you place the cell selector on a cell and press F2, the contents of the cell are returned to the input line, which now acts as the edit line. At the same time the mode indicator changes to EDIT. At the bottom left of the screen the worksheet name and window number are replaced by the address of the cell you are editing and the contents of the cell before editing. With the cell contents back on the edit line you can now make changes or additions and place the revised entry back in the worksheet by pressing ENTER.

When you are using EDIT mode several keys perform differently. Pressing HOME moves the cursor to the left side of the entry. Pressing END places the cursor back on the right side. You can also move around the contents of the cell with the LEFT ARROW and RIGHT ARROW keys. Suppose that in B2 you have mistakenly entered **Chidago Soth**, a left-aligned label, as shown in Figure 2-7. There are several ways to correct this error. You can press F2 to edit the cell, the effect of which is also shown in Figure 2-7. Note that the edit cursor is initially placed at the end of the cell contents.

Now you can press the LEFT ARROW key until your cursor is under the erroneous *d*, then press the DELETE key to remove it. You then type the letter **c** which will be inserted automatically into the text, to the left of the cursor. You can then move to the right with the RIGHT ARROW key to put the cursor under the *t*. There you type **u** to complete the editing. As soon as editing is completed you can press the ENTER key or click the

Editing an erroneous entry

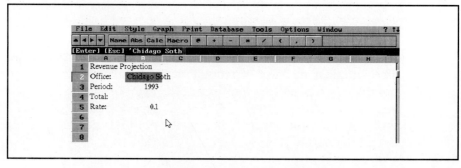

[Enter] button, regardless of where your cursor is within the data. The revised information on the edit line will be placed back in the cell.

Mouse users can click anywhere on the edit line to activate EDIT mode. As you can see from Figure 2-7, this also changes the SpeedBar, which now displays a set of buttons useful in cell editing, particularly when you are working with formulas.

Insert and Overstrike

While you are using EDIT mode, you are also using what is called INS or insert mode, where what you type is inserted beside the existing text instead of replacing what was there before. However, there is another method of typing, referred to as overstrike mode. You activate overstrike mode by pressing the INSERT key during editing. The message OVR appears in the status area at the bottom of the screen.

If you go into OVR mode when editing "Chidago Soth," placing the cursor on *d* and typing **c** replaces the *d*, without the need to press DELETE. However, OVR mode is not always helpful. Typing **u** when the cursor is on the *t* in "Soth" will replace the *t* with *u*. You can press INSERT a second time to get out of OVR mode. Note that Quattro Pro 4 automatically cancels OVR mode when you leave EDIT mode. In Table 2-1 you can see a list of other keys that are useful in EDIT mode.

Cell Delete

Sometimes you will want to erase the entire contents of a cell. If it is too late to use the Undo key (ALT-F5) the correct way to clear out a cell is with the Cell Delete key, which is DELETE. Simply move the cell selector to the cell whose contents you want to erase and press DELETE. If you are using a mouse you can click on Erase in the READY mode SpeedBar and then press ENTER to achieve the same effect. If you want to erase a whole group of cells, you can use the Extend key and select several cells before pressing DELETE, as explained in the section "Preselecting Cell Blocks" later in this chapter.

You may have learned another method of erasing a cell, used in spreadsheet programs that do not have a Cell Delete key. This involves placing the cell selector on the cell you want to delete and pressing the SPACEBAR, then ENTER. For example, with the cell selector in B4 type **50**

TABLE 2-1

Role of Keys in EDIT Mode

Key	Action
LEFT ARROW	Moves cursor 1 character left
RIGHT ARROW	Moves cursor 1 character right
HOME	Moves cursor to first character
END	Moves cursor to the right of last character
TAB	Moves cursor 5 characters to the right
CTRL-RIGHT ARROW	Moves cursor 5 characters to the right
SHIFT-TAB	Moves cursor 5 characters to the left
CTRL-LEFT ARROW	Moves cursor 5 characters to the left
DELETE	Deletes character at cursor
INSERT	Toggles between insert and overstrike modes
BACKSPACE	Deletes character to left of cursor
ESC	Cancels editing
ENTER	Enters contents of edited cell
DOWN ARROW	Enters contents of edited cell
UP ARROW	Enters contents of edited cell
PAGE DOWN	Enters contents of edited cell
PAGE UP	Enters contents of edited cell

Note: If you add a math sign to the end of a formula in EDIT mode, you can use the cursor-movement keys or mouse for the pointing method of formula writing. You can do this after typing a math sign in the middle of a formula if you press F2 before pointing.

and press ENTER. Now press the SPACEBAR and then ENTER. With this method it appears that the cell has been emptied. But if you look in the cell identifier you will see an apostrophe, which begins a left-aligned label. You have replaced what was in the cell with a blank label. Now press DELETE and the apostrophe is removed.

The SPACEBAR method of cell "deleting" is a bad habit to get into, because the cell is not really emptied. Such cells can affect some worksheet calculations, such as @AVG and @COUNT. Unless you place the cell selector on the "empty" cell and observe the cell identifier there is nothing to see. (You can use the Search & Replace feature, described later in this chapter, to find cells that have been erased like this.)

Automatic Editing

If you enter data that Quattro Pro 4 cannot read, pressing ENTER or clicking [Enter] to place the data in a cell causes your computer to beep and possibly displays a message box on the screen. For example, Quattro Pro 4 does not accept numbers that contain commas. In Figure 2-8 you can see the effect of trying to enter **8,000** in B4. The "Invalid character" message is displayed and the mode indicator has changed to ERROR. You can press ENTER or ESC to remove the message.

At this point, Quattro Pro 4 automatically switches to EDIT mode and tries to point out your error by placing the edit cursor at the first mistake it reads in what you tried to enter. In this case the cursor is placed on the superfluous comma so that you can press DELETE to remove it. The corrected data could then be placed into the cell with ENTER. In fact, you don't want any data in B4. Press CTRL-BREAK at the data entry error message or during cell editing to completely cancel the erroneous entry (if you did enter something into B4 select the cell and press DELETE to erase the cell).

FIGURE
2-8

Entering a value with a comma in it

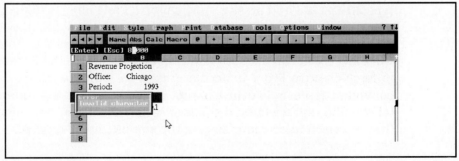

Quattro Pro 4 not only tries to show you the error but also gives you different error messages depending on the type of error. To use the example in Chapter 1, if you were trying to calculate a loan payment but misspelled the @PMT function, the result would be an "Unknown @-function" message. Many errors in entry give rise to the "Invalid cell or block address" message, which indicates that Quattro Pro 4 is attempting to read what you have typed as a formula.

Mixed Entries

The "Invalid cell" error arises when you want to enter a piece of text that begins with a number, such as **101 Main Street**. When you begin this entry Quattro Pro 4 assumes that you are entering a value, and the mode indicator changes from READY to VALUE. However, except in special circumstances, value entries cannot contain text. The result is that 101 Main Street is rejected as an invalid entry.

A related problem arises when you enter something like a phone number. Say that you enter **555-1212** you get –657 instead of a label that reads 555-1212. The problem here is that Quattro Pro 4 reads the hyphen as a minus sign and subtracts 1212 from 555. The simplest measure to avoid confusion between values and labels when you are working with entries that mix text and numbers is to begin label entries containing numbers by typing an apostrophe or other label prefix. This forces Quattro Pro 4 to accept the entry as a label. (You can also start phone numbers with a square bracket, as in **[415] 555-1212**, because a square bracket is a label indicator.)

A similar problem with a different solution is cell entries that represent dates, such as 12/25/93. Here Quattro Pro 4 reads the slashes as division signs and returns 0.0051613. The problem is not avoided if you type **25-Dec-93** and press ENTER. Quattro Pro 4 objects to the mixture of text and numbers. The solution with dates is to use the Date key, described later in this chapter. If you have a lot of data to enter in your worksheet, you can use the Data Entry command on the Database menu to force Quattro Pro 4 to accept entries as either labels or dates. This command is described in Chapter 5. The distinctions among values, labels, and dates will be discussed in greater depth in a moment, but first you need to consider storing the sample model on disk.

Storing Information

Further changes and additions to the sample model will be made as the chapter progresses, but at this point it is a good idea to store the worksheet on disk. Although there appears to be little connection between file saving and cell editing, it is important to remember that so far your cell entries only exist in RAM, the computer's random access memory. This means that the entries will disappear if the computer is turned off or suffers a power failure. A worksheet saved on disk will still be there after you turn the computer off. You have only made a few entries in the worksheet so far, but it is a good idea to use the File Save command fairly early in a session; it enables you to assign a name to the file, simplifying future save operations.

As you will read in Chapter 3, Quattro Pro 4 works in cooperation with DOS, the disk operating system, and follows DOS rules for file names. This means that you can choose the first eight characters of the name, and Quattro Pro 4 assigns the last three, known as the file extension. The file extension, which is normally .WQ1 for Quattro Pro 4 worksheets, is separated from the first 8 characters of the name by a period. As you can see from the files listed in Figure 2-9, files do not have to use all eight

The File Save list

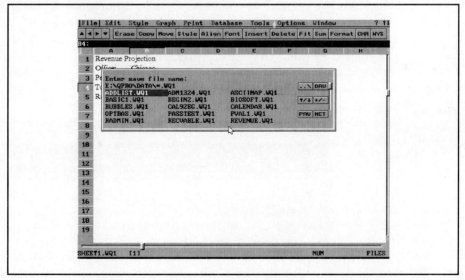

characters in front of the period. The file list shows all files that have
.WQ1 as the last three letters of their file name. This is what *.WQ1
means. (You can read more about file naming in Chapter 3.) To save the
sample model:

1. Type **/** and choose File from the main menu. Now select Save.
   Because the worksheet does not yet have a name, Quattro Pro 4
   automatically presents the file list, shown in Figure 2-9.

2. When Quattro Pro 4 presents the file list, the mode indicator at the
   bottom right of the screen changes to FILES. At the top of the list
   Quattro Pro 4 tells you where it plans to store the file, in this case
   the directory called E:\QPRO\DATA (your directory may well be
   different).

3. Below the directory name is a list of worksheet files currently stored
   in the directory. Type **ASAMPLE** and press ENTER. The worksheet
   will be stored in a file called ASAMPLE and you are returned to
   READY mode.

Note that the lower left corner of the screen now says ASAMPLE.WQ1
instead of SHEET1.WQ1. Also note that the next time you issue the File
Save command Quattro Pro 4 will know that a file called ASAMPLE.WQ1
exists and will ask whether you want to replace it, as shown in Figure
2-10. Choose Replace if you want to replace the contents of the file on
disk with the current worksheet. Choose Cancel if you do not want to
change the file already stored on disk. Choose Backup if you want to
replace the contents of the file on disk with the current worksheet but at
the same time create a copy of the existing file with a new name (the name

The Cancel/Replace/Backup dialog box

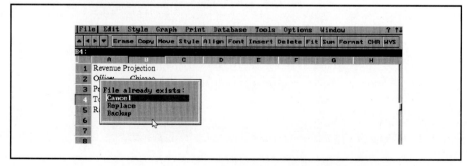

will be assigned automatically by changing .WQ1 to .BAK, as in ASAM-PLE.BAK). Quattro Pro 4 returns you to READY mode after all three of these commands.

In Chapter 3 you can read more about file operations. In Chapter 7 you can read about Quattro Pro 4's File Manager utility and the Transcript feature that helps you to re-create worksheets if your system suffers a power outage before your work has been saved.

Cell Blocks

Before you enter any more information in the sample worksheet it is important to introduce one of the most important concepts in spreadsheet work: cell blocks. This section describes techniques used throughout the rest of the book, so a few moments spent here will be helpful.

Defining a Block

A *block* of cells is a group of cells, rectangular in shape, on which you perform the same operation or command. The entries you have made so far in the sample model can be said to occupy a block extending from A1 to B5. You can refer to a block of cells by stating two diagonal coordinates. If you write this down it is normal to separate the two cells with a pair of dots. Thus you would refer to the block of cells from A1 through B5 as A1..B5. The diagram in Figure 2-11 shows what is considered to be a block, and what is not.

Blocks are used in many operations, including editing, applying styles and formats, and printing. For example, you cannot print your worksheet unless you first tell Quattro Pro 4 which block of cells you want printed. To see how Quattro Pro 4 handles cell blocks, try this exercise:

1. Type **/** to bring up the main menu and select Print.
2. The first item on the Print menu is Block. Select this option and the menu disappears, replaced by a prompt on the edit line asking for

FIGURE 2-11

What Quattro Pro 4 will accept as a block

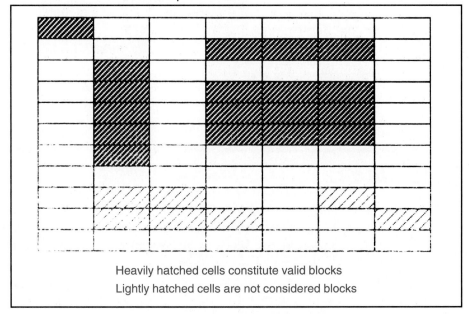

Heavily hatched cells constitute valid blocks

Lightly hatched cells are not considered blocks

the block of the spreadsheet you want to print. You can see this in Figure 2-12.

3. As you can see from Figure 2-12, the block prompt suggests a cell for you to start with. This is the cell that was current when you entered the menu system. Because you want to start the block at A1, press HOME and the prompt will change to A1.

FIGURE 2-12

A typical block prompt

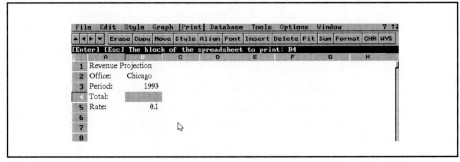

4. At this point you can move the cell selector quite freely, but what you want to do is extend the block from A1 down to B5. To do this you need to anchor the beginning point of the block at A1. Type a period or dot (.) and you will see that the prompt changes to A1..A1. (Note that you only typed one dot; Quattro Pro 4 supplied the second.)

5. A block marked by two cell coordinates on either side of two dots, as in A1..A1, is said to be anchored, and you can see why if you press the DOWN ARROW key once. This extends the highlighting to A2 so that the block prompt now reads A1..A2.

6. Now press END and then press the DOWN ARROW key. The highlighting extends down the column to the last consecutively occupied cell, A5. This extends the block so that it includes A1..A5.

7. Press RIGHT ARROW once and the highlighting will extend to the next column, making the block A1..B5, as shown in Figure 2-13.

At this point you could press ENTER to confirm the selected cells A1..B5 as the print block. However, it is worthwhile taking a moment to experiment with block operations.

Unlocking and Rejecting Block Coordinates

You may find that you want to begin your block at a point other than the current cell. You can press ESC or click [Esc] to unlock the block coordinates. This removes the second coordinate. You can then move the

Selecting or highlighting a block of cells

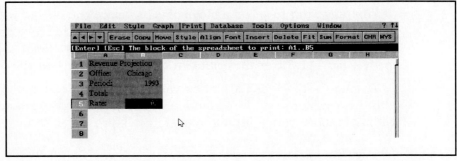

cell pointer to change the first coordinate. A slightly different action is performed when you press the BACKSPACE key.

Suppose that you have set A1..B5 as the print block and selected Quit from the Print menu to return to the worksheet. Now you move the cell selector to C1. If you go back to Print Block you will find that A1..B5 is retained as the block setting. When you press ESC, Quattro Pro 4 unlocks the coordinates so that A1..B5 changes to A1. However, press BACKSPACE and Quattro Pro 4 will reject A1..B5 completely in favor of the cell that was current when you entered the menu system, in this case C1.

Cell Blocks and Active Corners

When you have marked A1..B5 as the print block, you will notice that further use of the arrow keys changes the lower right corner of the block. In fact, you can adjust the block by moving any one of the four corners. The lower right corner is simply the default active corner. To change the active corner of a block you type a period (.). You will see the active corner change to the bottom left. This is shown by the block cursor and the block prompt, which changes (in this case from A1..B5 to B1..A5). Type another period and the top left becomes the active corner.

You can keep typing a period to move the corner all the way around the block. This is mainly useful in adjusting large blocks, when you want to adjust the top or left side of the block without completely rejecting the current block coordinates. It does not matter to Quattro Pro 4 whether you select a block as B5..A1 or A1..B5.

Preselecting Cell Blocks

You may want to select a block of cells before you choose a command that will affect them. For example, you can select A1..B5 before issuing the Print Block command. This selection tells Quattro Pro 4 to automatically accept A1..B5 as the print block as soon as you issue the command.

To select a block of cells when you are using READY mode, you can either use a mouse or the Extend key, SHIFT-F7. To select a block of cells with the mouse you point to the top left cell, press the left mouse button and hold it down while you are moving the pointer to the lower right cell. You can then release the mouse button, and the cells will remain selected. Note that you can also select from lower right to upper left if you want; Quattro Pro 4 is not fussy about the direction you use.

To select a block of cells without the mouse when you are using READY mode, you move the cell selector into the top left cell, then press the Extend key, SHIFT-F7. You will see the message EXT in the lower status line. Now use the cursor movement keys and note that the highlighting is extended in the direction you point. When you have highlighted the block you want, you can go to the menu to use a command. If you want to turn off the extended highlighting before using a command—in other words, to cancel it—you can press SHIFT-F7 to turn off the EXT message. The next cursor movement key you press removes the extended highlighting. In fact, pressing any noncursor movement key while the EXT message is displayed removes the message and enables you to press any cursor key to reject the extended highlighting.

Numbers, Formats, Dates, and the Style Menu

You have seen that Quattro Pro 4 distinguishes between value and label entries by the first character of a new entry. Anything that begins with one of the following characters is treated as a value: the numbers 0 through 9 . + − (@ # $. These items are called *value indicators*. If you do not begin an entry with one of these characters, Quattro Pro 4 treats the entry as a label. This section discusses entering values and changing their appearance.

Long Numbers

You have already seen that Quattro Pro 4 aligns numbers on the right of the cell, as in cells B3 and B5 of the sample model. Occasionally you will need to enter a large number into a Quattro Pro 4 worksheet. With the cell selector in B4, type **1234567890** and press ENTER. This entry causes 1.2E+09 to be displayed in the worksheet. The cell identifier lets you know that the number 1234567890 is still stored by Quattro Pro 4. What you are seeing is the scientific notation 1.2×10 to the power of 9.

The reason that Quattro Pro 4 alters the appearance of long numbers is that the default column width of nine characters can accommodate fewer than nine digits, due to the need to keep some space between the last digit on the right and the right edge of the cell. If Quattro Pro 4 did not maintain this space, long numbers in adjoining cells would appear to run together. Widening the column by using the Style Column Width command described later in this chapter restores the number to its normal appearance (note that in WYSIWYG mode the exact number of digits that will fit in a cell varies according to the font being used, whereas in character mode the maximum number of digits is always one less than the column width setting). If you regularly work with numbers in the millions and billions, you can use the Scientific numeric format, using the commands described next. Before you continue, press DELETE to clear cell B4.

Numeric Formats

The appearance of numbers in the worksheet is controlled by something called *numeric format.* You saw earlier that if you put commas in a number you are entering, Quattro Pro 4 will reject it. The idea is that you enter plain numbers and then dress them up with a suitable numeric format. When you create a fresh worksheet, it uses the General format to begin with. As you can see from cells B3 and B5 of the sample model, this format does not show decimal places unless you enter them. If you enter 1993, you get 1993 with no decimal digits. If you enter .1, you get 0.1.

The same is true when you enter formulas. If a formula results in a value with decimal places, the General format displays the decimal digits. However, the General format may not be able to show all of the digits to the right of the decimal point. If you enter 100/3 you will see 33 followed by a decimal point and as many 3s as will fit in the cell.

To see how numeric formats affect your work, you can make further entries in the sample worksheet. The entries will establish one of the sources of revenue that is being projected. Follow these steps, which will produce the results shown in Figure 2-14:

1. Move the cell selector to E2 then type **January** and press RIGHT ARROW.

2. In F2 type **February**, press RIGHT ARROW and type **March**.

3. Now move the cell selector to D3 and type **Hardware** then press RIGHT ARROW.

4. In E3 type **4567** and press RIGHT ARROW.

5. In F3 type a formula that will make the February sales in F3 ten percent larger than the January sales in E3, in other words, **1.1*E3**.

6. When you have entered the formula, move the cell selector to G3 and enter **1.1*F3**, which makes the March sales ten percent larger than the February sales.

If you enter a different starting value in E3, such as 5000, you will see that F3 and G3 both change. The value in F3 is 1.1 times whatever you enter in E3. The value in G3 is 1.1 times whatever value is in F3. Another way of describing the formulas in F3 and G3 is that they mean "1.1 times the cell to the left." When described like this, both formulas sound identical and this is exactly the way Quattro Pro 4 sees them. If you copy the formula from F3 to any other cell in the worksheet, it will still mean "1.1 times the cell to the left." This approach to formulas will be important later on when you use the Edit Copy command to expand the model.

As you can see from Figure 2-14, when you use the default format and the number of decimal places produced by the formulas varies, the

FIGURE
2-14

The next stage of the sample model

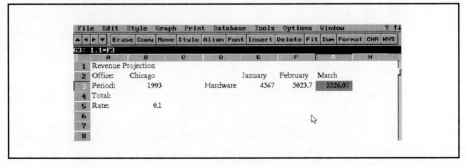

decimal point appears at varying positions in the cell. This may well be considered unprofessional, and next you'll see how to improve the appearance of numbers.

The Default Format

The default numeric format can be changed for a part of the worksheet or for all of it. For example, if most of the numbers in a worksheet represent money, you might want to choose either the Currency or the Comma format as your default format. To change the global or default format for the sample worksheet:

1. Type **/** then select Options, followed by Formats, and then Numeric Format. The menu you see in Figure 2-15 shows all of the Numeric Format choices. They are listed with examples in Table 2-2.

2. To select the Comma format, which uses commas as the thousands separator, simply type a comma (,).

3. To use the Comma format you must state how many decimal places should be used, so Quattro Pro 4 prompts you to supply a value

FIGURE 2-15   The Numeric Format choices

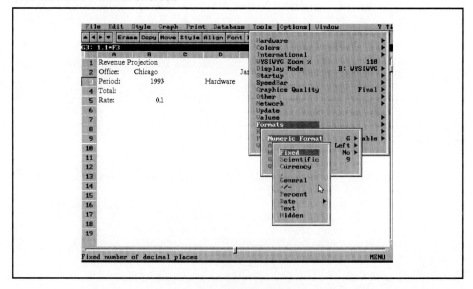

from 0 to 15, as shown in Figure 2-16. Quattro Pro 4 suggests two decimal places, but you can type your choice over this before pressing ENTER or clicking the Enter button to confirm the format selection. In this case simply press ENTER to accept the suggested two decimal places. Use the Quit option to return to READY mode and see the effect of the new format.

Figure 2-17 shows the result of using Comma as the default numeric format. The revenue figures are now consistent in their appearance and look more like financial values. However, the year in B3 no longer looks like a year. Note that only the appearance of the numbers has changed;

Format Choices

Format Name	Description of Format
Fixed	No commas in 1000s, negatives in parentheses, user-defined decimal places: 2000.99 (2000.99)
Scientific	Exponential notation, negatives in parentheses, user-defined decimal places: 2.00E+03 (2.00E+03)
Currency	User-defined currency prefix, commas in 1,000s, negatives in parentheses, user-defined decimal places: 2,000.99 ($2,000.99)
,(Comma)	Commas in 1,000s, negatives in parentheses, user-defined decimal places: 2,000.99 (2,000.99)
General	Varies decimal places; uses exponential notation for large numbers; negatives preceded by minus sign (–)
+/–	Represents positive numbers as plus signs (+), negatives as minus signs (–) for simple bar charts
Percent	Divides contents by 100; uses % sign as suffix
Date	Various options, described in Chapter 3, including formats for time values
Text (Formulas)	Displays formulas in cells rather than their values

TABLE 2-2

FIGURE 2-16

Deciding the number of decimal places

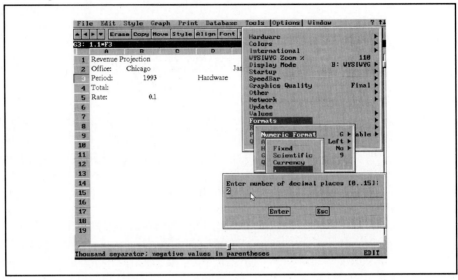

the underlying values in the worksheet are not altered. (In Figure 2-17 the cell selector was moved to B3 so that you can see that it still contains 1993.) When you change the default format with the Options Formats command, the change remains in effect for the current worksheet and is saved with the worksheet. Other worksheets are not affected.

FIGURE 2-17

Using Comma (,) as the default format, two decimal places

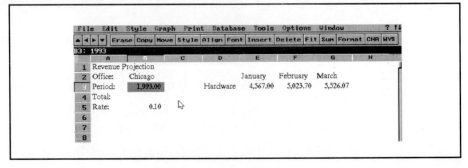

Style and Numeric Format

At this point, Quattro Pro 4 has to be told that some cells need a numeric format different from the default. Formatting individual cells or blocks of cells is the task of the Style commands, and you can see the Style menu in Figure 2-18. The second item on the menu is Numeric Format (the first item, Alignment, is discussed later in this chapter). The commands on the Style menu enable you to alter the appearance of a section of the worksheet.

You normally begin a Style command by placing the cell selector on the cell you want to change, or in the top left corner of the group of cells if there is more than one cell to be worked on. In this case you want to alter the appearance of B3 so select B3 before you type **/** to activate the main menu. When you pick Style and then Numeric Format you have the same format options as in the Options, Formats, Numeric Format menu, plus Reset, which you use to change a previously formatted cell back to the default format.

The Fixed format works well for entering years, because it omits the comma. When you choose the Fixed format you are asked for the number of decimal places. Type **0** and then press ENTER to confirm the format.

FIGURE
2-18

The Style menu

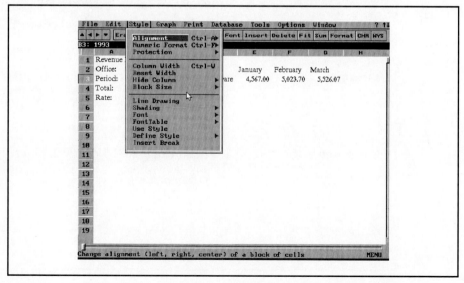

Now you will have to perform one more step: pointing out the cells that need to be modified. Quattro Pro 4 assumes that you want to format the cell that was current when you started the command. In this case, the cell is referred to as block B3..B3. You could extend this block, using the cursor keys to point out additional cells to be included. However, in this case you only want to change B3, so you simply press ENTER to confirm B3..B3. You can see the effect in Figure 2-19, which also shows you the result of using the Style Numeric Format command on B5, but choosing the Percent format, with two decimal places. (Go ahead and try this now if you want your worksheet to match the sample.)

As you can see from Figure 2-19, the cell identifier tells you that B3 has a Fixed format of 0 decimal places assigned to it (F0). If you select B5 you see that the cell identifier there says (P2) indicating that the Percent format has been used, with two decimal places. The full list of format identifiers can be seen in Table 2-3.

Cells formatted with the Style commands are not affected by changes to the default format assigned by the Options Formats command. Chang-

TABLE
2-3

Format Identifiers

Code	Format
F0 through F15	Fixed (0-15 decimal places)
S0 through S15	Scientific (0-15 decimal places)
C0 through C15	Currency (0-15 decimal places)
,0 through ,15	Comma/Financial (0-15 decimal places)
G	General (variable decimal places)
+	+/- (the bar graph format)
P0 through P15	Percentage (0-15 decimal places)
D1 through D5	Date formats
T	Text
D6 through D9	Time formats
H	Hidden

FIGURE
2-19

Using the Fixed format, zero decimal places

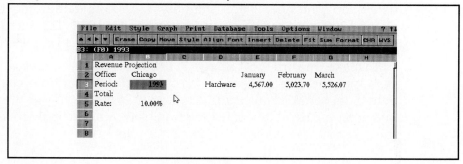

ing the default format at this point would affect the appearance of all values in the worksheet, *except* for those formatted with the Style Numeric Format command. In other words, E3 through G3 would change; B3 and B5 would not. If you were to select B3 and then issue the Style Numeric Format Reset command, the format in B3 would revert to whatever current default format was dictated by the Options Formats command.

Dates and Numeric Formats

You have already seen that Quattro Pro 4 has a problem with labels that begin with numbers and numbers that contain text. If you take a moment to think about dates you will see that they form a special category of problem entries. For example, if you enter **1/1/93**, Quattro Pro 4 thinks that you want to divide 1 by 1 and then by 93. However, if you enter **'1/1/93**, the apostrophe will force Quattro Pro 4 to see what follows as a label. The problem with this approach is that labels have no value. You may want to calculate the number of days between two dates, and you cannot do this if they are both labels.

As far as spreadsheet programs are concerned, dates are a special type of number. Quattro Pro 4 is designed to perform math with dates and times. For a computer program to read a date, such as 1/1/93, as something that has value, the date must be converted to a number. Quattro Pro 4 performs this conversion by calculating the number of days between the date involved and the end of the last century. This is the date's serial number. Thus, January 1, 1900 is date number 1. Move ahead 1000 days and you have September 27, 1902. The date 1/1/93 is day number 33,970, otherwise known as New Year's Day, 1993.

To make Quattro Pro 4 accept 1/1/93 as a date, you press CTRL-D and then type the date. When you press ENTER Quattro Pro 4 converts the date to its serial number and displays it as a date. If you press CTRL-D and enter a date in any of the following formats, Quattro Pro 4 converts the date to a number but displays it as a date:

	Date	Format
1.	25-Dec-93	DD-MMM-YY
2.	25-Dec	DD-MMM
3.	Dec-93	MMM-YY
4.	12/25/93	MM/DD/YY
5.	12/25	MM/DD

If you type in the date using formats 2 and 5, Quattro Pro 4 calculates the serial number based on the current year. Format 3 assumes you mean the first day of the month.

The formats just listed are the same as the ones presented by Quattro Pro 4 when you choose Date from the Style Numeric Format menu. After you have entered a date with CTRL-D you can change its appearance by applying any of the Date formats. Bear in mind that the first format, DD-MMM-YY, produces a date that is too wide for the default column width of nine characters. For more information about dates and times and the way they can be used in calculations, see Chapter 4.

Style and Alignment

The Style menu also enables you to alter the alignment of labels and values in a section of the worksheet. For example, the default alignment for the sample worksheet is left, but you might want the months in row 2 to be centered. To do this you use the Style Alignment command, as follows:

1. Move the cell selector to E2 and type **/** to activate the menu. Select Style.

2. From the Style menu select Alignment. You will see four options: General, Left, Right, and Center. The first option, General, aligns numbers on the right and leaves labels to follow the default setting established by the Options Formats Align Labels command described earlier.

3. The Left, Right, and Center options align values and labels on the side of the cell indicated by the name. In this case select Center. Quattro Pro 4 now asks which block of cells you want to align and suggests E2..E2.

4. To extend the block to G2, press END then press RIGHT ARROW. This extends the highlighting to the last occupied cell on the right, making the block E2..G2. Now press ENTER to return to the READY mode.

The results can be seen in Figure 2-20. The label prefix in all three cells has been changed from ' to ^. These and any other labels in the worksheet are not affected by any subsequent changes to the alignment made by the Options Formats Align Labels command. That command only affects new labels in the worksheet. However, if you want previously entered labels to revert to the default alignment, you can use the Style Alignment General option and select those labels.

There are many Style commands besides Numeric Format and Alignment. You will find the more advanced Style commands discussed in the next chapter. At this point it is important to look at the commands used to edit a worksheet.

FIGURE
2-20

The effect of centering labels

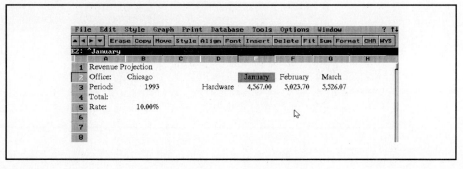

Spreadsheet Editing

One of the great advantages of an electronic spreadsheet over pencil and paper is the ability to copy and rearrange cells. In this section you will learn how to use the following commands from the Edit menu: Copy, Erase Block, Copy Special, Move, Insert, and Delete.

Edit Copy

In Figure 2-21 you can see the next stage of the sample model. A second line has been added to the revenue projection table. This represents revenue from software sales. Like the hardware sales, software sales are projected to grow by 10 percent per month. This means that the entries in D4 through G4 are very similar to those in D3 through G3. Only the label in D4 and the value in E4 are different. The formulas are essentially the same.

Earlier it was pointed out that the formula in F3, 1.1*E3, actually means "1.1 times the cell to the left." If that formula is copied from F3 to F4, Quattro Pro 4 changes the cell reference so that the formula in F4 means the same thing, 1.1 times the cell to the left. That is why the entry in F4 in Figure 2-21 reads 1.1*E4. What you will do now is copy D3..G3 to D4..G4 and then edit cells D4 and E4. The following steps will yield the results shown in Figure 2-21.

FIGURE 2-21

The next stage of the sample model

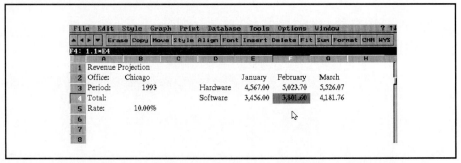

1. Place the cell selector in D3, type **/**, and select Edit. You will see the Edit menu shown in Figure 2-22. Select Copy (mouse users can simply click on Copy in the SpeedBar).

2. At this point Quattro Pro 4 wants to know the Source Block, the cells that you want to copy. The current cell is suggested, as in D3..D3.

3. Because this block is already anchored, you can simply press RIGHT ARROW to extend it to G3. A shortcut would be to press END, then RIGHT ARROW, extending the block to the last occupied cell on the right.

4. With the Source Block prompt reading D3..G3 press ENTER and Quattro Pro 4 will ask you to point out the Destination. Once again the current cell is suggested, but the block reference is not anchored. You can simply press DOWN ARROW to indicate the correct Destination, D4.

5. There is no need to anchor or extend the Destination Block. When you press ENTER to confirm D4 as the Destination, Quattro Pro 4 automatically copies the contents of D3..G3 into D4 through G4.

You can now proceed to edit the contents of D4 and E4. You can edit the label Hardware in D4 to read **Software** and replace 4567 in E4 with

FIGURE
2-22

The Edit menu

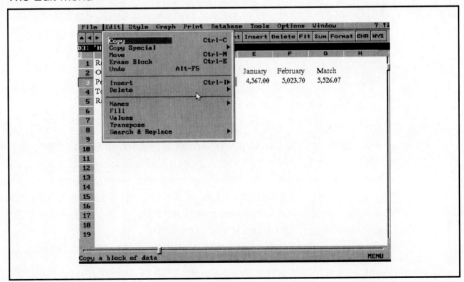

3456. The results will appear as in Figure 2-21. You can see that the formula in F4 is 1.1*E4. This is not an exact copy of the formula in F3, which was 1.1*F3, but Quattro Pro 4 translated the copied formula *relative* to its new location. This ability to work with relative cell references is a great help in many spreadsheet editing situations.

Note that Quattro Pro 4 made quite an assumption about the Destination for the copy. Whenever your Source Block consists of more than one cell and you point to a single unanchored cell as the Destination, Quattro Pro 4 will assume that the Destination cell is the top left corner of a block of cells equal in size and shape to the Source Block. This is generally a helpful assumption, but you need to be aware that the Edit Copy command can wipe out existing cell entries with the data it copies. For example, if there had been previous entries in F4 and G4, they would have been replaced by the copied cells.

To see how Quattro Pro 4 makes more than one copy of a group of cells, try the following steps that make two more rows for the revenue projection table:

1. Place the cell selector in D4; type **/**; and select Edit, then Copy. Alternatively, click Copy in the SpeedBar or press the Copy shortcut key, CTRL-C.

2. Quattro Pro 4 prompts for the Source Block and suggests D4..D4. Press END then RIGHT ARROW to select D4..G4 and then press ENTER.

3. Quattro Pro 4 prompts for the Destination and suggests D4. Press DOWN ARROW once to select D5 and type a period (.) to anchor this cell so that the Destination prompt reads D5..D5.

4. Press DOWN ARROW again to extend the Destination Block to D5..D6. Press ENTER to complete the copy. The result is two copies of D4..G4, as shown in Figure 2-23.

Note that when the Copy operation is completed the cell selector is left in the current cell—the one it occupied before the Copy command was started. The copies you have just created need editing, so go ahead and change D5 to Supplies and D6 to Training. Change E5 to 2345 and E6 to 1234. The results can be seen in Figure 2-24. As with the previous Copy operation, Quattro Pro 4 has adjusted the copied formulas so that their cell references are correct, relative to their location.

FIGURE
2-23

The effect of making two copies

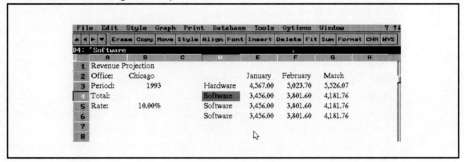

Multiple Copies

You have seen that Quattro Pro 4 makes a single copy of a Source block of cells if you identify a single cell as the Destination. If you select more than one cell as the Destination, Quattro Pro 4 can make multiple copies, as when you copy D4..G4 to D5..D6. You could use a similar operation to create additional columns for the table in Figure 2-24. For example, you could copy March, cells G2..G6, to H2..J2, and thus add three months to the table (there is no need to actually do this). Thus you can create multiple copies of a single column if the Destination is a number of columns. You can create multiple copies of a single row if the Destination is a number of rows.

FIGURE
2-24

The copies after editing

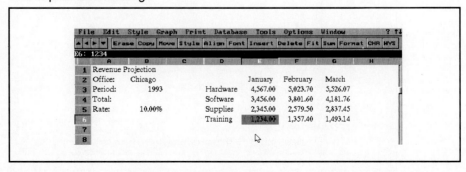

At times you may want to create multiple copies of several rows when the Destination is the same row. Consider the labels in D3..D6 in Figure 2-24. Suppose that you want two more sets of these labels, placed lower down in column D to form the basis of two more tables, as shown in Figure 2-25. If you select D3..D6 as the Source and D7 as the Destination, Edit Copy will give you one copy. The same is true however much you expand the Destination to include further cells in column D. The trick to making multiple copies of several rows in the same column is to expand the Source Block. If you use D3..D10 as the Source Block and then use D7 as the Destination, Quattro Pro 4 will fill D3..D14 with two copies of the entries in D3..D6.

The rule for this type of Copy operation is that you add cells to the Source Block in multiples of the number of cells you want to copy. Thus, if you add four cells to the four you want to copy, in essence doubling the Source Block, you get two copies. If you add eight cells, tripling the Source Block, you get three copies, and so on. The results shown in Figure 2-25 were achieved by copying with D2..D11 as the Source and D7 as the Destination. This repeated both the labels in D3..D6 and the empty cell, D2. Take the following steps to see how it works.

FIGURE 2-25

Extra copies of labels

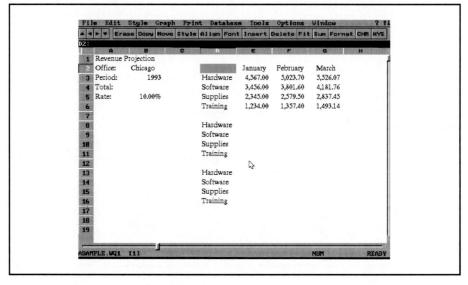

1. Place the cell selector in D2 and issue the Edit Copy command.

2. Extend the Source Block downward so that it is D2..D11, a total of ten cells—twice the number of cells you actually want to copy. Press ENTER to confirm the Source Block.

3. Select D7 as the Destination and press ENTER. The results will be the same as in Figure 2-25.

Although this technique for creating multiple copies may take a little getting used to, it is quite handy when you are building repetitive models. In fact, these extra labels are not needed in the sample model and so they will be erased, as described next. After that, you'll learn about the Copy Special command.

Edit Erase Block

You have already seen that you can erase the contents of a cell by selecting it and pressing the DELETE key. When you need to erase more than one cell you can use the Erase Block command from the Edit menu. As with other Edit commands, the first thing that Quattro Pro 4 wants to know when you issue the command is which cells are to be modified. Suppose that you had placed the cell selector in D8 before you issued the Edit Erase Block command. Quattro Pro 4 would suggest D8..D8 as the block of cells to be erased. You could then adjust or extend the block.

In the sample model you want to erase the extra labels in D8 through D16, as shown in Figure 2-26. With these cells highlighted you can press ENTER to confirm the command. The cell contents are immediately removed. The results mean that the sample worksheet will again look like Figure 2-24. Mouse users can access the Erase Block command by clicking on the Erase button in the SpeedBar. Note that Edit Erase Block is different from Edit Delete, which will be described later in this chapter.

If you have the Undo feature enabled, as described earlier in this chapter, you can reverse the Erase Block command. Otherwise, the entries are lost. There are several other precautions you can take when you use the Erase Block command. You can save the worksheet using the File Save command before you issue the Erase Block command. Then, if you erase the wrong cells, you can retrieve the saved version of the

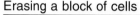

FIGURE
2-26

Erasing a block of cells

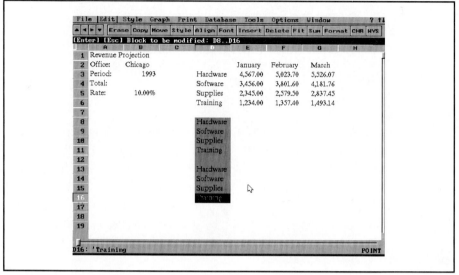

worksheet. Another way of recovering from a mistaken erase operation is to use the Transcript feature, described in Chapter 7.

Special Copies

All of the values copied in the previous examples were formatted with the default format for the worksheet (set with the Options Formats command). However, you may need to copy a cell, such as B5 in the sample worksheet, that has a special format applied with the Style command. Normally, Quattro Pro 4 copies both the contents of a cell and its format. This saves you going to the trouble of formatting the copied cell or cells.

There may be times when you want to copy just the contents of a cell. This means that the copy will not retain its format. At other times you might want to copy the way a certain cell looks, rather than copy its contents. In both of these scenarios, the Edit Copy Special command can be helpful. When you issue the Edit Copy Special command, Quattro Pro 4 asks whether you want to copy Contents or Format. Choose Contents if you want to strip the Source cells of their format and allow the format of the Destination cells to take precedence. Choose Format if you want to apply the formatting used by the Source cell in one or more Destination cells. The Copy Special command will be very useful when you are working with more complex formats, like those discussed in the next chapter.

Edit Move

There are times when you want to rearrange spreadsheet entries. The Edit Move command comes in handy for this. Suppose that you want the table in the sample worksheet in Figure 2-24 to be moved up one line so that the months are level with the label Revenue Projection in A1. Here is how the Edit Move command would handle the job:

1. Place the cell selector in D2. Type **/** and select Edit, then Move. Alternatively, you can activate the Edit Move command by clicking on the Move button on the SpeedBar or pressing the shortcut key combination CTRL-M.

2. Extend the Source Block from D2..D2 to D2..G6. A quick way to do this is to press RIGHT ARROW, then END, followed by RIGHT ARROW, followed by END and then DOWN ARROW.

3. Press ENTER to confirm D2..G6 as the Source Block and then move the cell selector to D1 for the Destination. When you press ENTER, the move is completed.

You can see the results of Edit Move in Figure 2-27, where the cell selector has been moved to F2 in order to illustrate the change that Edit Move makes to the formulas in the Source Block. You can see that the formula, which was 1.1*E3 in F3, has been translated into 1.1*E2 now that it is in F2.

Edit Insert

There are other ways of rearranging a worksheet besides moving cells. You can insert extra columns or rows. If you select Insert from the Edit

FIGURE
2-27

The effect of Edit Move

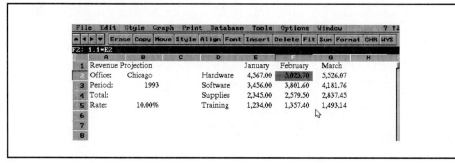

menu, you will see that there are four options: Rows, Columns, Row Block, and Column Block. The Row command inserts one or more new rows across the entire width of the worksheet. The rows are inserted above the current cell. The Column command inserts one or more new columns from the top to the bottom of the worksheet. The columns are inserted to the left of the current cell. The Row Block command moves a section of the worksheet down one or more rows. The Column Block command moves a section of the worksheet one or more columns to the right.

To see how the Edit Insert command works, you will insert several rows at the top of the sample worksheet. You can carry out these instructions with the cell selector anywhere in row 1, but for convenience press HOME to select A1:

1. Type **/** and select Edit and then Insert (you can click on Insert in the SpeedBar or press CTRL-I).

2. Select Rows and Quattro Pro 4 asks you to enter the row insert block. The initial suggestion is the current cell, in this case A1..A1. If you want to insert one row, you press ENTER at this point.

3. To insert more than one row, extend the row insert block. Press DOWN ARROW once so that the block is now A1..A2. If the row insert block is two rows long, two rows will be inserted. Press ENTER.

The result can be seen in Figure 2-28. Once again, Quattro Pro 4 has adjusted your worksheet formulas so that they are accurate in their new location. Bear in mind that a new row was inserted across all of the columns of the worksheet. This can means that you risk affecting tables that you have created elsewhere in the worksheet and that are not visible in the current screen. This is why Quattro Pro 4 enables you to move the cell selector to the left or right when you are pointing out the row insert block. By using the cell selector, you can move across the worksheet to check that no other entries will be affected.

Another way to prevent damage to adjoining areas of the worksheet when you insert rows is to use the Insert Row Block command. For example, suppose you want to move the table of numbers in Figure 2-28 down one row from D3..G7 to D4..G8, without affecting the entries in A3..B7. You can use Edit Insert Row Block and select D2..G2 as the row insert block. As a result, Quattro Pro 4 shifts all cells below D2..G2 down one row (do not actually do this now). Note that this command requires a lot of memory, so you may not be able to insert a very large Row Block unless you have extra memory in your computer.

The Edit Insert Columns command works the same as the Rows command, inserting one or more columns to the left of the current cell. The inserted columns cover all rows in the worksheet. The Column Block command performs a move operation similar to the Row Block command. All cells on the selected rows are shifted one or more columns to the right.

Edit Delete

Just as useful as the ability to insert complete or partial columns and rows is the ability to delete them. Select Delete from the Edit menu and

FIGURE 2-28

The effect of Insert Rows

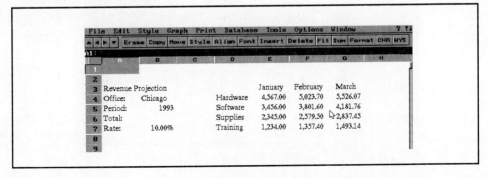

note that there are four options matching those for Edit Insert: Rows, Columns, Row Block, and Column Block. Follow these steps to remove row 2 from the sample model:

1. Place the cell selector in A2 (in fact, any cell in row 2 will work).
2. Select Edit Delete from the menu system or click on the Delete button in the SpeedBar.
3. Select Rows and Quattro Pro 4 will ask for the block of rows to delete.
4. Press ENTER to accept A2..A2 as the block. This will remove row 2, leaving the label Revenue Projection in A2.

Bear in mind that the Delete Rows command removes rows in their entirety, right across the worksheet. The Block options on the Delete menu remove only a portion of a row or column. To see how the Delete Row Block command works, follow these steps:

1. Press HOME to place the cell selector in A1. Select Edit Delete from the menu system and choose Row Block.
2. Select A1..B1 as the block and press ENTER.

The result can be seen in Figure 2-29. The contents of the cells below the deleted block are moved up one row, whereas the rest of the cells in the worksheet remain unchanged. At this point you can use the Insert Row Block command to move the cells in A2..B5.

The effect of Insert Row Block

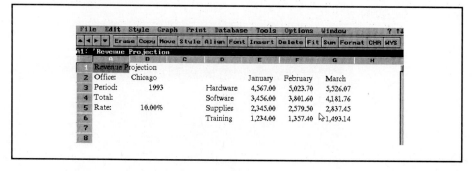

1. Place the cell selector in A2. Select Edit Insert from the menu system and choose Row Block.

2. Select A2..B2 as the block and press ENTER.

The result can be seen in Figure 2-30. The contents of the cells below the inserted block are moved down one row, but the rest of the cells in the worksheet remain unchanged. At this point you can save the sample model again using the File Save Replace command.

Using Formulas

Formulas are where much of the power of a spreadsheet lies. Whether you are simply adding cells together or calculating internal rate of return on an investment, the ability to establish a relationship between cells gives you tremendous number-crunching ability. The built-in formulas, such as the one used to calculate a loan payment in Chapter 1, are discussed in depth in Chapter 4. In this section you will create column and row totals and examine the problems of absolute and relative cell references.

Entering Formulas

In the sample model last seen in Figure 2-30, you want to total up the revenue for January and place the answer in E7. You might be tempted

FIGURE
2-30

The effect of further editing

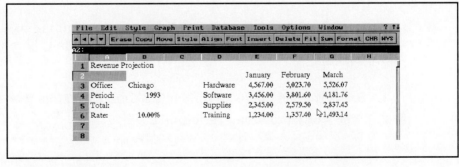

to enter the formula E3+E4+E5+E6. This is a good effort, but Quattro Pro 4 would reject it as a formula because it begins with E. Because this is a letter, Quattro Pro 4 reads the entry as a label. A better effort is **+E3+E4+E5+E6**. This is accepted as a formula because it begins with a plus sign (+), which is a value indicator.

The plus sign is very handy when you have to enter a formula that consists solely of cell references. When you entered the growth formula **1.1*E3** you did not need to precede it with a plus sign because the first character was 1, a value indicator. However, you could have entered **+E3*1.1**, and that would have been accepted.

Although the formula +E3+E4+E5+E6 gives the correct total for the revenue in January, there is an alternative method of adding these items. If you consider these cells to be part of a group, or block, you can apply a function that sums the contents of the block. The function that does this is @SUM. Like the other Quattro Pro 4 functions, the @SUM function consists of the @ sign followed by the function name, SUM, followed by parentheses that contain the function argument. The argument used by @SUM is the block of cells to which the function is applied. In this case, the block is E3..E6. The completed formula is thus @SUM(E3..E6).

To see how this works in the sample model, follow these steps:

1. Move the cell selector to E7.
2. Type **@SUM(E3.E6)**, noting that you only need to type one period.
3. Press ENTER and notice from the cell identifier that Quattro Pro 4 records this as @SUM(E3..E6), adding an extra period to make the block easier to see. The correct answer displayed in the worksheet is 11,602.00, as shown in Figure 2-31. (If your worksheet shows asterisks instead of this number, you need to widen the column using the procedure described in a moment.)

Instead of typing formulas, you can use the pointing method. This works either with keystrokes or with the mouse. First, here's the key-stroke method:

1. Select the cell that is to contain the formula, in this case F7.
2. Type **@SUM(** to begin the formula.

3. Press the UP ARROW key to select F3. Type a period (.) to anchor the block as F3..F3.

4. Press END, then DOWN ARROW to extend the block so that it is F3..F6.

5. Type a closing parenthesis and press ENTER to finish the formula.

Instead of typing the beginning of the formula as just described in step 2, you can use these two steps:

1. Press ALT-F3 to display a list of functions. Press F2 to search for the SUM function. Quattro Pro 4 will prompt you at the bottom of the screen, saying Search for: *.

2. Type **S**. Quattro Pro 4 highlights the first function that begins with S. Now type **U**; the highlighting moves to SUM. Press ENTER and Quattro Pro 4 displays @SUM(on the edit line.

Instead of typing formulas you can use the mouse. Here is how you would create the total in G7 using the mouse method:

1. Select the cell that is to contain the formula, G7.

2. Click on the edit line to activate EDIT mode and then click on the @ button. Click on the vertical scroll bar to bring the SUM function into view. Click on SUM and Quattro Pro 4 types @SUM(on the edit line.

FIGURE
2-31

The results of @SUM(E3..E6)

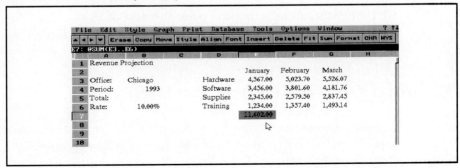

3. Point to G3, press the left mouse button, and hold it down while you drag down to G6, then release.

4. Click on the closing parenthesis button and then click on [Enter].

If you have tried all of these techniques, you have created formulas in E7 through G7. If not, create the formulas now. At this point you can create total formulas in column H to sum the rows of the table. The following technique illustrates how to create the first formula in H3, then copy it to H4..H6:

1. Move the cell selector to H3 and create the formula @SUM(E3..G3) using one of the methods just given.

2. The answer, 15,116.77, may not fit in the cell, so you will see asterisks instead. If this is the case, use the Options Formats command and select Global Width. Type **10** and press ENTER to set the normal column width to 10 instead of 9. Use the Quit command to return to the READY mode.

3. Type **/** and select Edit Copy, or press CTRL-C, or click on the Copy button in the SpeedBar. Press ENTER to accept H3..H3 as the Source Block.

4. Type a period to anchor H3..H3 as the Destination Block. Press DOWN ARROW four times to extend the Destination Block so that it is H3..H7. Press ENTER to complete the command.

The result, visible in Figure 2-32, is a series of formulas that provide row totals for the table, including the grand total in H7. Note that in this operation the single-cell Source Block was part of the Destination Block. Cell H3 was actually copied over the top of itself, but this poses no problem to Quattro Pro 4 and does not affect the formula result.

Tidying Up and Using TurboSum

Several steps are necessary to complete the current stage of the sample model, which can then be saved for use in later examples:

1. Enter the centered label, **^Total**, in H2.

FIGURE
2-32

Totals for columns and rows

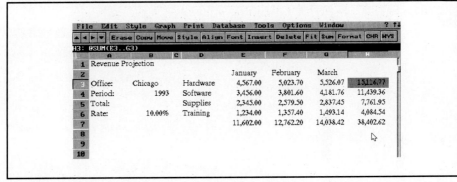

2. Enter the word **Total** as a left-aligned label in D7.

3. Because the model actually shows the first quarter revenue and not the whole year, move the cell selector to B4 and replace 1993 with **1st Quarter**, remembering to begin the entry with an apostrophe to make it a label.

4. In order to see the entire model in the width of your screen, narrow the width of column C. Move the cell selector to any cell in C, type **/**, and select Style then Column Width. Type **2** and press ENTER (the Column Width command will be dealt with in more detail in the next chapter).

5. To show the grand total from H7 in B5, move the cell selector to B5. Enter the formula **+H7**, which ensures that the value in H7 will always be reflected in B5.

The model should now look like Figure 2-33, and you can resave it with File Save Replace.

If you are using a mouse with Quattro Pro 4, there is a very quick procedure for creating @SUM formulas in model like this. This procedure was not introduced earlier because it is important to know how @SUM formulas are created the long way before you learn the shortcut. Quattro Pro 4's TurboSum feature automatically creates @SUM formulas for columns and rows.

In the sample model you could use TurboSum with the worksheet as it was in Figure 2-30. You would use the mouse to select the cells to be summed, E3..G6, plus a row and a column of blank cells at the bottom

FIGURE
2-33

The total from H7 displayed in B5

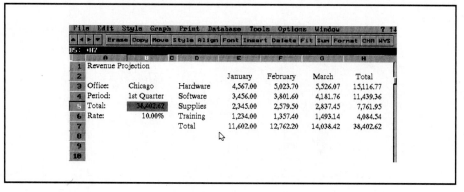

and to the right of this block. The complete block to be selected would thus be E3..H7. TurboSum will create @SUM formulas in the blank cells E7..H7 and H3..H7. To use TurboSum you click on the Sum button in the SpeedBar. The response is immediate: The column and row totals are created.

You can use the Sum button with single rows or columns as well as larger blocks. Just remember to include a blank cell at the bottom of the column or at the right of the row. This blank cell enables TurboSum to create the formula. It is possible to access TurboSum from the keyboard, but you must first create a macro, as described in Chapter 11.

Formula Errors

If you make what Quattro Pro 4 considers to be an error when creating a formula, using either the typing or the pointing method of formula building, pressing ENTER to place the formula in a cell will generate a beep and an error message. Sometimes the message can be quite specific, such as "Missing right paren" when you forget to close a pair of parentheses. Press ENTER at the message and Quattro Pro 4 switches to EDIT mode. Quattro Pro 4 points out your error by placing the cursor at the first mistake it reads in your entry. For example, entering @PMT(E1,E2,E3,) causes Quattro Pro 4 to place the edit cursor under the superfluous third comma so that you can press DELETE to remove it. The corrected formula can then be reentered.

Problems with Relatives

At this point the sample model shows revenue for the first quarter of the year growing at a rate of 10 percent per month. Because the growth rate is stated in B6, you might be tempted to change the formula in F3 from 1.1*E3 to (1+B6)*E3. You could then copy the new formula to all the calculated cells. That way you could simply change the growth factor in B6, and it would be reflected throughout the budget.

This sounds good in principle, but remember that a formula like 1.1*E3 in F3 means "1.1 times the cell to the left." The formula (1+B6)*E3, entered in F3, means "multiply the cell to the left by 1 plus the amount in the cell three down and four to the left." If you copy this formula from F3 to F4, you get (1+B7)*E4, which also means "multiply the cell to the left by 1 plus the amount in the cell three down and four to the left." However, that cell, B7, is empty, so the result is incorrect, as you can see from Figure 2-34. The same problem would occur with all other revenue figures for February and March if you copied the formula from E3 across the row and down the column.

The first lesson to be learned here is that whenever you copy a formula you should always check the results in its new location. If the answer looks wrong, move the cell selector to the cell with the first suspicious result and check the contents in the cell identifier. When you think about the formula in Figure 2-34, you can understand why it is wrong. The second lesson is how to prevent this problem. The solution lies in the difference between the relative cell references you have used so far and a different type of reference, discussed next.

FIGURE
2-34

A problem with formula copying

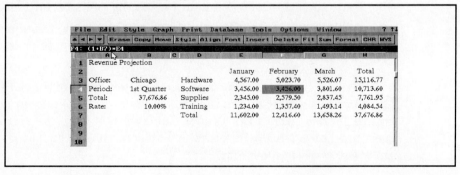

Absolute Solutions

The solution to the problem of copying relative cell references is to decide which references should not be relative and then change them. In the example just given, the formula (1+B6)*E3 refers to two cells. The first cell must not change, regardless of where the formula is copied or moved to. To fix a cell reference so that it does not change during move, copy, or insert operations, you make the reference absolute. All that is required to make a cell reference absolute is a dollar sign in front of the column letter and the row number, for example, $B$6. The correct formula for F3 of the sample model is thus (1+$B$6)*E3.

There are two ways to edit a cell reference to make it absolute. You can type in the dollar signs yourself, or you can use the Absolute (Abs) key, which is F4. When you are using EDIT mode and press F4, or click the [Abs] button on the SpeedBar, Quattro Pro 4 adds dollar signs to the cell reference, as long as the edit cursor is somewhere within the cell reference. If you keep pressing F4, Quattro Pro 4 will show you the four possible cell references:

$B$6	Absolutely column B, row 6
$B6	Absolutely column B, but any row
B$6	Any column, but absolutely row 6
B6	Completely relative

In the sample model, the reference to B6 must be completely absolute. Follow these steps to complete this stage of the sample model:

1. Create the formula **(1+$B$6)*E3** in F3.
2. Issue the Edit Copy command while the cell selector is in F3.
3. Use F3..F3 as the Source Block. Use F3..G6 as the Destination Block. (Do not copy over the @SUM formulas in column H or row 7.)

When the correct formula has been copied, each of the February and March values will be tied to the growth factor in B6. You can test this by entering a new rate in B6. Type **9%** and press ENTER. The results can be seen in Figure 2-35, where the cell selector has been placed on F3 to show the corrected formula.

Corrected formula with absolute reference to B6

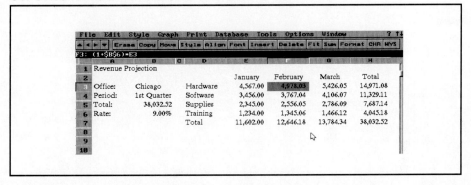

You can see that there are advantages to building models in this way, with the growth factor or other assumptions placed in separate cells. You can now adjust the growth factor by altering one cell rather than copying a new formula each time you want to see the effect of a different rate. The Abs key, F4, and the [Abs] button can be used when you are building formulas by the pointing method as well as when you are editing a formula. An absolute reference is necessary whenever you are writing formulas that are going to be copied but need to be referred to as a specific cell or block of cells in their new locations.

Rounding Out

If you take a close look at the model in Figure 2-35, you can see a slight problem. The totals in columns G7 and H7 do not seem to add up. Once again there is a lesson to be learned: Always check your spreadsheet work! Presenting this particular spreadsheet to the boss could be embarrassing, especially if you can't explain why the totals are off.

The reason for the anomaly in Figure 2-35 is the rounding operation that Quattro Pro 4 performs in order to display values in a format that has 2 decimal places. Quattro Pro 4 rounds numbers for the purposes of display, but it actually retains the full value of each calculation to 15 decimal places. You can see this very clearly if you change the global format back to General (using Options, Formats, Numeric Format). The results are shown in Figure 2-36.

FIGURE
2-36

The problem with rounding for display purposes

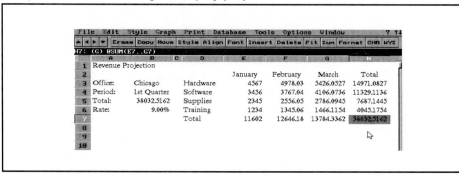

The solution here is to use the @ROUND function to round the results of a calculation to the number of decimal places you specify. This prevents the accumulation of minor fractions that eventually lead to the apparent inaccuracies of Figure 2-35. When the results of a formula need to be rounded, you make the formula the first argument of the @ROUND function. The second argument is the number of decimal places. Thus, the formula in F3 of the sample model, rounded to two decimal places, would look like this:

@ROUND(1+$B$6)*E3,2).

You can apply the @ROUND function in the sample model by following these steps:

1. Select cell F3 then press the F2 key to enter EDIT mode.

2. Press HOME to move the edit cursor to the beginning of the formula. Type **@ROUND(** and then press END to move the edit cursor to the end of the formula.

3. Type **,2)** to complete the formula and press ENTER.

4. Issue the Edit Copy command with the cell selector still in F3.

5. Use **F3..F3** as the Source Block. Use **F3..G6** as the Destination Block. (Do not to copy over the @SUM formulas in column H or row 7.)

The results can be seen in Figure 2-37, where the global format has been changed back to Comma, two decimal places (using Options,

Using @ROUND to solve rounding problems

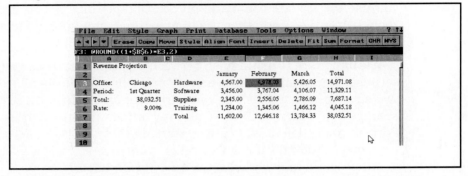

Formats, Numeric Format). The columns now add up accurately. At this point you can save the model again, in preparation for the next chapter, which explores more advanced style and editing commands, as well as printing and file linking. Note that in Figure 2-37 you can see more columns and rows of the worksheet than you did in earlier figures. This is because earlier figures enlarged the worksheet to make the entries easier to see. This is done with the WYSIWYG Zoom command, described next.

Zooms and Defaults

If you are using Quattro Pro 4 in WYSIWYG mode, you can shrink or enlarge your view of the worksheet to view more or fewer columns and rows. The setting that determines the scale of your worksheet view is called WYSIWYG Zoom %, and the default setting is 100 percent. On a normal VGA screen this setting shows you 22 rows and 9 columns. You can see the 100 percent setting in Figure 2-37, whereas Figure 2-36 shows a setting of 110 percent. Settings above 100 enlarge the cells, useful for detail work, whereas settings below 100 shrink them, helpful when you want to get "the big picture."

To change the WYSIWYG Zoom % you choose Options from the main menu and then select WYSIWYG Zoom %. You can then type a value between 25 and 200 and click Enter or press ENTER. Changes you make to the WYSIWYG Zoom % setting remain in effect until you exit Quattro

Pro 4. To fix the zoom setting so that it remains in effect in future sessions you use the Update command on the Options menu. This records the zoom percentage and other program settings in a special file known as the configuration file (the name of the file is RSC.RF).

It is important to distinguish between worksheet settings and program settings. The zoom setting is a program setting; it affects all worksheets you have open as well as any you retrieve or create during a session. The settings you adjust with the Options Formats menu, such as Numeric Format and Global Width, are worksheet settings, stored with the worksheet. They do not affect other worksheets. You will learn more about program and worksheet settings in Chapter 6.

Styles, Files, Links, and Printing

This chapter covers a variety of subjects that could be called "intermediate spreadsheet topics," because they build on the basic knowledge about spreadsheet making that you have acquired in Chapters 1 and 2. Now that you have seen how a single spreadsheet model is developed it is time to look at how you handle several worksheets at once, how you store worksheets, and how you print out information from Quattro Pro 4. This chapter also covers the finer points of worksheet formatting, including fonts and styles.

Of Files, Disks, and Directories

Before you begin working with several worksheets at once, it is important to fully understand the way Quattro Pro 4 stores your work. This section covers the File menu commands used when you work with multiple worksheets. If you are not yet familiar with the disk operating system (DOS), you will find useful tips in Appendix A.

The Filing Process

The File menu, shown in Figure 3-1, is used to store and retrieve your worksheet files. You have seen that the data that you enter into a worksheet is not immediately stored in a worksheet file on disk. Instead it is temporarily retained in the computer's random access memory (RAM). Think of RAM as an electronic desktop. Because it is electronic, the work that you do on this desktop, such as entering and calculating, is performed very quickly. By retaining most of your worksheet in memory while you manipulate it, Quattro Pro 4 can provide fast responses and rapid calculations. However, even an electronic desktop has its disadvantages, and the problem with RAM is that everything you have entered into it is erased when the power to your PC is turned off or interrupted.

Although Quattro Pro 4 uses the Transcript feature to record all of your keystrokes as you work, just in case you need to recover from a disaster like a power loss, it is still very important to use the File menu on a regular basis to copy the worksheet from memory to disk. The File menu is also useful when you want to create copies of a worksheet saved under different names or at different locations. For such a task you use

FIGURE
3-1

The File menu

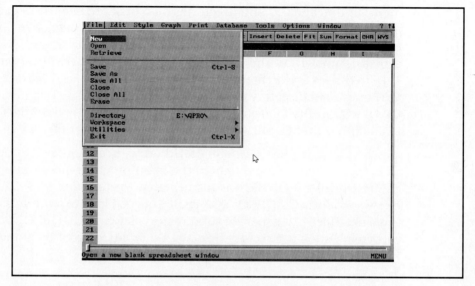

the File Save As command, described in a moment. For Quattro Pro 4 to safely store a copy of your worksheet file on disk, it needs two pieces of information: where to store the data and what file name to use.

Working with Subdirectories

Just as Quattro Pro 4 comes to you on disks, data created with the help of programs is also stored on disks. Information is stored on disks in files. As you work with your computer you quickly create many files. If you want to keep these files manageable, there is a practical limit to how many files should be stored on a disk. Large-capacity disks, particularly hard disks, are often divided into small, manageable parts called *subdirectories*. Subdirectories are an important part of organizing files on your hard disk (in fact, some versions of DOS limit the number of files in a directory to 512).

To understand subdirectories, consider a telephone directory for a large company. The directory lists departments and department heads but not every single person in the company. Consequently, each department has its own directory that lists each staff member in the department. In this analogy subdirectories on a disk are like the departmental directories. You can also think of subdirectories as being like limbs on a family tree, branching out from the root. In fact, the "main" directory of a disk is known as the root directory. This is where the first level of subdirectories are created. The root directory on drive C is referred to as C:\, and a subdirectory called QPRO on the same disk is described as C:\QPRO. (In the following examples you will see the hard disk referred to as both C and E, but your hard disk may have a different letter.)

When Quattro Pro 4 was installed on your computer a subdirectory called QPRO was created to hold the main program files. A subdirectory of QPRO, called FONTS, was also created to store font files. This would be referred to as C:\QPRO\FONTS. It is a good idea to store your Quattro Pro 4 data files in a separate subdirectory, such as C:\QPRO\DATA. You can create such a directory from within Quattro Pro 4 by using the File Utilities Dos Shell command:

1. Select Utilities from the File menu. Select DOS Shell.

2. Quattro Pro 4 prompts you to enter a DOS command. Type **MD \QPRO\DATA**, as shown in Figure 3-2. The command MD is short for "make directory."

3. Now press ENTER. Quattro Pro 4 will pass on the command to the disk operating system and then return you to READY mode.

If you get the message "Unable to create directory," you already have a directory by the same name or you do not have a QPRO directory (check the installation instructions in Appendix A for a more detailed look at directories).

Sometimes a program like Quattro Pro 4 needs directions in order to find a file. This information is the file's *path*. If you have a file called CHICAGO.WQ1 stored in a subdirectory called \QPRO\DATA on drive C, the path to that file is C:\QPRO\DATA. In Chapter 1 you saw that Quattro Pro 4 initially assumes that you want to save worksheets using the same drive and directory from which you started the program (typically C:\QPRO).

You can make a temporary change to this path by using the File Directory command. To do this, select Directory from the File menu. As

FIGURE
3-2

Selecting the DOS Shell command to use the MD command

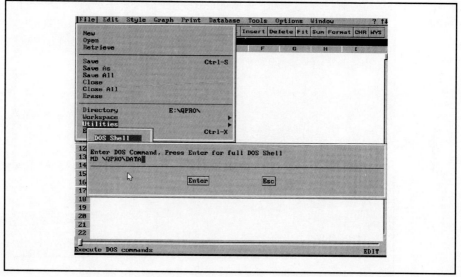

you can see from Figure 3-3, Quattro Pro 4 prompts you to "Enter name of directory:". The currently selected directory is shown, in this case, E:\QPRO. The cursor is under the first letter of the name. Simply type the path to the new storage area, for example, E:\QPRO\DATA, and it will replace the current one. Alternatively, you can edit the current name by pressing the EDIT key, F2. You can then press HOME to move the cursor to the end of the current name and add to it.

You press ENTER when you have typed the new name correctly. From now until you end the current session Quattro Pro 4 will store files to, and retrieve files from, this new path (unless you again use the File Directory command to select a different path). To make a more permanent change to the data directory setting, use the Options Startup Directory command (described in Chapter 6) and specify the directory you want Quattro Pro 4 to use. You can then use the Options Update command to add this preference to the program's configuration file that is read each time Quattro Pro 4 is loaded. To store just one file to an area other than the default directory, use the File Save As command, described in a moment, and edit the path that is used.

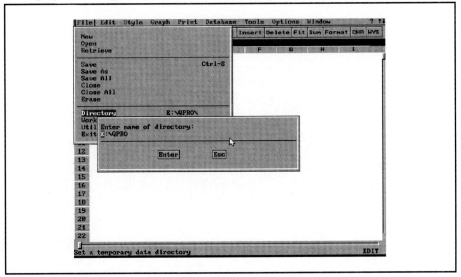

FIGURE 3-3

Changing the directory

Naming Files

Every file in the same directory of a disk must have a unique name. This name is composed of three parts: a file name, a period, and an optional extension. The file name consists of one to eight letters or numbers without spaces. You can use some punctuation marks in a file name, but it is usually easier to use numbers and letters rather than to try to remember which punctuation marks are acceptable. Valid punctuation characters in a file name are

( ) ! @ # $ % & - _ ' { } ~ ' ^

If you use invalid characters, DOS responds with "Invalid File Name" and so does Quattro Pro 4.

One punctuation mark has a special role in file names: the period. It connects the file name with its extension. The extension is usually three characters long and follows the same rules as those for file names. When they are used, extensions are often chosen to distinguish between types of files. For example, Quattro Pro 4 worksheets have the extension .WQ1. Earlier versions of Quattro used the extension .WKQ. 1-2-3 files use

.WKS, .WK1, and .WK3, depending on the version of the program (version 1 uses .WKS; version 2 uses .WK1, version 3 uses .WK3).

Quattro Pro 4 normally assigns an extension to the file name you create depending on what kind of data you are saving in the file. Table 3-1 is a list of extensions recognized or used by Quattro Pro 4. If you want Quattro Pro 4 to save to a format that can be read by another program—for example, 1-2-3—simply enter the file name and the appropriate extension. For example, Quattro Pro 4 would save BUDGET.WK1 as a 1-2-3 file. If you want Quattro Pro 4 to use a particular extension all the time, you can enter that extension as part of the program defaults using the Options Startup File Extension command described in Chapter 6.

When you are ready to save a worksheet that you have built from scratch, you select File Save. Quattro Pro 4 knows that the file has not yet been named and so responds by asking you to "Enter save file name:"

TABLE 3-1

Extensions Used with Quattro Pro 4

Extension	File Type
.WQ1	Quattro Pro worksheet (versions 1,2,3,4)
.BAQ	Backup of a Quattro Pro worksheet
.WKQ	Quattro 1.0 worksheet
.WSP	Quattro Pro workspace
.WKS	Lotus 1-2-3 worksheet (before Release 2)
.WK1	Lotus 1-2-3 worksheet (Release 2.xx)
.WK3	Lotus 1-2-3 worksheet (Release 3.xx)
.PRN	Print file (see Chapter 10)
.DBF	dBASE file
.LOG	Transcript log file
.MU	Quattro Pro menu file
.SND	Digitalized sound file
.CGM	Graphics metafile
.CLP	Clip-art file

FIGURE
3-4

The save file name prompt

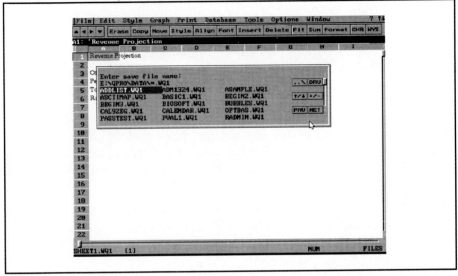

as shown in Figure 3-4. The file name prompt is immediately followed by the generic name prompt that uses the asterisk wildcard character, as in

```
E:\QPRO\DATA\*.WQ1
```

The asterisk means any file name in the E:\QPRO\DATA directory with an extension of .WQ1. This prompt creates a list of files already saved in the current directory.

The File List

The list of file names that Quattro Pro 4 shows you when you save a new worksheet enables you to see the existing names. You can pick an existing file from this list and save the current worksheet into it, but bear in mind that doing so will replace the contents of that disk file with the worksheet you are about to store. To pick a name from the list, use the arrow keys to highlight the name. If there are more than 12 files on the list, the list scrolls as you continue to press the arrow keys.

Mouse users can select a name from the list by pointing to it and clicking the left mouse button. Using the mouse you can scroll the list by either clicking on the scroll bar to the right of the box or dragging the "elevator" box down the scroll bar. Whatever method you use to find the file name you want, you can press ENTER to use the file name that is highlighted. There are several other keys that you can use to manipulate this list also, as listed in Table 3-2.

Note that you can search for a specific file name by pressing the Edit key, F2. This will return a prompt in the status line at the bottom of the screen, asking you what you are searching for. The search mechanism works the same way as in the function list, described in Chapter 2. Just type the first character of the name you are seeking. Quattro Pro 4 moves to the first file in the list that begins with that character or beeps to let

TABLE 3-2

File List Keys

Key	Action
DOWN ARROW	Down one row
TAB	Move to right column, then down one row
RIGHT ARROW	Right one column
UP ARROW	Up one row
SHIFT-TAB	Move to left column, then up one row
LEFT ARROW	Left one column
PAGE DOWN	Down one screenful of rows
PAGE UP	Up one screenful of rows
HOME	Top of list
END	Bottom of list
F3	Larger list/small list toggle
+ (numeric)	Detailed list
– (numeric)	Names only list
F2	Search for file
BACKSPACE	List parent directory
ESC	Edit path and file specification

you know that there are no names that begin with the character you typed. To continue the search type the second character of the name you are looking for, and so on, until it is located.

If you are unsure of the file name you are looking for, you might find it helpful to see the date and time all the files were last saved to the disk. Detailed file information is available by pressing the plus + on the numeric keypad, or clicking the +/− button. An example of the resulting display can be seen in Figure 3-5. Notice that this display also shows the size of the worksheet, useful information when you are attempting to decide which file contains the data you want. You can press the minus (–) on the numeric keypad to return to the names-only listing.

If you want to see more names in the list, in either the detailed or names-only format, you can press F3 or click on the button with the up and down arrows. This shows an enlarged file listing. Click on the same button to reduce the size of the file list box. When you have selected or typed a file name for your worksheet, press ENTER to confirm it. If the file name has already been used, you will have to confirm that you want the current worksheet to replace the contents of the existing file. You do this by selecting Replace, as described later under "Save Confirmation."

FIGURE 3-5

Listing file details

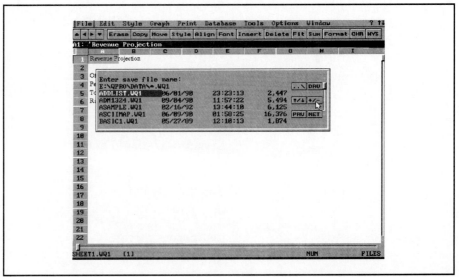

Saving Previously Named Files

You can use the File Save command if you want to save a worksheet that has already been saved. For example, the instructions in Chapter 2 showed you how to create a sample file called ASAMPLE.WQ1. Suppose that you have started a new session in Quattro Pro 4 and retrieved this file from disk with the File Retrieve command, discussed in detail later in this chapter. The file contains revenue projections for the Chicago office of a computer company, based on a certain rate of growth. You change the rate of growth to 8 percent and want to save the new version of the file. When you issue the File Save command Quattro Pro 4 knows that the worksheet already has a file name and immediately attempts to save the file. However, because the original version still exists on disk, Quattro Pro 4 asks you to confirm this operation by selecting Replace, as described in a moment under "Save Confirmation."

Instead of replacing the original version of the worksheet with the current one, you can use the File Save As command to save a worksheet file under a different file name. The File Save As command presents you with the existing file name, as shown in Figure 3-6, which you can proceed to edit. This is very useful when you are creating different versions of the same basic worksheet. You can follow these steps to make a copy of the sample file called ASAMPLE.WQ1, created in the last chapter:

1. After you start a new Quattro Pro 4 session, use File Retrieve to load the ASAMPLE.WQ1 worksheet.

2. Change the rate in cell B6 to 8% and then issue the File Save As command.

3. When the prompt appears, as in Figure 3-6, type **Chicago**, which will replace the current name.

4. Press ENTER to confirm the new name. The file will be saved to disk, and the name CHICAGO.WQ1 will replace ASAMPLE.WQ1 on the bottom left of the screen.

At this point you have two very similar files, one named ASAMPLE.WQ1 and the other called CHICAGO.WQ1. Later in this chapter you will learn how to link files together, and the example provided uses the

FIGURE
3-6

The File Save As command

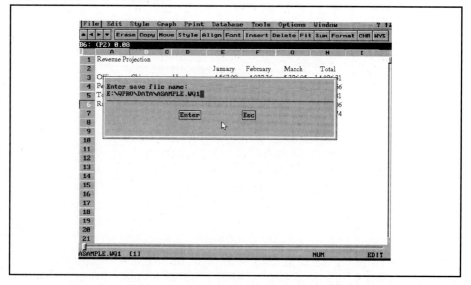

CHICAGO.WQ1 file plus three more worksheets that you can make now using the File Save As command and the following instructions:

1. With CHICAGO.WQ1 the current worksheet, change B3 to Dallas and B6 to 10%.

2. Issue the File Save As command and type **DALLAS.WQ1** to replace CHICAGO.WQ1. Press ENTER to save the new file.

3. With DALLAS.WQ1 the current worksheet, change B3 to Miami and B6 to 11%.

4. Issue the File Save As command and type **MIAMI.WQ1** to replace DALLAS.WQ1. Press ENTER to save the new file.

5. With MIAMI.WQ1 the current worksheet, change B3 to Combined and use Edit Erase to delete cells A6..B6.

6. Issue the File Save As command and type **COMBINED.WQ1** to replace MIAMI.WQ1. Press ENTER to save the new file.

In the section entitled "Linking Worksheet Files" you will see how to link these four files together.

File List Maneuvers

Note that instead of simply typing a new name at the save file prompt, you can edit the existing name. This is useful for situations in which the new name is similar to the existing name, for example, to save a file called SALES91.WQ1 to SALES92.WQ1. If you press the Edit key, F2, you can move the edit cursor through the file name and make changes in the same way that you edit entries in worksheet cells.

If you use File Save As with a previously saved file and want to see the names already in use, just press ESC at the save file prompt. You will get the generic file name (*.WQ1) prompt and the file list, as seen earlier in Figure 3-4. You have already seen that the up and down arrows button enlarges and reduces the size of the file list, whereas the +/- button switches between a detailed file list and the default, names-only list.

The Parent Button

The first button in the file list is marked with a pair of dots and a backward slash (..\). This button is used to display the "parent" directory, which is the directory above the current subdirectory. In Figure 3-7 you can see the effect of clicking the parent button. The parent directory of E:\QPRO\DATA is E:\QPRO (the parent directory to E:\QPRO is E:\, the root directory for drive E). An alternative to clicking the parent button is to press the BACKSPACE key, which also takes you "back" one level in the directory tree, toward the root.

As you can see from Figure 3-7, any subdirectories of the current directory are listed in alphabetical order at the bottom of the file list, after the worksheet files. If you highlight a subdirectory name and press ENTER, Quattro Pro 4 shows you a list of files in that subdirectory. You can select or type a file name for your worksheet whenever the directory you want to store it in is displayed.

The DRV and NET Buttons

If you want to store the worksheet on a different drive, you can click the DRV button, which displays a list of currently available drives. As

FIGURE
3-7

Viewing a parent directory

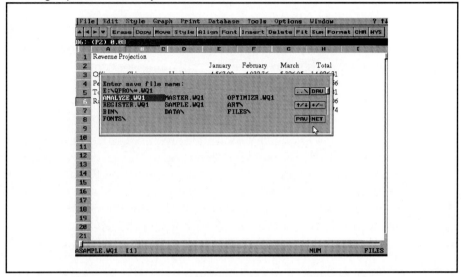

you can see from Figure 3-8, the drives are listed in alphabetical order, together with a description. Drives are described either as fixed, like a hard disk, or as removable, like a floppy disk or removable cartridge drive. By clicking on a drive letter you can list files and directories on that drive.

The NET button enables you to view the assignment of network drives. If a network drive has been set up, or "mapped" as a drive letter, it will appear in the list of drives displayed by the DRV button. (The mapping of network drives is carried out through the Options Network command, discussed in Appendix B.)

Manual Changes

If you want to save the current worksheet to a directory other than the current one, you can manually alter the path. You can press ESC when the file list is displayed and type the complete path name of the directory and the file name, as in

```
C:\SALES\BUDGET.WQ1
```

Listing available drives

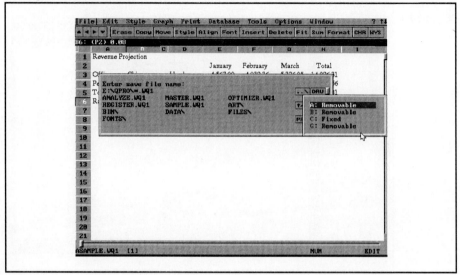

Another way to list files in a directory other than the current one is to press ESC to clear the save file name prompt and then type the path name of the storage area you are interested in *together with* the generic file specification, *.WQ1, and then press ENTER. For example, to list files in C:\SALES you would type **C:\SALES*.WQ1**. Quattro Pro 4 will respond with a list of files in the SALES directory (if you do not use a file specification, you cause Quattro Pro 4 to unintentionally save your file in the wrong area).

Save Confirmation

When you have the right path and file name entered for the worksheet you are about to save, press ENTER to confirm the name. If you are using either the File Save or File Save As command, Quattro Pro 4 does not immediately save the file but checks whether a file of the same name already exists in the current storage area. If such a file exists, Quattro Pro 4 responds with a three-line menu box offering these choices, shown in Figure 3-9: Cancel, Replace, and Backup.

FIGURE
3-9
The Cancel, Replace, and Backup options

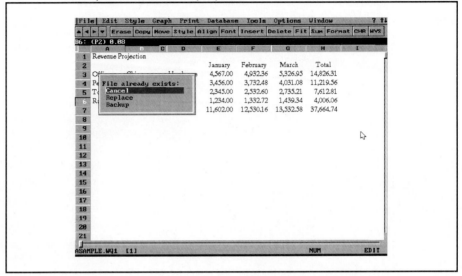

❏ **Cancel** The Cancel option is your chance to change your mind about the save operation. Selecting Cancel prevents the existing file from being overwritten and returns you to the READY mode.

❏ **Replace** Selecting the Replace option confirms that you want to overwrite the old file. You normally use this option when you are updating a file or when you are saving successive unfinished versions of a model you are building.

❏ **Backup** The Backup option preserves the existing file by changing the extension to .BAQ and then saving the new file with the name you requested.

Opening and Retrieving Files

When you want to bring back into memory a copy of a worksheet that you have stored on disk, you can use either the Retrieve or the Open command from the File menu. Both commands assume that you want to retrieve a worksheet from the drive and directory currently selected.

File Listing

When you select either File Retrieve or File Open, Quattro Pro 4 helps you to identify the file you want by displaying an alphabetical list of files, similar to the one you get when using the File Save and File Save As commands. You can see a typical File Retrieve list in Figure 3-10. The main difference from the File Save list is that the file specification is *.W?? and not *.WQ1. This is because Quattro Pro 4 enables you to retrieve more than just .WQ1 files. You can also retrieve .WK1 and .WK3 files created by Lotus 1-2-3 and these are listed.

You can use the keys in Table 3-2 to navigate the file list. When you have highlighted the file you want to retrieve, press ENTER and Quattro Pro 4 reads that file into memory. If you are using a mouse, you only need to click on a file name to select that file (you scroll the list with the scroll bar on the right of the box).

If you want to retrieve a file from a storage area other than the current one, you have several options. You can press ESC when prompted for a file name and then edit the path so that it accesses the area you want to retrieve from. You can press ENTER to see a list of the files in that area. Suppose you want to see all of the worksheets in the SALES subdirectory

The File Retrieve list

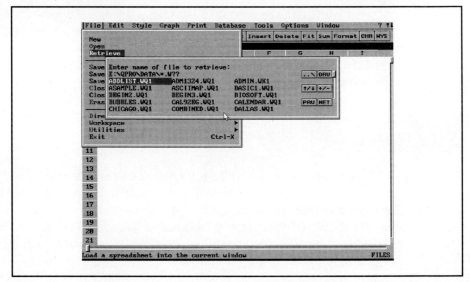

of the QPRO directory, but the DATA subdirectory is the current directory. The initial prompt is

```
C:\QPRO\DATA\*.W??
```

When you press ESC this changes to

```
C:\QPRO\DATA\
```

You can then press BACKSPACE five times to remove the DATA subdirectory from the path. Now you can type in the new directory, as in

```
C:\QPRO\SALES\
```

and press ENTER to see all of the worksheets in this directory. Quattro Pro 4 automatically adds the *.W?? specification.

Note the backslash at the end of the edited prompt. If you do not include this, Quattro Pro 4 assumes that you are looking for the file SALES.WQ1 in the QPRO directory. When you are at a file name prompt and want to change it completely, you can press CTRL-BACKSPACE. This removes the text of the prompt and enables you to type something completely different. Also note that all Quattro Pro 4 file lists have the same set of buttons for selecting different drives and directories. These were described earlier under "File List Maneuvers."

If you want Quattro Pro 4 to retrieve a foreign file (one that does not have an extension that begins with W), you can type a specific extension in the edited file name prompt, such as *.DBF for dBASE files. If you know the exact path and file name of the worksheet you want to recover, you can type that information and press ENTER.

File Retrieve

There is an important difference between the effects of the File Open and File Retrieve commands. When you read a file from disk with the File Retrieve command the data from the file is placed in the current worksheet window. If you have just started Quattro Pro 4, you have one worksheet window open, window number [1], named with the default name of SHEET.WQ1. Using File Retrieve reads the data from a file on disk into that window.

If you already have data in the current window and use the File Retrieve command, Quattro Pro 4 assumes that you want to replace the current contents of the window with the data you are going to read from disk. The data read from the file will replace all that was there before it, from cell A1 through cell IV8192. This means there is the potential to lose some of your work when you issue the File Retrieve command.

To prevent accidental loss of data, Quattro Pro 4 checks to ensure that your work in the current window is saved. If some of your work is not saved, Quattro Pro 4 asks whether you want to lose your changes, and you have to reply Yes or No before the File Retrieve command erases the current window contents and reads a data file from the disk. If you pick Yes, Quattro Pro 4 proceeds with the File Retrieve command, presenting a list of files from which to choose. If you pick No, you are returned to the File menu, where you can issue one of the save commands to store the current worksheet before you reissue the Retrieve command.

File Open

When you issue the File Open command and select a file name Quattro Pro 4 performs two operations, the first of which is to create a new worksheet window. The second operation is to read the requested file into the new window. For example, in Figure 3-11 you can see that the current worksheet is CHICAGO.WQ1. This worksheet is displayed in window [1]. The user now wants to work on a second set of figures for the Dallas office, stored in a file called DALLAS.WQ1. The File Open command is issued, and the DALLAS.WQ1 file is specified. The immediate result is that the newly opened file is displayed in window [2], completely obscuring worksheet window [1].

At this point you do not know whether window [1] is still open. You could use the Next Window key, SHIFT-F6, to see whether you switch to the other window. However, if you issue the Window Tile command you can clearly see that two windows are opened, as shown in Figure 3-12. When a window only takes up part of the screen, like those you see in Figure 3-12, it is referred to as a *reduced window*. A window that takes

FIGURE
3-11

Opening a second window

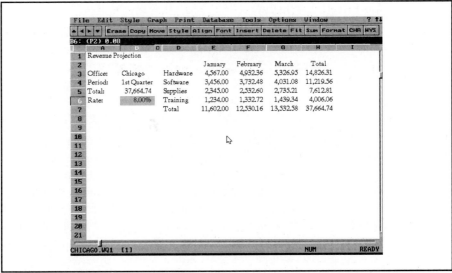

FIGURE
3-12

Two windows tiled

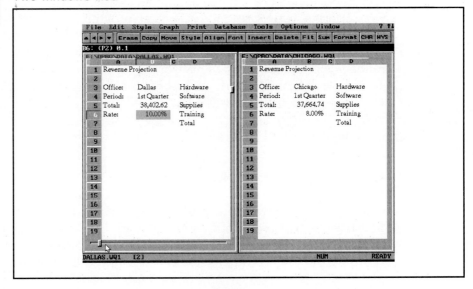

up the entire screen, like the one in Figure 3-11, is referred to as a *full-screen window.*

When windows are reduced the name of the file displayed in each window is shown at the top left of the window. The active window has vertical and horizontal scroll bars. The name of the file in the active window is shown in the bottom status line, along with the window number. The active window after you issue the Windows Tile command is the one that was current when you issued the command, and it is placed on the left (if there are more than three windows, it is placed in the upper left).

At this point you could issue the File Open command again to open a third window containing the worksheet you have requested. The more worksheets you work with at once, the more important the Windows commands become. The next section discusses these commands.

Multiple Worksheet Windows

When you have several worksheet windows open at once you will want to arrange them so that you can work effectively. In Figure 3-12 two windows are open, and they have been "tiled." If you are working in character mode you can also stack, resize, and move windows. This section discusses the commands for organizing multiple windows. The first commands to be examined are those that you use to create multiple windows.

Using Windows

You have seen that when you issue the File Open command Quattro Pro 4 creates a new window in which to display the requested file. You may want to create a new window without actually opening a file. For example, if you were working on the Dallas and Chicago worksheets seen in Figure 3-12, you might want to create a third worksheet to consolidate the two sets of numbers. To do this you can use the File New command. At first the new worksheet obscures existing windows. The new worksheet window is numbered; in this case it is window [3]. The default file name of SHEET2.WQ1 has been assigned to the new worksheet, showing that it is the second fresh worksheet of the current session.

If you issue the Window Tile command from this new window, you will see an arrangement similar to the one in Figure 3-13. Note that the Windows menu is displayed in Figure 3-13, although this menu disappears as soon as you issue the Tile command. If you are working in character mode, you can issue both the Window Tile and the Window Stack commands. The latter places the new window above the existing windows, as seen in Figure 3-14. The other windows are just partially visible behind the current window. Character mode, particularly with the higher resolutions such as the VGA 80x50 setting used in Figure 3-14, allows more flexibility as you arrange windows. In Table 3-3 you can see a comparison of commands and keys used when you work with windows in the two modes.

When you have several windows open in character mode, you have options when it comes to arranging them on the screen. You can use the Stack command to tell Quattro Pro 4 to arrange all open windows one on top of another with the worksheet name of each one displayed, as in Figure 3-14. The current window is displayed above the rest, and the windows are numbered in the top right of the window frame. The name

FIGURE 3-13

Additional windows tiled

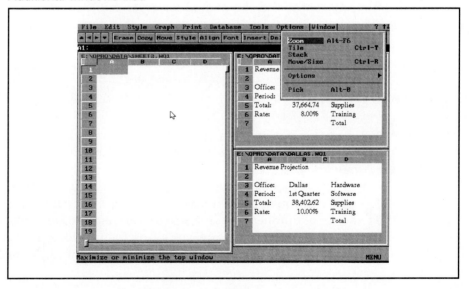

FIGURE
3-14

The Window Stack command in character mode

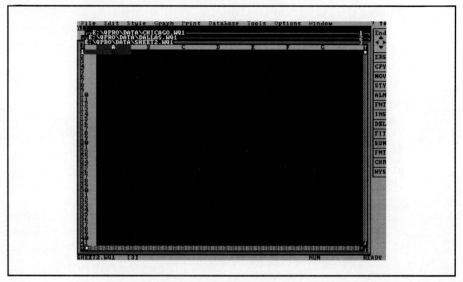

of the file in each window is given in the top left of the window frame. Note that whenever you switch display mode, from character to WYSIWYG or from WYSIWYG to character, Quattro Pro 4 returns all windows to full screen size, with the active window on top.

When several windows are displayed, the current window is indicated by a double frame as opposed to a single. As you move from one window to another, the cell selector jumps to a particular cell of the worksheet you are moving to. This is the cell that was active when last you left that window. Any window that has been reduced in size, by the Stack or Tile command, can be zoomed to full-screen size by moving to that window and pressing the Zoom key, ALT-F6. To reduce the window to its previous state, you can press ALT-F6 again, if you are using character mode. If you are using WYSIWYG mode, pressing ALT-F6 in a reduced window zooms all windows back to full screen. Use Window Tile to return zoomed windows to reduced size.

You can move from window to window with the Next Window key, SHIFT-F6. You can also click in a window with the mouse to make it active. To move to a window based on the number of the window, use ALT plus the window number. Thus, you can move to window 2 by pressing ALT and typing **2**. You can also select which window you want to move to by using the Pick command on the Window menu or the Shortcut key, ALT-0. This pops up a list of windows from which you can choose, either by clicking on the appropriate name or by typing the key letter (the first

Character and WYSIWYG Mode Commands

TABLE 3-3

Character Mode	WYSIWYG Mode
You can use Window Stack and Window Tile to reduce screens and arrange them	You can use Window Tile to reduce screens and arrange them.
You can use Window Move/Size to further adjust windows	You can press ALT-F6 in a reduced window to expand window to full screen, but this expands all other windows to full screen as well.
You can press ALT-F6 in a reduced window to expand window to full screen	You can only use Window Tile to return full-screen windows to reduced size.
You can press ALT-F6 in a full-screen window to shrink window to reduced size, if it has previously been reduced	You can use File Workspace Save to store a collection of windows, but they will be stored as full screen.
You can use File Workspace Save to store an arrangement of reduced windows	You cannot use File Workspace Restore to recreate an arrangement of reduced windows.
You can use File Workspace Restore to recreate an arrangement of reduced windows	You cannot use Window Stack to reduce screens and arrange them. You cannot use Window Move/ Size to further adjust windows.
	You cannot press ALT-F6 in a full-screen window to shrink window to reduced size, even if it has previously been reduced.

character in the worksheet name). You can see the Pick list in Figure 3-15, which shows the effects of the Window Tile command in character mode.

The Window Tile command tells Quattro Pro 4 to arrange all of the open windows on the screen at once, automatically adjusting their size to fit the available space. In Figure 3-13 you saw windows tiled in WYSIWYG mode. In Figure 3-15 you can see that the windows, which were stacked in Figure 3-14, have been tiled in character mode. The current window is marked by the double line border. Note the Pick list, displayed by pressing ALT-0.

You can enlarge any window to full screen size by pressing the Zoom key (ALT-F6). Press Zoom again to return the screen to its tiled size. The allocation of available display space is determined by the number of windows to be tiled. You can see several arrangements in the diagram in Figure 3-16. Mouse users can zoom a window to full-screen size by clicking on the up arrow in the pair of arrows at the top right of the screen. (This arrow is highlighted in Figure 3-15.) The Down Arrow will unzoom the current window if it is already zoomed.

FIGURE 3-15

Tiled windows in character mode with the Window Pick list

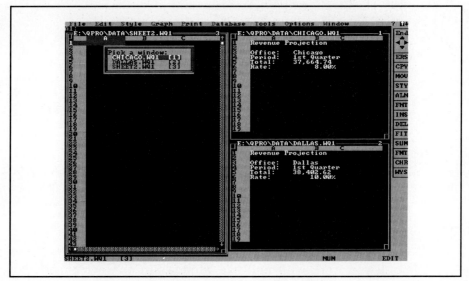

Adjusting windows in character mode

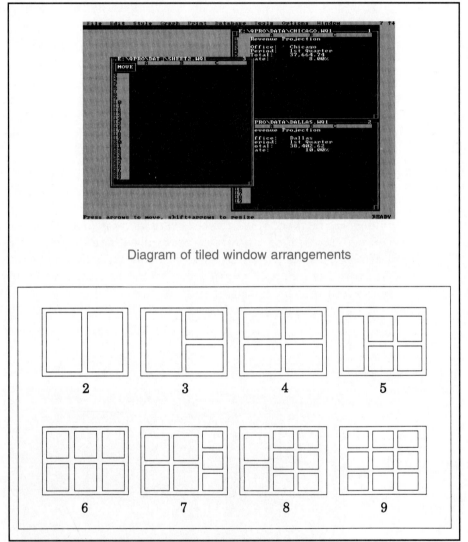

Diagram of tiled window arrangements

Sizing and Moving Windows

If you work with multiple windows in character mode you can use different arrangements of windows besides tiled and stacked. You may want to overlap certain parts of windows and obscure others. If you use a mouse in character mode, adjustment of windows is very easy. To alter the size of a window simply place the mouse pointer on the move/size box at the lower right of the window, then press the mouse button and drag. The window frame will change shape as you drag the mouse. When the shape is satisfactory, release the mouse button. Figure 3-16 shows window 3 has been reduced in size, as well as moved.

To move a window with the mouse, place the mouse pointer on the title of the window, in the top left of the frame, and then press the mouse button. The MOVE message will appear in the window and you can drag it to a new location. Release the mouse button when the new location is reached. Figure 3-16 shows window 3 being moved.

To move or size windows from the keyboard you will use the Windows Move/Size command. You can select Move/Size from the Windows menu or press CTRL-R. A box called MOVE appears on the screen to let you know that you are in Move mode, as seen in Figure 3-16. Use the arrow keys to move the box within the Quattro Pro 4 desktop. Press ENTER when the new location is reached. To change the size and shape of the window, press SCROLL LOCK after you have selected Move/Size and the MOVE box changes to SIZE. You can switch back and forth between MOVE and SIZE by using the SCROLL LOCK key.

Closing Windows

If you keep using the File Open and File New commands you eventually will reach Quattro Pro 4's limit of 32 windows, although you may well run out of memory in your system before reaching that limit. Bear in mind that neither the File Save command nor the File Save As command put away your work. The save commands store the contents of windows onto disk; they do not close the windows themselves. To close a window you need to use the File Close command. This command affects the current worksheet.

When performing a File Close, Quattro Pro 4 checks for unsaved changes in the worksheet, and, if none are encountered, the window is removed from the display. If unsaved changes are encountered, you are prompted to save them first. Mouse users have a quick way to close a window: Click on the square on the top left corner of the active window border. This closes the window immediately unless there are unsaved changes to be dealt with.

If you want to close all of the currently open windows, for example when you are moving from one project to another, you can issue the File Close All command. This checks each window for changes and closes each one in turn, prompting you to save work if you have not done so already. When you close all windows you are left with an abbreviated Quattro Pro 4 menu that shows just one item: File. When you select File with no worksheets open you have just five choices, as shown in Table 3-4. The first time that you see the reduced menu you may wonder what has happened, but as soon as you open a worksheet window the full menu will be restored.

Work Spaces

When you have set up the right arrangement of windows for your work you may want to preserve the arrangement. Quattro Pro 4 has a special type of file, called a *workspace file*, that will store information about a window arrangement, including the position of the windows and the names of the files that occupy them. To store the current arrangement of windows you issue the File Workspace command and pick the Save option. Type a name of up to eight letters. The extension .WSP, for workspace, is added automatically.

Choices on the Abbreviated File Menu

Item	Description
New	Opens a new worksheet window
Open	Reads a file from disk into a new worksheet window
Workspace	Restores a stored workspace
Utilities	Provides access to use the File Manager, from which files can be opened, or the DOS Shell
Exit	Closes Quattro Pro 4 and returns to DOS

Note that saving a workspace file (.WSP) does not save the data in the worksheet files that are displayed. Only the names of the worksheets and the arrangement of their windows are saved in a .WSP file. To save a Quattro Pro 4 session, preserving data as well as window arrangements, you would issue the File Workspace Save command, followed by the File Save All command.

When you start a new Quattro Pro 4 session and want to restore a workspace, you issue the File Workspace Restore command and select the workspace file you want. The windows and the files that were recorded in the workspace will be opened for you. Note that if you are working in WYSIWYG mode, the arrangement of windows is not restored. To arrange windows in WYSIWYG mode you must use the Window Tile command. Despite this limitation, the Workspace Restore command is still useful in WYSIWYG mode, because it opens the group of files you were working on, avoiding the need for repetitive use of the File Open command.

If you are working with multiple windows in character mode, you will quickly realize that Quattro Pro 4 stores the size and shape of a worksheet, as well as the data it contains, when you use File Save or File Save As. The location of the cell selector is the same when a stored worksheet is opened as when it was last saved, and so is the worksheet's desktop location and size. Sometimes this can be disconcerting. For example, if you have tiled a number of windows and then saved the worksheets in them, each one will be stored rather small. When you open one of these files in a later session you may not recognize it at first. There is an easy way to fix this: Zoom the window to full size. In fact, you might want to make a practice of zooming windows to full size before saving them, unless they are part of a special windows arrangement.

Linking Worksheet Files

Beyond the advantages offered for viewing several worksheets at once, Quattro Pro 4 provides the ability to link those worksheets, making data in one dependent on data from another. This creates new spreadsheet design possibilities. You may want to use this feature to split large and cumbersome worksheets into more manageable, interrelated units. Because you can copy or move data from one Quattro Pro 4 worksheet window to another, it is easy to disassemble a large worksheet into more manageable parts. Quattro Pro 4 supports links between worksheets by way of formulas, which enable you to follow more closely the traditional accounting model of consolidated sheets and supporting sheets. You can also link Quattro Pro 4 worksheets to files produced by other programs, such as 1-2-3. (Chapter 5 describes how you can link spreadsheets when working with database commands.)

Creating a Linked File Model

Suppose that you are the manager of a computer company that has three offices. You have requested revenue projections from each of the offices. The projections have been submitted in the form of Quattro Pro 4 worksheets, which you have copied into the data directory on your hard disk. Now you need to combine the figures from all three worksheets.

Earlier, in the section entitled "Saving Previously Named Files," you read how to make four copies of the ASAMPLE.WQ1 worksheet. These copied worksheets were called CHICAGO.WQ1, DALLAS.WQ1, MIAMI.WQ1, and COMBINED.WQ1. The first three worksheets contain revenue projection figures for the three offices, Chicago, Dallas, and Miami. The fourth worksheet, COMBINED.WQ1, will now be used to create a consolidation of the other three.

In Figure 3-17 you can see all four of the worksheets for this example opened and tiled. The WYSIWYG Zoom % setting has been changed to 90 to shrink the worksheets and show more of each one. Note that the WYSIWYG Zoom % has an equal effect on all worksheet windows. Also note that the Combined worksheet has no entries in A6 or B6, and the total in B5 is not correct at this point. The figures in the Combined worksheet will be supplied by worksheet links.

The links that you create with Quattro Pro 4 are actually formulas. For example, cell E3 in the Combined sheet should represent the revenue for Hardware in January for all three offices. In other words, cell E3 in the Combined sheet will add together cell E3 of the Chicago sheet, E3 of the Dallas sheet, and E3 of the Miami sheet. This is how the completed formula for cell E3 of the Combined worksheet will look:

```
+[CHICAGO]E3+[DALLAS]E3+[MIAMI]E3
```

This formula can be built quite easily using the pointing method. With the cell selector in E3 of the Combined worksheet press + and then press the Next Window key (SHIFT-F6). This will take you to the next window (Chicago) where you can point to cell E3, then press + again. You will be returned to the Combined worksheet where the formula so far on the input line will read something like this:

```
+[E:\QPRO\DATA\CHICAGO.WQ1]E3+
```

This looks a little intimidating, because Quattro Pro 4 states the full worksheet name and path of the cell you are working with. This will be abbreviated when the formula is completed.

The next step is to press SHIFT-F6 twice in order to move to the third window, the Dallas worksheet. Again you point to E3 and then press the plus (+) key. Quattro Pro 4 returns you to the Combined worksheet and you press SHIFT-F6 three times to move to the fourth window. After pointing to E3 you can press ENTER to complete the formula, which can

FIGURE 3-17

Four tiled windows in WYSIWYG mode

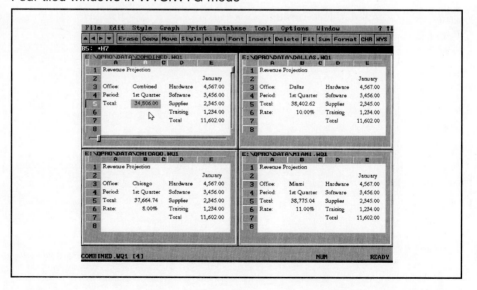

be seen in place in Figure 3-18. Note that only the worksheet name is included in the formula, not the full drive/path information.

At this point you have a formula that totals the values in three cells, each in a different worksheet. In other words, you have a total of the January Hardware revenue. What you want now is for every cell from E3 to G6 in the Combined worksheet to reflect the addition of the corresponding cells in the other three worksheets. This involves a copy operation and you might want to "zoom" the Combined worksheet so that it is full screen before you continue.

Just like other Quattro Pro 4 formulas, link formulas can be copied. To achieve the results you want in this example you copy the link formula in E3 of the Combined worksheet to the other categories and months. The Source Block for the Copy command will be E3..E3, whereas the Destination Block will be E3..G6. The results can be seen in Figure 3-19, where the worksheet has been zoomed to full screen size. The Combined worksheet will now reflect any changes to values in the other three worksheets. Note that there is no need to adjust the @SUM formulas in column H or those on row 7. These formulas continue to add up cells E3..G6.

Completed link formula

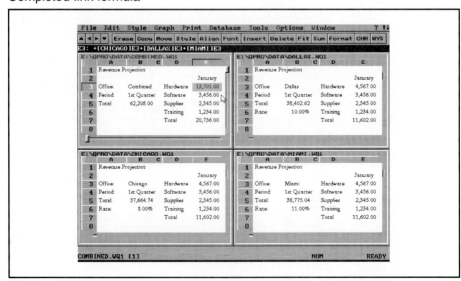

FIGURE
3-19

Link formulas copied

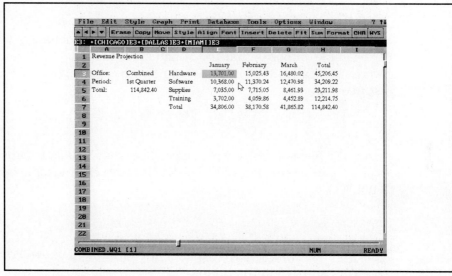

Working with Linked Files

The preceding is a fairly simple example of what can be done with linked worksheets, but the principles remain the same, even with much larger models. Formulas that refer to cells outside of the current worksheet are called *dependent formulas*. Values that are supplied to another worksheet are called *supporting values*. The COMBINED.WQ1 worksheet shown in Figures 3-18 and 3-19 depends on other worksheets for its values, so it is called a *dependent worksheet*. Worksheets like CHICAGO.WQ1 and DALLAS.WQ1 supply values to a dependent worksheet so they are called *supporting worksheets*.

When you establish a link with a supporting Quattro Pro 4 worksheet that is stored in the same directory as the dependent worksheet, the formula will only need to use the name of the supporting worksheet, enclosed in square brackets, as in

```
[CHICAGO]
```

rather that the full path, as in

```
[E:\QPRO\DATA\CHICAGO.WQ1]
```

If the file you are linking to is not a Quattro Pro 4 file with the default extension of .WQ1, your link reference will need to include the extension. For example, suppose that the Miami office is using 1-2-3 and supplies a worksheet called MIAMI.WK1. To link with cell E3 in this file you cannot just use

```
[MIAMI]E3
```

even if the file is in the current data directory. This is because Quattro Pro 4 will be looking for a file called MIAMI.WQ1. Instead, you will need to use

```
[MIAMI.WK1]E3
```

If you enter an invalid reference in a link formula, Quattro Pro 4 returns the error value NA in the cell.

In some versions of Quattro Pro an attempt to link to a file that the program cannot find will create an error message and a file name box. The problem may be that the file is not in the current directory or that the file does not have the default extension. If you press ESC at the file name prompt, you are shown a file list that you can browse until you find the correct name. Highlight the correct name and press ENTER to complete the link. If the file to which you want to link does not exist, you can press ESC several times to clear the error message and file list. You will end up in READY mode with NA as the result of the formula.

You might wonder why Quattro Pro 4 permits you to enter a link formula that refers to a supporting worksheet that does not exist. After all, the program objects to other invalid formulas, such as those that refer to nonexistent cells or functions. The reason can be seen in the case of the manager combining data from the three offices. Suppose that the Miami office is late in sending the worksheet. The Combined worksheet can still be loaded and worked on pending the arrival of the Miami worksheet. When the Miami worksheet arrives and is copied onto the hard disk the formula can be activated with the Update Links command on the Tools menu, described in the next section.

Loading and Refreshing

When you open a dependent worksheet Quattro Pro 4 checks whether the supporting worksheets are open. If they are not, Quattro Pro 4 responds with the Link options box, shown in Figure 3-20. The first option, Load Supporting, opens all worksheets referred to in formulas in the worksheet that is currently being loaded. This can be very helpful if you want to work on the supporting worksheets. The Load Supporting command saves repeated use of the File Open command.

If you do not want to load the supporting worksheets, you can use the second option, Update Refs. This tells Quattro Pro 4 to read from disk the values referred to by link formulas in the current worksheet. The supporting worksheets do not need to be opened for this command to work.

The third option in Figure 3-20 is None. This temporarily replaces link formulas in the dependent worksheet with NA. You might choose this option if you are doing design work on the dependent worksheet and do not need to see the results of the link formulas.

FIGURE 3-20

The Link options box

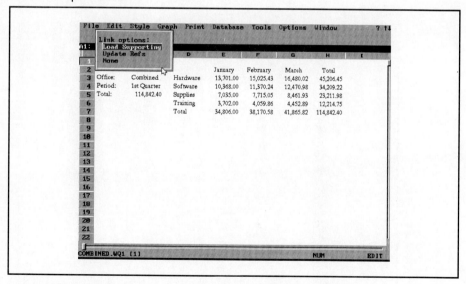

If you open a dependent worksheet and choose the Update Refs option, rather than opening the supporting files, it's possible that the supporting files will be altered and the changes not reflected in the dependent worksheet. For example, you might get an updated copy of a worksheet that is used to support the dependent worksheet you have loaded. If you are using Quattro Pro 4 on a network, another user might update a supporting file. If you alter the supporting worksheet on disk, the dependent worksheet does not automatically know this. To be sure that you are using the most recent figures in the dependent worksheet you can use the Tools Update Links command, shown in Figure 3-21, to refresh data links.

The Open command is similar to the Load Supporting option for retrieving a dependent worksheet in that it allows supporting files to be opened. The Refresh command corresponds to the Update Refs command in that it reads link data from disk instead of opening the supporting files. However, the Open and Refresh commands do not automatically open or read all of the supporting files. Instead, they give you a choice of which files you want opened or read.

When you select Open from the Update Links menu a list of supporting files is displayed. This list is shown in Figure 3-22, where files are being selected. You can select a single name by highlighting it and pressing

FIGURE
3-21

The Tools Update Links command

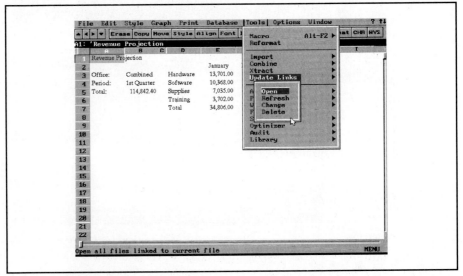

FIGURE
3-22

Supporting files listed

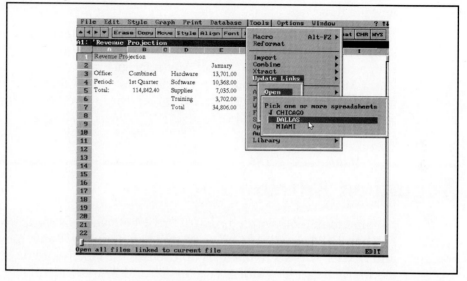

ENTER. To select more than one name from the list, highlight the first file you want to open and press SHIFT-F7. This places a check mark by the name. Now you can select another name. When all the files that you want to open are checked, press ENTER. Mouse users can simply click each file name to select it and then press ENTER.

The Refresh option operates in the same way as Open, enabling you to select which files you want Quattro Pro 4 to read values from. If you are using a dependent worksheet without the supporting sheets loaded into memory, it is a good idea to issue the Refresh command and get an update from all supporting worksheets before you print reports or base decisions on the values in the dependent worksheet.

The Change option on the Tools Update Links menu enables you to substitute a new supporting file for an existing one. This is handy if the name of a supporting worksheet has changed. For example, if the Miami worksheet arrives and is called MIAMIQ1.WQ1 instead of MIAMI.WQ1, you can change references to MIAMI.WQ1 to MIAMIQ1.WQ1 and do not have to edit and copy the formulas by hand. When you select Change you are given a list of the worksheets that support the current worksheet. Highlight the one you want to change and press ENTER. A file name box is presented, enabling you to type a new name or press F2 to edit the existing name. Alternatively you can press ESC to list files and choose the new file that way.

The Delete option on the Update Links menu enables you to remove supporting links. A list of linked files is presented, and you can choose which ones you want to delete. Any reference to a linked cell, such as [DALLAS]E3, is then replaced by ERR. This means that after the delete operation you can change the ERR to another reference, perhaps a cell within the current worksheet.

Advanced Editing Tools

Numerous tools within Quattro Pro 4 help you edit your worksheets. In Chapter 2 you saw the basic editing commands of Copy, Move, Insert, and Delete. This section shows how to use the last five items on the Edit menu: Names, Fill, Values, Transpose, and Search & Replace. Note that at this point in the book the step-by-step approach to examples gives way to a more descriptive approach. Commands are discussed in more general terms, with hypothetical examples. There will still be sufficient detail given for you to try out the commands, but instructions will be less explicit so that you can start to substitute your own data for that used in the text.

Edit Names

If you are making frequent use of a particular block of cells, you can save time by attaching a name to the block. Consider the revenue projection figures for the Chicago office in the sample worksheet, shown in Figure 3-23. The figures need to be totaled and the total may be used in several different places. If you attach a suitable name to the cells in the block E3..G6, such as CHICAGOQ1, you could then use the following formula in H7:

```
@SUM(CHICAGOQ1)
```

If you look closely at Figure 3-23 you can see that this formula has been used in H7. However, you cannot use a block name in a formula until you have created the name.

FIGURE
3-23

Sample worksheet using block name

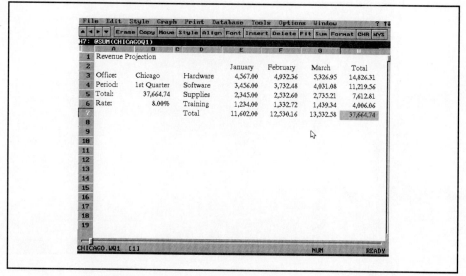

To name a block of cells you can begin by preselecting it. Either use your mouse or the keyboard to select the top left cell of the group block, press SHIFT-F7, then move the cell selector to the lower right cell. After you select the block, activate the menu, select Edit, and then select Names. You will see the menu shown in Figure 3-24. You use the Create command to assign a name. When you select Create, Quattro Pro 4 prompts you to type a name, for example, **CHICAGO**. Then you press ENTER to complete the command and return to READY mode. (If you did not preselect the cell block, you first have to point out the block, just as you do with other Edit commands, then press ENTER to complete the operation.)

As you might imagine, the names you use for blocks must follow certain rules. They can contain as many as 14 characters. You can use the letters A through Z and numbers 0 through 9 as well as punctuation characters. The names should bear some meaningful relationship to the contents of the cell but at the same time not be too long. Long names would negate some of the convenience of using the blocks. Block names should not be the same as any valid cell reference. For example, do not name a block Q4, because there is a cell called Q4 on row 4 in column Q. Using Q_4, or 4Q, or even FOURTH_QUARTER would be better. You can use any number of block names, and the blocks can overlap. For

FIGURE
3-24

The Edit Names menu

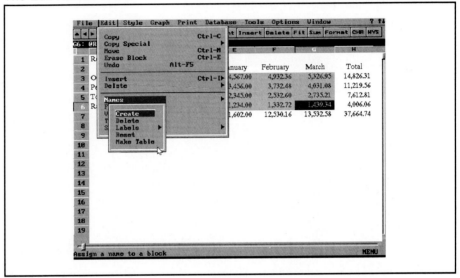

example, in Figure 3-23 you could name E3..G6 as both CHICAGOQ1 and QUARTER1.

When you use the Edit Names Create command and some cells have already been named you will see the names listed alphabetically, as Figure 3-25 shows. Here you can see that there is a block called RATE as well as one called CHICAGO. If you want to see the cell coordinates for the blocks that have been named, you can press the plus key (+) on the numeric keypad to get a detailed list like the one shown in Figure 3-26. Here the names are listed along with coordinates. You can see that RATE is the name attached to cell B6. If there are a lot of block names, you can press F3 to expand the names list and make it larger.

If you name a cell or block of cells and later decide that the name is no longer necessary, you can remove it by using the Delete command on the Edit Names menu. Quattro Pro 4 presents a list of names and you can highlight the one you want to delete and then press ENTER. Note that this deletes the block name without affecting the contents of the named cells. There is no confirmation of this command, but you can reverse it with UNDO. The Edit Names Delete command cannot delete more than one block name at a time. (The SHIFT-F7 key does not select names in the

FIGURE
3-25

The Edit Names Create command

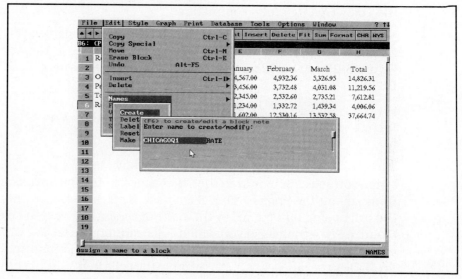

FIGURE
3-26

Detailed names list

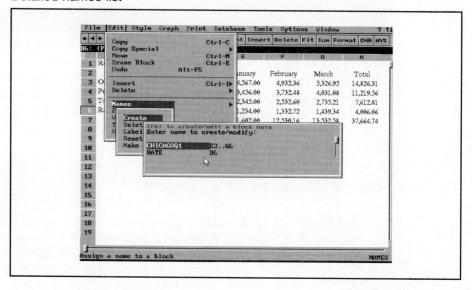

block names list the same way that it does in the file lists displayed by the Tools Update Links commands.)

The Labels command on the Edit Names menu enables you to assign names from labels in the spreadsheet. For example, in the worksheet in Figure 3-23 you could use the Labels command to name cells B3 through B6, like this:

B3	named	OFFICE:
B4	named	PERIOD:
B5	named	TOTAL:
B6	named	RATE:

When you select Labels from the Edit Names menu you are asked to select from among the choices of Right, Down, Left, and Up. In this scenario the cells being named are to the right of the labels, so you select Right. Quattro Pro 4 then asks you which cells contain the labels, which in this case are A3..A6. When you point out this block and press ENTER, Quattro Pro 4 uses the labels in A3..A6 to name the cells in B3..B6. In other words, the labels in A3..A6 name the cells to the right, B3..B6. This technique is particularly useful when you are working with macros and databases, and you will find it discussed further in Chapters 5 and 12.

The Reset command on the Edit Names menu deletes all block names at once. Because this step can accidentally erase names settings, Quattro Pro 4 requires you to confirm this action with a Yes/No response. The Make Table command on the Edit Names menu is used to create a two-column alphabetical list of the block names, together with their cell coordinates, in an area of the spreadsheet that you designate. This task is best done in an area set aside for worksheet housekeeping. Such a table is useful in larger worksheets for keeping track of block names you have used and their locations. However, the table is not automatically updated when block name assignments change, and you have to reissue the command to get a current table.

Using Block Names

Once a block has been named, you can use the name in a variety of ways. You can move the cell selector to a named block. When you press the GOTO key (F5) you can type the name of the block and press ENTER. In the example above, the location where B6 is called RATE, you could press F5 and enter **RATE**, and Quattro Pro 4 would select B6. If you have named E3..G6 as CHICAGOQ1, you can press F5 and enter **CHICAGOQ1** to select cell E3. This is because using F5 with a named block that is more than one cell has the effect of telling Quattro Pro 4 to select the top left cell of the block.

When you press F5 and are prompted for an address, you can supply a block name either by typing it or selecting it from a list. If you press the Choices key, F3, after pressing F5, you get a list of named blocks from which to choose. You can use the Choices key to create or edit formulas. For example, to create the formula @SUM(CHICAGOQ1), you can press the Functions key (ALT-F3) and select SUM, then press the Choices key (F3) and select CHICAGOQ1. All you have to do is add the closing parenthesis and the formula is complete. This highlights one of the primary advantages of block names over cell references. You can list and select names without typing.

Whenever you type information for Quattro Pro 4 you run the risk of making an error, plus it is often easier to remember a name, such as CHICAGOQ1, than a set of coordinates, E3..G6. Consider what happens if you enter E4..G6 by mistake, Quattro Pro 4 does not know you missed a line of numbers. But if you enter XHICAGOQ1 by mistake, Quattro Pro 4 beeps and tells you that the name is not correct.

Edit Fill

Quattro Pro 4 provides several methods for creating a series of numbers—1001, 1002, 1003, and so on. Such series are often needed to number consecutive columns and rows, as in the Item# column for the inventory items shown in Figure 3-27. With the Edit Fill command Quattro Pro 4 enables you to automatically fill a group of cells like this with consecutive numbers. You choose the starting number, the interval between numbers, and the ending number. For example, fill A4..A19 starting at 1001, incrementing by 1, and ending at 1016, as in column A of Figure 3-27.

When you select Edit Fill you are asked to define a Destination block of cells to fill. In Figure 3-27 the Destination block would be A4..A19. When you press ENTER to confirm the Destination, Quattro Pro 4 prompts you for a Start value. You can use the suggested default of 0 or any other

FIGURE 3-27

Inventory list with a numeric series

```
 File  Edit  Style  Graph  Print  Database  Tools  Options  Window        ? ↑↓
 ▲ ◄ ► ▼ │Erase│Copy│Move│Style│Align│Font│Insert│Delete│Fit│Sum│Format│CHR│WYS
 A4: 1001
      A      B            C              D         E        F        G
  1              TOA - Repair Shop Inventory Listing
  2
  3   Item#  Bin#     Description      Purchase    Sale    Purchased  InStock
  4   1001     9  Cone Nachelle, Left      1,340.56  1,675.70  08/09/93      7
  5   1002     5  Cone Nachelle, Right     1,340.56  1,675.70  07/13/93      9
  6   1003     1  Forward Bulkhead Unit      342.45    428.06  07/27/93      2
  7   1004     2  Cone Nachelle, Upper     1,340.56  1,675.70  09/07/93      5
  8   1005     2  Cone Nachelle, Lower     1,340.56  1,675.70  08/23/93      9
  9   1006     2  Nachelle, Retaining Flange  56.98     71.23  08/28/93     13
 10   1007     5  Cover Clamp               14.76     18.45  07/19/93     24
 11   1008     3  Wheel Brackets, Front    897.89  1,122.36  09/02/93     21
 12   1009     3  Wheel Brackets, Rear     980.67  1,225.84  08/28/93      7
 13   1010    10  Wheel Bracket Clip        45.89     57.36  07/31/93     28
 14   1011    11  Wheel Bracket Wing Nut     3.40      4.25  07/18/93     16
 15   1012     8  Wheel Bracket Washer       3.50      4.38  09/01/93    105
 16   1013     6  Strut Bracket, Left      978.56  1,223.20  08/20/93      4
 17   1014    12  Strut Bracket, Right     978.56  1,223.20  08/14/93     27
 18   1015     4  Wheel Bracket Seal        23.67     29.59  09/16/93     34
 19   1016     7  Wheel Rim Seal             3.50      4.38  09/06/93     32
 20
 FILLTEST.WQ1 [1]                                                    READY
```

number, such as 1001. Then press ENTER, and you will be prompted for the Step value. You can accept the default of 1, or use decimals or units larger than 1. You can use a negative Step value to create a series of declining values.

After entering the Step value, you have to specify the Stop value, which is the last value in the series. In this case you could use 16. When you enter the Stop value Quattro Pro 4 proceeds to fill the Destination block with a series of numbers that begins with the Start value and grows or decreases by the Step value (depending on whether the Step value is positive or negative). The last number in the series is determined by one of two factors: the Stop value or the size of the Destination block. For example, say you use as the Stop value the last number that you want in the series, for example 1016. In that case the series will end at 1016, provided that there are enough cells in the Destination block. If you had selected A4..A18 as the Destination block, the series would end at 1015, even if you had specified 1016 as the Stop value, because there are only 15 cells in A4..A18. In Figure 3-28 you can see a table of Edit Fill Scenarios that illustrate this point.

An alternative strategy for selecting a Stop value is to use a number beyond the last number in the series you are about to create (in this

FIGURE
3-28

The operation of Edit Fill

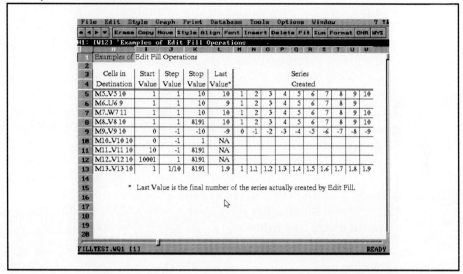

example you could use the default Stop value of 8191). Quattro Pro 4 will then create as many numbers as it can in the series until it has filled the Destination block. This is handy when you do not want to figure out the last number in the series but know how many cells you want to fill. Note that the default Stop number of 8191 comes from numbering all the rows from 0 to 8191. Also note that Edit Fill can also produce a horizontal series of numbers if you define a row as the fill block. You can even fill a rectangle with a series of values if you pick a rectangular fill block.

When you have used the Edit Fill command Quattro Pro 4 remembers the Destination, Start, Step, and Stop settings for that worksheet. The Edit Fill settings are stored with the worksheet. This means that if you want to re-create the same series or a slightly different one, the settings are all in place. You can press ENTER to accept Destination block and each of the value settings. If you want to alter a value setting, simply type over the previous value. However, if you want to create a fresh series in another location in the same spreadsheet, you will have to use ESC or BACKSPACE to reject the remembered Destination block. Pressing ESC will unlock the block coordinates, whereas BACKSPACE will unlock the block coordinates and move the cell selector to the cell that was current when you issued the Edit Fill command.

If you complete the Edit Fill command only to find that Quattro Pro 4 has not entered any values in the worksheet, verify that the Stop value is equal to or beyond the last number in the series. For example, if you start with 10001, increment by 1, and use the default Stop value of 8191, you will not get any values in the Destination block, because 8191 is less than 10001. Refer to Figure 3-28 for further examples of Edit Fill values. Note that you can use formulas or cell references for the values used by Edit Fill. For example, if you wanted a series of numbers that grew by a quarter, you could enter **1/4** instead of .25 as the Step value. If you want to grow a series of numbers by the value in B4, starting with the value that is in D6, you can enter **D6** as the Start value and **B4** as the Step value. If you decide to use cell references or formulas for Edit Fill values, you will find them converted to values the next time you use the command (for example, if you use 1/4 as the Step value, it will appear as .25 the next time you use Edit Fill).

You can select Edit Fill to create a series of dates, using date serial numbers, which were discussed in the previous chapter, or the @DATE function, described at the end of Chapter 4. For example, to create a series of dates representing successive Fridays you would begin by finding out the date serial number for the first day in the series. Do this by entering the date with the CTRL-D key. If you press CTRL-D and then enter **1/1/93**, which happens to be the first Friday in 1993, Quattro Pro 4 will display 01/01/93 in the current cell. From the cell identifier you can read that the date serial number in this case is 33970. You can now create the date series by using 33970 as the Start value and 7 as the Step value.

Note that Edit Fill does not supply the date format to cells. You will have to use the Style Numeric Format Date command to format the date serial numbers as dates. To create a date series with the @DATE function, refer to the section on date functions at the end of Chapter 4.

Another way of numbering consecutively is to use formulas. For example, to create the Item# entries in Figure 3-27 you could start by entering **1001** in A4, then enter the formula **1+A4** in A5. Copying the formula from A5 to A6..A19 will produce a series that looks just like the one created by Edit Fill. This has several advantages. You can create new numbers very easily. If you had to add a new item in row 20 at the bottom of the list, you could copy the formula from A19 to A20 and get 1017. Another advantage of a formula series is that you can change the whole series by altering the first number. By changing A4 from 1001 to 3001, you would change the numbers below accordingly, to 3002, 3003, and so on.

The advantages of a formula series are also its weaknesses. The numbers are not fixed, so copying an item from the inventory table to another part of the worksheet alters the Item#, rendering it incorrect. Fortunately, with Quattro Pro 4 you can create a series of numbers with formulas and then convert the formulas to their results, essentially "fixing" the values. This is done with the Edit Values command.

Edit Values

There will be times when you use formulas to generate numbers but no longer need the formulas. In other words, you want to "fix" the resulting values. You do this with the Edit Values command. Consider the worksheet in Figure 3-29, which is being used to calculate increased salaries. The formulas in column F create the new salary based on the percentage increase in E1. At this point a change to the percentage in E1 will alter all of the entries in F4..F19. When the rate of increase has been finalized there will be no need to make further changes to the New Salary figures.

FIGURE
3-29

Salary increase worksheet

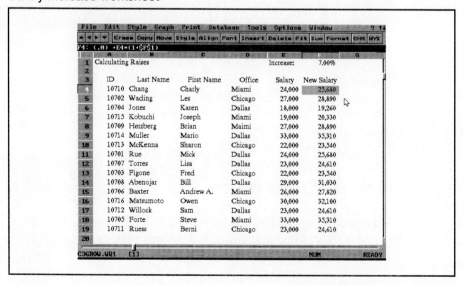

To replace the formulas in F4..F19 with permanent values you issue the Edit Values command and select F4..F19 as the Source Block. You will then be asked for the Destination. If you select F4 as the Destination, Quattro Pro 4 copies the values over the top of the formulas, directly replacing formulas with results. Alternatively, you can select a Destination outside of the Source Block and copy the resulting values to a different part of the worksheet.

Note that you can convert a single formula to its result by selecting the cell and pressing F2 followed by F9. This sequence of the Edit key followed by the Calc key is handy because it shows you the formula result on the edit line. This means you can press the ENTER key once to write the result over the formula or press the ESC key twice, which leaves the formula unchanged.

Edit Transpose

At times you may want to change the arrangement of information in a worksheet. For example, the table of employees in Figure 3-29 could be set up as in Figure 3-30, with one employee per column, rather than one row per employee. To move entries in this fashion you use the Edit Transpose command. The results in Figure 3-30 were created by issuing the Edit Transpose command and selecting A3..F19 as the Source Block, then choosing H23 as the Destination. You will probably want to use a Destination outside the Source Block to avoid confusing results.

Formulas that are transposed may not work properly. The formulas in column E of Figure 3-29 were converted to values before being transposed into Figure 3-30. The cell entries that you transpose will retain their cell formatting and alignment. In Figure 3-30 all of the cells were given right alignment after the Transpose command was used, making them easier to read.

Edit Search & Replace

Quattro Pro 4 offers a very useful Edit command called Search & Replace. Normally associated with word processing programs, the term *search and replace* refers to a program's ability to search for every

Transposed salary data

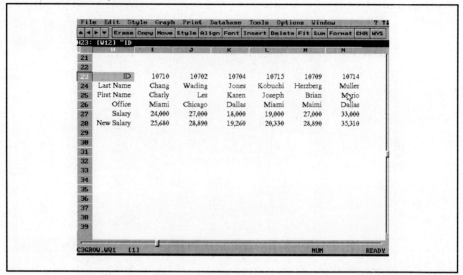

instance of one string of characters and replace it with another. For example, suppose that the Dallas office moves to Austin. The worksheet in Figure 3-29 would need considerable editing to change each instance of Dallas to Austin. This is a job for Search & Replace.

When you select Search & Replace from the Edit menu you get the menu shown in Figure 3-31. The first item to choose is Block. You then indicate the area of the spreadsheet to be searched. You should include all cells that you need to change. In this case the block is D4..D19. If you want to check all cells during a search and replace operation, you can use the following shortcut, which works whenever you want to select the entire worksheet at the block prompt:

1. Make sure that the starting coordinate is unlocked, that is, a single cell. The first time you use the Search & Replace block prompt this is the case, but at other times and with other commands the coordinates will be locked, as in D4..D4. You can use ESC to unlock coordinates.

2. Press HOME to move the cell selector to A1 and type a period (.) to anchor the coordinates there (A1..A1).

FIGURE
3-31

The Edit Search & Replace menu

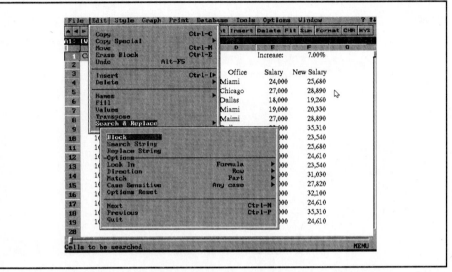

3. Press END and then HOME. This extends the block from A1 to the last column and row of the spreadsheet, that is, the ones furthest from column A and row 1 that contain any data.

4. You can now press ENTER to confirm the block.

After selecting the block of cells to be searched, you select Search String and type the characters you want Quattro Pro 4 to search for. These can be letters, numbers, math signs within formulas, or any character or string of characters you have entered into the cells. In this case you would type **Dallas**. Now you select Replace String and enter the characters to replace the ones you are searching for, in this case, **Austin**. If you do not wish to replace the item you are searching for but want to delete it, leave the Replace String blank. The Search & Replace options, listed in Table 3-5, enable you to fine tune the operation. In this case the default settings will work nicely.

To proceed with the Search & Replace operation, choose Next and Quattro Pro 4 will highlight the first cell it finds that contains the characters you are searching for. You then must make a choice, as shown

TABLE 3-5

Search & Replace Options

Type Option	Action
Look In:	
Formula	Looks for search string within formulas, cell references, block names, and so on. A search for 2 finds 2*2, B2, B52s, and so on, but does not find 6*7.
Value	Values the formula in each cell and looks for the search string in the result. Converts formula to value if result contains search string. Thus, a search for 2 with 5 as a replace string will find 6*7 and convert it to 45.
Condition	Enables you to set a condition in the search string, such as +B2>12, where B2 is the first cell in the search block and you want to find all cells with a value greater than 12.
Direction:	
Row	Searches the block from the current cell on, proceeding row by row.
Column	Searches the block from the current cell on, proceeding column by column.
Matches:	
Part	Searches for partial cell entries, so that a search string of **mar** would find **martian** and **market.**
Whole	Requires that the match be the entire cell contents, except for the label indicator, so that a search string of **mar** would not locate a cell containing **mars**.
Case Sensitive:	
Any-case	Does not require a match in cases, so that a search string of **erin** would find **Erin** and **ERIN**.
Exact-case	Requires that the match be exact as far as case is concerned. A search string of **ERIN** would not find **Erin**.

Note: A search initiated with Next moves forward through the block from the current cell, whereas a search initiated with Previous moves backward. Both choices search the entire block.

in Figure 3-32. You pick Yes to replace this instance of Dallas. Choosing No leaves this instance as it is. Selecting All tells Quattro Pro 4 to proceed with an automatic search and replace from this point on. Do not pick All unless you are certain about what will happen. If you are not careful about limiting the block to be searched, you could change instances of the search characters you did not anticipate.

The Edit option in Figure 3-32 is a very handy one, enabling you to interrupt the Search & Replace operation to edit a particular cell that has been found, for example, if you wanted to assign one of the employees from Dallas to Miami instead of Austin. The Quit option tells Quattro Pro 4 to stop the process before all instances have been changed. If you choose this option, the last cell found becomes the current cell. After the last instance of the searched characters has been reached and your decision has been entered, Quattro Pro 4 returns to READY mode. The next time you use the Search & Replace command for this worksheet in this session, it will remember the settings that you entered. In fact, the Search & Replace command will remember the settings even if you move to a different worksheet window, enabling you to repeat the same operation on similar spreadsheets, one after another. If you need to change the settings you can simply pick the Options Reset command.

Search & Replace in action

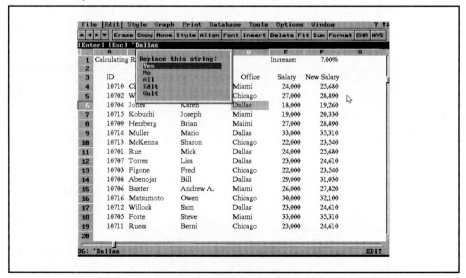

Draft Mode Printing

Using the Print menu, shown in Figure 3-33 you can produce anything from a single-page printout of your worksheet to a carefully formatted multipage report, complete with headers, footers, and other enhancements. If your printer supports graphic features such as fonts and line drawing, described later in this chapter, you can print reports that include these embellishments.

In fact, Quattro Pro 4 performs two quite different types of printing. The most direct method, supported by virtually all printers, is referred to as draft mode printing. The more complex method, which produces carefully formatted results including fonts and lines, is known as final quality printing. All printing, simple or complex, begins with the Print menu, and this section explores some of the basic Print commands. More advanced commands will be dealt with later, under "Final Quality Printing."

The Print menu

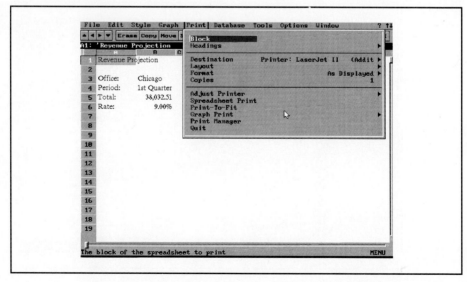

Basic Printing

There are numerous options available for print operations in Quattro Pro 4, but you can get results with just two commands on the Print menu: Block and Spreadsheet Print. The Print Block command is used to tell Quattro Pro 4 which group of cells are to be printed. As you might expect, Block on the Print menu works like any other Quattro Pro 4 block command. You specify the desired coordinates, either by typing them in or marking the cells. Spreadsheet Print is used to initiate the printing once you have specified a block.

Before you use the Spreadsheet Print command it is a good idea to check the Destination setting on the Print menu. In Figure 3-33 you can see that the Destination is

```
Printer: LaserJet II (Addit
```

The term "Addit" indicates that the printer has additional memory. The word "Printer" indicates that you will be using your printer in draft mode. If you select Destination from the Print menu, you see the options listed in Figure 3-34.

FIGURE 3-34

Destination options

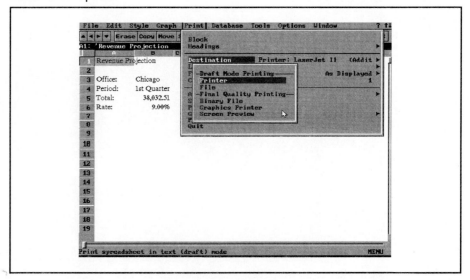

The Destination options are divided into two parts: Draft Mode Printing and Final Quality Printing. Under Draft Mode Printing you can choose between Printer and File. Under Final Quality Printing you have three choices: Binary File, Graphics Printer, and Screen Preview. These three options are dealt with later under "Final Quality Printing." For basic printing the Printer option under Draft Mode Printing will suffice. Note that you do not select the model of printer from the Destination menu. The Destination options merely tell Quattro Pro 4 how to deliver the printout, with the possibilities listed in Table 3-6.

To actually change the printer model you will need to use the Hardware command on the Options menu. When you have selected Hardware you need to choose Printers and then see what the Default Printer setting is. If the Default Printer setting is 1st Printer, which is usually the case, choose 1st Printer to alter the model, as shown in Figure 3-35. If the Default Printer setting is 2nd Printer, choose 2nd Printer from the Printers menu.

When you select Type of printer from either the 1st or 2nd Printer menu, Quattro Pro 4 prompts you to specify Make, Model, and Mode. When you have selected a Make (such as Brother or HP) you need to specify the Model (such as HL-8 PS or LaserJet II). There may be separate listings for the same model but with different amounts of printer memory or RAM. You may also need to select a print mode. This is a combination of page size (such as Letter, Legal, or A4) and resolution. The print resolution determines how tightly the dots of ink are placed on the page. For example "300 × 300 dpi" is 300 dots per inch, which is tighter, and thus smoother in appearance, than 150 × 150 dpi.

TABLE 3-6

Printing Possibilities

Type of Output	Destination
Basic characters on the printer	Draft Mode—Printer
Basic characters in a file	Draft Mode—File
Fonts, styles, and data in a file	Final Quality—Binary File
Fonts, styles, and data on the printer	Final Quality—Graphics Printer
Fonts, styles, and data on the screen	Final Quality—Screen Preview

FIGURE
3-35

Changing the printer model

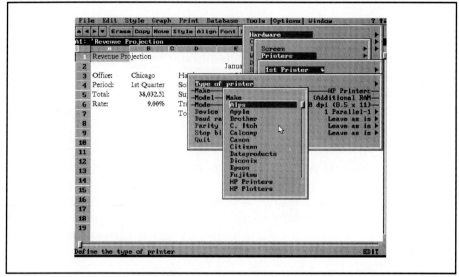

After you select the printer description that most closely resembles the equipment you plan to use, select Quit twice to return to the main Options menu. There you should choose Update in order to record your choice of printer. When you quit the Options menu and return to the Print menu the printer in the Destination setting should match the one you have just described under Options. Note that if you have a PostScript printer you may not be able to print in draft mode.

A Print Sample

Suppose that you want to print a sample spreadsheet called ASAMPLE.WQ1, described in Chapter 2 (or the CHICAGO.WQ1 worksheet seen earlier in this chapter). You can see the worksheet in Figure 3-36 where the Print Block is being defined. The basic printing operation is to select the cells to be printed, in this case A1..H7, and then issue the Spreadsheet Print command. You can select the cells with the mouse or keyboard prior to issuing the Print Block command. If you are using the keyboard, press HOME followed by SHIFT-F7 to activate EXT mode, then use the arrow keys to extend the highlighting to H7. With A1..H7 selected

Defining the Print Block

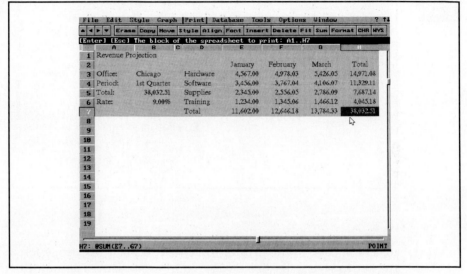

you can issue the Print Block command. Quattro Pro 4 immediately accepts A1..H7 as the Print Block.

If you issue the Print Block command before you have selected any cells, you will find that the initial block coordinate is not locked, so you can move the cell selector freely to identify the top left corner of the group of cells to be printed. You can then type a period to anchor the block and extend the highlighting to H7.

When the Print Block has been selected, Quattro Pro 4 returns you to the Print menu. At this point, if your printer is properly connected, turned on, and has paper in it, you can now select Spreadsheet Print. The MODE Indicator may flash the word WAIT for a moment. The completed print job will then start to appear at the printer, the results looking like Figure 3-37.

The type style in which the characters are printed will be determined by the printer. That is, the printer's default type style will be used. Some printers have a control panel that allows you to select a different type style. When you are using the Printer setting for Draft Mode Printing you can select a different type style with the printer, and Quattro Pro 4 will use it. Another technique you can use to perform Draft Mode Printing is

FIGURE
3-37

Initial print results

```
Revenue Projection
                            January   February   March     Total
Office:  Chicago    Hardware 4,567.00  4,978.03  5,426.05 14,971.08
Period:  1st Quarter Software 3,456.00  3,767.04  4,106.07 11,329.11
Total:      38,032.51 Supplies 2,345.00  2,556.05  2,786.09  7,687.14
Rate:          9.00% Training 1,234.00  1,345.06  1,466.12  4,045.18
                    Total    11,602.00 12,646.18 13,784.33 38,032.51
```

to send a code to the printer to activate a print feature, such as bold, via the setup string feature described in a moment. The point is that Draft Mode Printing enables the printer to determine the appearance of the characters. When you use Final Quality Printing, described later in this chapter, the appearance of characters will be determined by Quattro Pro 4 and the Style commands that you use.

Adjust Printer

With basic Draft Mode Printing all that Quattro Pro 4 sends to the printer is the contents of the Print Block, in this case seven rows. At this point Quattro Pro 4 has not even told the printer to move on to the next sheet of paper. This means that you can select a different group of cells as the Print Block and print them right below the last block. For example, you could load the Miami worksheet and print cells A1..H7, right below the Chicago printout. If you want a gap between the two printouts you can use the Adjust Printer command on the Print menu to advance the paper in the printer. There are three options:

Skip Line   Moves paper forward a line at a time. Skip Line is useful when you are using continuous feed paper and you want to print several blocks of cells one after another

Form Feed   Moves to next sheet of paper. When you are using continuous feed paper, Form Feed rolls the paper to the top of the next sheet. When you are using a paper tray or sheet feeder, Form Feed ejects the current sheet of paper (particularly useful with an HP LaserJet when the last page of a printout is not automatically ejected)

Align Paper   Tells Quattro Pro 4 that the current position of the paper in the printer is correct. In other words, the print head is at the top of the page. Using this command before each print job helps to ensure that results are properly placed on the page. This command also resets the page numbering to 1 so that page numbers in headers and footers are correct

Many printers' controls enable you to advance or eject pages. However, if you advance the paper with the printer controls instead of the Adjust Printer commands, Quattro Pro 4 will lose track of how many lines have been printed on the current page. This can lead to problems when you print a block of cells that extends past the end of a page. Quattro Pro 4 will add space for the page break in the wrong place. Use Adjust Printer commands to control paper positioning whenever possible and issue the Align Paper command if you have manually adjusted the paper.

Layout, Dialogs, and Defaults

When you use basic Draft Mode Printing your output is based on the size of the Print Block you define and the current Layout settings. As you can see from Figure 3-38, these settings include the length of the page and the margins that define the printing area. In other words, they are the parameters by which Quattro Pro 4 relates to a piece of paper.

Note that when you select Layout from the Print menu you do not get a normal submenu of options. What you get is referred to as a dialog box, a compact way of storing your preferences for a collection of settings. You will also find dialog boxes used in the Quattro Pro 4 Graph commands. Dialog boxes appear in both character and WYSIWYG display modes. If the dialog box shown in Figure 3-38 does not appear when you select Layout from the Print menu, you will have to change the settings through

FIGURE
3-38

The Layout dialog box

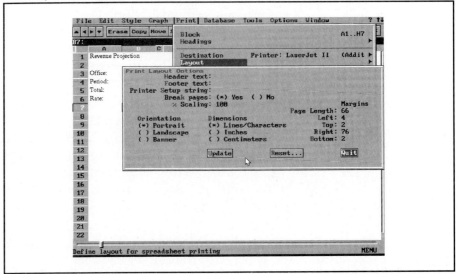

a series of menu choices. To make sure you have the dialog box, use the Startup command on the Options menu and select Use Dialogs. Choose Yes and then Quit. Choose Update from the main Options menu to record your preference.

Each setting or group of settings within the Layout dialog box has its own key letter. Some settings involve text entries, such as the header and footer, described in a moment. Other settings, such as Dimensions, only permit one of the options to be selected at once. For example, if you select Inches, Lines/Characters is automatically deselected. The settings shown in Figure 3-38 represent the default layout, diagrammed in Figure 3-39.

Lines/Characters or Inches and Centimeters

From the point of view of a software package, there are two different ways of looking at information printed on paper. You can see the words and numbers as so many characters on a line, and a certain number of lines per page. This is how the first PC programs treated printouts. Words

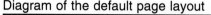

FIGURE 3-39

Diagram of the default page layout

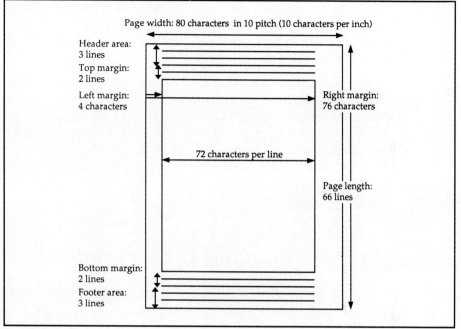

were printed at 10 characters to an inch (10 pitch). A piece of letter-size paper that is 8.5 inches wide could thus accommodate 85 characters. Leave half an inch or 5 characters margin on either side, and there was room for 75 characters on a line, which worked well with the 80-character width of early display systems.

Most early printers printed at 6 lines per inch, giving a page length of 66 lines when using letter-size paper that is 11 inches long. When you are using Draft Mode Printing you should use the Lines/Characters option for the Dimensions setting. Type **D** and then **L** to do this.

The alternative to the lines-and-characters approach is to measure the page in inches or centimeters and scale the words and numbers accordingly. This approach is used with Final Quality Printing when fonts are measured in point sizes rather than characters and lines per inch. Because Final Quality Printing means that Quattro Pro 4 controls the appearance of printed characters, you can set the margins in inches and not worry about exactly how many characters will fit on a page. Quattro

Pro 4 can shrink or enlarge output to fit the Print Block neatly into the space left on the page, within the margins. If you decide to use Final Quality Printing, you can change the Dimensions setting to Inches or Centimeters by typing D followed by either I or C. If you are using a mouse just click on the choice you want.

Note that if you are using an HP LaserJet series printer or one that's similar and you have Lines/Characters as the Dimensions settings, you should change the Page Length setting to 60 lines if you are using standard letter-size paper (8.5×11 inches). This is necessary to accommodate the fact that LaserJet series printers do not print all the way to the edge of the sheet of paper. You might also want to change the Left margin to 5 and the Right margin to 80 to better position the output across the page.

Changing Margins and Orientation

The margins are a critical factor when you adjust print settings. If you switch to wider paper, you must use the Margins settings to increase the right margin. The 15-inch-wide paper used in many wide-carriage printers calls for a right margin of 140. A sheet of 8 1/2- by 14-inch legal paper turned on its side, so the width is 14 inches, can use a 132-character right margin. To change a margin setting simply type the key letter of the item, such as L for Left margin. Then you can type the setting you want and press ENTER.

You should increase the Right margin setting if you reduce printer pitch to get more characters per inch. The condensed pitch of 17 characters per inch used on many dot matrix and laser printers provides for a right margin of 140 on 8 1/2-inch-wide paper and 250 on 15-inch-wide paper. You must set the margin yourself when you change paper size or print pitch.

You also have to change the margins and page length when you alter the direction of printing, referred to as the orientation. The choices for the Orientation setting are Portrait, which prints lines across the narrow dimension of the page, as in this book, and Landscape, which prints lines across the length of the page, at ninety degrees to portrait printing.

Printer Setup Strings

Many printers can be told to change their print style, print pitch, and other aspects by codes transmitted as part of the print data sent from the program. Quattro Pro 4 accommodates these codes with the Printer Setup string setting. The codes you enter here are sent ahead of the data being printed. For example, most IBM and Epson dot matrix printers respond to the characters \015 as meaning condensed print. Note that you should only use setup strings in Draft Mode Printing, not when the Print Destination setting is Graphics Printer. A setup string consists of one or more ASCII character codes, which are translated from the printer control codes listed in your printer's user manual. For example, Hewlett-Packard LaserJet printers understand the code

```
\027E\027(s16.66H
```

to mean compressed print (17 pitch). You can enter a setup string with the Printer Setup string option, or you can place the string in the worksheet by entering it in a cell in the leftmost column of the Print Block. If you enter a setup code in a worksheet cell, you must precede it with two of the special label prefix characters, the vertical line (¦), as in

```
¦¦\027E\027(s16.66H)
```

When it encounters this cell entry, Quattro Pro 4 sends the print instruction to the printer. Quattro Pro 4 does not print the line on which the entry occurs, which means that you should not place the code in a row that you want to print. The code does not have to be in the first row of the Print Block, and you can use several codes in the same Print Block, for example, to turn on condensed print, then turn it off again. (Note that you can use the ¦¦ code alone to hide a row during printing.)

Printer control codes can be sent in several forms. Most begin with the Esc character, which is entered as **\027**. This is followed by further codes that are either entered as a \ followed by a number or as a simple character like *E*. Your printer manual might tell you to use Esc 18 which is entered as **\027\018**. You can enter more than one code in a setup string as long as the printer supports it and the entire string does not exceed 254 characters. For example, the Epson FX-85 can print near-letter-quality, bold, and elite pitch characters, but it cannot print itali-cized characters in near-letter-quality mode.

Headers, Footers, and Headings

If you are creating a report that extends across several pages, you may want to repeat some information on each page, such as your company name, the report title, and a page number. You do this with the Header text and Footer text settings in the Layout dialog box. These commands provide areas into which you type the text to be printed, along with formatting instructions that tell Quattro Pro 4 how to align the text.

Special codes can be used in headers and footers to tell Quattro Pro 4 to print such information as the correct page number. The # sign tells Quattro Pro 4 to enter the page number in a header or footer. The @ sign causes the current date, according to your PC's clock, to be printed. The split vertical rule symbol, ¦, is used like a tab stop to position header and footer text across the line. Typing the header text with no ¦ symbol causes Quattro Pro 4 to left-align everything. Preceding text with one ¦ results in centering. Using two ¦ symbols places the text on the right. In Figure 3-40 you can see a report printed with the following entries for header and footer text:

Header text   Date: @¦¦Page #
Footer text   ¦Confidential

The report in Figure 3-40 extends to two pages. For this reason it repeats certain information on both pages. The worksheet that produced this report is shown in Figure 3-41. Basically, this is a combination of the three office worksheets used earlier, extended to cover six months. The Options WYSIWYG Zoom % was set to 75 so that the whole worksheet could be seen at once. The Print Block is cells A1..K25. Consider what would happen if you sent this Print Block to the printer with the default Print Layout settings shown earlier in Figure 3-38. Quattro Pro 4 would place as much of the Print Block on the first page as it could, then move to a second page and print the rest. In fact, A1..G25 would appear on the first page and H1..K25 would appear on the second. This would make the report somewhat difficult to read, as there would be no row titles on the second page.

FIGURE 3-40

Two-page report with header and footer

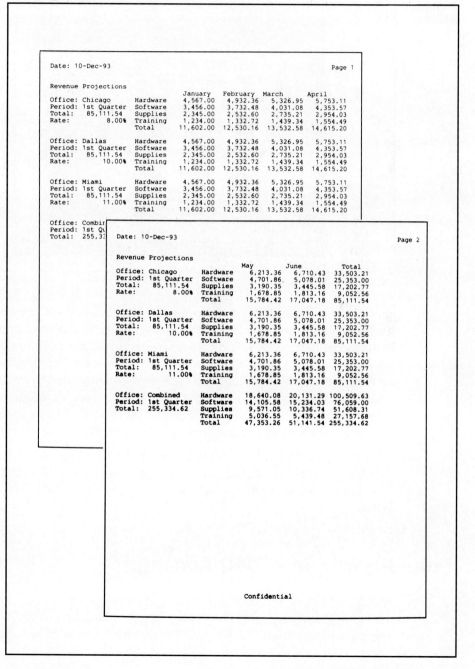

```
Date: 10-Dec-93                                                Page 1

Revenue Projections

                              January  February March      April
Office: Chicago    Hardware  4,567.00  4,932.36 5,326.95   5,753.11
Period: 1st Quarter Software 3,456.00  3,732.48 4,031.08   4,353.57
Total:    85,111.54 Supplies 2,345.00  2,532.60 2,735.21   2,954.03
Rate:        8.00% Training  1,234.00  1,332.72 1,439.34   1,554.49
                   Total    11,602.00 12,530.16 13,532.58 14,615.20

Office: Dallas     Hardware  4,567.00  4,932.36 5,326.95   5,753.11
Period: 1st Quarter Software 3,456.00  3,732.48 4,031.08   4,353.57
Total:    85,111.54 Supplies 2,345.00  2,532.60 2,735.21   2,954.03
Rate:       10.00% Training  1,234.00  1,332.72 1,439.34   1,554.49
                   Total    11,602.00 12,530.16 13,532.58 14,615.20

Office: Miami      Hardware  4,567.00  4,932.36 5,326.95   5,753.11
Period: 1st Quarter Software 3,456.00  3,732.48 4,031.08   4,353.57
Total:    85,111.54 Supplies 2,345.00  2,532.60 2,735.21   2,954.03
Rate:       11.00% Training  1,234.00  1,332.72 1,439.34   1,554.49
                   Total    11,602.00 12,530.16 13,532.58 14,615.20

Office: Combir
Period: 1st Qu
Total:   255,3
```

```
Date: 10-Dec-93                                                Page 2

Revenue Projections

                              May        June       Total
Office: Chicago    Hardware  6,213.36   6,710.43  33,503.21
Period: 1st Quarter Software 4,701.86.  5,078.01  25,353.00
Total:    85,111.54 Supplies 3,190.35   3,445.58  17,202.77
Rate:        8.00% Training  1,678.85   1,813.16   9,052.56
                   Total    15,784.42  17,047.18  85,111.54

Office: Dallas     Hardware  6,213.36   6,710.43  33,503.21
Period: 1st Quarter Software 4,701.86   5,078.01  25,353.00
Total:    85,111.54 Supplies 3,190.35   3,445.58  17,202.77
Rate:       10.00% Training  1,678.85   1,813.16   9,052.56
                   Total    15,784.42  17,047.18  85,111.54

Office: Miami      Hardware  6,213.36   6,710.43  33,503.21
Period: 1st Quarter Software 4,701.86   5,078.01  25,353.00
Total:    85,111.54 Supplies 3,190.35   3,445.58  17,202.77
Rate:       11.00% Training  1,678.85   1,813.16   9,052.56
                   Total    15,784.42  17,047.18  85,111.54

Office: Combined   Hardware 18,640.08  20,131.29 100,509.63
Period: 1st Quarter Software 14,105.58  15,234.03  76,059.00
Total:   255,334.62 Supplies  9,571.05  10,336.74  51,608.31
                   Training   5,036.55   5,439.48  27,157.68
                   Total     47,353.26  51,141.54 255,334.62
```

```
                         Confidential
```

FIGURE
3-41
Extended worksheet

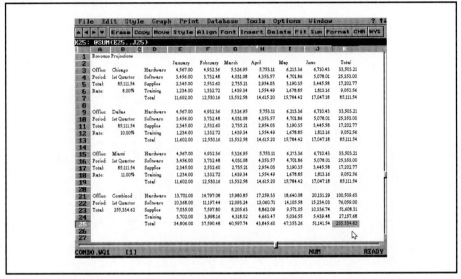

To correct this problem you can tell Quattro Pro 4 to repeat column and row headings in a printout. You use the Headings command on the Print menu to identify columns and rows containing cells to use as print borders that are repeated on each page. (If you do this, the Print Block setting must then be changed to exclude areas included in the headings.) The Print Headings command gives you two choices: Left Heading, which is one or more columns of cells repeated on the left of each page; and Top Heading, which is one or more rows of cells, repeated at the top of each page.

The results in Figure 3-40 were achieved by using cells A1..D25 as a Left Heading and changing the Print Block to E1..K25. Because the Print Block is not longer than a single page, it was not necessary to use a Top Heading.

Page Breaks and Cell Listings

The Break pages option in the Layout dialog box is normally set to Yes. This tells Quattro Pro 4 to insert page breaks according to the Page Length setting and how much of the Print Block will fit on each page. Figure 3-42 diagrams how Quattro Pro 4 creates page breaks when the Print Block is larger than a single page.

The page breaks automatically made by Quattro Pro 4 are referred to as soft page breaks, because they change position according to the size of the Print Block. However, you can place special page break characters in cells within the Print Block to force page breaks at chosen points in the printout. These hard page breaks consist of the vertical line character and two colons (|::) placed on an empty row. As mentioned earlier, the split vertical rule character, |, is a special label indicator that tells Quattro Pro 4 not to print what follows. These characters are stored as part of the spreadsheet and are not removed until they are individually deleted from the spreadsheet.

To create hard page breaks, either type in the codes or select Insert Break from the Style menu. In either case you should create a blank row first, because any other data on a page-break row will not be printed. Page breaks should not be inserted in heading blocks, which are described in a moment.

FIGURE
3-42
Diagram of page breaks for large Print Blocks

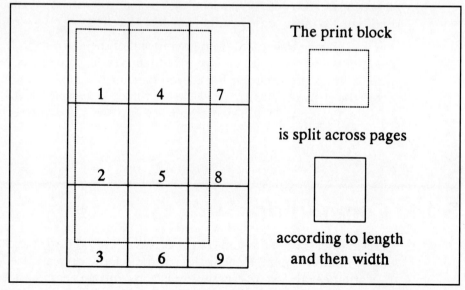

Quattro Pro 4 recognizes hard page breaks and inserts other, soft page breaks, as needed. Pages incorporate room for headers and footers. If you want a continuous stream of text, for example to print mailing labels, change the Break pages setting to No. Quattro Pro 4 will still respond to hard page breaks you have placed in the worksheet, but headers and footers are not printed and no other breaks will be made.

If you want a list of what is in every cell in a worksheet, including the cell format and width if they differ from the global setting, select the Cell-formula option from the Print Format menu. The resulting printout will include the cells that are in the Print Block down the side of the page. This is useful for reference or for communicating with other users.

Resetting Options and Storing Defaults

When you save a spreadsheet, the print settings in effect at the time you perform the save are stored together with the worksheet data. If you need to change the print settings completely, perhaps to print out a different section of the same worksheet, you can use the Reset command in the Layout dialog box. This pops up a menu with four choices: All, Print Block, Headings, and Layout. To clear the Print Block and return all settings to the defaults, select All. To clear just the Print Block, select that item. To clear print headings, select Headings.

If you choose Reset and then Layout, all of the settings in the Layout dialog box will revert to the program defaults. If you will be using the same settings on a regular basis, you can use the Update command to record the current settings in the Layout dialog box as part of the program defaults. Program defaults are described further in Chapter 6.

Style Commands

In Chapter 2 you saw some of the Style commands, such as Alignment and Numeric Format. They are used to alter the appearance of part of the worksheet and complement the Options Formats commands that can alter the appearance of all cells in the worksheet. This section demonstrates how to use the Style commands that affect the width and height of cells, as well as the fonts used to print cell contents and the line and shade enhancements you can add to cells.

Column Width

There are several ways to set the width of a single column. After placing the cell selector anywhere in the column you want to adjust, you can select Column Width from the Style menu or press CTRL-W, the Shortcut key for this command. In both cases Quattro Pro 4 prompts you to enter a width setting and displays the current setting, as in

```
Alter the width of the current column [1..254]: 9
```

This prompt reminds you that the column can be 1 to 254 characters wide. In response you can either type a number for the setting, which represents the approximate number of characters that will fit into the column, or you can use the LEFT ARROW and RIGHT ARROW keys to adjust the column one character at a time. Pressing RIGHT ARROW widens the column, while LEFT ARROW narrows it, one character for each time you press the arrow key.

If you use the arrow key method, you see the column width change on the screen. When the column is the right width or you have typed the desired width number, you can press ENTER to complete the command and return to READY mode. You will now see a code in the cell identifier that reminds you what the column width is set at, such as [10] for 10 characters.

Mouse users can alter the width of a column by pointing to the column letter and then holding down the left mouse button. This causes Quattro Pro 4 to display arrows on either side of the letter, as shown in Figure 3-43. You can now move the mouse pointer left or right to adjust the width. Release the mouse button when the width is correct.

FIGURE 3-43   Adjusting column width with the mouse

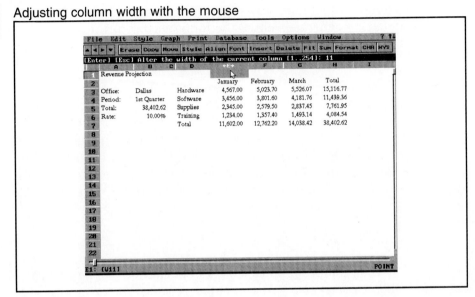

Reset Width

When you set the width of a column by using the mouse or the Column Width command, that width is no longer affected by the Global Width setting on the Options Formats menu. If you decide that you want a column to revert to the global width setting, you can place the cell selector anywhere in the column and select Reset Width from the Style menu. The column width will change to match the global width and the width code will disappear from the cell identifier.

The Block Size Commands

You can set the width of several columns at once by using the Block Size command on the Style menu. This presents four options: Set Width, Reset Width, Auto Width, and Height. The Set Width command prompts you for a block of columns that will all have their width set at the same time. After defining the block, you enter the width setting as you do with the Column Width command. You can return a group of columns to the default width by selecting the Reset Width option from the Block Size menu. After you indicate the block of columns to be adjusted, Quattro Pro 4 resets them to the width specified by Options Formats.

The Auto Width command enables you to make columns wide enough to contain the largest entry in the column. This is very handy when you are designing large worksheets, and having the width automatically set saves you from counting characters. When you select Auto Width Quattro Pro 4 prompts you to enter a number, between 0 and 40, that represents a measure of the number of characters of space to be left between columns. The default setting is 1. After pressing ENTER to accept the number of characters to be left between the adjusted columns, you are asked to indicate which columns you want to be adjusted. This can be a single column or a block of columns. When you have pointed out and confirmed the column selection, Quattro Pro 4 reads the cells' contents and widens or narrows the selected columns accordingly.

There are a couple of tricks you should know to use the Auto Width command effectively. At the column selection prompt you can indicate the block of columns with a single row block. This tells Quattro Pro 4 to adjust the columns based on the width of entries "in that row and any rows below it." This is helpful if you have some wide labels above columns of data and want to exclude the labels from the width setting calculation. However, if you have long entries that you want included in the width adjustment, make sure that they are on or below the row you use.

If you select a column block consisting of more than one row, either above or below the current cell, Quattro Pro 4 bases the width adjustment on the cells in that selected block and no others. This enables you to control exactly which cells are used to determine column width. Bear in mind that Auto Width narrows columns as well as widens them, depending on the width setting prior to the command and the size of cell entries.

When you use WYSIWYG mode and change the font used for letters and numbers, as described later in this chapter, Quattro Pro 4 automatically adjusts the height of rows to accommodate the change. For example, if you choose a 14 point font instead of a 12 point, the row height is increased to make room for the larger characters. The height of a row will thus be determined by the largest font used on that row. You can use the Height option on the block Size menu to adjust the height of one or more rows, but beware of setting a height that does not allow enough room for all of the fonts used on the row (undersizing row heights can result in strange display and printing effects).

When you select Height from the Block Size menu you can choose Set Row Height, which enables you to specify the rows you want to adjust and the height you want them to be. You can also select Reset Row Height, which restores the selected rows to the default height setting (large enough to properly display the largest font used on the row). After you select Set Row Height you select the rows to be changed, then use the UP ARROW and DOWN ARROW keys to adjust height. Alternatively you can type a number for the height and press ENTER. After you select Reset Row Height and the rows to be affected, you press ENTER. Quattro Pro 4 makes the adjustment for you.

Mouse users can alter the height of a column by pointing to the row number on the left of the screen and then holding down the left mouse button. This causes Quattro Pro 4 to display arrows above and below the number. You can now move the mouse pointer up or down to adjust the height. Release the mouse button when the height is correct.

You will find row height adjustments to be useful when you design more complex reports. You can increase the white space in a report by making a row much taller than it needs to be. You can also create a pleasant effect by making a row short and shading it with the Style Shading command, described later in this chapter.

Hiding Columns

Sometimes the data you see on the screen is not exactly the data you need. In such cases you can try hiding certain columns with the Style Hide Column command. Quattro Pro 4 lets you place selected columns in the background and closes up the ones in the foreground. This process is diagrammed in Figure 3-44. Thus, Quattro Pro 4 enables you to pick and choose which columns to view. The Style Hide Column command is also useful when you are dealing with confidential data or arranging a worksheet prior to printing. The hidden data is not lost, and hidden formulas continue to be active, but hidden columns do not print.

To hide one or more columns you place your cell selector on any row of the column and then select Style Hide Column. Your choices are Hide or Expose. Choose Hide and then press ENTER if you only want to hide

FIGURE 3-44 Hiding columns

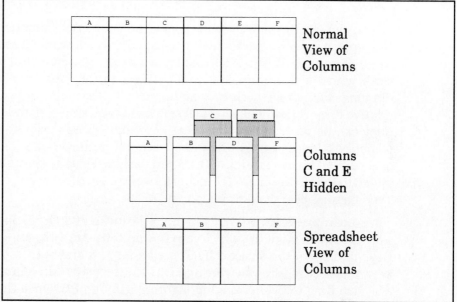

Normal View of Columns

Columns C and E Hidden

Spreadsheet View of Columns

the current column. To hide more than one column at once, type a period to anchor the beginning column, then press RIGHT ARROW to move the highlighting through to the last column you want to hide. When you press ENTER to confirm the selection of columns they disappear from view and cannot be accessed with cell selector, at least in READY mode. In Figure 3-45 you can see that columns E, F, and G have been hidden.

To return the columns to view, simply select Style Hide Column Expose. Asterisks next to the column letters indicate the columns that are currently hidden. To return some or all columns to the display, simply highlight them and press ENTER. If you press ESC and do not select any columns, the marked columns remain hidden.

Column width and format remain unaffected by the hide-and-expose process. When you carry out any command using the POINT mode to indicate cell references, Quattro Pro 4 temporarily reveals hidden columns, marked by asterisks, so that they can be considered in the command. For example, if you use the Edit Move or Edit Copy command or formulas built with the point method, the columns will be temporarily revealed so you can correctly complete the operation.

Line Drawing

You can use the Line Drawing command on the Style menu to enhance the appearance of worksheets. This command works regardless of whether you have a graphics display. However, you may find it easier to work with these commands in WYSIWYG mode. Quattro Pro 4's line drawing commands work by placing lines in locations that you specify, relative to cells that you select. The lines can be single, double, or thick. They can be placed all around a cell or block of cells, or just on the top or bottom. Lines can be drawn between columns or rows, or an entire grid can be drawn. In Figure 3-46 you can see several examples of lines added to the CHICAGO.WQ1 model as well as see the Placement and Line Type menus, described in a moment.

You can preselect cells to which you want to add lines. Suppose you were about to add the lines you see in cells A3..B6 in Figure 3-46. Keyboard users can select cell A3, press SHIFT-F7, and then use the arrow keys to select all the way through B6. Mouse users can simply click on A6, then drag to extend the highlighting through B6. Once this block of

Worksheet with columns hidden

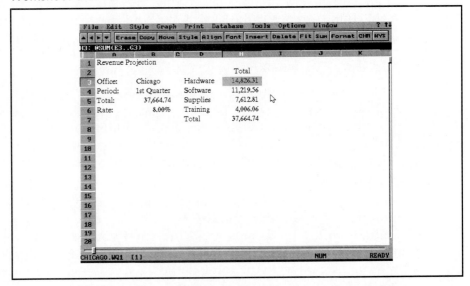

cells has been selected you can use the Style command and pick Line Drawing. The command you issue now will apply to the cells that you have preselected.

You do not have to use preselection with the Style commands. If you do not preselect cells or only have one cell selected, you are simply prompted for the block of cells after you have issued the Line Drawing command. When you pick Line Drawing and the cells to be affected have been indicated, you see the Placement options listed in Figure 3-46. This menu enables you to specify where the lines will be placed in relation to the cells you have selected. You can browse through the options on this list with the UP ARROW and DOWN ARROW keys, noting the explanations that appear at the bottom of the screen as you scroll.

When you pick any one of the placement choices, Quattro Pro 4 lists the types of lines you can use: Single, Double, or Thick. If you pick one of these types, Quattro Pro 4 draws the line and returns you to the Placement menu. For example, you could choose Left followed by Single. Quattro Pro 4 draws a single line on the left of all cells in the selected block, then returns you to the Placement menu so that you can draw more lines. When you have all the lines you want in the current block, select Quit to get back to READY mode. Alternatively, you can press ESC,

**FIGURE
3-46**

Lines and the Style Line Drawing command

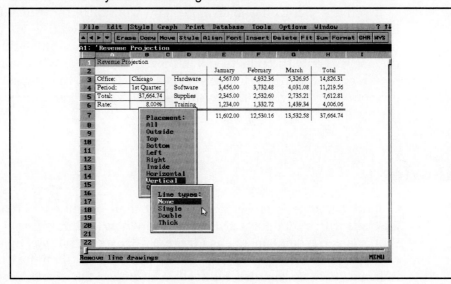

which gives you a chance to select a different block of cells and draw lines in them.

To create the example in Figure 3-46, the All option on the Placement menu was used on cells A3..B6. This option draws lines around all cells in the selected block. The double line on row 7 was created by selecting D7..H7 and then Top, followed by Double. Note that using a double line sometimes requires a manual adjustment to the row height, as described earlier in this chapter.

If you want to remove lines that you have added to a worksheet, you can select the cells, issue the Style Line Drawing command, and choose which lines to remove with the Placement menu options. Then you choose None instead of Single, Double, or Thick. For example, select Left, then None, to remove lines on the left of cells in the current block. Use All, then None, to remove all lines from the selected cells.

Note that although Quattro Pro 4 may appear to draw lines on all sides of a cell, it actually draws lines only on the left and top sides. The Right and Bottom options on the Placement menu actually draw lines in the left and top of the adjoining cells. This means that when you move cells only the top and left line formatting remains attached to the cells. When you are printing a worksheet that contains lines, you need to include one column to the right and one row below the cells to be printed to ensure that all of the lines are included.

If you are using character mode, you will notice that the addition of lines also adds space to the model. Unnumbered rows that are added do not affect any formulas or block commands. You cannot select lines themselves, only the cells to which they are attached. When you use the mouse or the SHIFT-F7 key to select cells, you will see that the cell selector increases in size when it encounters a cell with a line attached so that the line is included.

Shading

A further style improvement is to add some shading to a model. This fills cells with either grey or black, As seen in A2..H2 in Figure 3-47. Note that this is the same model as Figure 3-46, except that a couple of rows were added toward the top. Row 2 was shaded grey, then the height was reduced. Row 3 was also reduced to decrease the space between the

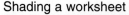

FIGURE
3-47

Shading a worksheet

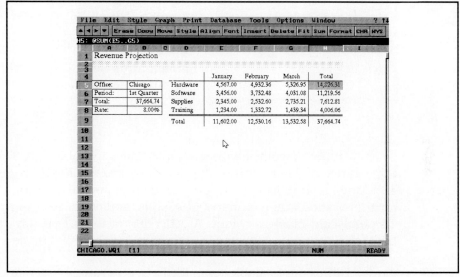

shading and the model. The label in A1 has a larger font, which is assigned by the Style Font command, described in a moment.

When you select cells and then issue the Style Shading command, Quattro Pro 4 offers a choice between None, Grey, or Black. If you choose Grey or Black, the command adds the shading and quits back to READY mode. If you choose None, Quattro Pro 4 removes any shading from the selected cells. The Shading command can be applied to cells containing values and labels, but this may make them hard to read.

Fonts

In Figure 3-47 the label in A1 is displayed in larger characters than the others. This is possible because Quattro Pro 4 offers a variety of fonts, applied with the Style Font command. These fonts will only appear in your worksheet if you are using WYSIWYG mode, but you can assign them to cells even if you are working in character mode. The fonts also appear when you are using the print preview feature, described later in this chapter.

TABLE 3-7

Fonts Supplied with Quattro Pro 4

BitStream Scalable Fonts	Swiss-SC, Dutch-SC, Courier-SC
BitStream Fonts	Swiss, Dutch, Courier
Hershey Fonts	Roman, Sans Serif, Old English, EuroStyle Monospace

Quattro Pro 4 comes with the fonts listed in Table 3-7. The printed appearance of some of these fonts can be seen in Figure 3-48. Strictly speaking, a font is a collection of characters all bearing the same characteristics, such as shape, size, style, and color. For example, Swiss 14 point bold black is a font. A collection of fonts that have the same basic appearance is a typeface or type style, so Swiss would be a typeface.

Note   BitStream Scalable fonts (SC) are generated on demand for both screen and printer and are generally faster and more convenient to use. Regular BitStream fonts are built separately on disk for every size used and font file creation can take several seconds. Hershey fonts are less accurate but much quicker to use, particularly if your printer has limited memory.

FIGURE 3-48

Font sample

> **Swiss 14 point**
> Dutch 18 point
> *Dutch 12 point italic underlined*
> **Courier 14 point**
> Roman 14 point
> Sans Serif 14 point
> **Old English 14 point**
> EuroStyle 14 point
> Monospace 14 point

When you want to assign a font to a cell you issue the Style Font command. Quattro Pro 4 asks you to confirm the cell that you want to format. At this point you can extend the block to other cells. When you confirm the cell or cells, you will see the menu shown in Figure 3-49. This shows you the current settings and the aspects of the font that you can change. When you want to assign a font to a group of cells you can preselect the cells and then issue the Style Font command. You will go directly to the menu in Figure 3-49. Note that a variety of fonts have been used in the worksheet in the background of Figure 3-49.

When you select Typeface from the menu illustrated in Figure 3-49, you are shown a list that includes the fonts supplied and installed by Quattro Pro 4 plus any that are installed on your printer. Simply select your choice from the list. The Point Size option works the same way, enabling you to choose from a list of available sizes. The Color option presents a palette of colors, and you can choose the one you want (bearing in mind that you cannot print in color unless you have a color printer).

The next three options (Bold, Italic, and Underlined) can be turned On—as is the case for Bold in Figure 3-49—or Off—as is the case with Italic in Figure 3-49. Simply highlight the item and press ENTER or click on it to toggle the attribute. The Reset option clears all attributes from

FIGURE
3-49

Changing the font

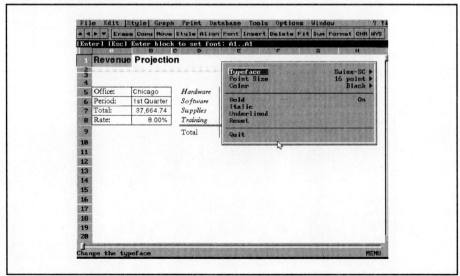

Bold, Italic, and Underlined. Note that Underlined creates lines under labels that extend only as far as the label, not across the whole cell occupied by the label. Select Quit when your font choices are complete. Quattro Pro 4 returns you to READY mode.

The Font Table

You might wonder how Quattro Pro 4 has been deciding which font to use up to this point, that is, before you began to use the Style Font command. In every worksheet there is a default font that is used for all cells until you use the Style Font command. This default font is determined by the Font Table command, which also offers a slightly different approach to font formatting than does the Style Font command.

When you select Font Table from the Style menu, you see a menu like that shown in Figure 3-50. The table lists 8 fonts. Font 1 is the default font, the font in which Quattro Pro 4 displays all entries unless you tell it otherwise. Suppose you want a group of cells to have a font other than the default. You can use the Style Font command just described, or you can select one of the fonts numbered 2 through 8 from the font table.

The Font Table command

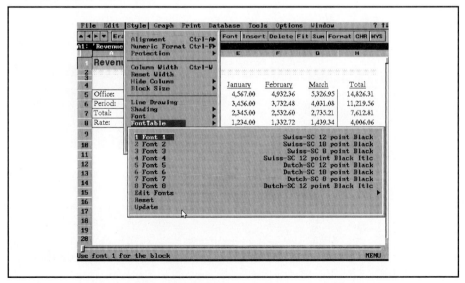

This leads to a block prompt, and you tell Quattro Pro 4 which cells to format. If you choose Font 2 in this example, the cells you choose will appear as Swiss-SC 18 point Black. However, what you have really done is format the selected cells with Font 2. You can edit the font table and change the font assigned to Font 2, in which case all cells formatted with Font 2 change to match the new assignment.

The Edit Fonts option shown on the menu in Figure 3-50 enables you to assign your choice of fonts to Font 1 through Font 8. If you change Font 1, all cells in the worksheet that have not otherwise been assigned a font automatically change to the font you have selected for Font 1. The Edit Font menu also offers Reset and Update options. The Reset option changes all font assignments back to the program defaults. The Update option makes the current font table assignments the new program defaults.

Defining and Using Styles

To help you manage the large variety of enhancements that Quattro Pro 4 can make to the appearance of cells, you are allowed to define any number of named styles. For example, a style named TOTAL might consist of the following information:

Name:	TOTAL
Font:	Swiss-SC 14 point Black Bld
Line Drawing:	Top
Shading:	None
Alignment:	Right
Data Entry:	General
Numeric Format:	Currency 2

You create such a definition with the Define Style option on the Style menu. The Define Style command displays a submenu with these options: Create, Erase, Remove, File, and Quit. When you select Create you see a list of previously defined styles. This enables you to select an existing style in order to change it, or type a new name and thus create a new definition. The menu that appears next contains the categories just listed. If you are creating a new style, the entries in the various categories are determined by the current style of the cell that was selected when you issued the Define Style command. In this way you can create a named style from an existing set of format attributes.

Select each style category that you need to change and make the appropriate adjustments. Select Quit when you have finished the definition. This returns you to the Create/Erase/Remove/File menu. Use the Create option to make or alter another style. Use Erase to get rid of unwanted style definitions. Use Remove to delete a style that has been used in the current worksheet. The File option is used with Retrieve or Save on a style library file. These files have the extension .STY and are used to store a collection of styles on disk. This feature enables you to give another user styles that you have designed. The File Retrieve option enables you to add styles from a library file to the current worksheet; the File Save command enables you to store the current worksheet's styles in an .STY file. You do not have to store styles in a library file. Style definitions are kept within the current worksheet, under the names you give them. They are automatically recorded with the worksheet the next time you use the Save option on the main File menu.

Whenever you want a cells or group of cells to take on the appearance defined as TOTAL, you can select the cells and choose the Use Style option from the Style menu. This option prompts you to choose from a list of previously defined styles. When you select the style and confirm the block of cells to be affected the format of those cells is changed. The cell identifier records the style you have used in square brackets, as in [TOTAL]. The appearance of cells formatted with the TOTAL style will reflect any subsequent changes to the definition of the TOTAL style.

User-Defined Numeric Formats

There is one aspect of the Define Style menu that has not been covered yet: user-defined numeric formats. In Chapter 2 you saw that the appearance of numbers in Quattro Pro 4 is determined by the format setting. This is imposed on all cells in a worksheet by the Numeric Format option on the Options Formats menu. However, individual cells or groups of cells can be varied from the global setting by using the Numeric Format option on the Style menu. You may want numbers to appear in a format other than those provided by these two options. For this you use the Define Style command. After you select Create and name the style, such as POUNDS to display currency with the £ sign, select Numeric Format, followed by User Defined. This option enables you to create a custom numeric format definition, as is being done in Figure 3-51.

FIGURE
3-51

Defining a custom numeric format

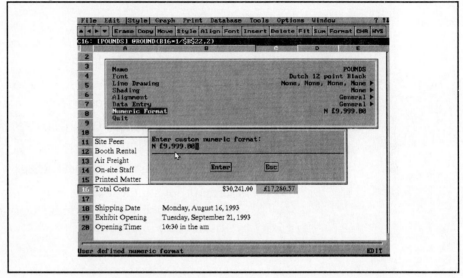

The definition consists of several codes and characters that tell Quattro Pro 4 how to display a value. These are listed in Table 3-8. In the background of Figure 3-51 you can see several examples of such formats. They enable you to add whatever text you like to describe values and can create attractive dates. By using a custom numeric format you can avoid a lot of unsatisfactory compromises in displaying values.

Final Quality Printing

If you have embellished your worksheet with lines, shading, and fonts, you will want to print out reports that include these features. You cannot do this with the Printer option under Draft Mode Printing, described earlier in the chapter. In Draft Mode Printing Quattro Pro 4 simply sends the contents of the cells—not the Style enhancements such as lines and fonts—to the printer. To print a worksheet with the full set of graphic enhancements, use the Print menu's Destination option. Choose Graphics Printer. Make sure that the printer model is the same as the one you

TABLE 3-8 The Custom Numeric Format Characters

Code	Description
N	Shows that the codes which follow constitute a numeric format, not dates or time
0	Displays a digit whether or not the number includes a digit in this position
9	Displays a digit unless the number lacks a digit in this position
%	Displays the number as a percentage
,	Inserts a thousands separator (a comma unless otherwise specified under Options International Punctuation)
.	Inserts a decimal separator (a period unless otherwise specified under Options International Punctuation)
E– or e–	Displays the number in scientific notation, preceding negative exponents with a minus sign. If the format includes at least one 0 or 9 after this symbol, you get the number in scientific notation, which uses E or e. If the exponent contains more digits than 9s or 0s following this symbol, the extra digits are displayed
E+ or e–	Displays numbers in scientific notation, preceding a negative or positive exponent with a minus or plus sign, respectively. If the format includes at least one 0 or 9 following this symbol, you get the number in scientific notation, which uses E or e. If the exponent contains more digits than 9s or 0s following this symbol, the extra digits are displayed
T	Shows that the codes which follow constitute a format for dates and times, not numbers

TABLE 3-8 Cont.   The Custom Numeric Format Characters

Code	Description
d(or D)	Displays the day of the month as a one- or two-digit number (1 through 31)
dd(or DD)	Displays the day of the month as a two-digit number (01 through 31). wday, Wday displays the day of the week as a three-character WDAY abbreviation, all lowercase, with the first letter capitalized, or all uppercase
weekday, Weekday, WEEKDAY	Displays the day of the week all lowercase, with the first letter capitalized, or all uppercase
m or M	If not preceded by h, H, hh, or HH, displays the month as a one- or two-digit number (1 through 12). Otherwise, displays the minute as a one- or two-digit number (1 through 59)
mm or MM	If not preceded by h, H, hh, or HH, displays the month as a two-digit number (01 through 12). Otherwise, displays the minute as a two-digit number (01 through 59)
Mo	Displays the month as a one- or two-digit number (1 through 12)
MMo	Displays the month as a two-digit number (01 through 12)
mon, Mon, MON	Displays the month as a three-character abbreviation, all lowercase, with the first letter capitalized, or all uppercase
month, Month, MONTH	Displays the name of the month all lowercase, with the first letter capitalized, or all uppercase
yy or YY	Displays the last two digits of the year (00 through 99)
yyyy or YYY	Displays all four digits of the year (0001 through 9999)

TABLE 3-1 Cont.   The Custom Numeric Format Characters

Code	Description
h or H	Displays the hour as a one- or two-digit number. If the format includes ampm or AMPM, the number will be between 1 and 12. If ampm or AMPM is not included, 24-hour format is used (0 through 23)
hh or HH	Displays the hour as a two-digit number. If the format includes ampm or AMPM, the number will be between 01 and 12. If ampm or AMPM is not included, 24-hour format is used (00 through 23)
Mi	Displays the minute as a one- or two-digit number (1 through 59)
MMi	Displays the minute as a two-digit number (01 through 59)
s or S	Displays the second as a one- or two-digit number (1 through 59)
ss or SS	Displays the second as a two-digit number (01 through 59)
AMPM or ampm	Displays the time in 12-hour format with characters for morning (AM) or afternoon (PM)
\	Displays the next character in the format, so to display a backslash, type \\
*	If the formatted entry is shorter than the column width, this fills the column by repeating the character to the right of the asterisk
""	Displays the characters inside the quote marks as part or all of the cell contents. Used when you want to use text that would otherwise be ambiguous, such as: T hh:mm "in the" AMPM. This formats time like this: 10:30 in the AM. Without the quotes, h would be read as the hours code

are using (see the earlier section on printing in this chapter for instructions on how to change the printer model).

When the print destination is set to Graphics Printer, the Spreadsheet command sends the cell contents and full formatting instructions to the printer. This may take some time, and a message will flash asking you to wait. You may also see a message about fonts being downloaded. Quattro Pro 4 sends the font information to the printer ahead of the rest of the print data. If you are doing a lot of printing with the Graphics Printer option, you might want to consider using the Print Manager, described in Appendix C. The Print Manager enables you to carry on working in Quattro Pro 4 while your work is being printed.

You might also want to have Quattro Pro 4 display an outline of the Print Block. This is only possible in WYSIWYG mode when the print destination is set to Graphics Printer or Screen Preview, described in a moment. When you select Window Options Print Block Display, Quattro Pro 4 displays a dotted line that shows the edges of the current Print Block. Perhaps more importantly, it also shows, as dotted lines, the location of soft page breaks, the ones that Quattro Pro 4 uses to divide large printouts into separate pages.

The results of using the Graphics Printer option can be checked before printing if you use the Screen Preview option on the Destination menu. When the Destination is set to Screen Preview the Spreadsheet Print command causes Quattro Pro 4 to display a miniature image of the document as it will appear on the printed page. You can see an example of this in Figure 3-52. When you first use the Screen Preview option Quattro Pro 4 shows you the first page of the printout and displays an entire page. You can use the Next command on menu at the top of the screen to move forward to subsequent pages and the Previous command to move backward through the document. The Zoom option brings you closer to the page, as in Figure 3-52, which shows the top half of the page. When you have zoomed in from the full-page view Quattro Pro 4 shows you a separate picture of the page and indicates the area being viewed with the ZOOM box. This can be moved with the arrow keys to view different parts of the page. Use ESC or the Quit command to leave Screen Preview and return to the Print menu. When you return to the Screen Preview you will get the same view as when you left. The options on the Screen Preview menu are summarized in Table 3-9.

Using Screen Preview for the Print Destination

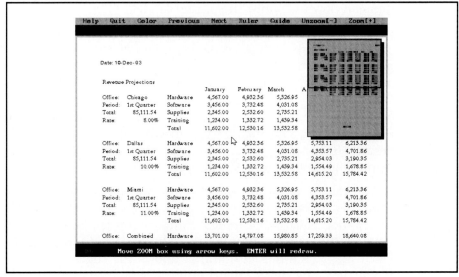

If your printout is just a little too large to fit on a single page, you can use the Print-To-Fit command instead of Spreadsheet Print. This command tells Quattro Pro 4 to scale down the printed output so that it fits on the page. You can use Screen Preview as the Destination setting to see the results before committing them to paper. The trick performed by Print-To-Fit can be replicated with the Scaling setting on the Print Layout menu. You can adjust this figure down from 100 to shrink reports or above 100 to enlarge them.

Window Options

In the course of using larger models, like the one shown earlier in Figure 3-41, you will encounter several situations that call for additional Quattro Pro 4 commands. In addition to the WYSIWYG Zoom % on the Options menu, which enables you to zoom out your view of the worksheet, Quattro Pro 4 provides a simple method for letting you see two parts of the same spreadsheet at the same time. You can also lock parts of a model so that they do not move and thus act as column and row headings. By

TABLE 3-9	The Screen Preview Menu

Option	Action
Help	Accesses the Help screens
Quit	Returns you to the Print menu
Color	Makes colors used in the display more appropriate to your hardware (cycles through these options as you press C: color screen/monochrome printer; color screen/color printer; monochrome for black and white displays; reversed monochrome for LCD and laptop displays)
Previous	Takes you to the previous page of the report (for example, from page 2 to page 1)
Next	Takes you to the next page of the report (for example, from page 1 to page 2)
Ruler	Displays a ruled grid of 1 inch squares to help you size the report
Guide	Displays the ZOOM box to show which section of page is displayed (you can turn this on and off with INS and DEL)
Unzoom	Reduces the level of zoom magnification
Zoom	Increases the level of magnification (three levels are available: 1x or 100% displays whole page; 2x or 200% displays half a page at twice normal size; 4x or 400% displays one eight of the page at 4 times normal size). You can use the numeric + and – keys to adjust zoom

turning on or off various window attributes you can adjust the display for different users.

Using Windows

Using the Window Options command you can split the screen either horizontally or vertically into two parts, called *windows*. Quattro Pro 4 uses the term "window" for two different features. The term "worksheet window" refers to the space within which each spreadsheet is displayed when more than one is open. You can also have a "split window" within a worksheet window. In each split window you can view a different part of the worksheet. As you move the cell selector in one window, you can scroll the view in the other one, or you can remove the synchronization from the windows to view each window independently.

When you select Options from the Window menu the first two options are Horizontal or Vertical splitting. Two new options, Sync and Unsync, enable you to switch between the default mode of synchronized split windows and the alternative, unsynchronized mode. The Clear option closes a split window if you have created one. The split occurs at the current position of the cell selector, which is why you moved to column E before issuing the command. Select Vertical, and the screen appears divided, as shown in Figure 3-53.

You can move between split windows by pressing the Windows key, F6. Press it several times, and you will see that this key toggles between windows. Pressing F6 returns you to the cell you left from. Initially, the split windows are synchronized. With a vertical split this means that pressing UP ARROW or DOWN ARROW scrolls the worksheet on both sides of

FIGURE 3-53

A vertical window

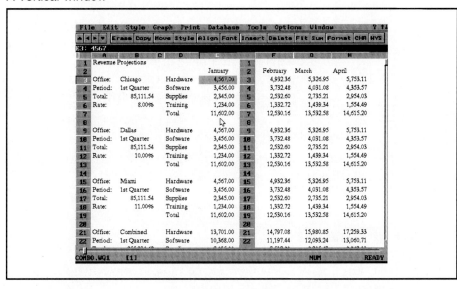

the split. You can see that the row numbers in the dividing line match those in the left border. With a horizontal window it means that RIGHT ARROW or LEFT ARROW moves the worksheet on the top and bottom halves of the screen, and the column letters in the dividing line match those in the top border.

Figure 3-54 shows the effect of unsynchronizing the windows. To unsynchronize windows, select Window Options Unsync. When this is done, place the cell selector on the right of the screen and move down to the bottom line of the model. The model is unmoved on the other side. You can see that the row numbers in the dividing line no longer match those in the left border. To clear windows, simply select Window Option Clear.

Titles

As you can see from Figure 3-54 the column headings disappear if the right side of the worksheet is moved down. In fact, you may have found this to be a problem when you have been working without windows. As

FIGURE 3-54

Unsynchronized windows

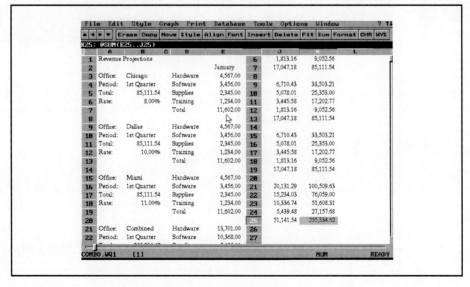

you move to the lower areas of a model, the column and row labels disappear, making it difficult to know which numbers you are viewing. Knowing where you are is particularly important when you have to update cells in the middle of a large spreadsheet. The Quattro Pro 4 solution is to freeze certain rows and columns for titles that you do not want to disappear.

To freeze titles, place the cell selector in the first cell that is below and to the right of the area that you want to freeze. When you use the Window Options Locked Titles command, you can choose Horizontal, which freezes the area above the cell selector; Vertical, which freezes the area to the left of the cell selector; or Both, which locks areas above and to the left of the cell selector. When you pick your Titles choice, you are returned to the spreadsheet. Now you can move around the model and the column and row headings remain on the screen, as seen in Figure 3-55.

After you lock titles, pressing HOME takes you to the cell in which you performed the title lock (in the case of Figures 3-54 and 3-55 that would be cell E3). You might wonder how you can make changes to the cells within the title area. You can either do this by unlocking titles or by using the Goto key, F5. When you press F5 and type the address of the title cell

FIGURE
3-55

Using locked titles (shaded in WYSIWYG mode)

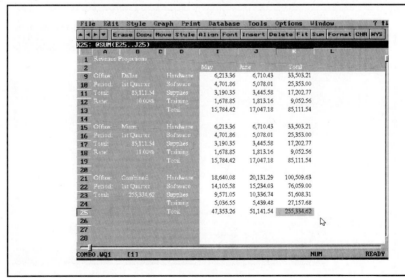

you want to edit, then press ENTER, the cell is placed on the edit line for you to change. Press F2 to edit the cell, then press ENTER to place the cell contents back in the cell. To put the updated title back into place, press PAGE DOWN, then TAB, and then HOME.

Row and Column Borders

In Figure 3-56 you can see a slightly different view of a Quattro Pro 4 worksheet. The column lettering and row numbering have been removed with the Window Options Row & Col Borders command. Change this setting to Hide and you can get more worksheet cells displayed on your screen. This view is attractive when you want to emphasize the content of a spreadsheet rather than the mechanics of its operation, for example, when you are making computer-based presentations with Quattro Pro 4. Use the Window Options Row & Col Borders Display command to return the column lettering and row numbering.

FIGURE 3-56

A worksheet with grid lines but no borders

| File | Edit | Style | Graph | Print | Database | Tools | Options | Window | ? ↑↓ |

| | Erase | Copy | Move | Style | Align | Font | Insert | Delete | Fit | Sum | Format | CHR | WYS |

A1: [W8] 'Revenue Projections

Revenue Projections

			January	February	March	April	May
Office:	Chicago	Hardware	4,567.00	4,932.36	5,326.95	5,753.11	6,213.36
Period:	1st Quarter	Software	3,456.00	3,732.48	4,031.08	4,353.57	4,701.86
Total:	85,111.54	Supplies	2,345.00	2,532.60	2,735.21	2,954.03	3,190.35
Rate:	8.00%	Training	1,234.00	1,332.72	1,439.34	1,554.49	1,678.85
		Total	11,602.00	12,530.16	13,532.58	14,615.20	15,784.42
Office:	Dallas	Hardware	4,567.00	4,932.36	5,326.95	5,753.11	6,213.36
Period:	1st Quarter	Software	3,456.00	3,732.48	4,031.08	4,353.57	4,701.86
Total:	85,111.54	Supplies	2,345.00	2,532.60	2,735.21	2,954.03	3,190.35
Rate:	10.00%	Training	1,234.00	1,332.72	1,439.34	1,554.49	1,678.85
		Total	11,602.00	12,530.16	13,532.58	14,615.20	15,784.42
Office:	Miami	Hardware	4,567.00	4,932.36	5,326.95	5,753.11	6,213.36
Period:	1st Quarter	Software	3,456.00	3,732.48	4,031.08	4,353.57	4,701.86
Total:	85,111.54	Supplies	2,345.00	2,532.60	2,735.21	2,954.03	3,190.35
Rate:	11.00%	Training	1,234.00	1,332.72	1,439.34	1,554.49	1,678.85
		Total	11,602.00	12,530.16	13,532.58	14,615.20	15,784.42
Office:	Combined	Hardware	13,701.00	14,797.08	15,980.85	17,259.33	18,640.08
Period:	1st Quarter	Software	10,368.00	11,197.44	12,093.24	13,060.71	14,105.58
Total:	255,334.62	Supplies	7,035.00	7,597.80	8,205.63	8,862.09	9,571.05

COMBO.WQ1   [1]   NUM   READY

Map View, Grid Lines, and Print Block

Another effect visible in Figure 3-56 is the display of spreadsheet grid lines, turned on with the Window Options Grid Lines Display command. Most screens in this book show the display with Grid Lines set to Hide, but you may find them useful in keeping track of cell entries. Also visible in Figure 3-56 is the dotted line showing the Print Block. This is displayed when you use Window Options Print Block and select Display rather than Hide. You will only see the Print Block border if you are working in WYSIWYG mode and have the Print Destination set to a Final Quality Printing option.

If you are auditing a spreadsheet to ensure that it is accurate you can use the Window Options Map View command. The normal setting is No, but if you change it to Yes Quattro Pro 4 shows you which cells contain labels, numbers, and formulas. You can see an example of this view in Chapter 9, which discusses spreadsheet auditing.

CHAPTER

Formulas and Functions in Depth

*I*n previous chapters you have seen that Quattro Pro 4 understands several formulas of varying complexity, from a simple formula that adds cells to a complex one that calculates a loan payment. In this chapter you will see the ways in which formulas can be applied to typical spreadsheet operations and the many built-in formulas, or functions, that Quattro Pro 4 provides to enhance your formulas.

Formulas Are Instructions

Although the word *formula* may remind many people of algebra and science classes, in the context of Quattro Pro 4 the term simply means an *instruction* written in a form that the program can understand. The way you give Quattro Pro 4 instructions can be as straightforward as "add cell A1 and cell A2." In fact, even complex instructions follow a consistent arrangement, or *syntax*. As you learn to manipulate formulas, you will want to use the program's built-in functions for more complex calculations. Quattro Pro 4 offers more than a hundred functions.

Formula Formats

Simple Quattro Pro 4 formulas combine values—like numbers or cells containing numbers—with operators, such as the division sign or the plus sign. The formula in cell H7 of Figure 4-1 can be diagrammed like this:

```
H7 = H5           *              H6
     Value         Operator      Value
```

If cells H5 and H6 are named as blocks, with H5 called WIDTH and H6 called LENGTH, the formula can be diagrammed like this:

```
H7 = Width         *              Length
     Value          Operator      Value
```

Quattro Pro 4 formulas are algebraic in format. Thus, within a formula you can use other formulas separated, or *delimited*, by pairs of parentheses, as in the following:

FIGURE
4-1

Example of formulas

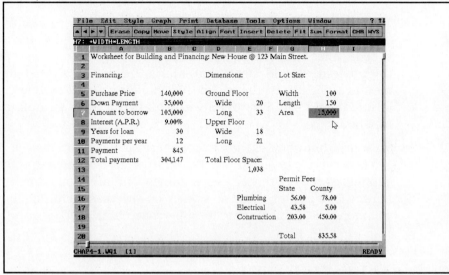

E13 = (E6*E7)+(E9*E10)

This formula in E13 means "multiply E6 by E7 and add that to the product of E9 multiplied by E10." The formula is used in E13 to calculate the total floor area of a two-story house with floors whose widths and lengths are in cells E6 through E10.

When you ask Quattro Pro 4 to make decisions about the data to be calculated, several elements are required, as in this formula:

B6 = @IF(0.25*B5<30000,30000,0.25*B5)

This formula tells Quattro Pro 4 that the down payment in B6 should be 25 percent of the purchase price in B5, unless the product of those two values comes to less than 30,000, in which case B6 should be 30,000. This formula is used in Figure 4-1 to calculate the down payment. The buyer must pay at least 25 percent of the purchase price and no less than $30,000.

An expense report that breaks down expenses for each week by type might contain the following formula.

G13=@IF(@SUM(WEEK)=@SUM(TYPE),@SUM(TYPE),@ERR)

This formula says that G13 will have one of two possible answers, depending on a decision made by the @IF function. If the sum of the block of cells called WEEK is equal to the sum of the block of cells called TYPE, the program should insert that sum; otherwise, it should give an error message (@ERR). By the end of this chapter you will be able to read such formulas and compose them with Quattro Pro 4's formula syntax and functions.

Notice that none of the previous formulas contain spaces. No spaces is a general rule in all Quattro Pro 4 formulas. Also note that the program capitalizes cell references, block names, and function names. It does not matter if you enter these as upper- or lowercase letters; Quattro Pro 4 will store and display them in uppercase.

Acceptable Values

The values in a Quattro Pro 4 formula can be cells containing values, as in +H5*H6. They can be a block of cells containing values, either stated as coordinates as in +G16..G18+H16..H18, or described by block names, as in STATE+COUNTY. They can also be functions like @PMT, which was used in Chapter 1 to calculate a car loan payment. The same function is used in Figure 4-1 to calculate a mortgage payment in cell B11. Note the use of a separate cell for number of payments per year. You can calculate the total payments to be made on a 30-year loan if you multiply the number of payments by the calculated payment amount, using the formula +B9*B10*B11. Many of the Quattro Pro 4 @functions that can be used in formulas are described later in this chapter.

Values in Quattro Pro 4 formulas can also be constants. A *constant* is a number, date, or piece of text that you enter directly, such as the 1 in 1+B3. Constants are used in formulas for projections; for example, a formula to calculate projected sales might be Sales*1.1. A constant is also used in calculations like finding the circumference of a circle (2*@PI*Radius).

Operators and Priorities

There are many different operators that you can use in Quattro Pro 4 formulas. First, there are the standard arithmetic operators: add (+), subtract (–), multiply (*), and divide (/). Another operator, the exponent (^), produces powers of a number. The formula +B2^3 returns 27 if the value in B2 is 3.

In Chapter 5 you will learn how to create database search conditions using logical operators, such as the greater-than sign in Rank > 5. All of the operators recognized by Quattro Pro 4 are listed in Table 4-1, where the order of operations in a formula is also shown. If all the operators are the same, as in 2*3*4 (=24), the calculation is performed from left to right.

TABLE
4-1

Operators and Order of Precedence (7 = Highest)

Operator	Used for	Priority
&	Placing text in string formulas	1
#AND#	Logical AND formulas	1
#OR#	Logical OR formulas	1
#NOT#	Logical NOT formulas	2
=	Equal in conditional statements	3
<>	Not equal in conditional statements	3
<=	Less than or equal to	3
>=	Greater than or equal to	3
–	Subtraction	4
+	Addition	4
*	Multiplication	5
/	Division	5
–	Negation (preceding a formula)	6
+	Positive (preceding a formula)	6
^	Exponentiation (to the power of)	7

You can affect the order of calculation by using parentheses, as in these two calculations:

2*3+4=10
2*(3+4)=14

When you nest calculations within several parentheses, the innermost calculations are performed first.

Using Formulas

Much of a spreadsheet's power clearly lies in formulas. Whether you are simply adding two cells together or calculating the sum of the year's depreciation of an asset, the ability to establish a relationship between cells gives you tremendous number-crunching ability.

Methods for Creating and Entering Formulas

You can create formulas in several ways. First, there is the literal method: you look at the worksheet and decide which cells are involved; then you type their addresses into the formula. For example, you can see that the total of the state permit fees in Figure 4-1 would be +G16+G17+G18. You can type this formula directly and Quattro Pro 4 will accept it, unless you type an invalid coordinate. The formula will be correct if the cells you have described are the correct cells for the formula.

For the more cautious spreadsheet user and the less adept typist, there is the pointing method of entering formulas. This method begins with the + sign or other value indicator, which places Quattro Pro 4 in VALUE mode. You then use the arrow keys or mouse to select the first cell you want in the formula. You have seen that, when you do this, Quattro Pro 4 types the cell address for you. You can then type the next math sign or value indicator, and the cell selector will move back down to the cell in which you are building the formula. The basic sequence is math sign, point, math sign, point. You can point to each cell that needs to go into the formula, and it is added on the edit line at the top of the screen as you build the formula. You place the completed formula into the original cell with the ENTER key. This method is very useful when you have lots of cells scattered throughout the spreadsheet and cannot remember the location of a particular number.

You can use the pointing method effectively with formulas that involve functions, as in the case of the loan payment. Separate each argument of the @PMT function from the next one with a comma. After you initiate the formula by entering **@PMT(**, move the cell selector to the cell containing the first argument. Then enter a comma to add that location to the formula and return the cell selector to the cell in which the formula is originating. When you then point out the cell for the second argument and type another comma, that location is pulled into the formula, and the cell selector is returned to the original cell. Lastly, point out the third and final argument, and with the cell selector on the third cell, type the closing parenthesis, which completes the formula. The cell selector is now back at the original cell. You can incorporate additional values into the formula by pressing the desired math sign (as in * to multiply this payment by a cell or number). Otherwise, press the ENTER key to place the completed formula in the cell.

Mouse users can add math signs to formulas by clicking on the appropriate button in the SpeedBar. In Figure 4-2 you can see a sum

Building a formula with the SpeedBar

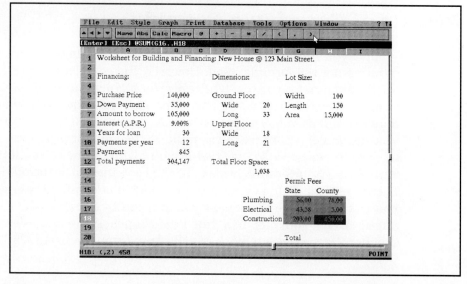

formula being created with the mouse. The SpeedBar enables you to insert the following characters: + – * / (,). You can also select from a list of @functions, as described later in this chapter.

Formulas and Blocks

Some formulas and functions use blocks of cells. You can enter blocks by typing the diagonal coordinates of the block directly as you create the formula. Alternatively, you can use the pointing method to block out the cells to be included, anchoring the upper left corner by typing a period and then using the DOWN and/or RIGHT ARROW as necessary to complete the highlighting of the block. You can also use the mouse to select a block. For example, after typing **@SUM(** you can point to the top left cell in the block, press the left mouse button, and hold it down as you drag the mouse pointer to the bottom right cell of the block. You then release the mouse button and type the closing parenthesis, or click on the closing parenthesis button in the SpeedBar, as shown in Figure 4-2. If the block is very large, you can click on the top left cell then use the scroll bars to bring the lower right cell into view. Now you can select the lower right cell by holding down the right mouse button and clicking on the left. This selects the entire block of cells.

Results of Entering a Formula

After you have entered a formula, the cell displays the *result* of the formula, not the formula itself. However, the cell identifier still displays the formula, not the value, whenever you highlight a cell that contains a formula. You may not want the value generated by the formula to be *dynamic* and therefore change when the worksheet is recalculated. To *fix* a value, you can convert the formula to the value it produces. This can be done in two ways. Press F2 while you highlight the cell containing the formula, and the formula is placed on the edit line at the top of the screen. Then press the Calc key (F9), and the formula is turned into its result. You can then place this result into the cell by pressing the ENTER key. Alternatively, you can use the Edit Values command, described in Chapter 2, to convert a block of cells from formulas to values.

Named Blocks

Naming blocks with the Edit Names command is very useful when you are developing formulas, because you can use block names instead of cell coordinates. Even attaching a name to a single cell is productive. It is often easier to type +LENGTH * WIDTH than +H5*H6, particularly if you are composing the formula in Q33. You do not need to check where these elements are and do not need to take the time to point them out. Furthermore, if you type +H555*H6 by mistake, Quattro Pro 4 will not tell you that this is an error. But if you try to enter an invalid block name, the program will beep and switch to EDIT mode so that you can correct the mistake. Many people find that block names are easier to use than cell coordinates, particularly because you can press the Choices key (F3) to pop up a list of block names from which to choose while you are composing a formula. In Figure 4-3 you can see the list of names that F3 creates during editing. In this example, several blocks, including the fees for State and County, have been named. If you press the plus key (+) on the numeric keypad or click the plus button on the SpeedBar while the

FIGURE 4-3

Block choices

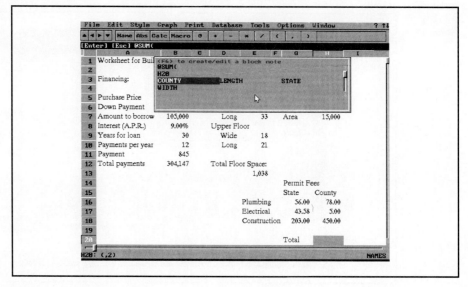

NAMES list is displayed, you get a more detailed list showing the coordinates of each block, as seen in Figure 4-4. At this point you can highlight the name you want to insert in the formula and press ENTER, or click on it. Press ESC or click outside the list to remove it.

Editing Formulas

If there is a mistake in a formula that you are creating, such as a misspelled block or function name or an invalid cell reference or unrecognized symbol, Quattro Pro 4 will not accept the formula when you press ENTER. Instead, it will beep and display a message. When you press ENTER or ESC to acknowledge the message, the program changes to EDIT mode and attempts to position the edit cursor near the error you have made. To edit an existing formula, you highlight the cell and press F2 to enter EDIT mode. The formula then is displayed on the edit line. To initiate editing with a mouse you simply click on the cell then click on the edit line.

FIGURE 4-4

Detailed version of NAMES list

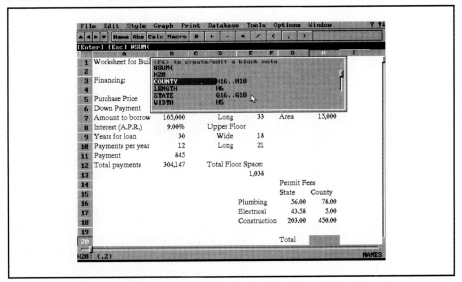

Common Formula Errors

If you type a formula correctly but used improper elements within it, Quattro Pro 4 displays an error message. The exact message depends on the error. For example, entering @SUM(B2..TC12) earns the response "Invalid Character," because there cannot be a cell TC12. When you see a message of this type, check the formula to find the error. The program attempts to put the cursor near the error, so look there first. You may have neglected to close a pair of parentheses or quotations, or omitted the @ sign before a function name. Table 4-2 lists error messages.

A common mistake is to enter spaces between the elements of a formula. Although the documentation occasionally appears to show spaces, they are generally not allowed in formulas. Unlike 1-2-3, Quattro Pro 4 does sometimes allow spaces in formulas, although you do not need to type any. To be on the safe side, however, you would do best to avoid spaces completely.

Named blocks must be spelled correctly. As you have seen, the Choices key (F3) enables you to select from a list of block names when writing formulas. Using the F3 key to insert block names in formulas helps to avoid typographical errors.

You may succeed in entering a formula only to see the message CIRC appear among the status indicators. This message tells you there is a *circular reference* in your formula, meaning that the formula refers to itself. You cannot ask Quattro Pro 4 to sum a block that includes H20 and put the answer in H20. This kind of problem, which usually becomes apparent as soon as you see what you have attempted to do, is solved by retyping the formula. If you see the CIRC message and cannot determine which cell is producing it, you can use the Options Recalculation command to find out. As you can see from Figure 4-5, the Options Recalculation command shows the location of the circular reference. You can then pick Quit to leave the menu and edit the cell in question.

A formula cannot refer to a named block of cells if the block is as yet unnamed. If you try to do this, Quattro Pro 4 makes you stop typing the formula to name the block. This is especially annoying when the formula is complex and lengthy. You can avoid the problem by defining a named block as soon as you create it and by using the Choices key (F3) to select block names.

TABLE
4-2

Common Entry Error Messages

Message	Problem/Solution
Formula too long	You exceeded the limit of 254 characters in a formula; break formula into several subformulas
Incomplete formula	You left something out; check for operators not followed by arguments
Invalid argument	You have tried to use an argument that does not fit the @function you are using; check the syntax of the argument
Invalid cell or block address	You entered something that is being read as a nonexistent cell reference or block name; check that you have typed formula correctly and defined all block names used in the formula
Invalid character	You used a character that does not fit the syntax; check for trailing commas or other punctuation that is out of place
Missing arguments	You forgot to supply an argument where one is expected; check your entry
Missing operator	You forgot to separate values or functions with an operator; check your entry
Missing right parenthesis	You opened one more set of parentheses than you closed; check for missing right parenthesis or extra left parenthesis
Syntax error	You have made an error that does not fall into the other categories; check spelling of your entry and syntax requirements of the functions you are using
Too many arguments	You have supplied more arguments than the function can accept; check syntax and punctuation of what you entered
Unknown @function	You used a function name that is not recognized; check spelling and try using Functions (ALT-F3) to list functions

FIGURE
4-5

Finding a circular formula

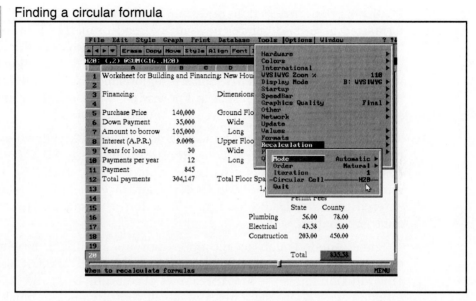

One trick to save the typing you have already done on a rejected formula is to press HOME when Quattro Pro 4 switches to EDIT mode and then type an apostrophe. This enables you to enter the formula as a label and then review it. When you edit the formula and are ready to reenter it as a value, press HOME and then DELETE to remove the apostrophe before pressing ENTER.

Functions Are Built-in Formulas

Quattro Pro 4 provides you with the basic building blocks of complex formulas in the form of functions. These built-in formulas are specially coded commands that facilitate typical calculations. Using functions, you do not have to enter lengthy instructions.

Function Arguments

Some functions simply generate values by themselves. For example, @PI gives the value of pi. The date function @NOW tells you what your

PC thinks the current date and time is (the results of @NOW must be formatted as a date before they can be read properly). However, most functions require additional information, called arguments. For example, the principal, interest, and term required by the @PMT function are said to be the arguments of @PMT. Some functions require just one argument, like @SUM, which only needs to know what block of cells you want to sum. Others, such as @PMT, require several arguments.

The arguments required by functions can be broken down into three types: *numeric,* such as cells containing numbers, as in @PMT(E1,E2,E3); *block,* such as a block of cells being summed with @SUM(B1..B3), or a named block, such as @SUM(COUNTY); and *string,* a label or piece of text entered into a cell, entered into a function in quotes, or produced by another function.

Some functions can accept more than one argument, in which case the arguments are separated by commas, as in @SUM (B1..B3,C1..C3,E1..E3). This function totals the first three rows of columns B, C, and E. Numeric functions can reference a mixture of cell coordinates and block names, as in @PMT(E1, INTEREST, TERM). Functions are often combined with operators and values in formulas, just like any other formula element.

Function Syntax

There are more than a hundred functions and several ways of classifying them. In addition to the distinction between numeric and string functions, which closely follows that between values and labels, functions can be grouped by the type of work they apply to: financial, date, logical, and so on. However, all Quattro Pro 4 functions are always entered in the same basic format, using a standard arrangement of parts, or *syntax:*

❑   Functions begin with the leading @ sign.

❑   Next is the name of the function, typed in upper- or lowercase or a combination and spelled accurately.

❑   The arguments, when required, follow the function name enclosed in parentheses.

❑   With more than one argument, you must separate one argument from the next with a comma; the arguments must be in proper order.

❏ There should be no spaces between the @ and the function name. (There may be spaces between the components, the left parenthesis, the arguments, and the commas, but they are not required.)

A function combined with any arguments is a *function statement*. If you try to enter a function statement that contains an error—for example, an incorrectly spelled function name—Quattro Pro 4 beeps, places the entry on the edit line, and attempts to place the edit line cursor in the area of the mistake. This can be very helpful if you have omitted a comma between arguments or left a pair of parentheses unclosed. See Table 4-2 for a list of error messages.

The Functions Key

One way to prevent errors like misspelled function names is to use the Functions key (ALT-F3). Pressing ALT-F3 when you are using either VALUE mode or EDIT mode pops up a list of the functions, as shown in Figure 4-6. The same list appears when you click the @ button on the SpeedBar. If you press ALT-F3 in READY mode, Quattro Pro 4 pops up the list of functions and switches to EDIT mode. You can then browse through this

FIGURE 4-6

The Functions list (ALT-F3)

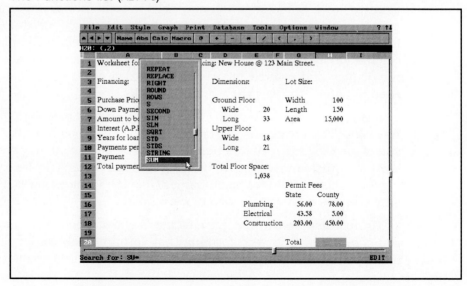

list with the arrow keys, moving a page at a time with PAGE UP or PAGE DOWN. When you see the function that you need, highlight it and press ENTER to place it onto the edit line. This avoids mistyping the name. Note that Quattro Pro 4 also types the @ sign for you. Mouse users can use the scroll bar on the right side of the list to view the functions.

You can also look up a function by spelling part of the name. When the functions list appears, press the Edit key (F2), and you will see the message "Search for: *" appear in the status line at the bottom of the screen. Just start typing what you can remember of the name and the list box will move to the closest match. For example, if you type **P**, then you will be taken to the first function beginning with *P*, which is PAYMT. Type **M** and you will get to PMT. To back up a step press BACKSPACE, and you will move back to PAYMT. Press ENTER to confirm your selection.

Mastering Functions

It would be hard to memorize all of Quattro Pro 4's functions. By using a few simple techniques, however, you can make full use of them.

First, you should *always assume there is an appropriate function.* Chances are that the calculation you want to perform is one that many other spreadsheet users need to perform, so it is probably provided by Quattro Pro 4. Sometimes you may need to combine several functions in one formula to do the job. Occasionally, you will need to use an intermediate cell to produce part of the answer before completing the calculation in another cell. Remember that columns can be hidden from the display and printed reports so that extra columns for calculations need not affect the way the worksheet looks.

It is a good idea to use the Functions key (ALT-F3) to look up and enter functions. The Functions key not only prevents typos but also reminds you of the wide range of functions that can be used. You may realize that there is a quicker way to structure your formula. When you are constructing formulas containing block names, use the Choices list (F3) to make sure you use correctly defined block names.

You will also want to save particularly useful function statements. When you come up with a good formula that you are likely to use often, you might consider saving the worksheet under a different name to keep a copy of the formula for reference. Chapter 9 discusses how to save portions of a spreadsheet to separate files and how to combine several files into one. This technique allows you to build a library of useful functions. You can also print useful formulas by highlighting the appropriate cell and pressing the PRINT SCREEN key. This will print the information from the whole screen, including the cell identifier (you may have to switch to character mode to use the PRINT SCREEN key).

If you follow these guidelines and are prepared to spend some time experimenting with and reading about functions, you will find that they offer tremendous power. A complete examination of each function is beyond the scope of this book. With three pages per function, this chapter alone would grow to 300 pages. What you will find in the rest of this chapter is a series of discussions on different sets of functions grouped according to their practical roles. Examples are given in most cases together with references to other parts of the book where functions are described.

You will find several commands for performing complex calculations on the Tools menu. These commands are described in Chapter 9 and include Solve For, which enables you to work backwards to an answer for a calculation. For example, in the revenue projection worksheet given as an example in Chapter 2, you calculated the total revenue based on a given rate of growth. Using Solve For you can determine the exact rate of growth required to create a target figure for total revenue. Also, the Tools menu's Optimizer command performs a complex analysis of problems with more than one variable. The Audit command on the Tools menu helps you to analyze the relationship between cells in complex formulas. The Tools Library command enables you to load additional @functions for specialized calculations.

Aggregate Functions

Aggregate functions perform some of the most commonly used calculations in spreadsheet work. In addition to @SUM, this group includes functions that aggregate a block of cells, count the contents and average the block, find the largest and smallest numbers in the block, and determine degree of variance. These functions also work with several different blocks at once or with numerous individual cells.

Sum

The @SUM function is one of the most frequently used functions. In Figure 4-7, @SUM is used to add the values in a block of cells—the earnings of a group of commodity brokers. You can use @SUM to total columns, rows, and blocks including columns and rows. All that @SUM needs to know is the coordinates or name of the block to be summed. Its syntax is

@SUM(*Block*)

The block does not need to contain values in every cell; the empty cells will be ignored. The @SUM function works well with block names. For example, @SUM(TOTAL) totals the values in the block of cells named TOTAL. You can sum several different blocks at once if you separate each from the next with a comma, as in @SUM(TA,TD), which sums two blocks, one named TA, the other TD.

There are several advantages to using @SUM to add up cells, rather than a "cell+cell+cell" formula. Rows or columns entered within a summed block are automatically included in the block. For example, consider these two approaches to adding up values.

@SUM and other functions

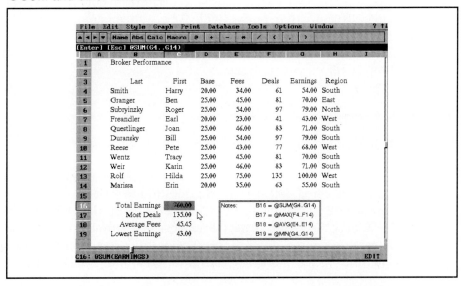

B2:	100		B2:	100	
B3:	200	or	B3:	200	
B4:	300		B4:	300	
B5:	===========		B5:	===========	
B6:	@SUM(B2..B4)		B6:	+B2+B3+B4	

In the formula on the left it will not matter if you need to insert an extra row into the spreadsheet to include another value in the calculation. For example, if you place the cell selector on row 4 and issue the Edit Insert Row command to include one more row, cells B4, B5, and B6 become cells B5, B6, and B7. The formula that was in B6 but is now in B7 becomes @SUM(B2..B5). If you enter a new value in B4 it will be included in the @SUM calculation.

The same is not true if you have used the cell+cell method of adding. Here you can see the results for both of the examples above, after a row and a new value of 250 was inserted at B4:

B2:	100		B2:	100	
B3:	200		B3:	200	
B4:	250	or	B4:	250	
B5:	300		B5:	300	
B6:	===========		B6:	===========	
B7:	@SUM(B2..B5)		B7:	+B2+B3+B5	

Inserting new rows within the summed range increases the range to include the new cells. Individually referenced cells are not automatically added to + formulas.

The integrity of the @SUM formula is preserved if you insert a row at B2, because the whole set of numbers is moved down. However, because Quattro Pro 4 inserts new rows above the current cell, the new B2 would not be included in the @SUM formula. If you were to enter a value into B2 at that point it would not be included in the sum. If you insert a row into the original example at B5, then the accuracy of the formula is preserved, but again, the new cell is not included. As a rule, then, you add a cell to a summed column if you insert the row while selecting the second cell of the block, the last cell, or any cell in between.

Because it is quite natural to add numbers to the bottom of a list, you might want to include the row below the last number when you create an @SUM formula. For instance, you could include cell B6 in the @SUM argument in the last example. Then you could place the cell selector on row 6 below the last number, insert a new row, and have that row be included in the summed block. When Quattro Pro 4 finishes calculating, the labels in the block would have a value of 0, and thus would not affect the answer.

Sum Product

Unlike @SUM, @SUMPRODUCT is a function that you will not find in all spreadsheet programs. This function is used to sum the results of multiplication between blocks of cells. For example, at the top of Figure 4-8 you have two sets of numbers in two columns and you want to know what you get if the pairs of numbers that are on the same row are multiplied together, and the results added up.

When you multiply 10 by 30 you get 300. When you multiply 20 by 40 you get 800. Add together 300 and 800 and you get 1100, which is the answer returned by @SUMPRODUCT. For its arguments the @SUMPRODUCT function requires two blocks of equal size, separated by a comma. This function does not work if any of the cells in the blocks are empty. As you can see from the lower half of Figure 4-8, the blocks used by @SUMPRODUCT can be either columns or rows, as long as their dimensions are equal.

Count

The @COUNT function counts the number of items or nonempty cells in a block of cells. This function is useful for such projects as inventory tracking, because @COUNT can tell you how many entries there are in a column, and thus how many inventory items there are in a list. You simply need to tell the function the location of the cells to be counted. The syntax is

@COUNT(*Block*)

Note that Quattro Pro 4 includes labels when calculating @COUNT. Thus the count for a summed range that includes a line of labels might be

FIGURE
4-8

@SUMPRODUCT function

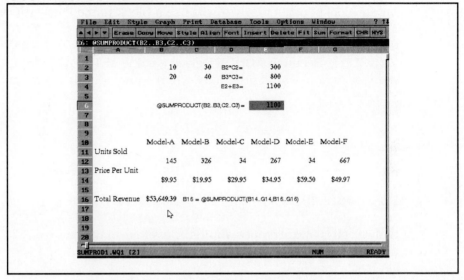

greater than you expect. For example, the following arrangement results in an answer of 6 when summed, an answer of 4 when counted.

B1:	2	B1:	2
B2:	2	B2:	2
B3:	2	B3:	2
B4:	============	B4:	==============
B5:	@SUM(B1..B4)	B5:	@COUNT(B1..B4)

Only if cell B4 was empty would the count be 3.

Average

@AVG gives the average of values in a block of cells. You can see the usefulness of this function in Figure 4-7, where it was used to calculate the average of fees earned by brokers. The function is simply

@AVG(*Block*)

Like @SUM, the @AVG function works well with columns, rows, and larger blocks, particularly if you use a block name. However, label cells are used in calculating the average. Essentially, the @AVG function combines @SUM with @COUNT; you could say that @AVG=@SUM /@COUNT. Because @COUNT gives a value of 1 to a label, the arrangement seen here would produce 6 when summed, but 1.5 when averaged.

B1:	2	B1:	2
B2:	2	B2:	2
B3:	2	B3:	2
B4:	=============	B4:	=============
B5:	@SUM(B1..B4)	B5:	@AVG(B1..B4)

Only if cell B4 were empty would the average of the values, 2, be correctly determined by @AVG.

Maximum

Shown earlier in Figure 4-7, this function finds the largest value in a specified block:

@MAX(*Block*)

Like the @SUM function, @MAX works well with block names. In Figure 4-7, for example, the block name DEALS was used for the cells F4..F14. The @MAX function is useful when you are evaluating projections, because it can tell you the largest number that results from a change in assumptions.

You can also use @MAX with a series of single cells if you separate each from the next with a comma. Thus @MAX(B5,G3,K7) tells you the largest amount in those three cells. This is handy when you want to perform a tax-form calculation and need to enter the larger of the numbers on two rows. You can also use @MAX to compare a cell to a number. Thus @MAX(G5,10) will return the value in G5 if it is greater than 10; otherwise, you will get the value 10. This is also useful for tax calculations, when a subtraction results in a negative number but you must enter 0 instead of the negative number. The formula @MAX(G5,0) will return either the value in G5 or 0, whichever is greater. If G5 is negative, the result is 0.

Minimum

Corollary to the @MAX function, the @MIN function returns the smallest value in a block of cells:

@MIN(*Block*)

This function can be used to identify low levels in projections and inventory lists. You can also use @MIN and @MAX to determine the highest and lowest balances for a customer's credit or checking account.

Standard Deviation

This function returns the standard deviation for a given block of cells that represent a population of data:

@STD(*Block*)

The standard deviation of a set of values is a measure of how much variation there is from the average of the values. The standard deviation is the square root of the variance. If you want to compute sample standard deviation, use the @STDS function, but be aware that this function is unique to Quattro Pro 4 and may not be compatible with earlier programs.

Variance

The @VAR function returns a measure of variance for a block of cells, that is, the amount of variation between individual values and the mean of the population.

@VAR(*Block*)

The result of this function is the square of the standard deviation of the same set of values. To calculate variance for a sample rather than a population, use @VARS, but bear in mind that this function is unique to Quattro Pro 4 and may not be compatible with earlier programs.

Arithmetic Functions

These functions affect the way numbers are calculated. They are often used when the outcome of a formula needs to be modified; for example, the outcome should be rounded, or a negative number should be turned into a positive number.

Absolute

To arrive at the absolute value of a number, you use the @ABS function. The syntax is

@ABS(*Value*)

For example, the formula @ABS(B5) returns the absolute value of the contents of B5. The absolute value of a number is its positive equivalent, so if B5 is –1.5, @ABS(B5) equals 1.5.

Integer

At times you need to drop the decimal places from a number, rather than round them up or down. This can be done with the @INT function. Its syntax is

@INT(*Value*)

Thus, the formula @INT(B5) returns 2, when cell B5 contains 2.75. The value is stripped of digits following the decimal place, rather than rounded up to 3.

Modulus

You use the @MOD function when you need the number that is left after two other numbers are divided. This returns the remainder of X divided by Y, as in

@MOD(X,Y)

Thus, the formula @MOD(B5,5) returns 1 when B5 contains the value 36. This function is very useful when you need to figure shipping factors. You could use, for example,

@MOD(*Cases In Order,Cases Per Truck*)

to determine how many cases will be left after a large order has been put on the trucks. Note that using zero as the value for Y is not valid, because you cannot divide by zero. Doing so produces an ERR message in the formula cell.

Random

When you need a random number in a cell you can use @RAND. This function takes no argument:

@RAND

@RAND produces a uniformly distributed random number greater than or equal to 0 and less than 1. You normally want to combine it with a formula to produce a random number within a certain range. You do this by putting the high end and the low end of the range, separated by a minus sign, in a pair of parentheses and then multiplying that by the @RAND function added to the low-end number. Thus, a random number from 3 to 12 would be produced by

(12–3)*@RAND+3

If you need to get a whole number from the @RAND function, you will need to use @INT or @ROUND.

Although random numbers might not seem to be very useful in a program that is designed to help you organize and accurately analyze information, they can be useful when you want to fill cells with numbers to test a spreadsheet design. Several of the models in this book were created from random numbers.

The @RAND function returns a new random number every time the worksheet recalculates. This can cause problems if you are trying to use the function to create values used elsewhere in the worksheet. Data generated by @RAND can be fixed by using the Edit Values command to change the formula to a value. This enables you to hide the fact that the numbers you have created with @RAND are just random numbers.

Round

In some models, you may need to round the numbers that are displayed and printed. Quattro Pro 4 retains up to 15 decimal places in calculations that result in fractions. When you use a display format that sets the number of decimal places to less than 1, these fractions are not displayed but are still active. This produces a visual problem when numbers containing fractions are summed but formatted for a small fixed number of decimal places. As the fractions accumulate, the total appears to be incorrect.

To solve this problem, the numbers being totaled need to be rounded with @ROUND. The format of the function is as follows:

@ROUND(*X, Y*)

The function rounds off the value of *X* using *Y* as the number of digits to round to. The value of *Y* should be between –15 and +15 and should be an integer (whole number). Quattro Pro 4 will round *X* to an integer.

The effect of the @ROUND was seen at the end of Chapter 2, where the rounding of numbers for display purposes produced an apparent discrepancy in column totals. In Figure 4-9 you can see three versions of the same set of numbers. The first version uses the Comma format with two decimal places and uses no @ROUND function in the growth formulas that increase February and March figures by 9 percent. The figures in column H do not add up properly.

FIGURE 4-9

Rounding function

File	Edit	Style	Graph	Print	Database	Tools	Options	Window		? ↑↓

| ◄ | ◄ | ▶ | ▼ | Erase | Copy | Move | Style | Align | Font | Insert | Delete | Fit | Sum | Format | CHR | WYS |

F16: (G) [W12] @ROUND((1+$B$5)*E16,2)

	A	B	C	D	E	F	G	H
1	**Comma format, 2 decimal places:**				January	February	March	Total
2	Office:	Chicago		Hardware	4,567.00	4,978.03	5,426.05	14,971.08
3	Period:	1st Quarter		Software	3,456.00	3,767.04	4,106.07	11,329.11
4	Total:	38,032.52		Supplies	2,345.00	2,556.05	2,786.09	7,687.14
5	Rate:	9.00%		Training	1,234.00	1,345.06	1,466.12	4,045.18
6				Total	11,602.00	12,646.18	13,784.34	38,032.52
7								
8	**General format, no rounding:**				January	February	March	Total
9	Office:	Chicago		Hardware	4567	4978.03	5426.0527	14971.0827
10	Period:	1st Quarter		Software	3456	3767.04	4106.0736	11329.1136
11	Total:	38,032.52		Supplies	2345	2556.05	2786.0945	7687.1445
12	Rate:	9.00%		Training	1234	1345.06	1466.1154	4045.1754
13				Total	11602	12646.18	13784.3362	38032.5162
14								
15	**General format, with rounding:**				January	February	March	Total
16	Office:	Chicago		Hardware	4567	4978.03	5426.05	14971.08
17	Period:	1st Quarter		Software	3456	3767.04	4106.07	11329.11
18	Total:	38,032.51		Supplies	2345	2556.05	2786.09	7687.14
19	Rate:	9.00%		Training	1234	1345.06	1466.12	4045.18
20				Total	11602	12646.18	13784.33	38032.51

ROUND2.WQ1   [1]   NUM   READY

In the second version, the same calculations are shown, this time in the General format. Now you can see the accumulated fractions created by the growth formula. The third version of the figures uses the @ROUND function as part of the growth formula, as seen in cell F16. The General formula is used to show that there are no further fractions beyond the two decimal places specified in the @ROUND function. This leads to a correct total in column H.

You can combine @ROUND with @RAND to produce a whole number within a specified range, as in the following formula:

@ROUND(((48–18)*@RAND+18),0)

This produces a number from 18 to 48 with no decimal places.

Exponent

The @EXP function returns the value of *e* (a constant, approximately 2.7182818) raised to the power of *X*, as in

@EXP(*X*)

where *X* is a numeric value less than or equal to 709. Thus, if *X* is 2, then *e* will be squared. This function is the inverse of a natural logarithm, @LN. If the value of *X* is greater than 709.85, then the @EXP function returns ERR.

Square Root

You can find the square root of a number or formula in Quattro Pro 4 with the @SQRT function. This function uses the syntax

@SQRT(*Value*)

For example, @SQRT(B5) returns the square root of the value in B5. Square roots of negative numbers produce the response ERR. Use the negation operator or the @ABS function to make the value a positive number.

One typical application of @SQRT is in the calculation of the hypotenuse, or slope, of a triangle. For example:

@SQRT(*Base*Base+Height*Height*)

Log and Log Base

The @LN(*X*) and @LOG(*X*) functions return the log base *e* of *X* and the log base 10 of *X*, respectively. Thus, @LN(100) equals 4.60517 and @LOG(100) equals 2. If the value of *X* is less than or equal to 0, these functions return the ERR message in the cell in which they were applied.

Database Functions

When you want to find the total of a column, you normally use the aggregate function @SUM. Likewise, to calculate the average of a column of numbers, you use the @AVG function. If you want to sum selected records, however, such as the fees for all brokers in the South, you would turn to the database functions shown in Figure 4-10. In the lower half of the figure you can see the seven database functions typed out in formulas, to the right of the answers that those formulas produce. In the upper half of the screen are the records referred to in the formulas as well as a small Criteria Table. The database functions use several of the concepts discussed in Chapter 5, such as Query Block and Criteria.

The basic operation of a database function is to tell Quattro Pro 4 which block of cells is involved, which column of the block you want the function applied to, and which records to include based on the Criteria Table. For example, in cell B16 in Figure 4-10 @DAVG averages only the records specified by the Criteria Table, in this case where Region = South. All database functions have the same syntax. In the case of @DAVG, it is

@DAVG(*Block,Column,Criteria*)

Block is the cell block containing the database, the rectangular group of consecutive rows and named columns that constitute a database, includ-

FIGURE
4-10

Database formula example

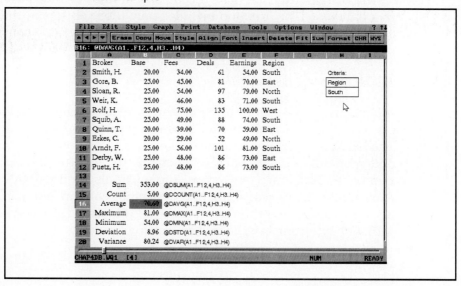

ing the field names at the top. *Column* is the number of the column containing the field you want to average, with the first column as 0, the second as 1, and so on. *Criteria* is a cell block containing search criteria.

The @DAVG function averages selected field entries in a database. It includes only those entries in the column number specified whose records meet the chosen criteria. "Criteria" refers to the coordinates of a block containing a Criteria Table that specifies search information, as in H3..H4. This is the Criteria Table for all the formulas in the lower half of Figure 4-10, which analyze the earnings for all brokers in the South region. (Criteria Tables are described in detail in Chapter 5.) The field specified in the criteria and the field being averaged need not be the same; you can average earnings for all brokers in the South Region or average fees for all brokers earning over 45. The field averaged is that contained within the column you specify with the column number. You can specify all or part of a database as the block, but field names must be included for each field you include in the block. All of the other database functions use the same three arguments: *Block*, *Column*, and *Criteria.*

Maximum Value

The @DMAX function finds the maximum value of selected field entries in a database. The function includes only those entries in the specified column whose records meet the criteria in the Criteria Table. Its syntax is

@DMAX(*Block, Column, Criteria*)

@DMAX is a very useful function when you are analyzing a large group of numbers, such as the broker earnings reports for each of four regions. The @DMAX function eliminates the need to sort through the records and manually choose ones to compare to find the largest earnings number for brokers in one region. You might also find @DMAX useful for determining the largest figure in the earnings column for all brokers who had earnings greater than a certain level. This would give you some basis with which to compare the higher-earning brokers.

Minimum Value

@DMIN finds the minimum value of selected field entries in a database. It includes only those entries in the specified column whose records meet the criteria in a Criteria Table. Its syntax is

@DMIN(*Block,Column,Criteria*)

You can use this function for such applications as inventory tracking. If one column in your inventory database is called Quantity On Hand and another is called Required Delivery Time, you can have @DMIN show the smallest current quantity on hand for all inventory items that need less than ten days' delivery time. By watching this number as inventory is added or deleted from the database, you know when to order more items.

Standard Deviation Measure

The @STD function finds the standard deviation value of selected field entries in a database. It includes only those entries in the specified column whose records meet the criteria in a Criteria Table. Its syntax is

@STD(*Block,Column,Criteria*)

If you want to compute sample standard deviation, use the @DSTDS function, but be aware that this function is unique to Quattro Pro 4 and may not be compatible with earlier programs.

Sum Value

The @DSUM function totals selected field entries in a database. It includes only those entries in the specified column whose records meet the criteria in the Criteria Table. Its syntax is

@DSUM(*Block,Column,Criteria*)

This function quickly returns such useful answers as the total earnings paid to brokers in one region.

Variance Measure

The @DVAR function calculates variance for selected field entries in a database. It includes only those entries in the column specified whose records meet the criteria in the Criteria Table. Its syntax is

@DVAR(*Block,Column,Criteria*)

To calculate variance for a sample rather than a population, use @DVARS, but bear in mind that this function is unique to Quattro Pro 4 and is not compatible with earlier programs.

Financial Functions

The functions provided for financial calculations in Quattro Pro 4 are extensive. You can calculate annuities, mortgage payments, present values, and numerous other figures that would otherwise require you to create a lengthy formula. Some basic terms and conditions are common to all Quattro Pro 4 financial functions. Table 4-3 lists the arguments that Quattro Pro 4 financial functions require and the abbreviations used for them. These abbreviations are used in the following descriptions.

Quattro Pro 4 stipulates that when interest rates are required in financial function arguments, they must be stated as a percentage per period. For example, when you are figuring monthly loan payments with the @PMT or @PAYMT functions, you state the interest argument as percentage per month.

A connoisseur of spreadsheet programs might describe the financial functions in Quattro Pro 4 as a subtle blend of the best from 1-2-3 and Excel. While retaining "backward" compatibility with 1-2-3 Release 2 and Quattro 1.0, Quattro Pro 2 and Quattro Pro 3, Quattro Pro 4 allows more sophisticated financial calculations, using optional arguments for the

TABLE
4-3

Financial Function Arguments

Argument	Definition
Rate	Interest rate, per period as defined in *Nper*, should be greater than –1
Nper	Numbers of periods—for example, 12 months or 1 year; an integer greater than 0
Pv	Present value; an amount valued today
Pmt	A payment; a negative cash flow amount
Fv	Future value; and amount to be accumulated
Type	Either 0 or 1. *Type* indicates the difference between ordinary annuity (0) and annuity due (1). Argument of 0 means payments are made at the end of each period; 1 means they are made at the beginning. The default assumption is that *type* = 0

timing of payments. In Table 4-4 you can see the older functions and the improved alternatives. Unless you are creating worksheets that need to be compatible with older programs you will probably want to employ the new Quattro Pro 4 functions.

Payment Functions

Several financial functions relate to loan payments. They are @PMT, @PAYMT, @IPAYMT, and @PPAYMT. They are considered as a group here, because they serve as a good example of the power and flexibility provided by Quattro Pro 4's financial functions. For example, the @PAYMT function can be used to perform several different calculations, depending on the number of arguments provided.

@PMT

As you saw in Chapter 1, the @PMT function calculates the amount required to pay back a loan in equal payments based on a given principal

TABLE	Older Functions and New Alternatives*
4-4	

Old Style Functions	**New Style Functions**
@CTERM(*Rate,Fv,Pv*)	@NPER(*Rate*,0,−*Pv*,0)
@FV(*Pmt,Rate,Nper*)	@FVAL(*Rate,Nper*,−*Pmt*,0,0)
@PMT(*Pv,Rate,Nper*)	@PAYMT(*Rate,Nper*,−*Pv*,0,0)
@PV(*Pv,Rate,Nper*)	@PVAL(*Rate,Nper*,−*Pmt*,0,0)
@RATE(*Fv,Pv,Nper*)	@IRATE(*Nper*,0,−*Pv,Fv*,0)
@TERM(*Pv,Rate,Fv*)	@NPER(*Rate*,−*Pmt*,0,*Fv*,0)

*Note that negative arguments indicate cash flows assumed to be negative.

or amount borrowed, a rate of interest, and a loan term. The format of the function is

@PMT(*Pv,Rate,Nper*)

Present value (*Pv*) is the principal, the amount being borrowed. *Rate* is the interest being charged, and number of payments (*Nper*) is the life of the loan. The values for *Pv*, *Rate*, and *Nper* can be numeric constants, numeric fields, or formulas that result in a number. Note that *Rate* must be greater than −1 and *Nper* cannot be zero.

Figure 4-11 shows a loan calculation worksheet, which demonstrates the argument requirements of the @PMT function. Because the rate is requested in percentage per period but is normally quoted as an annual percentage rate, the loan payment formula divides the contents of cell K3 by 12. Likewise, the term of the loan (*Nper*) is stated in years in K2 for convenience and then multiplied by the payments per year (12) in the formula. This value could be adjusted for quarterly (4), semiannual (2), or annual (1) payments. Note that Figure 4-11 includes a loan table, showing the progress of the loan. The first few rows have been formatted with the Text format to show the formulas used.

@PAYMT   A more sophisticated function for calculating loan payments and other values is @PAYMT. In its simplest form, the @PAYMT function

FIGURE
4-11

Loan calculation worksheet

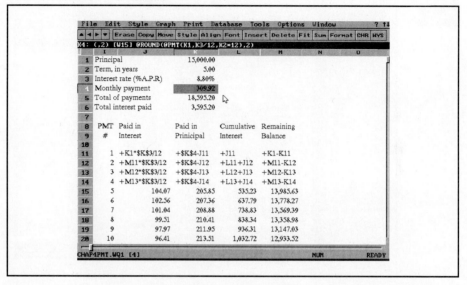

works like @PMT to return the size of payment required to amortize a loan across a given number of periods, assuming equal payments at a constant rate of interest. However, the first difference between the two functions is apparent in the order and number of arguments they use. The format of the @PAYMT function is

@PAYMT(*Rate,Nper,Pv,Fv,Type*)

The function's purpose can be defined as determination of the fully amortized mortgage payment for borrowing a present value amount at rate percent of interest per period over a specified number of periods.

You can use a numeric constant, a numeric field, or a formula that results in a number for the principal (*Pv*), *Rate*, and term (*Nper*) arguments. Note that the interest rate must be greater than –1 and that the term cannot equal 0. The last two arguments, future value (*Fv*) and *Type*, are optional and are discussed in a moment. Figure 4-12 shows an example of the @PAYMT function being used to calculate the payment required to repay $26,000 over 36 months when borrowed at 12.00% A.P.R. Here is where you can see the second major difference between the @PMT and @PAYMT; the latter produces a negative value. The reason

FIGURE
4-12

@PAYMT for loan calculation

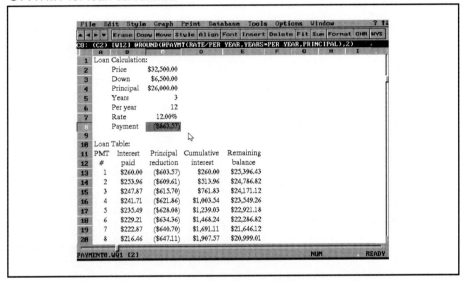

for this is the financial assumption that a payment is a negative item from a cash flow point of view.

In the example in Figure 4-12, the labels in column B are used to name and identify the figures in column C, using the Edit Names Create Labels command, described in Chapter 2. Note that the interest rate is stated as 12.00% in cell C7, meaning 12% per year. It is then divided by 12 when used as the *rate* argument in the @PAYMT function statement in cell C8. This is to comply with the Quattro Pro 4 requirement that *rate* be stated as interest per period.

Future Value and @PAYMT   The optional future value (*Fv*)argument in an @PAYMT function statement is used when you apply the @PAYMT function to the task of calculating the size of payments you need to make each month to accumulate a specific sum of money in the future. For example, suppose you want to accumulate $26,000 to purchase a new car. You are going to put away an amount of money every month for two years. That money will earn 8.00 percent interest. How large does the monthly payment have to be? You can see the answer in Figure 4-13, which shows two versions of the calculation. Note that when you use the future value argument you cannot just omit the present value argument.

A zero is commonly used as a placeholder for the present value argument, as in

@PAYMT(*Rate*/12,*Nper*,0,*Fv*,*Type*)

You might also note in Figure 4-13 the calculation of principal paid into the account and the amount of interest earned. These calculations are not automatically carried out by Quattro Pro 4 but provide a useful perspective on the @PAYMT function.

The Type Argument   The calculation on the right in Figure 4-13 uses the other optional argument for the @PAYMT function: *Type*. Quattro Pro 4 can calculate interest based on two types of payment arrangements. In Figure 4-13 you can see the effect of going to type 1 on a future value savings plan calculation. The effect is positive, because it assumes that you begin the savings plan by making the first deposit. On the left in Figure 4-13, the assumption was that the payment on the plan was at the end of the period, thus requiring larger payments to achieve the same goal. The *type* argument is likely to be 0 for such calculations as loans, but 1 for such items as annuities and savings plans.

FIGURE 4-13

Savings plan with type argument of 0

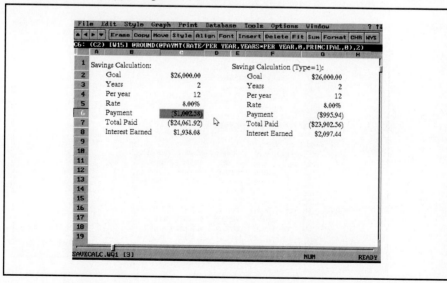

When you use @PAYMT the program assumes, as do many consumer loans, that payment is due at the end of the period. In other words, the first payment is due one month from when you receive the principal of the loan, and at the end of each one-month period after that. This assumption is type 0. If you omit a *type* argument, Quattro Pro 4 will assume type 0, as in Figure 4-12.

The alternative type, based on having the payment due at the beginning of each loan period, is type 1. You can force this assumption by including 1 as the *type* argument, as shown in the revised loan payment plan in Figure 4-14. You can see that the amount of each payment is less under a type 1 loan. Of course, the practical effect of going to a type 1 loan is to reduce the term of the loan by one period and pay the first payment from the proceeds of the loan, a practice once followed by some banks.

Loan Tables

You may want to see a table of payments for a loan, showing the split between interest and principal and the amount of principal left unpaid. A table of payments can be laid out below the loan calculations, as shown

FIGURE 4-14

Loan plan with type argument of 1

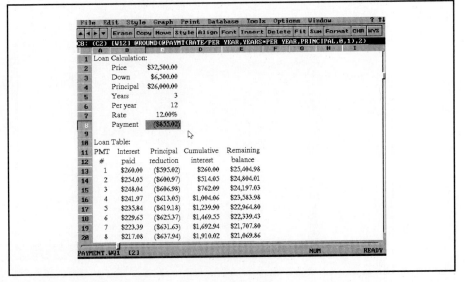

earlier in Figure 4-11 and again in Figure 4-15. Note that the @ROUND function is used to round the payment to the nearest cent (two decimal places). This is necessary when you are performing real-world loan calculations rather than just estimates.

The loan payment table consists of five columns, starting with the payment number, which runs from 1 to 60. In Figure 4-15 the Window Options Horizontal command has been used to show the bottom of the table as well as the top. Column J calculates the amount of each payment that is interest, while column K shows the amount paid to reduce the principal. In column L a running total of interest is maintained while the declining principal is tracked in column M. You can see the formulas that make up this table in Figure 4-15.

The total figures in K6 and K5 show the total interest and total payments, respectively. You might notice that the total principal reduction is actually 10¢ less than the amount of the loan. This is a result of the need to accept payments in dollars and whole cents. As any banker knows, there are several ways of dealing with this kind of minor imbalance in a loan amortization. (You might want to experiment with these using Quattro Pro 4; for example, the actual payment required to retire the sample loan in exactly 60 payments is 309.92135307589.)

FIGURE
4-15

Loan table

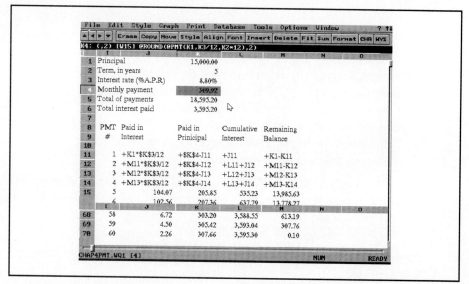

Finally, it should be noted that the method of calculating the remaining balance on the loan shown in Figure 4-15 is simple interest, the method commonly used by banks for mortgages and personal loans. Some lending institutions use the rule of 78 to determine the amount left unpaid. This method uses a system like sum-of-the-years-digits, shown later in the discussion of the @SYD function, to determine interest.

@IPAYMT and @PPAYMT

There may be times when you want to figure out how much of a loan payment is going toward interest and how much toward principal. Quattro Pro 4 has functions for both of these calculations. The interest portion of a payment is calculated with @IPAYMT, whereas the principal portion is calculated with @PPAYMT. Of course, if you already know the size of the payment, you can easily calculate these amounts from a loan table, or you can take the result of @IPAYMT away from the amount of the payment to get the result of @PPAYMT. However, both @IPAYMT and @PPAYMT can be used without first figuring the payment amount. They return the portion of the total payment for a specific payment, for example, for the 30th payment of 36. The form of both functions is the same:

@IPAYMT(*Rate,Period,Nper,Pv,Fv,Type*)

and

@PPAYMT(*Rate,Period,Nper,Pv,Fv,Type*)

where *Rate* is the interest rate, *Period* is the period of the loan you are calculating interest for, *Nper* is the total number of periods in the loan, and *Pv* is the principal of the loan. Quattro Pro 4 will assume the *Fv* argument to be zero if not supplied, and that *Type* is zero unless otherwise specified. The *Fv* argument is used when you are calculating an accumulated future amount.

To apply the @IPAYMT argument to the loan in Figure 4-15 and get the interest portion of the 59th payment you would use the formula:

@IPAYMT(K3/12,59,K2*12,K1)

The result would be –4.49599 to five decimal places, only slightly different from the result in the loan table, due to the rounding of the payment in the table. The @PPAYMT and @IPAYMT functions are handy for a number of lending related calculations.

@NPER

A great function for window shoppers is the @NPER function, which calculates the number of payments required to pay off a loan at a given payment amount. Suppose you want to buy a $10,000 car and can afford $200.00 per month. If the going rate of interest on car loans is 13 percent, you would use the formula

@NPER(0.13/12,–200,10000)

to calculate that just over 72 payments are required to pay off the loan. Note that the payment argument is entered as a negative value, because it is a negative cash flow item. The @NPER function uses the form

@NPER(*Rate,Payment,Pv,Fv,Type*)

and returns ERR if the *Payment* amount is not enough to amortize the loan. (As you might expect, the *Payment* amount must at least equal the interest rate per period times the principal.) The *Type* argument is used to indicate whether the payments are being made at the beginning or end of the period. The default, assumed if you omit the final argument, is 0, meaning at the end of the period.

The optional *Fv* argument is used when you want to calculate the payments required to create a future sum of money. For example, to calculate how many payments of $200 per month are required to reach a lump sum of $50,000 when you are earning 10 percent interest per year and have $2000 already invested, you would use the following:

@NPER(0.1/12,–200,–2000,50000,0)

The answer is roughly 132 payments. Note that this changes to 131 if you change the final argument from 0 to 1 to indicate that the payments are made at the beginning of the period. Also note that the current balance is a negative amount, as are the payments.

@TERM

An alternative function to use if you have a target figure or goal in mind for your investments is @TERM. Like @NPER, this function calculates how long it will take a series of equal, evenly spaced investments to accumulate to a target amount based on a steady rate of interest. The syntax of the @TERM function is

@TERM(*Payment,Rate,Fv*)

This function does not offer a present value or type argument and is provided in Quattro Pro 4 essentially for backward compatibility.

@CTERM

The @CTERM function calculates the number of periods it takes for a single investment to grow to some future amount. The @CTERM function has the following format:

@CTERM(*Rate,Fv,Pv*)

Rate is a numeric value representing the fixed interest rate per compounding period. The *Fv* argument is a numeric value representing the future value that an investment will reach at some point. The *Pv* argument is a numeric value representing the present value of the investment.

In Figure 4-16 you can see that the goal of reaching $1 million from an initial investment of $10,000 earning 12 percent per year will take 41 years to achieve.

Investment Functions

Quattro Pro 4 offers several financial functions that assist in the task of evaluating investments. These are @PV, @PVAL, @NPV, @FV, @FVAL, @RATE, @IRATE, and @IRR, and they are discussed here.

FIGURE
4-16
The @CTERM function

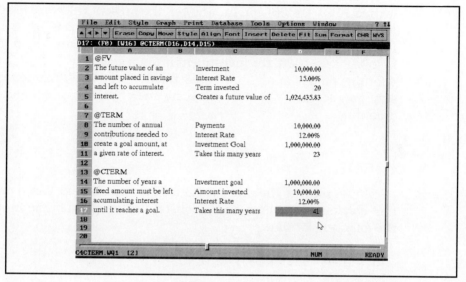

The Importance of Present Value

When you are evaluating a potential investment it helps to know the present value of the investment. Suppose you have been offered an investment opportunity that promises to pay you $1050 after one year if you invest $1000 now. You know that simply putting the $1000 in a good savings account will turn that $1000 into $1060, so the investment does not seem worthwhile. To put it another way, the investment promises a 5 percent yield whereas you can get 6 percent elsewhere. Another way of comparing the promised yield of an investment with your estimate of realistic alternative yields is to *discount* the payment from the investment. If the discounted value is greater than the amount you are considering investing, then the investment is a good one. Another term for the discounted value is *present value.*

Consider the present or discounted value of a venture offering a 12-month return of $1050 on an initial investment of $1000. You would take the $1050 and divide it by the number of payments plus the rate of return on the alternative investment, in this case 6 percent. The formula is thus 1050/(1+.06) and the answer, the present value of $1050 received a year from now discounted at a rate of 6 percent, is $991. Because the present value of the promised return is less than the price of the investment, $1000, the investment is not a good one. To use Quattro Pro 4 for this kind of analysis, you use the @PV and @PVAL functions, which can handle investments promising more than one annual payback amount.

@PVAL

@PVAL returns the present value of an investment based on periodic and constant payments and a constant interest rate. The function has the following format:

@PVAL(*Rate,Nper,Pmt,Fv,Type*)

Payments (*Pmt*), interest *Rate*, and term (*Nper*) can be numeric constants, numeric fields, or formulas that result in a number. Interest must be greater than or equal to –1. The future value (*Fv*) and *Type* arguments are optional.

An example of a @PVAL calculation is shown in Figure 4-17. The promised return on an investment of $150,000 is five annual payments

FIGURE 4-17

The @PVAL function

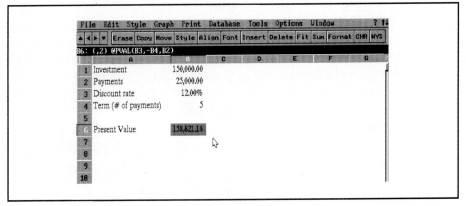

of $25,000. Entering the payments, the discount rate, and the term into the @PVAL function in B6 you get the result $158,821.18, the most you should consider investing to get the promised return. Note that Quattro Pro 4 treats payments as negative values. The entry of –B4 in the @PVAL statement causes the function to return a positive value for the present value rather than a negative value.

Because the present value of the promised return is shown to be greater than the proposed investment amount, you might want to approve the investment. However, while the @PVAL function enables you to take the time value of money into account when comparing investment opportunities, you must still bear in mind less readily quantifiable factors such as risk. Typically the discount rate represents a zero risk alternative such as CDs or Treasury notes.

Suppose that an investment of $100,000 was going to pay a lump sum of $150,000 at the end of the five years, rather than installments of $30,000. This can be calculated using the optional future value argument of the @PVAL function, as in

@PVAL(0.12,5,0,–150000)

The result is $85,114.03, considerably less than the amount of the proposed investment, indicating that the investment is not a good one. This makes sense, because you are deprived of the use of the money until the end of the investment period. You would have to get over $190,000 at the end of five years for the use of your $100,000 to exceed the return from the 12 percent discount rate. Note that the 0 in the @PVAL statement represents the missing present value argument.

Although the future value option makes the @PVAL function more versatile, most @PVAL calculations do not use the other optional argument, *type*. Quattro Pro 4 assumes that the payments from the investment will be made at the end of the periods, not at the beginning. To change the assumption to the beginning, include the argument 1 for type, as in

@PVAL(0.12,5,–30000,0,1)

The result of this formula is $121,120.48, indicating that the investment is more attractive if the return is paid at the beginning of the periods.

@PV   Another way to calculate the present value of a simple annuity—that is, a regular series of equal payments—is to use the @PV function, which takes the form

@PV(*Payment,Rate,Nper*)

The arguments can be numeric constants, numeric cells, or a formula that results in a number. Interest must be greater than –1.

An example of this calculation is shown in Figure 4-18. The promised return is five annual payments of $30,000, or $150,000. Entering the payments, the discount rate, and the term into the @PV function gives you the result of $108,143.29, the most you should consider investing to get the promised return. The @PV function enables you to take the time value of money into account when comparing investment opportunities. However, the @PV function is mainly included for backward compatibility with programs like 1-2-3.

Net Present Value

A function closely related to @PVAL is @NPV, which calculates the *net present value* of returns on an investment, based on a discount rate. The net present value of an investment should be greater than zero; otherwise, it offers no better return than investing at the discount rate. Whereas @PVAL assumes equal amounts of cash flow from the investment or a single lump sum, the @NPV function handles unequal amounts returned from the investment, using the format

Present value

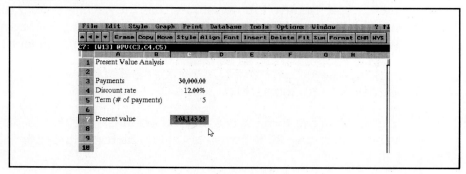

@NPV(*Rate,Block,Type*)

where *Rate* is the discount rate of interest and *Block* is cells containing the cash outlay and flows from the investment. Typically, the first value in the block is the amount invested, and further amounts are returns on the investment. The stream of cash is assumed to be constant, that is, at regular intervals, but the amounts can vary. For example, suppose you are promised three annual payments of $30,000, $40,000, and $50,000 in return for your investment of $100,000. The net present value of this proposition is calculated with the formula

@NPV(0.12,B1..B4)

The first argument is the discount rate of 12 percent. The second argument is the block of cells containing the values –100,000, 30,000, 40,000, and 50,000. The result is less than zero (–5,122.78 in fact), which suggests that this is not a good investment.

Suppose you are still interested in the investment and counter with an investment of $98,000 with returns of $35,000, $40,000, and $50,000. The result is positive ($648.90), suggesting that the investment is now much more profitable. In Figure 4-19 you can see two calculations

FIGURE
4-19

@NPV calculations

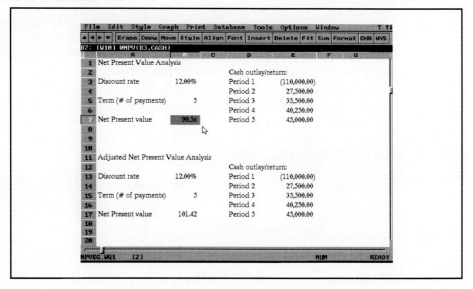

used to evaluate a further proposal that offers payments over a period of four years in return for an initial investment of $110,000. Note that you state the @NPV value arguments as a block, rather than as separate cells. In this case E3..E7 has been named CASH. The two different calculations show the effects of timing on financial transactions.

With all financial functions, including @NPV, you need to pay attention to Quattro Pro 4's assumptions about timing. When you use @NPV Quattro Pro 4 permits you to specify a type argument, which can be either 0 or 1, depending on whether the cash flows are at the beginning or end of the period. If you do not specify a type argument, Quattro Pro 4 assumes payment at the end of the period in @NPV calculations. This means that the formula in B7 in Figure 4-19 actually represents putting out $110,000 one year from the beginning of the project and receiving the first payment of $27,500 at the end of the second year. It is more likely that you will want to base calculations on paying out the funds for the investment at the beginning of the first period and receiving the first payment in return at the beginning of the second period. To accommodate this assumption you can specify a type argument of 1 as in B17 in Figure 4-19, where the formula is @NPV(B13,E13..E17,1). The result shows that the investment is slightly better under the new assumptions.

@IRATE

Suppose you are considering two investments. One offers to pay you four annual payments of $1000 in return for your investment of $3000. The other offers 48 monthly payments of $80 for the same $3000. You might want to calculate a rate of return for both of these investments in order to see which is the better deal. The rate at which your $1000 is expected to grow is the compound growth rate, calculated by the @IRATE function, using this format:

@IRATE(*Nper,Pmt,Pv,Fv,Type*)

The last two arguments are optional. In the case of the first investment the formula would be

@IRATE(4,1000,−3000)

The result is an annual rate of return percentage, because the *Nper* argument is entered as years. In this case the result is .125898325, or 12.59 percent when expressed with just two decimal places. The rate of return of the second investment is expressed as

@IRATE(48,80,–3000)

The result is .010562829, or 1.06 percent, which is a monthly rate of interest, because the *Nper* argument is expressed in months. To calculate an annual rate of return for the second investment you would use

@IRATE(48,80,–3000)*12

The result is 12.68 percent, which is marginally better than the first investment despite the fact that it pays less cash (48*$80=$3840 as opposed to $4000).

The @IRATE function arrives at its answer by performing a net present value calculation. Quattro Pro 4 guesses at the rate of return on the investment and figures the net present value of the investment at the guess rate. If the resulting net present value is greater than zero, the program guesses a higher rate and recomputes the net present value. If the guess rate results in a net present value lower than zero, a lower rate is used. In fact, the rate of return on an investment is the percentage that most closely results in a net present value of zero. Quattro Pro 4 repeats, or iterates, the calculation until it arrives at the correct rate or has completed 20 iterations. If it does the 20 iterations without getting the right rate, you see an error message.

@RATE

An alternative to the @IRATE function is the @RATE function, which takes the following form:

@RATE(*Fv,Pv,Nper*)

The @RATE function returns the rate of interest required to grow a present value sum into a specified target value over a stated term. This function is mainly provided for backward compatibility with earlier programs.

Internal Rate of Return

When you want to compare the payback you will receive from different investments, you can use the @IRR function to calculate the internal rate of return. This function uses the format

@IRR(*Guess,Block*)

where *Guess* is your estimate of what the answer will be and *Block* is a reference to a range of cells containing amounts of cash flow. Typically, the first number in the range will be a negative one, indicating the initial payment or investment. The @IRR function assumes that the payments occur at the end of the period. This function works much like the @IRATE function except that, like the @NPV function, it can handle a range of unequal cash flows.

Generally, an investment is attractive if it shows an internal rate of return greater than the rate you can obtain elsewhere, the rate known as *comparison* or *hurdle rate*. The @IRR function can be seen at work in Figure 4-20, where three different investments are compared. The third one offers the best return, because it results in the highest @IRR. Notice that the formula in I12 does not include a guess argument. This is

FIGURE 4-20

@IRR calculations

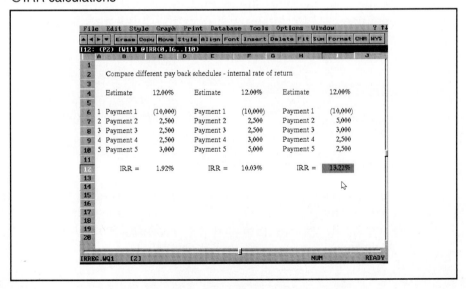

because the guess argument is optional and only required if Quattro Pro 4 has difficulty reaching an @IRR result. If you enter an @IRR formula and get an error in return, try altering or adding the guess argument, using a percentage close to what you would estimate the return to be.

@FVAL

To see what a series of payments will be worth over time, given that they earn interest, you use the @FVAL function. This is shown in Figure 4-21, where the @FVAL function returns the future value of the annual retirement fund contribution of $10,000, which earns 15 percent per year. The @FVAL function has the following format:

@FVAL(*Rate,Nper,Payment,Pv,Type*)

Rate is a numeric value greater than 0, representing the periodic interest rate. *Nper* is a numeric value, representing the number of periods of the investment. *Payment* is a numeric value, representing the amount of equal payments to be made. The @FVAL function calculates the future value of an investment where the payment is invested for a number of periods at the specified rate of interest per period. You can use @FVAL to see the effects of regular savings plans and evaluate such investments against alternative uses of funds. You can use the *Pv* argument to indicate an existing value in the program and the *Type* argument to indicate whether the payment is made at the beginning or end of the period. For example, you might want to put $1,000 into a savings account at the beginning of each of seven years, and you would like to know what the

FIGURE
4-21

The @FVAL function

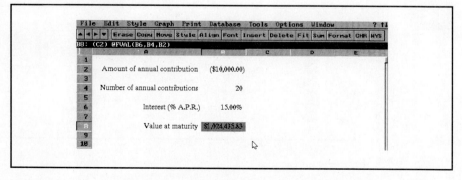

account would be worth at the end of the seven years. The account earns 8.5 percent per year, so the formula would be

@FVAL(.085,7,−1000,0,1)

which returns the answer of $9,830.64. If the account already had $2,500 in it when the plan began, the formula would be

@FVAL(.085,7,−1000,−2500,1)

which returns the answer of $14,255.99. If you decided to make the payments at the end of each period the formula would be

@FVAL(.085,7,−1000,−2500,0)

which yields $13,485.85.

@FV   Another function for calculating future value is @FV. This function is shown in Figure 4-22, where it returns the future value of an annual retirement fund investment of $2,500, earning 12.5 percent per year over a 10-year term. The @FV function has the following format:

@FV(*Payment,Rate,Nper*)

Payment is a numeric value representing the amount of equal payments to be made. *Rate* is a numeric value greater than 0 representing the periodic interest rate. *Nper* is a numeric value representing the number of periods of the investment. Although you can use @FV to see the effects of regular savings plans and evaluate such investments against alterna-

FIGURE 4-22   The @FV function

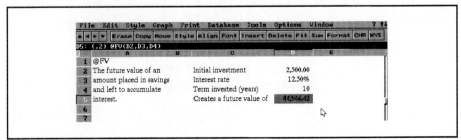

tive uses of funds, it is mainly provided in Quattro Pro 4 for backward compatibility. The assumption in @FV is that the payments are made at the beginning of the period.

Depreciation Functions

Quattro Pro 4 offers three different methods for calculating depreciation, all of which are shown in Figure 4-23. These methods are used because most goods lose value over time, and most state and federal tax laws allow businesses to deduct some of this lost value from taxable income, which in turn encourages new investment.

Straight-Line Depreciation

The straight-line method results in an equal amount of depreciation per period:

@SLN(*Cost,Salvage,Life*)

This is the simplest form of depreciation. As in all of the depreciation functions, *Cost* is a numeric value representing the amount paid for an asset; *salvage* is a numeric value representing the worth of an asset at the end of its useful life; and *life* is a numeric value representing the expected useful life of an asset.

FIGURE 4-23

The three methods of calculating depreciation

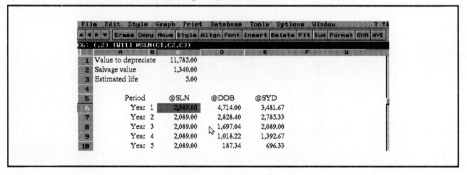

Sum-of-Years Depreciation

The @SYD function uses a method called the sum-of-years-digits to vary the rate at which depreciation is taken. This function requires knowing the year for each calculation and takes the form:

@SYD(*Cost,Salvage,Life,Period*)

An interesting application of the @SYD function is in the computation of a loan payout based on the "rule of 78," which results in a slower payoff for loans than the simple interest calculation shown earlier in Figure 4-15. The rule of 78 payout table is shown in Figure 4-24, with the @SYD formula highlighted in B11.

Double-Declining-Balance Depreciation

The @DDB function calculates depreciation based on the double-declining-balance method, using the following elements:

@DDB(*Cost,Salvage,Life,Period*)

FIGURE
4-24

Loan payout based on rule of 78

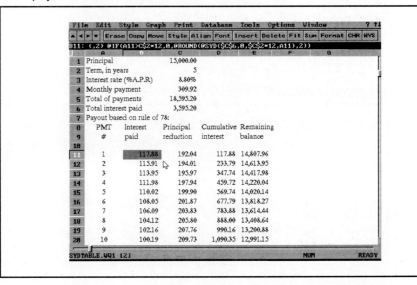

Period is a numeric value representing the time period for which you want to determine the depreciation expense. The @DDB function determines accelerated depreciation values for an asset, given the initial cost, life expectancy, end value, and depreciation period.

Accelerated Cost Recovery Some tax calculations no longer use the three methods of depreciation just described, but rather a method known as the modified accelerated cost recovery system (MACRS). The rate of depreciation allowed by MACRS varies each year of the asset's life and depends on when the asset was placed in service. There is no MACRS function in Quattro Pro 4, but you can use the @INDEX function to create IRS tables of depreciation rates, based on the month placed in service and the year of the asset's life. @INDEX is one of the logical functions, described next.

Logical Functions

Quattro Pro 4 provides a variety of functions that can be very useful in situations where logical arguments need to be entered into fields.

@IF

The @IF function instructs Quattro Pro 4 to choose between two actions based on a condition being either true or false. Suppose that you are budgeting quarterly revenue and expenditures for a computer store, using a spreadsheet like that shown in Figure 4-25. You have gotten good results from spending 5 percent of all sales revenue on advertising. Thus, advertising is normally Sales*0.05. However, you know that money spent on advertising beyond a certain dollar amount is not effective (say, $110,000, expressed as 110.00 in the model).

What you want to do is to budget your advertising expenditures with a ceiling of 110. You can do this by adding the @IF function to the advertising expense formula to tell Quattro Pro 4 that if Sales*0.05 is less than 110, Advertising=Sales*0.05; otherwise, Advertising=110. In the spreadsheet this is written as

@IF(0.05*B10<110,0.05*B10,110)

The format of the @IF function is as follows:

@IF(*Condition,True,False*)

This syntax means that if the condition is true, then the response is that stated in the *True* argument. Otherwise, the result is that stated in the *False* argument. True and false results can be constants, value or label cells, or other formulas, and they can be any type of data.

The @IF function is extremely versatile, because it allows the spreadsheet to become intelligent, that is, to do one of two things based on a condition that you establish. This conditional result can be used in numerous situations in a typical worksheet. For example, you can use @IF to test the integrity of a spreadsheet, as in the expense report worksheet shown in Figure 4-26. Anyone who has filled out expense reports knows that the sum of the rows should equal the sum of the columns. When you lay out this kind of report in Quattro Pro 4, the calculation is done for you. However, you should never assume that just because the work is done electronically it is always done correctly. The

FIGURE 4-25

Store budget

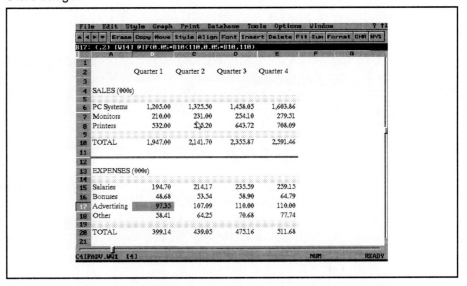

FIGURE
4-26

The expense report

@IF formula in cell G17 says that if the sum of the columns (TD) equals the sum of the rows (TA), the cell should contain the sum of the columns; otherwise, it should contain an error message (produced by the @ERR function) to show that a mistake has been made. When a mistake has been detected, the ERR message appears as a label in cell G17.

Suppose Quattro Pro 4 detects an error. You review the spreadsheet. Close examination reveals that someone typed a number over a formula in column G. This caused the sum of the columns to be incorrect. When the erroneous value is replaced by the correct formula, the ERR message disappears and the expense report is correct.

When you want to apply several conditions to a calculation, you can *nest* @IF statements. For example, in a large report you may want to allow a small margin of error in the figures. In the case of Figure 4-26 this would not exactly be appropriate, but you could amend the statement in G17 to read as follows:

@IF(@SUM(TD)>@SUM(TA)*1.01,@ERR,
@IF(@SUM(TA)>@SUM(TD)*1.01,@ERR,
@SUM(TD,TA)/2))

This tells Quattro Pro 4 that if the total down exceeds 101 percent of the total across, there is an error. Likewise, if the total across exceeds 101 percent of the total down, there is an error. Otherwise, the answer should be the average of the total down and the total across. If the figures are entirely accurate, the answer will be accurate. Otherwise, the answer will be within 1 percent of the correct total.

Another example of nesting @IF statements is shown in the formula used in Figure 4-27 to calculate commissions based on a percentage (4 percent to 6 percent) of sales. The statement in D5 reads

@IF(C5<40000,0.04*C5,@IF(C5<50000,0.05*C5,C5*0.06))

This formula says that if the sales in C5 are less than $40,000, the commission will be 4 percent (0.04) of sales; otherwise, if sales are greater than or equal to $40,000 but less than $50,000, the commission will be 5 percent. If sales are greater than or equal to $50,000, the commission will be 6 percent. The nesting of @IF statements takes a little planning, but if you write out the statement first, you can usually frame the actual formula to fit most conditional situations. The @IF function can return labels as well as values. For example, in the broker transaction record shown in Figure 4-28, the word Yes in cell K9 is the result of an @IF formula. The record needs to show if special handling is required. This

FIGURE 4-27

Results of nested @IF statement

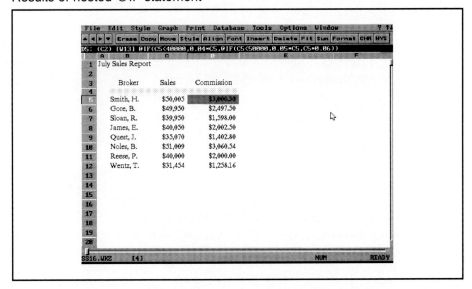

FIGURE 4-28

Using @IF to return text

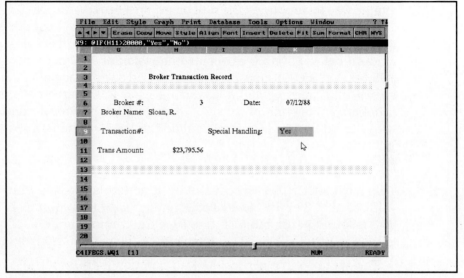

is based on the amount of the transaction, shown in H11. The formula in K9 states @IF(H11>20000,"Yes","No"). Thus, "Yes" is returned in this case, because the amount in H11 is greater than 20,000.

The name of the broker could also be entered with an @IF formula that looks for the broker number entered in H6 and responds with one of three names, like this:

@IF(H6=3,"Sloan, R.",@IF(H6=2,"Doe, J.",
@IF(H6=1,"James, E.",@ERR)))

This formula will result in the ERR message if the broker number is not 1, 2, or 3.

Lookup Tables

When you want to make a formula dependent on a range of conditions, you have an alternative to nesting @IF functions. You can have Quattro Pro 4 refer to a table of conditions, called a *lookup table*. This is a vertical or horizontal list of numbers or labels that you can use to look up related numbers or labels. Figure 4-29 shows a commission table that offers a simple way to determine the rate based on a broader range of sales levels. The vertical list of sales levels in column E and related commission rates in column F show the rate applicable to any given level of sales. Any sales amount below $35,000 earns a commission of 3.50 percent. Sales from $35,000 to $35,999 earn 3.75 percent, and so on. The bottom of the table shows that sales of $50,000 and up earn 8.00 percent. This table of numbers, consisting of cells E3 through F19, has been named TABLE with the Edit Names Create command. In cell D3 the formula reads

@VLOOKUP(C3,$TABLE,1)*C3

This means that the vertical lookup function is invoked to look up the value of cell C3 in the block of cells named TABLE in column 1. The value that is found in the table, in this case the commission rate of 8 percent, is then multiplied by cell C3 to calculate the commission amount.

The syntax of the vertical lookup function is thus

@VLOOKUP(*Index,Table,Column*)

The *Index* is the cell containing the value you are looking up in the table. The *Table* should be consecutive columns of values. The *Column* is the

FIGURE
4-29

Lookup table

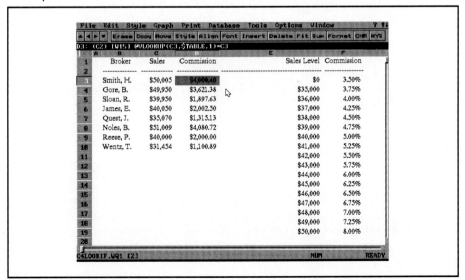

column in the table that the formula should look to for its result. The column numbering is 0 for the first column, 1 for the next column to the right, and so on. In the example, the contents of C3 and column 0 of the lookup table must be values. The column 0 values must be a consecutive range. However, the contents of column 1 and any additional columns in the table can be labels.

The lookup table can be laid out horizontally, as shown in Figure 4-30. The formula in H5 uses the @HLOOKUP function. This example supposes that each broker has a number and writes that number on sales transaction slips. A clerk then records the slips in the format shown in Figure 4-30. As the clerk enters the broker number, Quattro Pro 4 looks up that number in the horizontal table of names. (The table is shown on screen in Figure 4-30 for the purposes of illustration.) The first row of a horizontal table is row 0; successive rows are numbered 1, 2, 3, and so on. The syntax of the @HLOOKUP function is

@HLOOKUP(*Index,Table,Row Number*)

Row 0 must be a series of values or an alphabetical list of labels. Successive rows can be values or labels. Row 1, which the formula references in this case, is a set of labels.

FIGURE 4-30

Horizontal lookup table

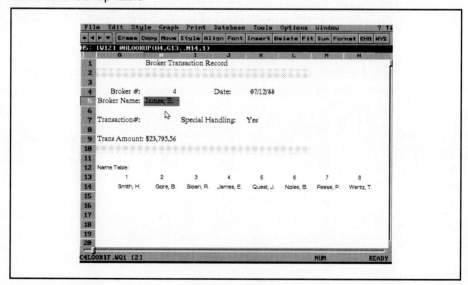

Note that you do not have to use a block name for the lookup table reference in the formula. None was used in Figure 4-30. However, a block name makes it easier to refer to the cells of the table than typing G13..N14, particularly if you want to copy the formula containing the reference to the table and thus need to make the cell references absolute, as in $G$13..$N$14. A reference to a block name can be made absolute simply by preceding it with a dollar sign, as in $TABLE.

Choose

A function directly comparable to a lookup table is @CHOOSE, which selects its responses based on a number. For example, if there were just a few brokers, you could use the @CHOOSE function in place of @HLOOKUP in cell H5 of Figure 4-30. If there were just four brokers, the formula in H5 could read

@CHOOSE(H4,"Smith, H.","Gore, B.","Sloan, R.","James, E.")

The number entered in cell H4 would thus determine the name placed into H5. The syntax of the @CHOOSE function is

@CHOOSE(*X, Case0, Case1,...,CaseX*)

If *X* equals 1, *Case0* is used. If *X* equals 2, *Case1* is used, and so on. The value of *X* must be a number between 1 and the total number of results in the argument. Values of *X* outside that range will cause an error. If *X* includes a decimal, Quattro Pro 4 rounds off the value. The *X* value can be a numeric constant, a cell, or a formula, as in the previous example, where this function is a compact way of handling small lists of results. The results can be constants or formulas of any data type. However, all results must have the same data type.

Error

When you want a cell to reflect an error you can use the @ERR function. This function takes no arguments; it is simply entered as

@ERR

@ERR returns the value ERR in the current cell and, in most cases, also creates the ERR message in any other cells that reference the cell in which you created the ERR condition. The exceptions to this are @COUNT, @ISERR, @ISNA, @ISNUMBER, @ISSTRING, @CELL, and @CELL-POINTER formulas. These formulas do not result in ERR if they reference a cell that contains ERR. The ERR value resulting from this function is the same as the ERR value produced by Quattro Pro 4 when it encounters an error.

@NA

The @NA function works the same as @ERR except that it returns the value NA, which distinguishes it from the ERR message that Quattro Pro 4 uses when a formula is typed incorrectly.

Index

The @INDEX function is a hybrid of the vertical and horizontal lookup tables. For this function you state the column number and row number for a value set in a table of values. The function has the syntax

@INDEX(*Range,Column,Row*)

There are a number of interesting applications for this function, including the accelerated depreciation schedule shown in Figure 4-31. This is a table of the allowed rates of depreciation for real property placed in service before March 15, 1984. The months are numbered across the top and the years of asset life are listed down the side. By answering the questions in rows 2 through 5 in column E, you provide the index data needed for the formula used in J5: @INDEX(A9..M17,E4,E5). The number 7 in E4 is the column coordinate; the number 4 in E5 is the row coordinate. The cell at which they intersect, H13, contains the value 9 percent returned by the @INDEX formula. Note that the number of the indexed block corresponds to the numbers you assign to the header column and row; not the 0, 1, 2, 3 numbering used in the @VLOOKUP function.

FIGURE 4-31

MACRS with @INDEX

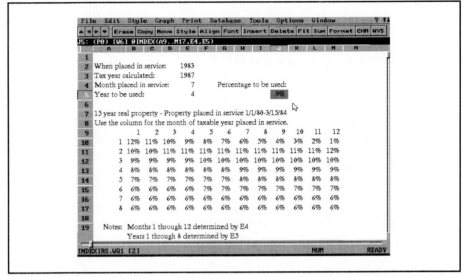

True and False

If you want to give a value to a conditional statement, you can use the @TRUE and @FALSE functions to provide a 1 and a 0, respectively. These functions require no arguments and are discussed in Chapter 13.

The @IS Functions

You will notice a series of functions in the Functions list (ALT-F3) beginning with @IS. They are @ISERR, @ISNA, @ISNUMBER, and @ISSTRING. Used in a variety of situations, these functions relate to errors and nonvalues for numbers and dates. They are described in detail in Chapter 13.

String Functions

A particularly powerful group of Quattro Pro 4 functions are those that help you manipulate strings. This is not an electronic version of marionettes, but rather a sophisticated way of handling sequences of characters or text. To Quattro Pro 4, a *string* is a sequence of characters with no numerical value. This can be words, like *Quattro Pro 4,* or a group of characters, like '*123,* because they are preceded by a label prefix. The words *John* and *Doe* entered into separate cells can be pulled together, or *concatenated,* by string formulas. As you can see in Figure 4-32, you can use string functions to create text from spreadsheet entries. The string functions can convert numbers to strings and vice versa. Because string functions relate directly to the way in which Quattro Pro 4 handles text, they are included in Chapter 10.

Special Functions

The complex set of functions referred to as miscellaneous or special functions are used in advanced worksheets and are explained in Chapter 13, where they are shown applied to practical situations. These functions are @@, @CELL, @CELLINDEX, @CELLPOINTER, @COLS, @ROWS, @CURVALUE, @FILEXISTS, @MEMAVAIL, @MEMMEMSAVAIL, @NUMTOHEX, and @HEXTONUM.

FIGURE
4-32

String example

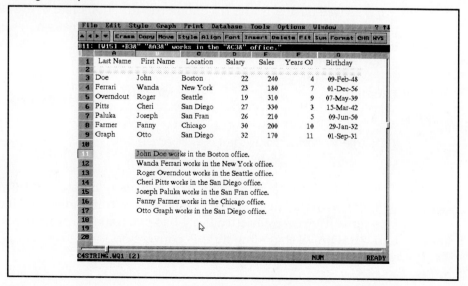

Trigonometric Functions

If you work with geometry and trigonometry, Quattro Pro 4 offers many useful functions. Although these functions are mainly used in engineering and scientific applications, they can be very handy in many situations.

Pi

The @PI function provides the value of pi to 11 decimal places. For calculations that require the value of pi, you can type **@PI**. The @PI function takes no argument; it simply returns the value 3.14159265359. The formula to calculate the circumference of a circle is thus 2@PI*Radius. The area of a circle can be calculated by combining @PI and the exponent function, @PI*(Radius^2), which calculates pi times the square of the radius.

Degrees and Radians

Another application of @PI is to convert radians to degrees. In Quattro Pro 4 as well as 1-2-3, the trigonometric functions like @SIN and @COS produce answers in radians. You can use pi to express angles measured in radians as degrees, and to convert degrees to radians, using the following formulas:

$$1 \text{ Radian} = \frac{360°}{\text{pi x 2}} \quad \text{or } 180/\text{pi}$$

$$1 \text{ Degree} = \frac{\text{pi x 2 x radian}}{360} \quad \text{or pi}/180$$

For trigonometric functions in 1-2-3, you must use 180/@PI and @PI/180 to make the necessary conversions from radians to degrees and vice versa. However, Quattro Pro 4 has two functions called @DEGREES and @RADIANS that simplify this conversion.

@DEGREES

Used to convert radians to degrees, the @DEGREES function is an alternative to using *180/@PI when you need to calculate an angle measurement. The syntax is @DEGREES(X), where X is a measurement in radians. You can see an example of this in Case 3 of Figure 4-33, where an angle is calculated by the @ASIN function from the measurements of two sides of a right-angled triangle.

@RADIANS

Used to convert degrees to radians, this function is an alternative to multiplying by @PI/180. The syntax is @RADIANS(X), where X is a measurement in degrees. You can see an example of this in Case 1 of Figure 4-33, where the @TAN function is being used to calculate the length of one side of a triangle.

Sine, Cosine, and Tangent

These three functions—expressed as @SIN(X), @COS(X), and @TAN(X)—return the trigonometric sine, cosine, and tangent, respectively, of X, an angle measured in radians. You can convert an angle measured in degrees to one expressed in radians by using the @RADIANS function. Thus, @SIN(@RADIANS(60)) returns the sine of a 60-degree angle. A result in radians can be converted to degrees with the @DEGREES function, so that the formula @DEGREES(@ACOS(a/b)) returns the angle between a and b expressed in degrees. These functions are shown in the problems in Figure 4-33.

Inverse Trigonometric Functions

The inverse trigonometric functions—expressed as @ASIN(X), @ACOS(X), @ATAN(X)—save you from having to create them from the @COS, @SIN, and @TAN functions. They return an angle measured in radians, given its sine, cosine, or tangent. The @ATAN2(X,Y) function

FIGURE
4-33
Flagpole example

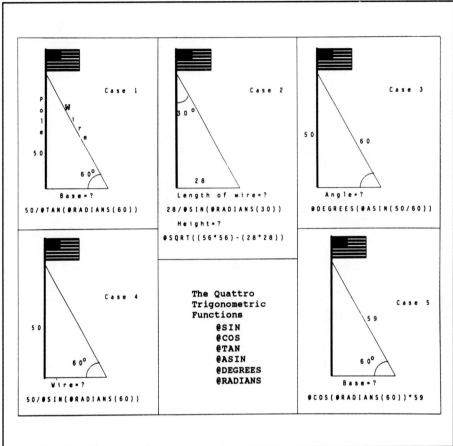

calculates a four-quadrant arctangent from the *X* and *Y* coordinates of a point.

Trigonometric Applications

Of course, there are a wide variety of ways in which the trigonometric functions can be used. You can use them to generate curves that show one set of values plotted against another. An example of this is a biorhythm chart, which is used to plot levels of physical, emotional, and mental energy on a time scale. The @SIN function is used to generate the curve shown in Figure 4-34, a simple biorhythm chart. The worksheet from which this was calculated is shown in Figure 4-35. The current date and the subject's birthdate are recorded and then extrapolated for the three different cycles: 22 days for the physical level, 28 for the emotional level, and 32 for the mental level.

Date and Time Math

Date and time information constitutes a special area of math. You saw in Chapter 3 that Quattro Pro 4 understands a date as a serial number, based on day 1 being December 31st, 1899. The first day of 1991 was serial number 33239. You can enter a date simply by pressing CTRL-D, typing the date in a recognized format, such as 1/1/91, and then pressing ENTER. However, there are other ways of creating dates, and plenty of ways of manipulating dates with Quattro Pro 4's @functions.

FIGURE
4-34

Sine curves on biorhythm chart

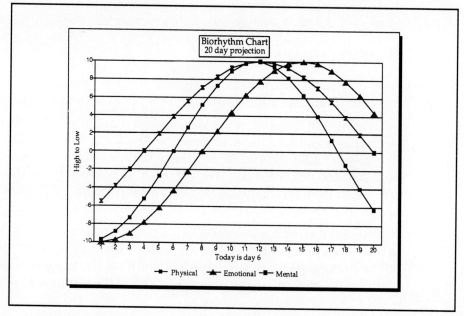

FIGURE
4-35

The biorhythm worksheet

Entering Dates with @DATE

In addition to the CTRL-D method of entering dates, you can create a date with the @DATE function. This function has the syntax

@DATE(YY,MM,DD)

where YY is a numeric value between 0 and 199, MM is a numeric value between 1 and 12, and DD is a numeric value between 1 and 31.

The @DATE function returns the serial number of the date specified with year, month, and day arguments. Thus, @DATE(90,12,25) returns the value 33232, or 25-Dec-90. Since Quattro Pro 4 can handle dates well into the next century, the year 2000 is referred to as 100, 2001 is 101, and so on. The highest date available is December 31, 2099, referred to as @DATE(199,12,31).

The number created by @DATE can be a whole number of days plus a fraction of a day expressed as a decimal. The whole number (to the left of the decimal point) in a date serial number is the number of days from January 1, 1900, up to the date referenced in the formula. The fractional portion of a date serial number is used for the time functions, which are discussed later in this chapter.

To display a date's serial number so that it looks like a date, you use the Style Numeric Format command and select one of the Date formats. This command suppresses the numeric display, showing instead the date in its more common form (Jan-1-87 instead of 31778). Any illegal dates, such as @DATE(87,2,29), return ERR as their value. This date corresponds to February 29, 1987, which is invalid since 1987 was not a leap year.

Using @DATEVALUE

Another method you can use to enter dates in Quattro Pro 4 is the @DATEVALUE function. There may be times when you will be working with spreadsheets that contain dates entered as labels. This often happens when data is transferred to Quattro Pro 4 from another program and the date values are converted to text in the process. The @DATEVALUE function produces a serial date value from a string of text or labels. This function has the syntax

@DATEVALUE(DateString)

where DateString is a string value in any valid date format. An example would be the label '25-Dec-90. If the value in DateString is not in the correct format, an ERR value is returned. There are five valid formats for labels to be read as values with the @DATEVALUE function:

❏ DD-MMM-YY (25-Dec-90)

❏ DD-MMM (25-Dec) (assumes the current year)

❏ MMM-YY (Dec-90) (assumes the first day of the month)

❏ The Long International Date format, the format specified as the system default: MM/DD/YY (12/25/90)

❏ The Short International Date format, the format specified as the system default: MM/DD (12/25). This format assumes the current year.

Provided they are written in these formats, dates entered as labels can be converted to values. You can display the resulting date values in standard date formats with the Style Numeric Format Date command. If you want to include the string in the function statement directly, you must enclose it in quotes. Thus, @DATEVALUE("25-Dec-90") returns the value 33232, which can be formatted to 12/25/90 using the D4 Date format. The statement @DATEVALUE(A1) returns the same value if A1 contains the label 12-Dec-90. For further discussion of strings and their conversion to values, see Chapter 10.

Date Deduction

When dates are stored as values, you can perform math with them. A typical application of this is tracking accounts receivable. If a payment is due on a date that has passed you can calculate how many days between then and now. Take the due date away from the current date since the serial value of dates increases the farther away they are from the turn of the century. Use the @TODAY function to find out the current date from your computer's clock. The practical value of knowing exactly how many days a payment is late comes calculating interest on the amount due. A late fee can calculated by multiplying the number of days past due by 1/365th of the annual percentage rate.

The @NOW and @TODAY functions reads your computer system's date from DOS and, if you have the system clock set correctly, will always show the current date. The @TODAY function returns a day serial number whereas @NOW returns the date and time, with the time being a decimal fractional of 1 day.

Date Series

With Quattro Pro 4 you can perform math with dates in order to create a series of dates. Instead of typing labels for January, February, and so on, months can be entered as date values. If you enter a starting date and then create the second date in the series with a formula that adds days to the start date, you can change the entire series simply by altering the start date.

To create a series of months with date values, you enter the start date as the first day of the first month of the series. Since you can format dates with the MMM-YY format, entering **1/1/90** and changing the format to MMM-YY produces Jan-90. You can then add 31 days to this date to produce the first of the next month, Feb-90, and so on. While the actual dates created by repeatedly adding 31 to the first of January are not the first of every month, because of the differing number of days in a month, the D3 format ignores the day of the month to give the date series just created an acceptable appearance. The technique of repeatedly adding 31 days to a beginning date of January 1 will produce acceptable consecutive MMM-YY dates for about 54 months.

An alternative method of creating a regular series of dates is to use the Edit Fill command. To use this method, you enter the first date of the series as a function, as in **@DATE(90,4,1)**. This function will display the number 32964 if you do not apply a Date format to the cell. Then, with the cell selector still on the number 32964, use the Edit Fill command and highlight a block with the number of cells you need. Then use 32964 as the start value and the number of days between dates as the step value. You can use the number 73050, the largest valid date number, as the stop value. The resulting numbers can then be formatted as dates. Note that a date series created with the Edit Fill command is not interactive and will not update when the first date in the series is changed.

These methods of creating date series by adding a fixed number of days to the previous date (either by copying formulas or filling a block) work in situations where the interval between dates is fixed. Thus, in the previous example, you assume that the payment schedule works on a fixed cycle of 30 days. When the cycle is based on calendar months, the calculations become more complex because of the differing number of days per month.

Date Part Functions

In addition to simple addition and subtraction, there are a number of other ways to manipulate dates. You have already seen how the @TODAY, @DATE, and @DATEVALUE functions are used to create dates and convert labels to dates. There are also date functions that allow you to extract parts of a date value for specialized calculations. Several Quattro

Pro 4 functions are designed to extract part of a date from a date value. The @DAY function extracts the day of the month from a date value. It has the syntax

@DAY(DateNumber)

where DateNumber is a number under 73050.9999999. This number represents the highest date possible, December 31, 2099. The @DAY function converts the date serial number you supply as DateNumber into the number (1-31) associated with that day. Thus, the formula @DAY(A1) would return the answer 25, if A1 contained the number 33232 or the formula @DATE(90,12,25).

The @MONTH function, which has the syntax

@MONTH(DateNumber)

@MONTH returns the number (1 through 12) corresponding to the month of the year represented by the DateNumber. Thus @MONTH(A1) returns 12, if the number in A1 is 33232 or A1 contains @DATE(90,12,25).

The @YEAR function returns the year of a date value and has the syntax

@YEAR(DateNumber)

The formula @YEAR(A1) would produce the answer 95, if A1 was any serial number or date within 1995. Likewise, the formula @YEAR(A1)+1900 would result in 1995.

The date part functions can be used with cell references or in combination with other date functions. Thus, the formula @MONTH(@DATE(90,12,25)) returns the answer 12. You can combine date functions with other functions for some useful formulas, such as this one:

@CHOOSE(@MONTH(B2)-1,"January","February","March","April",
"May","June","July","August","September","October",
"November","December")

This formula lets you create the full name of the month represented by the date serial number in cell B2. None of the built-in date formats produce the full name of the month. This formula uses the @CHOOSE function to pick a name from the list of names that are typed as labels in the formula. The syntax of the @CHOOSE function is

@CHOOSE(*N*,Case0,Case1,Case2,Case*n*)

where *N* is the number of the case to be selected from the list of cases, and Case0, Case1, and so on. The cases are either numbers or labels. Thus, the formula has the 12 months entered as the cases. Because they are labels, they are entered in quotes. The @MONTH(B2)-1 formula returns a number from 0 through 11 for the case number, which the @CHOOSE function then reads into the cell.

A similar formula is seen in the following, where the name of the day of the week for the date number in A1 is returned by dividing the number by 7 and looking up the remainder (0-6) in a list of seven cases:

@CHOOSE(@MOD(@DATE(B2),6),"Sat","Sun","Mon","Tue","Wed", "Thu","Fri")

Bear in mind that you can use the Define Style command on the Style menu to create a custom numeric format that shows names of days and months, as described in Chapter 3.

Another use of the date part functions is when you need to create a date series representing the first day of every month. This series cannot use the +30 method used earlier, because of the varying number of days in a month. The formula you see here uses the @CHOOSE function to pick the appropriate number of days of the month from a list of days:

@CHOOSE(@MONTH(B2)-1,31,@IF(@MOD(@YEAR(B2),4)=0,29,28), 31,30,31,30,31,31,30,31,30,31)

An @IF function statement is used for the second month number to determine if the year in question is a leap year and adjusts the number of days for February accordingly.

Time Functions

In addition to measuring calendar time, Quattro Pro 4 can calculate hours, minutes, and seconds. You can calculate clock time with the @NOW function, a more precise version of the @TODAY function. Suppose you enter @NOW into a fresh spreadsheet cell a little after eight thirty on the morning of December 10, 1993. The immediate result is a number like this:

34313.35449

This represents the day of the year (34313) and the part of the day taken up by eight and a half hours (.35449, the number of digits visible depending on the format used and the cell width). This figure will be updated every time you change the worksheet or use the Calc key (F9). To fix the number so that it is no longer updated but recorded as a static time value you press F2 followed by F9 and ENTER.

If you apply the first of the four time formats to the above number the results look like this:

08:30:28 AM

In other words, twenty-eight seconds past eight thirty in the morning. There are four Time formats. They are reached from the menu you get when you use the Style Numeric Format Date command. The first Time format, shown above, produces a display that is too wide for the default column width of 9 because it displays not only hours, minutes, and seconds, but also the AM or PM indicator. The second Time format only requires a column of 9 characters. There are two International formats, long and short, which correspond to your selection from the Options International Time menu.

You can record static time values in a worksheet with the @TIME function. The syntax of this function is

@TIME(HH,MM,SS)

where HH is the hours from 0 to 24, MM is the minutes from 0 to 59, and S is the seconds from 0 to 59.99999. Because the @TIME function works on a 24-hour clock, the time 11:35:00 PM is expressed as @TIME(23,35,00). However, if you want to use the shorter time format you need to add 30 seconds to the time as it is being entered. Otherwise, Quattro Pro 4 will round down the display to the previous minute.

Time values and math are useful when you need to calculate elapsed time between events, such as between hospital admission and discharge. Bear in mind that the basic unit is a day, and 1 day equals 24 hours.

Thus, 12 hours is represented by 0.5 and 1 hour by 0.04166, recurring. If you have times that are entered as labels, you can convert them to time values with the @TIMEVALUE function. Like the @DATEVALUE function, this process converts a string to a value if the string conforms to the standard Time formats. Thus, the syntax of the function is

@TIMEVALUE(TimeString)

where TimeString is a label in one of the following formats:

HH:MM:SS
HH:MM
Long International
Short International

The string must be enclosed in quotes if it is included in the function statement directly. Thus, @STRING("21:39:52") returns the value 0.902685, which is 9:39 PM when formatted with the second time format. The statement @TIMEVALUE(A1) returns the same value if A1 contains the label 21:39:52.

Time Part Functions

Just as Quattro Pro 4 can extract parts of the date from a date value, so it can extract the elements of a time value. The time part functions are

@HOUR
@MINUTE
@SECOND

Thus, @HOUR(@TIME(10,30,00)) produces 10 and @MINUTE(A1) produces 30, if A1 contains the value @TIME(10,30,00) or the number 0.4375, which is the serial number of 10:30 AM.

Database Commands

A database is a collection of information arranged in a meaningful way. Whether the information is laid out in a table of columns and rows or consists of a collection of separate forms, almost anything from a phone book to medical records to an inventory list can be considered a database.

Quattro Pro 4 As a Database

Programs designed to handle large amounts of information are called *database-management software.* In this chapter you will read about the database-management capabilities of Quattro Pro 4: how they enable you to enter, store, and then manipulate collections of data. Quattro Pro 4 has two database functions: sorting and selecting data. These two functions are referred to as a *database sort* and a *database query.* The sort capability enables you to reorder your data according to your specifications. The ability to query a collection of data means that you can ask the program to locate selected data. For example, the program can search the inventory database in Figure 5-1 for all inventory items that have the number 2 in the Bin# column. The query function also lets you extract information such as a list of all inventory items priced less than $1000. Many different software packages offer some level of database management. These programs can be divided into two groups: relational and simple.

Relational Databases

A *relational database* is one that can relate the data in several different files based on common elements. These programs can handle large amounts of data. Many of these programs also have a command language that can be used to compose complex sets of instructions in order to present users with complete menu-driven applications. Such programs are referred to as *programmable relational databases.* Examples of these kinds of databases are dBASE and Paradox from Borland International.

Quattro Pro 4 is not a relational database. However, it can keep a sizable amount of related information in one worksheet: more than 8000 records with as many as 256 fields, each one of which can be over 250

Inventory database

File Edit Style Graph Print Database Tools Options Window   ? ↑↓
◄ ◀ ▶ ▼ Erase Copy Move Style Align Font Insert Delete Fit Sum Format CHR WYS

A5: 110001

		A	B	C	D	E	F	G
1								
2				TOA - Repair Shop Inventory Listing				
3								
4	Item#		Bin#	Description	Purchase	Sale	Purchased	InStock
5	110001		9	Cone Nachelle, Left	1,340.56	1,675.70	08/09/92	7
6	110002		5	Cone Nachelle, Right	1,340.56	1,675.70	07/13/92	9
7	110003		1	Forward Bulkhead Unit	342.45	428.06	07/27/92	2
8	110004		2	Cone Nachelle, Upper	1,340.56	1,675.70	09/07/92	5
9	110005		2	Cone Nachelle, Lower	1,340.56	1,675.70	08/23/92	9
10	110006		2	Nachelle, Retaining Flange	56.98	71.23	08/28/92	13
11	110007		5	Cover Clamp	14.76	18.45	07/19/92	24
12	110008		3	Wheel Brackets, Front	897.89	1,122.36	09/02/92	21
13	110009		3	Wheel Brackets, Rear	980.67	1,225.84	08/28/92	7
14	110010		10	Wheel Bracket Clip	45.89	57.36	07/31/92	28
15	110011		11	Wheel Bracket Wing Nut	3.40	4.25	07/18/92	16
16	110012		8	Wheel Bracket Washer	3.50	4.38	09/01/92	105
17	110013		6	Strut Bracket, Left	978.56	1,223.20	08/20/92	4
18	110014		12	Strut Bracket, Right	978.56	1,223.20	08/14/92	27
19	110015		4	Wheel Bracket Seal	23.67	29.59	09/16/92	34
20	110016		7	Wheel Rim Seal	3.50	4.38	09/06/92	32
21								

INVENT2.WQ1 [1]   NUM   READY

characters in length. Because Quattro Pro 4 is memory-based, it quickly performs database operations like sort and find. Its database commands follow the same pattern as the spreadsheet commands, so you can perform database-management tasks without learning a new program. You have all the power of Quattro Pro 4's built-in functions and graphics on hand to help analyze your data. Furthermore, Quattro Pro 4 can read data from dBASE, Paradox, and other relational databases and export files to them as well. The adaptable user interface and macro command language of Quattro Pro 4 also make customized menu-driven applications a powerful possibility.

Simple Databases

The personal-computer equivalent of card files, simple databases are designed to make creating, sorting, and searching records as easy as possible. Simple databases, however, usually lack the graphics and math capabilities found in Quattro Pro 4. For this reason, if you are learning

Quattro Pro 4 for spreadsheet work anyway, you will also want to use it for simple database applications. In this way, you can easily add database-management capabilities to your repertoire of computer skills without learning another program, as well as keep all of your data in the same format.

The Quattro Pro 4 Database

Quattro Pro 4's fast and flexible spreadsheet makes it an excellent place to put together lists of information. There are just a few rules to follow in order for your lists to work with the program's database commands. These rules concern the fields and records by which the database is organized.

Fields

All information in a database is categorized by fields. *Fields* are the categories into which each set of facts, called a *record,* is broken down. In Quattro Pro 4, each field is a separate column, and each field has a name, which is placed at the top of the column. A Quattro Pro 4 database is composed of a series of consecutive columns. Each column typically contains consistent types of data; for example, each column should contain either all values, all labels, or all dates. Each column should have a unique title.

Records

Each set of facts about one item in a database is a record. Records correspond to each line on a list or to each card in a card file. In a Quattro Pro 4 database, each complete set of facts occupies one row. The rows of records are placed one after another with no empty rows between them. There should not be a blank row above the first record. Figure 5-2 shows examples of acceptable record layouts.

Acceptable and unacceptable fields, rows, and columns

First	Last	City	State
Fred	Jones	Bend	OR
Bill	Jones	Butte	MT
Frank	James	Hill	SD
Tim	White	Dallas	TX

Acceptable fields and records

First	Last	City	State
Fred	Jones	Bend	OR
Frank	James	Hill	SD
Tim	White	Dallas	TX

Blank row causes problems

First	Last	City	State
=====	=====	======	=====
Bill	Jones	Butte	MT
Frank	James	Hill	SD
Tim	White	Dallas	TX

Row of labels causes problems

Name	Name	City	State
Fred	Jones	Bend	OR
Bill	Jones	Butte	MT
Frank	James	Hill	SD
Tim	White	Dallas	TX

Invalid duplicate field names

Limits

Because a Quattro Pro 4 database consists of a block of consecutive rows and named columns, some limits apply to the database dimensions. The maximum number of fields is 256, the total number of columns. The maximum number of records is the total number of rows minus one row for the field names: 8191. The maximum field size is 253 characters, which is also the maximum column width minus 1 for the label identifier. As you might imagine, you will probably run out of memory before you get to the limits of Quattro Pro 4's database capacity. For more on memory size and usage, see Appendix A.

Database Creation

The Quattro Pro 4 database is not a special area of the program. As far as Quattro Pro 4 is concerned, any data entered into a worksheet and falling within the definition of consecutive rows and named columns is a database. You may already have created a database while you were working on a spreadsheet.

Spreadsheets as Databases

Consider the revenue projection figures used as an example in Chapter 2. The numbers for each category in the table occupy one row; thus, each row is a record. The columns containing the months plus the category names are the fields. This data can be rearranged with the Database Sort command, so that the categories are in alphabetical order, as shown in Figure 5-3.

Types of Data

Your entries in a database may be labels or values. The labels can be left-, right-, or center-aligned, because their alignment will not affect the operation of the database commands. In the example in Figure 5-3, the category names are labels. The values can be numbers, or they can be formulas and dates.

If the formulas you use refer only to other cells on the same row within the Sort Block, sorting cells containing formulas does not pose a problem. However, if you have formulas in a database that refer to cells outside the database, such as a cell containing the rate of growth, you must make

Categories in alphabetical order

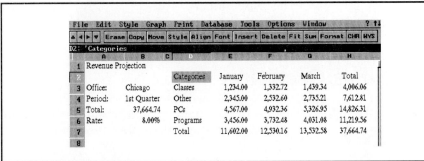

those cell references *absolute*. For example, in Figure 5-3 cell F3 contains the formula $B$6*E3. Placing the dollar sign in front of the column and row references prevents the coordinate from changing depending on its position. Thus, you can safely sort the block of cells D3 through H6 while retaining the rate of growth shown in cell B6. (Absolute referencing of cells was described in detail in Chapter 2.)

Quattro Pro 4's numeric dates, described in Chapter 3, are particularly important in databases, because often collections of information include dates. In many cases, records will need to be sorted or selected according to dates. Consider the inventory listing for the TOA repair shop shown earlier in Figure 5-1. The date that items entered the inventory is an important part of material and asset management. The same information can be sorted by date to show the oldest items on hand.

Problem Data

Many databases contain nonnumeric numbers, that is, numbers that are entered as labels. A typical example is ZIP codes in addresses. If you enter **01234** as a value, it will appear as 1234 in the cell because a leading 0 in a number does not register. You get around this problem and the ones created by 9-digit ZIP codes, telephone numbers, and part numbers that contain letters as well as digits by entering these numbers preceded by label prefixes. If you do not do so, the ZIP code **94109-4109** entered as a value would result in 9000, because Quattro Pro 4 will read the dash as a minus sign. Note that when you enter telephone numbers with area codes, beginning the entry with a square bracket will make it a label, as in **[800] 555-1212**. Quattro Pro 4 can still sort and search for numbers even if they are entered as labels.

The distinction between values and labels gives rise to another data entry problem, one that is immediately apparent when you try to enter a typical street address, such as 10 Downing Street. Quattro Pro 4 takes its cue from the first character of the entry, in this case the number 1. This is a value, and it leads Quattro Pro 4 to assume that what follows is also a value, an assumption that proves erroneous when you type the rest of the address and attempt to enter it. You will get the rather ironic error message "Invalid cell or block address." As with numbers such as ZIP codes, the answer is to place a label prefix at the beginning of any alphanumeric entry that is not a formula.

Remembering to type a label prefix in front of a nonnumeric number gets very tedious and can give rise to data entry errors. To overcome this problem, Quattro Pro 4 enables you to designate certain cells in a spreadsheet as Labels Only. To do this you use the Data Entry option on the Database menu. When cells are designated Labels Only, anything you enter into them will be automatically preceded by a label prefix. The Data Entry option also enables you to restrict entries to Dates Only, a means of avoiding errors in date fields. (Restricting data types is discussed in detail toward the end of this chapter, under the heading "Data Entry Techniques.")

Column Widths

Because the requirements of a database allow only one row for each record, fields containing lengthy information may require extensive widening of the column. Notice that the Description field in Figure 5-1 had to be made significantly wider than the others. In order to compensate for widening, you can narrow the columns containing short data, such as the Bin# field in Figure 5-1. Keep in mind that you do not have to make each column wide enough to show all the data that it contains in order for Quattro Pro 4 to store long entries. However, if you want all of the data to print, you will need to expand columns prior to printing.

One solution to this dilemma is to use the Auto Width command. This command enables you to set the width of a group of columns all at once, making each column wide enough to display its longest entry, plus a fixed number of blank spaces. A typical use of this command would be after you enter data into the database but before you print out reports. Rather than checking each column to make sure it is wide enough, simply select the field name cell in the leftmost column of the database. Then type **/** to activate the menu and select Style, followed by Block Size. You can now pick Auto Width, and Quattro Pro 4 will prompt you to enter the extra space between columns, as shown in Figure 5-4. The space is measured in characters. In most cases the default of 1 character is sufficient. When you press ENTER you are prompted for the block of columns that you want to adjust. Highlight the columns with the cursor keys or the mouse and press ENTER to confirm. You will immediately see that all of the columns within the block have their column widths set

Using the Auto Width command

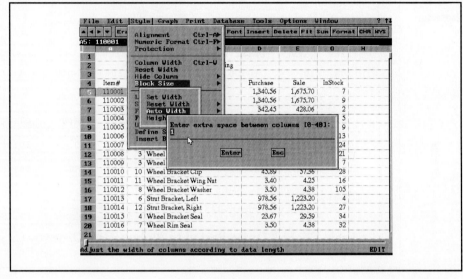

automatically. You need only indicate one row within each column, but the columns must be in a contiguous block. To auto-adjust nonadjacent columns you need to issue the command for each column in turn.

Note that the Style Hide Column command, described in Chapter 3, will let you temporarily remove selected columns from view if necessary. Notice that in Figure 5-4 column F is missing. This is because column F is currently hidden.

Sort

Sorting is the process of rearranging rows of information according to alphabetical or numerical order. Typically, sorting is used for placing the records in a database into a new order, as diagrammed in Figure 5-5. For example, the airline flights listed in this figure can be sorted numerically according to flight number as shown on the left, or alphabetically according to the city of their destination as shown on the right. However, you do not need field names to sort spreadsheet information with Quattro

FIGURE
5-5

Database sort menu

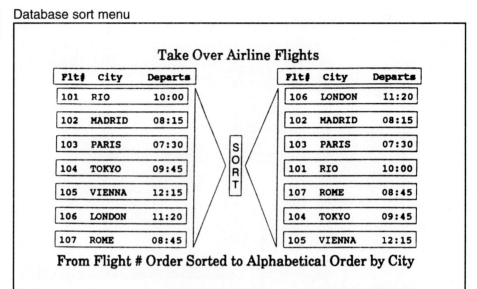

Pro 4. For example, you could sort the list of things to do shown in Figure 5-6 according to the priority numbers, without bothering to provide any field names.

Providing Sort Information

To change the order of records in a worksheet, Quattro Pro 4 needs to know two things:

Where the data is located	The Sort Block of cells contains the records but not the field names.
How you want the data sorted	The columns that are the keys on which to sort. You can use up to five keys.

You define the Sort Block and the sort keys by using Database menu items. Quattro Pro 4 will then remember them and enable you to resort the database after editing the records.

FIGURE
5-6

The Database menu

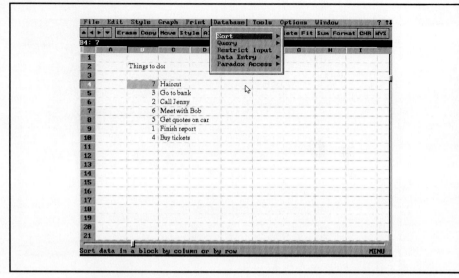

The Database Menu

To perform a sort you activate the menu bar, then select Database as shown in Figure 5-6. When you pick Sort from the Database menu, you are prompted in logical order for the information that Quattro Pro 4 needs to perform a sort—Block, 1st Key, 2nd Key, and so on—as shown in Figure 5-7. When you have provided this information, you select Go to activate the sort. In Figure 5-7 you can see the result of sorting the block B4..C10 using B4 as the key with ascending (A) as the order. When the Sort Go command is executed you are returned to READY mode. You can use Reset on the Database Sort menu to move from sorting one area of a worksheet to another. Selecting Quit from the Database Sort menu returns you to READY mode.

The Sample Database

Figure 5-8 shows a collection of information that will be used to demonstrate the database features of Quattro Pro 4. The worksheet lists

FIGURE 5-7

The Sort menu

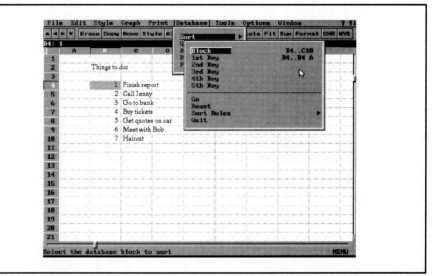

FIGURE 5-8

A sample database

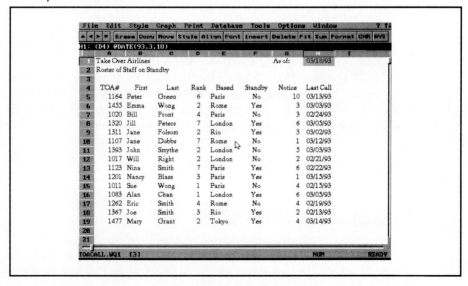

employees at Take Over Airlines who are on standby to work. Their names and ranks, employee numbers, together with relevant data such as where they are based and how many days notice they must have before working, are recorded. To practice the database commands, enter this database into a blank Quattro Pro 4 worksheet. Enter the names as labels and the numbers as values. Enter dates in MM/DD/YY format after you first press CTRL-D to set the date format. Although this is only a small collection of data, it is a typical Quattro Pro 4 database in form and application and will be an effective model for learning the database commands. Note that the column titles or field names have been centered, as have the entries in column D and F. The width of column D has also been reduced to six characters. The remaining columns are all nine characters wide.

The Sort Block

The first item of information that Quattro Pro 4 needs in order to sort a database is the block of data to be sorted; that is, all of the fields of all of the records. This block consists of the entire database *except* for the field names. In Figure 5-8, the block of data is cells A5 through H19; all of the employee names, their locations, and so on. When you select Block from the Sort menu, you are prompted to point out the cell block containing the records. The easiest way to point out this block is to place the cell selector in the top left corner of the block (the first record of the first field) before you enter the menu system. The initial coordinate in the Sort Block prompt is the cell occupied by the cell selector before you enter the menu system. The first time you set the Sort Block this coordinate is not locked. Make sure the cell selector is in A5, then type a period. Quattro Pro 4 responds by showing you the locked cell coordinates, in this case, A5..A5.

The END Key and the Mouse

To complete the highlighting of the Sort Block, you can use the END key. Press END once and the word END appears in the lower right of the screen. Now press RIGHT ARROW. You will see the highlighting move to the last column on the right. The END message will disappear. Next press END again and then DOWN ARROW. Now the highlighting runs through to the last row, completely highlighting the data (cells A5..H19 in this case). Press ENTER to confirm this block, and you will be returned to the Sort menu for the next step. The END key is particularly useful in this instance, because it automatically encompasses the entire block of data.

You can preselect the Sort Block, either using your mouse or by pressing SHIFT-F7 and using the cursor movement keys. When you preselect a block of cells and then issue the Database Sort Block command, the preselected cells are automatically accepted as the Sort Block. However, if you preselected the cells by dragging or extending the highlighting from A5 to H19, Quattro Pro 4 will assume that you want the cell selector to stay in H19 when you exit the menu system. In fact, it is more likely that you will want the cell selector to be in A5 when you leave the menus. For this reason you may want to preselect cells by extending the highlighting from bottom right to upper left. This will mean that the upper-left cell of the block is current when you exit the menu system. Alternatively, you can preselect from top left to bottom right, but then press the period key (.) twice to move the active corner of the block back to the top left.

You should avoid defining the data to be sorted as just one or two fields. In other words, do not think "I am going to sort last names," but rather think of the entire database as one entity and decide, "I am going to sort the database according to last names." By defining the Sort Block, you have told Quattro Pro 4 where the data to be sorted is located. You then need to tell Quattro Pro 4 how you want the sort to be ordered.

The Sort Keys

To tell Quattro Pro 4 in what order to put the records, you select *keys*, which are devices for pointing out which column is the key to the sort. For example, to sort the TOA staff alphabetically by last name, you would select the Last column as the first key. If you wanted a complete sort by name so that the several Smiths were sorted by first name, you would select a second key, the First column. When two or more items have identical entries in the field chosen for the first key, the second key acts as a tie-breaker.

To select keys, simply pick the appropriate number from the Sort menu. As you can see, five keys can be used. This number is sufficient to sort a customer account database by first name, last name, middle initial, ZIP code, and date of last purchase. When you type **1** for the first key, you will be prompted for the column to be used.

The cell location is not anchored; it is the initial cell your selector occupies prior to entering the menu system. Place the cell selector on the first record in the desired column; in this case it is cell C5, the first item in the Last field. There is no need to anchor the cell with a period. When you press ENTER to confirm the location, you are prompted for either Descending or Ascending order. Descending is, of course, from highest to lowest (3, 2, 1 or C, B, A); ascending is from lowest to highest (1, 2, 3 or A, B, C). Thus, to sort from A to Z you select Ascending. Remember that Quattro Pro 4 is thinking numerically, that is, A=1 and Z=26. After picking Descending or Ascending, you are returned to the Sort menu. However, the data has not yet changed. You must select Go to initiate the sort. When you do so, Quattro Pro 4 reorders the database and returns you to the Sort menu. You can see the results of an Ascending sort based on C5 in Figure 5-9.

FIGURE 5-9

Sorted list

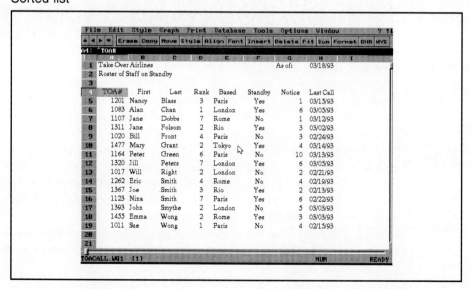

Successive Sorts

If you are performing a series of sorts—for example, as you edit names and you want to check that the alphabetical order is correct—you do not need to redefine the Sort Block or the sort keys already set. Quattro Pro 4 remembers the locations of these items. For example, if you decide to add a second key column to the sort, such as the First Name column in the TOA staff database, you do not need to redefine the Sort Block. The block is retained in memory. If you pick Block and find the correct block of cells is already defined, simply press ENTER to reconfirm it. Do not press ESC, because this will unlock the block coordinates.

The ability to resort a block of cells without having to redefine the sort parameters is convenient, but it can pose a problem when you want to sort several different blocks of cells within the same worksheet. For example, suppose you have sorted cells A5..H19 based on columns B and C. Then you create another table of information in cells A25..D35 of the same worksheet. this might be a list of flights that require staffing. You want to sort this block based on the flight numbers in column A. Because there can only be one Sort Block in each worksheet, you know you have to redefine the sort Block from A5..H19 to A25..D35. You also have to redefine the 1st Key setting. What is not so obvious is that you should not simply redefine these settings, but you should use the Reset option on the Sort menu before entering the new settings.

The reason for using Reset when you change Sort Blocks is that there is no other way to clear a sort-key setting. In the example just given, you were going from a sort where two keys were used, B5 and C5, to a sort where only one is required. The Reset command is the only way to clear B5 from the second key setting, and this is something you may overlook if you do not need a second key in this particular sorting operation. If you do not do something about the second key, you will get the error message "Key column outside of Sort Block." At this point you will have two choices: to define a second key that is appropriate to the new Sort Block or to use the Reset option on the Sort menu. The Reset option affects all five keys *and* the Sort Block, so using Reset at this stage means that you lose all of your settings. For this reason you should use Reset whenever you decide to sort a separate area of a worksheet. A more radical approach to this problem is to use the multiple-worksheet capability of Quattro Pro 4. If you have two databases to sort in one worksheet, you can always copy one of them to another worksheet and avoid having to reset sort settings.

Sort Block Expansion

When you add data to the bottom of a database Quattro Pro 4 does not automatically include the added data in the Sort Block or place the data in the correct alphabetical order. For example, suppose you are adding new staff names to the bottom of the list in Figure 5-9. After adding the new names, you need to redefine the Sort Block and issue a command to sort the new records into the database.

Quattro Pro 4 will automatically extend the Sort Block to cover new additions to a database if you insert a row before the end of the database. Rows inserted into the worksheet within any named or recorded block of cells become part of that block. The coordinates of the block expand to accommodate the new cells. Inserted rows are added to the Sort Block if you use Edit Insert Rows with your cell selector on any row in the database except the first one. Thus, if you want to add new employees in their correct alphabetical locations within the list, you can normally do so with Edit Insert Rows. In Figure 5-10 you can see a new employee being added to the list. The Sort Block will automatically expand to A5..H20. If you want to insert a row into the database without affecting the arrangement of cells outside the database, use Edit Insert Row Block, which does not insert rows all the way across the worksheet. (This command was described in Chapter 2.)

Rules of Order

You may wonder how Quattro Pro 4 decides exactly in what order to place the rows when the Database Sort Go command is issued. The program looks at the column that is designated as 1st Key, sorts it, and the rest of the cells are moved according to their entries in the key column. Typically, a column will consist of all labels or all values, in which case the order is fairly easy to predict. If you have picked Ascending, numbers go from lowest to highest and words go from those beginning with A to those beginning with Z. Dates go from the oldest to the most recent.

FIGURE
5-10

Adding a new employee

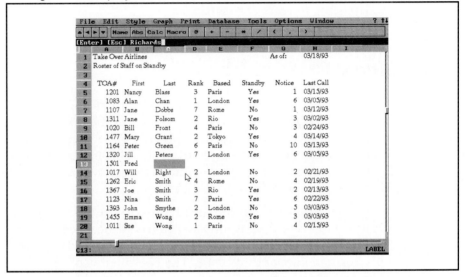

However, there are some subtleties to alphabetical order and some rules that Quattro Pro 4 uses to determine sort order when a key column contains a mixture of values and labels. The default sort order used by Quattro Pro 4 in an ascending sort is listed in Table 5-1.

In a couple of situations, the order may not be what you expect. Accidental spaces at the beginning of a label will cause that label to be placed at the top of a list. You can change the rules slightly using the Sort Rules option on the Database Sort menu. There are two areas that you can affect, as shown in Figure 5-11. The Numbers Before Labels option is either Yes or No, with No being the default. When changed to Yes, the effect is to change the order of items in Table 5-1 to 6, 1, 2, 3, 4, 5.

The Sort Rows/Columns setting is normally Rows. This means that the rows in the Sort block are recorded (according to the key columns that you select). If you change the Sort Rows/Columns setting to Columns, you can change the order of columns in a database. For example, you could reorder the sample database so that the columns are in alphabetical order (Based, First, Last, and so on). To do this you first change the Sort Rules setting for Sort Rows/Columns to Columns, then

TABLE 5-1 Ascending Sort Order

Item	Description
Blank cells	These appear at the top of the list, even before cells that contain only blank spaces.
Labels beginning with spaces	These are arranged according to the number of spaces preceding the first character, with more spaces preceding fewer; then alphabetically from A to Z, according to characters after an equal number of spaces.
Labels beginning with numbers	These come before labels that begin with words and are arranged numerically.
Regular labels	These are arranged according to the alphabet, from A to Z, according to the rules in the following description.
Labels beginning with special characters	Such characters as @ and $ come after Z. When two labels begin with the same special character they are arranged according to the second character, so that $NEW comes before $OLD. There is a consistent order among special characters that goes, from lowest to highest: ! " # $ % & ( ) * + - ./ : ; <=> ? @ [\ ] ^ ' {	}~.
Numbers from lowest to highest	This applies to the value of the number, not its formatted appearance. Thus 10 and 1.00E+01 are equal, as are 0.1 and 10.00%.

you expand the Sort Block to take in the column labels on row 4. You would then choose A4 as the 1st Key. When you pick Database Sort Go, Quattro Pro 4 reorders the columns based on the row you indicated for the 1st Key. Another example of column sorting is supplied later in this chapter.

The Label Order option can either be set to Dictionary or to ASCII. The Dictionary setting means that Quattro Pro 4 sorts labels alphabetically,

The Sort Rules option

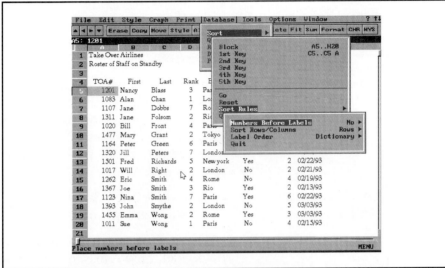

with those that begin with special characters coming after those that begin with ordinary letters. In ascending order the Dictionary sort will place words with uppercase letters before identical words with lowercase letters, as in FRED, FREd, FRed, Fred, fred.

The ASCII order uses the ASCII code of the first character of the label as the basis of the sort. *ASCII* stands for American Standard Code for Information Interchange, a system of codes in which each printer or screen character has a numeric value, from 0 to 255. (You can use the @CODE function described in Chapter 10 to explore ASCII codes.) The effect of selecting ASCII order for sorting a list based on a column of labels is likely to be surprising if you are not familiar with ASCII. For example, all labels beginning with capital letters will come before those beginning with lowercase letters, and some special characters will also come before lowercase letters. In ascending sorts, labels beginning with numbers will precede any labels beginning with letters.

You can also alter the sort order by using a Sort Table. By using a Sort Table you can determine the priority given to foreign characters. To use a Sort Table, select Options from the main menu and then choose International. This feature is described in Chapter 6. The selections you make under the Sort Rules option on the Database Sort menu are recorded as program defaults when you use the Options Update command, also discussed in Chapter 6.

Applying the Sort

Having seen Quattro Pro 4's ability to sort information, you are ready to consider some applications of this feature. Placing data in order can be especially useful when you are attempting to analyze or report it.

Analytical Sorting

Suppose you have a list of sales statistics for a company's sales force. Instead of having them arranged alphabetically, you may want to sort these numbers according to the Total column to see which people are turning in the best overall performance. To see who is selling more of a particular product you could sort by the product column. Later in this chapter you will learn how to find specific records within a database using the Data Query command, but it is important to bear in mind that simply sorting data makes it easy to find your way around it and to draw conclusions from it.

Prereport Sorting

In addition to analyzing a database, sorting is useful when you are creating reports from a database. A budget report will look better if the items are placed in some order rather than arranged haphazardly. If you were a manager using the database of TOA standby personnel, you might need to produce lists of TOA staff who are available to work at any given time. Placing the list in alphabetical order makes it easier to read as well as more professional looking.

A related use of the Sort command is to tidy up data entry errors. For example, it is quite possible to enter the same record into a database several times. Duplicate records can be found by sorting the database and then browsing through it.

Nondatabase Sorting

A further application of the Sort command was mentioned earlier: sorting lists that are not databases. This means that you can use the Sort command when you are building or organizing a spreadsheet project that is not intended to be a database. For example, suppose you are creating a budget and are entering figures for a number of expense categories, as shown in Figure 5-12. You might decide that they will look better in numerical order, from largest to smallest, so you use the Sort command to arrange them that way. The quick way to do this is as follows:

1. Select the cells: Using SHIFT-F7 and the cursor keys or the mouse, highlight from cell A4 down through B14. This will probably leave the cell selector in B14, which is fine.

2. Issue the Database Sort Block command. This will pick up A4..B14 as the Sort Block.

3. Pick 1st Key and press ENTER. This will select B14 as the 1st Key, which is what you want. Press ENTER.

Expenses before sorting

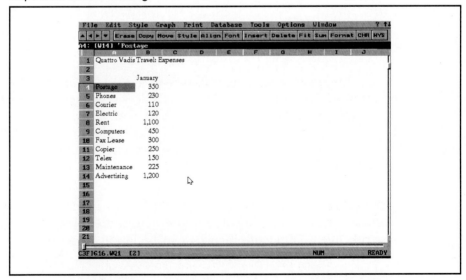

4. Now pick Go. This will produce a descending list, as shown in Figure 5-13. Note that you do not have to type **D**, because this is the default sort order.

In this example there are two shortcuts: preselecting the Sort Block and using a cell other than the first cell in the column as the sort key. You can also see that you do not need field names for a sort to work. If you now decide that an alphabetical list might be better, you can change the 1st Key to any cell from A4 through A14 and pick A as the sort order.

Sorting Columns

With Quattro Pro 4 you can sort columns as well as rows. This can be useful in a number of situations. Consider the table of sales figures in Figure 5-14. At the moment the columns representing sales for each of the three salespersons are in alphabetical order (Fred, Jane, Sue). If you would like the columns placed in order of sales totals you can reorder them with the Database Sort command.

FIGURE
5-13

Expenses after sorting

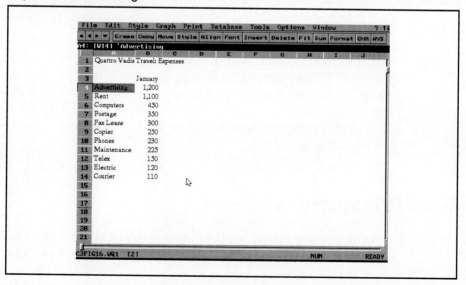

FIGURE
5-14

Table of sales figures

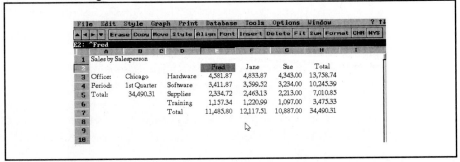

To do this you first change the Sort Rules setting for Sort Rows/Columns to Columns. Then you set the Sort Block as E2..G7, the columns that you want to reorder. Note that you exclude the labels in column D and the total formulas in column H. You then choose E7 as the 1st Key and type **D** for Descending as the sort order. When you pick Go from the Database Sort menu, Quattro Pro 4 reorders the columns based on the entries in row 7. The results can be seen in Figure 5-15. When you have finished sorting columns, remember to change the Sort Rules setting for Sort Rows/Columns back to Rows.

Sort Saving

When the sort operation is performed, a large amount of information is moved. Unless you are very sure of the effects of the sort, you should always save a worksheet before sorting it. Another safeguard is to make sure that the Undo feature is enabled. (Select Options, Other, Undo, and Enable.) This enables you to reverse the effect of a sort just by pressing the Undo key (ALT-F5).

Sort Precautions

As mentioned earlier, do *not* think of sorting one column in a database, because if you sort a single column, information will become detached

FIGURE 5-15

Sales figures results

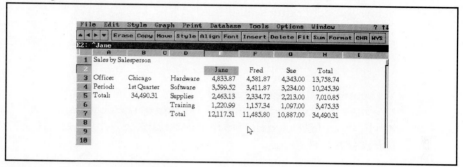

from its records and cannot be put back together. To guard against unwanted changes to data, always save the file before a sort. That way, if the sort produces an effect you do not want, you can retrieve the presort version of the file. You might also want to check the Sort Block setting on the Sort menu before issuing the Go command. If you cannot see the Sort Block coordinates on your menu, press the plus key (+) on the numeric key pad. This will give you a wide version of the menu, showing the settings.

Database Printing

To print a database, you simply need to define the database as the block of cells to be printed. Quattro Pro 4 arranges the data on pages according to the quantity of information and the size of the page. To print the data in sorted order, be sure to use the Sort Go command before you issue the Print Spreadsheet Print command.

Quattro Pro 4's print commands were covered in detail in Chapter 3. Several commands are pertinent to printing databases. Using field names as a heading that will appear across the top of each page is very useful when the list runs onto several pages. Multiple-page listings will also benefit from headers that number the pages.

Once you have defined a print block, Quattro Pro 4 continues to print from those same cells; you don't have to redefine them. Thus you can sort, print, and then resort and print without redefining the print block.

You may want to add a separator line printed at the top of your database below the field names, like this:

First   Last   Rank   Based   Standby   Notice   Last Call

You can use the Line Drawing option on the Style menu to create a line like this, placing the line on the bottom of the field name cells. This avoids having to add an extra line to the database, which could get sorted into the rest of the data.

Making Inquiries

Quattro Pro 4 can not only sort a collection of data in a worksheet, but, with the Database Query feature, it can also locate specific records or groups of records. Having located records, you can browse through and edit them. You can even copy matching records to a separate list. (The Database Query feature is not the same as the Edit Search & Replace feature described in Chapter 3.)

Lines of Questioning

As an example of the Database Query feature, imagine you are the personnel manager at TOA. You need to find employees at a specific location and then you want to know which employees are available. You can phrase this need as a question or query. A typical query would be "Find employees based in Paris who are available." Using the TOA standby database for this management function, you can address this query to the program. The conditions you place on requests to find specific data in Quattro Pro 4 are called *criteria*. In this example, the criteria can be expressed as "Find all employees whose records have Paris in the Based column and Yes in the Standby column." When given this command in the appropriate manner, Quattro Pro 4 will respond either by highlighting records that match the criteria or by placing a list of matching records in a separate area of the worksheet.

In order to find data that matches certain conditions or criteria, Quattro Pro 4 needs to know two things:

Where the data is located | The Query Block contains the entire database, including the field names

Which data to find | The Criteria Table is used to specify the criteria of your search,that is, what data to match

After you have given Quattro Pro 4 these two pieces of information, the program locates matching records by highlighting them. If you provide a third piece of information, called an *Output Block,* Quattro Pro 4 extracts a list of items and places the list in that area of the worksheet.

Where Data Is Located

To undertake any query operation, you first need to tell Quattro Pro 4 about the Query Block, that is, which block of cells contains the data you want to search. If you have just sorted the database, you might think that you have already answered the question "Where is the data?" After all, the Sort menu asked you to define a block of data. However, although the procedure used in a query is similar to that used in a sort, there is a difference: The Query Block includes the field names; the Sort Block does not.

To define the Query Block, select Database from the menu bar and then Query. You will see the menu shown in Figure 5-16. When you select Block, Quattro Pro 4 prompts you to point out the cells containing the database records. This is the entire database, including the field names. When you first pick Block, the prompt for the cells containing the database records is not anchored, and you should move the cell selector to the top left corner of the database if it is not already there. Anchor the cell by typing a period. Just as in sorting operations, you can use the END key very effectively to highlight the Query Block. Press END and then RIGHT ARROW. Press END again and then DOWN ARROW. This will highlight the entire database. Press ENTER to confirm this block. Now you are ready to tell Quattro Pro 4 what records you want to find.

FIGURE
5-16

The Query menu

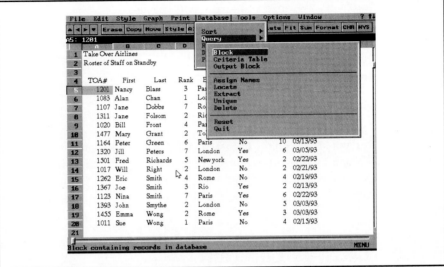

Note that you do not have to include the entire database in the block to be searched. You can leave off some records from the bottom of the block. However, you must include field names for the columns you are searching.

Which Data to Find

To tell Quattro Pro 4 which data you are looking for, you establish a *Criteria Table*. In its simplest form a Criteria Table consists of a field name above a piece of data. For example, suppose you want to find all personnel in the sample database who are based in London. The Criteria Table would be as follows:

Based   (this is the field name)

London   (this is the data to match)

You enter this information into cells of your worksheet. You then tell the program the location of that criteria and ask it to locate the records.

Quattro Pro 4 does this by trying to match what you have specified in the criteria to each row of the appropriate column in the Query Block. In this example, the program looks in the field or column that is called or headed by the word *Based*. The program checks for the text *London*. When a match for such text is found, the record that contains the matching text is selected.

The data that you ask Quattro Pro 4 to match can consist of formulas as well as simple text or value entries. You can also use multiple criteria, checking up to 256 fields at once.

Creating a Criteria Table

A typical Criteria Table is shown in Figure 5-17. As you can see, this table consists of two field names, with values from those fields entered beneath them. This particular table is being set up to locate anyone based in Paris who is on standby. This means that Quattro Pro 4 will look in two fields, Based and Standby. The program will look for *Paris* in the first field and *Yes* in the second. Only when it encounters a record that meets both of these criteria will it accept the record as a match.

FIGURE 5-17

Setting the Criteria Block

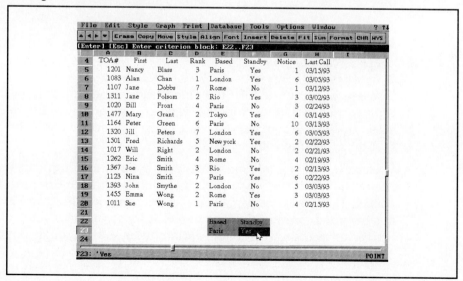

To build a Criteria Table, you type the field names of the columns in which you want to match data, followed by the data you want to match, in a separate area of the worksheet. The actual positioning of the Criteria Table on the spreadsheet is not critical to performance of the Locate operation, but the Criteria Table should be set apart from the database in an unused portion of the worksheet. However, there are some practical factors regarding location that you should consider. Do not place the Criteria Table directly to the right or left of the database if you expect to be deleting records or rows from the database with the Edit Delete Row command. Do not remove the Criteria Table too far from the database, because this needlessly consumes memory.

You define the Criteria Table to Quattro Pro 4 by selecting Criteria Table from the Query menu. You highlight the appropriate block of cells, as shown in Figure 5-17. Be careful not to include any blank lines in the Criteria Table, because this causes Quattro Pro 4 to find everything in the database. When you have selected the correct cells, press ENTER or click [Enter].

If the entries beneath the field names in a Criteria Table are all on the same line, as they are in Figure 5-17, the relationship between them is AND. This means that a record must meet both criteria to be included in the Locate operation. If the entries are on separate lines, the relationship is OR, and the program locates records that match any one of the criteria. For example, the arrangement in Figure 5-18 selects everyone who is based in Paris, plus everyone who is on standby.

Locating Data

When you have defined the Query Block and the Criteria Table, you are returned to the Query menu. To find the records meeting your criteria, select the Locate command. Locate causes Quattro Pro 4 to highlight the first item meeting your criteria.

However, before issuing the Locate command you might want to set Locked Titles in the worksheet. You will recall from Chapter 3 that the Locked Titles prevent part of the screen from scrolling, and in this case it is helpful to prevent the field names from scrolling as you look through the list of records. To set appropriate titles in the sample database you

FIGURE
5-18

Criteria Table with OR relationship

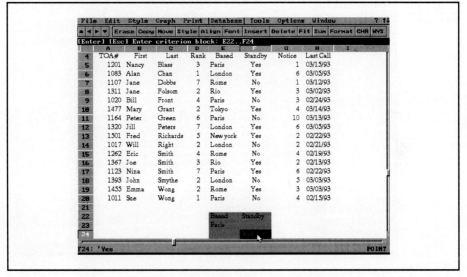

would place the cell selector in A5 or any other cell in row 5, then issue the Window Options Locked Titles command. Select Horizontal and the area above row 5 will be set as a title area.

If you are currently using WYSIWYG mode, the title cells will be shaded, as shown in Figure 5-19, which shows the results of the Locate command, based on the criteria in Figure 5-17. Quattro Pro 4 has moved the cell selector to the first record that meets the criteria, which also happens to be the first record in the database. In the lower right of the screen you can see that the mode indicator has changed to FIND. If you are currently using character mode, you will see that instead of indicating matching records with the cell selector, a highlighting bar runs the full length of the record. You can then move to the next record that meets the criteria by pressing the DOWN ARROW key. When you get to the last matching record and try to go further, Quattro Pro 4 will beep. You can move back up through the records with the UP ARROW key and continue to browse through the matching items by using the UP ARROW and DOWN ARROW keys. The END key takes you to the last record, while HOME takes you to the first. If there are no records meeting your criteria, Quattro Pro 4 beeps in response to the Locate command and returns to the Query

FIGURE
5-19

Results of Locate

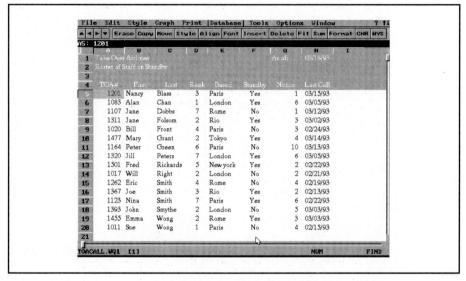

menu. This is an opportunity to check that you have specified the criteria correctly.

If you are using character mode the cursor flashes within the Locate highlight bar. In either mode you can move the cell selector across the bar with the RIGHT ARROW and LEFT ARROW keys. To change any cell on the Locate row, select the appropriate column, type the new entry, and press ENTER. Alternatively, you can press F2 and edit the cell contents, returning them to the cell with the ENTER key.

After you have used Locate, you return to the other areas of Quattro Pro 4 by pressing ESC. If you entered the FIND mode, ESC takes you back to the Query menu, where you can make changes. If you entered the FIND mode by pressing F7—described in a moment—ESC takes you directly to READY mode. Remember that to get from any mode or menu back to READY mode, regardless of how you got there, press CTRL-BREAK.

The Locate feature is very useful for quick searches when you do not want to print out a separate list, for example, to perform a quick check of a specific item in stock or an employee record. If you want to copy the records that have been located to another part of the worksheet or to another worksheet, you need the Extract command, which is described later in this chapter.

Advanced Criteria

So far you have seen that a Criteria Table offers a simple but effective way of indicating the parameters of your search for data. You can take the Criteria Table even further by using formulas and block names to create detailed search specifications.

Assigning Names

An option on the Database Query menu called Assign Names enables you to give block names to each cell in the second row of your database, using the field names in the first row. Why would you want to do this? You have already seen that you can query your database without carrying out this operation. The value of the Assign Names command appears when you start to develop more sophisticated search criteria. So far, you have seen how to search for something that is an exact match, telling Quattro Pro 4 to match *Paris* and *Yes*. You have also seen that placing criteria on separate rows creates an OR match. When you come to search for a range of values, such as *Rank greater than 5*, block names come in very handy.

The Assign Names command is very easy to use. After you have defined the Query Block, just select Assign Names. You will not see anything happen. However, if you exit the Query menu and use the Edit Names Create command, you see a list of the block names you have just created. If you press the plus key (+) on the numeric keypad, you will see the cell coordinates listed next to the names, as shown in Figure 5-20. You can then use these names in search formulas. Note that block names are stored in capital letters. In fact, Quattro Pro 4 is not at all case-sensitive when it comes to the Query command. A query based on *YES* also finds *yes* and *Yes*. When you put together Criteria Tables and formulated criteria it will not matter if you refer to field names in upper- or lowercase.

FIGURE
5-20

Names Create list after Assign Names

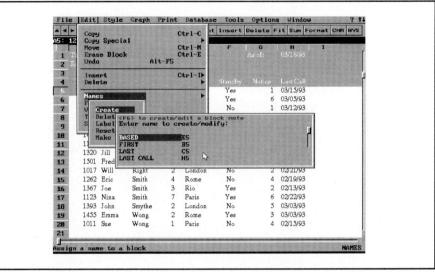

Formulated Criteria

You can enter numbers and labels into a Criteria Table, and you can also use formulas. These formulas use *comparison operators*. They also use the block name associated with each column by the Assign Names command. Thus, you could enter **+RANK>5** in the Rank column of a Criteria Table to find all persons with a rank greater than 5.

Each Criteria Table formula includes three elements: field, comparison operator, and value. These tell Quattro Pro 4 which field contains the value you are attempting to match, whether you want to match an exact value or a range of values, and the value itself. For example, suppose you need to find all staff with a Rank above 5. This can be expressed as +Rank>5. Note that the plus sign is used here because this is a formula. Rank is the field name, > is the comparison operator (meaning greater than), and 5 is the value. The comparison operators you can use are as follows:

> Greater than (+Rank>5 means 6, 7, 8, and so on)

< Less than (+Rank<5 means 4, 3, 2, and so on)

>=	Greater than or equal to (+Rank>=5 means 5, 6, and so on)
<=	Less than or equal to (+Rank<=5 means 5, 4, 3, and so on)
<>	Not equal to (+Rank<>5 means anything other than 5)
=	Equal to (+Rank=5 means only 5)

Note that you generally will not use an expression like +Rank=5 unless it is part of a larger formula, because there is no need to use a formula if the criterion is a single case. Simply use 5 as the criterion.

You can create formulas using block names with the List key (F3). For example, to create the formula +RANK>5 you first type **+** and press F3. Select RANK from the list by highlighting it and pressing ENTER. Now you can type **>5** and press ENTER to complete the formula. This avoids typing errors such as incorrect spelling of block names.

Complex Formulated Criteria

To place additional qualifications on the criteria you use for querying items, you can add *logical operators,* which set up more categories to match. The logical operators shown here set up two or three criteria for the personnel list:

AND	as in Based="Rome"#AND#Rank>5
OR	as in Based="Rome"#OR#"Paris"
NOT	as in Based="Rome"#AND#Rank>5#NOT#First="Joe"

The logical operator must be placed in the formula within # signs as shown in the examples. You create multiple conditions with logical operators to make your search more specific. For example, to locate all staff based in Paris with a rank greater than 5, you would type **+BASED="paris"#AND#RANK>5** as shown in Figure 5-21. This Criteria Table would find Peter Green and Nina Smith.

Notice that the field name in the Criteria Table in Figure 5-21 is Based, but the Based field is not the only one referred to in the formula. In fact, you can use any field name from your database when you are using

FIGURE 5-21

A Formula Criteria

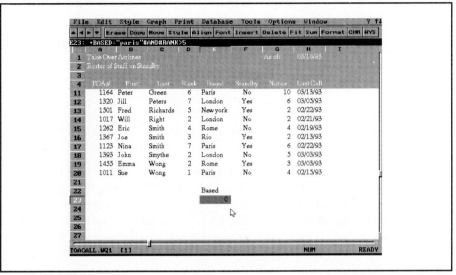

formula criteria that reference named cells in the database. For example, you can use a formula referencing Rank and Notice that is entered under the field name Last.

Criteria Techniques

A quick way to create and use a Criteria Table is to copy the entire set of field names to a new location and then define those names and the row beneath them as the Criteria Table. Enter the data you want to match under the appropriate field name prior to a search and then delete it when the search is completed. You do not have to have an entry in every column of the Criteria Table for it to work.

For example, in Figure 5-22 you can see an example of the full set of field names used for a Criteria Table. The entire block A22..H23 can be set as the Criteria Table. The current criteria are entered in D23 and E23.

You can also set up more than one set of cells to be used as criteria in a worksheet. Although only one block at a time can be specified as the Criteria Table, you can quickly switch settings by using block names. For example, in Figure 5-23 you can see three different sets of criteria located

FIGURE 5-22

Criteria Table

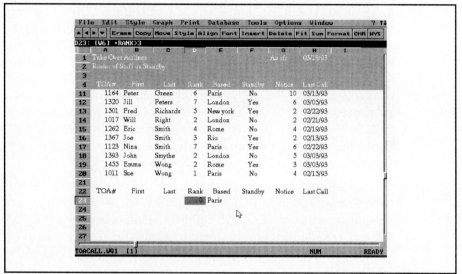

FIGURE 5-23

Three separate Criteria Tables

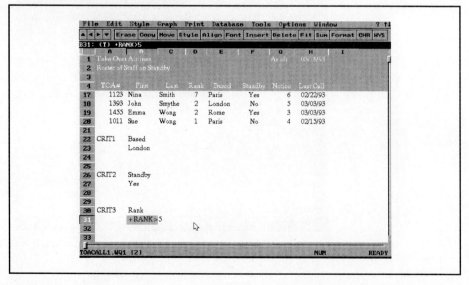

in blocks B22..B23, B26..B27, and B30..B31. These blocks have been called CRIT1, CRIT2, and CRIT3, respectively. Suppose you have just performed a Locate operation with B22..B23, otherwise known as CRIT1, as the Criteria Table and now you want to use CRIT2. You simply type **/** to activate the menu, select Database, Query, and then Criteria Table. When prompted for the Criteria Table coordinates you press F3 for a list of block names. Highlight CRIT2, as shown in Figure 5-24, and press ENTER to confirm. You can now select Locate to perform the search on CRIT2. Note that when you use a named block for your Criteria Table, the name of the block (rather than the coordinates) appears in the menu settings, as shown in Figure 5-25.

Another technique that is helpful when you work with formula criteria is to format cells with the Text format. In the last few figures you can actually read the formula in cell B31. This is because the Style Numeric Format Text command was used to apply the Text format to the cell. This causes Quattro Pro 4 to display the text of the formula rather than the result.

FIGURE 5-24

Selecting named Criteria Block

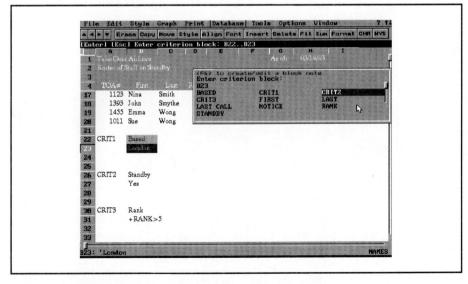

FIGURE
5-25

Named Criteria Table setting

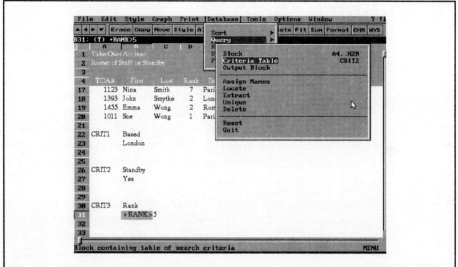

Matching Text

If what you are looking to match in a criterion is a piece of text—that is, something that has been entered as a label—and you want to incorporate it into a formula, you must place it in double quotes. For example, "paris" will find *PARIS, Paris,* and *paris.* When you use the comparison operators with labels, Quattro Pro 4 interprets > as meaning higher in the alphabet. This means that you can use these operators with nonnumeric fields like ZIP codes to specify codes equal to or greater than, say, 94100, which would be written as +ZIP>"94100".

To add scope to your searches for a text match, you can use *wildcards.* These are the question mark (?), the asterisk (*), and the tilde (~). The question mark stands for any character in that position in a string, as in *V?LE,* which would find *VALE, VOLE, VILE,* and so on. The asterisk means anything from this character to the end of the label, as in *VERN*, which would find anything beginning with VERN,* like *VERNAL, VERNON,* and so on. Tilde means "not," as in *~Paris,* which would find everything but *Paris.*

Repeating a Query

The F7 key repeats the last query you performed. Suppose you have to look up different employee records on a regular basis, and you have a Criteria Table with Last and First as headings. You would type the name of the employee you were looking for under the Last and First headings in the Criteria Table and select Locate. The next time you needed to look up an employee's record, you would type the name of the employee in the Criteria Table and press F7. The same Criteria Table and Query Locate are used, but with the new entry in the Criteria Table. In this way you can find a succession of employees from a long list with relative ease.

After performing a Query Locate, you will get the same results again when you press F7 if you are working in the same spreadsheet during the same session. If you last performed a Query Extract, which will be discussed next, an Extract is performed the next time you press F7.

Query Extract

So far you have seen that Quattro Pro 4 is adept at locating records in a database. At some point you will probably want a list of items matching your criteria. You do this once you have established the database and the criteria. You can then place the list anywhere in the worksheet.

Providing the Data

You create a list of data selected from a Quattro Pro 4 database by using the Extract command, which copies data meeting your criteria into a separate area of the spreadsheet. The Extract command needs the following four pieces of information:

Where the data is located   The Query Block

What to extract   The Criteria Table

Where to output   The cells in which to place the extracted
                           data

What data to output   The names of the fields to be included in
                           the list

If you have already used the Locate feature, you will have used the first
two items. The last two involve moving to an empty part of the worksheet
and typing in the names of the fields you want reported.

The Output Block

Once you have decided which pieces of information you want and
where to have Quattro Pro 4 output the matching records you can extract
the information. For example, in Figure 5-26 you can see the results of
the Extract function, using the fields Last and Last Call. This figure shows
the names of the staff that meet the criteria plus the date they were last
called.

Extract results with two field names

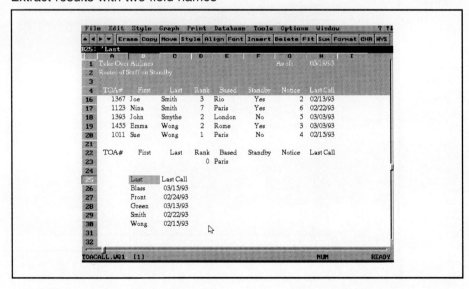

There is no limit to the number of fields you can include in the Output Block, and you do not need to include fields that were part of the criteria. Of course, as you can see from Figure 5-27, you can include all fields in the output if you want to.

When you have entered the names of the fields you want reported, you must next record the Output Block. Place your cursor on the leftmost field name and select Output from the Query menu. Anchor the cell you are in and press END and RIGHT ARROW to include all of the field names. Press ENTER to confirm the output block. You may want to extend the Output Block of cells. If you do not extend it beyond the row of field names, you will be telling Quattro Pro 4 that it can use any number of rows below the field names for the output. If you press PAGE DOWN once, you will be saying that there are 20 lines available, and Quattro Pro 4 will highlight this area. As your worksheets get crowded, it is a good idea to limit the Output Block like this so that the program is prevented from copying output into cells that already contain data.

**FIGURE
5-27**

Extracting complete records

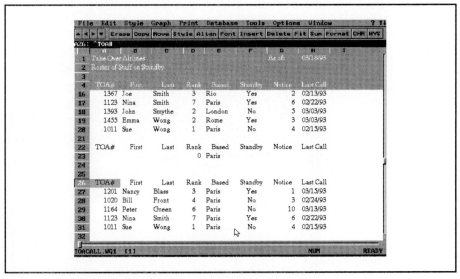

The Extract

With the Output Block defined, select Extract to tell Quattro Pro 4 to place the items identified by your criteria into the output cells. Quattro Pro 4 reads the Criteria Table and copies all matching records to the output block. When you have performed the extract, the data can be printed, copied, or further manipulated. As with the Locate command, you can repeat the last query with F7. Thus, you can change the name of the city you are looking for, for example, and press F7 to get a new list in the output block.

Note that when Quattro Pro 4 extracts numbers from the database to an output range, they are only numbers. Formulas in the database are converted to their numeric value upon extraction.

Unique Records

There may be situations in which you want to extract only the unique values in one or more fields. For example, suppose you have a database of wines classified according to Country, Region, and Year. You want a list of all regions of France represented in the database. You can use a criterion of Country=France and an output field with the heading Region. When you issue the Extract command, however, the resulting list will contain one region name entry for every record that has France in the Country field, meaning there will be many duplicates in the list. In a situation like this, when what you want is each unique region name listed only once, use the Unique option on the Database Query menu. The Unique option lists any item that will be identical to another item in the output block once. In other words, the Unique option lists unique values, whereas the Extract option lists all values.

Sorting Extracted Data

Extracted data is a series of consecutive columns and rows; in fact, by extracting data you have created a new database. This database can now be sorted. If you were asked to provide a list of all the staff, you would want the list alphabetized or put in some other order. You can do this by defining the Sort Block as the output data minus the field names. Remember that Quattro Pro 4 remembers the last Sort Block and keys you used, so it is wise to select the Reset command from the Sort menu before performing a sort on a new block.

Deleting Records

When you are cleaning up or maintaining a database, you may need to get rid of records. One way of doing this is to find the record and then delete it with the Edit Delete Row command. However, this has the possibly negative side effect of removing any data that is on the same row as the deleted record, all the way across the worksheet. Quattro Pro 4 has an automated alternative, called Query Delete, that does not interfere with cells outside the database.

The Query Delete command has the effect of an Edit Erase operation on cells containing records to be deleted, followed by an Edit Move to close up blank cells in the database. At the same time it adjusts the Database Query Block setting to make sure it is correct.

To use this command you set the criteria for the records you want deleted and then select Delete instead of Locate or Extract. You will be prompted to confirm this action, because the program removes cells from the worksheet. Query Delete can be dangerous; be careful that your criteria are correct before using this command and perform a File Save beforehand. You can always perform a Query Locate before a Query Delete, just to make sure that your criteria are working as intended. Another safeguard is to make sure that the Undo feature is enabled (by selecting Options, Other, Undo, and Enable). This will allow you to reverse the effect of Query Delete just by pressing the Undo key (ALT-F5).

Databases and Multiple Worksheets

You can see that managing a database requires several elements in addition to the data itself. Querying the database requires a Criteria

Table. An Output Block is required for an Extract to be performed. One way to manage these elements is to divide them between worksheets. For example, you can keep the database in one worksheet and the Criteria Table and Output Block in a separate worksheet. You can see this arrangement in Figure 5-28 where two worksheets, DATABASE and REPORT, are tiled side by side. The REPORT worksheet is where the user is specifying the criteria and extracting the data.

With the REPORT worksheet active you set the Query Block by defining the cells occupied by data in the DATABASE worksheet. When you get the prompt "Enter database block," use SHIFT-F6, the Next Window key, to make DATABASE the active worksheet; then highlight the database cells. When you confirm this, the setting in the Query menu looks something like: [DATABASE]A4..H20. Keeping the REPORT worksheet active, you proceed to define the Criteria Table and Output Block using cells in the REPORT worksheet. You can see that this has been done in Figure 5-29.

To extract data from the DATABASE worksheet into REPORT you make REPORT the active worksheet and then issue the Extract command. Records from DATABASE that meet the criteria in REPORT will be copied into REPORT. You can also use the Locate command from REPORT. In this case, Quattro Pro 4 takes you to the DATABASE worksheet and

FIGURE 5-28

Extracting from a separate file

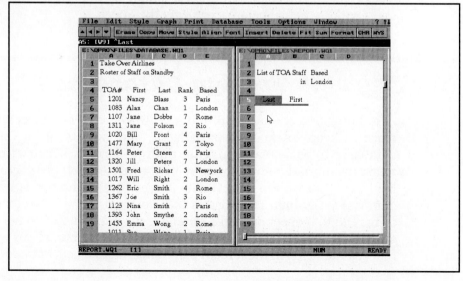

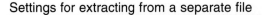

FIGURE
5-29

Settings for extracting from a separate file

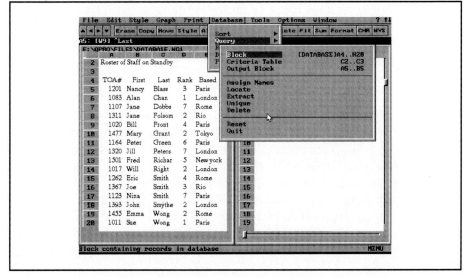

shows you the selected records there. When you leave FIND mode you are returned to the REPORT worksheet.

An extension of the multiple-worksheet approach would be to have several different worksheets for reporting on the same database. This would enable you to switch criteria simply by making a different worksheet window active before executing the query.

Working with Foreign Databases

Although many users find that a Quattro Pro 4 worksheet is the ideal place to keep track of their data, no one expects all of the world's databases to be available in Quattro Pro 4 format. Because there is so much useful data stored in databases created by other programs, Borland gave Quattro Pro 4 the ability to read files created by other popular database programs. This means that you can use the Database Query command to inspect data in a database file created by another program such as dBASE or Paradox. You can establish criteria in your worksheet that refer to fields in the foreign file. Using the Extract command you can read a selection of data from the foreign file into a Quattro Pro 4 worksheet.

You can also use Quattro Pro 4 to update a foreign database. For example, suppose that your company uses Paradox to maintain a central database of expenses and that you keep track of your expenses in a Quattro Pro 4 worksheet. You can store your expense records in a file that can be saved as a Paradox database. You can read about how to query foreign databases in Chapter 13, which covers importing and exporting Paradox data, as well as the Paradox Access command on the Database menu.

Data Entry Techniques

Spreadsheets used as databases take far more keystrokes than regular spreadsheets, in which the bulk of the entries are created by formulas that are copied. In addition, databases often need extensive editing to be kept current. If you are maintaining a sizable database, you may wish to employ a typist to edit or input the data. Following are some steps you can take to make the work easier for someone unfamiliar with Quattro Pro 4.

Input Form

If you are having people who are not well versed in spreadsheets perform data entry for you, you can make an input form to assist them. The first step is to protect the entire spreadsheet. To do this you issue the Options Protection command and select Enable. This prevents any data from being altered. Then you can use the Style Protection command to Unprotect cells in which the data will be entered or edited. When you are ready to have someone work on the database you can issue the Restrict Input command from the Database menu. You highlight a block of the worksheet that includes the unprotected cells. When you press ENTER this area becomes the *Input Block*. User access is now limited to any unprotected cells in the Input Block. The diagram in Figure 5-30 shows how the Input Block and unprotected cells work together to create a *mask* over the worksheet.

FIGURE
5-30 Diagram of input range

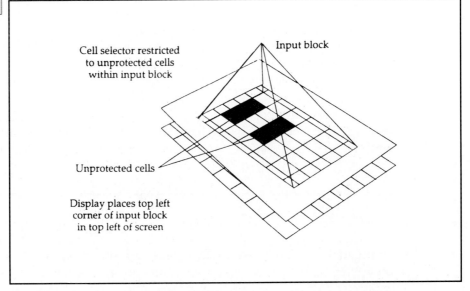

The effect of the Restrict Input command is considerable. The message INPUT appears in the mode indicator. The cursor keys will not take you outside of the defined Input Block of cells and will only move to those cells within the Input Block that are unprotected. You can type data and press ENTER, or edit data with F2 and reenter it. The program menu is not available, so typing / begins a new label instead of activating the menu.

To break out of the INPUT mode you press ESC or ENTER while the INPUT message is displayed. This means that it is very easy to override the Restrict Input command. In fact, the command is most effective when used in macros that further control the user's access to commands, as described in Chapter 12.

Data Control

Earlier, this chapter mentioned the need to type a label prefix when you enter nonnumeric numbers such as ZIP codes. Another chore for data-entry workers is making sure that dates are entered as dates. To overcome this problem, Quattro Pro 4 enables you to designate certain cells in a spreadsheet as Labels Only. To do this you use the Data Entry option on the Database menu. When you select the Labels Only command, you highlight an area—usually a field or column—to be affected by the command. From then on, anything entered into those cells will be automatically preceded by a label prefix. You will see the word *Label* in front of the cell address on the input or status line to remind you that the cell has a forced data type.

The default label prefix, usually the apostrophe for left-alignment, is added to what you type into a label cell. If the cells you selected with the Labels Only command already contain numbers or formulas entered as values, these cells retain their status. However, if you edit and then reenter one of these cells, it will be converted to a label.

The Database Data Entry command also enables you to restrict entries to Dates Only, a means of avoiding errors in date fields. You can see this in operation in Figure 5-31. You see the word *Date* in front of the cell address in the input and status lines to remind you that what you enter must be a date. Cells selected by the Dates Only command accept dates typed in any of the standard date formats, which were described in Chapter 2. You do not have to press CTRL-D before entering a date in a Dates Only cell.

FIGURE
5-31

Forced data type: Date

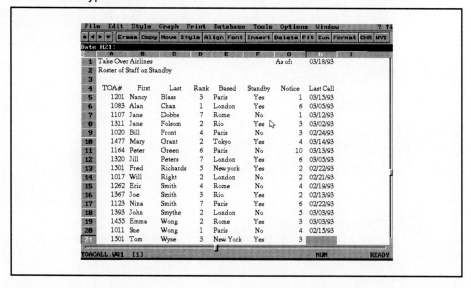

CHAPTER

Working with Defaults

*T*his chapter shows you how to customize many aspects of Quattro Pro 4. In Chapter 1 you learned that the program automatically detects several aspects of your computer system and provides default settings for many commands. Quattro Pro 4's installation procedure gives you an opportunity to select some hardware defaults, such as the make and model of the printer. Using the Options menu after installation, you can change the ways the program runs on your system. You can also adjust default settings of individual worksheets to fit your needs and preferences. In fact, the extent to which the details of Quattro Pro 4 can be tailored is quite exceptional. You can create customized menus and even add macros to menus. Some of these advanced features are covered in Chapter 12. However, you can begin with a number of simple changes that can make your work more efficient and more effective.

The Menu of Options

The changes to Quattro Pro 4 discussed in this chapter are made from the Options menu shown in Figure 6-1. The first ten commands deal with such basics as coloring the screen and the display mode used. The Update command stores the current settings from the first ten commands

FIGURE
6-1

Options menu

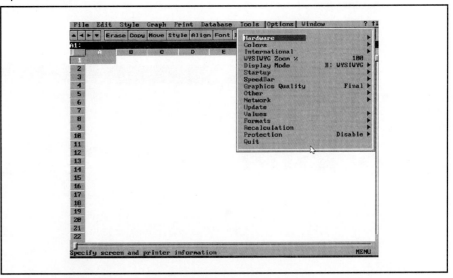

into a special file so that they can be used in the next session. The Values command displays a list of current default values. The next three commands are concerned with default settings that apply to the current worksheet, as opposed to the program operation as a whole. The last command, Quit, returns you to READY mode.

About Defaults

A computer program's defaults are what the program does unless you tell it to do something differently. Most programs have defaults of one kind or another because the program has to make some basic assumptions about how you will be using it. For example, most word processing programs arrange text between margins and tabs, and so they begin with default margin and tab settings. In the same way, Quattro Pro 4 has default column and format settings that determine how wide the columns will be and how numbers will be displayed. The starting defaults—the ones that the program uses when you first install it on your computer— are listed in Table 6-1. This list does not include hardware defaults, which depend on equipment you are using.

Worksheet Defaults

As you can see from Table 6-1, the defaults for Quattro Pro 4 can be divided into two categories: worksheet and program. The program defaults affect all program activity. If you use the Update command, the changes carry over to the next session when you reload Quattro Pro 4.

The worksheet defaults are set for a specific worksheet. They do not affect new worksheets created in the same session or in any following sessions. Thus you can display a spreadsheet called SALES.WQ1, change the default label alignment to Right, and all new labels that you enter will be automatically right-aligned. However, the next worksheet you open with File Open or create with File New will revert to left-alignment of labels. This grants you maximum control over the formatting of your worksheets without unpredictable results. Altering worksheet defaults with Quattro Pro 4 will not change formats that you have already established for specific cells.

| TABLE 6-1 | Starting Defaults |

Worksheet Settings	
Column Width	9 characters
Currency	$ prefix (in U.S. version)
Font	Font 1
Grid Lines	Hide
Hide Zeroes	No
Label Alignment	Left
Numeric Format	General
Protection	Off
Recalculation	Background
Program Settings	
Autoload File	QUATTRO.WQ1
Clock	None
Default Printer	1st Printer
Expanded Memory	Spreadsheet data
File Extension	WQ1
Label Order	Dictionary
Macro Supress Redraw	Both
Macro Recording	Logical
Startup Macro	\0
Transcript Recording	Active
Undo	Disabled
Use Dialogs	Yes
WYSIWYG Zoom %	100

Configuration File

The program defaults for Quattro Pro 4 are stored in the configuration file called RSC.RF. When you start the program, it reads the default settings from this file. You can update the configuration file to reflect your preferences. Suppose that you want on-screen display of the current date and time while you are working with Quattro Pro 4. You activate the menu and select Options followed by Other and then Clock. Your choices are Standard, International, or None. You pick Standard. Quattro Pro 4 returns to the READY mode, and the date and time are displayed on the status line. They remain there throughout your Quattro Pro 4 session. However, when you exit from Quattro Pro 4 and reload the program, they will not be displayed, *unless* you use the Options Update command.

To make your default selections permanent, you select the Update option from the Options menu. Selecting Update writes the current settings into the configuration file, so Quattro Pro 4 can reload them the next time you start the program. The work that you do may fall into two or more different categories so you may want to have several different sets of default choices. If you want to preserve a set of default choices, you can copy the RSC.RF file to another file, such as MY-RSC.RF, before you select Update. When the RSC.RF file is updated, the MY-RSC.RF copy will not be overwritten. This enables you to keep two different sets of defaults. You can keep many different sets of defaults in separate files and select the one you want for a particular session just prior to loading Quattro Pro 4. This process is described in Appendix A.

Format Options

The first default options discussed here are those that determine how your data appears on the worksheet. Careful manipulation of the format defaults can save a lot of time when you are applying formats to individual cells. The Formats menu contains the following options: Numeric Format, Align Labels, Hide Zeroes, Global Width, and Quit.

Numeric Format

The Numeric Format option enables you to determine the default format for the display of values. These choices are listed with examples in Table 6-2. Many of the formats prompt you to specify the number of decimal places (from 1 to 15). Although the Numeric Format option can be very convenient, saving you the trouble of formatting blocks of cells

TABLE
6-2

Format Choices

Format Name	Description of Format
Fixed	No commas in 1,000s, negatives in parentheses, user-defined decimal places: 2000.99 (2000.99)
Scientific	Exponential notation, negatives in parentheses, user-defined decimal places: 2.00E + 03 (2.00E + 03)
Currency	Commas placed in 1,000s, negatives in parentheses, user-defined decimal places, user-defined currency symbol; default is $: $2,000.99
,(Comma)	Commas placed in 1,000s, negatives in parentheses, user-defined decimal places: 2,000.99
General	Varies decimal places; uses exponential notation for large numbers
+/−	Represents positive numbers as plus signs (+), negatives as minus signs (−) for simple bar charts
Percent	Multiplies contents by 100; uses % sign as suffix
Date	Various options, described in Chapter 9, including formats for time values
Text (Show Formulas)	Displays formulas in cells rather than their values
Hidden	Hides cell contents from view; shows contents only on the descriptor line

separately, you should exercise some care. For example, if you select Fixed format with zero decimal places and then you have to work with values of less than 1, you might find it confusing to enter such values and see Quattro Pro 4 display 0. A value of less than 1 will appear as 0 until the cell it occupies has a format of at least one decimal place. As a rule, you will not want to use a default format that has no decimal places.

Align Labels

You have seen that you can align labels and values to the left, right, or center of columns by using the Style Alignment command. The alignment of labels is determined by the leading character: ' for left, " for right, or ^ for center. To avoid making you start every label with one of these signs, Quattro Pro 4 enables you to select one of them as the default. Normally, this is left-aligned, but you can change it to right or center.

Making a change to Align Labels under the Options menu can save time if you think you will be using the Style Alignment command to realign most of your labels after they are entered. However, changing the default alignment does not affect labels that are already entered. Typically, you will use the Options Formats Align Labels command before you build your worksheet. If your worksheet is already built, you can use the Style Alignment command to change the alignment of a whole group of labels at once. Alignment set with Style Alignment is not affected by the Options Formats Align Labels command.

If you are working with long labels, these are generally easier to use if they are left-aligned. Also, the alignment of values cannot be altered with the Options Formats Align Labels command. Values in your worksheet are usually right-aligned by default, but you can use Style Alignment to center- or left-align them on a cell-by-cell or block basis. String functions that create labels from values create left-aligned labels by default. You can individually center or right-align them with the Style Alignment command.

Hide Zeroes

You may have noticed that a formula resulting in zero is displayed as 0 in the worksheet. Some worksheets have a lot of zeroes in them to show that no values have yet been entered in those cells. When you are preparing a worksheet containing many zero entries, you may want to hide or suppress them. To do this, issue Options Formats Hide Zeroes command and select Yes.

Bear in mind that Quattro Pro 4 will hide only true zeroes, not numbers like 0.01 that a display format has rounded to 0. Also Quattro Pro 4 does not erase the contents of cells containing zero that are hidden. The zeroes return when you change the Hide Zeroes option to No. Because many of the cells producing zeroes may actually be formulas that need to become active if certain other cells receive values, be careful not to accidentally overwrite these apparently empty cells. To prevent accidental overwriting of cells, you can use the protection commands described later in this chapter.

Global Column Width

You have already seen that the column width can be changed for a single column with the Style Column Width command, or for all columns in a block with the Style Block Size command. To change the global width of the columns in the current and successive worksheets, use Options Formats Global Width.

Recalculation Options

One of the great features of a spreadsheet is that you can enter numbers and formulas and immediately see the effect of changes. This feature is known as *automatic recalculation*, the constant rechecking of all cells affected by each new entry into the worksheet. However, such a powerful feature has its drawbacks: As your worksheet grows, the time taken for each new item to be checked against the other cells increases. This recalculation time can take so long that it slows down the entry of new data. To avoid this problem Quattro Pro 4 has an added feature called *background recalculation*. This enables you to carry on working while the program is recalculating in the background. You have three options for the mode of recalculation in Quattro Pro 4: Automatic, Manual, and Background. You are presented with these options when you select Mode from the Options Recalculation menu which is shown in Figure 6-2.

FIGURE
6-2

The Options Recalculation menu

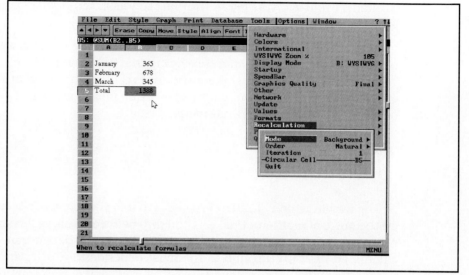

Because background recalculation does your math automatically while you work on other things, you may wonder what is the point of the other two choices. You use the Manual option when you do not want new worksheet entries or changes to old ones to affect other cells. This is valuable when you have a lot of data to enter into a large worksheet that is beginning to slow down Quattro Pro 4's normally fast response time. Time is saved because in manual mode, the program does not check whether a newly entered formula affects other results on the worksheet.

Although manual mode means that your spreadsheet is not always up to date, Quattro Pro 4 has safeguards to prevent errors. Even when you are using manual mode, the program will calculate a formula as it is entered. It will also recalculate formulas that are edited or copied. Although Quattro Pro 4 will not update other cells when in manual mode, it does know when you make changes to the worksheet. It reminds you that you have made changes that may affect the contents of other cells by displaying the CALC message in the status area. Whenever it is convenient, for example, after entering a new set of data, you can press the Calc key (F9), and Quattro Pro 4 will perform a complete recalculation of the worksheet. The CALC message is removed to let you know all changes have been accounted for. If you use manual mode you should make sure that before you print, save, or make decisions based on the worksheet figures, you press the Calc key (F9). Otherwise, you may be working with inaccurate data.

The automatic mode of recalculation is primarily used as an alternative to background, the difference being that automatic mode will not let you proceed with further data entry until recalculation is complete. This can be annoying when your spreadsheet begins to grow and yet you do not want to switch to manual mode.

Order of Recalculation

The way in which Quattro Pro 4 calculates your spreadsheet is based on the natural mathematical relationship between cells in formulas. This is referred to as *natural recalculation.* The least dependent cells are calculated first, on through to the most dependent. Earlier spreadsheet programs could only calculate row by row down the spreadsheet or column by column across. These methods were called row-wise and column-wise, respectively, but they were not always that "wise." For example, row-wise calculations can produce errors if row 5 is based on the outcome of a calculation in row 10. Users of these programs usually worked around this problem and produced spreadsheet models that worked correctly if they were calculated in the correct order, either by column or by row. As you can see when you select Order from the Recalculation menu shown in Figure 6-2, Quattro Pro 4 enables you to emulate these earlier programs and so can accommodate spreadsheets designed to use these methods of calculation. Unless you know a specific reason why the worksheets you are working on will not be accurate unless calculated in a specific order, you will not need this option. Most Quattro Pro 4 users can enjoy the benefits of natural recalculation.

Iteration

Many of the problems of row-wise and column-wise calculations can be solved by repeating the calculation process a number of times. The repetition of calculation is called *iteration.* You can use the Iteration option on the Options Recalculation menu, shown in Figure 6-2, to repeat the recalculation process as many as 255 times each time you press F9. If you have selected row-wise or column-wise as the method of calculation, you should set iteration to at least 2 to avoid errors. If you are constructing complex financial formulas containing circular cell references that require a specific number of iterations to produce a correct answer, you can enter this number on the Iteration menu.

If you are using natural recalculation, Quattro Pro 4 refers to the iteration number only if you have circular references in the worksheet. The last item on the Options Recalculation menu is Circular Cell. As you can see from Figure 6-2, this option shows you the location of a circular cell reference in the worksheet if you have the CIRC message in the bottom status area of your screen. The CIRC message means you have entered a formula into a cell that uses the result of the cell to solve the formula. For example, @SUM(B1..B5) entered into any cell from B1 through B5 would create a circular reference. Sometimes it is difficult to see what is causing a CIRC message from just viewing the spreadsheet. Use Options Recalculation Circular Cell to see which cell contains the circular reference.

Note that the calculation preferences you select are specific to the worksheet, and the setting is stored with the worksheet. This helps to prevent errors and inconvenience. Whenever you retrieve that large spreadsheet in which you set recalculation to Manual, the mode is already set. But when you switch to a small worksheet where the recalculation is Background or Automatic, the correct mode will be in operation.

Protection

To preserve the hours of work that go into making a good worksheet and to allow less proficient users to enter data into a spreadsheet without undue risk of damaging its underlying formulas, Quattro Pro 4 provides several methods of cell and worksheet protection. When you select Protection from the Options menu you have three choices: Enable, Disable, and Formulas. Selecting Enable is like placing a sheet of glass over the current worksheet. You will be able to see the data but you will not be able to change it. New data cannot be placed into the worksheet, and none of the cells can be edited. Selecting Disable turns off this protection. Saving a file with protection enabled means that anyone who retrieves the worksheet will have to turn off the protection before changing the data. The Formulas option allows you to assign a case-sensitive password to all formulas in the worksheet. This means that anyone using the worksheet will have to enter the correct password before they are allowed to edit formulas. To remove formula protection from a worksheet you must select Formulas from the Options Protection menu, then choose Unprotect and enter the password.

If you want to allow limited changes to cells on the worksheet, for example, for data entry work, you can turn on protection with Options Protection Enable and then unprotect specific cells with the Style Protection Unprotect command. This will mean that you can move around in the spreadsheet but only change those cells formatted with the Style Protection Unprotect command. These cells will appear highlighted or in a different color, making it easy for data entry personnel to locate them. You can adjust the shading of unprotected cells with the Options Colors command described later in this chapter.

Going International

Having looked at the defaults that can be established for a particular worksheet, it is time to examine those aspects of Quattro Pro 4 that can be altered for an entire session or permanently. This section begins with the International options.

Quattro Pro 4 is used in many different countries that use various notations for numbers and dates. When you select International from the Options menu, as shown in Figure 6-3, you can see that there are several areas of the program that can be changed to accommodate the needs of users in other countries. In fact, you may want to use some of the options even if you are working in the United States. For example, when you are using Quattro Pro 4 for calculations in currencies other than U.S. dollars, you may want to change the way the Currency format displays your values. The values shown in Figure 6-3 are default settings for U.S. users.

FIGURE
6-3

International options

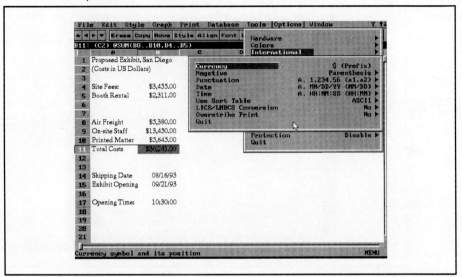

Currency

Users of the U.S. edition of Quattro Pro 4 will have seen that when you first install the program and select the Currency format, numbers are displayed in the form of U.S. currency. The dollar sign precedes the number, as in $50. You can change the symbol for currency from the dollar sign to any other character. For example, you could change it to F for French francs or £ for British pounds, as shown in Figure 6-4.

When you select Currency from the International menu, you type the character you want for the monetary symbol in the dialog box that appears and press ENTER. You are then asked whether this is to be a prefix, preceding the value, or a suffix, following the value. When you select one of these two options, you are returned to the International menu.

If the foreign character you want to use is not on your keyboard—such as the pound sign (£), which is not on American keyboards—you can

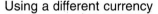

FIGURE
6-4

Using a different currency

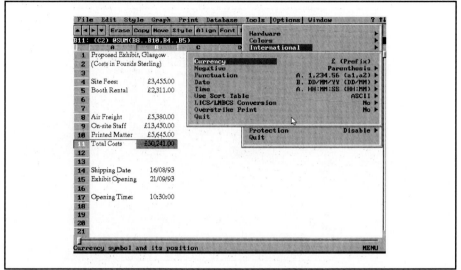

choose the appropriate ASCII character from those shown in Figure 6-5. When prompted for the currency symbol, hold down the ALT key and type the number corresponding to the character you want from the numeric keypad (not the numbers across the top of the keyboard). Note that £ is 156, and 157 is the symbol used for Yen. Also note that Figure 6-4 shows dates in British format, with days listed ahead of months. This is a function of the Date setting, described in a moment.

Punctuation

If you are preparing a spreadsheet for users who are French, you may want to make changes to the numbers in addition to changing the currency symbol. The French and other Europeans use different notations for thousands and decimals. Selecting the Punctuation option from the International menu reveals an extensive list of options, as shown in Figure 6-6. You can see that option A is the default, whereas option B, which uses dots for thousands and commas for decimals, was used in the underlying worksheet.

FIGURE
6-5

An ASCII table (in character mode)

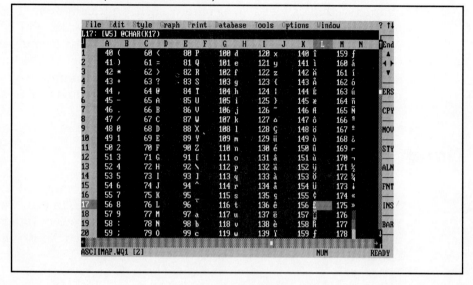

FIGURE
6-6

Punctuation options

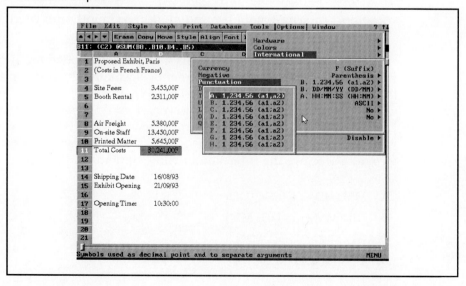

The second column of the list of punctuation options refers to the character that is used to separate each argument from the next in functions. Instead of the comma between arguments, you can use a period, as in options B and F. You can see this in the formula in B11 of the worksheet in Figure 6-6. The first block in the @SUM function is separated from the next by a period instead of a comma. You can also use semicolons for argument separators, as in options C,D,G, and H.

Date

The way that dates are written varies greatly throughout the world. You can change the way Quattro Pro 4 displays dates in your worksheet. When you use the Style Numeric Format menu and select Date to assign a date format to a cell or group of cells, you have the following date style options:

1. DD-MMM-YY
2. DD-MMM
3. MMM-YY
4. Long International (day, month, and year)
5. Short International (day and month, or month and year)

The actual format used by items 4 and 5 will depend on the selection you make from the International menu. Normally, the Date option in the International menu is set to MM/DD/YY, which is how dates formatted with style number 4 appear. However, if you change the International Date setting to one of the other three possibilities, all dates in the current worksheet formatted with the D4 format will change to reflect the new format. These are the International date options:

A. MM/DD/YY (MM/DD)
B. DD/MM/YY (DD/MM)
C. DD.MM.YY (DD.MM)
D. YY-MM-DD (MM-DD)

You can see that each one has a long and short version. Dates formatted with the Short International format from the Style Numeric Format menu (D5) will appear in the short format shown in parentheses in the lettered list above.

Remember that the format you select from the International Date menu is the one used by the on-screen calendar and clock display when you select International from the Clock option on the Options Other menu. This format is also used by the CTRL-D date entry command. You can see the B option in Figure 6-6.

Time

Just like dates, the way that times are written also varies considerably from country to country. When you are working with time values in a worksheet and want to format a value as a time, you select Time from the Style Numeric Format Date menu. These are the options:

1. HH:MM:SS (D6)
2. HH:MM (D7)
3. Long International (24-hour clock—hours, minutes, and seconds) (D8)
4. Short International (24-hour clock—hours and minutes) (D9)

These options, when applied to cells, are shown in the status line as D6 through D9. The choice you make in the Time option of the International defaults is reflected in the D8 and D9 time formats used in the worksheet, as well as in the on-screen calendar and clock display. Thus, the format you get when selecting items 3 and 4 will depend on the choice you make with the Options International Time command. Selecting Time from the International menu reveals the options shown in Figure 6-7. All of the international options for time use 24-hour notation, and each has both a long (D8) and a short (D9) form. You can see option A in cell B17 of Figure 6-6 and option D in Figure 6-7.

FIGURE
6-7

Time format options

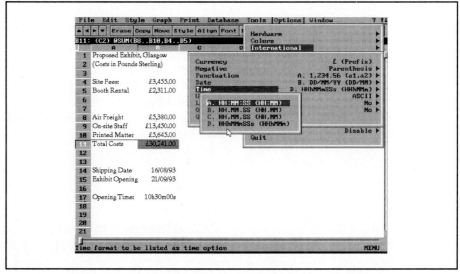

Custom International Formats

The ability to use foreign currency and data/time formats is very handy, but the settings made with Options International have one drawback: They apply to all numbers, dates, and times in a worksheet. In fact, they apply to all worksheets you load. This means that if you use Options International to change the currency symbol to £, perhaps because you are working on a quotation for a British company, you will see £ signs in all the other worksheets you load that use the Currency format, even if they were originally created when the currency symbol was the $ sign. The same principle applies to dates and times that use the international formats. The solution to this problem is to create custom numeric formats for foreign data, leaving the Options International option set to the way you normally format currency, dates, and times.

Creating custom numeric formats was described in Chapter 3. In Figure 6-8 you can see that cell C4 has a style called POUNDS applied to it. This style, which includes a numeric format using the £ symbol,

FIGURE
6-8

Using a custom numeric format

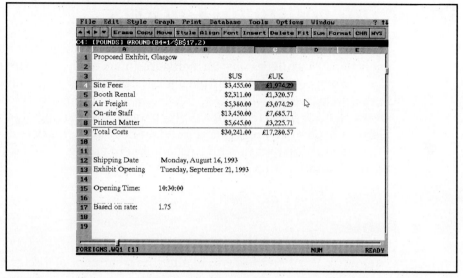

enables the worksheet to display both $ and £ signs for currency. The currency style seen in C4 was created like this:

1. The format of the dollar amount in B4 was copied to C4 to provide the basis of the style in terms of font, alignment, and so on (use Edit Special Copy and choose Formats to copy the format of a cell but not the contents).

2. The Define Style Create command was issued from the Style menu. At the prompt to name the style, the name POUNDS was entered.

3. None of the style settings were changed except Numeric Format. After selecting Numeric Format, User Defined was selected, and the following custom numeric format code was entered:

```
N £9,999.00
```

4. After quitting the style definition, the Use Style command was issued and the POUNDS style was selected for C4..C9.

The custom style created in these steps is automatically stored with the worksheet. Note that Figure 6-8 also includes an example of custom date formatting, showing the full name of the day and the month.

Other International Options

As businesses become increasingly cosmopolitan in their outlook and operations, it is necessary for software to accommodate the needs of a wider range of users. Quattro Pro 4 incorporates several enhancements in this area. These include Use Sort Table, LICS/LMBCS Conversion, and Overstrike Print on the Options International menu. Together with other features of Quattro Pro 4 they should make it easier for users everywhere to work with the program and for anyone to create more authentic and accurate foreign language documents.

Sort Tables

Quattro Pro 4 enables you to alter the treatment of foreign characters during Database Sort operations. The Use Sort Table command provides four options, which represent four different files with the extension .SOR. These are files in which sorting order tables are stored. Select the one that is most appropriate to your needs.

ASCII.SOR

In an ascending sort this places uppercase letters before lowercase. This is because the capitals have lower ASCII values than lowercase letters. For the same reason, accented letters, which have high ASCII values, appear after z.

INTL.SOR

Short for "international," this table places uppercase and lowercase and accented letters into a continuous sequence just like that used in a dictionary: a, A, b, B, c, C, and so on. A letter u with an umlaut appears with the u's as opposed to after the z's. This is the table most people will use unless they need ASCII sorting or wish to segregate certain foreign characters.

NORDAN.SOR

This is just like the international sort except that special characters used in Norway and Denmark, such as æ and ø, follow the regular alphabet.

SWEDFIN.SOR

Again, this is like the international sort except that special characters used in Sweden and Finland, such as å, follow the regular alphabet.

The .SOR files used by Quattro Pro 4 are the same as those employed by Paradox and other Borland products. If you have any other .SOR files in the Quattro Pro 4 program directory, they will be included in the list displayed by the Use Sort Table command. Bear in mind that the Sort Rules command on the Database Sort menu also affects the sort order. You should coordinate the two settings. If you set Use Sort Table to ASCII you should use the ASCII setting for Label Order under Sort Rules in the Database Sort menu. If you set Use Sort Table to anything other than ASCII, you should use the Dictionary setting for Label Order under Sort Rules in the Database Sort menu.

International Characters

There are several enhancements involving the printing of foreign characters, which are necessary for accuracy and authenticity in foreign documents.

Overstrike Print

Some printers, such as the Epson FX-80 and Diablo 630, can print accented characters *if* they are allowed to back up a space and overstrike the letter with the accent symbol. If you set Overstrike Print to Yes, this facility on your printer will be enabled. Other printers, such as the HP LaserJet series, print accented letters as distinct characters and do not need this option turned on.

International Character Set

When installing Quattro Pro 4 you have the option of using an international character set as opposed to the normal U.S. character set. If you select the international set, the Bitstream fonts generated by Quattro Pro 4 will include 42 additional foreign characters. This option increases the time required to create each font and uses up more disk space. However, the international option gives you the ability to print characters that may be important if you need to prepare documents in foreign languages. The additional characters are shown in the Quattro Pro 4 manual. To switch between international and U.S. character sets, do the following:

1. Delete all existing font files. These files have the extension .FON and are stored in the \FONTS subdirectory below the Quattro Pro 4 program directory. Enter the following command at the DOS prompt in the \FONTS directory:

    DEL *.FON

2. To change from U.S. to international rename all files with the .SFO extension in the Quattro Pro 4 program directory to ones using .SFR, entering the command:

    REN *.SFO *.SFR

3. To change from international to U.S. rename all .SFR files in the Quattro Pro 4 program directory to .SFO, using the command:

    REN *.SFR *.SFO

Using LICS/LMBCS

The need to provide spreadsheet users with a means of representing foreign characters led Lotus to come up with a variation on standard ASCII. Known as the Lotus International Character Set (LICS), it can present a problem when you are reading .WK1 spreadsheets into Quattro Pro 4. If you set LICS/LMBCS Conversion to Yes, Quattro Pro 4 will read LICS/LMBCS characters into the equivalent ASCII characters when retrieving a .WK1 file. Quattro Pro 4 will then convert the character back to LICS/LMBCS characters when saving the file in the .WK1 format.

Startup Options

The Options Startup menu shown in Figure 6-9 covers several areas of Quattro Pro 4's operation that are effective when the program is first loaded. You can also use this menu to change some aspects of how the menu system works.

Directory Options

In Chapter 1 you saw that the first time you use the File Save command, Quattro Pro 4 assumes you want to store your worksheet in the same area as the program files. You can use the File Directory command to change this choice for the current session. To use a new default area for storage at all times, you use the Directory option on the

FIGURE
6-9

The Startup menu

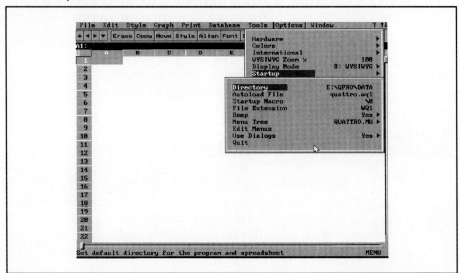

Startup menu. When you pick this option you get a dialog box like the one shown in Figure 6-9. The directory you set in this dialog box is the area in which you want the program to store your worksheets. It can be the name of any drive that you have available on your system, such as A:, B:, C:, D:, E:, and so on. You can follow the drive name with the name of the subdirectory that has been set up on that drive, such as \DATA or \QUATTRO\DATA.

If you want to use a directory that has not yet been created, use the File Utilities DOS Shell command to leave Quattro Pro 4 temporarily. This command returns you to the disk operating system, which you can use to create a directory. You can also create directories with Quattro Pro 4's File Manager, which you access from the File Utilities menu. Operating system commands are discussed in Appendix A, while the File Manager is described in Chapter 7.

Instead of creating a default Startup Directory, you can leave this setting blank. The effect is to allow Quattro Pro 4 to use whatever directory you start the program from. Thus, if you switch to a directory called D:\DATA while using DOS and then start Quattro Pro 4 from there, the File commands will assume D:\DATA as the default directory. This approach gives you considerable flexibility; however, in order to load Quattro Pro 4 from a directory other than the program directory you must have the program directory in your AUTOEXEC.BAT file's PATH statement. (For more about the PATH statement, see Appendix A. Quattro Pro 4 adds its program directory to the PATH statement in your AUTOEXEC.BAT file during installation, unless you ask it not to.)

If you want to clear the Startup Directory setting so that Quattro Pro 4 is free to load from different data directories, you select Directory from the Startup menu, then press ESC followed by ENTER. Be sure to use the Update command on the main Options menu to record this change.

Automatic File Loading

You may find that your work with Quattro Pro 4 involves extensive use of one particular worksheet. For example, if you are almost exclusively pricing contracts, you may start with the same pricing spreadsheet every time you work with the program. To simplify your work, you can have Quattro Pro 4 retrieve a file automatically whenever the program is loaded. When you pick Autoload File from the Startup menu, you are asked to enter the name of the worksheet you want loaded whenever the program is started.

For example, if the file is a pricing spreadsheet called PRICING.WQ1, you simply type this name and press ENTER. You will immediately see the file listed on the menu. However, you must use the Update command on the Options menu to record this change and to make the autoload feature effective the next time the program is loaded. After you pick Update and reload Quattro Pro 4, the PRICING.WQ1 file will be retrieved. You can then enter the necessary data and save the new file under a different name, leaving the standard pricing worksheet unchanged on disk.

The autoload feature is always active. Whenever you load Quattro Pro 4 it looks for the file name that is recorded in the Startup menu. As you can see from Figure 6-9, the default name is QUATTRO.WQ1. If Quattro Pro 4 finds that file in the default directory when the program is loading, it retrieves the file. You can use the autoload feature either by changing the file name as just discussed, or you can save the file you want to autoload as QUATTRO.WQ1. This file can contain not only commonly used data, but it can also be a file of instructions. You could even produce a setup file for a novice Quattro Pro 4 user. You can also place macros, stored keystrokes, commands, and even custom menus in the autoload file to further assist the spreadsheet user. (If you also use 1-2-3, you can make the file called AUTO123.WK1 the autoload file name in order to use existing spreadsheets designed around this feature.)

Automatic Macro

You can designate a specific set of stored keystrokes (a macro) to be played back as soon as Quattro Pro 4 loads any spreadsheet containing the macro named in this section of the Startup menu. This autoload macro is initially called \0 (backslash zero). You can change the name to any valid macro name. (See Chapter 11 for more details on naming macros.) To supply a macro name, pick Startup Macro from the Startup menu. You can then type the name of the macro and press ENTER. Remember that to record this change to the automatic macro, you must use Update.

Each worksheet can have a macro with the designated autoload name. If you create an autorun macro in the autoload worksheet, you can have Quattro Pro 4 carry out a whole series of commands every time the program starts. This process enables you to provide automated applications for other users and is described in Chapter 12.

File Extensions

The file name used by Quattro Pro 4 when it stores your worksheets on disk consists of two parts. The first part of the name can be as many as eight characters long. The second part, separated from the first part by a period, can be three letters long and is called the *extension.* Initially, the program assigns the extension .WQ1 to your worksheets. However, if you are sharing worksheets with a 1-2-3 user, you will want to save files with the .WK1 extension so that 1-2-3 can read the files. You can make .WK1 the default extension by selecting File Extension from the Startup menu, typing **.WK1**, and pressing ENTER. Note that you can always see both .WQ1 and .WK1 files on the file lists used by the File Open and Retrieve commands since Quattro Pro 4 looks for *.W??, which means any file name with *W* as the first letter of the extension and any other characters as the second and third. This wildcard pattern also lists files from earlier versions of Quattro, which have the extension .WKQ.

To Beep or Not to Beep

If you press HOME and then UP ARROW while you are using READY mode, Quattro Pro 4 will beep to let you know that the key you pressed was not appropriate, because you cannot go up from the home position. The beep is designed to be helpful, and many users appreciate knowing they have pressed the wrong key when entering data and formulas. However, if you find this beep annoying, or if those around you object to it, you can turn it off by selecting Beep from the Startup menu. A small No/Yes box pops up.

You choose Yes to turn on the beep and No to turn it off. Turning off the beep can be helpful as a temporary measure when you are working on an airplane or in other close quarters where the noise of the beep would be distracting to others. If you want to keep the beep turned off in future work sessions, remember to use the Update option from the Startup menu to record your preference.

Menu Trees

As mentioned in Chapter 1, Quattro Pro 4 enables you to customize your menus. The feature of the program that does this is called the Menu Builder. A set of menus is called a *menu tree* and is stored in a file with the extension MU. You can create your own personalized menu tree and store it in an MU file. For example, if Debbie redefined her menu system, she could call it DEBBIE.MU. The Quattro Pro 4 program comes with two menu trees: QUATTRO.MU, the one that the program uses to begin with and that is pictured in most of the illustrations in this book; and 123.MU, which is designed for those who are familiar with 1-2-3 and want to operate Quattro Pro 4 with similar groupings of menu choices. You can see from the Startup menu in Figure 6-9 that the current selection is QUATTRO.MU.

To activate a user menu tree other than the default QUATTRO.MU, you select Menu Tree from the Startup menu. You are presented with a choice between the 1-2-3 menu tree and the standard Quattro Pro 4 menu tree. To change to the 1-2-3 menu tree, highlight 123 and press ENTER. You will be returned to the READY mode and the 1-2-3 menu will be in effect. In Figure 6-10 you can see the 1-2-3 menu with the Range option selected. To return to the Quattro Pro 4 menu, you pick Worksheet, Global, Default, Files, and Menu Tree, as shown in Figure 6-11. Then you can select the QUATTRO file from the list. You are returned immediately to the normal arrangement of menus. A change to the menu tree will remain in place after the current session only if you select Update to write the change to the RSC.RF file. To do this from the 1-2-3 menu system you select Worksheet, Global, Default, and Update. Note that the 1-2-3 menu tree shows Quattro-only commands with a small square next to them. All other menu items match those available in 1-2-3. However, the 1-2-3 menu tree does show the Quattro Pro 4 shortcut keys.

FIGURE
6-10

The 1-2-3 menu tree in action

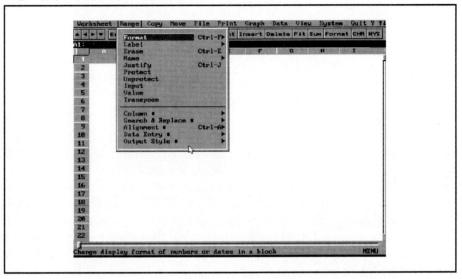

FIGURE
6-11

Using the 1-2-3 menus

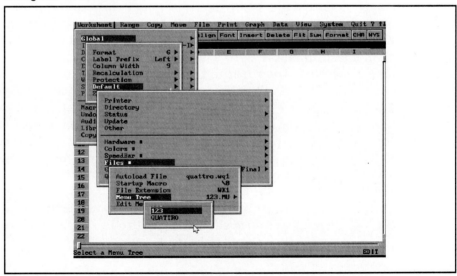

Edit Menus

Not only does Quattro Pro 4 enable you to choose from among a range of alternative menu trees, but with the Edit Menu feature you can create your own. To alter your system's menus, select the Edit Menus command on the Options Startup menu. Suppose that you want to be able to select the Spreadsheet Print command from the File menu rather than from the Print menu. Using procedures that are described later in Chapter 12, you can use the Menu Builder to redefine the File menu and change Spreadsheet Print on the Print menu to Print on the File menu.

About Your Hardware

The Hardware option on the Options menu is where you tell Quattro Pro 4 about your screen and printer. You can also use this menu to check the status of various aspects of your system, as you can see from Figure 6-12.

FIGURE 6-12

The Hardware menu

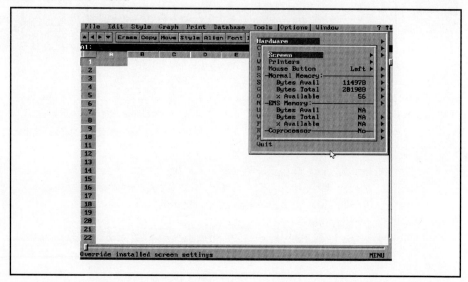

Screen Questions

When you installed Quattro Pro 4 on your PC, you may have noticed that you did not have to specify what kind of display you were using. Quattro Pro 4 automatically detects the kind of display you have. In fact, if you are running Quattro Pro 4 on a system that has a color display and you need to move to a computer that has a monochrome display, you do not need to make any changes to the program disks.

When you pick Screen from the Hardware menu, you are presented with the menu shown in Figure 6-13. The menu has four commands besides Quit. The only time you will need to select the Screen option from the Hardware menu is if you are using a display system that Quattro Pro 4 does not know about or if you want to override the autodetect feature. If you want to change the color or shading of your display, you use the Colors command from the Options menu, rather than the Hardware command. If you want to change from character display to graphics display you use the Display Mode command described later in this chapter in the section of the same name.

FIGURE 6-13

Screen options

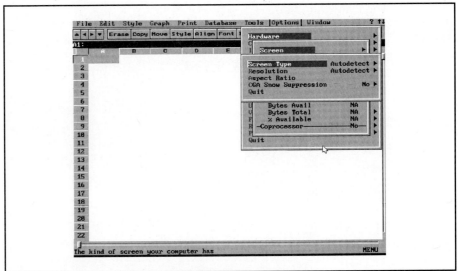

Screen Type

The first Screen setting is Screen Type, and this is normally Auto-detect. If your PC is displaying spreadsheets clearly, you do not need to change the screen type. If you want to force Quattro Pro 4 to consider your display system to be a particular type, you can change to one of the listed alternatives.

Resolution

Graphic display systems create images from a collection of dots. The number of dots on a screen is referred to as the display's *resolution*. The resolution determines the sharpness of the displayed image. Resolution is measured by the number of dots across the screen and the number of lines of dots going down it, as in 640 x 200. Because some displays can operate at different resolutions, Quattro Pro 4 provides the Resolution option, which lets you choose between them. Note that you cannot change the screen resolution while in WYSIWYG mode. You must be in character mode to change resolution. The display modes are discussed in a moment.

The Resolution setting only affects the display of graphs. By default Quattro Pro 4 autodetects your display adapter and uses the highest resolution available. Change the Resolution setting only if you want to use a lower resolution.

Aspect Ratio

The ratio of the width of your monitor to its height is called the aspect ratio. This ratio affects the monitor's ability to show circles as truly round. Although Quattro Pro 4 can detect the display method used by your screen, it has no way of knowing the physical dimensions of the display. Dimensions vary from model to model. In fact, many models actually enable you to change the height of the screen display area, so different users of the same model can have different screen dimensions. For

Quattro Pro 4 to display circles, such as those used in pie graphs, as circles and not as ellipses, you need to tell Quattro Pro 4 the aspect ratio of your screen. In some ways this is merely a cosmetic concern, because Quattro Pro 4 will print round pie graphs regardless of this setting. However, if you are using a screen capture system to make Quattro Pro 4 graphs part of a presentation, then entering the ratio can be important. When you are setting Aspect Ratio, you use the UP ARROW and DOWN ARROW keys to adjust the test circle, then press ENTER to accept the new ratio. Press ESC to abort the process.

Suppressing Snow

If you are using a CGA display system, that is, one based on the old IBM Color Graphics Adaptor, you may find that certain actions in Quattro Pro 4 produce a fuzzy effect on the screen. This is referred to as "snow" and can usually be eliminated by setting CGA Snow Suppression to Yes.

About Printers

At the Hardware menu you can select Printers to let Quattro Pro 4 know about the equipment you will be using for hard copy. As you can see from Figure 6-14, you can define two printers and select one of them as the default.

When you pick 1st Printer you see the menu shown in Figure 6-15. This lists the current settings, including Make and Model. If you selected a printer during installation, it will be listed here. If you did not select a printer during installation, you can do so now by selecting the first menu item, Type of printer. If you want to define a second printer, use the 2nd Printer option on the Printers menu and select Type of printer.

When you select Type of printer, you will see a list of brand names, such as Apple, Epson, and HP. After you pick the correct brand name for the printer you want to use, pick the exact model name. In some cases, such as the HP LaserJet II, you will also need to pick the print resolution that you want to use. When you have selected the type of printer, you are returned to the menu shown in Figure 6-15.

Printer options

FIGURE
6-14

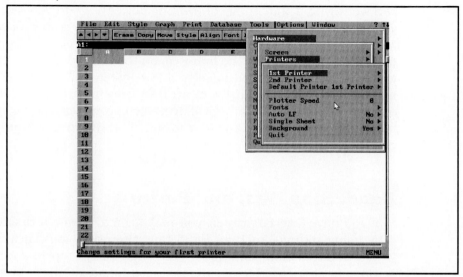

Selecting printer type

FIGURE
6-15

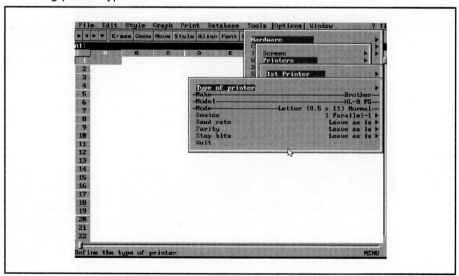

The options on this menu allow you to modify Quattro Pro 4 so that it can work with a wide range of printing devices. When you select Device you have 11 options, which represent a variety of ports on your computer, as well as a network printer queue. Most printers are parallel printers on port number 1, which is the first item on the list. If you are printing over a network, you may need to select LPT1 instead of Parallel-1. The EPT option sends printed output to an IBM laser printer. The PRN option sends printed output to an ASCII print file. If you pick a serial option you must select various parameters to match your printer input requirements.

Baud, Stop Bits, and Parity

If you have a serial printer, you may need to match it to Quattro Pro 4 by using settings such as Baud rate, Stop bits, and Parity. Consult your printer manual for the correct baud rate, stop bits, and parity setting. You may need to use the DOS command MODE to prepare your serial printer for use with Quattro Pro 4; this will be described in your printer manual. The "Leave as is" setting tells Quattro Pro 4 to use the current DOS Mode settings.

Printer Control

Having selected the correct settings on the 1st Printer menu, you return to the main Options Hardware Printers menu. Here you can choose 2nd Printer and define a completely different printer model. The Options Hardware Printer menu is also where you decide which of the two printers will be the Default Printer. Quattro Pro 4 lets you redefine printers during a session, but it needs to know which printer is the one to use. The printers are defined as either 1st Printer or 2nd Printer. For example, suppose you defined a laser printer as 1st Printer and a dot matrix printer as 2nd Printer, and you normally print on the laser. You would set Default Printer to 1st Printer. If you had to print invoices with carbon copies using the dot matrix, you would use Options Hardware Printers and select Default Printer. You would then select 2nd Printer. The 2nd Printer would remain the current printer until the end of the current session. Bear in mind that if you issue the Options Update command while Default Printer is defined as 2nd Printer, then the 2nd Printer will be the default in the next session as well.

When Quattro Pro 4 is printing it needs to know how certain aspects of print operations will be controlled. These options relate to plotter operation, fonts, line feeds, and sheet feeding.

Plotter Speed

This setting enables you to slow down the speed at which the plotter pen moves if you are using a plotter. This can be helpful when you are plotting onto some materials that are apt to smudge when written on at high speed. The default setting of 0 is the fastest plotter speed. Using a higher number will slow the plotter down.

Fonts

As you saw in Chapter 5, Quattro Pro 4 provides extensive support for fonts, allowing you to print and display text in a variety of typefaces, sizes, and styles. You can print out a mixture of fonts in a worksheet report when you use Spreadsheet Print after setting the print destination to Graphics Printer. You can see a worksheet report formatted with fonts if you set the print destination to Screen Preview. You can view fonts in a graph if you use the Graph View command (F10). You assign fonts to graphs with the Graph Text command, described in Chapter 8. Fonts for worksheets are assigned under the Style Font menu, discussed in Chapter 3.

Your font-printing capability depends to a certain extent on your printer. If you have installed a printer that uses font cartridges, such as the HP LaserJet series, then Quattro Pro 4 enables you use the Fonts option to specify which cartridges are installed. For example, the HP LaserJet II has a left and right cartridge. When you select the Left Cartridge you get a list of possible cartridges from which to select, a list that will be familiar to users of the LaserJet. You can use the cursor movement keys to scroll down the list. To tell Quattro Pro 4 about your printer, simply highlight the name/letter of the cartridge that you have in the left cartridge slot of your printer and press ENTER. Quattro Pro 4 returns you to the Printers menu. You can repeat the process for the right cartridge if you have a set of fonts installed there. The same menu is also used to set the level of gray used when your LaserJet printer prints the Style Shading format.

The other option on the Fonts menu is Autoscale Fonts. This controls Quattro Pro 4's automatic font scaling option. The default setting is Yes, which means Quattro Pro 4 adjusts font point size to fit the dimensions of the printed report. If you set this option to No, Quattro Pro 4 prints fonts in exact point size regardless of page dimensions. This option must be set to Yes if you want to use the Print-to-Fit feature.

Auto LF

Most printers today do not have an automatic line feed. Instead, the software tells the printer to advance the paper after each line of text. However, if you have a printer that adds a line feed after a line of text, you may find your output is unintentionally double spaced. If this is the case, change the Auto LF setting to Yes to solve this problem.

Single Sheet

You activate this option by picking Yes from the Yes/No choice box. Picking Yes will cause Quattro Pro 4 to pause and then prompt you to insert paper in a single-sheet printer. Note that this is only required for manual feed printers; do not select Yes for this option if you are using an HP LaserJet or some other printer that continually feeds sheets from a paper tray, unless you want to feed special sheets, such as envelopes.

Other Hardware

At the Hardware menu in Figure 6-12 you can see three items with a line through them that cannot be selected. These items are simply status reports. Several Quattro Pro 4 menus use this display style to show that the items are not active choices.

Normal Memory

The random-access memory, or *RAM*, in your computer is the area in which most of your work with Quattro Pro 4 takes place. The size of this area is measured in bytes, and the normal memory indicator on the status line tells you how much RAM is still available. When you turn on your PC, the RAM area is empty, but shortly after the system starts up, the core of the disk operating system (DOS) is loaded into RAM. The amount of memory DOS takes depends on the version of DOS you are using. When you load Quattro Pro 4 it takes up space in RAM. As you enter data into a worksheet, the amount of available RAM decreases. You can monitor your use of RAM by periodically using the Options Hardware command or the @MEMAVAIL function described in Chapter 13.

Expanded Memory

A lot of computers have 640K of RAM, because that is the most that can be recognized directly by DOS. However, numerous hardware and software manufacturers have designed ways of adding memory that can be recognized by programs. This is called *expanded memory*, or EMS. If you have such memory installed, Quattro Pro 4 will recognize it and report its status on the EMS section. If you have expanded memory in your PC but it is not shown on this menu, check that you have installed the drivers that came with the board. You can use the @MEMEMSAVAIL function to report available memory in a worksheet, as described in Chapter 13. For more on the types of memory and how to utilize memory effectively with Quattro Pro 4, see Appendix A.

Coprocessor

There is one computer chip inside your PC that does most of the processing of data. This chip is called the *CPU*, or *central processing unit*. Typically these units are called 8088, 80286, 80386, and 80486. However, many PCs have room for additional chips that can share the processing load. These are called *coprocessors*, and Quattro Pro 4 will detect and use one if it is installed. The most common type of coprocessor helps the CPU take care of mathematical calculations. Called numeric or math coprocessors, these units are typically named 8087, 80287, or 80387. You can see from the Hardware menu whether Quattro Pro 4 has found a coprocessor in your system. If you have a coprocessor physically installed in your system but it is not listed on the Hardware menu, recheck the installation instructions for the chip.

Display Mode

On today's PCs there are two basic technologies for displaying information on the screen: character mode and graphics mode. In basic character mode the display is made up of 2000 characters arranged in 25 lines of 80 characters each. This is the default mode used by Quattro Pro 4 if you select character mode instead of WYSIWYG mode during installation. The alternative to character mode is a graphics mode known in Quattro Pro 4 as WYSIWYG, where the screen is composed of a series of dots that draw shapes, including numbers, text, and circles. The WYSIWYG mode offers advantages when it comes to drawing pictures such as charts. The disadvantage is that WYSIWYG mode requires a lot of memory and responds more slowly than character mode does.

Quattro Pro 4 has the unique ability to switch between different modes of display, as described in Chapter 1. This means that typical spreadsheet operations such as data entry and calculation can take place in the faster environment of character mode. However, when you want to design a high-quality report or a graph, you can switch to WYSIWYG mode. The mode that Quattro Pro 4 uses when you load the program is determined by the Options Display Mode setting. The first option on the Display Mode menu is 80x25, which is the most basic form of character mode. The second option is WYSIWYG mode. If you use the Options Update command, the current Display Mode selection becomes the default setting. However, the two mouse buttons, WYS and CHR, enable you to switch display modes without using the Options menu or altering the default setting.

In addition to the 80x25 character mode, some EGA and VGA systems support advanced character modes with more characters and lines, such as 80x43. If your screen is one of these, you can choose a higher density character display mode. However, such modes are not WYSIWYG and will not show font changes and grid lines. If you want to have the CHR button activate one of these advanced character modes instead of 80x25, see the later section, "The SpeedBar."

Changing Attributes and Colors

Through the Options Colors command, Quattro Pro 4 provides tremendous flexibility in the way the various elements of the program are displayed on your monitor. As you can see from Figure 6-16, a system of menus enables you to choose how each part of the screen is displayed. If your screen can display colors, Quattro Pro 4 enables you to customize the colors used by the different parts of the spreadsheet. For example, you can have a brown background with the cell selector in blue with white letters, or a white background with blue letters. The number of possible combinations are far too numerous to describe. If you have a monochrome display, you can control the video attributes of the screen,

FIGURE 6-16   Setting colors

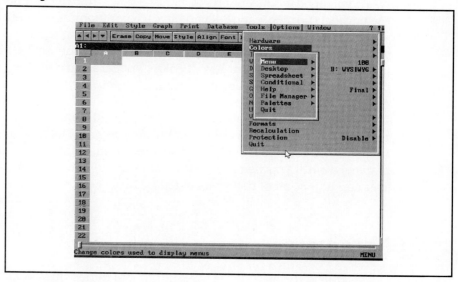

choosing between Normal, Bold, Inverse, Underlined, and Empty attributes.

At first the ability to change shades and colors may seem somewhat frivolous. However, such changes can improve efficiency. For example, special shading can be assigned to negative numbers, thus making them easier to locate. Labels can be displayed differently than values and make the spreadsheet easier to read. You can even tell Quattro Pro 4 to highlight values outside of specified ranges, thus alerting users to incorrect answers.

If you have a color display system or one that emulates a color system and a black-and-white or LCD screen, changing the shading can be very useful. For example, if you are using a laptop computer with an LCD screen, you will probably find the standard Quattro Pro 4 colors hard to read when they are interpreted by your system. Changing them can enhance their legibility.

Changing Colors

When you pick Colors from the Options menu the first item is Menu. When you choose this option you can see how Quattro Pro 4 breaks down the parts of the menu and—if you have a color monitor—the current color settings. The breakdown of menu parts can be seen in Table 6-3. Suppose you want to alter the color of the menu frame. You select Frame and immediately a small paint box of colors appears with the current setting marked by a rotating cursor. By using the cursor-movement keys you can move around the paint box. Each band of color is a different background hue and each dot is a foreground shade. When you have placed the cursor on the choice you want you press ENTER. The choice is immediately reflected in the text of the menu setting but may not be displayed until you use the Quit commands to leave the menu system. You can adjust all of the areas listed in Table 6-3.

Fill Characters

Desktop is the area of the screen that is behind your worksheets. The Fill Characters used in Menu and Desktop refer to the way Quattro Pro 4

TABLE 6-3

Color Settings

Menu	Spreadsheet WYSIWYG
Frame	Unprotected
Banner	Drawn Lines
Text	Shaded Cells
Key Letter	Locked Titles Text
Highlight	Titles Background
Settings	Row and Column Labels
Explanation	Highlight
Drop Shadow	Shadow
SpeedBar	Face
Fill Characters—Shadow	Text

Desktop	Conditional
Status	On/Off
Highlight-Status	ERR
Errors	Smallest Normal Value
Background	Greatest Normal Value
Fill Characters—Desktop	Below Normal Color
	Normal Cell Color
	Above Normal Color

Spreadsheet	Help
Frame	Frame
Banner	Banner
Cells	Text
Borders	Keywords
Titles	Highlight
Highlight	
Graph Frames	File Manager
Input Line	Frame
Unprotected	Banner
Labels	Text
Shading	Active cursor
Drawn Lines	Inactive cursor
WYSIWYG Colors	Marked

Spreadsheet WYSIWYG	
Background	Cut
Cursor	Copy

makes up the pattern behind your worksheet windows and menus in character mode. The pattern is simply a repetition of the shading character. You can·use the ASCII chart in Figure 6-5 to choose an alternative character, and enter the number under Fill Characters. For example, you could use 156 to fill the desktop with £ signs.

Spreadsheet

The parts of the spreadsheet that you can color are listed in Table 6-3. Two areas that deserve special attention are Unprotected and Labels. The Unprotected option lets you choose a special color or shading scheme for cells that are specifically protected or unprotected. This coloring helps you distinguish these cells more clearly. Note that Quattro Pro 4's initial color and shading settings already distinguish these cells. You may also find it helpful and attractive to see cells that contain labels displayed with a different color or attribute. The Labels option enables you to do this. You can make column and row headings form a contrasting frame around the calculation areas.

Another interesting option on the Options Colors Spreadsheet menu is WYSIWYG Colors. This option helps you fine tune the appearance of your screen in WYSIWYG mode. The possibilities here are extensive, with all areas of the screen adjustable, as listed in Table 6-3.

Conditional

Possibly the most exciting of Quattro Pro 4's colorization options is Conditional. The Conditional menu enables you to change the color or attributes of cells based on the value of their contents. Thus, negative numbers could be shown in bold, ERR cells in an eye-catching inverse, and so on. You can even set value parameters so that Quattro Pro 4 will highlight excessively high or low numbers.

On/Off

Because the use of different colors or shadings for cells based on the value of their contents can be disconcerting to those not used to this feature, it can be turned off. When you select On/Off from the Conditional menu, you can select either Enable or Disable to activate or deactivate the conditional coloring of cells.

ERR

You can bring errors to people's attention more dramatically by setting a special coloring for any cell that has the contents ERR. When the error is resolved and the ERR content is changed to a correct result, the cell color will return to normal.

Value Colors

If you select Smallest Normal Value or Greatest Normal Value from the Conditional menu, you can set value limits beyond which Quattro Pro 4 alters the color of cells selected with the Normal Cell Color, Below Normal Color, and Above Normal Color options. This feature is particularly helpful for data-entry personnel because it can visually alert them to data-entry mistakes that result in numbers that are outside of expected ranges.

Because a set of conditional parameters can be disabled with the On/Off option, you can easily activate it temporarily to help inexperienced users. For example, highlighting of error cells and abnormally low or high entries can be turned on to help data-entry personnel, possibly by using a macro, as will be described in Chapter 11. The conditional coloring can be turned off for more experienced users. Remember that conditional color settings, like all the other customized color settings, are not permanently stored until you use the Update option on the Default menu to write the current settings to the configuration file.

Help

You can customize the appearance of the help screens with the Help option on the Colors menu. This option divides the help screen into five areas. The Frame is the edge of the help screen; Banner is the heading for the screen; and Text is the actual wording of the help information. The Keywords are words that are used to select further help screens, and the Highlight is the shading you move around the help screen to pick keywords.

Color Palettes

The Palettes option on the Colors menu lets you select from a collection of standard color settings. This option is useful when you want to restore the original settings. When you select Palettes from the Colors menu, the choices are Color, Monochrome, Black & White, Gray Scale, Version 3 Color, and Quit. You could use this menu, for example, to temporarily switch between a customized set of colors that were stored in your RSC.RF file and the standard color palette.

The SpeedBar

If you are using a mouse, you may want to alter the selections available to you in the SpeedBar. There are 15 buttons to which you can assign keystrokes on both the READY mode and EDIT mode SpeedBars. You can see the READY mode SpeedBar settings in Figure 6-17.

FIGURE
6-17

The default READY mode SpeedBar settings

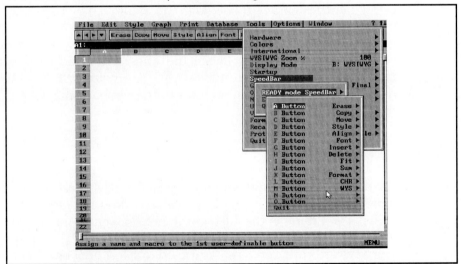

You can alter all of the buttons, but this is not recommended unless you are sure you know what you are doing. Many of the buttons use macro codes, so some familiarity with macros (discussed in Chapters 11 and 12) is helpful. The default EDIT mode SpeedBar settings can be seen in Figure 6-18.

Suppose that you make very little use of the Fit button and decide to replace it with something else. After selecting SpeedBar from the Options menu, you choose the READY mode SpeedBar and pick item I. In Figure 6-19 you can see how the settings for a button are stored. There is a Short name, used in character mode, and a Long name, used in WYSIWYG mode. Then there is the action performed by the button, which you enter in the Macro field.

You decide to change the Fit button so that it acts as a Home button, moving the cell selector to A1. First change the Short name to HOM (you are limited to three letters). Then change the Long name to Home. Now change the Macro to {HOME}. When you quit back to the READY mode, you will see the revised button in place, as shown in Figure 6-20. Clicking on the Home button will execute the command {HOME} which is macro language for pressing the HOME key.

The default EDIT mode SpeedBar settings

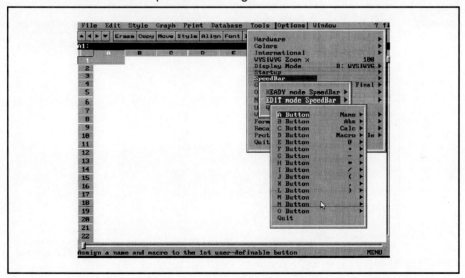

FIGURE
6-19

Typical button settings

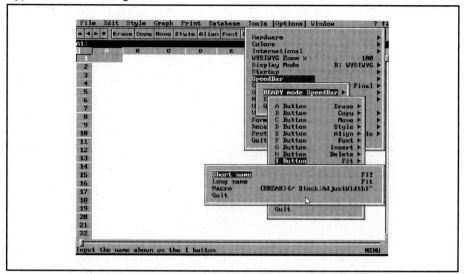

FIGURE
6-20

Revised SpeedBar in place

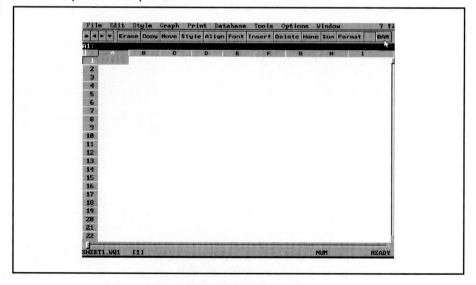

In Figure 6-20 you can see another feature of the SpeedBar. If the display of buttons you create gets too big for the display area on the screen, Quattro Pro 4 splits the buttons into two sections and displays a BAR button. Clicking on the BAR button switches you between the two sections. What has happened in Figure 6-20 is that Home button is longer than the Fit button and so caused the Char and Wys buttons to be moved off the screen.

You can avoid this if you shorten one of the other buttons. For example, if you change the Long name setting for the Delete button to Del, all of the buttons can be displayed, as shown in Figure 6-21. Remember that you can change or add buttons in both the READY and EDIT mode SpeedBars. Also remember that you must select Update from the main Options menu if you want to record the changes you make to the SpeedBars.

Graphics Quality Control

The Options Graphics Quality command enables you to control when Quattro Pro 4 creates or renders Bitstream high-quality fonts. Select the

Shortened SpeedBar displayed

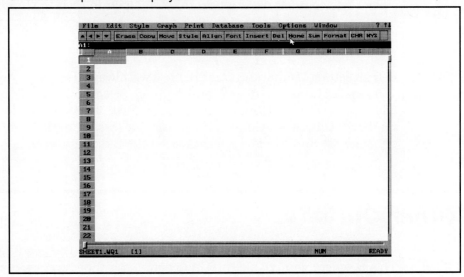

TABLE 6-4   Actions That Can and Cannot Be Reversed with Undo

The following items can be reversed with Undo:

❏ Making a new spreadsheet entry

❏ Changing a spreadsheet entry

❏ Deleting a spreadsheet entry

❏ Deleting a named graph

❏ Deleting a block name

❏ Retrieving a file

❏ Erasing a spreadsheet with File Erase

❏ Using Undo

The following cannot be reversed by Undo:

❏ Command settings

❏ Style and format settings

❏ File Manager operations

Note that Undo always reverses the last undoable action. If you retrieve a file (undoable) then use the Style command to format cells (not undoable) then press UNDO, the File Retrieve will be reversed, not the Style commands. Just press UNDO again to reverse Undo.

default setting of Final and Quattro Pro 4 will always use the Bitstream fonts you request for screen display and printing. Select Draft and Quattro Pro 4 will only use the Bitstream fonts you request if they have already been rendered. Otherwise, Quattro Pro 4 uses the less detailed Hershey fonts to simulate the approximate appearance of the Bitstream fonts.

Other Options

There are several useful options grouped under the heading "Other." This is where you enable the Undo command that reverses many of the commands and actions that you perform with Quattro Pro 4. When

Undo is Enabled the Undo key, ALT-F5, can undo the actions listed in Table 6-4.

You can use the Macro command to adjust screen updating during macros for faster execution. The choices are Both, Panel, Window, and None. The Both option gives the fastest macro operation, but it can make macros hard to follow when you are debugging them. The None option is the slowest. The Expanded Memory command determines what information can be placed in extra memory if you have such memory installed.

The Clock command enables you to turn on and off the display of the date and time in the lower left corner of the screen. You can either display the date and time in Standard format or in International format, which will be the format currently in effect from the International Date and Time options. The Paradox command helps you to fine tune the use of Paradox data files over a network. You can tell Quattro Pro 4 where to look for data and for the PARADOX.NET file. For more on network operations, see Appendix B. For more on working with Paradox, see Chapter 13.

FIGURE
6-22

Options Value menu

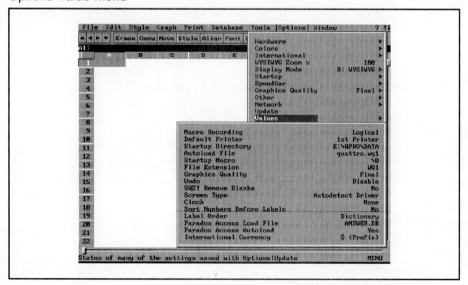

Conclusions

The Quattro Pro 4 Options menu is a powerful tool for extensive personalizing of the program. You can save a lot of time by making your preferred choices permanent program choices with the Update option. When you want a summary of the default settings, use the Options Values command. This produces the display shown in Figure 6-22. You will note two items that are not covered in the Options menu: Macro Recording and SQZ! Remove Blanks. The Macro Recording setting is determined by the Tools Macro menu, described in Chapter 11. The SQZ! settings are controlled by the File Utilities SQZ! menu, discussed in Chapter 7.

CHAPTER

File Management

*I*n this chapter you will learn how to use the File Manager, a complete hard disk management program that is built into Quattro Pro 4. You can use the File Manager to load worksheets, copy files, and make directories, all without leaving Quattro Pro 4. This chapter also describes password protection of worksheet files and SQZ!, the automatic file compression feature in Quattro Pro 4 that enables you to store worksheets in less space.

Overview of the File Manager

Quattro Pro 4's File Manager works as a shell between you and DOS to give you easy access to your files. You can use it to work with Quattro Pro 4 spreadsheet files or any other files located on either your hard disk or floppies. With the File Manager, you can display a list of files in any directory or disk drive and open a file by choosing its name. You can use wildcards to filter the file list, for example, *.WQ1 to display only Quattro Pro 4 spreadsheet files. You can turn this around to apply a negative filter, creating a list that shows all files except those specified in the filter. Thus, the filter [*.WQ1] shows all files except Quattro Pro 4 spreadsheet files.

File Manager also enables you to sort file lists by name, extension, size, original order, or timestamp. You can display a directory tree that reveals the structure of all directories on your disk. You can move in and out of directories in the tree and use the GoTo key (F5) to search through the tree for a specific file. You can move or copy a file from one directory to another, rename files, and delete them from disk.

The File Manager Window

Quattro Pro 4's File Manager works within a File Manager window. This is like a worksheet window except that it displays only file names and directories. To open a File Manager window, choose File Manager from the File Utilities menu. Quattro Pro 4 displays a window, as shown in Figure 7-1. Note that the choices in the menu bar change slightly when a File Manager window is active. The choices are now File, Edit, Sort, Tree, Print, Options, and Window (as opposed to File, Edit, Style, Graph, Print, Database, Tools, Options, and Window).

If you have not used the File Manager during the current session, the window displays information about files in the current directory. Otherwise, the directory displayed in the File Manager window is the one that was there the last time you used File Manager in the current session. Similarly, the screen position of this window is taken from the last open File Manager window. Note that you can use SHIFT-F6 to switch from this window back to the worksheet windows. You do not have to close the File Manager before returning to a worksheet. You use File Close if you want to put the File Manager away. Also note that if your File Manager window is not shown full-screen, you can press ALT-F6 to zoom the window so that it appears as in Figure 7-1.

The File Manager window shown in Figure 7-1 is actually divided into two sections. These are called *panes*. The top pane, called the *control pane,* displays prompts that accept your changes in four areas: drive, directory, filter, and file name. In Figure 7-1 the settings are

Drive: E
Directory: \QPRO\DATA
Filter: *.*
File Name: _

FIGURE
7-1

File Manager window

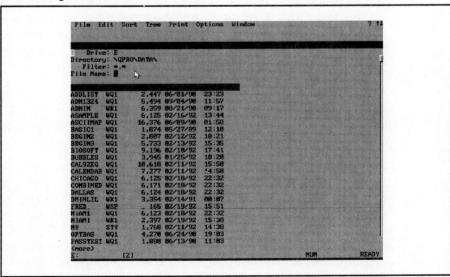

You move between these items with the UP ARROW and DOWN ARROW keys. The cursor will mark which one is active. You can change the active item by pressing ESC to erase the entire entry, or by pressing BACKSPACE to erase one character at a time. You can then type the new setting and press ENTER to confirm it. When you press ENTER, Quattro Pro 4 immediately reads in a new list based on your changes. When you are entering new subdirectories, be sure to precede the subdirectory in the path name with a backslash (\). For example, to view the files in D:\ SALES\REPORTS you would change Drive to D and then change Directory to \SALES\REPORTS. There is no need to enter the final backslash; Quattro Pro 4 will do that for you, changing \SALES\REPORTS to \SALES\ REPORTS\.

Underneath the control pane is the *file list pane.* This is the list of files and subdirectories in the specified directory. You can browse this list with the UP ARROW and DOWN ARROW keys as well as PAGE UP and PAGE DOWN. You can also change the directory being displayed in the File Manager window by selecting another directory from within the file list pane. If you want to see one of the subdirectories included on the list, just highlight it and press ENTER. You will find subdirectories listed below file names in the file list. If you want to see the parent directory of the current subdirectory, select the double dots (..) at the top of this list, which are shorthand for the parent directory.

A third pane, called the *tree pane,* is created when you use the Tree Open command. Figure 7-2 shows a File Manager window with a tree displayed by the Tree Open command. The tree pane gives a visual representation of the directory system on the currently specified drive (E). The tree diagram shows how subdirectories branch from parent directories. The path to the current directory is highlighted.

Before you can work in a particular pane of the File Manager window you must activate that pane. To activate a different pane, press the Pane key (F6) or the TAB key. You will cycle through the control, file list, and tree panes as you continue to press F6.

You can have two or more File Manager windows open at the same time. Opening a second File Manager window is simply a matter of repeating the File Utilities File Manager command. To move between File Manager windows and the spreadsheet itself, use the Next Window key

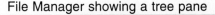

FIGURE
7-2

File Manager showing a tree pane

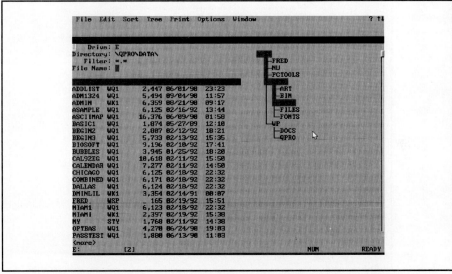

(SHIFT-F6). Alternatively, you can move from window to window with the ALT-*number* technique, for example, use ALT-5 to move to window 5. You can use the Move/Size command from the Window menu to alter the size or position of File Manager windows.

To close the active File Manager window, use the File Close command. If you want to return to the worksheet you were using but do not want to close the File Manager window, press the Next Window key (SHIFT-F6) or select the worksheet from the Window Pick list. You can return to the File Manager window at any time by selecting the window from the Window Pick list. File Manager windows are described in the Window Pick list according to the drive that is being viewed. You can see this in Figure 7-3 where the File Manager window is shown alongside a worksheet window (this arrangement was created by the Windows Tile command, described in a moment). The Window Pick list is presented when you press ALT-0 or SHIFT-F5 or choose Pick from the Window menu. You can see that the File Manager window is displaying files on drive E and so the window is shown in the Window Pick list as E.

FIGURE 7-3

A File Manager window and worksheet window

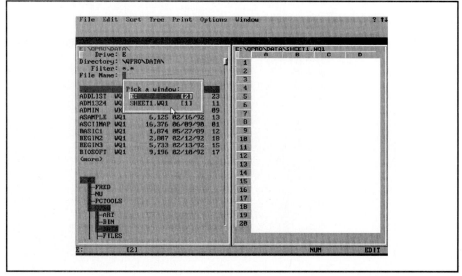

As you can see from Figure 7-3, it is possible to view a File Manager window alongside a worksheet window. The amount of detail you will see in each window depends on your display system. If you are working in WYSIWYG or an advanced character mode it is possible to view several windows at once, each containing useful amounts of information. Any File Manager windows you have open are adjusted whenever you issue the Windows Stack or Tile commands.

In Figure 7-4 you can see one worksheet window and two File Manager windows arranged with the Windows Tile command (remember that WYSIWYG mode only allows Windows Tile, whereas character mode permits the Windows Stack screen layout as well). You can use ALT-F6 to zoom any reduced window to full size (remember that in WYSIWYG mode you switch between full-screen and reduced windows with the Windows Tile command, whereas in character mode you can use ALT-F6 to switch in and out of full-screen size, as well as adjust your display of windows with the Windows Move/Size commands, described in Chapter 3). A complete list of the special File Manager keys is provided in Table 7-1. Note that there is no SpeedBar for the File Manager.

TABLE 7-1

File Manager Keys

General Windowing Keys	Name/Function
SHIFT-F5	Pick Window; accesses other windows.
ALT-0	Pick Window; accesses other windows.
F6 or TAB	Pane; activates the next File Manager window pane in the following order: control pane, file list pane, directory tree pane.
SHIFT-F6	Next Window; activates the next open File Manager window.
ALT-F6	Zoom Window; zooms an open window to full screen and back again. If the window is already expanded, this key shrinks it again, as with Window Zoom.
ALT-n	Jumps to window number n. The window number appears on the top edge of each frame.
Keys for the Control Pane	
F2	Rename; prompts for a new a file name and renames the current file list selection to the file name you specify (same as Edit Rename).
F5	GoTo; finds the file name (or combination of wildcard characters) typed at the file name prompt.
ESC	Clears the entry at the prompt. When you move the highlight bar away from the prompt and make no new entry, restores the original entry.
DELETE	Deletes the character under the cursor.
ENTER	Moves the cursor to the blank file name prompt or, if the cursor is at the file name prompt, opens the file or subdirectory highlighted on the file list.

TABLE 7-1 Cont.

File Manager Keys

Keys for the Control Pane	
HOME	Moves the cursor to the beginning of the prompt entry.
Keys for the File List Pane	
F2	Rename; renames the current (highlighted) file (same as Edit Rename).
SHIFT-F7	Select; selects the current (highlighted) file in the list so you can open, move, copy, or delete it. If the file is already selected, this key deselects it.
ALT-F7	All Select; selects all files on the list for moving, copying, or deleting. If some files on the list are already selected, deselects those files.
SHIFT-F8	Move; marks the selected file to be moved.
F9	Calc; reads the disk and refreshes the file list pane (same as file Read Dir).
SHIFT-F9	Copy; copies the selected files into the paste buffer for copying to another directory or disk, keeping them on the list.
SHIFT-F10	Paste; inserts the files in the paste buffer at the cursor position in the current directory's file list.
ESC	Escape; returns all selected files to normal. Activates the control pane and moves the cursor to the file name prompt.
ENTER	Opens selected files or the file at the cursor. If the highlight bar is on the .., opens the parent directory. If the highlight bar is on a subdirectory, moves to the subdirectory.

TABLE 7-1 Cont.	File Manager Keys

Keys for the File List Pane	
HOME	Moves the highlight bar to the .. parent directory item.
END	Moves the highlight bar to the end of the file list.
PAGE UP	Moves the file list display up one screen.
PAGE DOWN	Moves the file list display down one screen.
In the Tree Pane	
ESC	Returns all selected files to normal; then activates the control pane and moves the cursor to the file name prompt.
DELETE	Deletes all selected files or the highlighted file in the file list.
F9	Calc; rereads the current disk/directory.

In Figures 7-3 and 7-4 you can see that when you reduce the size of a File Manager window Quattro Pro 4 moves the tree pane underneath the control pane and the file list pane. The amount of space taken up by the directory tree can be adjusted, as described in a moment. You can also see that the two File Manager windows in Figure 7-4 show two different drives. File Manager windows can also show different paths the same drives, helpful for moving or copying files, as described later in this chapter. The next discussion describes the File Manager menus. A complete list of the special File Manager keys is provided in Table 7-1.

The File Manager Menus

When you are in a File Manager window, you have access to a set of menus by typing **/** or pressing F3. Quattro Pro 4 activates a variation of

FIGURE
7-4

Three windows tiled

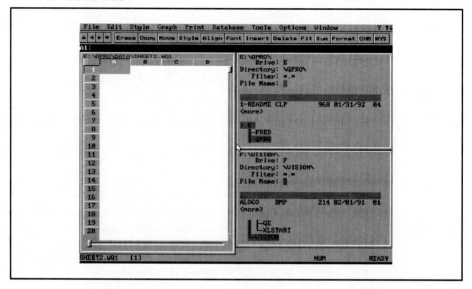

the main menu as shown in Figure 7-1. This menu contains a subset of the usual menu commands with some new ones added.

By using options from the File menu in File Manager you can create a new worksheet window or open an existing worksheet. You can close the current File Manager window or close all windows, both File Manager and worksheet. You can tell File Manager to reread the current directory specified in the control pane, making sure that the list is up to date. You can also use the File menu to save and restore workspaces or access the file utilities (issuing the File Utilities File Manager command opens a fresh File Manager window). If you want to close all windows and exit Quattro Pro 4, you can do so from the File menu in File Manager.

The Edit command lets you copy, move, rename, duplicate, or erase files from the displayed directory. The Sort command lets you reorder the list of files by name, extension, timestamp, size, or DOS order. With the Tree command you can display the directory tree in a pane below or to the right of the file list, as well as resize the tree pane and close the tree pane.

The Print command displays a menu for printing lists of files and directory trees. This menu works much the same as the standard Print menu. The Options command lets you switch the file list display between names only and names and file status. You can also reset many system options, such as the Startup directory and screen colors. Finally, the Window command enables you to adjust the size and position of the windows, expand the current window, or move to a different window.

Working with the Control Pane

Suppose that you want to view all 1-2-3 worksheet files in the directory called FRED on drive E. First, make sure that the control pane of the File Manager window is active. This means that the cursor will be in one of the top four fields (press F6 or TAB to change active windows). Move the cursor to the drive field and then type **E** and press ENTER. In the directory field type **FRED** and press ENTER. Now move the cursor to the filter prompt. The filter lets you restrict the files shown in the file list pane. This setting accepts DOS wildcards: * to take the place of any number of characters and ? to take the place of one character. The default filter setting (*.*) displays all file names with any extension. To narrow down the files listed, you change the filter to exclude files you do not want to see. In this example, you can enter *.**WK**? to list all files with *WK* as the first two letters of their extension. This includes .WKS and .WK1, as well as .WK3. To be more specific, for example, to find all spreadsheet files beginning with *SALES*, you would enter **SALES???.WK?** You can also specify a negative filter to display all files except those that meet the filter specifications. To indicate a negative filter you enclose the wildcard specification in square brackets. For example, to display a list of all 1-2-3 spreadsheet files except those beginning with *SALES*, enter the following specification:

[SALES???.WK?]

You can also combine filter specifications to create one filter. Just separate the specifications with commas. For example,

.WK?,[SALES.*]

displays all 1-2-3 spreadsheet files except for those beginning with *SALES*. The filter limits the files displayed in the File Manager window and remains in effect until you change it, even if you change directories. To erase the current filter and return to the default of *.*, highlight the filter prompt and press ESC and then ENTER.

Selecting Files

When you open the File Manager window the file name prompt is blank. At the same time, the control pane is active and the file name prompt is highlighted. You can use this prompt to open a worksheet file or look for a specific file on your disk. To open a worksheet file you type the name at the file name prompt and press ENTER. If Quattro Pro 4 finds a file by this name, the File Manager window disappears and the worksheet is displayed. Note that if Quattro Pro 4 does not find the file you have named in the current directory, it creates a new spreadsheet with that name and displays it even if the name is not suitable for a worksheet, such as FRED.EXE. For this reason you may want to locate the file in the file list, as described in a moment, rather than risk a mismatched file name entry. Table 7-1 provides a list of the special keys you can use in the control pane and their functions.

If you do not know where on a disk a particular file is located you can type in the file name at the file name prompt and press the GoTo key (F5). Quattro Pro 4 searches through every directory on the disk until it finds a file with that name. It then changes the file list to show the directory containing the file you specified, with the file name highlighted and marked by a check. If there are other files with the same name, press F5 again to move to the next. If you do not know the exact name of the file, you can use wildcards to search for near matches. For example, to find a worksheet file with a name that begins with *FRED* you type **FRED*.WQ1** in the file name field. Then you press F5. Quattro Pro 4 locates the first file that match this specification. there may be other files that match, so you can press F5 again to highlight the next matching file name. When the file you want is highlighted, press ENTER to open it.

Note that you could search for any file name beginning with *FRED* by simply typing FRED in the File Name field and pressing F5. In Figure 7-5 you can see the results of a search like this. This figure also shows the Wide View of files, described next.

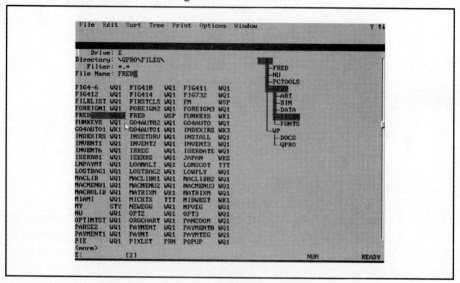

FIGURE
7-5

The Wide View of files, showing search results

The File List Pane

The file list pane catalogs all files and subdirectories that pass through the given filter in the specified drive and directory. File names are listed first, followed by subdirectory names, in alphabetical order. The first column shows file names, the second shows file name extensions, and the third shows file size measured in bytes. The last two columns show the date and time the file was last altered. If there are more files in the directory than will fit in the pane, Quattro Pro 4 displays "<more>"at the bottom of the screen. You can press PAGE DOWN to display the next page of names or END to move to the end of the list.

Moving to the end of the list is useful, because there you can find a directory status that shows the number of files in the current directory and the number of files displayed in the file list, which may be less if you have used a filter. This status line also shows how many bytes of the disk have been used together with the total number of bytes available on the disk. If you do not need datestamp and file size information, you can use the Options File List Wide View command to allow room for more file names in the list, as shown in Figure 7-5. Table 7-1 lists the special keys you can use in the file list pane. The Options File List Full View option restores a detailed listing of files.

Sorting File Lists

By default, Quattro Pro 4 lists all files and subdirectories in the file list in alphabetical order. This is the Sort Name option. To change the order of the file list you choose Sort from the File Manager menu and then select the sort order you want from the list. When you choose Name or DOS Order, Quattro Pro 4 also sorts subdirectories listed in the tree pane. You can sort by Timestamp, which lists file names and subdirectories chronologically according to their timestamp. This order reveals when files were last modified. The oldest file is listed first. This command sorts by time, even when the Options File List command is set to Wide View. The Extension option sorts the file list alphabetically, first by extension, then by file name. The Size option sorts file names and subdirectories by size (in bytes). The smallest file appears first in the list. The DOS Order option sorts file names in the same order that the DOS command DIR would list them (usually in the order of original creation).

Navigating with the File List

The Options Startup Directory setting in the File Manager menu determines which directory is displayed when you first open a File Manager window. To change the directory displayed at startup you choose Options Startup Directory. Then select either Previous (the default) to display the last directory you looked at in your last Quattro Pro 4 session or Current to show the directory you were in when you loaded Quattro Pro 4.

If the file you want is not in the directory shown in the file list, you can access different directories by choosing subdirectories. These are normally found at the bottom of the alphabetical file list and distinguished by a backslash after the directory name. You can also move up in the directory system by using the item denoted by two dots (..), which is the parent directory of the current directory. To display files from one of the subdirectories in the file list pane, just move the highlight bar to the directory's name and press ENTER. The directory prompt changes to show the subdirectory name, and the file pane changes to list files in that subdirectory.

To move out of the current directory and into its parent directory press HOME to highlight the double dots denoting the parent directory at the top of the file list pane, and then press ENTER. Quattro Pro 4 takes you back one level in the directory and displays file names and subdirectories in the parent directory. Table 7-1 lists the keystrokes you can use in the control pane of a File Manager window.

The Directory Tree

By choosing subdirectories or the parent directory (..) item in the file list you can get to any file stored on your disk. But if you expect to traverse many directories or are not sure what files are in your directories, you may want to use the directory tree, which Quattro Pro 4 can display in a third File Manager pane, as shown in Figure 7-5. The directory tree lists all directories and subdirectories on your disk in alphabetical order. You can move the cursor around the tree to display different directory contents in the file list pane. When you want to use a directory tree, choose Tree Open from the File Manager window.

To display the directory tree just choose the Tree Open command. Quattro Pro 4 opens a tree pane below or to the right of the file pane in the File Manager window. The root directory is at the top. Subdirectories branch to the right and down. Quattro Pro 4 highlights the current directory on the tree. If there are more directories on your disk than will fit in the tree pane, you can use the direction keys to scroll the list. When you use the cursor keys to move the highlight bar, Quattro Pro 4 displays files in a different directory. As you move the bar the directory prompt changes to show the name of the highlighted directory, and the file list changes to display the files in that directory.

Sizing the Tree

The first time you display a directory tree, Quattro Pro 4 divides the available File Manager window space equally between the file pane and the tree pane. You may want to give more or less space to the tree pane. To change the size of the tree pane, select Tree Resize from the File Manager menu. Quattro Pro 4 prompts you for a percentage. Enter a larger percentage to increase the amount of space devoted to the tree, a smaller percentage to reduce the space used by the tree.

In future sessions, when you display the tree pane, it will be the size you last specified. Table 7-1 lists some keystrokes that let you select, delete, open, and refresh the display of file and directory information in the directory tree pane. If most of your work is in one directory, you can give more space to the file list by closing the directory tree pane. To do this, use Tree Close. Quattro Pro 4 removes the directory tree and expands the file list pane to fill its space.

Printing File Information

The File Manager menu bar contains a print option. You can use this specialized Print menu to print parts of the File Manager window. The Print Block command gives you three options instead of a cell block prompt. The default option is Files, which prints a list of all files in the file list pane, even those you have to scroll to display. To print the directory tree, choose Tree. To print the file list followed by the directory tree, choose Both. You can send the output to a printer or to a file. Use the Destination command on the Print menu to choose between Printer, the default print destination, or File.

You can use the Go command on this Print menu to send data to the chosen destination. The Adjust Printer option enables you to carry out the Skip Line, Form Feed, and Align commands described in Chapter 3. Note that printed output from the File Manager does not use WYSIWIG fonts but rather the standard print characters.

Managing and Loading Files

With the File Manager, you can move, copy, rename, or delete files on your disk without accessing DOS. You perform these actions from the File Manager Edit menu.

Selecting and Pasting Files

The first option on the File Manager Edit menu, shown in Figure 7-6, is Select File. This marks the highlighted file on the file list so that it stays highlighted even when you move the highlight bar away. You can see that SALES1.WK1 in Figure 7-6 is selected even though the highlight bar is on USPRICES.WK1. You can use the Select File command when you want to select a group of file names. The All Select option highlights all files on the file list or, if some files are already selected, deselects all files.

The Copy option stores a copy of the selected files in the paste buffer. You can then paste the copy into any other directory. The Move option moves the selected files into the paste buffer and from there you can paste them into another directory. The Erase option deletes the selected files from the disk. The Paste option inserts the files in the paste buffer in whatever directory you select.

If you want to copy a file from one directory to another, you first have to highlight the file in the file list pane. Then you can mark the file as selected using Edit Select File (or by pressing SHIFT-F7 or by clicking on the file name). Once the file is selected you can issue the Edit Copy command, and the File Manager will know which file you want to copy (you can use SHIFT-F9 for the Edit Copy command). The color of the

FIGURE
7-6

The Edit menu in File Manager

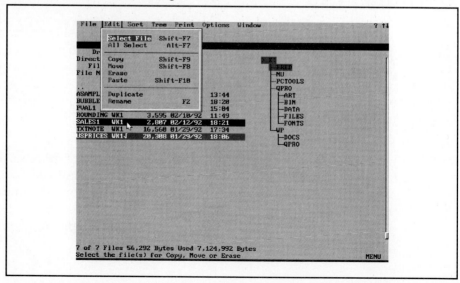

highlighting on the file changes when you issue the Edit Copy command. The File Manager keeps track of the file name in the paste buffer.

Now you can use the tree to locate the directory into which you want to copy the file. If you do not have a directory tree displayed you can use the Tree Open command to create a tree of the current drive. Alternatively, you can use the control pane to select a different directory or drive. When the directory into which you want to copy the file is displayed you can use Edit Paste or SHIFT-F10 to complete the copy operation.

If you use Edit Move instead of Edit Copy and then use Edit Paste, the File Manager will erase the source file after first making a copy in the destination directory. You can perform Copy and Move with more than one file by selecting a number of files before you issue the Edit Copy or Edit Move command. You can select all of the files in a directory at once by using Edit All Select (ALT-F7).

The Duplicate option performs double duty, copying and renaming a file, then storing the copy in the same or a different directory. The Rename option enables you to change the name of a file. Table 7-1 lists the special keys used in the file list pane for moving around, as well as for renaming, moving, copying, opening, and deleting files. Note that you can rename any file simply by highlighting it and pressing F2.

Opening Files

You can use the File Manager to open a spreadsheet file and display it in a new spreadsheet window. Just select the file name on the file list and press ENTER. Quattro Pro 4 removes the File Manager window from view and displays the spreadsheet, overlaying any existing spreadsheet windows. To open a file using a mouse, move the pointer to the file name and click the button to highlight the name; then click again to open the file.

To open several spreadsheet files at once, use the Edit Select command or SHIFT-F7 key to select each file on the file list and then press ENTER. Quattro Pro 4 opens a new spreadsheet window for each and loads the file. Remember that you can also open a file from within the File Manager window by entering a name at the control pane's file name prompt and pressing ENTER.

Managing Directories

The File menu that you access from within a File Manager window contains a New command that opens a new worksheet window, and a Close command that closes the current window. The Read Dir command reads and redisplays the files on the current directory. The Make Dir command creates a new directory or subdirectory with the name and location you supply at the prompt. As in a worksheet window, the Workspace command enables you to save the current setup of windows in a file or retrieve a saved workspace setup. The Utilities command enables you to open another File Manager window or access DOS without leaving Quattro Pro 4, as with the DOS Shell command on the regular File Utilities menu. The File Utilities command also allows you to adjust the SQZ! settings discussed later in this chapter. The Exit command puts away Quattro Pro 4 and returns you to DOS.

The File Read Dir command rereads the files in the specified directory and updates the file list accordingly. A typical use for this command would be when you have inserted a new disk in a floppy drive. The Calc key (F9) performs the same function as File Read Dir, by "recalculating" the directory display.

File Manager Options

Selecting Options from the File Manager menu displays an adjusted Options menu. This menu lists some of the same system options available within a worksheet window and two options that deal directly with File Manager windows. The Hardware, Colors, Beep, Display Mode, and Update choices are the same as when you are in a worksheet window. The Startup option contains the Menu Tree and Edit Menus commands plus a special command called Directory. This allows you to choose between a File Manager display of the directory you were in when you last used Quattro Pro 4, and the directory from which you just loaded Quattro Pro 4. The File List option lets you choose between Wide View, just the file names in the file list—in several columns, or Full View which is a single column that includes size, date, and time information for each file.

Using SQZ!

A very useful file management feature that is built into Quattro Pro 4 is the ability to compress files when you store them on disk. This conserves valuable disk space. To use this feature you simply add the file name extension .WQ! when saving a worksheet. When storing files with the .WQ! extension, Quattro Pro 4 uses a piece of software called SQZ! to pack the data tightly. When you retrieve a file with the .WQ! extension the SQZ! program, which is contained within the main Quattro Pro 4 program, automatically unpacks the data. You can still use password protection with SQZ! files. With Quattro Pro 4 you can read compressed 1-2-3 Release 2 worksheet files that have the extension .WK!, as well as compressed files from earlier versions of Quattro that have the extension .WKZ.

The File Utilities SQZ! menu shown in Figure 7-7 enables you to adjust the way SQZ! operates. The Remove Blanks option increases the effectiveness of SQZ!. The Yes choice implements the added space saving of Removing Blanks. The default choice of No leaves blank cells in the compressed file. The Storage of Values option has three choices: Exact, Approximate, and Remove. The Exact option retains all formulas and

FIGURE 7-7

The File Utilities SQZ! menu

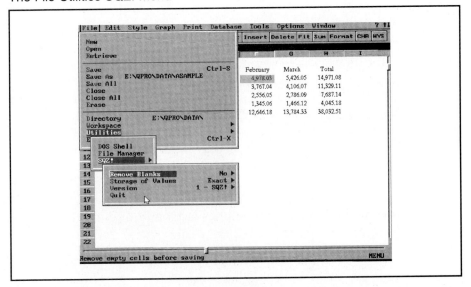

values in the compressed file. Leave this default setting in place if you plan to share the file with other programs. The Approximate choice retains formula results to 7 digits instead of the usual 15. The Remove option takes result values out of the worksheet and calculates results when the file is retrieved again.

The Version option on the SQZ! menu enables you to use either SQZ! or SQZ! Plus. The default is the less efficient SQZ! so that you can pass on a file to a user who only has the first version of SQZ!. The most efficient settings for space saving are as follows:

Remove Blanks:	Yes
Storage of Values:	Remove
Version:	SQZ! Plus

To make saving in SQZ! format automatic, use Options Startup File Extension from the worksheet menus to make WQ! the default extension.

Out-of-Space Problems

When you are building a large worksheet, it is surprising how fast it can grow in size. The Edit Copy command in particular quickly generates a lot of data. This can result in space problems, both on disk and in memory.

Disk Space

When you attempt to save a file that is too large to fit in the remaining free space on your disk, Quattro Pro 4 displays a "disk full" error message. You can respond to this in several ways.

Save to a Floppy Disk

If you have been saving to a floppy disk and the current disk cannot accommodate the worksheet you are trying to save, you can retry the save after inserting a disk with more free space on it. Note that a worksheet file cannot be split across two floppy disks. You can use the DOS Shell command on the File Utilities menu to temporarily exit to DOS and format a fresh floppy disk if you need one. The DOS Shell command, does not affect your unsaved work. If you have been saving to a hard disk that has now filled up, you might consider saving to a floppy disk as a temporary measure. Remember that some floppy disks can now store over a megabyte of information.

Clean Up Your Hard Disk

If you are trying to save to a hard disk that has run out of space, you can either use DOS via the DOS Shell command or the File Manager to erase unwanted files from your hard disk. This will make more room available and help to accommodate the worksheet you are trying to save.

Convert Values

The amount of space required by formulas in a worksheet is greater than that taken up by values. If you convert numbers that are generated by formulas into their values, using the Edit Values command, the worksheet can be stored in less space.

SQZ! the Worksheet

If saving a worksheet in the regular .WQ1 format results in a "disk full" message, you might want to try the SQZ! option, described earlier in this chapter. You do this by using the file extension .WQ! instead of .WQ1. This causes Quattro Pro 4 to compress the worksheet, sometimes by as much as 75 percent, and thus store it in a smaller file.

Divide the Worksheet

When you attempt to save a worksheet and get a "disk full" message you may want to consider splitting the worksheet into separate, smaller worksheets. To do this you can open a new window and use the Edit Move command to move data from the current worksheet to the new one.

Memory Space

Quattro Pro 4 displays the message "memory full" when you attempt to retrieve a file that is too large to fit in currently available memory. You get a similar message when you expand the current worksheet beyond the limits of available memory. If you want to check on the amount of memory you have available, use the Options Hardware command and read the current memory status from the Hardware menu. If you have a worksheet loaded when you read the Hardware menu, you can see how much room there is for expansion. If you have a blank worksheet, you can tell how large a file you can retrieve. Quattro Pro 4 needs enough free memory to read in the file from disk and to manipulate the data within the worksheet. Thus, if you had 82,944 bytes available, you would be unwise to try to retrieve anything larger than 80,000 bytes.

When you use a command that results in the "memory full" message you should save parts of the worksheet to separate files using the Tools Xtract command, described in Chapter 9. This enables you to store the data safely so that you can redesign the worksheet, perhaps free more memory, or add more memory to the system. You can free memory by saving the current worksheet, exiting Quattro Pro 4, and removing any memory-resident programs you might have loaded.

If it was an Edit Copy command that caused the "memory full" message, you will probably find that only part of the block was copied. However, the data you had before the copy operation should still be intact. Likewise, if you tried to retrieve a file that was too large, only part of the file will be in your worksheet, but the entire file will still be safely stored on disk.

Password Protection

To prevent unauthorized access to a worksheet stored on disk, you can assign a password to the worksheet while you are saving it. Select File Save As and then type in the file name followed by a space and the letter **P**. When you press ENTER Quattro Pro 4 prompts you for a password. Actually, this can be several words, numbers, and spaces up to a total length of 15 characters. Pick a password that you can remember. Neither Borland nor anyone else can retrieve the data if you forget the word. No one can see the letters of the password as you type, because Quattro Pro 4 displays only a blank rectangle for each letter as shown in Figure 7-8. When you have typed the password, press ENTER. You are then asked to verify the word by typing it again. The theory is that if you can type the word twice, you know what it is and did not make a mistake the first time you entered it. After typing the word a second time, press ENTER. The file-saving process continues as usual.

When you attempt to retrieve or open the password-protected file, you are prompted for the password. This time you need only type the password once and then press ENTER to access the file. If you type an incorrect password, Quattro Pro 4 beeps and gives you the message "Invalid password." When you save a file with password protection Quattro Pro 4 *encrypts* the file; that is, it scrambles the data to make it unintelligible, even to a sophisticated, well-trained programmer. Do not expect to be able to get the data back if you forget the password. Trying to get around the password by using the partial file retrieval command, Tools Combine, does not work either. You should leave a copy of the password in a secure place such as a locked desk drawer or in another password-protected Quattro Pro 4 file.

FIGURE 7-8   Adding password protection

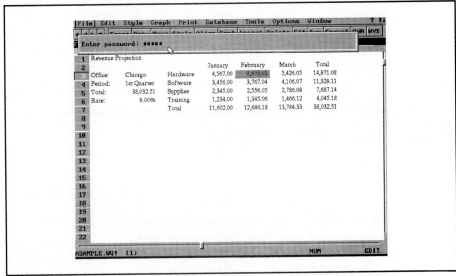

When you want to remove password protection from a file, you first open the file, and then use the File Save As command. Quattro Pro 4 will remind you that the file is password protected, as shown in Figure 7-9. You can press BACKSPACE to remove the protection message. Press ENTER to complete the file save and the file is no longer protected. Unless you remove the password protection with File Save As, the file will continue to be password protected.

If you are using Quattro Pro 4 to read 1-2-3 files, as described later in this chapter, and those files are protected by 1-2-3 password protection, Quattro Pro 4 will be able to decode the files, provided you supply the correct password.

Using passwords can be a nuisance, so you should decide whether the need for security is real. If it is, then you will want to make sure you use proper passwords. A password is of little use if it is a useless password such as *password, pass, your first name, the filename,* and so on. Believe it or not, you can buy lists of common passwords, and the serious data thief is likely to guess most words that do not have the following features.

❑   At least eight characters

❑   A mixture of text and numbers

**FIGURE
7-9**

The password reminder

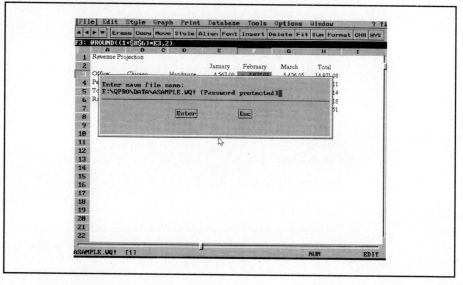

❏   Some odd characters, like @, spaces, and commas

❏   A mixture of uppercase and lowercase

❏   A lack of logic

Although some applications are not sensitive to upper- and lowercase distinctions, Quattro Pro 4 is, which is an important point to remember when recording your passwords. The password *Fred's File* will not be accepted if it is supplied as *FRED'S FILE*, and even *Fred's file* will be rejected. To use the last feature—a lack of logical connection between the content of the file and the password protecting it—you need to be imaginative. For example, a banker might use the names of birds to protect a series of salary recommendation files. Combined with the other features, something like this would be difficult to guess:

Robin@5769

Because such a name would also be difficult to remember you must also make proper provision for recording and securing passwords. A sheet of paper locked in a drawer is usually a good technique. You can use a spreadsheet or word processor to list files and their passwords. The more paranoid might want to code the passwords on the printed listing.

Data Loss and Recovery

The best approach to prevent data loss is the same one you can use for steady monetary accumulation: save on a regular basis. This means saving every 15 minutes. You should also save your files before you do any of the following:

❏   Perform a file retrieve

❏   Exit Quattro Pro 4

❏   Leave your PC unattended

❏   Move or copy a large block

❏   Sort data or perform an extract or block fill operation

❏   Combine files

However, even if you try to live by these rules, there is always a possibility that something will go wrong. Quattro Pro 4 has a built-in method of helping out.

Using Transcript

If you have lost data, you can rely on the Quattro Pro 4 *keystroke log*. This is a transcript of your recent activity that is created by a built-in feature of Quattro Pro 4 called Transcript, which automatically keeps track of your keystrokes on disk. The keystrokes are saved to a special log file with the name QUATTRO.LOG. If your machine malfunctions or you accidentally delete data, you can recall this data by replaying your actions from the Transcript log. Several thousand actions can be recorded in one log before Quattro Pro 4 copies the log to a backup file called QUATTRO.BAK and continues with a new QUATTRO.LOG. This means that between the files QUATTRO.BAK and QUATTRO.LOG you can keep an extensive record of what has been done during your Quattro Pro 4 sessions.

To gain access to the Transcript log file and review or restore keystrokes from it, use the Tools Macro command and select Transcript to display a log of data like that shown in Figure 7-10. You can browse through this list with the highlight bar, which you move by means of the UP ARROW and DOWN ARROW keys. Use the PAGE UP and PAGE DOWN keys to move through this list. The line on the left side of the log groups commands that occurred since the current session started.

To use the recorded keystrokes, type **/** and you will see the Transcript menu, shown in Figure 7-11. You use this menu to mark blocks or sections of commands for playback. Alternatively, you can have Transcript play back the commands up to the point marked by the highlight bar.

Suppose you start working with Quattro Pro 4 and have loaded Transcript. The first piece of work you do is retrieve a budget file. You are busy updating the budget numbers when there is a power outage. You have lost the changes to the budget file; however, the original file is still on the disk. When power returns you simply reload Quattro Pro 4 and run Transcript. The log file then comes up and the commands from it may be replayed. These will include the retrieval of the budget file and

FIGURE 7-10

The Transcript Log

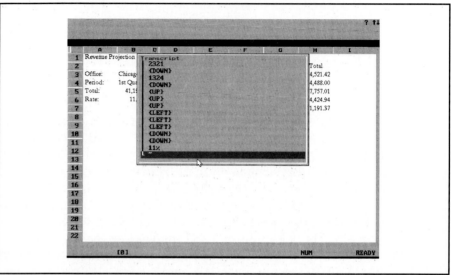

FIGURE 7-11

The Transcript menu

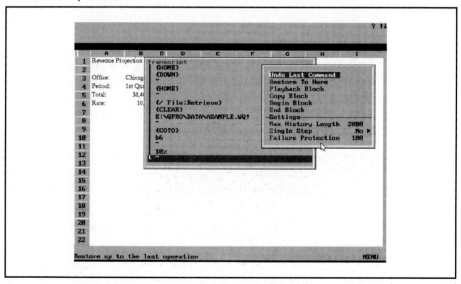

the changes you made. If you have lost data because of an inadvertent command, such as Edit Copy, you can run the log up to, but not including, that command. Of course, if you have enabled Undo, as described in the next section, you can reverse the consequences of many typical spreadsheet actions. However, Transcript enables you to undo a whole series of actions, which Undo cannot.

Note the Settings part of the Transcript menu. The Max History Length determines how many lines of recorded actions will be held in the log file before it is backed up and a new one created. The Single Step option enables you to play back your Transcript commands one at a time. The Failure Protection feature determines how many keystrokes Quattro Pro 4 should wait before recording them to disk. The smaller you set this number the more complete your recovery from disaster will be. However, lower numbers also mean more frequent disk writing. For more on Transcript commands, see Chapter 12.

Activating Undo

Sometimes you can overcome errors and accidents without resorting to Transcript. If you activate Quattro Pro 4's Undo feature you can press ALT-F5 after a command to reverse its effects. This is very handy after a mistaken Edit Erase Block, or a disastrous Data Sort. To activate Undo, you use the Options Other command and select Undo. Select Enable and be sure to use the Options Update command to record this change if you want it to be in effect in the next session. You may notice a slight slowing of Quattro Pro 4's reaction time when Undo is in effect. This is due to the extra work that the program is doing to keep track of your actions, but it is a small price to pay for the ability to reverse critical actions. Table 7-2 lists actions that cannot be reversed with Undo.

TABLE 7-2	Actions That Cannot Be Undone

Commands that make settings such as Sort Block (but Sort Go and Data Query Extract can be undone)

Print commands that send a document to the printer (use CTRL-BREAK to stop printing)

File menu commands

Copy, move, and delete operations in the File Manager

Format commands from the Style or Options menu

Note: To undo some commands you need to return to READY mode from the menu first. Repeat the Undo key to reverse an Undo operation.

Special Files

Quattro Pro 4 can read and write not only its own worksheets but also data files created by several other popular programs. If you have 1-2-3 or Symphony files on your directory, they will automatically be listed by Quattro Pro 4 because the *.W?? pattern includes .WRK and .WK1 files. You do not have to do anything special to retrieve one of these files. Highlight the name, press ENTER, and the file is read into Quattro Pro 4. When you go to save the file, Quattro Pro 4 will assume that you want to store it in the original format, using the same extension. For example, if you open SALES.WK1 and then use the File Save As command, the suggested name will be the same, SALES.WK1, and the file will be stored as a 1-2-3 worksheet. However, when you use the File Save As command you can alter the file extension to .WQ1 to match the Quattro Pro 4 format you require.

You can read other types of files with the File Retrieve or File Open command if you enter the full file name or alter the *.W?? prompt to *.* to list them. Files that can be read in this manner are listed in Table 7-3. When you open a 1-2-3 worksheet with the .WK1 or .WK3 extension, Quattro Pro 4 checks whether there is an accompanying format file created by the two 1-2-3 add-in programs called Impress and Wysiwyg. These format files contain information about advanced formatting such as fonts and lines and have the extension .FMT or .FM3. For example, if you have used Wysiwyg to format the SALES.WK1 worksheet, a file called SALES.FMT will have been created. Quattro Pro 4 can read many, but not all, of the settings in this file and can translate them to the corresponding Quattro Pro 4 settings. Table 7-4 lists the features that Quattro Pro 4 recognizes. Bear in mind that the .FMT or .FM3 file must be in the same directory as the .WK1 or .WK3 file when you retrieve the worksheet.

TABLE
7-3

Files That Can Be Retrieved by Quattro Pro 4

Extension	Type of File
WKQ	Worksheets from Quattro 1.0
WKZ	Worksheet from Quattro 1.0 compressed with SQZ!
WK1	1-2-3 Release 2 worksheet
WK3	1-2-3 Release 3 worksheet
WK!	1-2-3 Release 2 worksheet compressed with SQZ!
WKS	1-2-3 Release 1 worksheet
WRK	Symphony worksheet
RXD	Reflex database
DB	Paradox database
DBF	dBASE II or III database, dBASE IV database without memo fields
DIF	Data Interchange Format

Writing to Foreign Files

You can save data into some foreign file formats simply by changing the file extension. For example, to save a file in the .WK3 format that can be read by 1-2-3 Release 3, you use the File Save As command to change the worksheet extension to .WK3 and proceed with the save. If you want to save data from a Quattro Pro 4 worksheet to a database format such as dBASE or Paradox, you need to consider the location of the data that you are going to save. You can only save fields and records to a database format. For this reason you will probably want to use the Tools Xtract command to perform the save and specify only those cells that contain records and field names.

The Tools Xtract command enables you to save just part of a worksheet, rather than the whole thing. For example, in Figure 7-12 the cells to be exported to dBASE are A4 through H20. When you use the Tools Xtract command you must specify whether you want to save values or

TABLE 7-4   How WYSIWYG/Impress Files are Handled

Quattro Pro 4 Recognizes	Quattro Pro 4 Does Not Recognize
Fonts, including, boldface, italic, underline, and colors	Column page breaks and column width
Inserted graphs	Formatting embedded in text
Named styles	Display options such as colors, mode, and zoom
Text alignment (except left of cell overlap)	Line shadow and line colors
Row height page breaks	Inserted clip art and drawings
Print range, configuration and orientation, and print-to-fit compression	Page size and bottom borders breaks
	Grid or frame printing
Print layout margins and titles	Printer type

formulas and values. When you are storing to other worksheet formats you can save formulas, but when you are saving to a database format you will want to save values. In Figure 7-12, the Tools Xtract Values command was issued and the file name was entered with the .DBF extension. The block of cells to be saved was then pointed out. When you have pressed ENTER to confirm the selection of cells, Quattro Pro 4 knows you are exporting data to dBASE because of the .DBF extension, and you get the opportunity to check the structure that Quattro Pro 4 has assigned to your data. You can see this from the specific format review menu displayed in Figure 7-13.

The first option on this menu, View Structure, shows the Field-name, Type, Width, and Decimals settings, as seen in Figure 7-14. Note that the field names have been altered to match the limits of field naming in dBASE. Every name has been capitalized and underlines are used in place of spaces. If a Quattro Pro 4 field name contains a punctuation character not acceptable to dBASE, the letter *A* is used instead. All unacceptable field names are thus replaced with the letters of the alphabet.

FIGURE
7-12

File Xtract to dBASE format

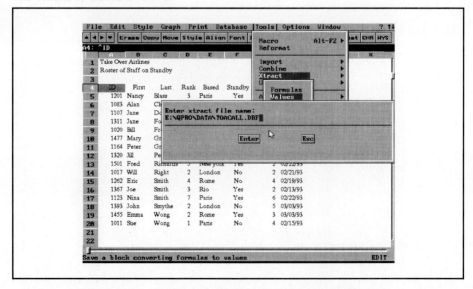

FIGURE
7-13

dBASE File Save menu

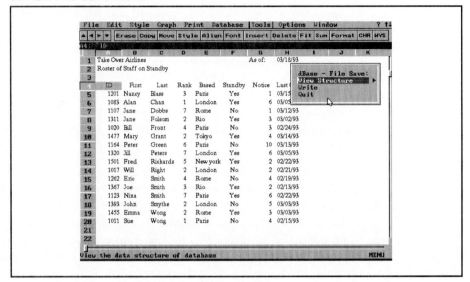

FIGURE
7-14

View Structure menu

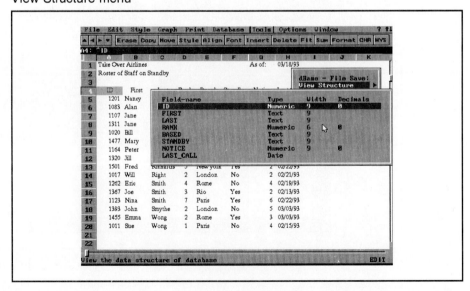

To alter settings for a particular field, you highlight the field and press ENTER. For example, you might want to change the Number field to a text field. A small menu appears from which you can select Name to change the name of the exported field, or Type to alter the type of the field. When you select Name you are prompted to edit the current name and enter the results. The Type option lists four possibilities for field types in dBASE: Text, Numeric, Logical, and Date, as shown in Figure 7-15. Note that the fifth type of data in dBASE, the Memo field, is not supported either when you are writing or reading from the .DBF format. If you pick Numeric, you are prompted for a decimal place setting. When the structure is acceptable, press ESC to return to the dBASE File Save menu, shown in Figure 7-13, and select Write. This creates the dBASE file on disk.

When you are performing extracts to another database format, such as Paradox or Reflex, a menu tailored to the structural requirements of that database is presented.

FIGURE 7-15

Changing the field type

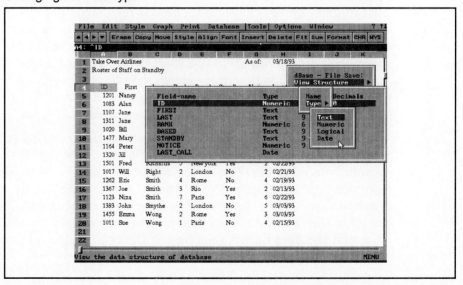

Autoload Files

You may find that your work with Quattro Pro 4 involves heavy use of one particular worksheet. You can have Quattro Pro 4 retrieve a file automatically whenever the program is loaded by means of the Options Startup command (described in the previous chapter). Autoload File is the second item on the Startup menu. When you select it, Quattro Pro 4 asks you to enter the name of the worksheet that you want to have loaded whenever you start the program. When you enter the file name, you will immediately see the file listed on the menu. However, you *must* use the Update option from the Options menu to record this change and have the autoload feature effective the next time the program is loaded.

The autoload feature is always active. Whenever you load Quattro Pro 4, it looks for the file name recorded from the Startup menu. The default name is QUATTRO.WQ1. If Quattro Pro 4 finds that file in the default directory when the program is loading, it retrieves the file. You can use the autoload feature either by changing the file name in the Startup menu, or you can save the file you want to autoload as QUATTRO.WQ1.

Extracting from Foreign Files

You can also read selected data from foreign database files by using the Database Query command. You will recall that the Database Query command requires three pieces of information: the Query Block, the Criteria Table, and the Output Block. The Query Block is the database, the collection of information you want to query. The Criteria Table is the set of conditions that determine which records are read from the database Quattro Pro 4. The Output Block is an area of a worksheet into which the selected records from the database are written.

In Figure 7-16 you can see a worksheet set up to extract records from a dBASE file. The dBASE file is called QSALES1.DBF and is stored in the current data directory. The Criteria Table in B22..B23 tells Quattro Pro 4 to look in the SALARY field of the QSALES1.DBF file for all salaries greater than 30000. Records with salaries greater than 30000 will be read into the Quattro Pro 4 worksheet below the field names in row 26. Note that the field names used in the Criteria Table and Output Block must match those in the .DBF file.

FIGURE
7-16

Data Query from a dBASE file

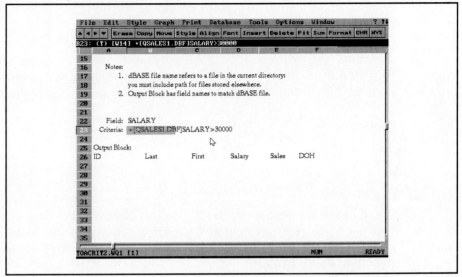

FIGURE
7-17

Results of querying a dBASE file

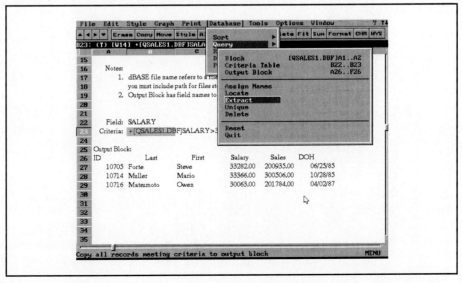

When you want to extract records from a file other than the current worksheet, you refer to the file by name in the Query Block setting. In this case the setting will be [QSALES1.DBF]A1..A2. The file name requires the full path if it is in a directory other than the current data directory. The cell reference of A1..A2 is used with any foreign format file to tell Quattro Pro 4 to begin at the top of that file when searching for records. The complete Database Query settings for this operation are

Query Block: [QSALES1.DBF]A1..A2

Criteria Table: B22..B23

Output Block: A26..F26

You can see the results of the Extract in Figure 7-17. Note that the link you have created here between Quattro Pro 4 and the .DBF file is not dynamic and the extracted records will not be updated automatically if the .DBF file is altered.

CHAPTER

Graphing

Quattro Pro 4 offers exceptional graphics features. You can design a graph that is automatically updated when you change the numbers in the underlying spreadsheet. You can quickly create graphs with just a few keystrokes by using the Fast Graph option. You can place graphs within spreadsheets and create charts using data from multiple worksheets. But that is only the beginning. Quattro Pro 4 also offers a wide range of graphing options to produce well-designed, professional-quality graphs. In this chapter you will learn how to generate graphs from your data and apply the graphing options to improve and enhance those graphs.

Because Quattro Pro 4 provides so many options for customizing your graphs, illustrating every possible combination is beyond the scope of this book. The main options will be described, however, with suggestions for their application to your specific graphing needs.

Fast Graphs

Quattro Pro 4 can automatically generate graphs from spreadsheet numbers. This provides a quick way to make a graph; you can enter with one command the main settings from which you can develop a variety of customized graphs.

Using the Fast Graph Feature

Consider the spreadsheet in Figure 8-1. This is a record of year-to-date sales by the three agents at the Van Ness office of Quattro Vadis Travel. To make a graph of this data will take only one command. However, before issuing the command, place the cell selector in the top-left corner of the set of data to be graphed. In the case of Figure 8-1, this is D3. With D3 selected you can simply press CTRL-G, the default Shortcut for the Fast Graph feature. Alternatively, you can select Graph from the main menu and then select Fast Graph. You can see the Graph menu in Figure 8-2.

When you issue the Fast Graph command, either as a Shortcut or as a menu command, you are prompted for a Fast Graph block. This is a block of cells that includes the numbers to be graphed. Do not include

Spreadsheet data to be graphed

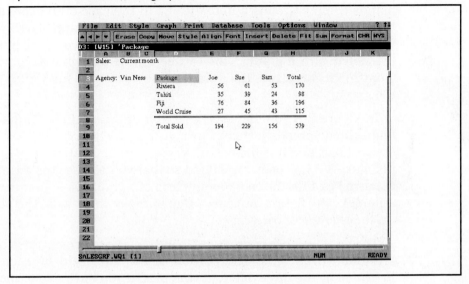

Graph menu

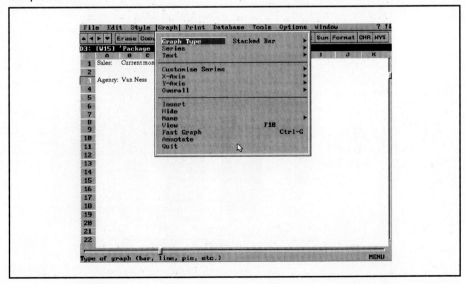

totals for rows or columns of numbers being graphed—the graph commands compute totals automatically. In the case of the spreadsheet in Figure 8-1, the correct cells to include in the Fast Graph block are D3..G7. When you press ENTER to confirm this block, you are immediately presented with a graph. This can be a little alarming at first, because Quattro Pro 4 replaces the worksheet screen with a full screen display of the graph.

In Figure 8-3 you can see the graph drawn by Fast Graph from the highlighted spreadsheet cells in Figure 8-1. This type of chart is called stacked bar, and it is the default graph type in Quattro Pro 4. The graph in Figure 8-3 has been annotated so that you can see the terms used by Quattro Pro 4 for the component parts of a graph. Note that the program automatically figures out how large to make the y-axis, the scale going up the left side of the graph.

The total number of products in each of the four categories of product are graphed as bars. The portion of the total sold by each agent is indicated by the three different shadings. If you have a color monitor you will see the agents differentiated by color as well. The legend box outside

FIGURE 8-3   Stacked bar graph drawn by Fast Graph

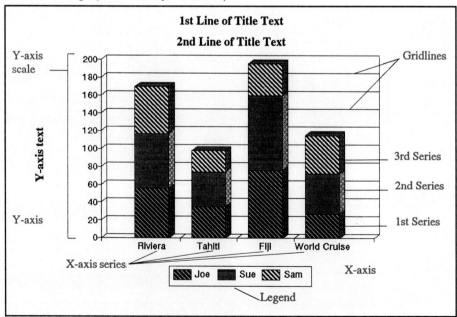

the main body of the graph explains which bar represents each agent. In Figure 8-3 and other figures in this chapter, the shading of the legend may not exactly match that of the main graph. This is due to the process used to reproduce the graph screen for purposes of illustration; the legend will be accurate in graphs printed and displayed by Quattro Pro 4.

To return to the spreadsheet you can press ESC or the SPACEBAR. In fact, most keys will take you from the graph view back to the worksheet, but typing / as you view a graph takes you to the *graph annotation screen*. To leave the graph annotation screen, which will be described in detail later, you type / again and then **Q** for Quit. You will be back at the graph view. You can use CTRL-BREAK to go from the annotation screen to the regular graph view and use it once again to go from the regular graph view to READY mode.

Working with a Graph

As you review this first graph, note that in graph terminology the numbers for each agent constitute a series. These are measured on the y-axis, which is sometimes called the *value axis*. Each category of product is listed across the x-axis, which is sometimes called the *category axis*. Each value in the cells E4..G7 is represented by a different bar segment, which is referred to as a *data point*. The box that explains the shading is called a *legend*. Quattro Pro 4 enables you to remove the legend if it is not required (for example, when only one series of data is defined). In fact, there are many changes and embellishments you can make to this basic graph, and they will be dealt with in the course of this chapter. Bear in mind, however, that making this first graph took just one command, and the results are very respectable. Furthermore, the graph you have made is dynamically linked to the data in the spreadsheet. For example, suppose that Sam actually sold 63 trips to Fiji rather than 36. You exit the graph view and change cell G6 from 36 to 63. To immediately see the difference in the graph you do not even need the menu; just press the Graph key (F10). This displays the current graph, which is the graph that the current settings generate. (Later you will see how Quattro Pro 4 stores a variety of graphs in one spreadsheet, but there is only one current graph.)

The graph of the corrected figures is shown in Figure 8-4. Notice how the y-axis has been altered to account for the increase in the size of the

FIGURE
8-4

Corrected stacked bar graph

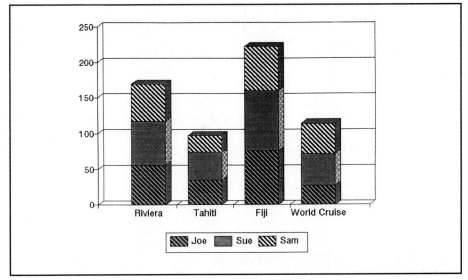

largest bar being graphed. If you have a printer that is capable of printing graphs you can easily print this graph. In READY mode, select Print from the main menu and then pick Graph Print. Select Destination and choose Graph Printer. Then select Go. Quattro Pro 4 should print out the graph, using the default values for size and layout. Graph printing can take several minutes, so do not be alarmed if your printer does not react for a little while.

Inserting a Graph

With Quattro Pro 4 you can insert the graph you have made into the spreadsheet that generated it. If you have either an EGA or a VGA display system, you can actually view the graph and worksheet together. On other display systems, you can insert graphs into worksheets in order to print them together on the same page, but you cannot view them together on the screen.

To insert a graph, select Insert from the Graph menu. You will be asked to specify a graph to be placed into the spreadsheet. Unless you have already defined other graphs, there will be only one graph in the list, the one that is current and appears when you press F10. This is listed as <Current Graph>. Highlight this and press ENTER. You will then be prompted for the location at which the graph is to be inserted. You might want to place the cell selector in a cell below the numbers that generate the graph. In fact, you can insert the graph over the numbers (or anywhere in the worksheet) without affecting them; in this case, cell B11 will work nicely. Anchor the block coordinates by typing a period, then press the RIGHT ARROW and DOWN ARROW keys to move the highlighting to paint out an area of suitable size for the graph, in this case through to cell H23. This is the area that the graph will occupy. Press ENTER to complete the Graph Insert command.

Unless you have an EGA or a VGA display system and are using the WYSIWYG mode, you will not see much of a result from this command. A section of the worksheet will simply be blocked out to show the area occupied by the graph. If you have an EGA/VGA system and you want to see the graph displayed in the spreadsheet, use the Options Display mode command to select WYSIWYG or click the WYS button. The graph will be drawn as the screen is rewritten. You can see the results in Figure 8-5. Note that B11 now displays Graph B11: <Current Graph> in the cell identifier. A similar notation appears in all the cells of the block that you

FIGURE 8-5

Graph displayed in spreadsheet (WYSIWYG mode)

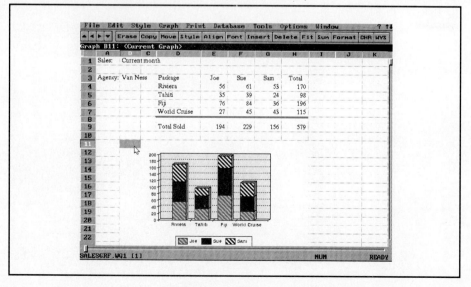

highlighted for the Graph Insert command. Data in any of these cells is not damaged, but it is obscured by the graph. In Figure 8-5 the worksheet gridlines have been turned on to show the area occupied by the graph (using Window Options Grid Lines Display).

When you insert a graph into a spreadsheet it is dynamically linked to the data in the spreadsheet. Any changes you make to the spreadsheet entries that generated the graph are reflected in the graph. For example, suppose that the name of the World Cruise is changed to Mega-Cruise and that Joe realizes his Tahiti figure should be 53. Making these changes in the worksheet updates the graph, as you can see in Figure 8-6.

Working with Inserted Graphs

Displaying a graph in WYSIWYG mode can be quite a test of your computer's processing ability. Quattro Pro 4's response time slows down considerably when you are working in WYSIWYG mode on a spreadsheet that contains an inserted graph. Movement of the cell selector and cell editing will be slower because of the constant need to redraw the graph. You will probably want to insert graphs toward the end of the design

FIGURE 8-6   Updated graph in spreadsheet (WYSIWYG mode)

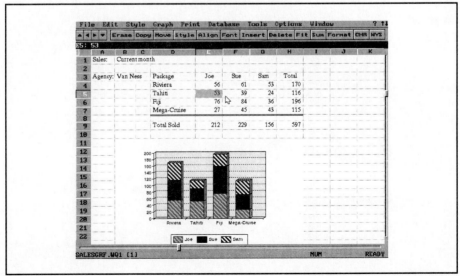

process and switch to character mode when you need to make a lot of changes to a worksheet that contains inserted graphs. To switch to character mode, click the CHR button or use the Options Display Mode command to select a character mode, such as 80x25.

Note that you can insert more than one graph in the same worksheet. Later in this chapter the procedure for naming graphs will be reviewed. When you have named a graph you can insert the named graph as well as the current graph, and the graphs will all be updated to reflect changes in the worksheet.

To remove a graph that you have inserted in your worksheet you use the Graph Hide command. This shows a list of all the inserted graphs from which you select the one you want to remove. Highlight the graph name and press ENTER, and the graph will be removed. The graph will still be available for display.

To print a worksheet together with a graph you use the Spreadsheet Print command from the Print menu, but you set the Print Destination to Graphics Printer. You must include the graph cells (B11..H23) in the Print Block. An example of the combined output is shown in Figure 8-7. Obviously, the results of the combined print operation will depend on your printer and its capabilities; indeed, the graph-making side of spreadsheet work depends heavily on your choice of equipment. The next section reviews some of the hardware considerations in making graphs.

Graphics Equipment

Displaying and printing graphs imposes more demands on your hardware than printing spreadsheet text. As was discussed in Chapter 6, there are two different ways of displaying and printing information: character mode and graphics mode. The type of display adapter and printer that you have will affect your ability to produce graphs with Quattro Pro 4.

Graphics Display

In the character mode of display, each screen you view is made up of many separate characters typically arranged in 25 lines of 80 characters

FIGURE
8-7

Combined spreadsheet and graph output

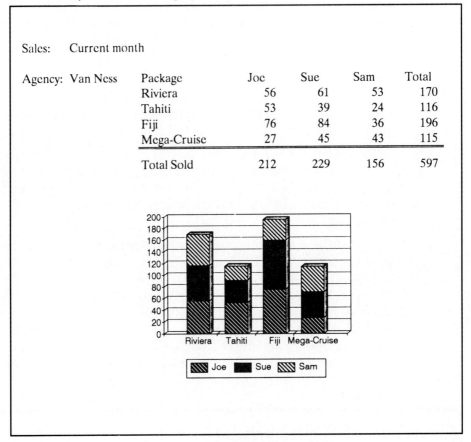

Sales: Current month

Agency: Van Ness

Package	Joe	Sue	Sam	Total
Riviera	56	61	53	170
Tahiti	53	39	24	116
Fiji	76	84	36	196
Mega-Cruise	27	45	43	115
Total Sold	212	229	156	597

each. The alternative is a graphics mode referred to in Quattro Pro 4 as WYSIWYG mode, where the screen is composed of a series of dots that draw shapes, including numbers, text, circles, and so on. This is the mode shown in most of the screens in this book. Quattro Pro 4 can switch between different modes of display. This means that typical spreadsheet operations such as data entry and calculation can take place in the faster environment of character mode. However, when you want to design a high-quality report or a graph, Quattro Pro 4 can switch to graphics or WYSIWYG mode, shown in Figure 8-6.

If you have an IBM Color Graphics Adapter, a Hercules graphics card, an IBM Enhanced Graphics Adapter, or a VGA system, you will be able to display Quattro Pro 4 graphs on your screen when you press the F10 key and use the Annotate feature to embellish graphs. If your system does not support graphics displays, you can still create a Quattro Pro 4 graph; however, you will not be able to see the results until they are printed.

In addition, if you have a VGA display you can use the WYSIWYG mode to display additional columns and rows in the work space, as well as graphs that have been inserted within worksheets using the Graph Insert command. The WYSIWYG mode enables you to increase or decrease the number of spreadsheet columns and rows so that you can zoom in for greater detail or zoom out to see the bigger picture. The command for this is Options WYSIWYG Zoom%. Note that users of monochrome, Hercules, and CGA systems cannot view inserted graphs or use WYSIWYG mode.

Graphics Printing

To print a Quattro Pro 4 graph, you need a graphics *output device*; that is, a printer or plotter capable of reproducing graphics images. Most dot matrix, laser, ink-jet, and thermal printers can produce graphs; however, daisy-wheel printers cannot produce Quattro Pro 4 graphs. Quattro Pro 4 graphs can be reproduced in color with a color printer or plotter. You initially tell Quattro Pro 4 about your graphics output device through the installation program. If you did not specify a printer then or you need to change printers, use the Hardware command on the Options menu, as discussed in Chapter 6. When you select Printers from the Hardware menu you will see that Quattro Pro 4 enables you to define two printers, 1st Printer and 2nd Printer. You define one of these two printers as the default; this is the one that is used when you issue a print command from the Print menu.

There are two ways of printing graphs with Quattro Pro 4. You can send just the graph to the printer, or you can insert the graph in a spreadsheet Print Block and print the graph as part of the spreadsheet. As you saw from the Graph menu in Figure 8-2, there is no Print option.

In Quattro Pro 4 you print graphs from the Print menu shown in Figure 8-8. As you can see, the Print menu has a Destination option. However, this affects only the direction of spreadsheet output sent to the printer with the Spreadsheet Print command, not the printing of graphs. The Graph Print command has its own Destination option, as shown in Figure 8-8.

The three options on the Graph Print Destination menu are File, Graph Printer, and Screen Preview. Graph Printer is the default selection; this is the option to use when you are sending a graph to the printer on its own, as opposed to being part of a combined spreadsheet/graph print job.

To clarify the printing procedure, consider the following example. Suppose that your printer is one of the HP LaserJet series. This printer is capable of printing text and graphics. Using the Options Hardware menu, you have chosen the correct model in the LaserJet series as 1st Printer and made sure that 1st Printer is the Default Printer. You have used Fast Graph to create a graph. You have made sure that the numbers are correct. You pressed F9 in READY mode to make sure that the spreadsheet is calculated up to date. You have pressed F10 to view the graph. The graph looks good and you want to print it. Back in READY mode, you select Print from the main menu, then Graph Print. You make

The Destination option

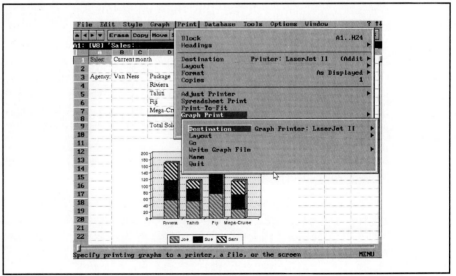

sure that Graph Printer is chosen as the Destination. You check that the Layout settings are correct. You then pick Go. Quattro Pro 4 sends the graph to the Default Printer—your 1st Printer, which Quattro Pro 4 knows is a LaserJet.

Now suppose that the graph came out nicely and you want to print a quick draft of the spreadsheet that generated the graph. You pick Print from the main menu and define the Block. You check that the Destination setting on the Print menu is Printer. You check the Layout settings and then pick Spreadsheet Print. Now suppose that you decide you would like a presentation-quality print of the same area of the spreadsheet. You select Destination from the Print menu, change it to Graphics Printer, and then select Spreadsheet Print.

Suppose that you decide to insert the graph in the spreadsheet as described earlier. You complete the Graph Insert command. You use the Print Block command to select an area of cells in the spreadsheet that includes the inserted graph. You make sure that the Print Destination setting is Graphics Printer, and select Spreadsheet Print. Both the spreadsheet cells and the inserted graph are printed on the same page. Details of the other graph printing commands, Layout and Write Graph File, are described in the section on "Finer Points of Graph Printing" later in this chapter.

Manual Graph Commands

Although the Fast Graph feature is a powerful one, you will probably want to learn more about the different commands that you can use to create a graph. This will enable you to use the commands to create graphs from scratch and also to customize graphs that you have started with the Fast Graph feature.

To demonstrate how you use Quattro Pro 4 to build a graph from scratch, a typical scenario is presented here. As the manager of Take Over Airlines you are called on by the owner to review the year's performance. Immediately, you turn to the worksheet in which you have been accumulating the passenger volume figures in each of these three classes: First, Business, and Coach. This worksheet is shown in Figure

8-9. The number of passengers in each class in each of the four quarters can be easily transformed into a graph.

An example of what the numbers might look like as a graph is shown in Figure 8-10. In the following sections you will find the basic elements of building graphs described in the order in which they arise in the building process. As you have already seen in the section on Fast Graph, Quattro Pro 4 requires very little information to build a very presentable graph. However, because most elements of a graph can be customized to enhance the graph's appearance and accommodate unusual types of data, many of the menus you will use contain several options. Not all of these options will be examined as the graph is built, but they will be presented later.

Preparing to Graph

The basic procedure for creating a graph with Quattro Pro 4 is to indicate the spreadsheet coordinates of the data to be graphed. Usually this data is readily available in your spreadsheet, as in the case of the sales statistics shown earlier in Figure 8-1, or the passenger statistics shown in Figure 8-9. In both cases, the numbers are in consecutive columns that form a block. In fact, Quattro Pro 4 requires that each set of values for your graph be in consecutive cells in the worksheet. Occasionally, prior to building a graph, you will need to rearrange data to comply with this requirement. You can use either the Edit Copy or Edit Move command to accomplish this, or you can develop a new spreadsheet that references the cells from the main model in a compact block suitable

FIGURE
8-9

Passenger volume by class as spreadsheet

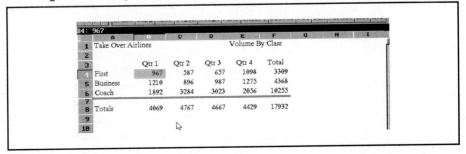

FIGURE
8-10

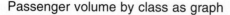

Passenger volume by class as graph

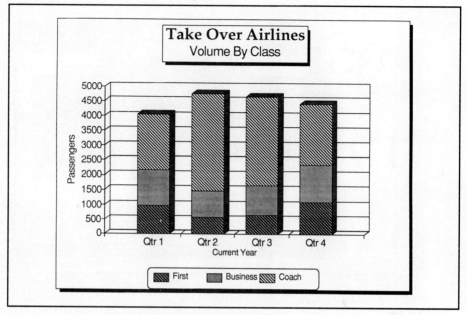

for graphing. In most cases, however, you will probably be graphing data that is already arranged in suitable blocks of cells.

Although the position of your cell selector before you display the Graph menu is not critical, you should place it near the data that is to be graphed, in this case, in cell B3 or B4. To build a graph from the spreadsheet in Figure 8-9, you first select Graph from the main menu. The Graph menu, shown earlier in Figure 8-2, shows you the main options involved in graphing. The first option, Graph Type, refers to the kind of graph that you want Quattro Pro 4 to produce. The default type is the stacked bar shown in all of the graphs so far in this chapter. When you select Graph Type, you will see a list of the available types. If you are using the graphics display mode, the list of types will appear as a diagram illustrating the different possibilities with the current selection shown highlighted. In Figure 8-11 you can see the Graph Type diagram with stacked bar selected. Whichever type of list you are using, use the arrow keys to move the highlighting to the graph type you want and press ENTER to select it.

The Graph Type option in WYSIWYG mode

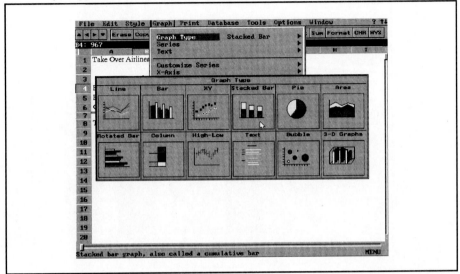

You do not have to make your final selection of graph type before creating the graph; the type can be changed later. Unless you have a specific type of graph in mind, leave the setting at the default stacked bar. Next, you need to tell Quattro Pro 4 the various pieces of information it needs to build the graph. Refer to Figure 8-3 for some of the basic terminology used.

Series Values

The numbers you are charting in the graph are called the *series values*. The series values must be values; they *cannot* be labels. You can graph as many as six sets of values at once. In this example, the three series values to be graphed are the volume figures for First, Business, and Coach class. When you select Series from the Graph menu, the Series menu lists 1st Series, 2nd Series, and so on. There is also a command on this menu to specify the x-axis cells; that is, the numbers or labels displayed along the x-axis to identify the different series. The Group option is used to specify more than one set of values at a time, as described in the next section.

When you select 1st Series, you are prompted to enter the cell coordinates of the first set of values. You can highlight, or paint, the cells as you do with other blocks of cells in Quattro Pro 4. First move the cell selector to make sure it is on the first value in the series; in the example in Figure 8-9 this is cell B4. Then enter a period to anchor the beginning coordinate. The screen will respond with B4..B4. Now you can select 2nd Series and use the cursor-movement keys to move to the second coordinate and highlight the column or row of values. Because values for a series must all be in consecutive cells, the END key may work well to highlight the cells you want. However, you do not need to include the total for the column or row that is being specified as a series, because Quattro Pro 4 will calculate the total of the values in the block for you. Thus, the example uses B4..E4 as the 1st Series.

Of course, if you know the cell coordinates, you can just type them, instead of pointing to the cells. When you press ENTER to confirm the coordinates, you are returned to the Series menu where you can indicate the next series. After you have entered all three of the series values, press ESC to return to the Graph menu. Note that the menu shows the settings for the series as you establish them, as shown in Figure 8-12. If you need to change the spreadsheet coordinates of the series values, you select Series and pick the number of the series you want to check. You will see the currently recorded block of cells highlighted. Press ENTER to confirm this block, or press ESC or BACKSPACE to unlock the coordinates and redefine them. If you want to remove a series, you must use the Reset option, which is described later in this chapter.

Reading and Grouping Series Values

You may wonder why it is necessary to use the Series command when the Fast Graph command reads all of the series for you, including the x-axis. Unfortunately, the Fast Graph command does not know that it

The Series option

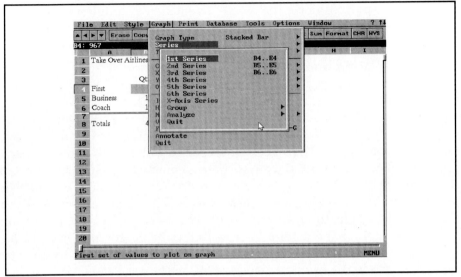

should avoid empty cells in a block. For example, Fast Graph applied to the worksheet in Figure 8-13 would produce the graph shown in Figure 8-14. You can see that there are gaps between the data points in each series, leading to greater separation between the bars.

Another aspect of the Fast Graph command that is not immediately apparent is the way it interprets the block of data to be graphed. The series values in a block can either be read column-wise or row-wise. In the first example in this chapter the three agents, Joe, Sam, and Sue, were read as the series, and the four different packages they sold were read as the x-axis. That is, the data was interpreted column-wise because the series was read from the columns. However, you might have wanted the agents to be the x-axis and the packages the series. You can see a manually constructed graph of the same data in Figure 8-15, where Quattro Pro 4 has taken the series from the rows rather than the columns.

FIGURE
8-13

Spreadsheet with gaps

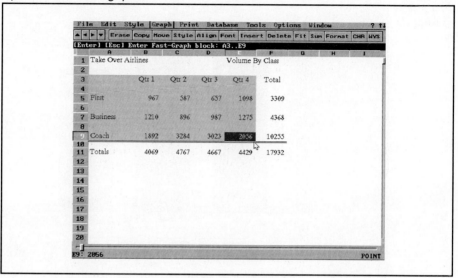

FIGURE
8-14

Fast Graph applied to the worksheet in Figure 8-13

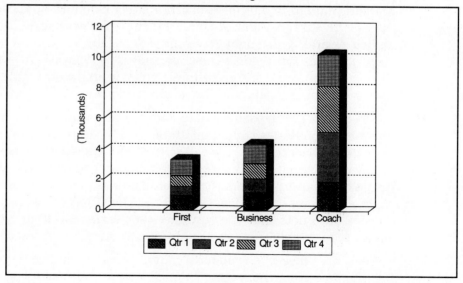

FIGURE
8-15

A row-wise reading of data

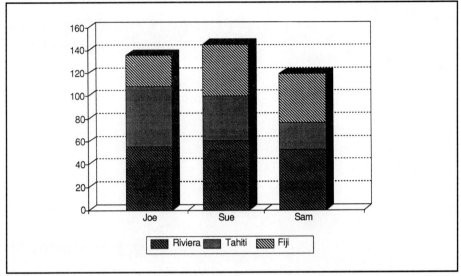

The individual selection of series is also a necessity when you are graphing data from multiple worksheets. For example, suppose that the data for the graph was not combined into one worksheet, but spread across several. You might have three separate worksheets, each one storing figures for a single class, as shown in Figure 8-16. In a fourth worksheet you could graph the total figures from the other three without having to copy the data into the fourth worksheet.

To create a graph that refers to data in other worksheets, you simply use the Graph Series command and for each series move to the appropriate worksheet to make the cell selection for the series values. Clearly, you need to specify each series separately so you cannot use the Fast Graph command. Note that the current graph is the one that is displayed when F10 is pressed. In Figure 8-16 the TOAGRAF1.WQ1 worksheet is current. Also note that you can have the x-axis read from a column of values even though the series values are in rows.

There are times when you have your data series arranged conveniently but separate from the x-axis. In such cases, you can speed up series entry by choosing the Series Group option. When you choose this option you have a choice between Columns and Rows, as shown in Figure 8-17.

FIGURE 8-16

Three spreadsheets compiled by class

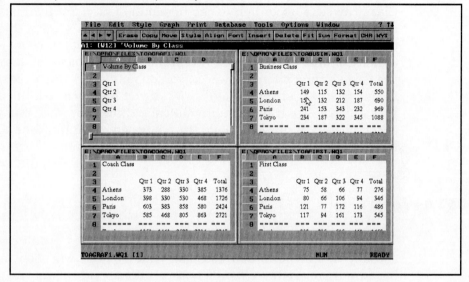

FIGURE 8-17

The Group option

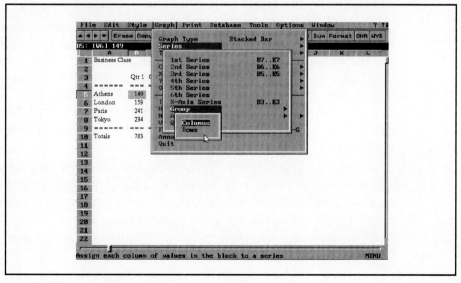

This worksheet contains quarterly passenger numbers for Business Class travelers according to the destination city. You can assign each column of values in the block to a series, or each row. In this case, to create a quarterly graph you would use the Rows option. When you select either Columns or Rows you are prompted for a block of data (as with the Fast Graph option). However, you do not include the x-axis or labels in this block—just series values. When you have selected the block you press ENTER. No graph is automatically drawn for you, but you have accomplished in one command the equivalent of setting four series, one for each city. All you need do now to get a basic graph is to set the x-axis.

X-Axis

As soon as you have provided at least one series of values, you can actually view the graph. In this case, Quattro Pro 4 will show three bars, because there are three parallel observations made about each series of data. However, until you specify the x-axis values to be displayed along the bottom of the graph, Quattro Pro 4 cannot tell you what these bars represent. The x-axis values can be numeric values or labels and should be entered before viewing the graph. This enables Quattro Pro 4 to identify the observation points along the x-axis. In the case of the statistics shown in Figure 8-9, the x-axis values are Qtr 1, Qtr 2, and so on.

To define the x-axis you select Series from the Graph menu and then select X-Axis Series, which is one of the last options on the menu. You are prompted to enter the values as coordinates. You highlight the cells containing the x-axis data (cells B3 through E3 in this case) or type the coordinates, just as you did with the 1st Series command. When you press ENTER to confirm the x-axis coordinates, you are returned to the Graph menu. The coordinates are shown on the menu for reference purposes.

You can have from 1 to 8192 separate data points on the x-axis, if they are stored in a column; or from 1 to 256, if they are stored in a row. However, you will encounter limitations of display space, which may make more than 30 data points difficult to see. In such cases, you do not need to enter any x-axis coordinates. Quattro Pro 4 will simply show a check mark for each set of data.

Viewing the Graph

To produce a basic graph, all Quattro Pro 4 needs is at least one series of values. A set of x-axis values helps only to clarify the chart. The Graph menu contains the View option. When you select View, your screen switches to graphics mode and displays the latest version of the graph you are working on. You cannot change the figures represented in the graph while you are viewing it. After you have viewed a graph, press ENTER or ESC or SPACEBAR to return to the menu you left. In Figure 8-18 you can see a graph based on the settings in Figure 8-12 plus a set of x-axis values.

Although this graph still needs a title to describe what the bars represent, it is important to see how much work has been done so far. Quattro Pro 4 has totaled the figures for each quarter and represented the total as a large bar. It has proportionately divided the bar according

FIGURE 8-18

Quarter volume graph

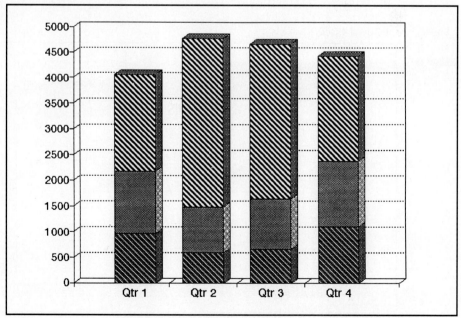

to each class of traveler. The scale on the left has been selected to accommodate the largest quarterly volume total. The x-axis values—in this case, the labels Qtr 1, Qtr 2, and so on—are shown along the bottom. At this point the graph lacks a legend. When you are constructing a graph manually, any legend text that you want displayed has to be entered one series at a time. You may also want to enter text for titles and to describe the x- and y-axes.

Adding Text

As you can see from Figure 8-19, there are several areas of the graph to which you can add text. These were diagrammed in Figure 8-3. These pieces of text are fixed to specific points of the graph and should not be confused with the free-floating text that can be added with the Annotate feature, which is described toward the end of this chapter.

FIGURE
8-19

The text option

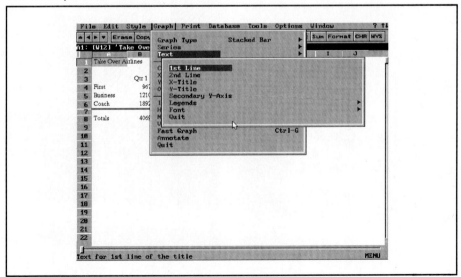

Text Sources

All of the text added to a Quattro Pro 4 graph can be supplied by worksheet cells. This capability was used by the Fast Graph feature to label the first graph. Using a cell reference for text, rather than simply typing the text, has the advantage of being easy to update. As you saw in Figure 8-6, altering the name from World Cruise to Mega-Cruise automatically updated the graph.

To manually enter text for the graph you select the appropriate item on the Text menu and then type the text you want displayed in the graph, or you can type the coordinates of the cell containing the label you want used as text in the graph, preceded by a backslash (\). Thus, to supply the title Take Over Airlines as the 1st Line of the graph title, you would enter **\A1**. Note that there is no facility for pointing to cells to enter their coordinates in the Text menu. Furthermore, the cell references are not dynamic. If you move the label from A1 to B1, Quattro Pro 4 will not know, and the label will essentially disappear from the graph.

Title Text

Most graphs need a title. To supply one you first select Text from the Graph menu. The item called 1st Line is the one that heads the graph. Select 1st Line from the Text menu and type the text you want, such as **Take Over Airlines**, in the box provided, as shown in Figure 8-20. Alternatively, because this same text has been entered as a label in worksheet cell A1, you can type **\A1**. The title can be 39 characters long. You can use BACKSPACE to correct any errors as you type. If you want to edit the title, the LEFT ARROW and RIGHT ARROW keys move the cursor through the text of the title. You can insert new characters to the left of the cursor just by typing them. Pressing ESC while you are typing a title removes the text you have entered. Pressing ESC with nothing on the title edit line returns you to the Text menu. When you have typed the title correctly, press ENTER to confirm it. Quattro Pro 4 returns you to the Text menu, where all or part of the text of the title is visible. This helps you to keep track of text you have entered. Note that when you use a cell reference for text, the cell reference and not the text itself is visible on the Text menu.

FIGURE
8-20

The 1st Line option

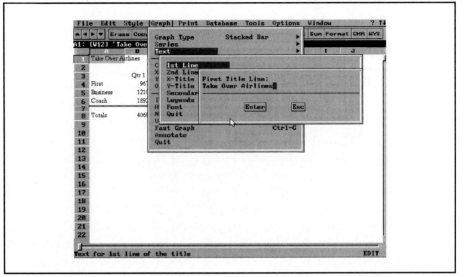

You can add a 2nd Line title, such as Volume by Class, or type **\E1** to use the text from the worksheet. Text to label the x-axis is called the X-Title. In the case of the graph in Figure 8-18 this could be Current Year. The Y-Title labels the y-axis, and the graph in Figure 8-18 should include text that explains what units of measurement are displayed, in this case Passengers. Although the x-axis title may sometimes be omitted, a y-axis title is often essential to properly document the graph. Note that if you use a second y-axis, as described later in this chapter, you can label it with the Secondary Y-Axis option.

Each of these pieces of text has a maximum length of 39 characters. You can see the graph from Figure 8-18 labeled in Figure 8-21. Note that this figure was produced by using a screen print program, not the Graph Print option on the Print menu. Because the clarity and dimensions of displayed graphs vary according to display types, this graph may not be an exact replication of what you will see on your screen. Also note that the style of lettering used is the default—the font options for your lettering may be different.

FIGURE
8-21

Labeled graph

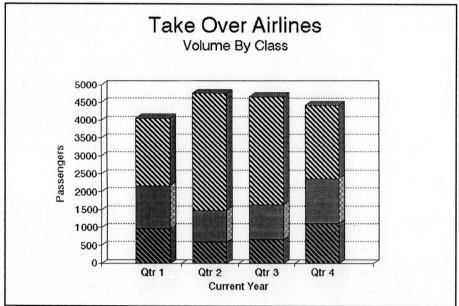

The Legend

The one element still lacking in the graph in Figure 8-21 is an explanation of what the different data values represent. You cannot tell from the graph which shading represents which class. The key to a graph is its legend, which you set through the Text Legends option. The legend text for each series consists of either manually entered text or a reference to a cell where the text can be found. When you select Legends from the Text menu you will be shown a list of six series, one for each of the maximum six sets of values. You enter text here as you do with the other text items. To label the first series, the First Class passengers, you pick 1st Series and either type the text **First Class** or use the cell reference **\A4**. Remember that the first series appears at the bottom of a stacked bar graph.

The Text Legends menu includes the Position option, which enables you to decide whether to display the legend at the Bottom of the graph, to the Right of it, or not at all. The default setting is at the Bottom, so that as soon as you enter some legend text a legend will be displayed below the actual graph. You select None from the Position menu to turn off the legend display without erasing the text that you have entered in the legend series. By switching between None and one of the other two choices for Position, you can turn the legend on and off. Note that the Annotate feature, described later in this chapter, gives you complete freedom to place the legend wherever you like on the graph.

The maximum number of characters you can enter as the legend text for a series is 19. The number of characters of legend text displayed by the graph will vary according to the dimensions and proportions of the graph. Tall, narrow graphs can accommodate only nine or ten characters in the legend, while wide graphs can show the full 19. After typing the legend text and pressing ENTER, you can proceed to the other series and name them accordingly. After setting up the legends, you can view the results by pressing the F10 key. The resulting graph will look like the one pictured in Figure 8-22.

FIGURE 8-22

Graph titles and legend (in bottom location)

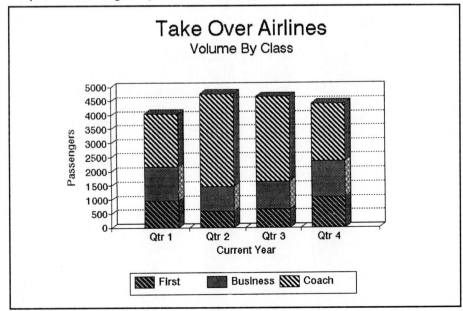

Fonts

You may notice that the text of your titles is displayed in a different typeface, or font, from that seen in Figure 8-22. There are many different fonts available for graphing, including all of those available for enhanced spreadsheet printing (described in Chapter 3). You can adjust the font settings for each piece of text in the chart by using the Font option on the Text menu. When you select Font from the Text menu you see these choices:

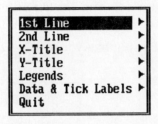

Text in each of these areas of the graph can be individually adjusted to achieve the best visual effect. All of the options are the same as in the Text menu, except for Data & Tick Labels. These are the numbers that Quattro Pro 4 adds to the y-axis to document the scale of the graph as well as the x-axis labels.

When you select any of the options on the Font menu you are shown a menu of four characteristics that can be adjusted to alter the displayed and printed appearance of your graph, as follows:

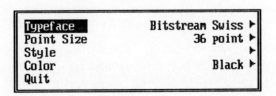

Note that selecting the Color option, which leads to a list of colors that can be assigned to the text, does not affect the printed version of your graph unless you have a color printer.

The Typeface option on the font characteristics menu leads to a list of available typefaces, with the current selection already highlighted. The list includes the Bitstream fonts, plus the Hershey fonts. In addition, there may be typefaces for specific printers such as those available to LaserJet series printer users. To see the full range of typefaces, scroll down the list. To assign a typeface you highlight your choice and press ENTER. To leave the list without altering the current typeface setting you press ESC.

When you have chosen a typeface you will also want to assign a point size. The Point Size option leads to a list that goes from 8 point to 72 point. To give you an idea of the relative size of these measurements, take a look at Figure 8-22. The 1st Line title is in 36 point and the 2nd Line is in 24 point. The x-axis title is in 18 point.

The Style option enables you to select from the following list of font styles:

```
┌─────────────────┐
│ Bold            │
│ Italic          │
│ Underlined      │
│ Drop Shadow     │
│ Reset           │
│ Quit            │
└─────────────────┘
```

Some items may have the word "On" next to them, indicating that the style has been chosen for the current piece of text. You can turn on one or more of the items by highlighting and pressing ENTER, or by typing the first letter.

The Bold and Italic options are useful for adding emphasis to a piece of text. The Underline option causes the text to be displayed with a line below it. The Drop Shadow option places a shadow behind letters to highlight them. The Reset option enables you to turn off all of the attributes.

You can see the effects of font choices while you are still in the menu structure just by pressing F10. Although it may take you a while to get used to the effect of different sizes on the text of your graph, you will find that an appropriate choice of font will enhance your graph's appearance and effectiveness.

Graph Keys

When you have designed a graph and returned to READY mode, any changes you make to the cells that make up the x-axis values or the series values will be reflected in the graph and visible the next time you view it. You can try this now by leaving the Graph menu, either with ESC or the Quit option, and typing a new number, 833, for First Class passengers in the third quarter. To see the change that this new number has made to the graph, you can either choose View from the Graph menu or from READY mode press the Graph key (F10), which displays the current graph. You can have only one graph at a time in memory, and this graph is referred to as the current graph. The next key you press will return you to the Graph menu if you used the Graph View command or to READY mode if you viewed the graph from READY mode with F10.

The F10 key works either in READY mode or MENU mode, whether or not you are using the Graph menu. Bear in mind that when you have no graphs defined in a worksheet, pressing F10 will cause Quattro Pro 4 to display a blank screen with the message "No series selected." The one exception to this is if you select Text as the Graph type. In this case you get a blank graph screen on which to place text with the Annotate feature.

There is one special key to use while you are viewing a graph: the / key. This activates Quattro Pro 4's Annotate feature, which is a complete drawing program built into the Graph feature. With this feature, described later in the chapter, you can enhance your graphs with a virtually unlimited range of images. You can even use Annotate to create pictures that are not graphs but shapes and symbols, like the ones in Figure 8-23, that can be printed from Quattro Pro 4 or inserted into spreadsheets. However, before exploring these exciting possibilities it is important to learn the mundane but vital commands needed to save and organize your work with graphs.

Pictures created by using Annotate

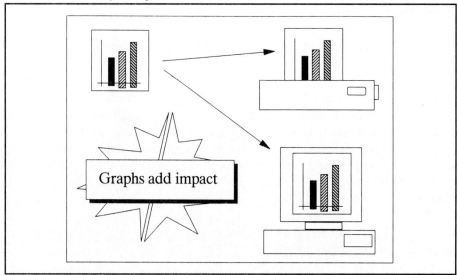

Naming and Storing Graphs

Having viewed your graph and decided that it is acceptable, you might be tempted to rush to print the graph. But before proceeding, you should take a moment to save your work. So far, none of your graphing work has been stored by Quattro Pro 4. The settings for the x- and y-axes, your titles, the choice of font, and so forth are still only in memory. You must issue the File Save or File Save As command to save the worksheet and the graph settings.

Storing Graph Names

If you design a graph and then store your worksheet, you will be able to see the graph the next time you retrieve the file simply by pressing F10 or by using the Graph View command. Having built one graph, however, you may wish to go on to create another. Because Quattro Pro 4 can have only one graph in memory at a time, changing the graph settings at this point would alter the graph you just designed. To store the collection of settings that together produce the graph you have just viewed so that you can recall them later, you assign a name to the graph, much the same as you do when naming a block of cells. Select Name from the Graph menu and you will see the seven options: Display, Create, Autosave Edits, Erase, Reset, Slide, and Graph Copy.

Select Create to see a list of any previously stored graphs. Whether or not there are any previously stored graphs, you will be prompted with "Enter graph name:". You can highlight one of the existing names and press ENTER to replace that graph with the current one, or you can simply type a new name and press ENTER. Here you can see that a couple of graphs have already been named:

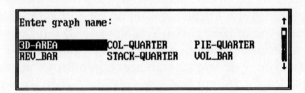

When you enter a name, you are returned to the Graph menu. If you want to see a previously named graph, select Name again, and then select Display. Finally, select a name from the list. You can remove names from the list with Erase or completely remove all graph names with Reset. The Reset command requires that you answer Yes or No to the question "Delete all named graphs?", because the command is a destructive one, wiping out all named graph settings.

The Graph Name Create command attaches a name to whatever graph is current. If you display a graph called BAR with the Name Display command and then make changes to it, you must be careful if you want to keep the changes. If you use Name Create and select BAR, Quattro Pro 4 updates the BAR graph to reflect the changes. But you must do this before you display another graph or the changes will be lost. Alternatively, you can set the Autosave Edits option to Yes. This will ensure that changes made to a named graph are stored under that name.

An exciting option on the Graph Name menu is Slide. Using this option you can create a *slide show* with Quattro Pro 4. This consists of a series of graphs displayed one after the other. See the section "Slide Shows" in Chapter 13 for more on this command.

The last option of the Graph Name menu is Graph Copy, a powerful tool for users who need to create a lot of graphs. With Graph Copy you can paste a graph from one spreadsheet into another. Linking cell references are automatically created for you. You can use the graph as is or edit it. This enables you to transfer a whole range of graph settings from one set of data in one spreadsheet to a completely different set of data in another.

Suppose you are working on a spreadsheet to predict revenue for the next year for Take Over Airlines. You want to use this revenue spreadsheet as the basis for a presentation to the board of directors. You know that in the spreadsheet containing last year's volume figures there was a super graph of volume by class of passenger. You want to use that volume graph in the revenue projection spreadsheet but do not want to import all of the figures. You can use Graph Copy to paste the graph into the revenue projection spreadsheet, just as you would a block of cells. First you open the spreadsheet containing the graph you want to use, in this case, the volume spreadsheet. Then you issue the Graph Copy command and select from the list of named graphs that is displayed. When you have entered the name of the graph you want to copy you are asked to indicate the target spreadsheet—the one into which the chosen graph will be pasted. In this case, you indicate the revenue projection spreadsheet. Simply select the spreadsheet, either with SHIFT-F6 or the Window Pick command, then press ENTER to complete the Graph Copy command. The graph is now a named graph in the revenue projection spreadsheet.

You must move to the target spreadsheet and issue the Graph Name command to actually see the graph. Select Display and you will see the copied graph named in the list. Select the graph to show it, and make it the current graph. You can keep the graph as is or change the settings. For example, if you like the style of the graph, you can change the data series to cells within the current spreadsheet and then give the new graph a different name. This enables you to copy the style of graphs from one worksheet to another. Note that unless you edit the copied graph it will continue to draw its data from the source worksheet. This means that when you load the worksheet containing the copied graph you will get the chance to select one of the Link options (Load Supporting, Update Refs, or None). Choose either Load Supporting to open the file that supplies the data for the copied graph or Update Refs to read the correct current values for the linked graph. If you choose None, the supporting links will be temporarily disabled.

Remember, even though you have assigned a name to a graph you still must save the worksheet file to store the graph names on disk. Also bear in mind that placing graphs in worksheets with the Graph Insert command has a bearing on graph changes. In effect, a graph inserted in the worksheet becomes the current graph if you enter the Graph menu while your cell selector is within the inserted graph. For example, if you have inserted the graph called BAR in A21..H30, you will see Graph A21:BAR and similar notations in all of those cells. If you press F10 or select a command from the Graph menu while your cell selector is in one of these cells, then BAR will become the current graph. However, if you return to the READY mode and move your cell selector to a nongraph cell, the previous current graph will be reinstated.

Storing Graph Files

There may be times when you want to store a graph as a *picture file,* which contains the necessary data for other programs to read the graph as an image and display it, edit it, or print it. To save a graph in this type of file, you print it to a file with the Graph Print option on the Print menu. You then use the Write Graph File option, which is described in the next section.

Finer Points of Graph Printing

When you have stored the worksheet containing the current graph settings, you can proceed to print the graph. You do not have to store before printing, but it is advisable. The Graph Print option on the Print menu prints out the latest version of the current graph if the Destination setting is Graph Printer. You should press F10 once more before printing to make sure that the graph you are about to print is the correct one.

Telling Quattro Pro 4 About Printers

When you select Graph Print from the Print menu you will see a menu listing the following: Destination, Layout, Go, Write Graph File, Name, and Quit. The Destination is normally set to Graph Printer and the name of the printer model will be shown, as you can see in Figure 8-24. The Layout option leads to a submenu of settings that describe how you want the graph sized and placed on the page. The Go option actually initiates the printing process. The Write Graph File option is for creating files from graphic output.

Destination

When you select Destination from the Print menu, you can choose to send the graphic output to one of three places: File, Graph Printer, or Screen Preview. The last option, Screen Preview, shows you what the graph will look like when printed, including the dimensions and place-

FIGURE 8-24

Graph Print Destination

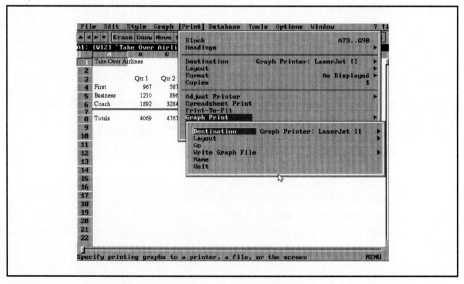

ment on the page. The preview system for graphs works in the same way as that for spreadsheets (described in Chapter 3).

If you want to store a Quattro Pro 4 graph as a text file that can be printed later or used by another program, select File as the destination of the print operation. Quattro Pro 4 prompts you to enter a file name of up to eight letters for the graph. When you enter the file name, Quattro Pro 4 sets the destination to which a .PRN file containing a data image of the current graph would be written. To create this graph, execute the Graph Print Go command. An alternative file format for storing graphic images is the .EPS type, which you can create by using the Write Graph File option on the Graph Print menu.

Write Graph File

To store your graph in a special file that can be read by other programs, you select Write Graph File from the Graph Print menu. The options are EPS File, PIC File, Slide EPS, and PCX File. The .EPS format is Encapsulated PostScript. This can be read by a number of other programs, and can be printed on a printer that understands the PostScript page description language, such as the Apple LaserWriter. For example, when you are using the TOPS network to connect IBM PCs to Apple Macintoshes and LaserWriters you can use the TOPS commands to send your .EPS file to a LaserWriter on the network. The .EPS format preserves all of the graph's visual qualities; however, none of the graph file formats are dynamic. This means that once a graph is written to a file it does not automatically change when the worksheet that generated the graph is updated.

The .PIC format is compatible with Lotus 1-2-3, which enables 1-2-3 to print Quattro Pro 4 graphs. However, 1-2-3 graphs are limited in scope. Thus, features unique to Quattro Pro 4—such as special fonts, free-floating text, and drawn objects—are lost when a file is stored in the .PIC format. The Slide EPS option is used when sending files to a slide preparation 35mm service bureau, as described in your Quattro Pro 4 manual. The .PCX format allows the graph to be edited and used by paint programs such as PC Paintbrush or Microsoft Paint running under Windows 3.

To create a specialized file of either of the two types, you select the correct type from the list. For example, to create an .EPS file you select EPS File from the Write Graph File menu and then enter a file name of up to eight letters. Quattro Pro 4 will add the .EPS extension. When you press ENTER the file is created on disk.

Layout

When you have selected Graph Printer as the Destination on the Graph Print menu and picked Go, Quattro Pro 4 prints the current graph with the current page layout. The default page layout produces a graph that covers the width of a regular sheet of paper and is positioned halfway between the top and bottom of the paper.

Although the default setting is acceptable in many cases, there will probably be times when you want to alter the size and shape of the finished graph. You do this with the Layout option of the Graph Print

FIGURE
8-25

The Layout menu

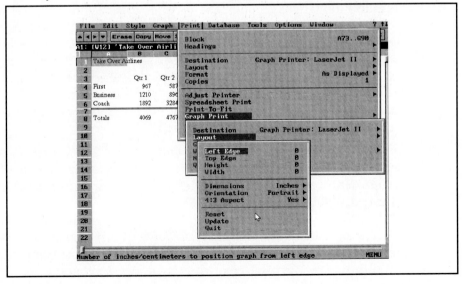

menu. As shown in Figure 8-25, the Layout menu lets you define the dimensions of the printed graph in either inches, which is the default, or centimeters. The Left Edge setting indicates the graph's left margin, the number of inches or centimeters from the left edge of the paper. The Top Edge setting indicates the top margin, where Quattro Pro 4 should start printing the graph.

In Figure 8-25 you can see that the dimensions of the graph are not defined. The effect of a setting of 0 for the edges, height, and width is to tell Quattro Pro 4 to fill the page with the graph. If you do enter height and width measurements, Quattro Pro 4 gives you the option of either preserving a standard ratio of width to height (4:3) or allowing the actual ratio of height to width measurements to determine the proportions of the finished graph. For example, if you enter 4 inches for both height and width then Yes for the 4:3 Aspect option on the Layout menu, Quattro Pro 4 will not print the graph as a square. Instead the rectangular shape of the graph is preserved within the space you have allotted. For example, a graph that is laid out as 4 inches by 4 inches will have an x-axis side that is 4 inches long, but the y-axis side will be about 3 inches. However, if you select No for the 4:3 Aspect option, Quattro Pro 4 will scale the graph to the dimensions you have specified, and in this example, you will get a graph that is literally square.

Some printers take a long time to produce full-page graphs, particularly at high resolution. Consequently, you may want to limit their size when printing the first few versions until you have the design ready for a final printing. Note that laser printers must print full-page graphs at 150 dpi or print half-size graphs at 300 dpi unless they have at least 1MB of memory.

The Orientation setting on the Layout menu is where you choose between Landscape placement of the image at right angles to the print path and the alternative, which is Portrait, or vertical placement. In Figure 8-26 you can see a diagram—drawn with Quattro Pro 4—of the difference between Landscape and Portrait. If you print the graph in Portrait orientation, the height measurement is the y-axis of a stacked bar graph and the width measurement is the x-axis. In Landscape orientation the height measurement is the x-axis and the width is the y-axis.

Choices of graph orientation

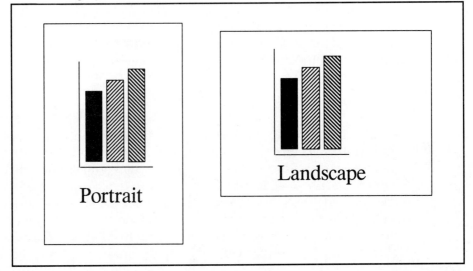

The Printing Process

With the Destination and Layout information recorded, you can initiate printing with the Go command on the Print menu. Because your printer or plotter has to translate the screen image into a series of dots or pen strokes, some time can pass before the image of the graph appears. The "Now Printing" message appears along with the message "CTRL-Break to stop". Note that you can use the Print Manager, described in Appendix C, to print graphs in the background while you continue to work with Quattro Pro 4.

The Options Hardware Printers menu has an item called Plotter Speed. This enables you to adjust the speed of your plotter. You may need to do this because some surfaces you plot onto, such as plastic overheads, accept ink better at lower speeds. When you select Plotter Speed, you can enter a value from 0 to 9, with 0 being the fastest, or current speed.

If you use the Options Hardware command to select a PostScript printer model, you will see two options for each paper size: Normal and

Patterns. The Patterns options will print graphs in which the shading matches the hatch patterns of your graph; the Normal option allows the PostScript printer to substitute its own shading.

Changing Graph Types

The examples so far in this chapter have featured the default graph type, Stacked Bar. There are many more types of graph available in Quattro Pro 4 and you can mix types within a graph. The type of graph is easily changed. Once you have selected appropriate values, you can see them graphed in each of the different graph types. The main types of graph were shown earlier in Figure 8-11.

Bar Types

Four of the Quattro Pro 4 graph types are variations of a bar graph. The stacked bar graph you have seen so far is a good way to show relative performance across the x-axis for cumulative values. For example, you can clearly see in Figure 8-22 that total volume varied from quarter to quarter.

To see the plain bar graph, select Graph Type from the Graph menu and then select Bar. This version of the graph can then be displayed with the View option or the F10 key. It will look like the graph shown in Figure 8-27. Each piece of data is represented by a separate bar. This graph makes gauging the overall performance in each quarter more difficult, but it makes comparing the relative performance per quarter in each class somewhat easier. Notice that the scale for a bar graph does not need to be as large as that of the stacked bar graph shown earlier. Quattro Pro 4 automatically adjusts the y-scale.

The third type of bar graph produced by Quattro Pro 4 is the rotated bar, shown in Figure 8-28. This chart is very effective when you want to highlight the performance of different categories. The viewer's eye is immediately drawn to the longest bar. Note that the x-axis is the vertical axis in a rotated bar graph.

Plain bar graph

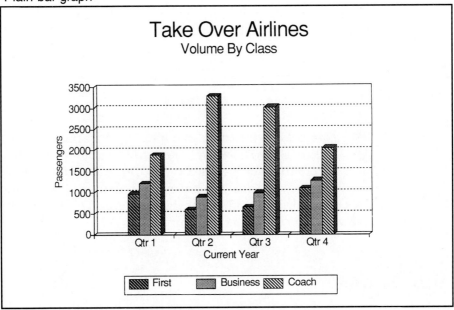

Rotated bar graph

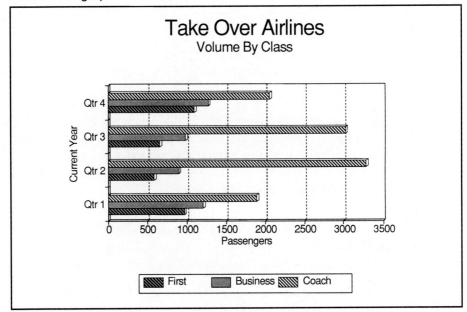

The fourth type of bar graph is called column, which is also known as the 100% bar. This graph type displays a single column that gives a percentage breakdown of a single series of values. If you select the Column option for the same series used in Figure 8-28, you will get a breakdown of the first series—the volume of First class passengers—by quarter, as shown in Figure 8-29. Seeing a chart of the percentage of annual volume attained in each quarter is probably not that useful. The percentage breakdown that you would probably like to see is the total volume for the year according to class. For this task the column graph is ideal, although the series needs to be redefined. The first series would be cells F4..F6 of the worksheet in Figure 8-9. There would be no other y-axis series. Column charts do not use legend text. Instead, you use the x-axis series to label the data. Thus, the x-axis series would be cells A4..A6. When the graph is drawn, the percentage breakdown of the total will be provided next to the names, as you can see from the resulting graph on the left of Figure 8-30. Notice the similarity of a column graph to a pie chart. A column graph is essentially a rectangular pie chart. The shading of column charts is actually controlled by pie chart commands.

FIGURE
8-29

Column graph

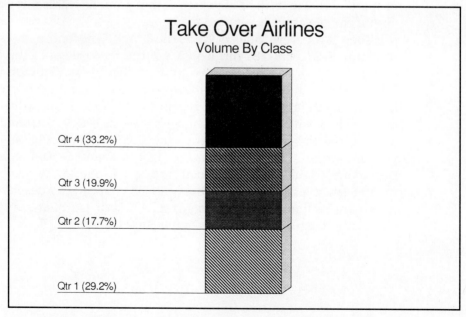

FIGURE
8-30

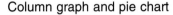

Column graph and pie chart

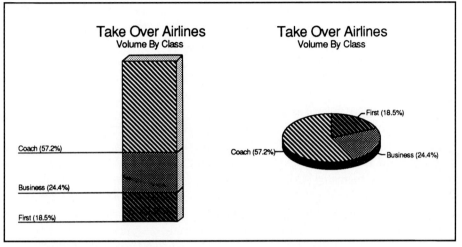

Pie Charts

The pie chart is an effective image when you want to display the proportional distribution of values within a single whole. Like a column graph, the pie chart is a one-dimensional graph; it uses only one series of values. If you were to select Pie as the Graph Type for the series graphed in Figure 8-27 or 8-28, you would see the breakdown of the first data series; that is, the First Class volume broken down between quarters. What you probably prefer is to show the total volume for the year, broken down by class. This is done by redefining the first series as cells F4..F6 of the worksheet. There would be no other y-axis series. You would use the x-axis series to label the data. Thus the x-axis series would be A4..A6. As you can see from the results on the right of Figure 8-30, the percentage breakdown of the total is provided next to the names. This is one of the many elements of a pie chart that can be changed, as described in the upcoming section, "Customizing Graphs." Both pie charts and column charts are controlled by the Customize Series menu.

Line Graphs

When you want data values to appear as points, and lines to be drawn connecting the points, you need the line graph type. This is used effectively for showing changes in data over time, as in the chart seen in Figure 8-31, which graphs the volume figures. You can use different symbols for the *markers* that represent data points, or you can turn them off and just use lines to connect the points. Alternatively, you can turn off the lines and just use markers for the data. You make these changes through the Customize series command. Note that in Figure 8-31 the second title is printed in drop shadow text.

FIGURE 8-31   Line graph

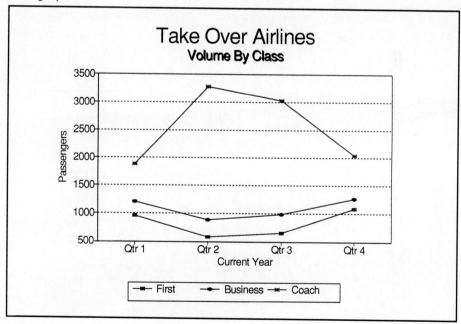

Area Graphs

When you want to represent data as an expanse of space rather than as a line or bar, you can use the area graph, an example of which is shown in Figure 8-32. Note that this type of chart does not allow accurate comparison of relative series values but does give a strong visual impact.

Hi-Low Graphs

To graph stock prices and trading in other commodities in the classic format of hi-low charts, you select the Hi-low option. In its basic form this graph uses two series, one for the highest price during each trading period and the other for the lowest. Each pair of prices is represented by a vertical line from the high number down to the low number. Two further series can be added for the closing price and opening price of the period. These are represented by small horizontal lines, as shown in Figure 8-33.

FIGURE 8-32   Area graph

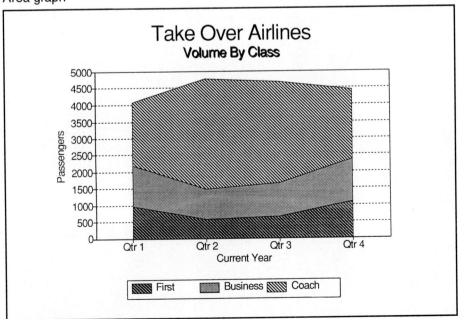

Hi-low graph

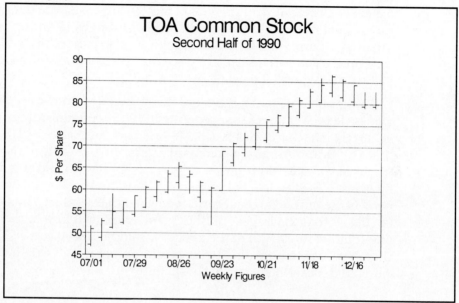

Text Graphs

The diagrams in Figures 8-23 and 8-26 were created with the Graph Annotate command. This enables you to place free-floating text, arrows, shapes, and symbols on a graph. You can actually choose a type of graph, Text, that does not require a data series. This allows you to use a blank graph area for designs created entirely with Graph Annotate. The Annotate command is described in greater detail at the end of this chapter. In Chapter 13, you can read how to use Annotate and other commands to create slide shows.

Bubble Graphs

Quattro Pro 4 introduces a new type of graph that is a variation on the XY graph. Whereas an XY graph uses points to plot two series of values, a bubble graph uses circles. The size of the circle is adjusted according to a third series. For example, with an XY graph you could plot the relation between revenue and costs for an airline route. With the x-axis measuring revenue and the y-axis measuring costs, the data points for each would route would be positioned accordingly. However, as you can see from Figure 8-34, a bubble graph can also plot a third value, in this case profit. You can immediately see that costs and revenue are high for flights to Asia, *and* the profit is substantial.

The graph in Figure 8-34 has been inserted into the spreadsheet alongside the numbers that generate it. In this example the x-axis series is B3..B6, the 1st Series is C3..C6 and the 2nd Series is D3..D6. Note that the Graph Annotate command, described later, was used to label the bubbles and add a boxed title to the graph. Data labels could also have been used to labels the bubbles. Quattro Pro 4 sizes bubbles as a percentage of the x-axis according to the largest value. The default size is 10% so that the largest bubble in the graph will have a radius that is one-tenth of the length of the x-axis, with other bubbles sized relative to that. You can adjust the 10% setting by using the Customize Series command, described later in this chapter.

**FIGURE
8-34**

A bubble graph

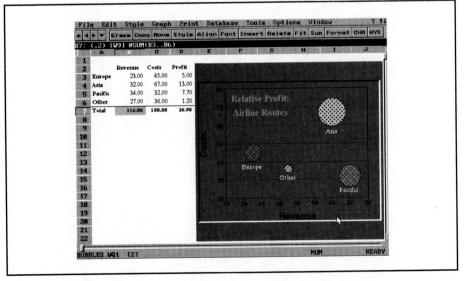

3-D Graphs

You will find some very effective graph types grouped under 3-D Graphs at the bottom of the Graph Type menu, or under the 3-D Graphs icon if you are working in graphics display mode. There are four 3-D graphs: Bar, Ribbon, Step, and Area. You can see a 3-D bar graph in Figure 8-35. Note that instead of being displayed next to each other as in an ordinary bar graph, the bars are ranked across a third axis. This is what distinguishes 3-D graphs from the mere impression of perspective used by Quattro Pro 4 to draw other graph types, as seen earlier in Figures 8-27 and 8-30. The perspective used in regular graphs is a setting adjustable from the Graph Overall dialog box, where the Add Depth option can be set to Yes or No. The default setting is Yes.

The 3-D graphs can be very effective in conveying information and are visually striking, a cut above ordinary charts. In Figure 8-36 you can see a 3-D step graph of the same data as in Figure 8-35. A step chart is

FIGURE
8-35

A 3-D bar graph

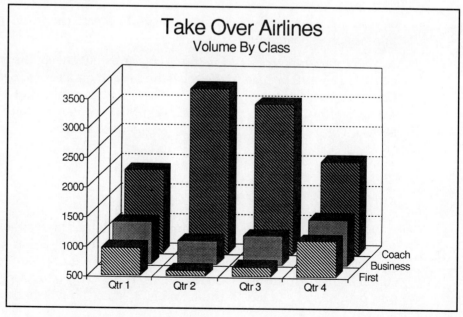

A 3-D step graph

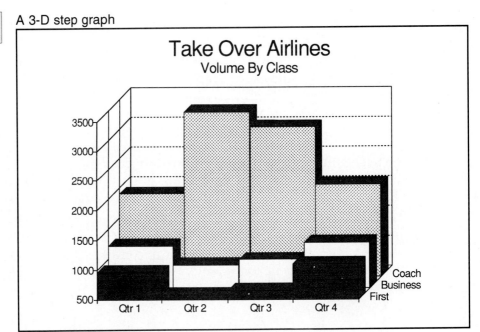

essentially a bar chart with no spaces between the bars, giving an impression of solid data.

There are some tricks to using 3-D graphs effectively. In particular, attention should be paid to the selection of each data series, because the first series is the one shown at the back of the graph, that is, further along the third axis. You will note that in the regular stacked bar chart seen in Figure 8-22 and earlier, the series were as follows:

1st Series	First
2nd Series	Business
3rd Series	Coach

While this led to a slightly top-heavy set of bars, the results were still legible. If you were to use the same settings for a 3-D bar chart, the smaller bars of the Business and First series would be lost behind the much higher volume of the Coach series. You will need to review the data you plan to show in a 3-D graph and give some thought to the selection of series. In this example the series were changed to the following to produce the graphs seen in Figures 8-35 through 8-38:

1st Series	Coach
2nd Series	Business
3rd Series	First

Another area requiring attention in 3-D graphs is the placement of the legend. You will note that the graphs in Figures 8-35 and 8-36 both have the legend in the bottom right corner. This is the only legend location permitted in a 3-D Graph. However, you can leave out the legend and use alternative means to label the graph. In Figure 8-37 you can see a 3-D ribbon graph that has no legend. The ribbon graph is effective for showing changes over a period of time, as in a line chart, but with more visual interest.

The text describing the series was added by means of Interior Label Block, an option in the Customize Series dialog box. The three names for

FIGURE 8-37 A 3-D ribbon graph

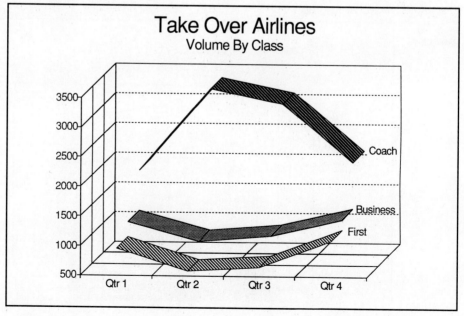

the legend were placed in cells E11 through E13, as in E11:Coach, E12:Business, and E13:First.

From the Customize Series dialog box the Interior Label Block option was selected to mark these cells to label the graph, as follows:

Series	Cell Block	Location
1st	B11..E11	Right
2nd	B12..E12	Right
3rd	B13..E13	Right

The Location setting determines the position of the labels with respect to the data points. The relative position of the labels in the Label Block determines how far along the x-axis the labels will be placed. The Text Legends Position command was used to turn off the regular legend.

There is one more 3-D graph type, the area graph, an example of which is shown in Figure 8-38. This is an effective type for use with cumulative data or situations in which you can rank each series according to size.

A 3-D area graph

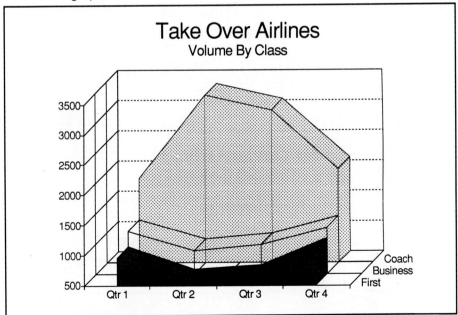

Note that the 3-D area graph is not automatically cumulative, that is, the series are not added together or stacked, as they are in a regular area graph. Also note that the second series of the graph in Figure 8-38 was given an empty shading to produce the "wire frame" effect.

XY Graphs

The XY graph is mainly used to show the distribution of values, and thus it is helpful when you are analyzing statistical data. XY graphs are described in the context of other Quattro Pro 4 statistical features in Chapter 9.

Customizing Graphs

Quattro Pro 4 is so rich in features for customizing graphs that an entire book could be devoted to the subject. Just about every aspect of a chart can be fine tuned to your personal whim. There are two main approaches to customizing graphs with Quattro Pro 4. You can use the Annotate feature, described later in this chapter, and you can use the Graph menu, as described in this section. You have already seen that text can be presented in a variety of typefaces, styles, and sizes. The four items in the second section of the Graph menu are used to customize other aspects of a graph: Customize Series, X-Axis, Y-Axis, and Overall. All four use dialog boxes instead of pull-down menus. To make sure you get dialog boxes use the Options Startup command and set Use Dialog to Yes.

Customize Series

In Figure 8-39 you can see the Customize Series dialog box. Across the top of the dialog box you can see check boxes for each of the six possible series. Check the series you want to adjust before you alter the settings for Color, Fill Pattern, Bar Width, and Interior Label Block. The first column enables you to select the colors for each of the six series on the graph. The current choice is marked with an asterisk. You can use your mouse or type **C** and then use arrow keys to select another color.

The Customize Series dialog box

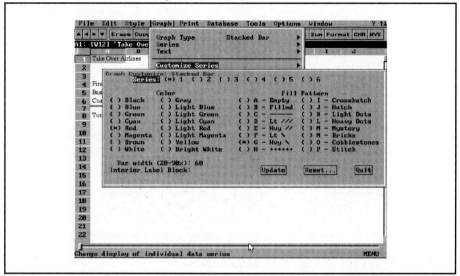

The Fill Pattern columns enable you to pick a pattern to fill in the bars of bar graphs, the areas of area graphs, and the slices of pie charts. There are 16 different patterns to choose from. When you are creating a bar graph, the spacing between bars may not be to your liking. You can use the Bar Width option in the Customize Series dialog box to alter the spacing. You can make the thickness of the bars anything from 20%, which is very thin, to 90%, which leaves virtually no gap between the bars. When you select Bar Width, just type in the desired number and press ENTER.

Quattro Pro 4 uses a different dialog box for the Customize series command to enable you to control the appearance of line and XY graphs by varying three elements for each of the six series. As you can see from Figure 8-40, you can vary Line Style, Marker, and Format. The Override Type setting enables you to change the chart type for one or more series. This is how you create a graph that mixes lines and bars. The three chart types that can be mixed in this way are XY, line, and bar. If you want a series to be given its own y-axis on the right of the chart, you can select Secondary under the y-Axis option in the lower right of the dialog box.

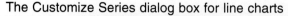

**FIGURE
8-40**   The Customize Series dialog box for line charts

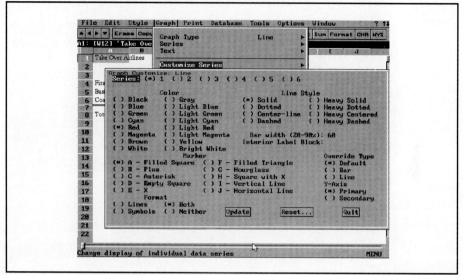

The Customize Series dialog box for a pie chart can be seen in Figure 8-41. You saw a pie chart in Figure 8-30 and another one is shown later in Figure 8-47. Instead of adjusting each series in a pie chart, you adjust each slice. This is because there is only one data series in a pie chart, the 1st series (you can use an x-axis series to supply names that match the values being charted). The first slice represents the first value in the series and in the chart it is drawn extending clockwise from the 12 noon position. You can adjust color and fill pattern for each and choose whether to have it explode. The explode option moves the slice out from the body of the pie, which is very useful for emphasis.

You can also choose whether the labeling of the slice shows the value represented by the slice (Value) or the percentage of the whole that the slice constitutes (%). You can show the value as a dollar amount ($) or choose no labeling (None). The Tick Marks option draws a line connecting the pie label to the slice it describes.

When the Graph Type setting is Bubble you get the Customize Series dialog box shown in Figure 8-42. The settings are straightforward except for the Max Bubble Size. Quattro Pro 4 sizes bubbles as a percentage of the x-axis according to the largest value with the default being 10% (the

FIGURE
8-41

The Customize Series dialog box for pie charts

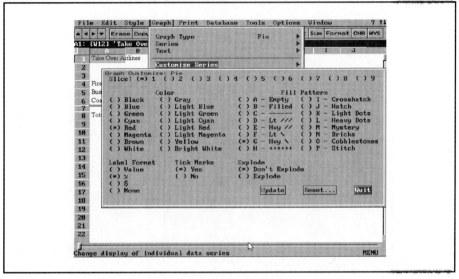

FIGURE
8-42

The Customize Series dialog box for bubble charts

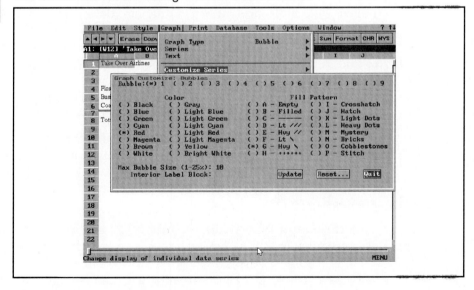

largest bubble in the graph will have a radius that is one tenth of the length of the x-axis, with other bubbles sized accordingly). You can use a size setting from 1% (small bubbles) to 25% (large bubbles).

All of the Customize Series dialog boxes have Update and Reset buttons. Use the Update button to record a set of options as the program defaults to be used as the basis for any further graphs that you create. Use the Reset button to cancel any changes you have made to the settings and return them to the program defaults.

Y-Axis Customizing

There are times when the automatic scale applied to the axes by Quattro Pro 4 does not give the desired effect. On the right side of Figure 8-43 you can see the effect of graphing First Class volume figures with an upper limit on the y-axis of 2000. This makes the performance look pretty poor compared to the graph on the left. Both graphs use the same numbers, but the graph on the left uses the automatic scaling of the y-axis, whereas the one on the right has had the y-axis customized. This was done because the company goal is 2000 First Class passengers per quarter. This adjustment puts the performance into a different perspective.

FIGURE 8-43   Relative y-axis scales

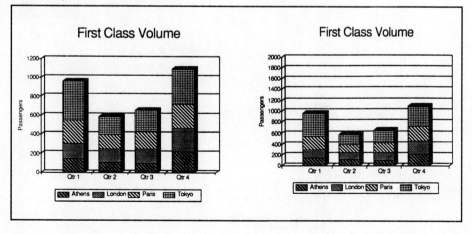

You adjust the y-axis by selecting Y-Axis from the Graph menu and using the options shown in Figure 8-44. The Scale setting is either Automatic, which is the default, or Manual. When you alter the other settings on the Y-Axis menu to create a customized scale you can turn this scale on by selecting Automatic, or turn it off by using Manual.

The Low and High settings determine the boundaries of the scale—normally from 0 to a round number larger than the largest number you want to graph. A typical example of setting the graph's *origin* (the beginning point of the y-axis) is seen in weekly charts of average stock prices. These are often shown with an origin larger than 0 to emphasize the day-to-day variation of the figures. You can see an example of this in Figure 8-33, where the origin is set at 45. Note that area and stacked bar charts cannot have their origin made less than 0.

The Increment option affects the numeric gap between the values on the y-axis scale. For example, for the numbers graphed on the left in Figure 8-43 the automatically selected values for the y-axis were 0 to 1200 in 200-unit increments. The manually adjusted graph on the right of Figure 8-43 also uses 200-unit increments.

FIGURE 8-44   Customize Y-Axis options

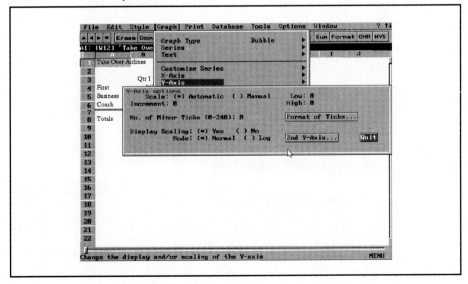

The Format of Ticks is a rather strange sounding option that is in fact very important. The numbers on the y-axis can be formatted using any of the worksheet formats, such as Currency or Fixed. For example, in the previous illustration, the Comma format is used to place commas as thousands separators. This format will also enclose negative numbers in parentheses.

The No. of Minor Ticks option enables you to create small lines on the y-axis scale instead of numbers. For example, if you set the increment to 50 you will have this series of numbers: 0, 50, 100, 150, 200, and so on. If you request a No. of Minor Ticks setting of 1, Quattro Pro 4 will skip every other number, showing 100, 200, and so on, and place tick marks at 50, 150, and so on. Every third scale number is displayed by using a setting of 2.

When Quattro Pro 4 graphs large numbers that run into the thousands or millions, those units are displayed as text on the axis, and the actual axis numbers are adjusted accordingly. You can turn off the display of this text if you want, by selecting No for Display Scaling. Although some graphs may appear to need no explanation of the scale, you should use this option to avoid graphs that are deceptive or hard to read.

When you are dealing with large numbers or scientific data you may want to use a logarithmic scale rather than a normal scale. To turn the y-axis scale to log mode, select Mode and then Log. Select Normal to go back to a regular scale. Be sure to document the use of a logarithmic scale on the graph to avoid confusion.

Quattro Pro 4 enables you to set a second y-axis for mixing graph data. When you do this you can completely customize the second axis by choosing the 2nd Y-Axis option. You can also use this option to turn off the display of scaling for the second y-axis. An example of a graph with dual y-axes is given later in this chapter.

X-Axis Customizing

There are times when you also want to customize the x-axis. In Figure 8-33 you saw a graph of stock prices. The x-axis consists of a series of dates that are all seven days apart. If every date was displayed on the x-axis, they would be unreadable. There are two approaches to clarifying the x-axis when it is crowded. You can have the x-axis series represented on two rows instead of one, and you can skip some of the values. The latter approach was taken in Figure 8-33, where only every fourth 7-day period was shown with a date.

You typically use the X-Axis option on the Graph menu to adjust the x-axis when it consists of numbers and the graph type is XY. Customizing the x-axis may be redundant when the x-axis series is labels, as is the case when you graph quarterly volume. You can see from Figure 8-45 that the X-Axis options closely match those on the y-axis menu. The Scale can be set to Automatic to have Quattro Pro 4 design the x-axis, or you can create your own design by setting the Scale to Manual and using the other menu options. The Alternate Ticks option is set to Yes when you need to use two rows for your x-axis data. The No. of Minor Ticks option is adjusted to replace labels in the x-axis with minor tick marks. In the example in Figure 8-33, this was set to 3 to produce a date every fourth label.

FIGURE
8-45

Customize X-Axis options

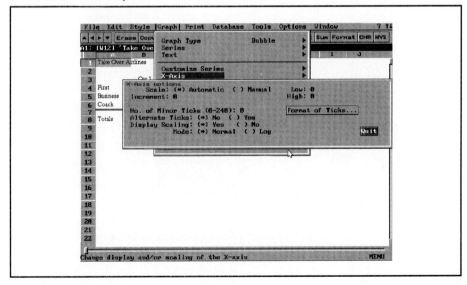

Overall Customizing

The options for Overall customizing can be seen in figure 8-46, which shows the dialog box displayed by the Overall command. The Use Colors option was set to No for creating the graphs in this chapter. When you pick No, the colors in your graphs are turned to black and white so that you can print in black and white as opposed to color. The nice part of the Use Colors option is that after you have used No you can turn the color back on, and Quattro Pro 4 will reinstate all of the default color choices. Do not select the No option, however, if you have customized colors that you want to save. Even if you do not have a color printer, you may not need to set Use Color to No. Laser printers and some high-resolution dot matrix printers can convert color output to shades of gray. Try printing with Use Color set to Yes and check the results.

The Grid option enables you to place lines on your graph. You can use Horizontal, Vertical, or Both. Use the Clear option to remove the lines. The grids you create can be customized by choosing Grid, Line Style, and

The Graph Overall dialog box

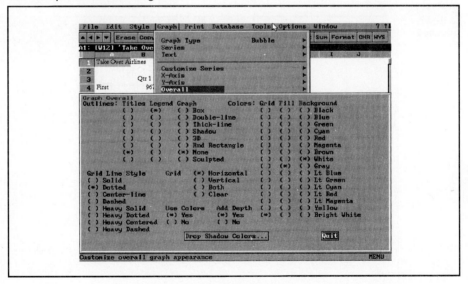

changing the color for both Grid and the Fill. Fill Color is the color that lies behind the bars in a bar graph.

The Outlines option is used to put boxes and other demarcation around three elements of the graph: Titles, Legend, and Graph (the entire chart, including text and legend). Each of these elements can be outlined by using the following options: Box, Double-line, Thick-line, Shadow, 3D, Rnd Rectangle, or Sculpted. The None option will turn off the outline. The 3D option draws a perspective box behind an object to give it an appearance of depth. The Shadow option is rather effective for text and is used in Figure 8-47. You can use the Drop Shadow Colors button to change the color used by this option. The Sculpted option creates a box like those used for menus in WYSIWYG mode.

The Background color setting in the Overall dialog box simply enables you to choose the color used for the background of the graph, whereas the Add Depth option adds perspective lines to the chart box to give an impression of depth. You can see the effect on a pie chart in Figure 8-30 and again in Figure 8-47. This chart has the Overall option called Three-D set to Yes. The first slice of the pie is exploded from the rest, and the labels show the data values.

FIGURE
8-47

Pie chart in 3-D

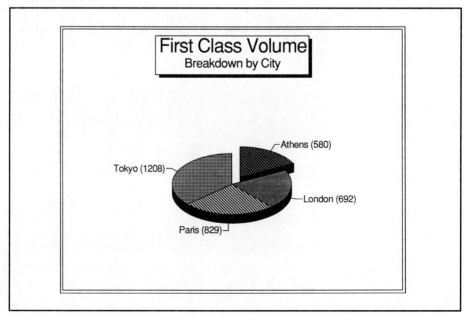

Interior Labels

The graph in Figure 8-48 shows the First Class volume figures in a rotated bar graph. The remarks for each city are displayed on the graph by means of graph labels. Such a display can be helpful and also enhances the graph's visual effect.

When you select Interior Label Block from the Customize Series menu, you can specify the spreadsheet coordinates of the data to be used to identify points of the series on the graph. The labels for your graph can be the values in the chart; they can be any set of numbers or labels. For example, you could use the city names to label the bars by using the cells that are the X-Axis series. Alternatively, as in Figure 8-49, you can enter into the worksheet a series of remarks about the values represented in the chart and then display them as interior labels. The labels in column G have been selected as labels for the graph. The results are as shown in Figure 8-48. Note that you do not have to label every data point. If you erased cells G5, G7, and G8 but still used the block G5..G8 for the interior labels setting, the graph would only show the comment for London.

Remarks as interior labels

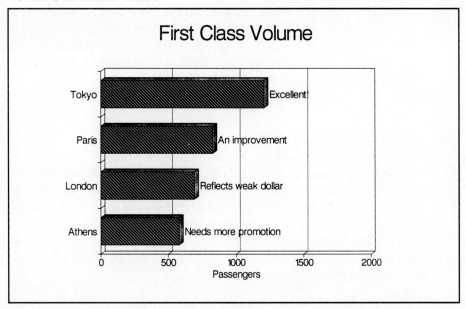

FIGURE
8-49

The Interior Labels option

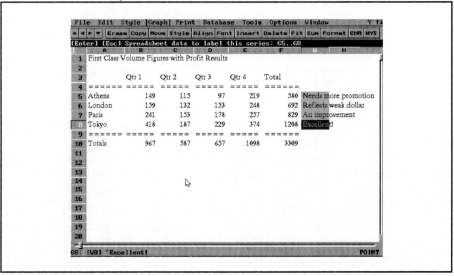

When you have entered the cell coordinates for interior labels, you are prompted for the position of the labels on the graph. Your choices are Center, Left, Above, Right, Below, or None. The None option suppresses display of that set of labels. When you have chosen an appropriate position, you are returned to the Interior Labels menu to work on the next series. The labels in Figure 8-48 are shown with a position setting of Right. Also note that the graph has customized y-axis settings that elongate the graph to make room for the labels.

Multiple Graph Types and Y-Axes

In Figure 8-43 you saw two graphs of passenger volume. The one on the right was customized to show that the passenger volume was not as great as it might appear in the graph on the left, relative to expectations. You might want to create a graph that shows the expectations or goals relative to performance. You can see an example of this in Figure 8-50. The total volume for each quarter is shown as a bar, whereas the goal for the quarter is shown as a line.

FIGURE
8-50

Combined bar and line graph

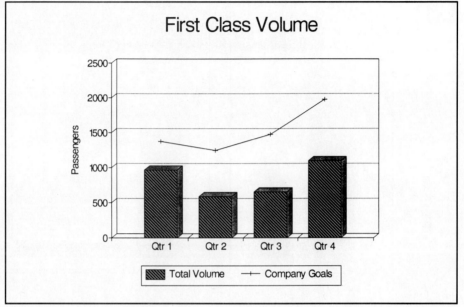

To create this graph from the worksheet in Figure 8-51 you need to establish the totals in cells B10..E10 as the first series and the goal figures in B13..E13 as the second series. The x-axis series is cells B3..E3. If you already have data series established, you can use the Graph Customize Series Reset command to delete the previous series settings. You highlight the series you want to reset and press ENTER. Bear in mind that this action cancels the series coordinates but does not change such items as graph type and graph text. Also bear in mind that the Graph option on this menu removes all graph settings, including text.

Having established the correct data series you can select Bar as the Graph Type. This will show both series of data as bars. In order to show the first series as bars but the second as a line you need to use the Override Type option in the Customize Series dialog box.

At first all six series are set to Default, meaning whatever you have selected as the current graph type. You can then choose between Default, Bar, and Line. In this case, Line will be chosen for the second series. The results are shown in Figure 8-50.

FIGURE
8-51

Spreadsheet showing goals

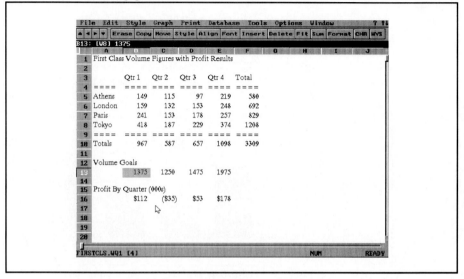

Although the ability to mix graph types increases your options for making a clear presentation of the facts, it does have limitations. You cannot mix stacked bar, pie, column, or area graphs. You can mix only line, marker, and bar graphs. Mixing graph types does not get around the problem posed by mixing numbers of completely different types. For example, what if you wanted to add the profit figures to the graph in Figure 8-50? These numbers, in row 16 of the worksheet in Figure 8-51, are in dollars and bear little relation to the other numbers. To help you graph such unrelated numbers, Quattro Pro 4 provides the ability to add a second y-axis.

To graph the profit numbers on a second y-axis you first add cells B16..E16 as the third series. Then you select the Y-Axis option in the Customize Series dialog box. This enables you to assign each series to either the Primary or the Secondary axis.

In this case the third series is assigned to the Secondary axis. Because the current graph type is bar, the profit will initially appear as a bar. To change this to a more suitable line type you would use the Override Type option, selecting Line for the third series. The results are shown in Figure 8-52.

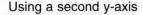
FIGURE
8-52

Using a second y-axis

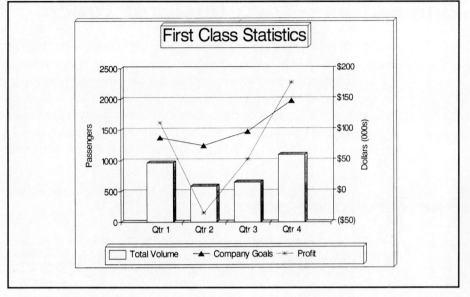

Note that the graph in Figure 8-52 has been customized slightly from the default settings. The Fill Pattern option in the Customize Series dialog box was used to clarify the bars for the first series. The Marker and Line Style options were used to alter the third series display. First, the Line Style command was used to alter the style of line for the series, in order to distinguish it from the goal line. Then the Marker option was used to make asterisks the symbol for the profit line. The Text Secondary Y-Axis command was used to add the words Dollars (000s) to the graph. The actual scale of the secondary axis was set automatically by Quattro Pro 4, but the 2nd Y-Axis command from the Y-Axis dialog box was used to change the format of the numbers to Currency with zero decimal places. Finally, the Overall command was used to add boxes around the legend, the title, and the entire graph. The box style was set to 3D as was the overall style of the graph.

By carefully mixing features as shown in this example it is possible to use Quattro Pro 4 to graph most information in an attractive and effective manner. When you want to go further in your customization, you can use the Annotate feature described next.

Annotation—The Finishing Touch

The Graph Annotate feature in Quattro Pro 4 is really a full-featured built-in drawing program. You can use it to turn ordinary worksheet-generated graphs into stunning visuals or even to create drawings that are not related to figures in the spreadsheet. In this area of Quattro Pro 4, a mouse—although not mandatory—is certainly a great plus, making quick work of drawing and coloring shapes and lines, as well as moving elements of the graph and performing cut-and-paste operations.

The Annotate Screen

You can see the Annotate feature at work in Figure 8-53, where a piece of text is being added to a stacked bar graph. Note that this level of

FIGURE 8-53

Text added by using Annotate

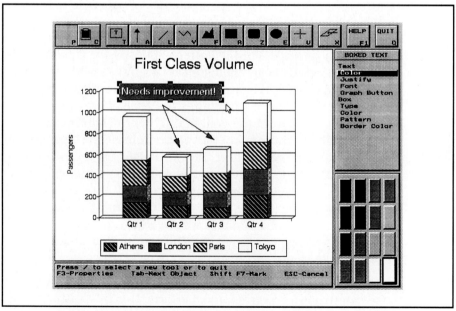

customizing goes beyond the use of interior labels. The text that has been added here can be floated to any point on the graph, resized, or even enclosed in a variety of box styles. The elements of the graph that you have created with the other graph commands can also be moved about. The legend can be moved to a new location, as can any graph text.

There are two ways to get to the Annotate feature. When you view a graph you can press the / key. You can also use the Annotate option from the Graph menu. In both cases the current graph is placed into a window and a panel of tools is provided. If you have used paint or draw programs with a mouse before, the operation of the Annotate feature will be familiar. Basically, you click on the pointer box labeled P in the top left corner of the screen to make your mouse or cursor keys act as the selector. Then you click on objects in the graph to select them or press the TAB key to move from one item to another.

You click on the various tools in the top menu bar to select them and draw lines, polygons, rectangles, and circles by the click-and-drag method. Each object in the graph has a set of handles on it (the small boxes around the boxed text in Figure 8-53). If you point to one of these boxes and then click and drag, you can alter the size and shape of the object. If you click within the selected object, you can move it to another location on the screen. The menus and palettes on the right side of the screen are used for editing the colors, patterns, and other attributes of the objects you select. You click on the Clipboard, the second box, when you want to copy and paste elements of the graph and move them to the front or back of the picture. You also use this tool to paste pictures from the clip art files (with the extension .CLP). You can click on the Text tool to type free-floating text for the graph.

In the lower part of the screen a very helpful set of instructions guides you through the appropriate actions and provides keystroke alternatives to the mouse commands. In Figure 8-54 you can see the way that the Annotate feature transforms a good but basic graph into a stunning visual. The legend was moved to the top of the chart; the title was moved to the bottom. A piece of boxed text was added, along with two arrows. Then a polygon in the shape of an aircraft was drawn and placed below the main graph area using the Clipboard. In Chapter 13 you will find further discussion of this feature and how it can be applied.

Graphics created by using Annotate

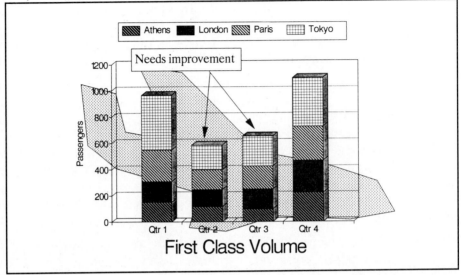

Annotated Text Charts

When you want to use the Annotate feature to create charts like the ones shown earlier in Figures 8-23 and 8-26 that are not based on any numbers in a worksheet you simply open a new worksheet and select Text as the graph type. You can then select Annotate and a fresh canvas appears, ready for you to add text, shapes, or whatever you desire. The capability to perform these actions from within what is ostensibly a spreadsheet program makes Quattro Pro 4 one of the most versatile software packages around. In Figure 8-55 you can see an example of a text chart, which shows that the term really does not do justice to the results. This graphic can even be inserted into a spreadsheet to make a very interesting effect.

Intelligent Graphs

You have already seen that Quattro Pro 4 does more than just graph your data. When you use a pie chart Quattro Pro 4 totals the values being

FIGURE
8-55

A text chart

graphed and calculates what percentage of the total each value represents. The same type of math occurs when you create a stacked bar chart.
Quattro Pro 4 totals each set of values and displays each individual value
as a portion of the total. Yet Quattro Pro 4 can do much more with the
data that you graph, creating periodic and cumulative values, as well as
moving averages. You can even tell Quattro Pro 4 to create a table of the
values that it calculates from your graph.

An Analytical Example

In Figure 8-56 you can see a worksheet that is graphing daily water
consumption. The dates in column A generate the x-axis, whereas the
values in column B form the 1st Series, shown as the line and markers
on the inserted graph. There are 90 readings, from the first of the year
to the first of April. Apart from the problem of excessive data points, which
renders the dates at the bottom of the chart unintelligible, the current
graph settings make the overall trend difficult to assess. You can see that

consumption is probably rising, but there are wide variations from day to day. Compare the graph in Figure 8-56 to the one in Figure 8-57 and you will see a clearer picture of the trend in consumption. This is because Figure 8-57 graphs weekly aggregate consumption instead of daily consumption for the same three-month period.

To create an aggregate graph like this you first establish the x-axis and the data series you want to work with. Then you select Series from the Graph menu and choose Analyze. In this example you analyze the first series, but if you have several series in your graph you can choose any one of them. When you have selected the series you get the menu shown in Figure 8-58, which is referred to as the Analyze Series menu. To graph an aggregate value, choose Aggregation. You will then need to determine three settings: the series period, aggregation period, and function.

Series Period

The Series Period setting tells Quattro Pro 4 what the values in the series represent—for example, daily readings, weekly sales figures,

FIGURE 8-56

Worksheet and chart of water consumption

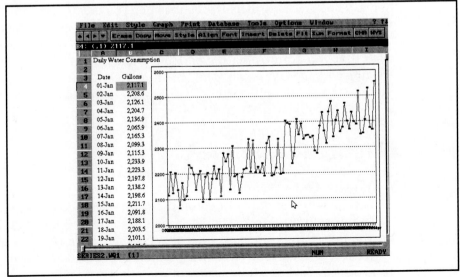

FIGURE
8-57

Chart of the weekly aggregate water consumption

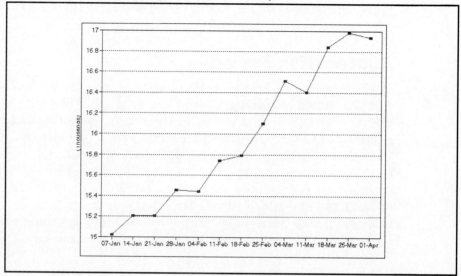

FIGURE
8-58

The Analyze Series menu

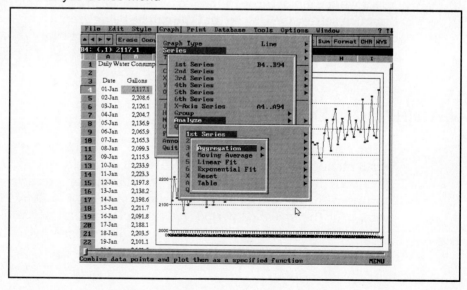

monthly returns. The options are Days, Weeks, Months, Quarters, or Years. In Figure 8-57 the Series Period setting is Days.

Aggregation Period

The Aggregation Period setting indicates how many data points you want combined for each point on the new graph. For example, choosing Weeks combines 7 data points in the original series to make one data point in the new graph. The Aggregation Period in Figure 8-57 is Weeks. The other options are Months (30 points), Quarters (90 points), Years (360 points), and Arbitrary, which enable you to set the number of original data points make up one new point at a figure other than 7, 30, 90, or 360. For example, if you want to graph the aggregate weekly price of a commodity from daily trading figures, but the commodity is only traded five days of the week, you should use Arbitrary and enter **5**.

Function

The Function setting determines what kind of math Quattro Pro 4 does with the figures in each of the periods. The options are represented as functions: SUM, AVG, STD, STDS, MIN, and MAX. See Chapter 4 for more about what each of these functions does. In the graph in Figure 8-57 the Function setting is SUM, so that the values being graphed represent total consumption in each week. If the AVG function was used, the data points would show the average for the week.

Analytical Possibilities

The Aggregation command is only one of six available on the Analyze Series menu shown in Figure 8-58. The Moving Average option is used to smooth fluctuating data points by plotting progressive averages. Starting with the first point in the series Quattro Pro 4 calculates the average for the specified period, for example the first seven days in an analysis of daily data by week. At each following point Quattro Pro 4 recalculates the average for a similar length of time but drops one point and adds a new one, as in January 1 through 7, followed by January 2 through 8, and so on.

The effect on the daily water consumption data is reflected in the wavy line in Figure 8-59. The graph shows as many data points as Figure 8-56, but the curve is less erratic. There are two settings to make with the Moving Average option. The Period setting determines the length of time over which the averaging will occur. In Figure 8-59 this is 7. The Weighted Average setting is normally No, but you can change it to Yes if you want Quattro Pro 4 to place greater emphasis on more recent numbers within the period being averaged.

The straight line that appears in Figure 8-59 was created with the Linear Fit option. This uses simple linear regression to draw a line that best fits the data. Use the Exponential Fit option to generate a curve that fits data that increases or decreases exponentially. Bear in mind that when you select a series and change the Analyze setting the new analysis is graphed instead of the previous one. If you want to see several different

FIGURE 8-59

A graph of moving average and linear fit

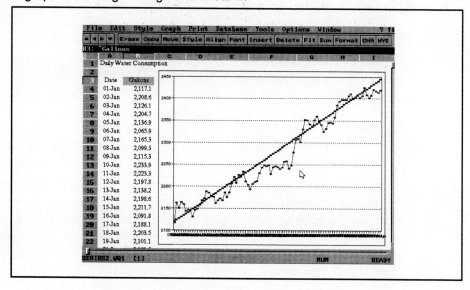

analyses of the same data, you must graph the data in two different series. In Figure 8-59 the values in B were graphed as both the 1st Series and the 2nd Series. The Moving Average was applied to the 1st Series, whereas Linear Fit was applied to the 2nd Series.

The Reset option on the Analyze Series menu clears the analysis settings for the currently selected series. The Table option enables you to select a block of cells into which Quattro Pro 4 will then copy the results of the analysis. For example, in the case of Figure 8-57 the table consists of the 13 weekly totals calculated and graphed by the Aggregation command. Even if you do not need to graph data, the Table command is a very handy tool to calculate values that would otherwise require a series of formulas. If you are graphing data, you can use the values in the table as data labels for the graph. In fact, the possibilities presented by the Analyze command are almost unlimited. To what extent you exploit them depends on your need to get to grips with large amounts of data and present it graphically. Bear in mind that you do not have to use line charts for graphical analysis. You can also use bars.

Working with Large Graphs

Although you can only graph six data series at once with Quattro Pro 4, you can graph a large number of data points. As you saw in Figure 8-56, this feature enables you to chart detailed information, such as daily figures, over extended periods of time. However, displaying such information on a single screen is difficult, so Quattro Pro 4 has a special feature that enables you to establish how much of the graph you see in each screen and to move through sections of a graph one screen at a time.

This feature is referred to as Zoom and Pan. After you have pressed F10 to view a graph, or selected View from the Graph menu, you can press both mouse keys at once to get the Zoom and Pan controls. These appear at the top of the screen, as shown in Figure 8-60. The button on the left, marked by a pair of plus signs (++) zooms in on the chart, reducing the number of data points graphed each time you click it. The next button,

FIGURE 8-60

The Zoom and Pan controls

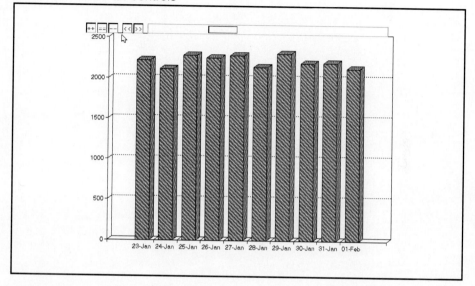

with the pair of equal signs (==) returns the graph to the original view, that is, with all data points graphed. The button with the two minus signs (--) zooms away from the chart, adding more data points to the view. The buttons with left and right chevrons (<< and >>) pan your view of the chart, moving your view to left and right, respectively.

The Zoom and Pan controls are not just useful for viewing the chart. When you exit the graph view the Zoom and Pan settings remain in effect. They will be used when the graph is printed or when it is displayed in the worksheet.

CHAPTER

Advanced Tools

*T*his chapter explores advanced commands on the Tools menu. These include Optimizer, Solve For, What-if, and Advanced Math—tools designed to help you analyze information within your Quattro Pro 4 spreadsheets. The Library command, which you use to increase the range of @functions in Quattro Pro 4, is described. Because the Advanced Math command includes matrix arithmetic and regression, XY graphs that plot regression are also explored. Ways to check the accuracy and integrity of your spreadsheets with the Audit command are discussed, along with the related Map View command from the Window Options menu. The chapter ends with two commands on the Tools menu that help you move data between files, Xtract and Combine.

Relating with Regression

When you have a large collection of related facts you may want to see how strong the relationship is between them. For example, you may want to evaluate the relationship between goods sold and the amount of money spent on advertising them, see the connection between earnings and levels of education, and so on. One method of analyzing the connection between such facts is called *linear regression.* Quattro Pro 4 provides a built-in method for performing this through the Regression option on the Advanced Math menu. The subject of regression analysis is complex, and a complete discussion is beyond the scope of this book. A reference such as *Modern Business Statistics* by Ronald L. Iman and W. J. Conover (New York: John Wiley & Sons, 1983) provides complete coverage of all aspects of the field as they relate to typical business situations.

A Regression Example

Regression is a measurement of how different factors relate to each other. For example, how does the amount of advertising done by a company relate to its sales? Standard business philosophy states that the amount of advertising a company does is related to the sales level it achieves. Regression can help you determine the strength of this relationship in the case of your company.

Suppose you have compiled the marketing data shown in Figure 9-1. Column B is the number of full-page newspaper advertisements placed during the year, listed by month. The numbers in column C represent sales, in thousands, for those same months. You may want to know how these two sets of numbers relate. Once you measure the relationship, you can use that measure to predict future sales based on different levels of future advertising.

Setting Up Regression

When you select Regression from the Advanced Math menu, you see the menu shown in Figure 9-2. Note that before this menu was selected, the cell selector was placed in E3. This was done because the Regression command produces a table of results that occupies an area of the worksheet. It should be a block of blank cells set apart from the data being analyzed.

The first two items on the Regression menu refer to the variable factors in the regression calculation. The effect of the independent variable on the dependent variable is being calculated. In this case, Pages, in cells B4..B15, is the independent variable. Its effect on Sales, in cells C4..C15,

TOA Marketing Figures

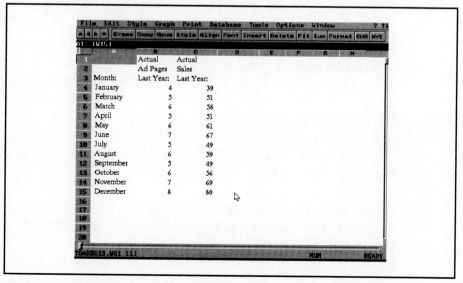

FIGURE
9-2

Regression menu

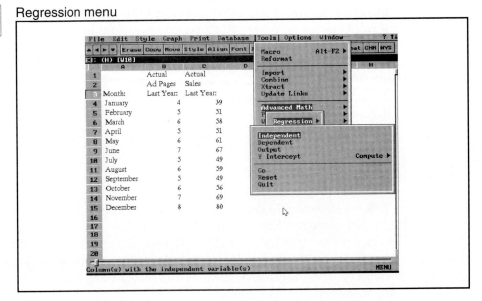

the dependent variable, is what is to be calculated. Both variables must be situated in matching columns and rows of the worksheet and must contain an equal number of data, as is the case in this example. When you select Independent and Dependent, you can enter the cell coordinates either by typing them or by pointing to them. (There can be more than one independent variable, as will be shown in a later example.)

The completed entries for the regression calculation will appear in the menu. The Output block is referred to as E3..E3, although the results of the calculation will occupy four columns and nine rows. You need only define the top left corner of the cells of the Output block. Use the Go option to tell Quattro Pro 3 to complete the regression calculation. The results are shown in Figure 9-3.

Regression Results

The result of a regression calculation is a column of numbers that represent the numeric relationships between the variables, and labels describing these numbers. The heading Regression Output will appear more centered if you output to wider columns than the default width of

FIGURE 9-3

Results of regression

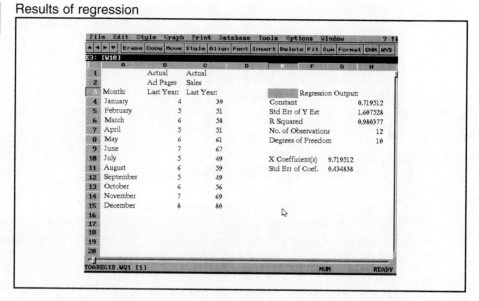

9. Note that outputting to columns any narrower than 9 will make the data difficult to read.

Interpreting these results involves understanding numerous statistical concepts. The No. of Observations is how many data points were observed for the variables—in this case 12, one for each month. Degrees of Freedom represents the number of observations minus one for each variable observed, in this case 10. The value R Squared is sometimes referred to as the coefficient of determination, a measure of the extent to which the variables are related, with 1 being the optimal value. In this example, where the sales are clearly very closely related to the pages, the value of R Squared is nearly 1.

The Std Err of Y Est is the estimated standard error of the Y values. With this you measure the certainty with which the independent variables predict the dependent variables. In general, the larger this measure, the less reliable the relationship between the independent and the dependent variables. This measure, like R Squared, is useful as you decide among different independent variables as predictors of the dependent variables. The Std Err of Coef. gives an error measurement of the coefficients. The larger this measurement, relative to the X coefficient, the less certain the relationship among the variables. This measurement will often be smaller when more observations are included in the calculation.

Probably the most useful numbers in the regression output are the constant and the X coefficient. The constant can be described as the y-axis intercept of the regression line that describes the relationship between pages and sales. The X coefficient tells how much the dependent variable, sales, will change for a single unit increase in the independent variable, pages. As you can see in the output in Figure 9-3, this is close to 10, and most of the sales figures are, in fact, about ten times the pages figures.

Using Regression Results

The constant and X coefficient readings can be used to predict the value of sales based on different numbers of pages. In Figure 9-4 a calculation has been entered in column D, representing the formula *Constant+X Coefficient x Independent variable*; in this case, cell D4 is **$H$4+$G$10*B4**. This formula was copied down the column to produce the predicted results, which are fairly close to the real results. The value of this calculation can be seen when the pages in column B are changed from actual to planned and the sales for the next year are predicted. You can see this in Figure 9-5, but remember that the prediction is only a statistical inference, not a guaranteed basis for a business decision. However, it is a suggestion that more advertising will produce more sales.

FIGURE 9-4

Predicting sales from regression results

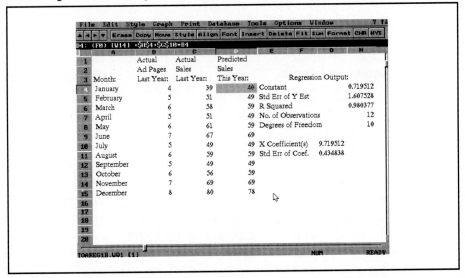

FIGURE
9-5

Adding predictions

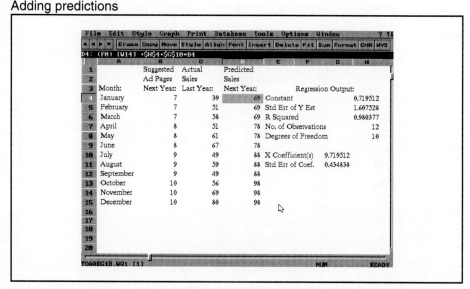

Multiple Variables

You can include more than one independent variable in the regression calculation. An example of this is the analysis of the survey questionnaire shown in Figure 9-6. This set of questions was sent to all of Take Over Airline's corporate accounts. The worksheet shows a sample set of responses. The results of the survey were entered into the worksheet in tabulated columns, as shown in Figure 9-7. The company names are in column A. Column B shows the number of employees at the company. The numbers entered in column C refer to a code for the company's type of business. There are just over a hundred responses to the survey. The analyst wants to know whether there is a significant relationship between the size of the company, as measured by the number of its employees; the type of business the company is in, as signified by the code; and the number of flights made to Europe in 1990, listed in column H. This means that the independent variables are columns B and C, and column H is the dependent variable.

Note that coded data must be shown as numeric values if it is to be used as a variable. Also note that when you are using two or more independent variables they should be in adjacent columns, as with the number of employees and business codes used in this example.

FIGURE 9-6

Completed corporate survey form

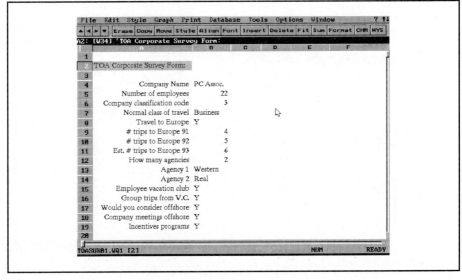

FIGURE 9-7

Table of survey results

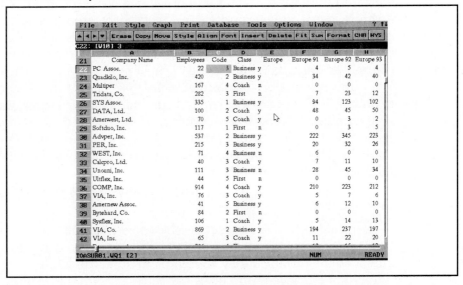

The settings would thus be B22..C124 for Independent and H22..H124 for Dependent. The result of this regression example, using P2 as the Output can be seen in Figure 9-8. Note that there are two X coefficients, one for each of the independent variables. The measure of R Squared is 0.65642, which shows a moderate relationship between the two independent variables and the dependent one.

Frequency Distribution

When you are handling large quantities of data, such as that shown in the last example, you often need to analyze the distribution of the data. For example, someone might ask "How big are the companies that responded?" Measured in terms of employees, you could say that they range from 22 to 914, and you could see this from simply browsing column B. But this response would be rather vague. If you were to categorize the companies based on number of employees and count how many fell into each category, you would get a better understanding of the survey's respondents. This is the role of the Frequency command on the Tools menu.

FIGURE 9-8

Results of regression from survey data

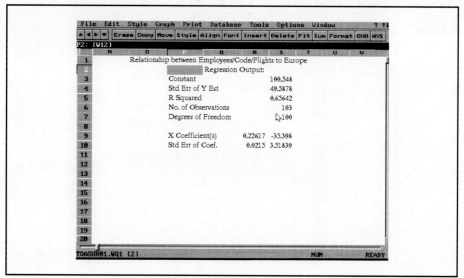

Performing a Distribution

To perform a frequency distribution with Quattro Pro 4, you need to supply two pieces of information. The first is the block of values that are to be categorized. The second is the column of numbers representing the range over which the values are to be distributed—the categories, as it were. The group of cells containing these category numbers is called the *bins block*, as though each number in the values block was tossed into the appropriate bin for counting. The result of the Tools Frequency command is a list of the totals of that count placed in the column to the right of the bin numbers.

To see this in action, consider the response to the TOA survey, which you want to analyze according to the number of employees at each company. First, a series of numbers for the bins block must be entered. The first number will represent from 0 to the number, so that 100 would represent from 0 to 100. For the employee numbers you could use 100 through 1000 in intervals of 100. This series of numbers can easily be entered with the Edit Fill command, as shown in Figure 9-9.

Be sure that the cells you use for the bins block have empty cells immediately to the right of them. When you select Frequency, you are first

FIGURE
9-9

Edit Fill

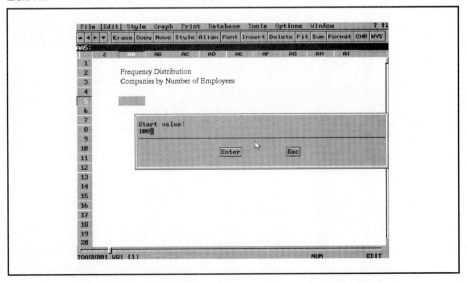

prompted for the values block, in this case, cells B22..B124. As soon as you enter this, you are prompted for the bins block, as shown in Figure 9-10. Here you can see that the bin numbers range from 100 to 1000 and are being defined. When you enter the bins block, Quattro Pro 3 immediately responds with the count of numbers shown in Figure 9-11. From this result you can see that 35 of the companies responding to the survey had from 0 to 100 employees. There were 14 companies with 101 to 200 employees. These results provide a valuable picture of the survey data. Frequency distributions are a good basis for many graphs, an example of which is shown in Figure 9-12.

Improving the Distribution

Because the bin numbers are somewhat difficult to interpret, you can add a second column, as shown in the worksheet in Figure 9-13. This is a list of sales figures for travel agents. The sales from column C are distributed in column H. The bin numbers are shown in column G. The numbers in column F show the range of numbers implied by the distribution performed by the Frequency command.

FIGURE
9-10

The bins block

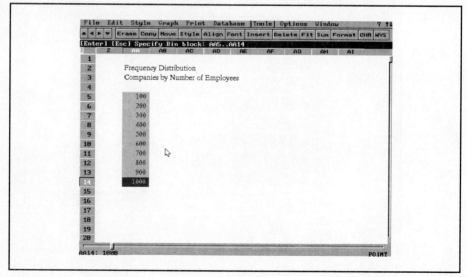

FIGURE 9-11

The completed distribution

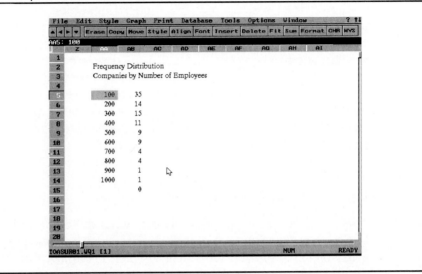

FIGURE 9-12

Distribution graph

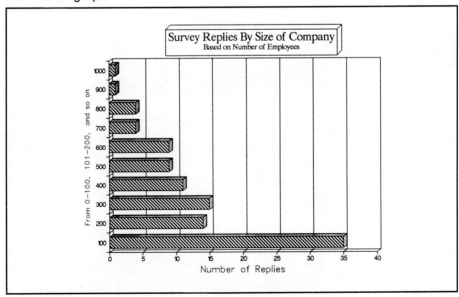

Improved bin numbers

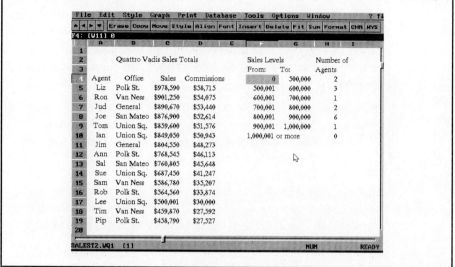

What-if Analysis

When making projections, you will want to experiment with values to see what effects different actions will have. This is called *what-if analysis.* After you have established the formulas that relate the different cells in a worksheet, you can change the numbers on which the formulas are based. For example, you can set up a worksheet to calculate sales for the next 12 months based on a starting volume of 2000 units increasing at 5 percent per month. By adding up the sales for the year, you can see what kinds of sales are possible with a 9 percent growth rate starting at 2000 units. By changing the starting figure, you can calculate sales beginning at 2500 instead of 2000. Then, you might want to create a table of total sales achieved by different starting numbers. Such a table is sometimes referred to as a *one-way data table,* because it lists the results obtained from varying one factor in a calculation. You could create a *two-way data table* by varying both the beginning figure and the rate of growth. This kind of what-if analysis can be automated to a certain extent by the What-if selection on the Tools menu.

A One-Way What-if Example

Suppose you are thinking of buying a car. The spreadsheet shown in Figure 9-14 includes some of the calculations involved. The cells are shown in the text format to reveal the formulas they contain. The total price of the car is calculated and the down payment subtracted to show the amount you would need to finance.

The figures in D1, D2, and D3 show the principal, interest, and term of the loan. You may want to know how large the payments on the loan will be at different rates of interest. For example, the list of rates that begins at 10 percent in cell A11 could be extended all the way to 19 percent by the Edit Fill command, filling cells A11 through A20 with values starting at 0.1, incremented by 0.01 to stop at 0.19. The Percent format could then be applied to the cells. The formula in cell B10 simply refers to the loan payment calculation cell. This is the cell whose answers you want to see in the completed table.

You can see from Figure 9-14 that the What-if option has been chosen from the Tools menu. You can actually vary two items with the What-if selection by choosing 2 Variables. The Reset option simply clears any previous settings. The action performed by the first item on the menu, 1

Calculation formulas

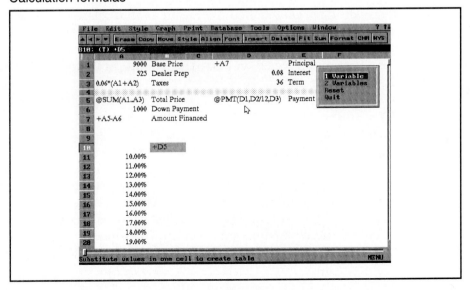

FIGURE
9-14

Variable, is to replace one cell with cells from the left edge. This is what is needed to see the loan payment calculated for each rate of interest.

When you select 1 Variable, you are prompted for the block of cells to be used as the data table. In this case the block is cells A10 through B20, as shown in Figure 9-15.

The table is all of the numbers to be fed into the formula, plus the formula, represented in this case by +D5. When you have entered the data table block, the program prompts "Input Cell from column," meaning "Into which cell do you want to read the values from the left column of the data table?" In this case, the interest cell, D2, is the input cell, as shown in Figure 9-16.

When you have entered the input cell, the results are tabulated. Quattro Pro 3 feeds each of the values from column A into cell D2 and reads the resulting answer in D5 into the table, creating the output shown in Figure 9-17. This output consists of numbers, not formulas, and so it is not interactive. Changing the terms of the loan on the spreadsheet would not cause any change in the cells of the data table. You must repeat the What-if command to take into account changes in the model. The data table is a quick way to perform a repetitive series of calculations, and pressing Table (F8) repeats the last table command.

FIGURE
9-15

Marking the block

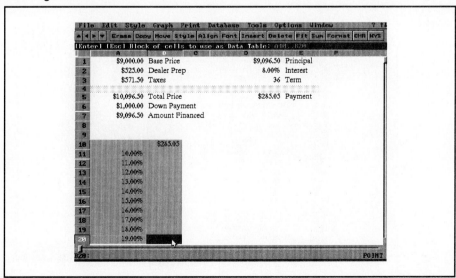

FIGURE
9-16

Setting the input cell

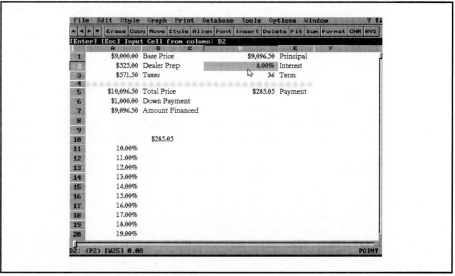

FIGURE
9-17

A What-if loan data table

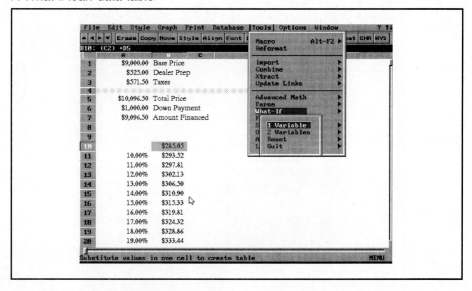

Two-Way What-if Calculations

The next step is a two-way data table, shown in Figure 9-18. This table shows the payments on the loan based on a variety of interest rates and five different payment terms. The table varies both the interest in D2 and the term in D3. The operation is performed by first setting the interest rates down the side of the worksheet and then the terms across the top. The What-if command is then selected from the Tools menu, and 2 Variables is chosen. The data table is defined as the block formed by the column of variables and the row of variables, A10 through F20, in this case. You are then prompted "input cell from Column," which is the interest in D2. Finally, you are prompted for the input cell from the top row, the term in cell D3, as entered in Figure 9-19.

The results are then created by Quattro Pro 4 as shown in Figure 9-18. You can use this table to decide what terms are best suited to your budget. You could easily produce a different table with various prices and interest rates to see how expensive a car you could afford to finance. Use the Reset command to clear out the current settings for the data table and input cells. Remember that the data table is not interactive and will not be updated when you change other factors in the model. To update the table, you must reissue the What-if command or press F8, the Table key.

FIGURE 9-18

Two-way data table

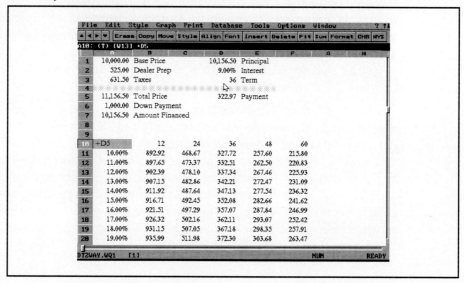

FIGURE
9-19

Input cell

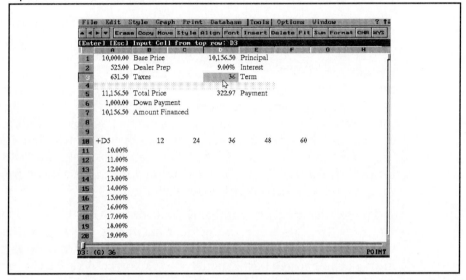

Matrix Arithmetic

Two items on the Advanced Math menu, Invert and Multiply, provide tools for performing matrix arithmetic. If you know what the inverse of a matrix is and need to perform matrix arithmetic in your work, the following account of the Invert and Multiply commands will get you started applying Quattro Pro 4 to the task. If you are not familiar with inverting matrices, the following example will give you an idea of how they are used to solve practical problems.

Matrix arithmetic is used in linear programming, a technique for determining the optimal allocation of limited resources. This has practical application in many areas, notably economics, which has been defined as "the science that studies human behavior as a relationship between ends and scarce means which have alternative uses." Although a discussion of economic theory and linear programming concepts is clearly beyond the scope of this book, you can get an idea of how matrix commands work and how linear programming is applied with Quattro Pro 4 from a relatively simple example.

At Take Over Airlines, management needs to determine the optimal mix of cargo on a plane, choosing between packages and people. The data from which this mix must be calculated is the amount of fuel needed to fly each package and each person, plus the amount of handling time involved for each package and each person. This data is laid out in the worksheet shown in Figure 9-20.

The profits per package and per person are also listed in the worksheet. The numbers are pure data, not formulas. You can, however, set up a similar worksheet very easily by setting the width of column A to 16 and the rest to 10. Enter the numbers as values. In cell F3, the words **Matrix Output** have been entered to label the results of the first set of calculations, which will be created by Quattro Pro 4's Invert command. The calculation that must be performed to determine the optimal mix of packages and persons involves the following equations:

2750*Packages+9250*Persons=80,000 Gallons
3*Packages+2*Persons=40 Hours

These equations will yield the number of packages and persons you should load to optimize allocation of the given resources. Once you have entered the data in the worksheet, as shown in Figure 9-20, you can have Quattro Pro 4 calculate an inverse of the matrix of numbers in B4..C5.

FIGURE
9-20

The cargo worksheet

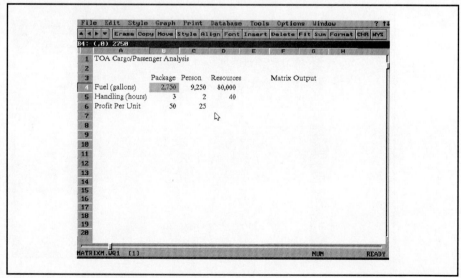

Matrix Invert

When you select Invert from the Advanced Math menu, you are prompted for the source block of cells. In this case the block is B4..C5. The cell coordinates can be pointed out or typed in, just as you do at other Quattro Pro 4 block prompts. The matrix to be inverted must be square; that is, it must have the same number of columns as rows. When you have entered the Source Block coordinates, you are prompted for a Destination Block. In this case F4 will be used. The Destination Block will be the same size as the Source Block, so you must use an adequate area of your spreadsheet for this. However, you need only point out the top left corner of the Destination Block. When you enter the Destination Block coordinates, the inverse matrix is produced, as shown in Figure 9-21.

This example shows how Quattro Pro 4's default General format displays long numbers. The number in cell F4 is –0.000076294277929. But because the column is only ten characters wide, the number is shown in scientific notation, standing for -7.63×10^5. Unless you need to observe the details of the inverse matrix results, you will probably want to leave the output cells in General format. Otherwise, you may have to use a format with a large number of decimal places and a wide column width to see the numbers.

FIGURE 9-21

The inverse matrix

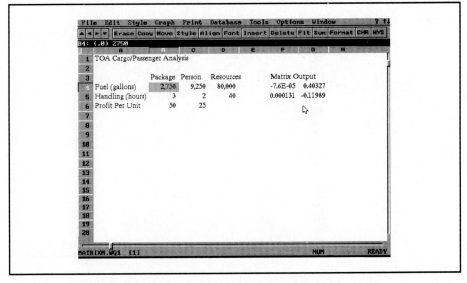

Matrix Multiply

Having calculated the inverse matrix of the numbers, you can use the Advanced Math Multiply command to multiply the original resources of 80,000 gallons and 40 hours by the inverse matrix. The resources, which were the constants in the equations, constitute a matrix. The Multiply command enables you to multiply two matrices together. In this case the results will be the number of packages and persons that make the most efficient use of your limited resources. When you select Multiply from the Matrix menu, you are prompted to "Specify 1st Matrix," which will be the output of the inverse matrix, cells F4..G5.

When you enter these coordinates, you are prompted to "Specify 2nd Matrix," which will be the resources in D4..D5. After entering the second matrix coordinates you are prompted for a "Destination for cells." In this example cell B10 is named, as shown in Figure 9-22, where some additional labels have been added to identify the results. When you enter the destination coordinates, the results of the calculations are seen. In this case a mix of 10.03 packages and 5.67 persons is the most efficient use of the resources available.

Note that cells B10 and B11 in Figure 9-22 have been formatted to two decimal places with the Comma format. Because you cannot have

FIGURE
9-22

Profit calculation

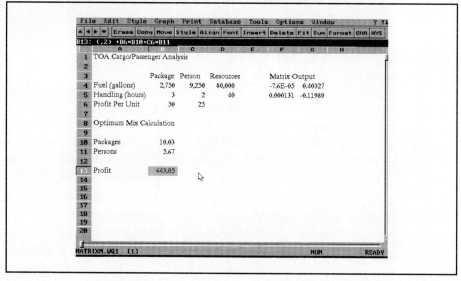

5.67 persons, you might want to display the result without any decimal places. However, if you are going to use the result in another calculation, you may want to use the @ROUND function to eliminate the decimal places.

In Figure 9-22 there is one additional calculation in the worksheet. This figure shows the amount of profit made by the mix determined in B10 and B11, using the profit figures from row 6. The formula +B6*B10+C6*B11 is used to multiply the per-unit profit by the optimal number of units. You might modify the formula as follows, in order to use whole units of packages and persons:

+B6*@ROUND(B10,0)+C6*@ROUND(B11,0)

XY Graphs

Because this chapter has discussed some advanced features of Quattro Pro 4 for analyzing and determining relationships between collections of data, this is an appropriate place to address the subject of XY graphs. This type of graph was not included with the other graphs in Chapter 8 because it is a specialized type. Used to plot the relationship between data points that have two coordinates, XY graphing can be used for such tasks as analyzing measurements and displaying regression lines.

Making an XY Graph

Figure 9-23 shows a worksheet of size and weight measurements for a number of packages. The weight is in kilos and the size is the sum of the length plus the circumference of the package in centimeters. These packages were picked at random from the airport loading dock in an effort to learn more about the relationship between package size and weight. You decide to graph the size of these packages relative to their weight.

If you set the weight figures in B2..B14 as the x-axis and the sizes in C2..C14 as the 1st Series Value, and use the Marker graph type, you get a graph like the one in Figure 9-24. Each measurement is displayed as a point on the graph, a square box in this case. The x-axis numbers are

FIGURE
9-23

Parcel data

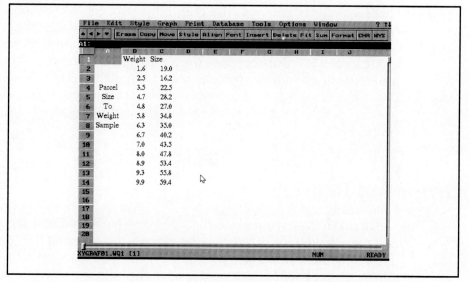

FIGURE
9-24

Unsorted Marker graph

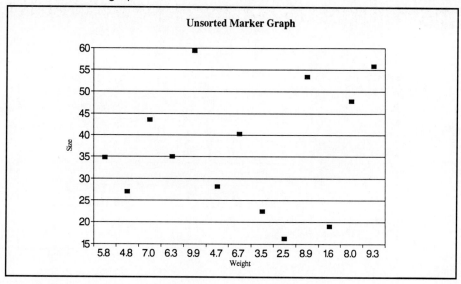

displayed in the order in which they exist in the worksheet. Although each package is graphed, the graph does not tell you much about the relationship between the two axes. However, if you change the graph type from Marker to XY, the graph is much more informative, as you can see in Figure 9-25. This is because the XY graph *sorts the data* on the x-axis into order of magnitude. You can see a fairly strong relationship between the size and weight. As size increases, so does weight. If you were told a package weighed 6.5 kilos, you could guess that the size is probably 35 centimeters.

Graphing Regression

There is a close relationship between the display of data in an XY graph and the calculations in regression analysis. If you look at the revised TOA marketing figures shown in Figure 9-26, you will see the monthly advertising page count next to the sales for the month (in thousands) and the projected sales based on the regression analysis on the right. If the pages were graphed as the x-axis in an XY graph, and if the sales were graphed as the 1st Series value, you could see the relationship between them.

**FIGURE
9-25**

XY graph

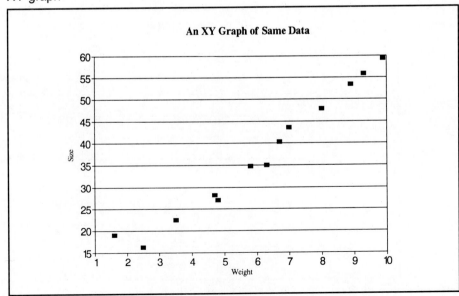

FIGURE 9-26

The updated marketing figures

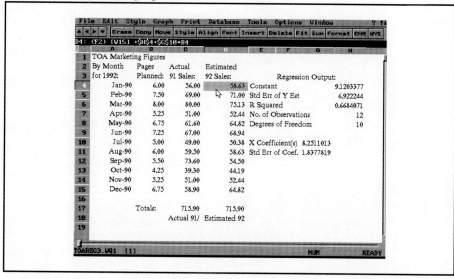

Figure 9-27 shows how this has been done. The actual sales are seen as boxes. The projected sales calculated from the regression figures are also graphed, as the 2nd Series value, and displayed as a line rather than as data points. You can see that the data points produced by the regression calculation represent a straight line drawn to fit as closely as possible to the relationship between sales and pages.

Using Solve For

Quattro Pro 4 provides a simple but powerful command, Solve For. It enables you to specify an answer to a formula and determine the appropriate value for one of the formula inputs. For example, consider a simple loan repayment calculation:

A	B
1 Principal	5000
2 Interest	.12
3 Term	36
4 Payment	@PMT (B1,B2/12,B3)

**FIGURE
9-27** Regression graph

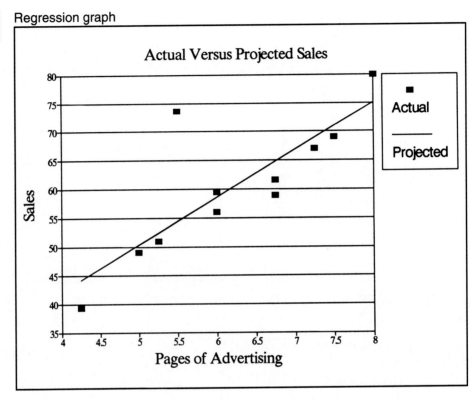

The formula in B4 returns the amount required to pay off a loan of $5,000 paid in 36 monthly installments at 12.00 percent A.P.R. The answer, to two decimal places, is $166.07. Suppose you can only repay at $150 per month. This means you cannot afford to borrow as much as $5,000. However, you want to know the largest amount you can borrow given the same term and rate of interest. The Solve For command can tell you this very quickly.

Before using the Solve For command, it is a good idea to save your spreadsheet and to turn on the Undo feature (using Options Other Undo Enable). This enables you to experiment with the possible answers without disturbing the original data.

To solve the payment formula for a given payment you select Solve For from the Tools menu. You must provide three pieces of information: Formula Cell, Target Value, and Variable Cell. The cell information can be provided either by typing in a cell reference or by pointing to the cells in the worksheet. In this example the Formula Cell is B4 and the Variable Cell is B1. The Target Value is simply typed, in this case 150. After setting these three items you select Go. This tells Quattro Pro 3 to change the value in the Variable Cell so that the formula cell results in the number specified as Target Value, in this case 4516.13, when given to two decimal places.

If you select Quit from the Solve For menu, you can press ALT-F5 to change the contents of B1 back to the former value. In this manner you can switch between two possible values and see the effects in the formula cell. This is a basic example, but it shows the usefulness and simplicity of this command. You can apply Solve For to larger models. In Figure 9-28 you can see the revenue projection worksheet used in Chapter 2. The figure for total revenue for the quarter is displayed in H7, where there is an @SUM formula adding up all of the revenue. The revenue grows from month to month based on a factor, currently 8 percent, recorded in B6.

You would like to know what rate of monthly increase would result in a total revenue figure of $40,000. You enter this as the Target Value in the Solve For menu, as shown in Figure 9-29. You then enter H7 as the Formula Cell and B6 as the Variable Cell. When you select Go you get the answer seen in Figure 9-30. If you have the Undo feature enabled

FIGURE 9-28

The revenue projection

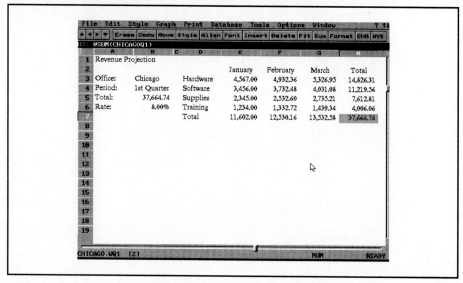

FIGURE 9-29

The Solve For menu

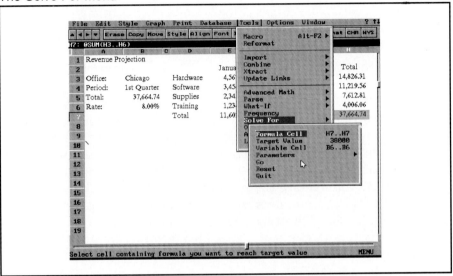

FIGURE 9-30

New revenue projection

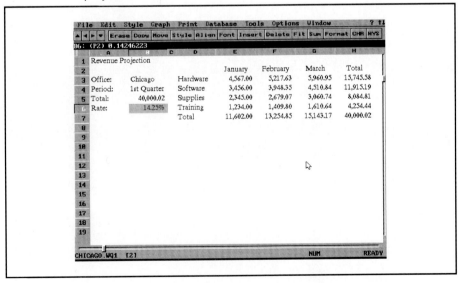

you can easily switch back to the original value in B6 and try a different entry in Target Value. As you can see, this type of backward solving of equations is very useful when you are dealing with projections and what-if scenarios.

When you want to move on to solve a different formula, you can use Solve For Reset to clear the current settings. The Parameters command enables you to specify two settings: Max Iterations and Accuracy. Because Solve For works by repeatedly guessing the answer, the Max Iterations setting determines how many times Quattro Pro 4 guesses before giving up. If your variable has only an incremental influence on your target value, then you may need to increase this setting from the default value (for example, using a target value of 100,000 in this example results in the warning message "Maximum iterations reached"). If you get this message you should try Solve For again, using a larger iteration setting. The Accuracy setting determines how close Solve For must get to a perfect answer before it stops guessing. The default value should be acceptable in most cases.

Optimization

The Tools menu provides another technique for analyzing data and solving problems. This is the Optimizer feature, which performs sophisticated linear programming and is used to minimize or maximize a combination of variables, subject to various constraints. The calculations are based on data in your spreadsheet that you specify through a series of settings. In the context of the Optimizer, *constraints* are the limitations placed on your variables. The ability to deal with constraints makes optimization particularly useful in analyzing economic problems, because economics is based on the relationship between ends and scarce means that have alternative uses. Suppose you want to optimize a manufacturing operation. The resources available are a constraint; you do not have endless supplies or an infinite number of person-hours per month. Plant capacity is also a constraint, because you cannot make an unlimited number of products.

An Optimizer Scenario

If you are already familiar with the general procedures used in solving complex nonlinear problems with multiple variables and constraints most of the items on the Optimizer menu, shown in Figure 9-31, will be self-explanatory. However, if you are not familiar with this type of problem solving, the best way to understand it is through an example. In the background of Figure 9-31 you can see part of a model that will be used as an example of the Optimizer commands.

The purpose of the model, shown in Figure 9-31 and again in Figure 9-32, is to calculate the profit for a company selling package tours to Alaska through direct mail advertising. The model shows a year's worth of business, broken down into quarters. The second line of the screen shows two of the values used in the calculations. The price charged for each ticket is in cell D2, block named PRICE. The wholesale cost to the seller for each ticket is in cell G2, block named COST. On row 6 there are four numbers that represent the seasonal factor in tour bookings. These factors have been established by analysis of past years' business. For example, sales are weak in the first quarter but strong in the third quarter.

FIGURE
9-31

The Tools Optimizer menu

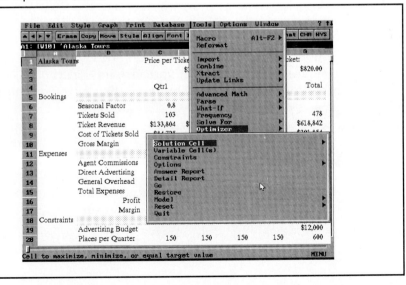

FIGURE
9-32

The sample spreadsheet

		Price per Ticket:			Cost per Ticket:	
Alaska Tours						
		$1,295.00				$820.00
		Qtr1	Qtr2	Qtr3	Qtr4	Total
Bookings						
	Seasonal Factor	0.8	0.9	1.1	0.9	
	Tickets Sold	103	116	142	116	478
	Ticket Revenue	$133,804	$150,529	$183,980	$150,529	$618,842
	Cost of Tickets Sold	$84,725	$95,316	$116,497	$95,316	$391,854
	Gross Margin	$49,079	$55,213	$67,483	$55,213	$226,988
Expenses						
	Agent Commissions	$8,028	$9,032	$11,039	$9,032	$37,131
	Direct Advertising	$3,000	$3,000	$3,000	$3,000	$12,000
	General Overhead	$16,056	$18,063	$22,078	$18,063	$74,261
	Total Expenses	$27,085	$30,095	$36,116	$30,095	$123,392
	Profit	$21,994	$25,118	$31,367	$25,118	$103,597
	Margin	16.4%	16.7%	17.0%	16.7%	16.7%
Constraints						
	Advertising Budget					$12,000
	Places per Quarter	150	150	150	150	600

The seasonal factor is used to project the number of tickets sold, using the formula shown in cell C7. This formula takes the into account the seasonal factor (C6), the level of advertising for the quarter (stated in C13), a basic level of sales (300 tickets), and an exponential growth limit (stated as ^0.6). The formula acknowledges the positive effect of advertising on ticket sales but also imposes the law of diminishing returns on each additional dollar of advertising spent. (If you were to calculate the formula in C7 with a range of values representing increasing levels of advertising and graph the results, you would find that eventually each additional dollar in advertising produces only a marginal increase in ticket sales.)

Rows 8 through 10 of the model calculate the gross margin from the projected sales, based on the selling price of the tickets and their cost to the seller. The Agent Commissions in row 12 are calculated at 6 percent of the revenue in row 8. The Direct Advertising figures in row 13 are simply the annual advertising budget of $12,000 spread evenly over all four quarters. The General Overhead in row 14 is 12 percent of revenue. By adding up these expenses and subtracting them from the Gross Margin, the model figures the Profit on row 16. On row 17 the model figures the percentage of profit margin. The bottom part of the model, labeled Constraints, will be discussed in a moment.

A Simple Problem

At this point the model embodies the past experience of the company in that seasonal factors are reflected in the sales, as are the effects of advertising. If advertising increases, so will revenue. Suppose you want to boost revenue in the first quarter to $150,000 and would like to know the level of advertising that will be require to reach this goal. This is a simple problem that could be addressed by the Solve For command, but the Optimizer can handle it as well. The first step is to select Solution Cell from the Optimizer menu. This leads to a menu with two options. The first is Cell, which in this example is C8, the ticket revenue for the first quarter.

As you can see from Figure 9-33, the second option is called Max,Min,Equal. In a simple problem like this where there are no constraints the setting must be Equal. When you select Equal you are prompted to enter a target value, in this case **150000**. When you have

FIGURE 9-33

Setting the Solution Cell

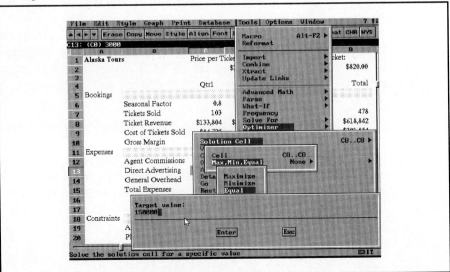

entered the target value you are returned to the Optimizer menu, which begins to reflect the settings you have made.

After establishing the solution cell and the target value you need to indicate the Variable Cell. This is the cell that the Optimizer should vary to reach the target value. In this example the cell is C13, the amount spent on advertising. When the variable cell has been set, the Optimizer has all of the information it needs to solve this particular problem and you can issue the Go command. After a brief wait the figures in the worksheet will change. The Optimizer menu will remain on screen and this may make it hard to see the results. You can either select Quit from the Optimizer menu or press the F6 key to temporarily hide the menu and view the worksheet.

If you use F6 to hide the menu you will not be able to move the cell selector, which will be frozen in the cell it occupied when you entered the Tools Optimizer menu. However, you will be able to see the worksheet, as shown in Figure 9-34. There you can see that the value in the variable cell, C13, has been changed from 3000 to just over 3692. This is the amount of advertising that produces the target revenue figure of 150000.

At this point you can press the F6 key to return to the Optimizer menu and, if you wish, change the settings. Alternatively, you can use the Restore command on the Optimizer menu to undo the changes to the

FIGURE 9-34

Viewing the results after Tools Optimize Go

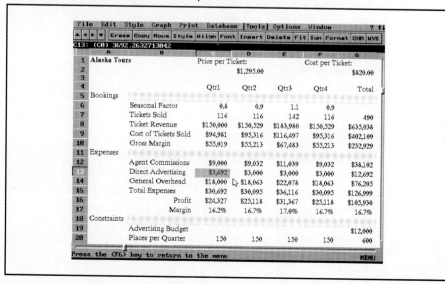

worksheet made by the Optimizer. The Restore command always reverses the effects of the last optimize operation, regardless of whether you have enabled Quattro Pro 4's Undo feature. In fact, because the Optimizer uses a lot of memory you may want to disable the Undo command, which increases the amount of memory available to Quattro Pro 4, before using the Optimizer. You can then rely on the Restore command to reverse the effects of optimization on the spreadsheet.

How you use the results of optimization will depend on the type of work you are doing. You can use the Optimizer to test different scenarios and play "what-if." In this case you may not need to save the results of each different optimization. Alternatively, you may want to use the Optimizer to create the final version of a worksheet, in which case you can save the file after performing optimization. A third option is to use the File Save As command to store several different versions of the worksheet under different names, reflecting different scenarios. A fourth option is to use the Model command on the Optimizer menu, described later in this chapter.

An Example of Constraints

In the previous example the Optimizer sought a simple goal with a single variable cell. A more powerful type of optimization involves more than one variable cell, and the use of constraints. You use constraints to determine which cells fall within upper or lower limits or meet a target. Constraints take the form of an equation or relationship between two cells, stated in the following format:

constraint cell	relation	constraint value
G13	<=	12000

where G13 is the constraint cell,, the relation is "less than or equal to," and the constraint value is 12000.

Constraints are easier to understand when put in practical terms. In the sample model you might want to find out how best to spend the annual advertising budget of $12,000. In other words, you would like to maximize the annual revenue value in G8, within the constraints imposed by the advertising budget of $12,000. Because the figure of $12,000 is stated in cell G19 you can supply the constraint value as a cell reference rather than a number. Note that cell G19 is a value, not a formula. Cells referred to as constraint values should contain values and not formulas.

Before you perform an optimization based on these parameters you may need to reset the Optimizer settings. You do this with the Reset command on the Optimizer menu. This enables you to clear any of the following settings: Solution Cell, Variable Cell(s), Constraints, Options, Answer Report, Detail Report, and All. Use the last option, All, when you want to establish a completely new optimization scenario.

To optimize revenue by varying the amount of advertising dollars spent in each quarter within the constraints of a total advertising budget of $12,000 you would, after resetting all of the Optimizer settings, do the following:

1. Set the Solution Cell to G8. This is the Ticket Revenue for the year.

2. Set the Solution Cell Max,Min,Equal option to Maximize, because you want to maximize the revenue figure.

3. Set the Variable Cells to C13..F13, because these represent the advertising expenditure that you are interested in adjusting.

4. Select Constraints followed by the <Add New Constraint> item. You will be prompted to supply a cell. In this case you want the total advertising in G13 to be limited so select G13.

5. You are now prompted for a relation, and you have three choices:

   Less than or equal to   <=

   Equal to   =

   Greater than or equal to   >=

   In this case you want <=, because the advertising budget is limited to $12,000 or less.

6. You are now prompted to enter a constraint value. This can be a cell containing a value, such as G19, or a value that you type, such as 12000. Typically a cell is preferable, because you can easily alter the value in the cell to perform the optimization with a different constraint value.

7. The Constraint is thus recorded as either G13 <= G19 or G13 <= 12000, depending on whether you have supplied the value as a cell or number. You can now issue the Go command to perform the optimization.

8. After a moment or two the values in the spreadsheet will be altered and you can press F6 to view the results. In this case they will appear as shown in Figure 9-35.

The Optimizer has varied the marketing values in the variable cells and increased the revenue by $6,470 (from $618,842 to $625,312). However, this has been done without exceeding the constraint of $12,000 for the total advertising budget. As you can see from Figure 9-35 the advertising expenditure is concentrated in the quarters with highest seasonal factor, but the calculation that Quattro Pro 4 has performed is considerably more subtle than simply prorating expenditure based on the seasonal factors. If you based advertising solely on the seasonal factors, the breakdown and resulting revenue would be as follows:

Equal values:	Optimized values:	Prorated values:
$3,000	$1,937	$2,595 (G19*D54/D58)
$3,000	$2,702	$2,919 (G19*D55/D58)
$3,000	$4,658	$3,567 (G19*D55/D58)
$3,000	$2,702	$2,919 (G19*D55/D58)
Revenue:	Revenue:	Revenue:
$618,842	$625,312	$622,639

FIGURE
9-35

Results of optimization with a constraint

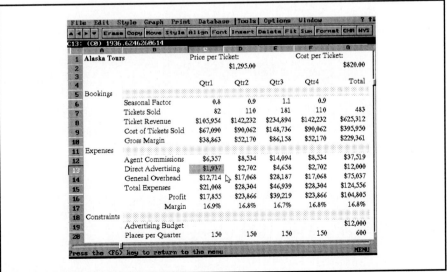

The gain in revenue from optimizing the advertising as opposed to prorating is thus $2,673 ($625,312–$622,639).

This is a good example of how the Optimizer can arrive at solutions that would otherwise take a lot of trial-and-error calculations. Of course, you can still play "what-if" with the Optimizer. For example, suppose that you wanted to know the effect of allocating more resources to advertising, increasing the annual spending to $18,000. If you enter the constraint value as cell G19, you can simply change the value in that cell from 12000 to 18000 and issue the Go command from the Optimizer menu (this is one reason why it is better to use a cell rather than a number for the constraint value).

In this particular scenario the results lead to annual ticket sales of 605. You will note that the bottom row of the model lists 600 as the maximum number of tickets available for the year. In other words, it is possible to spend so much on advertising that demand exceeds supply. The number of tickets that can be sold represents a constraint that is not accounted for in the previous example. Indeed, if you look at Figure 9-35 you can see that ticket sales for the third quarter exceed 150, which is the limit stated in E20.

Fortunately, the Optimizer can take into account additional constraints. Suppose that the supply of tickets is not limited to 150 per quarter, but is limited to 600 per year. With a ticket limit of 600 entered in G20 and an advertising limit of 18000 in G19 you can add a second constraint to the model. Select Constraints and choose <Add New Constraint>. This will be defined as G7 <= G20. When you select Go, the Optimizer produces the results shown in Figure 9-36. There you can see that with additional advertising, revenue reaches $777,000 by the time all of the 600 tickets are sold. The advertising required to reach this point is $17,787, slightly less than the $18,000 you were prepared to spend.

Optimizer Limits and Options

By this point you should be able to see that the Optimizer has tremendous ability to assist in the solution of practical problems facing organizations that must work with limited resources. However, there are times when issuing the Go command on the Optimizer menu results in an error message. When this happens, you can press the Help key (F1)

FIGURE
9-36

Results of optimization with multiple constraints

to get an explanation of the error. One such error message states "Problem is unbounded." This usually implies that the solution to which the Optimizer is working is too good to be true, and probably based on unrealistic parameters. The key to successful use of the Optimizer is giving it realistic tasks.

Another error message you might see is "Objective function changing too slowly." This means that Quattro Pro 4 can only adjust the solution cell a small amount or not at all, no matter how much it adjusts the variables. You should check that variable cells actually contribute to the solution. If they do, try different starting values. The message "No feasible solution can be found" suggests that the constraints are not consistent or have been set incorrectly. Once again you should check that the starting values are realistic. Another response is to alter the Precision setting.

The Precision setting is found on the Tools Optimizer Options menu, shown in Figure 9-37. There are eight settings that you can adjust in order to alter the way that the Optimizer performs when you issue the Go command. The Max Time setting controls the length of time, in seconds, that Quattro Pro 4 has to come up with a solution. You might

FIGURE
9-37

The Tools Optimizer Options menu

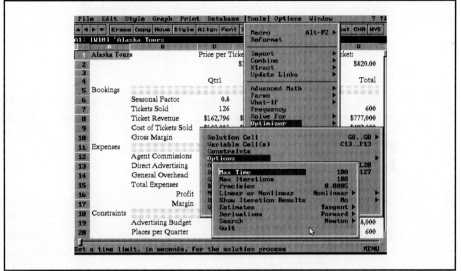

consider increasing this setting if the Optimizer fails to give you an answer. The default setting for Max Time is 100 seconds.

The Max Iterations setting controls how many times the Optimizer runs through the calculations required to arrive at a solution. Increasing this setting may allow the Optimizer to solve a problem that would otherwise take too many iterations. The default setting for Max Iterations is 100. The Precision setting is a value between 0 and 1 that determines how accurate the Optimizer is required to be. The default setting is .0005. If you add zeroes to this decimal value you increase the precision required. Values closer to 1 imply less precision but this may be required to solve more difficult problems.

The Linear or Nonlinear setting can be altered from the default of Nonlinear to Linear if you know that the problem is linear. This results in faster solutions to problems. A problem is considered to be linear when there is one optimal solution or no solution at all. More complex problems can have several different solutions and are referred to as nonlinear. If you are trying to solve a nonlinear problem you should start with values that are as realistic as possible. Run the Optimizer several different times with different starting values and compare the solutions.

You might find it helpful to watch the Optimizer working towards a solution. You can do this by changing the Show Iteration Results setting from No, the default, to Yes. When you issue the Go command with Show Iteration Results set to Yes, Quattro Pro 4 will pause after each attempt to solve the problem, enabling you to see the solution. You are then prompted to continue with the next iteration or stop the optimization.

The following advanced items on the Options menu can alter the way that the Optimizer does its calculations: Estimates, Derivatives, and Search. Experienced mathematicians will be familiar with the options that these settings provide. The default setting for Estimates is Tangent, which means that the initial estimates of the basic variables in the problem are derived by a linear extrapolation from a tangent vector. The alternative setting is Quadratic, an alternative form of extrapolation that may be more successful in solving highly nonlinear problems. The Derivatives setting is normally Forward, but the alternative setting, Central, may succeed if an optimization results in the "All remedies failed to find better point" message. Note that the Central option may require more iterations to complete the solution. The Search setting is usually Newton, which is a method of determining the direction of the search for a solution. Try the alternative setting, Conjugate, if you get the "Objective function changing too slowly" message.

Optimizer Models

You may want to use the same model to try out several different scenarios with the Optimizer. To switch from one set of parameters to another you do not have to reset the Optimizer and enter new values from scratch. You can actually store parameters in the worksheet with the Model Save command and load them with the Model Load command.

When you select Model from the Optimizer menu you must choose either Load or Save. When you select Save you are prompted for a section of the worksheet into which Quattro Pro 4 will write the current parameters from the Optimizer. In Figure 9-38 you can see the result of choosing N4 as the cell for the Model Save command, based on the last optimization example, just described, maximizing revenue in G8 by increasing advertising from $3,000 per quarter to an annual maximum of $18,000 (G19)

FIGURE
9-38

Results of the Model Save command

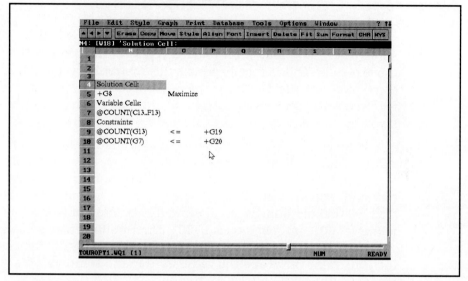

with a limit of 600 on ticket sales (G20). You can see that Solution Cell, Variable Cells, and Constraints, are all listed.

In N5 the Solution Cell is stated as G8. Note that in fact this is a cell reference formula (+G8) formatted with the Text format. In O5 the Min,Max,Equal setting is stated. If you have specified a target value for the solution the entry in O5 would be Equal and the value would be placed in Q5. The entries that appear as @COUNT are formulas formatted in the Text format. If you change these cells to a numeric format you will see how many cells there are in each case.

Once you have saved a model into the worksheet, as in Figure 9-38, you can copy the solution cells to another section of the worksheet and change the cells in the copy so that they represent a different set of parameters. You can then use the Model Load command to read the new parameters from the worksheet into the Optimizer. You can create a set of model cells without using the Model Save command, but the model cells must match the general arrangement shown in Figure 9-38. Note that when you use the Model Save command Quattro Pro 4 adjusts the width of the worksheet columns to accommodate the results.

Reporting Optimization Results

In addition to seeing the results of the Optimizer command in your spreadsheet, you may want to get a report of the process that achieved those results. This is the purpose of the Answer Report and Detail Report commands on the Optimizer menu. These commands create reports within a worksheet, and you can then format them and print them out if you so desire.

The Answer Report tells you how many constraints are met, including variable and constraint dual values. You can see an example of an Answer Report in Figure 9-39. The contents of the report are fairly self-explanatory and represent maximizing revenue in G8 by increasing advertising from $3,000 per quarter to an annual maximum of $18,000 (G19) with a limit of 600 on ticket sales (G20). The Binding entries show whether the constraints were met. The Slack entries show any differences between the constraint value and the value used in the solution. This report was created with cell H4 as the destination.

The Detail Report lists the variables and solution cell values at each iteration. You can see how variable cells change throughout the solution process. This is useful when you are doing a lot of "what-if" testing using

FIGURE 9-39

An example of the Answer Report

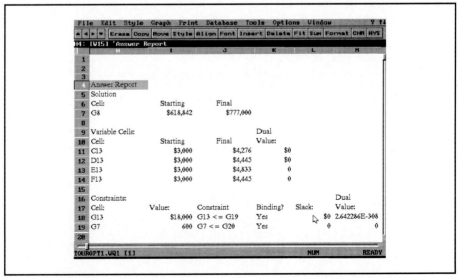

the Optimizer with different starting values. You can see an example of a Detail Report in Figure 9-40. The contents of the report represent maximizing revenue in G8 by increasing advertising from $3,000 per quarter to an annual maximum of $18,000 (G19) with a limit of 600 on ticket sales (G20). You can see that the Optimizer took only three iterations to find the solution. This report was created with the cell H22 identified as the destination.

The reports are produced during the optimization process so you must select the type of report you want before you select the Go command. After choosing either Answer Report or Detail Report you are prompted for a block of cells in the spreadsheet into which the report will be written. You can indicate a single cell to give Optimizer the maximum freedom in producing the report. The report will take up as much space as is necessary, so make sure there are no important entries in cells below the cell you indicate. As a guideline for report blocks, the Answer Report uses six columns and ten more rows than there are variable and constraint cells.

The Detail Report takes up two more columns than there are variable cells, plus three more rows than there are iterations in the solution process. Because the number of iterations is hard to predict the best approach for a Detail Report is to indicate a single cell with nothing below

FIGURE
9-40

An example of the Detail Report

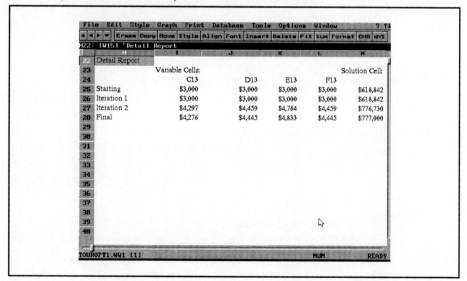

it (you cannot use a separate worksheet as the destination for Optimizer reports). You can create both types of report during the same optimization process. Select each report in turn and specify separate blocks for the results before you select Go.

Additional Functions

The Tools Library command enables you to increase the number of @functions available within Quattro Pro 4. Additional @functions can be stored in a library file with the extension .QLL. A sample library file, called SAMPLE.QLL, is shipped with some versions of Quattro Pro 4. When you select Library from the Tools menu you must choose Load or Unload. The Unload command is used to remove a library you have already loaded. A list of loaded libraries appears, and you can select the one you want to unload. Unloading libraries increases the amount of memory available in Quattro Pro 4.

The Tools Library Load command is used to read a library of @functions into memory. You are presented with a file list box with which to specify the file. Library files use the extension .QLL. Once a file has been selected the @functions it contains are available for the rest of the current session and in future sessions, until the Unload command is used to remove the library from memory. To use a library @function you enter the function like this:

@SAMPLE.LAST_DAY(A1)

The name SAMPLE comes from the name of the library file, in this case SAMPLE.QLL. The name of the library function, in this case LAST_DAY, follows the library name, separated from the name by a period. Any arguments that the function requires can then be stated. In this case the argument is A1, and the function returns the date serial number of the last day of the month in any valid Quattro Pro 4 date. Thus the function returns the serial number for January 31st, 1993 if the date in the argument cell is any day in January 1993.

You will find that a growing number of @function libraries are available for Quattro Pro 4, including specialized financial and scientific formulas.

Programmers can write these libraries using a high-level programming language and the Quattro Pro Developers Toolkit, available from Borland International. If you use library @functions in your spreadsheets you may want to use the @ISAPP function to a check for the presence of a particular library. For example, you can use the following formula to check that the library called SAMPLE.QLL is loaded:

@ISAPP("SAMPLE")

The result is 1 if the library is loaded, 0 if it is not. Such a formula can be used in a macro designed to load the library if it is not already loaded (for more on macros, see Chapters 11 and 12). To check whether a specific function is available, you can use the @ISAAF function, as in the following example, which returns 1 if the LAST_DAY function is available:

@ISAAF("SAMPLE.LAST_DAY")

Spreadsheet Auditing

The golden rule of business computing is this: "Never rely on the answers that the computer gives you." This doesn't mean you shouldn't be using a program like Quattro Pro 4; it simply means you should know enough about what you are asking Quattro Pro 4 to do to tell right answers from wrong. In its simplest form spreadsheet auditing means proofreading the spreadsheet, checking that the results given by formulas make sense. You can take this a step further by including formulas that check results for you (an example was given in Chapter 4 of a cross-footing formula created with the @IF function). This section describes two tools in Quattro Pro 4 that assist with auditing: Window Options Map View and Tools Audit.

The Map View

Consider the screen shown in Figure 9-41. This is a map view of a spreadsheet that projects revenue for several computer sales offices. The

FIGURE
9-41

A spreadsheet displayed in Map View

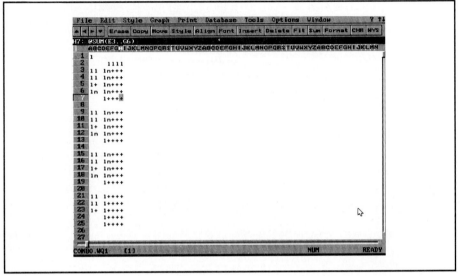

columns have been narrowed to fit more of them on the screen. Each letter *l* represents a cell containing a label. Each letter *n* represents a cell containing a numeric value that is not calculated by any formula or function. The plus signs represent cells containing formulas, such as H7. This cell, as you can see from the cell identifier, contains a total.

The map view is created by selecting Map View from the Window Options menu and choosing Yes. You return the display to normal by using the same command and choosing No. While Quattro Pro 4 is in map view you can still enter and edit data in the worksheet. However, the main purpose of the map view is to let you check the integrity of the worksheet. For example, in Figure 9-42 you can see a normal view of the same worksheet (in fact, this is a view with the WYSIWYG Zoom % set to 80 in order to show all of the cells). It is clear that the numbers in column H should be calculated from formulas. If you went to the map view and found that column H had an *n* in it, you would know that something was wrong. Entering a number over the top of a formula is a common spreadsheet error. If the number is equal to the initial result of the formula, the problem may not be apparent. However, when the values that give rise to the formula change, the number will be wrong.

FIGURE 9-42

A normal view of the spreadsheet shown in Figure 9-41

The Tools Audit Commands

When you select Audit from the Tools menu you get the list of options shown in Figure 9-43. Before you use any of the commands, you may want to check that the Destination is set to Screen. This enables you to see the results of the audit commands on your screen. The alternative Destination setting is Printer, which ends results directly to your printer (in draft mode).

The Tools Audit Dependency command asks you to select a block of cells to audit. Suppose that you want to check the totals in cells H21..H25 of the worksheet shown in Figure 9-42. When you have selected the cells the Dependency command produces the audit screen shown in Figure 9-44. Here you can see that the dependencies of the first cell in the block are diagrammed. For example, H21 sums E21, F21, and G21. The dependencies for these cells are also listed and the diagram extends off the screen. If you press /, a short menu appears with the items that are listed in Table 9-1. Each menu item has a shortcut key. Using the menu or the shortcut keys you can navigate the audit screen and return to the spreadsheet.

FIGURE
9-43

The Tools Audit menu

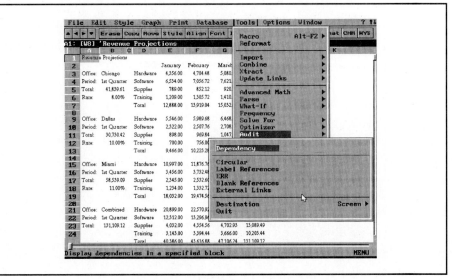

FIGURE
9-44

The Audit screen

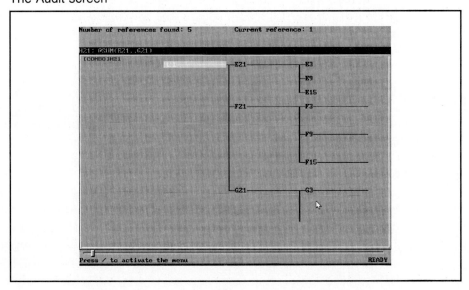

TABLE 9-1

The Audit Screen Menu

Menu Item	Shortcut	Action
Next	PGDN	Move to next screen of the diagram
Previous	PGUP	Move to previous screen of the diagram
GoTo	F5	Move to the spreadsheet and select the cell currently highlighted in the audit screen
Begin	ENTER	Lists the cells that are dependent on the currently highlighted cell
Quit	ESC	Returns you to the Audit menu and the spreadsheet

The other next five items after Dependency on the Audit menu are used to check specific situations in a spreadsheet. These are circular formulas, formulas that refer to labels, formulas that result in ERR, formulas that refer to cells that are currently blank, and formulas that link to other spreadsheets. Circular formulas were discussed in Chapter 4, and—except in very specialized situations—they are to be avoided in spreadsheets.

Formulas that refer to labels or blank cells should be checked in case they are erroneous. For example, if a cell containing a space label has been included in an @AVG function argument it might produce an incorrect answer (a "space label" is created by pressing the SPACEBAR and then ENTER, an action that is sometimes used to delete a cell but which in fact creates a hard to see label that can distort the results of some functions). The problem with empty or blank cells is that they can create "divide by zero" errors, because a value cannot be divided by an empty cell.

By using the Audit commands you can perform a thorough check on the integrity and design of a worksheet. By changing the Destination setting to Printer, you can print the results of the audit, thus creating a permanent record of the audit for later reference.

Tools for Files

In Chapter 7 you read how the Tools Xtract command can be used to copy data from within a Quattro Pro 4 worksheet to a file on disk. There are several other file-related commands on the Tools menu, and they are described here. The Tools Import command is also discussed in Chapter 10, which describes the Tools Parse command in detail.

Tools Xtract

The Tools Xtract command copies a block of cells from the current worksheet to a file on disk. This is helpful when you need to share a portion of a worksheet with a colleague or if you want to divide a large worksheet into several smaller worksheets. For example, suppose you have developed a worksheet like the one seen earlier in Figure 9-42, which adds up the revenue projections for three regional offices. You want to send the manager of the Chicago office a spreadsheet that only covers that office's revenue, in other words, cells A2..H7. You can use the Tools Xtract command to copy A2..H7 to a new file on disk.

When you issue the Tools Xtract command you must choose between Formulas and Values. When copying database records to a foreign file format you should choose Values. You can also choose Values if you do not need to preserve the spreadsheet formulas in the file you are about to create. Choose Formulas if you want the new file to be a working model rather than simply a collection of fixed values. After choosing between formulas and values you are prompted to enter a file name. If you want the file to be a normal Quattro Pro 4 worksheet, simply enter up to eight letters for a file name. The default .WQ1 extension will be added automatically. If you want to export data to a foreign file format, add the appropriate file extension (such as .DBF to create a dBASE file). Check the relevant section in Chapter 7 for more on exporting data.

After you have selected or entered a file name you are prompted for the block of cells to be copied to the new file, in this example, A2..H7. When you select the block and press ENTER the file is written to disk (if a file of the same name already exists you will have a chance to cancel the command or replace the existing file with the new data). If the block of cells you copy to the file is "self-contained," the new file can immediately be loaded and used. A self-contained block is one that includes all of the values necessary to carry out the calculations that occur within the block. For example, in Figure 9-42 the values in columns F and G are created by multiplying by a factor stored in column B. This means that extracting D2..H7 would not create a working model, because the cell with the growth factor would be excluded.

Tools Combine

The Tools Combine command reads all or part of a worksheet file into the current worksheet. Unlike File Open, the Tools Combine command does not open a separate window for the data that it reads from disk. Unlike the File Retrieve command, Tools Combine does not replace the current worksheet when it reads data file from disk. Instead, the Tools Combine command writes the incoming data into cells within the current worksheet. Because the Tools Combine command has the ability to overwrite data within the current worksheet, you should use the command with care.

In fact, the Tools Combine command was developed to help users consolidate worksheet data before the advent of multiple spreadsheets and spreadsheet links. Consider the manager working with the spreadsheet in Figure 9-42. This could easily be split into four separate spreadsheets, one for each of the three offices plus a fourth used for consolidation of the other three. Such a scenario was described in Chapter 2. In that scenario the staff at the Chicago, Dallas, and Miami offices sent in their projection worksheets to the head office where they were consolidated by using link formulas to read the values into a master spreadsheet. However, the Tools Combine command does allow each of the supporting worksheets to be copied into a master worksheet.

Before you issue the Tools Combine command, make sure that the cell selector is in the top left cell of the area you plan to use for the incoming data. When you issue the Tools Combine command you first have to choose from among the Copy, Add, and Subtract options. The Copy option simply brings in all of the entries from the supporting worksheet. The Add option actually adds the values in the incoming data to existing values within the receiving worksheet. This happens if the incoming data is placed over existing data. This allows a series of identically formatted worksheets to be added together in a master worksheet, as in the case of monthly sales reports being added together to create year-to-date figures. The Subtract option does the same thing as Add, except that the incoming values of subtracted from the existing value. This allows such operations as subtracting monthly sales from a yearly quota figure to determine the amount of quota still unmet.

After you have selected Copy, Add, or Subtract, you must choose between File or Block. The File option means that the entire contents of the file will be read into the current worksheet. Note that empty cells in the incoming worksheet will not overwrite cells of the current worksheet that are already occupied by data. The Block option enables you to read in a selected block of cells from a file. This is useful if you only need to read in part of a file. However, if you select Block you must provide Quattro Pro 4 with either the block coordinates, such as A1..H20, or a valid block name that was assigned to the cells in the source file. After selecting File or Block you must name the file that you want to read from. This is done through a standard file list box. When the file has been selected the data is read into the current worksheet beginning at the current cell.

Tools Import

Like the Tools Combine command the Tools Import command is used to read data into the current worksheet. However, whereas the Tools Combine command reads worksheets, the Tools Import command reads text files. Many programs can store data in text files so that they can be read by other software. You will find a discussion of text files in the next chapter. Basically there are three types of text file that Quattro Pro 4 can read. When you issue the Tools Import command Quattro Pro 4 presents the choices listed in Table 9-2.

An ASCII text file is read line by line. This is useful when you need to add a lot of text to a worksheet. You can create the text in a word processing program, store it in a text file, then read it into the worksheet with the Tools Import ASCII Text File command. When you issue the command you simply identify the file that you want to read. Note that the file will be read into the current cell of the worksheet and additional cells in the same column. The incoming text will appear as a series of long labels.

TABLE 9-2 The Text Import Options

File Type	Description
ASCII Text File	Created by most word processors and also communications programs that capture screen data on disk
Comma & "" Delimited File	Data stored in rows, with each row split into delimited groups. Each group is separated from the next by a comma, with text groups enclosed in quotes. Typically used where rows are database records and groups are database fields
Only Commas	Data stored in rows, with each row split into groups. Each group is separated from the next by a comma, with quotes used to enclose entries that contain commas. Typically used where rows are database records and groups are database fields

Be aware that the incoming data will overwrite entries within the current worksheet at or below the current cell. The other two categories of imported text are split into cells. Each delimited group is entered into a separate cell; groups in quotes form labels, and numbers create numeric values.

CHAPTER

Managing Text

Although spreadsheets are designed primarily to manipulate numbers, in some situations you can use them to manipulate text as well. In this chapter several Quattro Pro 4 commands that apply to text will be examined, and Quattro Pro 4 will be used to produce paragraphs of text. Quattro Pro 4 can convert spreadsheet data to text files that can be read by word processors and can also read text files from other programs. This process of data exchange will be examined. Finally, the string commands that manipulate labels will be discussed.

Quattro Pro 4 as a Text Editor

Most spreadsheets require that you enter at least some text—words or phrases that describe the values in the model. Sometimes these pieces of text can be fairly lengthy. Consider the spreadsheet of projected expenses shown in Figure 10-1. The designer of this model felt that it was necessary to explain several of the assumptions at work in the calculations. This is a good practice to adopt, especially if the spreadsheet is going to be used or read by others.

Annotated expenses

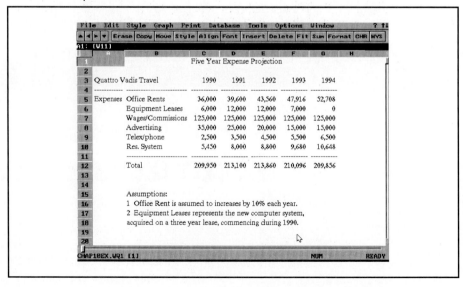

Entering Blocks of Text

Entering a piece of text, like assumption 1 in Figure 10-1, is simply a matter of typing a long label. You type the text and then press ENTER. Once you have entered the text, you may need to edit it, for which you use the F2 key, as described in Chapter 2. Remember that you can move your cursor through a long label by using the CTRL-RIGHT or CTRL-LEFT ARROW key combinations, which move the cursor five character positions to the right or left. Use CTRL-\ to delete to the end of the entry.

Text like that in assumption 2 is handled a little differently. It begins as a long label. When you type a label longer than 66 characters, Quattro Pro 4 actually moves the worksheet display down a line to make the text visible as you type it. This is shown in Figure 10-2. Note that in some display modes you may be able to type more characters before going to a second line. Also note that the program does not know that you are typing a series of words. The word *on* is split between two lines because the sixty-sixth character on the first line of the label is the *o* in *on*. Quattro Pro 4 does not perform the word processing function known as word wrap while you enter a long label.

FIGURE 10-2

Typing a long label

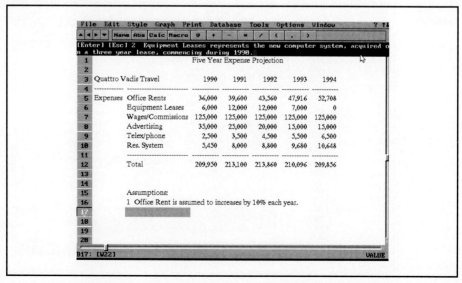

When you complete the label and enter it, the label initially spreads across the columns of the worksheet in a long, somewhat hard-to-read line of words. In fact, before you can enter this label you will have to insert an apostrophe to the left of the first character, otherwise Quattro Pro 4 assumes it is a value.

You can see the long label in Figure 10-3, which shows the next stage: changing a long label like this into a paragraph. Quattro Pro 4 does this by breaking the long label into several shorter labels in a process called *block reformatting.* You perform this process with the Tools Reformat command, which wraps the text within an area of the spreadsheet that you designate. Place your cell selector on the cell containing the long label that you want to adjust to a more compact size, in this case B17. Select Reformat from the Tools menu and, when you are prompted for the block to be modified, point out the area into which you want the long label rearranged. In this case, the block of cells B17..F18 is highlighted, as shown in Figure 10-3.

The highlighted area should be empty except for the cell being reformatted. It should be as wide as you would like the paragraph to be and may stretch several rows below the original cell, so that there is room for the formatted text. When you press ENTER, the long label is divided into a series of shorter labels as wide as the block you highlighted. Notice

FIGURE
10-3

Reformat block

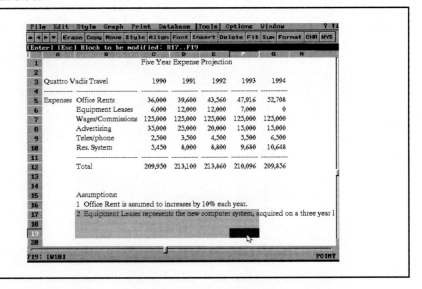

that the label is divided without breaking the words. The results can be seen in Figure 10-1. The second line of the second assumption is a label formed in the cell below the original label.

If you need to edit the text that you have reformatted into shorter labels, you highlight the cell containing the text to be edited and press F2. However, if you make any line in the middle of a paragraph (such as line 18 in this example) much shorter or longer than it was before editing, you will have to reissue the Reformat command. In this way you can compose short documents, letters, and memos from a series of long labels using the reformatting command. You can use macros to simplify successive reformatting of text. Macros will be described in Chapter 11.

Printing to a File

Because Quattro Pro 4 is not really equipped to work as a word processor, you may want to copy words and numbers from Quattro Pro 4 to your word processor. This is done with a special file that the word processor can read. Different word processing programs store their documents in different file formats. In other words, the way in which the actual letters are stored on disk varies from program to program. However, all popular word processing programs can read files that are stored in ASCII, the American Standard Code for Information Interchange. One reason word processing programs can read information stored this way is that they communicate with printers in ASCII. Printers receive the letters and numbers of your documents as ASCII characters.

In fact, that is how Quattro Pro 4 sends your spreadsheet cells to the printer. By diverting data intended for the printer to a file on disk, you can create an *ASCII file,* or *print file,* of the spreadsheet data. Quattro Pro 4 creates this file through the Print Destination command, which changes the target of the print block from the printer to a file. The file name usually has the extension .PRN to distinguish it from other files. The data in the file is simply strings of letters, numbers, and spaces. Formulas are converted to their values and the values become text, including any formatting such as the dollar signs of the Currency format. The resulting file is often called a *text file.*

Suppose that you want to put the numbers from Figure 10-1 in a memo that you have been writing with your word processing program. Retyping the numbers from Quattro Pro 4 into a word processing document would be a chore, and typos could arise from retyping. Instead, you decide to export the figures as an ASCII file.

Preparing for Printing

In order to make the data coming from Quattro Pro 4 easier for your word processor to read, you may want to use the Print Layout command to change some of the options prior to printing to disk. By selecting the Margins option from the Layout menu, you can change the left margin from 4 to 0 characters. This number will prevent Quattro Pro 4 from adding four spaces to the left of the data in the file. Similarly, entering 0 for a top margin will stop Quattro Pro 4 from adding lines to the top of the print block. The right margin setting needs particular attention, because the data in the file will be split into sections if you have set the right margin narrower than the width of the print block. In general, you will not want to use a right margin wider than 80 for a text file that will be read by a word processor that is using a normal 8 1/2-by-11-inch page. Otherwise, your text file will contain more data than will fit between the word processor's margins.

Making Print Files

Having selected the Print options you want to use, you can proceed to indicate the print block, the cells whose contents will be placed in the print file. You decide to use cells B3 through G12, because the numbers are the most important part of the worksheet and the rest of the titles can be added in the word processing document. You do not want to include any extra columns and rows in the print block, because they will only add empty space to the word processing document.

The next step is to select Destination from the Print menu. The possible print destinations are separated into Draft Mode and Final Quality. As you learned in Chapter 3, Draft Mode is simple character output with no complex formatting such as fonts. Final Quality printing includes detailed instructions to the printer about fonts, lines, and other enhancements. Each print mode has its own file option. If you select File from the Draft Mode Printing section you will be creating a pure ASCII file, stripped of all format information. This can be read by just about any word processing program. The Binary File option under Final Quality Printing creates a file containing text plus a detailed set of print instructions. Do not choose this option if you are exporting text to another program.

When you select File from the Draft Mode Printing section of the Print Destination menu, Quattro Pro 4 presents a file name prompt so that you can name the file to be used. If there are any files with the .PRN extension in the current data directory they will be displayed, as shown in Figure 10-4. Otherwise, you will simply see the file name prompt with no files listed. Type the name of the file you want to create, leave off the extension if you want Quattro Pro 4 to add .PRN for you. If there are already .PRN files in the default data directory, you can select one of them as the destination for the print job.

If you select an existing name, the program asks whether you want to replace the data in an existing print file with new data or append the new data to the old. Appending new data is useful for accumulating data from various parts of a spreadsheet or from different spreadsheets into one

FIGURE
10-4

The print block

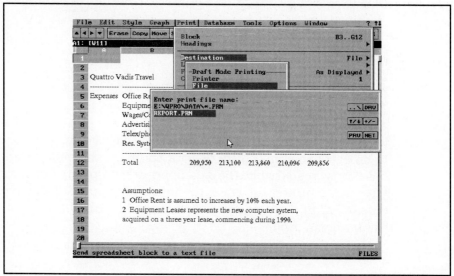

text file. You can also choose to cancel the overwriting of an existing file or to back up the data already in it to a file with the .BAQ extension.

Once you have selected or typed a name, that file is opened on the disk and space is set up to receive the print data. When you select Spreadsheet Print from the Print menu, the data is actually written into the file. When you quit the Print menu, the file is closed. In a moment you will read how to use the file with your word processor.

Binary Print Files

Before you deal with the transfer of a spreadsheet text file to a word processor, it is important to distinguish between the two types of print files that Quattro Pro 4 can create. The File option under Draft Mode Printing on the Print Destination menu creates a pure ASCII file that can be read by a wide range of programs. The Binary File option under Final Quality Printing creates a file that contains detailed instructions on the formatting of the data. With one exception, discussed in a moment, the binary print files created by this option are not intended to be read by other programs. What you can do with binary print files is send them directly to the printer using the DOS command COPY. For example, you could direct a lengthy report to a binary print file and then copy the file to a floppy disk. You could take that disk to another computer and use DOS to output the report on a printer attached to that computer, without running Quattro Pro 4.

The COPY command is used at the DOS prompt and would look like this:

COPY REPORT.PRN /B LPT1:

where REPORT.PRN is the name of the binary print file and the printer is attached to the computer's first parallel port (which most printers are). In order for this procedure to work correctly, the binary print file must have been created when the default printer in Quattro Pro 4 was the same type as the printer on which the report is to be printed. Otherwise, the detailed print instructions stored in the file will not make sense to the printer being used.

Another reason for creating binary print files is that you can send a series of such files to the printer, one after another, in a print queue. However, the Print Manager built into Quattro Pro 4 takes care of queuing print jobs, completing them in the background while you carry on working in Quattro Pro 4. The Print Manager is described in Appendix C.

There is one exceptional case when you are working with print files. If the default printer is a PostScript printer, you cannot create a plain ASCII print file. PostScript is a special method of describing information to a printer, known as a page description language. The first printer to popularize PostScript was the Apple LaserWriter, but these days there are many printers that use PostScript, often denoted by the letters PS in the model name, such as the Brother HL-8PS. The advantage of Post-Script is that it is extremely accurate. One disadvantage to most Post-Script printers is they insist on receiving information in the PostScript language, rendering them incapable of Draft Mode printing. This is why you cannot create a plain ASCII file when the default printer is a PostScript printer, even if you select File as opposed to Binary File from the Destination menu.

If you need to create an ASCII file you should select a different printer model, such as Epson FX-80, as the default printer before you print to a disk file with the Destination File setting. If the PostScript printer was defined as your 1st Printer with the Options Hardware Printers command, you can choose 2nd Printer and select the Epson model. Then you only need to use the Default Printer command to select 2nd Printer before you use the Print Destination command.

There may be times when you will want to take advantage of the way that Quattro Pro 4 handles PostScript printers. If you create a print file when the default printer is a PostScript printer, you can use this file in programs that support the .EPS (Encapsulated PostScript) file format. .EPS files represent a complete description of an image, whether it is a single graph or an entire report. Some desktop publishing programs can read .EPS files and display them as images. This means that you can export a table from Quattro Pro 4 to a desktop publishing program using EPS. You create an .EPS file from Quattro Pro 4 cells by using the Print command with Binary File as the Destination setting and a PostScript printer as the default device. When you select Binary File from the Destination menu you can name the file with .EPS as the extension, as in REPORT.EPS.

Editing the Results

Once you have created a print or text file from a Quattro Pro 4 file, you can edit it with a word processor. Make sure that you have saved any necessary changes to your worksheet; then quit Quattro Pro 4 and load your word processing program. You can type text as you normally would, up to the point where the print file is to be included. Before issuing the command to read in the print file, you may want to set the margins wide enough to accommodate the incoming data. How word processors read in ASCII text varies. Some programs, such as WordPerfect 5.1, can simply read ASCII files with the Retrieve command. Others require a special command. In Figure 10-5, you can see the .PRN file retrieved into a WordPerfect document. Note that the text "is Travel" is left over from the long label in cell A3 of the worksheet. This can be edited out.

At this point the text is a series of characters and spaces. There are no tab settings or columns inserted. If you want to import a table from Quattro Pro 4 into WordPerfect, you might prefer to use the Spreadsheet option on the Text In/Out menu. This enables you to import a group of spreadsheet cells as a WordPerfect table, or even to Link to a spreadsheet. The Link option creates a table in WordPerfect that is updated when the spreadsheet on which it is based is changed. This feature is supported in WordPerfect 5.1, and Quattro Pro 4 spreadsheets are among those WordPerfect can read directly. You can see the sample worksheet as a linked table within WordPerfect in Figure 10-6.

FIGURE
10-5

The .PRN file in WordPerfect

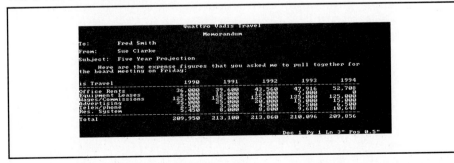

FIGURE
10-6

Quattro Pro 4 spreadsheet as a linked WordPerfect table

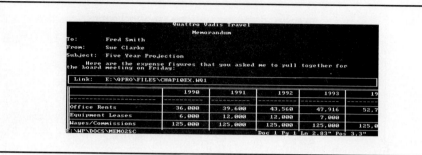

Reading Text into Quattro Pro 4

Having seen how Quattro Pro 4 creates a text file that can be read by word processing programs, you will see next how Quattro Pro 4 reads text files into a spreadsheet. At times you may have useful information stored in files created by another program, but Quattro Pro 4 cannot read the format of those files. You might like to bring this information into a Quattro Pro 4 spreadsheet. One way of doing this is to convert the data into a text file by using the other program's equivalent of Quattro Pro 4's Print Destination File command.

Importing ASCII Text Files

Suppose your company has an accounting program for accounts receivable. You would like to create a spreadsheet of accounts receivable data. The accounting program should be able to print a text file to disk. Quattro Pro 4 can then read this file using the Tools Import command. In Figure 10-7 you can see the Tools Import command about to be issued with the cell selector in A4 of a blank worksheet.

You will probably want to try your first experiments with importing text files using a blank spreadsheet, because the data that is brought in can have unexpected effects on existing data in the spreadsheet. Your choices when importing files are ASCII Text File, Comma & "" Delimited File, and Only Commas. The ASCII Text option is for importing a file name

FIGURE
10-7

Selecting a text file with Tools Import

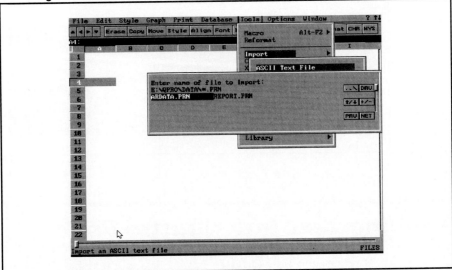

that consists simply of lines of data separated by spaces, not punctuation. The Delimited File option is used for bringing in data from programs that create files in which the pieces of information are separated by either commas, quotes, or both. The Only Commas option is for files in which commas are used to separate sections of text.

When you issue the Tools Import ASCII Text File command, you must specify the name of the file. That file is then read into the worksheet at the current position of the cell selector, as shown in Figure 10-8. Note that Quattro Pro 4 assumes your text file will have the .PRN extension. You can edit the file prompt to list other files.

The information in cell A4 of Figure 10-8 looks a lot like a spreadsheet entry arranged in cells, but if you carefully observe the contents of cell A4, you will see that it is one long label. There is no data in columns B, C, D, and so on. There are two techniques you can use to help Quattro Pro 4 make sense of data like this. The first is called *parsing*, which involves breaking up the lines of data according to a set of interpretation rules. The second approach is to use the string functions, described later in this chapter.

FIGURE
10-8

Imported file

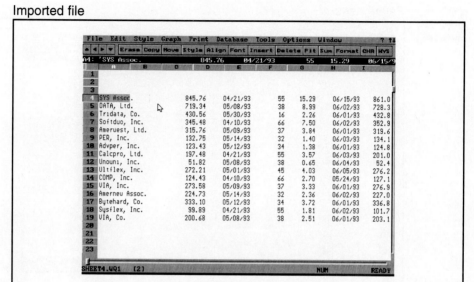

Using the Tools Parse Command

To give Quattro Pro 4 a set of rules by which to break up the long labels of data into separate cells of information, you place your cell selector on the first cell containing a label to be parsed. You then issue the Tools Parse command, which displays the menu shown in Figure 10-9. Next, select the third option, Create. This option inserts a new row into the worksheet above the current row. Quattro Pro 4 places a line of symbols, called the *parse line*, into this row, as shown in Figure 10-10.

After the special nonprinting label indicator (¦) the parse line contains a mixture of different characters, including L, V, D, *, and >. Above what Quattro Pro 4 understands to be the beginning of a new cell within the first line of labels the parse line will contain one of the following: L, V, D, or T. These stand for the type of data that Quattro Pro 4 thinks the cell should contain, with L for Label, V for Value, D for Date, and T for Time. After the type character comes a number of > signs. Quattro Pro 4 uses the > signs to show how wide it thinks the entry will be. Add the type character to the number of > signs to get the total number of characters. The asterisks in the parse line simply fill in the spaces between entries.

FIGURE
10-9

Parse menu

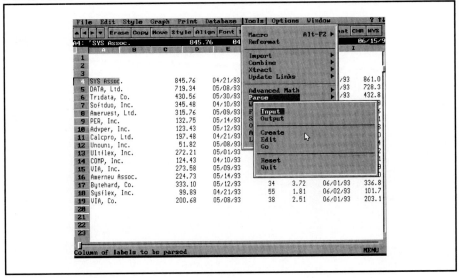

FIGURE
10-10

Parse line

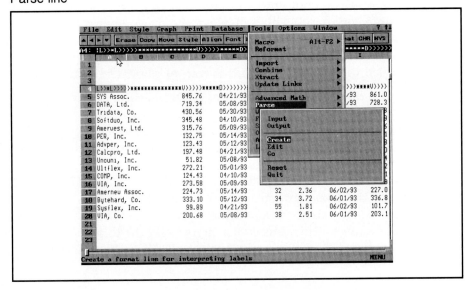

Parse Editing

If you look closely at the way this parse line reads, you can see that the text of the first company name has been read as two labels. This will create two cells instead of one. This is why the Parse menu has the Edit option. There are many situations in which the parse line created by Quattro Pro 4 does not interpret the text as you would like it to. After all, it is a complex logical task to determine how this long label should be divided into cells.

When you are still at the Parse menu, you can select Edit immediately after issuing the Create command, and the menu will disappear so that you can make changes to the symbols. Notice that you are automatically placed into OVERSTRIKE mode, as indicated by the bottom status line message, OVR. The reason for this mode is that, although the symbols on the parse line may be wrong, there are just the right number of them to describe the line. Instead of adding and deleting symbols, you type the ones you want over the top of the incorrect ones. In this case the only change needed is to change the beginning of the parse line from |L>>*L>>>>> to |L>>>>>>>>>. When you have edited the line, press ENTER to return to the Parse menu. You can also edit a parse line from READY mode by using the F2 key, because the parse line is simply a label.

Parse Completion

When the parse line is acceptable (and it may take several attempts to perfect) you must identify the input and output cells. The *input* is the column of labels that contain the data to be parsed including the parse line, in this case A4..A20. The *output* is the top left corner of the area of the spreadsheet you want the parsed data to occupy, in this case, cell A22 will work fine. When you have specified the input and output cells, the settings are displayed in the Parse menu. If they are correct, as shown in Figure 10-11, you can issue the Go command.

The results are shown in Figure 10-12, Although not all of the company names are readable because the column widths are currently set at the default of 9, you can see that the numbers were read as numbers and the dates as serial numbers. You can format the dates as described in Chapter 3.

FIGURE
10-11

Parse settings in place

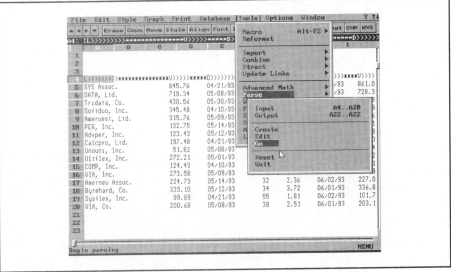

FIGURE
10-12

Parse results

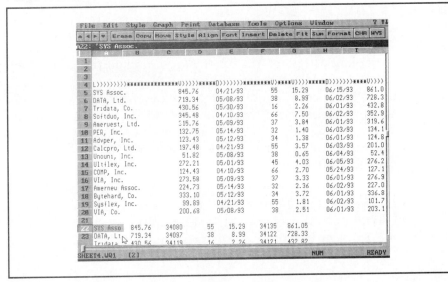

Note that in this example, the parsed data from A5..A20 was copied to an empty section of the worksheet (the Input setting was actually A4..A20 because it has to include the parse line). This means that the original labels remain in the worksheet. If the parse operation is a success, the labels can be erased (you can delete the rows if there is nothing else on them or delete the row block if you want to protect other areas of the worksheet).

When you are comfortable with the Parse command you can have Quattro Pro 4 copy the results of the parse operation over the original labels. To do this you make the Output setting the first label cell (in this example A5). When you issue the Parse Go command the labels are replaced by the cell entries. You can then delete the parse line. If you need to parse a lot of similar data you might want leave the parse line in place, because it can be reused and will not appear in any printouts, because it begins with the nonprinting character (|).

Once data has been converted from text to cell entries you can add further formatting, such as lines, and descriptive labels, such as column headings. Although the text file you import may include headings and even column totals, it is not worth parsing these. Simply make a note of them and enter them by hand after you have parsed the data. Even though Quattro Pro 4 enables you to create several different parse lines within a collection of long labels, such as one for the headings, one for the data, and one for the column totals, it is usually best to parse only the data. Column headings are easy to add after parsing. Column totals will not parse into formulas, so you will have to re-create the necessary formulas anyway.

In Figure 10-13 you can see that the original labels have been erased. Cells have been formatted. Column total formulas and column headings have been added to the worksheet. Bear in mind that the values in the late fee and total past due columns are not calculated amounts, but simply values. You could replace these values with formulas, but the main purpose of the parse command is bring in data that would otherwise need to be entered by hand.

Parsing text is not a particularly common operation for most spreadsheet users, but it can be a great time-saver when you need to work with data from other programs.

FIGURE
10-13

Parse results after formatting

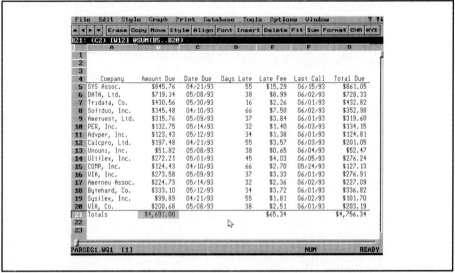

Text in Formulas

Text entered into a cell in Quattro Pro 4 is a label and has no numeric value. However, the program can still use labels in many formulas. This means that you can handle a variety of data in your spreadsheet. Text formulas are particularly useful when you are developing macro commands, as described in Chapter 12.

Labels in Logical Functions

You can use text in several of the @functions. Quattro Pro 4 can enter a label in a cell by means of an @IF formula. The formula

@IF(A1>1000,"Expensive","Cheap")

returns the answer "Expensive" if the contents of A1 are greater than 1000, or "Cheap" if not.

You can use text in the @CHOOSE function to supply a label for a number. As with the @IF function, text in an @CHOOSE statement must be enclosed in quotes. For example, the formula @CHOOSE (A1, "Bill", "Fred", "Sue") returns "Bill" if cell A1 is empty or contains 0. The same formula returns "Fred" if cell A1 contains 1 and "Sue" if A1 contains 2.

Combining Labels

Quattro Pro 4 formulas can reference labels in other cells as well as values, as you can see in Figure 10-14. The formula +B5 has been placed in cell B19. This formula cross references the name Emma from the list of names into the Availability Report. There are a number of situations where it is useful to relate label cells in this manner. Using the formula +C5 in cell C19, you could bring the last name into the cell next to B19.

If you are preparing an information report from a spreadsheet, you may want to connect the two names with just one space between them, as in Emma Wong. You might be tempted to use the formula +B5+C5 to do this, but that formula results in 0 because Quattro Pro 4 thinks you are trying to add two labels together, and labels have a value of 0.

FIGURE
10-14

Referencing text

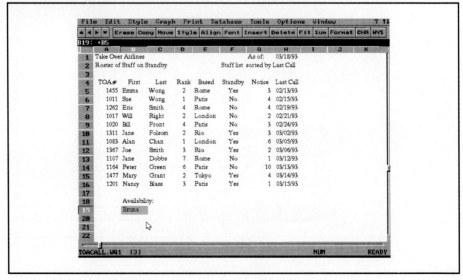

However, you can combine labels with the & sign. The formula +B5&C5 produces EmmaWong.

The & sign adds labels together. This process is called *concatenation*. As you can see, +B5&C5 brings the two parts of the name together without a space between them. You can add a space and other text, such as words and punctuation, to a concatenated formula by enclosing it in quotes ("). You must add the text in quotes to the formula with an & sign. Thus,

+B5&" "&C5

produces the desired result, shown in Figure 10-15.

The & sign is not acceptable as the first character in a formula, but you can use it between cell references and strings of text in a formula. The previous formula is simply three pieces of information: a cell reference, B5; text placed in quotes, in this case, a space " "; and another cell reference, C5. The formula begins with a + sign to let Quattro Pro 4 know

Improved concatenation

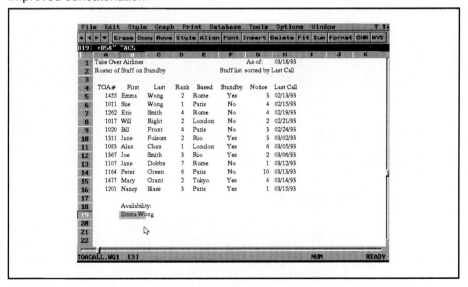

this is a formula. The & sign simply works as an addition sign for text data.

You can create some useful formulas by using these elements for cell referencing (the & sign and quoted text preceded by a + sign). In Figure 10-16 you can see that the Availability Report can take on the appearance of a written statement using a string formula with the top two entries the staff list. If the list is sorted by the Standby column, in descending order, the employees with "Yes" in this column will be at the top. If you sort by Rank as the second key, the list will be headed by the top-ranking staff on standby.

The benefit of using a formula like this, rather than simply typing a statement, is that the cell references in the formula are dynamic. When staff availablity changes, the text is updated. When new names appear in B5 through C6, then they will also appear in the formula. This means that you can create invoices, letters, and other documents that have the appearance of static text but are, in fact, dynamically related to the contents of the spreadsheet.

Lengthy string formula

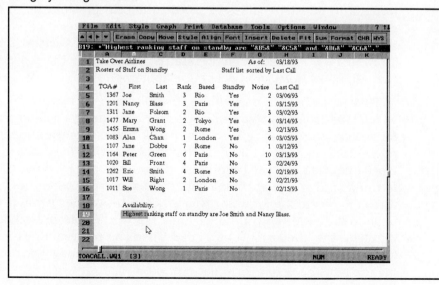

Label Formulas to Labels

If you ever want to change a formula that results in a label to the label produced by that formula, you can use the Edit Values command. This command requires that you indicate the cell or block of cells that is being converted to values and a destination. The destination can be a separate area of the worksheet, if you want to preserve the original formulas; or the original cells themselves, if you want to convert them permanently to their result.

Numeric Formulas to Labels

In several situations you will find it useful to convert a numeric formula to a label. Suppose you have developed a lengthy formula containing numerous relative references to cell locations. The formula is correct but located in the wrong cell. When you copy or move a formula with the Edit commands, the relative cell references change relative to the new location of the formula. To prevent this from happening, you first convert the formula to a label and then copy or move it. Finally, you convert it back to a formula. The easiest way to do this is to highlight the formula in question, press F2 to edit the cell, press HOME to move the cursor to the beginning of the formula, and then type an apostrophe ('). When you press ENTER, the formula will appear as a left-justified label. To return the formula to active status, you reverse the procedure: edit the cell, press HOME, and delete the apostrophe.

This procedure is particularly useful when you enter a formula to which Quattro Pro 4 objects, that is, one containing a syntax error. If the formula is lengthy, the error might not be immediately apparent and you might need time to find it. If the formula contains a reference to a named block that has not yet been created, you will not be able to enter the formula, and you might think that you have to abandon the typing that it took to create the formula. This loss can be avoided if you press HOME to go to the beginning of the formula, type an apostrophe ('), and press ENTER to store the formula as a label. Then you can examine the formula, find the problem, and create any necessary block names before converting the label back to a formula.

String Functions

A specialized means of working with labels in formulas in Quattro Pro 4 is through the use of @functions specifically designed for manipulating text. These functions are called the *string functions*, because a string in Quattro Pro 4 is a series of characters that results in a label and not a value. String functions are valuable when you are working with data imported from other programs in the form of text files. They can also be used effectively with some advanced macro commands, as described in Chapter 12.

@CHAR

Earlier you saw that many programs can share information by using ASCII characters. There are 256 ASCII characters, numbered from 0 to 255. Many of them are symbols not found on the keyboard, such as graphics characters. The @CHAR function can display these codes in Quattro Pro 4. @CHAR returns the ASCII character corresponding to a given ASCII code. Its syntax is

@CHAR(*code*)

where *code* is a numeric value between 0 and 255. Since Quattro Pro 4 will truncate any values entered as *code* to an integer, you should always enter the *code* argument as an integer.

Although your DOS manual probably has a standard ASCII table for numbers corresponding to the ASCII codes for each character, you can use the @CHAR function instead to create or refer to such a table within Quattro Pro 4. In Figure 10-17, the numbers 80 through 255 have been entered in alternating columns. The @CHAR function has been used to show the character corresponding to that code number. For example, the pounds sterling sign is code 156. You can print this as a reference for the codes, although some printers will not print all of the characters.

Note that Figure 10-17 shows Quattro Pro 4 in character mode. This is because character mode best reveals the ASCII characters. If you use WYSIWYG mode, some of the ASCII characters may not appear. This is because many of the fonts used in WYSIWYG cannot, and do not need

FIGURE
10-17

ASCII table

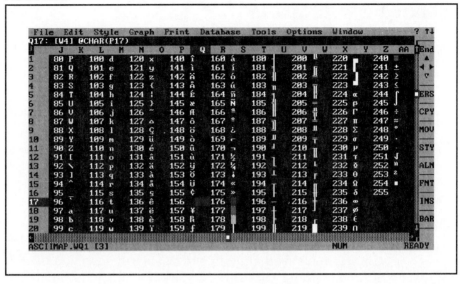

to, support all of the ASCII characters. If you ask for an ASCII character in WYSIWYG and the current font does not support it, a question mark will be displayed instead. You will find that Monospace font does support a wide range of ASCII characters. Later in this chapter you will see a number of screens shot in character mode, because they better illustrate the way Quattro Pro 4 handles strings of text.

The usefulness of the @CHAR function depends on how much of your work requires looking up ASCII codes, or on how much imagination you want to use in designing your spreadsheets. You can use ASCII characters for making simple pictograms. A *pictogram* is a chart that represents numbers as pictures. In a pictogram one picture usually equals one unit of measure. For example, you can use the @REPEAT function to repeat the male symbol, @CHAR(11), as shown in Figure 10-18. The upper bar shows the number 28 by repeating the male symbol 28 times. The lower bar shows the number 21 as the female symbol, which is @CHAR(12). This method of making a chart is an alternative to selecting the +/− bar chart format from the Style Numeric Format menu. You can see the numbers 28 and 21 formatted with this style in the lower pair of pictograms in Figure 10-18.

@REPEAT

The @REPEAT function repeats a string of characters a specified number of times. Its syntax is

@REPEAT(*string,number*)

where *string* is a string value and *number* is a numeric value greater than or equal to 0. @REPEAT returns as many copies of the *string* as you specify with *number*. The result is a label.

Although this function is somewhat similar to the repeating label prefix (\) that is used to produce dashed lines in a cell, the main difference is that with @REPEAT you can specify exactly how many times you want the string to be repeated. Also, the label prefix adjusts the number of repeated characters to fit the column, even when the width is changed. The @REPEAT function can display a fixed number of characters that does not change. When you specify a text string with @REPEAT, you must surround it with double quotes (").

The *number* argument in the @REPEAT statement can be a formula or a cell reference. This argument can be used to repeat a character or characters according to a variable factor. This is one way of making a pictogram, as shown in the top half of figure 10-18.

@CODE

A reverse of the @CHAR function, the @CODE function tells you the ASCII code of a special character. Why would you want to know this? Sometimes data that you import from another program is corrupted by odd characters. Identifying them with the @CODE function could help you determine their origin. Its syntax is

@CODE(*string*)

where *string* is a string value, and the first letter is evaluated by @CODE to return the ASCII code.

FIGURE
10-18
Creating bar charts and pictograms

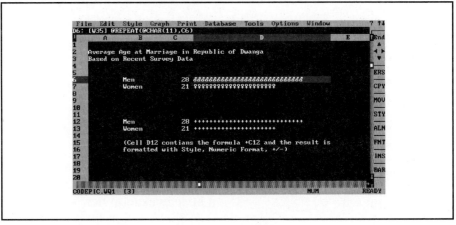

@FIND

The @FIND function uses three arguments to find characters within a string. Its syntax is

@FIND(*substring,string,startnumber*)

where *substring* is a string value representing the target value to search for, *string* is a valid string value representing the source value to search within, and *startnumber* is a numeric value of 0 or greater representing the character position to begin searching with. The @FIND function returns the character position at which the first occurrence of the target was found.

The number 0 represents the first character in the string, the second is 1, and so on. Thus, @FIND("t",A1,0) returns the value 3 if A1 contains the label *Quattro Pro 4,* because the letter *t* first occurs at position 3. Note that the *startnumber* value tells the program to begin the search at that number of characters into the string. You will receive an error if the value of *startnumber* is more than the number of characters in *string* minus 1. You will also get an error if @FIND fails to find any occurrences of the *substring.*

Consider the spreadsheet in Figure 10-19, prepared by the Union Square office of Quattro Vadis Travel. The users in this office are new to spreadsheets and enter the agent name and office name as one long label, rather than as separate facts in separate cells. You need to convert the data to a more useful format.

This example will be used several times in the following sections to demonstrate string functions. The most likely source of problem entries like this is either a new user or a set of data imported from another program. The first three names of agents are exactly the same length, and all of the labels have a hyphen in them. The hyphen might help break the labels into their separate parts. You can use the @FIND function to measure the position of the hyphen, as shown in Figure 10-20.

Although this is not exactly vital data, it shows how the function can be used to compare labels, a function that might prove useful with larger collections of labels.

@EXACT

Another way to compare labels is to use the @EXACT function. This function has the syntax

FIGURE
10-19

Entries as long labels

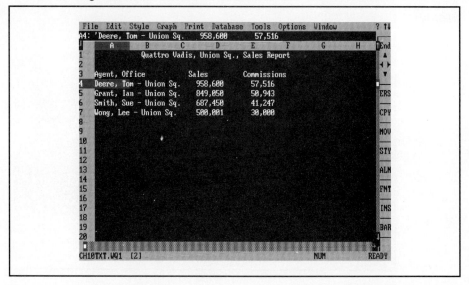

@EXACT(*string1*,*string2*)

where *string1* is a string value or a reference to a cell containing a string, and *string2* is a second string value or cell reference.

The @EXACT function compares the values of *string1* and *string2*. If the values are exactly identical, including capitalization, it returns a value of 1. If there are any differences, it returns a 0 value. As you can see in Figure 10-21, the text in strings that you are comparing must be surrounded by double quotes unless the text is a cell entry.

Because @EXACT returns a value of 1, you can use it to activate mathematical calculations. Thus, agents who have not answered Yes in this example could be paid commissions times the value in column H, in other words, no commission if the response in G is not exactly "Yes". You can compare only the contents of label cells with @EXACT. If you attempt to compare one or more numbers or empty cells, the result is ERR. Label prefixes are ignored.

To compare strings or cell contents without regard for capitalization, you can use the @IF function. The @IF function is not case-sensitive. For example, @IF(A1=A2,1,0) will return a 1 value, meaning true, if the

@FIND results

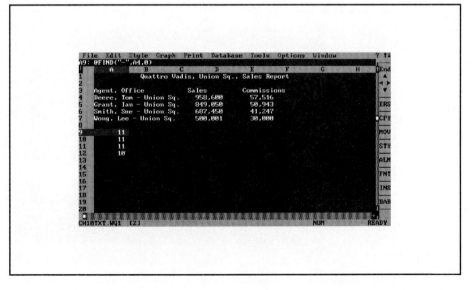

contents of the cells are the same but capitalized differently (for example, if A1 contained YES and A2 contained Yes). Another formula that you can use to check for a spelling match that disregards capitalization in a string is +A1="Yes", which returns 1 for both Yes and YES.

@REPLACE

You can use the @REPLACE function with four arguments to replace a string of characters within a label. The syntax is

@REPLACE(*string,startnumber,num,newstring*)

where *string* is a string value, the label to be worked on; *startnumber* is the character position to begin with; *num* is the number of characters to delete; and *newstring* is a string value, the characters to insert at the position marked by *num*. In Figure 10-22 you can see @REPLACE used to update the spelling of *Sq.* to *Square*.

This formula would not work for Mr. Wong, because the twentieth character in his label is a period, not *q*. Thus, the result for him would be *Union Sqquare*. The @FIND function works well with @REPLACE to locate the first occurrence of *Sq* in order to replace it with *Square*. This can be seen in Figure 10-23, where the string *Sq* is being used as the place to make the replacement. The only time this would cause a problem is when an agent has a last name like Squib, because @FIND is looking for the first occurrence of *Sq* and would replace *Squib* with *Square* rather than *Sq* with *Square*. Other uses of @REPLACE are to add one string to

FIGURE 10-21

The @EXACT function

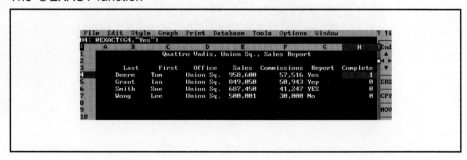

the end of another. You do so by specifying as the *startnumber* a number that is one greater than the number of characters in *string*. To delete part or all of a string, specify " " as *newstring*. Remember that you can also use the Edit Search & Replace command to perform search-and-replace operations instead of @FIND and @REPLACE.

@LEFT, @RIGHT, and @MID

The @LEFT, @RIGHT, and @MID functions are used to find strings of characters within labels based on the position of those characters. These functions follow the same basic syntax:

@LEFT(*string,number*)

where *string* is a string value and *number* is a numeric value of 0 or greater.

The @LEFT function returns the leftmost characters of *string*, the number of characters returned being that specified by the *number*

The @REPLACE function

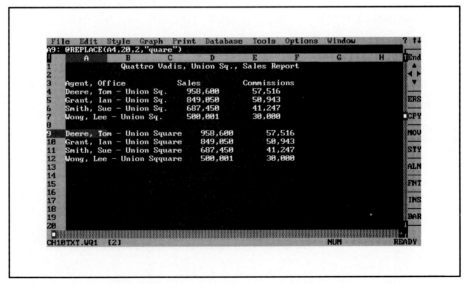

FIGURE
10-23
@FIND with @REPLACE

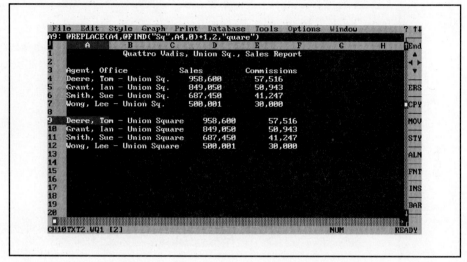

argument. In Figure 10-24, @LEFT returns the characters *Deere* from cell A4, because they are the five leftmost characters.

This function can be used to extract the agent names from the label where the agent name and office are mixed. However, the problem of varying label lengths appears once again due to cell A7. You can solve this problem by using the @FIND function. You use it to specify how far the reading of the leftmost characters must go. In this case, that is as far as the comma. In Figure 10-25 the comma is being found by the @FIND function. The @RIGHT function is sometimes easier to apply, as is the case when you want to extract the commission figure from the labels. You could use the function statement @RIGHT (C4,6) to extract the last six characters of the label in C4.

@TRIM and @LENGTH

The @TRIM function has the syntax

@TRIM(*string*)

The @LEFT function

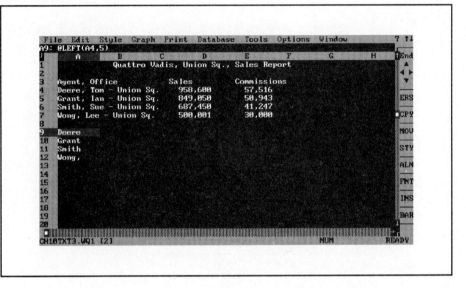

It is used to remove any extra spaces from *string*. These extra spaces include the trailing spaces following the last nonspace character. It can also mean spaces preceding the first nonspace character plus duplicate spaces between words. Normal strings are not affected. If *string* is empty or contains a numeric value, the @TRIM function returns ERR. This function is particularly useful when you are working with data from other programs that pad some data to equal lengths by using trailing spaces.

The @LENGTH function is used to measure the length of a label. It uses the syntax

@LENGTH(*string*)

Thus, @LENGTH(A1) returns 13 if A1 contains the words *Quattro Pro 4*.

@LOWER, @UPPER, and @PROPER

These three functions change the case of a string. Their syntax is as follows:

FIGURE
10-25

@FIND with @LEFT

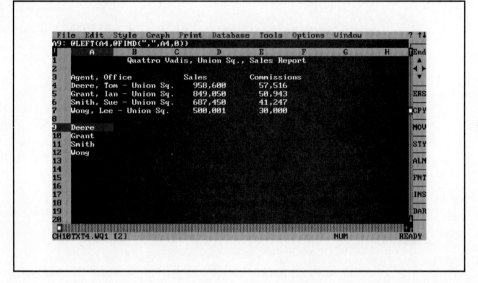

@LOWER(*string*)
@UPPER(*string*)
@PROPER(*string*)

You can use @LOWER to turn a string into all lowercase characters. The @UPPER function returns all uppercase characters; that is, it capitalizes the string. The formula @UPPER(B4) returns YES if B4 contains either yes or YES.

The @PROPER function converts the first letter of every word in the string to uppercase and the rest of the characters to lowercase. In Quattro Pro 4 a word is defined as an unbroken string of alphabetic characters. The @PROPER function considers any blank spaces, punctuation symbols, or numbers as marking the end of a word. You can use the @PROPER function to produce better looking text from heavily capitalized text entries. Thus @PROPER(B4) returns "William Shakespeare" if B4 contains WILLIAM SHAKESPEARE.

In all three functions, numbers and symbols within the string are unaffected by the function. If the string is blank or is a numeric or date value, the result is ERR.

@STRING

Used to convert numbers to labels, the @STRING function has the syntax

@STRING($x, decplaces$)

where x is a numeric value and *decplaces* is a numeric value between 0 and 15 representing the number of decimal places to the right of the decimal point. Thus, for example, @STRING(A1,2) converts 2.001 to a label, rounding it and then returning the decimal precision indicated by the *decplaces* argument. The label returned is 2.00.

@VALUE

The @VALUE function converts a label to a numeric value. The syntax is

@VALUE(*string*)

where *string* is a string value that can contain any of the arithmetic operators, but must not contain dollar signs, commas, or embedded spaces. One period, interpreted as the decimal place, is permitted, and leading and trailing spaces are ignored.

The @VALUE function—together with @DATEVALUE and @TIME-VALUE—is useful for converting data that was imported as text with the Tools Import command but was not automatically converted into values. You can also use this function to return values for numbers that have been turned into labels.

More Text Tips

The possibilities for text manipulation with Quattro Pro 4 are extensive. Using the string functions and text in formulas, you can handle many tasks beyond the traditional number crunching for which spreadsheets were originally designed. As a final example, consider the Quattro Pro 4 Business Name Generator shown in Figure 10-26. The

Name generator

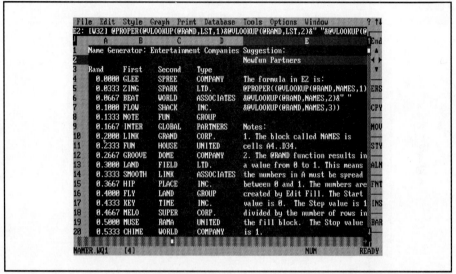

plausible-looking company name in E2 was produced by the formula at the top of the screen. The @VLOOKUP function was used to look up a random number in the table of name parts from A4..D46. The table consists of a column of numbers roughly spaced across the possible value of @RAND, from 0 to 1.

Columns B and C are typical business names. Column D contains several types of companies repeated down the list. The @PROPER function is used to turn the actual business name into a capitalized word. The & sign is used to connect the three @VLOOKUP statements, and the comma and space separate the name from the type. By repeatedly pressing F2 to edit the cell containing the formula and then pressing ENTER, you can cause Quattro Pro 4 to reselect the random numbers and keep producing new combinations of names.

If you make the lookup table references absolute in the formula, you can copy the formula to many cells in a column to produce a list of possible names. By extending the table with phrases that fit the kind of business for which you are trying to create a name, you can produce some very interesting results. Many of the company names shown in the examples in this book were produced by a formula of this kind.

FIGURE
10-27

Printed certificate

FIGURE
10-28

Worksheet used to create diploma

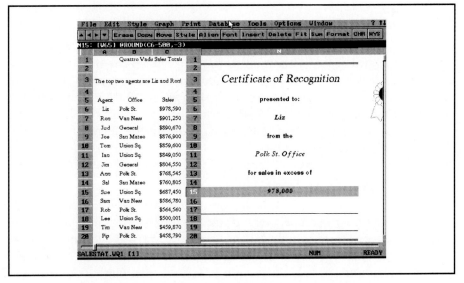

You can combine text formulas with the tremendous formatting capability of Quattro Pro 4 to achieve impressive results. For example, consider the printed certificate in Figure 10-27. This was produced from a Quattro Pro 4 spreadsheet. In fact, you can see the data that forms the basis of the certificate in Figure 10-28. The word "Liz" in Figure 10-27 was produced with a simple cell reference, +A6. The worksheet area occupied by the certificate can be seen on the right in Figure 10-28.

The block L2..P20 was formatted with Style Line Drawing using the Outside and Double options. A variety of fonts was used in the wide, center-aligned column N. The formula in N15 was designed to produce a round number slightly less than the actual sales figure in Figure 10-28, cell C6. The formula uses a negative value for the @ROUND function's decimal place argument:

@ROUND (C6-500,-3)

The –3 argument rounds up to the nearest 1000th so the –500 constant is used to make sure the result is actually the next lowest 1000th, as you can see from Figure 10-28.

The rosette graphic in the Annotator

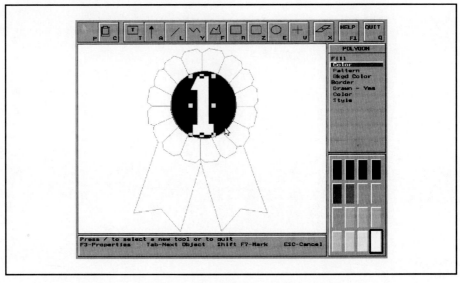

The text "Polk Street Office" is supplied by the text formula +B6&"Office", which adds a space and the word *Office* to the name in B6. The print block that produced Figure 10-27 was L2..P20.

The rosettes were created from clip art (the file AWARDRIB.CLP) to which the number 1 was added. The clip art was added to a text chart in Annotate. The graph was named ROS1 and again ROS2. Two graphs had to be created, because Quattro Pro 4 can only insert each named graph once. Using Graph Insert, ROS1 was placed in L3..M8, and ROS2 was placed in 03..P8. Note that a full screen graphic can be made small by inserting it in a small block. You can see the rosette graphic in the Annotator in Figure 10-29 (for more on Annotator see Chapter 13).

By combining text formulas, spreadsheet Style commands, and Graph Annotate work, you can produce a wide range of results that go far beyond the bounds of traditional spreadsheet work.

CHAPTER

Shortcuts and Macros

As you become familiar with Quattro Pro 4 and apply it to more tasks, you will want to take advantage of several shortcuts to frequently used menu items and to use macros to reduce repetitive typing. In this chapter you will read how to use, modify, and create Quattro Pro 4 Shortcuts; and how to record and use basic macros.

You may be somewhat in awe of the term *macros,* because they have traditionally been in the realm of power users and spreadsheet aficionados. However, with Quattro Pro 4 it is easy to create and use macros. Macros are no more complex than other spreadsheet tasks, and they do not require you to be highly proficient with everything else in the book to this point. If you plan to use more than a few macros, you should have a good grasp of naming blocks, described in Chapter 3. Perhaps the most important requirement for using macros is that you are already using Quattro Pro 4 for a task that you want to simplify or speed up.

In the Quattro Pro 4 menu system, the most commonly used commands are grouped in a logical way, making them easily accessible. The size of menus is kept manageable. Because different types of spreadsheet work require different sets of commands, however, you may often use commands that are several layers down in the menu structure. Quattro Pro 4 addresses this problem in two ways. First, you can create Shortcuts. A Shortcut enables you to use a single keystroke to select any menu item. The second approach, described in the next chapter, is to redesign the menu system. Quattro Pro 4 allows you to regroup and rename menu items to match your pattern of work with a feature called the Menu Builder.

Shortcuts

You may have noticed that several of the Quattro Pro 4 menus have notations on the right, such as the CTRL-C and CTRL-M on the Edit menu shown in Figure 11-1. These represent Shortcuts or *hot keys* that are already incorporated into Quattro Pro 4. A Shortcut enables you to access a menu item with a single keystoke, bypassing the menu system. Little mention has been made of these keys so far in order to concentrate on the purpose of the menu items rather than quick ways of selecting them. However, once you are familiar with what a particular menu item does you may want to start selecting it with the assigned Shortcut. You can

Edit menu Shortcuts

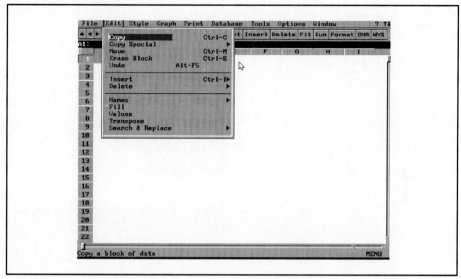

see all of the preassigned Shortcuts listed in Table 11-1. Perhaps the most useful is CTRL-C for the Edit Copy command. This takes you directly to the Source Block prompt, ready to perform a copy operation. Another very convenient Shortcut when you are building worksheets is CTRL-W for Style Column Width. One special Shortcut, CTRL-D does not represent any single menu item but is used to enter dates, as described in Chapter 3.

Note that some Shortcuts, such as CTRL-A for style Alignment, take you to a program menu. However, menus displayed by a Shortcut key do not appear above the corresponding parent menus. Instead they pop up as shown in Figure 11-2, which shows the CTRL-A Shortcut in action.

Creating Shortcuts

The more spreadsheet work you do, the more you will appreciate an opportunity to reduce keystrokes, and Shortcuts do just that. However, you may not like or use all of the preassigned Shortcuts. Fortunately, Quattro Pro 4 enables you to reassign or eliminate them. Suppose you are designing a large spreadsheet. You find you are repeatedly using the

TABLE
11-1

Default Shortcuts

Shortcut	Command
CTRL-A	Style Alignment
CTRL-C	Edit Copy
CTRL-D	Date Prefix
CTRL-E	Edit Erase Block
CTRL-F	Style Numeric Format
CTRL-G	Fast Graph
CTRL-I	Edit Insert
CTRL-M	Edit Move
CTRL-N	Edit Search & Replace Next
CTRL-P	Edit Search & Replace Previous
CTRL-R	Windows Move/Size
CTRL-S	File Save
CTRL-T	Window Tile
CTRL-W	Style Column Width
CTRL-X	File Exit

FIGURE
11-2

Using the CTRL-A Shortcut

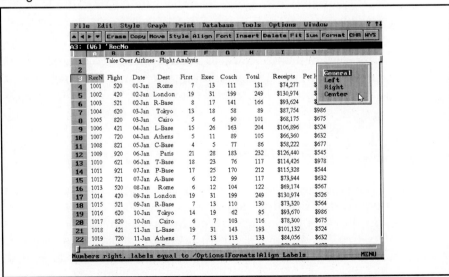

Window Options Locked Titles Both command to set titles in the worksheet. (Recall that this command freezes the cells above and to the left of the cell selector, so that row titles and column headings do not scroll off the screen when you move around the worksheet.) Using Quattro Pro 4's Shortcuts feature, you can execute the Window Options Locked Titles Both command with a single keystroke, such as CTRL-L. The same feature can be applied to the Window Options Locked Titles Clear command, assigning it to CTRL plus a different letter. This will enable you to set and remove titles with just two keystrokes instead of eight.

To make a shortcut for a menu item, you first highlight the menu item you want. For example, Figure 11-3 shows the Locked Titles Both command being highlighted. You then press CTRL-ENTER, and Quattro Pro 4 prompts you at the bottom of the screen for the keystroke combination to which you want this menu item assigned. Press the letter L, and the prompt disappears. The menu remains on the screen. The menu item you assigned to CTRL-L has not been selected, but the menu now shows the name of the assigned Shortcut, as seen in Figure 11-4. You do not have to select the menu item just to assign it to a CTRL-letter key combination. If you do not need the menu item at this time, use ESC or CTRL-BREAK to leave the menu. Whenever you are ready to set titles in the

FIGURE
11-3

Setting the Locked Titles Shortcut

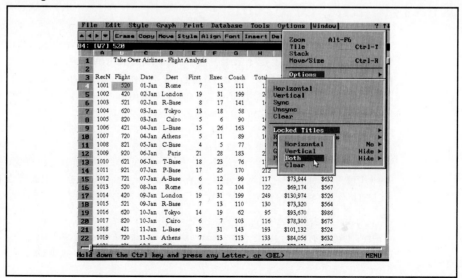

FIGURE
11-4   Assigned Shortcut CTRL-L

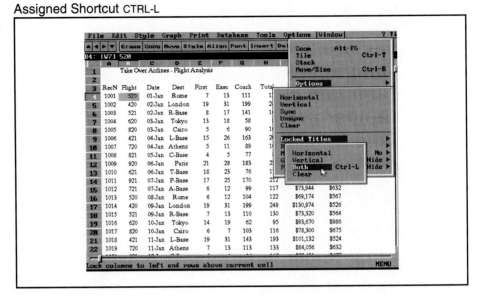

worksheet, press CTRL-L. The command is instantly executed without any need to use the menu system.

Reassigning Shortcuts

To match the Locked Titles Both Shortcut you might want to assign Locked Titles Clear to a different CTRL-letter key combination, for example, CTRL-C. You do this by highlighting the Clear command on the Locked Titles menu and pressing CTRL-ENTER followed by CTRL-C. You can then clear titles simply by pressing CTRL-C. However, this new Shortcut conflicts with the preassigned use of CTRL-C for Edit Copy. In fact, you must first remove the current assignment of the CTRL-C shortcut before reassigning it to another task. To remove CTRL-C from Edit Copy you highlight Copy on the Edit menu and press CTRL-ENTER followed by DELETE. You will be prompted to press DELETE again to confirm the action.

If you highlight any menu item and press CTRL-ENTER, then DELETE, then CTRL-ENTER again, you can delete any of the Shortcuts by typing the letter. This enables you to remove a Shortcut letter from a menu item without locating the item. If you press CTRL-ENTER, DELETE, CTRL-ENTER you can delete all Shortcut assignments by pressing DELETE instead of a single letter. However, this is not advisable, because the process is difficult to reverse. You will have to reinstall the QUATTRO.MU file, described in the next chapter.

Managing Shortcuts

If you try to reassign an existing Shortcut without first deleting the current assignment, Quattro Pro 4 will warn you "Shortcut key is already in use." Quattro Pro 4 has no built-in means of displaying a list of current Shortcut assignments. However, you can see the Shortcuts on the menus from which they operate. You can use the Help system to find a list of the default or preassigned Shortcuts. Just highlight a menu item, press CTRL-ENTER, and then press F1. This will take you to Help for Shortcuts. There you will see an option called Preset Shortcuts. This list does not change to reflect new Shortcuts you create or changes to existing Shortcuts.

You might want to keep track of active Shortcuts by noting them on a piece of paper or in a worksheet file. If you share a PC system and Quattro Pro 4 with other users, you should inform them of the Shortcuts you have set up. This will help prevent problems that arise from accidental activation of a Shortcut. Quattro Pro 4 automatically records Shortcuts in the current configuration file. See Appendix A for more about configuration files.

Note that you cannot assign a Shortcut to a menu item if it has been "popped up" instead of "pulled down." For example, if you wanted to make CTRL-K the key for Style Alignment Center, you would have to display the Alignment menu pulled down from the Style menu first, not from CTRL-A, which produces the small pop up menu seen in Figure 11-2.

Macros

When you find yourself repeating the same keystrokes over and over, but they are not simply menu items you can assign to Shortcuts, you need the power of macros. Originally developed for word processing programs as a way to record and play back frequently used phrases, macros store multiple keystrokes under a single key or name.

Macros in Quattro Pro 4

The macros you create in Quattro Pro 4 enable you to record and play back any series of keystrokes, including labels, numbers, formulas, menu choices, and even Shortcuts. For example, you could create a macro for setting titles in your worksheet. In addition to simply picking the Locked Titles Both command from the menu, the macro could move the cell selector to the correct cell prior to issuing the command, thus eliminating the need for you to position the cell selector yourself. If you have to format a lot of separate cells to Percent format you could create a macro to perform that action. You might have noticed that the Numeric Format option on the Style menu already has a Shortcut, CTRL-F. But this only takes you to the list of formats. If you assigned a Shortcut to the Percent format, you would still need to specify decimal places and select the block to be formatted. A macro can complete the whole command, including selection of decimal places, without having to go through the menus every time.

A Quattro Pro 4 macro can be defined as a set of keystrokes or instructions stored as labels. Numbers and letters are stored as numbers and letters; commands are stored as special symbols or words within brackets. For example, you can have a macro that consists of the label **Report~**. This macro tells Quattro Pro 4 to type the letters **R-e-p-o-r-t**, then press ENTER (represented by the tilde symbol, ~). You can use this macro to enter the word "Report" into a cell. In fact, you can easily create this macro in a blank worksheet, as follows:

1. Place the cell selector in A1, type **Report~**, then press ENTER. The cell identifier will show 'Report~ as the contents of the cell.

2. Move the cell selector to A3, where the word "Report" will be typed by the macro.

3. Press ALT-F2 for the Macro menu, shown in Figure 11-5. Select Execute from the Macro menu. You will be prompted for the cell

FIGURE
11-5

Macro menu

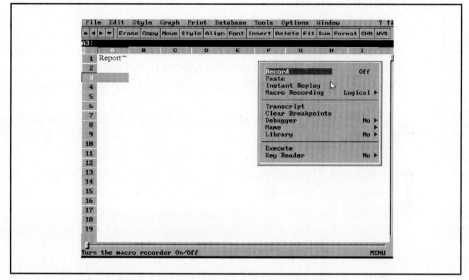

coordinates of the block of macro commands that you want to execute.

4. Type or point to A1 and press ENTER. The word "Report" is entered in cell A3. You have just created and used your first macro.

Obviously, this is a simple example; the macro is of limited use and sophistication. Macros can consist of much longer instructions. When a macro contains many instructions, the instructions are placed on successive rows of the same column. A macro that consists of more than one line of instructions is executed by indicating the first cell in the macro. Quattro Pro 4 reads the instructions in that cell, then the instructions in the next cell down, and so on until a blank cell is encountered. One problem with the simple macro just described is that it is not particularly easy to use. Executing it involves several steps, including entering the location of the macro. You can make a macro easier to execute by using the Macro Name command to name the cell containing the macro. You can use several types of macro names.

Macros by Name

When you have attached a name to a cell containing a macro, you can use F3 to execute that macro. For example, if cell A1 were named RP with the Macro Name command, the macro could be executed more easily. To name a macro and use the name to execute the macro, follow these steps:

1. Place the cell selector in the cell that contains the first line of the macro, in this case A1.

2. Press ALT-F2 for the Macro menu (you can also use the Macro command from the Tools menu). Select Name and then Create and type the name **RP**, as shown in Figure 11-6. Press ENTER.

3. Quattro Pro 4 prompts you to specify coordinates for the block and assumes the current cell, in this case A1..A1, as the block. This is correct, so press ENTER.

4. To execute the newly named macro, move to a blank cell into which you will enter the word "Report" and press ALT-F2. Select Execute and then press F3. You will see RP in the list of named blocks.

FIGURE 11-6

Naming a macro

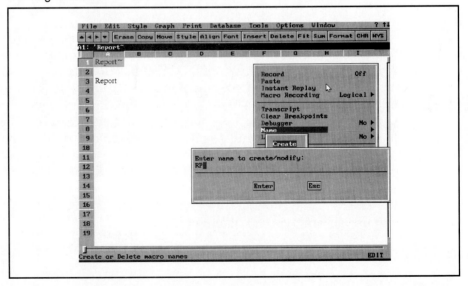

Highlight RP and press ENTER. The macro in the cell named RP will execute.

Macro Shortcuts

One Shortcut you can use to improve the macro-execution process is to issue the Macro Execute command with CTRL-Q. The CTRL-Q key is not used in the default set of Shortcut keys. To assign it to Macro Execute, select Tools from the main menu, then Macro (do not pop up the Macro menu with ALT-F2). Then highlight Execute and press CTRL-ENTER. Now type Q and the Execute command is assigned to CTRL-Q. Whenever you want to run a named macro simply press CTRL-Q followed by F3 and then select the macro name from this list.

If you want instant access to a macro, you should name the macro with a special combination of characters: the backslash (\) together with a letter. You can then execute the macro by holding down the ALT key and pressing the letter you used in the name. To make an instant macro, use the following steps, which describe the procedure in the case of the Report macro. This macro can be called \R, so that it can be executed with ALT-R.

1. Place the cell selector in the cell that contains the first line of the macro, in this case A1.

2. Select Name from the Macro menu, pick Create, and type the name **\R**. Press ENTER.

3. Quattro Pro 4 prompts you to specify coordinates for the block, but it will assume the current cell, in this case A1..A1, as the block. This is correct, so press ENTER.

4. To execute the newly named macro, move to a blank cell and press ALT-R. The macro will execute.

Note that block names can overlap, as in this case, where the names RP and \R were both assigned to cell A1. Because \R is a block name, you can execute this macro with the Macro Execute command as well as with the ALT key. You can create 26 instant macros named from \A to \Z. These names are usually reserved for frequently used macros. The letter used in the macro name should have some mnemonic relationship to the action of the macro, such as \R for the Report macro.

Applying Macros

In practical applications, macros are used for common operations and repetitive tasks, particularly ones that involve many settings. Good examples are database operations and printing. You will recall that Quattro Pro 4 can remember only one Sort Block and one set of sort keys at a time. Similarly, the Print command can remember only one Print Block at a time. Sorting two different databases on the same spreadsheet or printing two different blocks of the spreadsheet involves changing a lot of settings. You can use macros to specify all of the details about two different sort or print jobs, reducing many keystrokes and many chances for error to just one accurate set of instructions.

You can even create macros that contain conditional statements. Such statements as If-Then-Else enable you to have a macro choose among several different actions based on user input or spreadsheet conditions. The ability to include special command language statements in macros transforms macros into the equivalent of a programming language. With this capability you can create custom menus, data input forms, and specialized applications. The Quattro Pro 4 command language and its use in macros is explained in greater detail in the next chapter.

Ways to Create Macros

When you consider creating practical macros you will quickly face the question of how to tell Quattro Pro 4 to perform typical actions such as EDIT or END, or UP ARROW. You have seen that a macro is essentially a label or series of labels stored in a worksheet cell. When you created the macro to enter "Report" into a cell you used the tilde (~) to represent pressing ENTER. This is because you cannot type "ENTER" as a label. In fact, if you are typing a label and you press ENTER, what you are typing is simply entered into the cell. Consequently, there is a whole system of codes for those actions that cannot simply be typed as labels. These codes are listed in Table 11-2.

There are also special ways of describing menu actions in macros. If you wanted a macro to execute the Spreadsheet Print command, you could use the characters "/PS" but Quattro Pro 4 has a better way than this, as you will see as you examine the different ways to create macros.

TABLE
11-2

Macro Equivalents and Keys

Macro Equivalent	Key Represented	Macro Equivalent	Key Represented
Function Keys		**Movement Keys**	
{ABS}	F4	{HOME}	HOME
{CALC}	F9	{END}	END
{CHOOSE}	SHIFT-F5	{LEFT} or {L}	LEFT ARROW
{COPY}	SHIFT-F9	{RIGHT} or {R}	RIGHT ARROW
{EDIT}	F2	{UP} or {U}	UP ARROW
{FUNCTIONS}	ALT-F3	{DOWN} or {D}	DOWN ARROW
{GOTO}	F5	{PGUP}	PAGE UP
{GRAPH}	F10	{PGDN}	PAGE DOWN
{MACROS}	SHIFT-F3	{BIGLEFT}	CTRL-LEFT
{MARK}	SHIFT-F7	{BACKTAB}	SHIFT-TAB
{MARKALL}	ALT-F7	{BIGRIGHT}	CTRL-RIGHT
{MOVE}	SHIFT-F8	{TAB}	TAB
{NAME}	F3	{WINDOW*n*}	Selects window *n*
{NEXTWIN}	SHIFT-F6		
{PASTE}	SHIFT-F10	**Status Keys**	
{QUERY}	F7	{NUMON}	NUM LOCK
{STEP}	SHIFT-F2	{SCROLLOFF}	SCROLL LOCK off
{TABLE}	F8	{SCROLLON}	SCROLL LOCK on
{UNDO}	ALT-F5	{CAPOFF}	CAPS LOCK off
{WINDOW}	F6	{CAPON}	CAPS LOCK on
{ZOOM}	ALT-F6	{INS}	INSERT

TABLE 11-2 Cont.   Macro Equivalents and Keys

Macro Equivalent	Key Represented	Macro Equivalent	Key Represented
Other Keys			
{BREAK}	CTRL-BREAK		
{BACKSPACE} or {BS}	BACKSPACE		
{DATE}	CTRL-D		
{DEL}	DELETE	{INSOFF}	INSERT off
{DELEOL}	CTRL-\ (delete to end of line)	{INSON}	INSERT on
{ESC}	ESC		
{CLEAR}	ESC		
{CR} or ~	ENTER		
{?}	PAUSE (for user input		
{/} or {MENU}	Displays menu		

The method you use for a particular macro will depend on the purpose of the macro, its level of complexity, and your level of familiarity with the macro process. You can combine all three methods of making macros when you are creating large macros.

Macro Recording

The simplest method of creating useful macros is to record them. Even novice users can make macros in this way to simplify commonly used tasks. Recording a macro simply means telling Quattro Pro 4 to keep a record of your actions while you use the program. This is done by placing the program in RECORD mode and then typing the necessary keystrokes to perform the actions that are to be part of the macro. Quattro Pro 4 holds a record of the actions you carry out in memory until you either paste the macro into a worksheet or record a new macro. You do not have to paste the recorded macro into a worksheet in order to use it. However, if you do paste the recording into a worksheet you can examine it, edit it, and add to it. For example, suppose you have recorded the following actions:

❏ Move the cell selector to B4 with the GoTo key (F5)

❏ Set both vertical and horizontal locked titles

The recorded macro would look like this:

{GOTO}B4~
{/ Titles;Both}

From this macro code you can see what the macro is supposed to do, and you can see that Quattro Pro 4 has provided the codes for special keys and menu items. The next section presents a complete macro recording example.

Macro Writing

The sample macro that enters the word "Report" was created by simply writing it into a cell. When you become familiar with how macros work, you can use this method to write macros. Use Table 11-2 to find the equivalents that Quattro Pro 4 uses for common commands when you are writing macros.

Quattro Pro 4 provides a very useful feature for those who want to write macros. The SHIFT-F3 key, known as the Macro List key, displays a menu of macro commands from which you can choose, just as you list and pick @functions with the ALT-F3 key. When you press SHIFT-F3, while you are using either READY mode or EDIT mode, the first thing you see is a menu dividing the macro commands into six areas: Keyboard, Screen, Interactive, Program Flow, Cells, File, and / Commands.

Some of these options lead to further menus. For example, when you select Keys you see the following choices: Movement keys, Function keys, Status keys, and Other keys. In Figure 11-7 you can see the list that is presented when you select Movement keys. When you have highlighted the command you want, you can press ENTER to place it on the edit line. the curly braces are added for you. The SHIFT-F3 key saves a lot of typing and prevents you from misspelling macro commands. It is particularly useful when you are writing more advanced macros.

Macros from Transcript

The record of your keystrokes maintained by Transcript (described in Chapter 7) is compatible with Quattro Pro 4's macro terminology. Thus, you can call up the Transcript log and copy sections of the keystroke record to your spreadsheet. An example of the Transcript log is shown in Figure 11-8. You can see that the line-drawing command was used in two instances since the file was retrieved. You could use this code to create line-drawing macros. You call up the Transcript log by using the Macro Transcript command. When the log is on screen, you can type **/** for the Transcript menu and mark a block for copying to the spreadsheet. This process is described in detail at the end of this chapter.

Recording a Macro

To see the macro-recording process in action and to get a better understanding for the potential of macros, try the macro design example in this section. This macro enters the current date in the worksheet.

FIGURE
11-7

List presented when Movement keys is selected

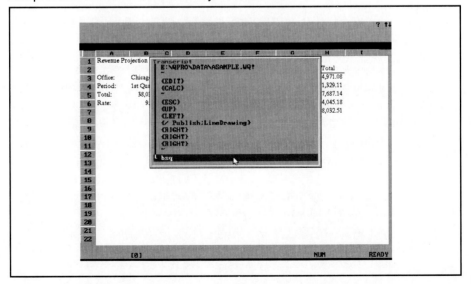

Transcript log

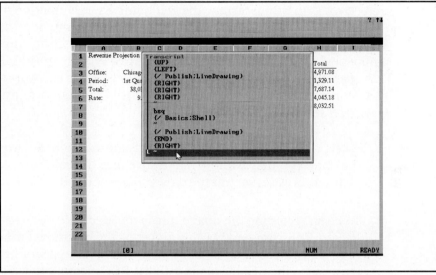

Macro Design

Whenever you create a macro, you need to give some thought to what its role will be. You can use macros to enter values and labels, to select menu items, and to activate function keys. You can execute macros in READY mode, in EDIT mode, and from within the menu system. Of course, if you make a macro that works from READY mode, you must execute it in READY mode and not in the middle of a menu. Also, you need to be careful about the action of the macro and the cells it will affect. Keep in mind that there is a possibility of losing data through any of these actions: Copy, Move, Fill, Transpose, Output, Erase, or Delete. For example, if the macro is designed to perform a particular action on a cell, you must remember to move your cell selector to a suitable cell before executing the macro.

Suppose you need to enter today's date at several different places in a spreadsheet used for recording sales calls. If the choice of date format is not important, you can press CTRL-D, type @**NOW**, and press ENTER. This action enters the current date in the D4 format.

To enter the current date with the D1 format, you would type **@NOW,** press ENTER, and then format the cell using Style Numeric Format Date 1. Doing so requires a dozen keystrokes, and it is a tedious operation if you have to repeat it often. To make a macro to perform this task, you simply perform the steps once while Quattro Pro 4 is in RECORD mode. This operation is presented in Figure 11-9 in a sales call worksheet used by salespersons. Of course, you can try this operation in any practice worksheet.

1. Select any empty cell on a spreadsheet into which you want to enter the date. You may want to make sure that the column is at least ten characters wide, so that the date you are about to create can be seen properly.

2. To begin recording the macro, press the Macro key (ALT-F2) and select Record. This command begins and ends the macro-recording process. After you select Record, the Macro menu disappears and you are returned to the READY mode with the REC message in the status line.

3. Type **@NOW** and press ENTER. Then select Style Numeric Format Date. Select the D1 format and press ENTER to confirm that the current cell is the one you want to format.

4. Press ALT-F2 and select Record to end the recording. The REC message will disappear. Your macro is ready to use. You can see the results shown in Figure 11-9.

There are two ways to stop the macro recorder other than using the ALT-F2 key with Record. You can select Instant Replay, or you can select Paste from the Macro menu. These options will be described next.

Instant Replay

As soon as you are back in READY mode you can use the macro that you have just recorded. Move the cell selector to an empty cell, press ALT-F2, and then select Instant Replay. The macro instructions are carried out, and the date is entered and formatted. Instant Replay plays back the most recently recorded macro. Quattro Pro 4 stores what you record in a small area of memory called a *buffer*. When you begin a new recording the contents of the buffer are cleared out to be replaced by the new

FIGURE
11-9

Actions completed

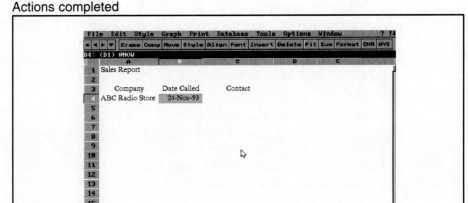

recording. For this reason Instant Replay is best used for one-shot macros that you will not need again. Using Instant Replay saves you the trouble of naming a macro if you will need it only for a short while. You can assign a Shortcut to Instant Replay to execute the recorded macro with a single keystroke.

Macro Paste

Another way to stop macro recording is to use ALT-F2 followed by Paste. This command enables you to paste the recorded macro into a worksheet where you can examine, name, and store it. In fact, before doing more work with the @NOW macro you have just created, you might want to take a look at the way it has been recorded by Quattro Pro 4. You can do this by selecting Paste from the Macro menu. You will be prompted for a name to create or modify, as shown in Figure 11-10. This is the name of the macro and the block of cells it will occupy. In this case, use the backslash and the letter *T* (for Today), as shown in Figure 11-10. Now press ENTER to confirm the name. Next, you will be prompted for the coordinates of the block of cells in which to store the keystrokes that make up the macro. Quattro Pro 4 assumes you want to use the current location of the cell selector. This location is not correct, because the current position of the cell selector is the cell in which you actually want to enter the date. You change the cell coordinates by first unlocking them with ESC.

Move the cell selector to an empty cell away from the rest of the worksheet—one that has at least two empty cells directly beneath it. For example, you could press HOME and then TAB. Using these keys is a quick way to move to a position away from the main work area with only two keystrokes. Press ENTER to confirm the location. You have now named the macro so that it can be executed with ALT-T. Before you use the macro, you might want to examine it.

An easy way to move to the cell you named to store the macro is to press the GoTo key (F5) and then the Name key (F3). You should see \T on the name list along with the names of any other blocks of cells that have been named in the spreadsheet. Highlight \T and press ENTER. Your cell selector will be placed in the top cell of the block you named \T. In Figure 11-11 you can see the record that Quattro Pro 4 made of your keystrokes in RECORD mode. The first cell is the function @NOW, as you

FIGURE 11-10

Naming a recorded macro

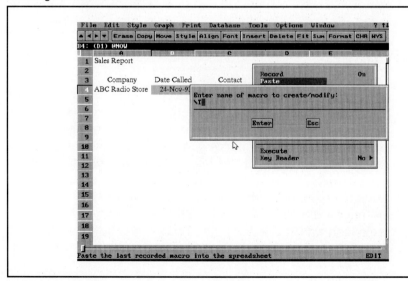

typed it, followed by the tilde (~), which is the macro language symbol for
ENTER. Below this is a record of the menu items you chose. These are
stated in terms that Quattro Pro 4 calls *menu equivalents.* Instead of
simply saying /SND1, which were the actual letters for the menu items
you selected, Quattro Pro 4 shows you the nature of the menu commands
you chose.

To use the \T macro you have created, first place the cell selector on
the cell into which you want to enter the date. Then press ALT-T and the
date will be entered and formatted for you.

Macro-Naming Strategies

If you had named the macro using the word DATE instead of \T, you
could execute it by first using the Macro Execute command and then
pressing F3 for a list of named blocks. Selecting DATE by highlighting it
and pressing ENTER would execute the macro commands stored in that
block. As was mentioned earlier, you can create as many as 26 instant
macros named with ALT plus a letter *A* through *Z.*. Although this method
limits you to 26 macros, you can use any valid block name for a macro
and thus create an unlimited number of macros. The chances are that
as your applications become more complex and your procedures more
streamlined, you will use both macro-naming methods, together with
Shortcuts. Thus, you could have 26 menu items assigned to CTRL-A/Z, 26
common operations assigned to ALT-A/Z, and then a selection of macros
accessible with Macro Execute.

Macro code

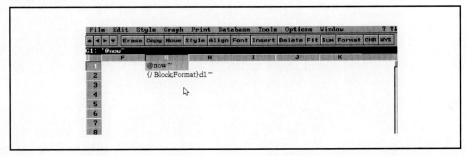

Expanding Macros

Recall that in the previous example, only cell G1 was named as \T. The macro record occupied more than one cell, however, so Quattro Pro 4 split the record of your keystrokes to prevent the creation of very long labels that are hard to read and edit. Because Quattro Pro 4 reads macros from the first cell, then from the next cell below that, and so on until it reaches an empty cell, you can easily add steps to the end of an existing macro. For example, when you are entering the date with the @NOW function, which was the purpose of the ALT-T macro described previously, you may want to add a step to convert the date in a function statement to a fixed date value.

The @NOW function returns the current date from your system clock. If you load the same spreadsheet the next day, the @NOW date changes. What you would probably want in a record of sales calls is a permanent date that does not change. You can set this with the Edit Values command. To add another set of instructions to the existing macro in G1 and G2 using the record method, follow these steps:

1. Place the cell selector in the cell that contains the @NOW function (B4 in this example). This location is where the actions to be recorded will be carried out.

2. Press ALT-F2 and pick Record to initiate the record feature.

3. You are now using RECORD mode. Use the Edit Values command and press ENTER to confirm that the cell containing the @NOW function is the one you want to transform into a value. Press ENTER again to copy the value to the same cell.

4. Press ALT-F2 and select Paste to terminate RECORD mode. Quattro Pro 4 prompts for the "name of macro to create/modify" and displays a list, as shown in Figure 11-12. Do not pick \T, but press ESC once and then press ENTER. This will result in a prompt for a paste location.

5. Press ESC to unlock the prompted coordinates, move the cell selector to G3, and press ENTER. The recorded action is now pasted into the worksheet below the existing macro code.

If you look at cells G3 and G4 now, you will see the action you just performed recorded as

{/ Block;Values}~~

Because this instruction is directly below the last cell of the \T macro, it will be read as part of the \T macro. You can now move to the cell into which you need to enter today's date and press ALT-T; the date will be entered and converted to a value that will not change when the worksheet is reloaded at a later date.

Note that you could have replied to the prompt in Figure 11-12 by typing a new name, such as **VALUE** or **\V**, which would then have been attached to the recorded code even as it became a part of the other macro. However, placing macros within macros is not recommended. If you want to use the code in G3 and G4 in a separate macro, the best approach is to copy it to another location, which brings up the question of macro management.

Name macro prompt

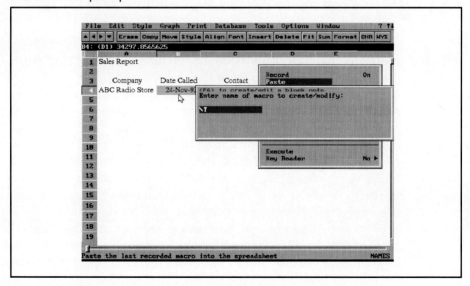

Macro Management

Macros are such powerful and useful tools for spreadsheet users that once you start to develop them you will probably begin to accumulate many of them. Placement of macros within a worksheet, conventions used for assigning names, and sharing macros between worksheets are important factors to consider as you organize your macros.

Macro Placement

If you want to store additional macros close to the ones already entered into the worksheet, but you do not want them to become part of the existing macros, you should make sure that at least one blank cell separates each macro from the next. In Figure 11-13 you can see that several more macros have been added in the same area of the worksheet as the \T macro. The macro in G7 is the Edit Values macro that turns a formula in a cell into a value. In cell G10 is a macro that widens the current column by one character, whereas the macro in G14 narrows the current column by one character. Because each of these macros is separate from the others, they are not activated by another macro.

Where you place macros on your spreadsheet not only affects how they relate to other macro instructions but also the rest of your work. Consider the location of the macros in the previous example, that is, to the right of the work area. This location is acceptable until you decide to delete a row from the work area. Because the macros and the work area are probably not going to be in view at the same time, it is all too easy to delete a row from the work area and accidentally delete a row of macro code. Macros run until they encounter a blank row, so even deleting a blank row or inserting a new row can cause problems for macros stored to the right of the work area. One way to avoid damaging these macros is to use the full movement of the cursor when you use the Row Delete or Row Insert command. You can press not only the DOWN ARROW key when deleting or inserting rows but also the RIGHT ARROW and the TAB key. Doing so allows you to move to the right of your work area to check for macros before deleting or inserting the rows.

FIGURE
11-13

Additional macros

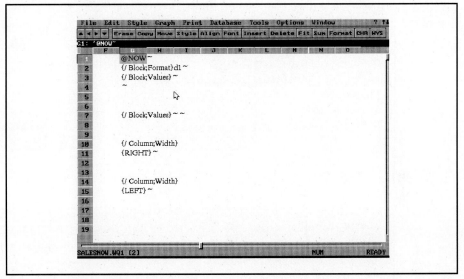

Another way to avoid problems for macros caused by deleting rows is to store the macros below the work area. You are less likely to delete columns and adding columns is less likely to disrupt a macro, because the instructions are stored in single columns. Some users like to place their macros above the main work area and to the left of the spreadsheet, that is, around the home position. Here they are safe from row deletion and easy to find. Such considerations are a part of worksheet aesthetics or spreadsheet design. The three preferred arrangements—below, to the right and below, and to the left and above—are shown in Figure 11-14. You will probably develop your own style of organizing your spreadsheets.

Organizing Macros

If you want to rearrange your macros within a worksheet, keep in mind that you can easily move a macro without affecting its operation by using the Edit Move command. This command retains the integrity of block names, so that Quattro Pro 4 knows where a named block is, even after it has been moved.

FIGURE
11-14

Macro layout diagram

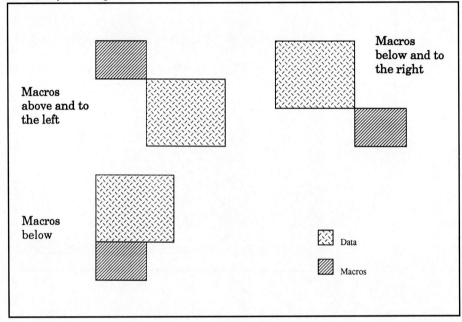

When you are designing macros, remember that you can use the TAB and PAGE DOWN keys to quickly move your cell selector a number of columns and rows at a time. By using HOME before TAB and PAGE DOWN, you can consistently move to the same location from anywhere on the worksheet. Thus, if you are working in normal character mode with 20 rows per screen you can set up a macro area at cell A61 that you can reach from anywhere on the worksheet with just four keystrokes: HOME, PAGE DOWN, PAGE DOWN, PAGE DOWN. But keep in mind that while this method is convenient, it is unreliable if you have to add or delete many columns or rows. The series of cursor keystrokes you have been using to get to a specific area may no longer be accurate. This is also true if you switch to a different display mode with more rows per screen.

An alternative way of moving to a specific area is to name the area with the Edit Names Create command. You could assign the name MACROS to the entire macro storage area. Then you can move to the named block by pressing GoTo (F5), typing **MACROS**, and pressing ENTER. You could also use GoTo followed by F3 to list the names and then select the name from the list. (One way to move quickly to an important block is to name it with a block name, such as AAA, that is alphabetically prior to any other names you have used. In this way the name becomes the top name on the F3 list. Then you can move to the block with GoTo, F3, and ENTER.)

Using cursor-movement keys to move to a specific location can be a problem in macros themselves. When you are designing cursor movement into a macro the best approach to locating a specific area is first to name the cell in the top left corner of the area you want to get to and then, in the macro instruction, to use {GoTo} and the block name. Subsequent changes to the location or size of the block will not affect the macro instruction.

Macro Layout

In addition to the possible danger to the macros in Figure 11-13 from deleting rows, there are other problems with the layout of these macros. You cannot see what their names are from looking at them. One way of finding out the names and locations of all named blocks in a worksheet is to use the Edit Names Make Table command. This command produces a two-column list of the block names and their corresponding coordinates, as shown in Figure 11-15.

In the figure, the Edit Names Make Table command was issued with the cell selector in K1. The table occupies columns K and L and as many rows as are needed to list all the current block names. You should always issue this command after you have prepared enough room for the resulting table to appear; otherwise, the table will overwrite the contents of existing cells. Note that the table is not dynamic; that is, it is not linked to the Edit Names Create command and will not be automatically updated when new names are created.

As useful as the Make Table command is in many situations, particularly when you have many block names to keep track of, it does not really tell you what you want to know about the macros in the worksheet. Consider the layout of the macros shown in Figure 11-16. These macros were moved to an area of the spreadsheet below the main work area. This arrangement follows the 3-column convention that has been widely adopted by many spreadsheet users. The first column contains the block names of the macros. The second column contains the actual lines of macro instructions. The third column contains a series of labels briefly

Edit Names Make Table results

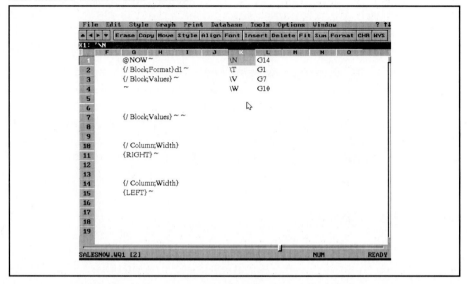

describing what each macro does. (Note that entering \T as a label requires a label prefix character.)

One reason for the popularity of this arrangement is that it works well with the Edit Names Labels command that assigns names to blocks based on labels in adjacent cells. For example, with the @NOW macro in cell B22 and the label \T in cell A22, as in Figure 11-16, you can use the Edit Names Labels Right command to name cell B22 as T. Similarly, you could use the Edit Names Labels Down command to attach the names Name, Code, and Action, to cells A22, B22, and C22. When you use the Labels command to assign names, you must include all the cells on the row or in the column that contain the names you want to use. Blank cells do not create blank names; they are simply ignored.

Macro Libraries

Macros stored in a regular spreadsheet are specific to that spreadsheet. Unlike Shortcuts, macros initially consist of labels stored in the cells of a single worksheet. Macros are saved with that worksheet

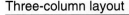

Three-column layout

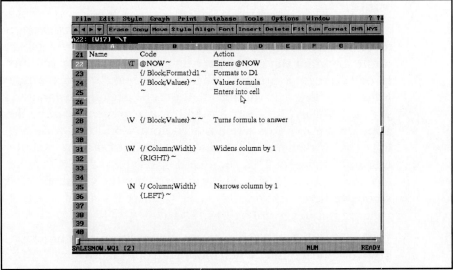

and are not immediately available when you move to a new worksheet. However, chances are that you will want to use some macros in many different worksheets. You can easily copy macros from one worksheet to another by using the Edit Copy command, but when you copy a named block from one worksheet to another the block name does not go with it. This means that to make a macro active in the worksheet to which it has been copied, you must issue the Edit Names command. If you use the 3-column layout you can use the Labels Right method described in the previous section.

Creating a Macro Library

You may want to collect macros from several worksheets into a single worksheet file called a *macro library*. A macro library is a very useful file to maintain in an office with several users developing Quattro Pro 4 macros. You can share macros and avoid duplication of effort if a common macro library is maintained. A prerequisite to this is adherence to some basic standards of layout, such as the 3-column method. In Quattro Pro 4 a macro library is not just a useful collecting place for macros. You can open macro libraries so that the macros they contain can be used in other worksheets.

A macro library is a document that typically consists of nothing but macros. Whenever you execute a macro Quattro Pro 4 looks for the name of the macro in the current worksheet. If the macro you have called on is not there, the program checks whether there are any open macro libraries. These are worksheets that are specially designated as libraries with the Macro Library command. Any worksheet can be designated as a macro library. To make a macro library out of a worksheet you must load the worksheet and make it current, and then execute the Macro Library command. This command gives you a Yes/No choice, as shown in Figure 11-17. Choose Yes and then save the worksheet. From now on, whenever this worksheet is loaded Quattro Pro 4 will look to it for macros that are not in the current worksheet.

There is no special name for a macro library document; you can use any worksheet name. When more than one macro library is open, Quattro Pro 4 will look into them in the order in which they were opened. Remember, Quattro Pro 4 only looks outside of the current worksheet for a macro if the current worksheet does not contain the macro you have asked to execute.

Applying Macro Libraries

There are numerous advantages to placing most of your macros into one or more macro libraries. Earlier, the question of protecting and preserving macros was discussed. From an organizational point of view, macros are much safer from accidental corruption when they are stored separately in a macro library, and they are generally easier to keep track of.

Because Quattro Pro 4 enables you to have more than one macro library, you can develop libraries for specific types of work. A macro library for spreadsheet design work could contain 26 instant macros plus many others that you have developed to speed design work. When it comes time to move on to data entry you can close the design macro library and open the data entry macro library, containing 26 different instant macros plus other macro routines. You can save a macro library as part of a workspace so that it is available immediately when you get down to work. You can use some special macros, described later in this

FIGURE
11-17

Macro Library command

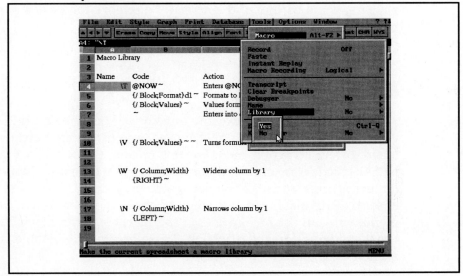

chapter, in a macro library to initiate a whole chain of events and provide real power over your Quattro Pro 4 environment.

Macro Control

Quattro Pro 4 contains numerous features for controlling macro execution. You can use these features to determine why a macro does not work the way you expect it to.

Stopping Macros

If you give the command to execute a macro and the effects immediately appear to be different from what you expect, you may want to stop the macro. You do this with CTRL-BREAK (CTRL-SCROLL LOCK on some keyboards). When you press CTRL-BREAK during macro execution, Quattro Pro 4 responds with "Macro Error at *Location*." *Location* is the cell containing the macro instruction that was interrupted. This message appears at the bottom of the screen. To remove the error message and return to READY mode, just press ESC.

Debugging Macros

Quattro Pro 4 macros execute quickly, so it may be hard to tell what goes wrong when a macro misbehaves, and it may be hard to stop the macro before it is completed. For this reason, Quattro Pro 4 provides a DEBUG mode of macro execution. This mode is both a sophisticated tool for identifying errors in advanced macro programming and a simple way of seeing your macro run one step at a time. Using the Macro Debugging menu, you can set *breakpoints* in the macro—points at which Quattro Pro 4 will pause during playback. These breakpoints enable you to see sections of the macro at a time.

As an example of how the macro debug feature can help in a relatively simple macro, consider the worksheet in Figure 11-18. This worksheet is a monthly expense projection. The expenses are listed in columns by month. The columns are being summed on row 11 using an @SUM formula like the one in B11. The macro visible on the worksheet is designed to sum a column. The macro is supposed to do this by first typing the @SUM function and the opening parenthesis. The macro then moves the cell selector to the top of the column, anchors the block to be summed at that point with a period, and includes all the cells down to the bottom of the column. Finally, a closing parenthesis is added and the formula is entered in the cell with a tilde.

The idea behind the \S macro is that the user will place the cell selector in C11 and press ALT-S to activate the macro and sum the column. But as you can see from Figure 11-18, the results are not as expected. Cell C11 contains the formula @SUM(C10..C8192), which is not only incorrect but also a circular reference, as noted by the message CIRC at the bottom of the screen. The debug feature should help show where the problem lies.

To activate DEBUG mode, press the Step key (SHIFT-F2). The message DEBUG appears at the bottom of the screen. From this point until you reissue the SHIFT-F2 command, any macro you execute will cause the debug windows to appear. Before executing the macro you want to debug,

FIGURE
11-18

\S macro in trouble

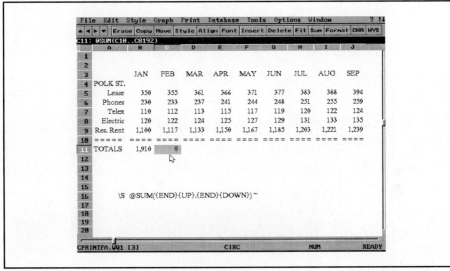

however, you should make sure that the conditions are correct. For example, in the case of the worksheet in Figure 11-18, the incorrect formula needs to be deleted from cell C11 before the macro is retried. If you then issue the command to run the sample macro \S that needs to be debugged, Quattro Pro 4 opens up two windows in the lower half of the screen, as shown in Figure 11-19. In the upper window, called the *debug window,* Quattro Pro 4 shows the location of the macro you are executing and places the cursor on the first instruction. (The apostrophe is not an instruction, merely the label indicator.) The lower window, the trace window, shows you any trace cells that you have specified. This feature is used in advanced debugging, which is described in Chapter 12.

The SPACEBAR is used to play back the macro one step at a time. Pressing the ENTER key tells Quattro Pro 4 to run the macro until the next breakpoint. For a simple investigation of a malfunctioning macro you will not need to set breakpoints; you can use the SPACEBAR to play back the macro one step at a time. (Breakpoints are discussed further in Chapter 12.)

In Figure 11-20 you can see that the problem with this macro has become apparent. The END, UP ARROW combination took the cell selector only to cell C10, and the END, DOWN ARROW combination is about to take the cell selector to the bottom of the worksheet. You can abort the macro at this point by typing **/** for the Macro Debugging menu, shown in Figure

FIGURE
11-19

The DEBUG screen

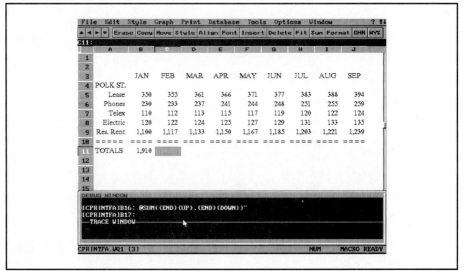

11-21. Select the Abort option from the menu then press ENTER to clear the error message and return to READY mode. Note that this action does not reverse the effect of SHIFT-F2, which will continue to cause macros to be executed in DEBUG mode until you press it again. The other options on the Macro Debugging menu will be examined in Chapter 12, which explores more advanced macro applications.

Special Macros

You have seen that you can create an unlimited number of named macros that you can select with ALT-F2 and F3. You can create 26 instant macros named \A through \Z. In addition to these, there are several special types of macros which are described in this section.

Automatic Macros

You can have Quattro Pro 4 activate a macro as soon as the file in which it is stored is retrieved. This *Startup macro* is normally called \0,

FIGURE
11-20

The problem revealed by DEBUG

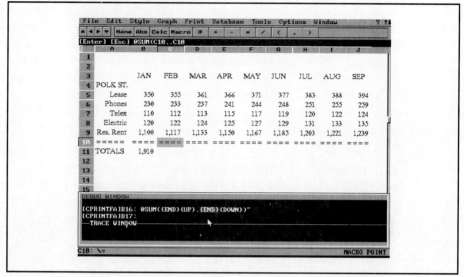

FIGURE
11-21

The DEBUG menu

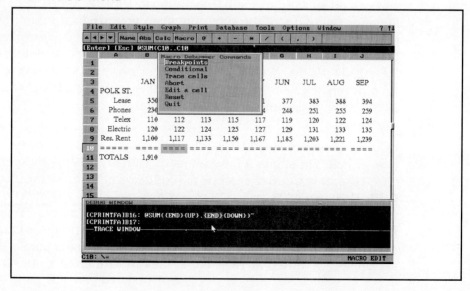

but you can use a different name, such as FIRST, as long as you record your choice with the Options Startup and Options Update commands. The Startup macro works well with the autoload file, which is a worksheet file that is retrieved from disk as soon as you load Quattro Pro 4. The name of the file that the program looks for when it is loaded is normally called QUATTRO.WQ1, but you can change it to another name (such as FIRST.WQ1) by using the Options Startup menu. If you create a Startup macro in a worksheet named as the autoload file, you can initiate any series of events that macros can control.

A simple application of the Startup macro feature is to have Quattro Pro 4 display a list of files every time you load the program. To do this, enter the label **'/FR** or {**/ File;Retrieve**} into an empty worksheet and name the cell as the Startup macro, **\0**. Then save the file using the name QUATTRO.WQ1 or whatever name you have selected as your autoload file. When you next start up Quattro Pro 4, the first thing you will see is a list of files from which to select. Note that the label '/FR is the exact key equivalent of the command, whereas the words in braces are the menu equivalent of the command.

Command-Line Macros

If you want to load Quattro Pro 4 and then a particular spreadsheet, you can do so without using the autoload feature. Type the name of the file after the name of the program when you are loading from the DOS prompt or the command line. For example, suppose you have to respond to an urgent request for a price quote. Your pricing calculations are in a file called PRICING.WQ1. You have turned on your PC and are at the DOS prompt ready to load Quattro Pro 4. Simply type **Q PRICING** and press ENTER. The program will load and immediately retrieve the pricing worksheet.

You can go one step beyond this by naming a macro on the command line as well. Thus, if you have a macro in the PRICING worksheet called QUOTE that is a series of steps to produce a price quote, you could type **Q PRICING QUOTE** at the DOS prompt and press ENTER. The program would then load itself, the worksheet, and the macro. This level of flexibility, together with the speed with which Quattro Pro 4 loads, opens a wide range of possibilities for your applications. For example, you could set up several different DOS batch files to load Quattro Pro 4 together with different worksheets. (DOS batch files are described in Appendix A.) The automatic and command-line macro-loading options take on particular significance when you work with the macro commands described in the next chapter.

You can also load a workspace from the command line. You do this by specifying the full name of the workspace file, as in **Q PRICING.WSP**, which loads a workspace called PRICING.WSP. If this workspace includes a worksheet that has been designated as a macro library, and includes an autoexecute macro, then you can initiate a whole series of events from the command line.

A Macro-Executing Macro

When you have created a number of named macros and want a quick way to execute them, you can develop a macro that will help you select one macro from a macro list. You could create this macro-executing macro by entering the label

{/ Name;Execute}{NAME}

into a blank cell. If you use the Edit Names Create command to name this cell with an instant macro, possibly \M for macro executing, the next time that you need to execute a named macro, you can simply press ALT-M. The macro uses the Macro Execute command and the F3 function {NAME} to display a list of named macros from which you can choose.

Macro Writing and Editing

As you have seen, there are several ways to create macros in Quattro Pro 4. You can record your keystrokes. You can use sections of the log of your keystrokes recorded by Transcript, as described later in this chapter. You can also write the macro yourself, using your knowledge of Quattro Pro 4 to compose a set of keystrokes. You can combine sections of macros that you have written with sections produced by the other methods. Writing or editing macros becomes more important as your macros become more complex. The chances are that you will need to edit lengthy macros to improve their performance, streamline their arrangement in the worksheet, or correct bugs in their operation.

Composing Macros

Before you compose a macro, it is helpful to make notes of the operations you want the macro to perform and sketch out the required steps. When you enter the macro instructions into the worksheet, remember that you can use either direct keystrokes for menu selections or the menu equivalents. Thus, you could enter a macro to convert the current cell into a value, such as **/EV**, or {**/ Block;Values**}~~. Although the first approach might seem quicker, it is more difficult to read. The second approach does not require that you memorize all of the menu equivalents. You can look these up by using SHIFT-F3 and selecting /Commands from the menu. The commands are logically grouped together and easy to find.

Often you will be able to put together a macro from several sources. For example, you can use the record method to capture the keystrokes for part of an operation and then add those recorded keystrokes to the rest of the macro with the Edit Move command. When you are combining macro instructions, you may want to use several of the techniques described here.

Repeating and Abbreviating

When you use the record method to capture keystrokes, you sometimes get rather cumbersome lines of instructions like this one:

{/Block;Copy}{DOWN}{DOWN}{DOWN}{DOWN}{DOWN}{RIGHT}{RIGHT}

Quattro Pro 4 records each cursor movement as a separate keystroke, repeating the keystroke representation over and over. However, you can refer to a series of repeated keystrokes by the name of the key representation and a number. That is, the key representation takes a numeric argument enclosed within braces, as in {DOWN 5}. You can use this system with any of the macro key representations listed in Table 11-2 except for {CR} and {MENU}.

The number used as the argument can be a number you type in or a number in a cell referenced by the cell coordinate or a block name. Thus, {DOWN A1} causes the DOWN ARROW action to be repeated five times if A1 contains the number 5 or a formula that results in 5. Likewise, the instruction {DOWN TIMES} causes the action to be repeated five times if the block TIMES contains the number 5 or a formula that results in 5.

You can further shorten your macros if you refer to the arrow keys as follows: DOWN as {D}, UP as {U}, LEFT as {L}, and RIGHT as {R}. Also, you can use {ESC} instead of {ESCAPE} and {BS} instead of {BACKSPACE}. Thus, {DOWN 5} becomes {D 5} and the lengthy instruction just given can be reduced to this:

{/ Block;Copy}{D 5}{R 2}

This abbreviated version is easy to read and much more compact. However, you will probably want to look carefully at the use of multiple cursor-movement keystrokes in your macros. In general, you will find macros more reliable if you use block names wherever possible, instead of the pointing method of identifying cell coordinates.

Splitting Macro Lines

At times you may not be able to reduce the length of recorded macro instructions by using the abbreviation method. However, you may still want to split the macro line into more manageable sections. One way to do this is to copy the line that needs to be split and then edit both versions. For example, you might want to split the following line:

{/ Sort;block}{BS}.{END}{RIGHT}{END}{DOWN}

To split this line of instructions, first copy the line from its current cell to the one below it (assuming that the cell you are copying to is empty or contains expendable data). Then highlight the original instruction and press F2 to edit it. Use the BACKSPACE key to erase all the text to the right of the period. Then press ENTER to return the edited line to the cell. Move your cell selector to the copy of the original line and press F2 to edit it. Press HOME and then press DELETE to remove all of the text up to and including the period. Press ENTER to return the edited contents to the cell. The resulting cells will look like this:

{/ Sort;block}{BS}.
{END}{RIGHT}{END}{DOWN}

You now have the macro instruction in two short labels rather than one long one. This technique often helps to make macro instructions more manageable.

There may also be times when it is prudent to combine lines of macro code. For example, earlier in Figure 11-13 you saw that Quattro Pro 4 recorded a single tilde on one line at the end of a macro. This was later added to the line above to make the macro easier to copy and keep together.

Transcript Macros

The Transcript feature keeps track of all your keystrokes while you are using Quattro Pro 4. It saves the keystrokes to a log file on disk so that you can reconstruct your work after a power outage or a serious operator error. The format in which Transcript records your keystrokes is the same as that used in macro recording. You can actually copy sections of the Transcript log to your worksheet for use in macros.

Using the Transcript Log for Macros

If you have loaded Quattro Pro 4 and have performed an operation that you would like to incorporate into a macro, you can access the Transcript log of your actions by using the Tools Macro command or by pressing the Macro key (ALT-F2). From the Macro menu, select Transcript. A window showing the Transcript log will open in the middle of the screen. You can see this window in Figure 11-22, which shows an accounts receivable worksheet in which a new column for Total Owed is being added. The most recent actions are at the bottom of the list. You use the UP ARROW or LEFT ARROW key to scroll back up through the log to view earlier actions. Mouse users can click the mouse pointer on the word Transcript to produce the Transcript log. Hold down the mouse button to continuously scroll up the list.

The line in the left margin of the Transcript window marks the activity since the last File Retrieve, Open, Save, or New command or since the last time Transcript saved the log. Transcript uses the files you save on disk as a basis for the re-creation of your work in the event of data loss. You can see the File Retrieve command in Figure 11-23, where the log has been scrolled and the Transcript menu activated by typing /.

Suppose that you copy the new formula created in cell G9 of the accounts receivable worksheet down to the bottom of the model, using the END key. Having performed the action, you would like to make a macro out of it. Press ALT-F2, select Transcript, and you will see that the action has been recorded, as shown in Figure 11-24, where it occupies the last two lines of the log. To copy a section of the log to your worksheet, first place the highlight bar on the first line of instructions you want to copy, as was done in Figure 11-24. Then type / for the Transcript menu. Select Begin Block from the menu. The menu will disappear and leave a triangle marking the beginning point of the block. You can move the highlight bar to the last line of the section you want to copy. Type / and select End Block. This marks all of the commands chosen from the beginning to the end of the block with a triangle, as you can see in Figure 11-25.

FIGURE
11-22

Transcript window

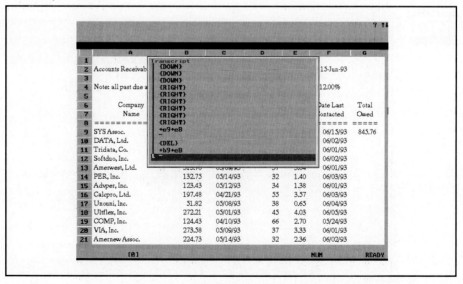

Having marked the block of Transcript code, type **/** again and select Copy Block from the Transcript menu. You will be returned to the worksheet and prompted for a macro name to create or modify, as shown in Figure 11-26. This enables you to name the worksheet cell into which you are about to paste the Transcript code. You can enter a name if you have one picked out already or just press ENTER to continue with the copy operation without naming the destination cell. When you press ENTER or enter a name you will be prompted for a cell location, just as you are when you use the Macro Paste command. You can paste the code into the current worksheet or into a macro sheet by entering the worksheet name in brackets before the address. After you specify the first cell of the block to which you want the instructions copied, press ENTER; the copy is completed. In Figure 11-27 you can see the results of copying from the Transcript Log with S2 as the destination.

Bear in mind that the destination cell must be above enough empty cells to accommodate the number of lines you are copying into the worksheet. The Transcript log records the copy action as a Macro Paste and remembers the block markers. You can move these to other parts of the Transcript log with the Begin Block and End Block commands.

FIGURE
11-23

The Transcript menu

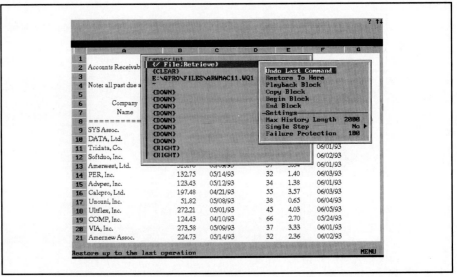

FIGURE
11-24

Action recorded

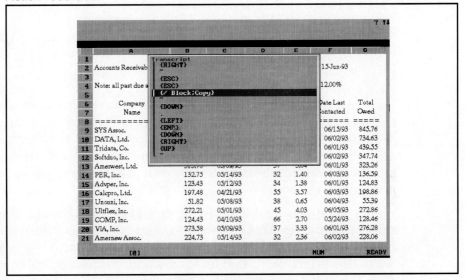

FIGURE
11-25

Marked block

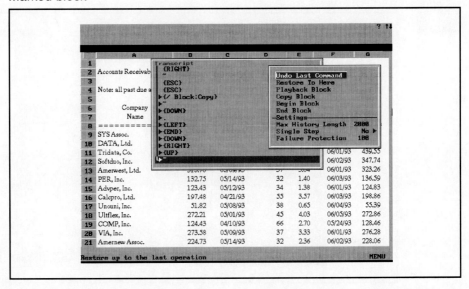

Other Transcript Commands

The Undo Last Command option at the top of the Transcript menu is useful when you do not have the regular Undo feature activated. To use this command and the Restore To Here command successfully, maintain your position in the spreadsheet before you issue the command. When you issue the Restore To Here command, Quattro Pro 4 carries out all of the actions since the last file save or retrieval. If you make an error and then move all over your worksheet trying to fix it before remembering Transcript and selecting Restore To Here, you can get unexpected and chaotic results. It is best to use this command as soon as you realize you have made a mistake.

You might wonder how far back you can go to get code for macros from the Transcript log. Notice the Settings section of the Transcript menu in Figure 11-25. The Max History Length option is currently set at 2000 lines. This is how many lines of instructions Transcript will record before discarding line 1. You can increase this setting to store more of your actions, resulting in larger Transcript log files on disk, or you can shorten the setting to conserve space. The maximum setting is 25,000 lines. To change this setting, simply highlight the menu option and press ENTER.

FIGURE 11-26

Name prompt

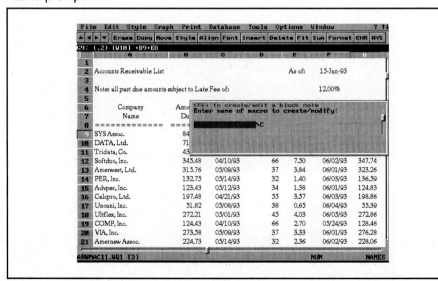

Posted Transcript code

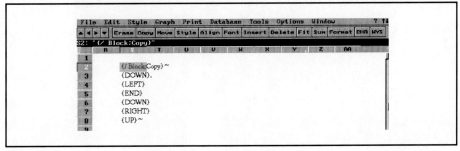

Note that adding to Max History Length increases the memory area used by Transcript.

In Figure 11-25 you can see that the option called Single Step is currently set to No, meaning that if you use the Playback Block command the code in the log will be played back one step at a time, similar to the DEBUG mode of macro execution. Setting this option to Yes provides a greater level of control when playing back Transcript with the Restore To Here or Playback Block commands.

Under the Transcript settings, the Failure Protection option refers to the number of lines recorded before Transcript saves the log to disk. Currently this is set to 100. Failure Protection carries the same limit as the Max History Length, 1 to 25,000. If you decrease this number you will notice more disk activity, but recovering from a disaster will likely be more complete. Bear in mind that the Undo feature will reverse some actions if you use it immediately, providing a front line of defense ahead of Transcript.

CHAPTER

Further Macros and Macro Commands

*T*his chapter explores the more advanced aspects of creating Quattro Pro 4 macros, including automatic macros and macro libraries. You will learn about the macro commands that allow you to create menu-driven applications with Quattro Pro 4. You will see examples of macros that prompt for user input and review advanced @functions, such as @CELL. You will also learn how to customize the actual program menus of Quattro Pro 4, using the Edit Menus command to cut and paste menu items and arrange them the way you want, thus developing a unique program interface.

Macro Commands

In addition to using macros for a fixed set of instructions that replicate keystrokes as if they were entered manually from the keyboard, you can use special macro commands to access features and functions that are not available from the keyboard. This section discusses the theory of macro commands and reviews the individual commands. These range from {BEEP}, which sounds your computer's beep to alert the user, to {GETLABEL}, which prompts for user input, to {MENUBRANCH}, which branches to the data for a custom menu.

The Role of Macro Commands

The basic purpose of macro commands is to add logic to macros, thus enabling you to create macros that evaluate conditions and choose between different courses of action based on parameters you specify. For this reason the macro commands are a lot like programming statements. This does not mean that macro commands are just for programmers. Typical users are quite capable of taking advantage of this facility, either to simplify their own work or to prepare Quattro Pro 4 applications for others. However, the macro commands do permit you to develop macros to such a high level of sophistication that complete texts have been devoted to programming in macro command languages. Because the Quattro Pro 4 macro commands closely follow the syntax and format of the 1-2-3 macro command language you will find that texts on that subject are generally applicable to Quattro Pro 4. You should bear in mind that there are some commands in Quattro Pro 4 that do not exist in 1-2-3 Release 3, and that the design of Quattro Pro 4 has alleviated the need for some of the programming steps necessary in 1-2-3. These differences will be pointed out as the commands are described in this chapter.

Using the {BRANCH} Command

A simple, yet typical situation where a macro command can be very effectively applied is the need to repeat a series of operations. Suppose you have a column of values that need to be rounded to two decimal places with the @ROUND function. You edit the first cell and place **@ROUND(** in front of the value. Then you place **,2)** at the end of the value and enter the new information into the cell. You could use a macro called \R to do this:

{EDIT}{HOME\@ROUND({END},2)~

After performing this action on one value you would move down to the next. Alternatively, you can add this movement to the macro. Because the DOWN ARROW key enters data from EDIT mode, you could amend the macro to read:

{EDIT}{HOME}@ROUND({END},2){DOWN}

If the column of values is long, you will need to repeat the macro many times. Instead of repeatedly executing the same macro, you can incorporate this repetition into the macro by means of the macro command {BRANCH}. The {BRANCH} command tells Quattro Pro 4 to go to a new cell and read the instructions from there. Like @functions, many of the macro commands require arguments. Include these within the braces, separated from the name of the command by a space. Connect multiple arguments with commas, just as you do in @functions.

The following \R macro tells Quattro Pro 4 to go back and repeat the macro. When the first line of code is read the second line tells Quattro Pro 4 to return to the first, the actual cell named \R:

{EDIT}{HOME}@ROUND({END},2){DOWN}
{BRANCH \R}

Once you execute ALT R the macro will loop continuously until you stop it, or it reaches an empty cell or a label. You can stop the macro with CTRL-BREAK. Although this is a fairly crude way of controlling macro execution, it is simple to implement. If the macro reaches an empty cell or a label it causes an error which you can clear with CTRL-BREAK.

Using the @CELL Function

The @CELL function and its companions, @CELLPOINTER and @CELLINDEX, are very useful in macros when you need to get information about a cell. For example, suppose you want to know whether cell A1 is blank. There are several methods you could use, but the simplest is @CELL("type", A1). This returns "b" if the cell is blank, "v" if it contains a value, or "l" if it contains a label. The codes you can use in the @CELL function and more examples of the function are provided later in this chapter. The information returned by the @CELL function covers address, row, column, contents, type, prefix, protection status, width, and format.

Bear in mind that the @CELL response itself may be a label, so an {IF} or @IF statement using @CELL may need to refer to the result as a string in quotes, like the "b" in this formula, which returns VACANT if A1 is blank:

@IF(@CELL("type", A1)="b", "VACANT", "OCCUPIED")

The categories of information dealt with by @CELL are described later, in the section entitled "Advanced Functions." There you will find a table of the codes that can be used as the first @CELL argument. The @CELLPOINTER function works like @CELL except that it always refers to the current cell. This means that @CELLPOINTER does not require a cell argument. If you enter @CELLPOINTER("type") in A1 the result is "v" for value, because the cell contains the formula you have just entered. However, if you move the cell pointer to A2 and enter a label, the result in A1 changes to "l", because A2 is now the current cell and it contains a label.

This ability to reflect the status of the current cell makes @CELLPOINTER very useful in macros. For example, the sample \R macro that rounds values could use @CELLPOINTER to test for the presence of a value in the current cell. The following code, the first line of which is named \R, represents a macro that works down a column of values, adding the @ROUND function until it reaches a cell that is not a value, at which point the macro stops:

```
{EDIT}{HOME}@ROUND({END},2){DOWN}
{IF @CELLPOINTER("type")="v"}{BRANCH \R}
{QUIT}
```

This macro uses the {IF} command, which is described in detail in a moment.

Using the {GETNUMBER} Command

Many macros are designed to make a worksheet easier for novices to use. Often, you would like a macro to prompt the user for the required data. An example of this is shown in Figure 12-1, in which an automobile loan is being calculated. The basic calculations take place on the left of the screen. On the right is an area set aside for a loan payment table. The calculations in column e stem from the price of the automobile.

A macro has been designed to ask the customer the price on which they want to base the loan. In Figure 12-2 you can see some of this macro code and a table of block names used in the worksheet. The first line of the macro places the price of the automobile into the cell named PR, using the {GETNUMBER} command. In Figure 12-1 you can see the user being asked to supply the price. The macro is activated by pressing ALT-C. It is also activated whenever the worksheet is retrieved, because it is also called \0.

A {GETNUMBER} statement needs two pieces of information: the text of the prompt or question, enclosed in quotes; and the location into which to place the response. This location can be a cell coordinate or a block name. Block names are preferable, because they are more constant than cell references. When you activate this macro you are prompted with the text in the prompt argument of the /{GETNUMBER} command, as shown in Figure 12-1.

When you type a number and press ENTER, the number is placed into the designated cell, in this case, PR or C4. If you enter something other than a number, you get an ERR message.

FIGURE 12-1

Vehicle loan calculator

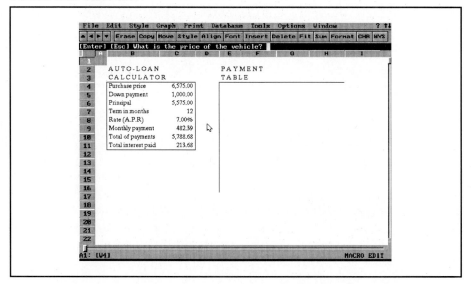

FIGURE 12-2

Macro code loan calculator

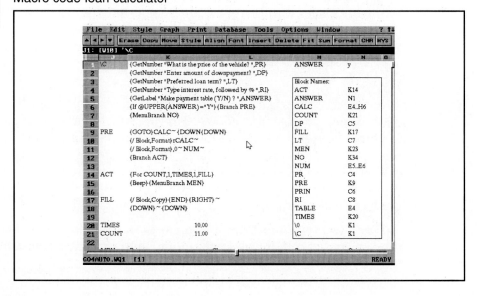

Finding Commands

You can use Quattro Pro 4 to look up macro commands as you are writing macros. The Macro List key (SHIFT-F3) shows a list of different types of macro commands, as listed in Table 12-1. The commands that prompt for user input are called the *interactive commands*. If you select Interactive from the SHIFT-F3 list, you will see the possibilities shown in Table 12-2. Highlight the one you want to use in your macro and press ENTER to place it on the edit line.

User-input commands can be used one after the other to prompt for all of the variables in the loan calculation. The {GETLABEL} command you see in cell K5 of Figure 12-2 handles label input in a continuation of the \C macro. This command has been set up to place the response in a location stated as a named block, ANSWER. You can see that the cell called ANSWER is N1.

Using the {IF} Command

The sample macro has been designed so that the responses to the price, down payment, and term questions of the loan calculation are placed in their respective cells. The {GETLABEL} command asks the user

TABLE
12-1

The Macro Categories Listed by the Macro List Key (SHIFT-F3)

Category	Description
Keyboard	Macro names for keystrokes (grouped as Movement, Function, Status, Other)
Screen	Commands to control screen updating
Interactive	Commands to control user input
Program Flow	Commands to control macro flow
Cells	Commands to control cell contents and calculation
File	Commands to read and write ASCII data files
/ Commands	Macro equivalents of menu commands

TABLE 12-2   Interactive Macro Commands

Command	Description
?	Pauses and accepts keyboard input
BREAKOFF	Disables CTRL-BREAK
BREAKON	Restores CTRL-BREAK
GET	Accepts single key input
GETLABEL	Accepts lable input
GETNUMBER	Accepts numeric input
GRAPHCHAR	Stores single character input
IFKEY	Determines macro key assignment
LOOK	Stores next keystroke
MENUBRANCH	Branches to custom menu
MENUCALL	Runs custom menu subroutine
MESSAGE	Displays message box
PLAY	Plays digital sound files (SND)
STEPOFF	Turns off single-step mode
STEPON	Activates single-step mode
WAIT	Pauses for a time period

whether to display a payment table and places the response in a cell named ANSWER. The next line of the macro, on row 6 of the worksheet, evaluates the contents of the ANSWER cell, using the very powerful {IF} command. This command is used to make the macro evaluate a specific condition before proceeding. Like the @IF function, it is followed by a condition statement. If the cell named ANSWER contains the label Y, the macro branches to a macro cell called PRE. The {BRANCH} command moves the flow of the macro to the cell specified in its argument. If the condition is not True, the macro continues with the next line, which is a {MENUBRANCH} command. In this case the {MENUBRANCH} command directs the macro to a cell called NO.

The Payment Table Macro

The PRE macro in Figure 12-2 is activated if you type **Y** in response to the prompt in line 5 for a payment table. The instructions in PRE start the payment table. This is done by first reformatting a block of cells called CALC. This is the area at the top of payment table in Figure 12-1, from E4 through H6. As you can see from Figure 12-3, these cells contain information, but it is disguised. After resetting the format of those cells so that they can be seen, the macro branches to ACT.

The cell contents are disguised by the special numeric format known as Hidden, denoted by the format identifier (H). This format allows a cell to contain data but not display it. The exposed cells can be seen in Figure 12-4. The cell contents are exposed by using the Style Numeric Format Reset command. This causes the format of the cells to change from Hidden to whatever is the global or default format, set by the Options Formats command. In this worksheet the global format is Comma, with two decimal places.

The idea behind the use of the Hidden format is that the contents of E4..H6 remain unseen until the user requests a payment table. This gives the worksheet in Figure 12-1 a clean and uncluttered appearance. Then, when the user requests a table, the first three lines are already written.

FIGURE 12-3

The hidden contents of H6

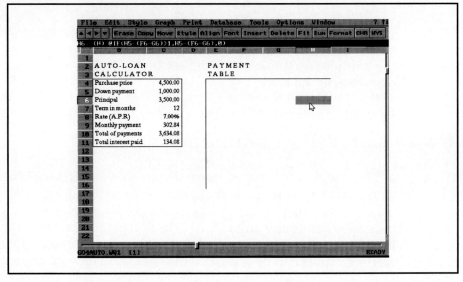

FIGURE 12-4   The exposed contents of E4..H6

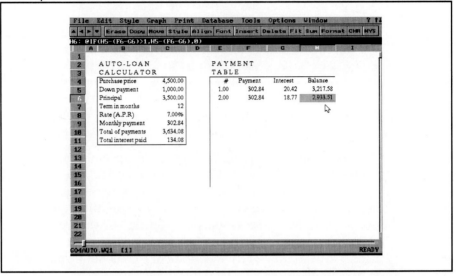

The column titles are in E4..H4. The first row of calculations is in E5..H5. In E6..H6 are the formulas for the second row of the table. These can be copied as many times as it takes to complete the table. The rather complex formula in H6 merely ensures that when the remaining balance on the loan is 1 or less, the entry in the Balance column will be 0. This avoids having a few cents left over at the end of the loan.

The copying of the formulas on row 6 of the table is done by a separate macro, called ACT. The task of this macro is to make as many copies of the formulas as it takes to complete the table, based on the number of payments in the loan.

Using the {FOR} Command

The macro called ACT, shown in Figure 12-2, uses the {FOR} command to control repetition of a task. In this case the task it repeats is a macro called FILL, which copies a line of the payment table once. The {FOR} command has several arguments. The first is the location of the counter, in this case a cell named COUNT, as K21. The second argument is the starting number to be placed in the counter. The next argument is the stop, the total number of times the command repeats, in this case the cell called TIMES. Located at K20, this cell is the number of periods in the term of the loan, minus two because of the lines already entered and hidden in the worksheet. The fourth argument is the step, the amount to increment the counter after each iteration. The last argument is the cell address or block name containing the macro routine to be executed. The result of a complete execution of the \C macro, in which the user responded **Y** to the payment table question, is shown in Figure 12-5. Note that there is a menu in the top left of the screen. This will be discussed in a moment.

Evaluating Input

When you are designing applications to be used by others, there are many factors to consider that do not arise when you are simply creating macros for your own use. For example, the macro command used to prompt for the payment table in the loan calculation model might have been written as

{If ANSWER="Yes"}{Branch PRE}

FIGURE 12-5

Completed payment table

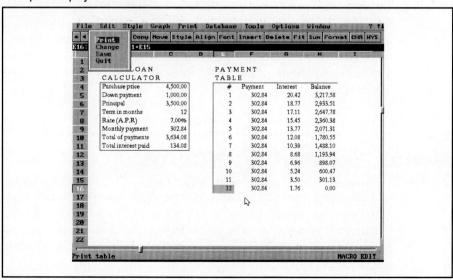

This would require the user to enter three characters, thus increasing the chance of mistakes. The {IF} command is not case sensitive, so **YES** and **yes** will be accepted as well as **Yes**. You could make the response requirement a single letter (Y or N) to simplify the user's role. There is actually a redundant function in the statement used in this example:

{If @UPPER(ANSWER)="Y"}{Branch PRE}

The @UPPER function, which turns the contents of ANSWER into capitals, is not required, because {IF} evaluates y and Y as the same response. However, there may be situations in which you would like to maintain tight control of the input to ensure accuracy. You can demand an exact response by using @EXACT, as in

{If @EXACT(ANSWER,"Yes")}{Branch PRE}

Here, the user would have to type **Yes** to proceed. Entering **YES** would not be acceptable.

Providing Feedback

In Figure 12-2 you can see that the {BEEP} command is used in the ACT macro. This sounds the beep when the payment table is completed. Tasks that take more than a few seconds to complete and keep the user waiting can benefit from a {BEEP} to alert the user of the task's completion. Although {BEEP} simply uses the speaker in your PC to make a simple sound, you can use more complex sounds by employing the {PLAY} command which operates the digital sound files that come with Quattro Pro 4. For example, {PLAY "DRUMS.SND"} will activate the DRUMS.SND file, if it is stored in the current directory.

Menus Created by Macros

Following the completion of the ACT macro in the loan payment example, the macro branches to a menu by using the {MENUBRANCH} command. You can see the menu in Figure 12-5. One of the most popular uses of the macro commands is to create customized menus within a spreadsheet to simplify its operation, either for yourself or for other users.

You can place macro menus in macro libraries to make them available in any worksheet. The menu in Figure 12-5 named MEN is called from within the loan calculation macro. This menu offers the user three choices: printing the loan table, changing the figures in the loan calculation, or saving the worksheet. The code that generates this menu is shown in Figure 12-6. This figure also shows the macro code for the menu called NO, which appears when the user decides not to create a payment table.

Writing Macro Menus

Macro-generated menus follow the same format as regular Quattro Pro 4 menus, with a vertical list of the options, descriptions of the options at the bottom of the screen, and the first letter method of selection. Quattro Pro 4 automatically places the menu on the screen in a suitable location, based on the position of the cell selector when the menu is invoked, as well as the size of the menu. To let you know that you are still in the middle of a macro, and not in a Quattro Pro 4 menu, the program automatically displays the MACRO message at the bottom of the screen.

FIGURE
12-6

The code for the MEN Menu

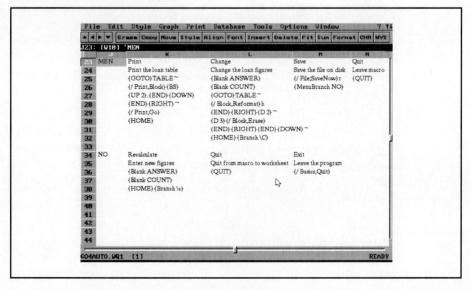

When the user selects one of the items on the menu in Figure 12-5, macro commands are activated to carry out the menu item. You can easily create such a menu to operate macros in your worksheets. However, remember that this menu is part of this worksheet, not a part of the overall Quattro Pro 4 menu system. You can use the Options Startup Edit Menus command to splice macros into the system menu, as described later in this chapter. You can place macro menus in a macro library if you would like to access them from any spreadsheet.

All of the instructions that make up the menu macro in Figure 12-5 are shown in Figure 12-6. Each menu item is in a separate but contiguous column, listing the parts of the macro on consecutive rows. The first row is the name of the item as it is to appear on the menu. Quattro Pro 4 can normally display about 12 menu items in a single level of a menu macro out of a total of 256. The actual number of menu items displayed depends on the position of the cell pointer when the macro is called. Quattro Pro 4 dynamically adjusts the menu size to fit the available space on the screen and to avoid obscuring your work.

You can create multiple-level menus just as in the Quattro Pro 4 menu system itself. Each menu item at the same level should begin with a different first letter if you want to be able to use the first-letter method of picking them. The second line is the explanation of the item that appears at the bottom of the screen when the item is highlighted. In 80 × 25 display mode, menu item names can be up to 55 characters long, and the explanation line can be up to 72 characters long. (In normal practice, make the menu name brief and the explanation lengthier.) Below the explanation text are the macro commands that are executed when an item is chosen. To refer to a menu like this in a {MENUBRANCH} command, the top left cell of the menu is named. In the example in Figure 12-6 the cell is K23.

Note that in cell L30 of Figure 12-6 the command {D 3} is used instead of {down}. This is an abbreviation that you can use with all of the direction commands. It helps to shorten the macro and makes it easier to change should the number of repetitions be incorrect.

You can see from Figure 12-6 that the placement of macros in adjacent columns stipulated by the menu macro command syntax could make it difficult to see all of the commands on a given line, particularly if you could not widen the columns. However, this is not a problem for the execution of the macro, because Quattro Pro 4 does not care if the entire command is visible.

Macro Menu Control

When the user selects any one of the macro menu items in Figure 12-5, the commands beneath that item are executed. As you can see from the code in Figure 12-6, several different actions are performed at the end of each menu item macro. The Print item simply ends after defining the Print Block and sending the table to the printer. The user is returned to READY mode with the cell selector in A1 (as a result of the {HOME} command). The Change item ends by returning the user to the main \C macro, after blanking out the cells used by the {FOR} command and clearing the loan table (hiding the first three rows and deleting the rest). The Save item stores the file on disk and then brings up the NO menu. The Quit item simply returns the user to READY mode.

If you were designing the loan calculation application yourself, you might want to alter the way that the MEN choices work. For example, you might like them to be more consistent. One way to control macro menu options is to end each one with the {MENUBRANCH} command. For example, if each item except Quit ended with {MENUBRANCH MEN}, the user would keep returning to the MEN menu after the macro actions of the menu item were completed.

When you want to control the user's options in macro menus there is an alternative to {MENUBRANCH} known as {MENUCALL}. The effect of {MENUCALL} is to return macro flow to the macro that called the menu. This is useful when you want to use a second level of menu. A macro selected at the first level can call a second menu. The user chooses from the second menu and after the chosen item on the second menu is completed the first menu is restored. An example of this technique can be seen at work behind the macro menu shown in Figure 12-7. This worksheet is an employee database, and the macro menu is used to enter employee records, sort them, and print them out.

With the exception of Quit, all of the menu options in Figure 12-7 lead the user to a further menu. You can see much of the code for this menu system in Figure 12-8. The main macro, called ADMIN, begins with the {HOME} command, which ensures that the database is displayed on the

FIGURE 12-7

Another example of a macro menu

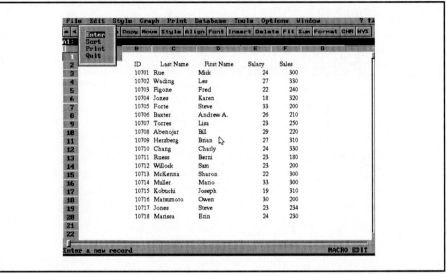

FIGURE 12-8

Macro code for the menu in Figure 12-7

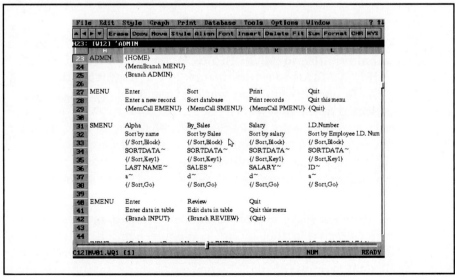

screen. The macro then performs a {MENUBRANCH} to the MENU code. Note that the third line of the ADMIN macro tells the macro to return to ADMIN. This ensures that even if the user presses ESC while the menu in Figure 12-7 is displayed, the menu will stay on the screen.

The MENU code, which produces the menu shown in Figure 12-7, leads the user to three separate menus by means of {MENUCALL} statements. You can see two of the menus in Figure 12-8. The SMENU enables the user to choose between several different sort orders. The macro code refers to the data to be sorted as the block named SORTDATA, and the keys for sorting are also set with named blocks. When the user selects one of the SMENU items the sort is performed and the user is returned to the menu shown in Figure 12-7. This is because the SMENU is called with {MENUCALL} and not {MENUBRANCH}.

The EMENU contains three items: Enter, Review, and Quit. The Enter option uses the macro code seen in Figure 12-9. The INPUT routine asks a series of questions and places the answers in groups of cells named ENT1, ENT2, and so on, through ENT5. These cells are arranged in a column elsewhere in the worksheet. The area where they are stored is called PREVIEW. At the end of the INPUT routine the macro proceeds to PROCESS. This displays the results of the user input in the PREVIEW

The INPUT and PROCESS macro code

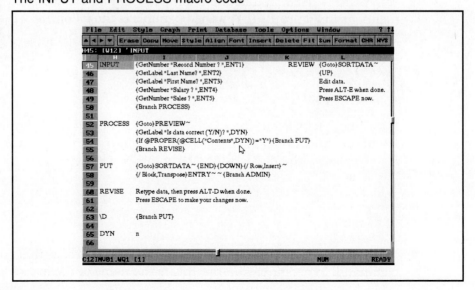

area and asks whether the data is correct. If the user replies **Y** for Yes, the macro proceeds to the PUT routine. This inserts a row in the SORTDATA block, which is the employee database, and copies the column of user input onto a new row as a fresh record. This is done with the Edit Transpose command, which turns a column of cells into a row. After the record has been added to the database macro control is returned to the ADMIN macro.

If the user does not reply Y to the PROCESS question about the accuracy of the data, the macro branches to REVISE. This code displays a message and asks the user to press ESC to clear the message, to make changes to the data, and then to press ALT-D when the data is correct. The ALT-D macro simply activates the PUT routine. A similar system is used by the Review option on the EMENU. This code displays the database and presents a message that gives the user a chance to alter data. The ALT-E macro referred to in the REVIEW code shown in Figure 12-9 is in fact the ADMIN macro, which displays the main menu.

Note that menu macro code can get crowded. The SMENU code in Figure 12-8 was actually abbreviated for the purposes of illustration. You may not want to enter all of the code for a macro menu item directly beneath the menu item. The approach used in the EMENU is often better. Each menu item consists of three lines: menu item name, menu item description, and a command. For lengthy menu items the {BRANCH} command is used so that the main code can be located away from the menu, as in Figure 12-9. Another example is the following arrangement, which gives menu access to macros called PD and SD:

```
Print               Sort                Quit
Print data          Sort data           Leave the menu
{BRANCH PD}         {BRANCH SD}         {QUIT}
```

If the user picks Print, the PD macro is executed. If the user picks Sort, the SD macro is executed. If the user picks Quit, the macro ends, whether it was called with {MENUBRANCH} or {MENUCALL}.

Subroutines

An alternative to this approach is to call on macros with a subroutine command. In its simplest form, this is the name of the macro in braces, as in {PD}, entered on a line by itself. When Quattro Pro 4 encounters this statement in a macro it looks for the macro called PD and executes it. The difference between a subroutine and a branch is that the macro flow after a subroutine is back to the place from which the subroutine was called, whereas flow after a branch does not return but continues in the new direction. The subroutine is normally referred to as {subroutine} in lowercase to indicate that the only argument is a variable. You can actually add data to a subroutine, a technique described later under the heading "The {subroutine} Command."

In the case of {BRANCH PD}, the flow is directed to PD when the user picks Print and it terminates there (unless the menu itself was generated with {MENUCALL}, which essentially runs menu choices as subroutines; or unless the PD macro redirects the flow). In the following example the selection of List runs a macro called SORT_DATA and then the PRINT_DATA macro. The SORT_DATA macro does not have to contain any statements directing macro flow. Quattro Pro 4 automatically returns to the line after the SORT_DATA call in the macro.

```
List
Sort and print list
{SORT_DATA\
{PRINT_DATA}
```

Note that Quattro Pro 4's ability to refer to macros by full block names makes it easy to read and write macro statements, particularly as they begin to approach a programming language in their complexity of flow control. However, it is important to make a distinction between names used to refer to blocks of data cells, names used for macros, and the names of macro commands. You may want to establish some conventions for naming to help you distinguish between the various parts of macro code. As you can see from the examples so far, block names, macro names, and macro commands can all be given in either upper- or lowercase. This means you could use a system such as all uppercase for block names, all lowercase for macro names, and initial capitals for macro commands. Also, you should avoid using two-part names for blocks or macros, unless you connect them with an underline. For example, SORT_DATA is better than SORT DATA, because the latter is ambiguous and might be taken to mean two blocks, SORT and DATA.

One of the main appeals of the {subroutine} command is that it provides the ability to assemble macros from reusable parts. Thus, the

SORT_DATA macro might be a sorting operation that is used in several other macros. Instead of repeating the same code each time sorting is required, the SORT_DATA macro can simply be referenced as a subroutine. A simple subroutine can store commonly used commands such as the standard steps for printing:

```
{CALC}                          Recalculate spreadsheet
{/ Print;Align}                 Align printer
{/ Print;ResetAll}              Reset printer settings
```

Placing this macro in a subroutine called PRE_PRINT would enable you to insert these commands into any print macro in the spreadsheet with the simple statement {PRE_PRINT}.

Links and Flow

When you are designing and running more complex macros you need to consider the question of current cell location. The macro command {GOTO}B52~ directs Quattro Pro 4 to make B52 of the current worksheet the current cell. This means that the next action will affect cell B52 of the worksheet. This is radically different from the command {BRANCH B52}, which directs macro flow to cell B52 of the worksheet. You might want to think of macros as establishing two movable pointers, one being the regular cell selector, the other being a macro cell selector. As the macro executes, both pointers are moved. The regular cell selector goes from one cell to another based on the macro commands, whereas the special macro pointer goes from cell to cell of macro code, based on the rules of flow and any subroutine or branching commands.

This concept of two independent pointers is particularly important in multiple spreadsheets. Before the advent of linked spreadsheets and macro libraries, a subroutine could only call macros from the current spreadsheet. However, when you are running macros from a macro library file, additional questions about macro flow need to be addressed. A standard method of operation with Quattro Pro 4 is to keep macros in a library file that has been saved with a Tools Macro Library setting of Yes. With the library file open, any open worksheet can call macros from the library. If you press ALT-M while SALES.WQ1 is the current worksheet and there is a macro named \M in an open library file called MACLIB.WQ1, that macro is run. (If there is a macro called \M in the

SALES.WQ1 worksheet, that macro will run first, giving you an opportunity to preempt your library macros on special occasions.)

When the \M macro in MACLIB.WQ1 is running, the flow of command moves the macro pointer through the library worksheet. The regular cell pointer is maneuvered in the regular worksheet. However, there is nothing to stop the macro from using links, either for worksheet actions or macro flow. The command {GOTO}B52~ tells Quattro Pro 4 to make cell B52 the current cell of the current worksheet, whereas {GOTO}[BUDGET]B52~ makes cell B52 of the open worksheet BUDGET.WQ1 the current cell. The macro command {BRANCH [MACLIB1]B52} directs macro flow from the current macro library to the worksheet called MACLIB1. You can even direct flow to the worksheet that called up the macro to begin with. This is done by referring to the worksheet with empty square brackets. For example, if you execute \M while SALES.WQ1 is current and \M runs from a macro library, but you want to direct flow to a section of code at cell B100 of SALES.WQ1, you use:

{BRANCH [ ]B100}.

If you bear in mind the difference between the active cell of the worksheet and the current location of the macro pointer, you can keep track of macro action even while it crosses several worksheets. However, you will probably find it easier to put most subroutines in one place, rather than skip from worksheet to worksheet. One advantage of running macros from a macro library is that you can copy to your favorite library subroutines that you have developed in other worksheets. You can name these and then pull them into new macros whenever you need them with the {*subroutine*} command.

Syntax of Macro Commands

Having explored the ways in which some of the more popular macro commands are used, it is time to review all of the commands. Quattro Pro 4's macro commands can be categorized in several ways. There are those that do not have arguments, and those that do. Both types include a keyword in braces. Subroutine calls are an exception, because they invoke another macro, making the name of the called macro (rather than a keyword) the item that is placed in the braces. The format of the nonargument commands is simply a keyword enclosed in braces, { }.

These braces are recognized as label indicators by Quattro Pro 4. A subroutine call also follows this pattern except that the characters inside the braces represent a macro name instead of a keyword. The format of the argument type of command consists of the keyword followed by a blank space and a list of arguments separated by commas. As with @function arguments, no spaces are allowed between or within arguments. The entire statement complete with arguments is enclosed in the braces.

Screen and Response Commands

You can use macro commands to control updating of the display screen and the Quattro Pro 4 control panel. If you leave such commands turned on, you can follow the progress of the macro on-screen; when you turn them off, the screen does not change. The macro commands in this group also enable you to customize the mode indicator and to give audible feedback to the user.

The {BEEP} Command

The {BEEP} command produces a sound from your computer's speaker, somewhat like the one Quattro Pro 4 makes when you press an invalid key (such as BACKSPACE in the READY mode). The format for the {BEEP} command is {BEEP *number*}, where *number* is an optional argument that you can use to affect the tone of the sound. The *number* argument can have any value from 1 to 4; 1 is the default value when no number is specified.

You can use the beep to alert the operator to an error, indicate that you expect input, periodically show that a macro is still functioning during a lengthy set of instructions, or signify the conclusion of a step. Try using several beeps of different tones to really grab attention and to distinguish between actions. Because each PC seems to make a different sound in response to the {BEEP} command, you may want to test your system's beeper. This is easy to do in a blank spreadsheet with the value **1** entered in A1 and the following formula entered in B1:

+"{BEEP "&@STRING(A1,0)&"}"

This formula produces the result {BEEP 1} in B1 and is an excellent example of how string functions can be used to generate dynamic macros, that is, macros that depend on the contents of other cells. Now enter the numbers **2**, **3**, and **4** in cells A2, A3, and A4. Copy the formula from B1 to B2..B4. Your spreadsheet should look like Figure 12-10, a macro created with a string function.

Now use the ALT-F2 key or Tools Macro menu to select Macro Execute and then point to B1 as the cell to execute. You will hear all four tones from your computer's speaker. By varying the number in column A you can compose short jingles that add a personal touch to your macros. (Try the sequence 1,1,2,2,3,3,2, which sounds like "Twinkle Twinkle Little Star" on some systems.)

The {INDICATE} Command

The {INDICATE} command enables you to customize the mode indicator in the lower right corner of the screen, which normally says READY. The format of the {INDICATE} command is

{INDICATE *string*}

where *string* is any character string. Actually, the screen can show only five characters for the mode indicator, so {INDICATE} will use only the first five characters of the string. You can blank out the indicator by using an empty string (that is, {INDICATE ""}). You can return the indicator to READY mode by omitting the string argument (that is, {INDICATE}).

FIGURE 12-10

Macro code created with string functions

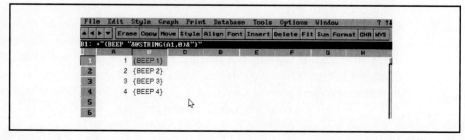

Another way of blanking out the mode indicator is to adjust the colors of the status line so that the text is not visible.

The indicator you establish with {INDICATE} remains in effect until you use the command again, either to establish a new setting or to return it to the default, READY. In fact, the {INDICATE} setting continues beyond the completion of a macro. Setting the indicator to PAUSE in a macro causes the word PAUSE to remain on the screen even if you are back to the READY mode. Use {INDICATE} without any argument to restore Quattro Pro 4's normal indicator display at the conclusion of the macro.

The {INDICATE} command is useful if you have a series of menu selections. You can use it to supply a string that reflects the menu selection, providing positive feedback as to the user's selection. Thus, the command {INDICATE "SORT"} can be inserted near the beginning of a macro that performs a sort operation. The user can then see that Sort has been selected.

The {PANELOFF} and {PANELON} Commands

These two commands control redrawing the control panel, the upper and lower areas of the screen that normally show you the progress of an action or command. The format for the {PANELOFF} command is simply {PANELOFF}. The {PANELON} command restores the default setting, instructing Quattro Pro 4 to update the control panel with each instruction executed. The format for the {PANELON} command is {PANELON}. These commands have no arguments.

You can use these commands to temporarily obscure the details of a macro's execution. After a macro reads the {PANELOFF} command, the entries on the input line are not visible as they are typed by the macro. When the macro reads {PANELON} the normal display is restored. One reason for these commands was to control the annoying screen jitters that occurred when 1-2-3 executed macro instructions, particularly those involving menu choices. This is less of a problem in Quattro Pro 4, because the menu equivalents bypass menu selection. The commands are still useful if you do not want the operator to be aware of the macro code being run. Even if a user invokes DEBUG to slow down the operation of the macro so that the instructions can be read, the control panel will not be updated while {PANELOFF} is in effect.

The {WINDOWSOFF} and {WINDOWSON} Commands

The {WINDOWSOFF} command freezes the entire screen, except for the control panel. It has the format {WINDOWSOFF}. The {WINDOWSON} instruction returns the normal mode of screen updating and has the format {WINDOWSON}. Neither command uses an argument. Like the panel commands, the window commands reduce the flicker that occurs on the screen with some macro instructions. They can also speed execution of long macros, because Quattro Pro 4 does not have to redraw the screen every time the macro moves the cursor or changes data. You can use {PANELOFF} and {WINDOWSOFF} together with {INDICATE "WAIT"} to flash the WAIT message and simply suspend further screen change until a macro is complete. Of course, you should use {WINDOWS-ON} near the end of a macro to have the screen updated with the current results.

Interactive Macro Commands

When you want user input during a macro's execution, you need to use the interactive macro commands. These commands can streamline data entry and add flexibility to macro designs.

The {?} Command

The {?} command is one of the most convenient and powerful of the macro commands, and it is often the first macro command that users learn beyond simple replaying of keystrokes. Its purpose is to allow the operator to enter information from the keyboard. This command has no arguments and uses the simple format {?}. Place this at any point in a macro where you need to obtain information from the user. After a macro encounters a {?} command, program control is handed to the user who can type a label or number, make a menu selection, or highlight an area of the spreadsheet. However, as soon as the user presses ENTER, the macro resumes control. For this reason, the {?} is followed by an ENTER (~ or {cr}) to actually enter or confirm the user input.

If you want to prompt for input of values or labels, then {GETNUMBER} and {GETLABEL} are more useful. These commands provide prompts as a part of the instruction to clarify the exact information you want. {GETNUMBER} tests the response to see if it is indeed a number. If you use the {?} instruction, you can use an instruction before it to place a prompt message in the current cell. For example, this instruction places the cell selector in the cell called AGE, enters the message "Type Age and Press Enter," and then replaces that message with the number when the user types it and presses ENTER:

```
{GOTO}AGE~Type Age and Press Enter~{?}~
```

One disadvantage of such a macro is that the user is free to access the menu system (and potentially destructive options) as long as they don't press ENTER. Some power users would say that {?} is better suited to your own macros than to applications for beginning users.

The {GET} Command

The {GET} command is designed to accept the entry of a single character from the keyboard. The format of the {GET} command is {GET *location*} where *location* is the storage location for the single character you enter from the keyboard. Thus, you could use {GET ANSWER} to place the response letter **Y** or **N** into the cell named ANSWER. The response to {GET} can be any key, letter, number, or function key. This command is yet another option to consider when you need to incorporate keyboard input in a macro. For example, you could use the following to prompt for a single-letter piece of information:

```
Type Y/N
{GET ANSWER}
{ESC}
```

The text "Type Y/N" will appear on the input line. The next character typed will be placed in ANSWER. The input line will be cleared.

The {GETLABEL} Command

You use the {GETLABEL} command to handle entering a label from the keyboard in response to a prompt message. The format for the {GETLABEL} command is {GETLABEL *prompt message, location*}. The *prompt message* argument is a word or words. The *location* is the cell into which the label is placed when the user presses ENTER. You must enclose the prompt text in double quotation marks if you use a comma or a semicolon because these characters are used as argument separators (as in {GETLABEL "Enter Name:",D1}). You must include a space at the end of the prompt text if you want a space to appear between the text and the cursor on the input line.

The length of text in the prompt is limited by the space at the top of the screen, which is used by the macro when it displays the {GETLABEL} instruction. If you use a string longer than 76 characters, the text will wrap to the next screen line and may be difficult to read, because Quattro Pro 4 will not wrap the text of the prompt by complete words. However, you can use spaces after the 76th character to push text onto the next line, and you can use up to three lines at the top of the screen for the prompt. The prompt text string can be stored in a separate cell and referenced if you construct the macro as a formula. Thus

+"{GETLABEL "&C3&"?,E3}"

will give you the prompt "Last Name?" if cell C3 contains the label **Last Name**. This is very convenient when you have a series of field names and want to provide prompts for each one.

The *location* argument in {GETLABEL} is a reference to the cell, block, or block name where the information entered from the keyboard will be stored. Up to 80 characters will be accepted as input. If a named block is supplied for the location argument, the character string entered will be stored in the upper left cell of the block. The {GETLABEL} command stores your entry as a left-justified label in the specified location. This is true regardless of the current default label alignment setting. If the entry is a number it is still stored as a label.

The {GETNUMBER} Command

The {GETNUMBER} command is very similar to the {GETLABEL} command and is used to elicit numeric information from the user in response to a prompt message. The format for the {GETNUMBER} command is {GETNUMBER *prompt message, location*}. The rules for the *prompt message* argument are the same as for {GETLABEL}. The elements of the prompt text string can be stored in a separate cell and referenced by constructing the macro as a formula. When you use a whole series of data cells, your formula can even determine whether to use the {GETLABEL} or {GETNUMBER} command. Thus, the formula

+"{GET"&@IF(@CELL("type",D3)="v","NUMBER","LABEL")&"}"

returns {GETNUMBER} if cell D3 contains a value or {GETLABEL} if it contains a label. You can combine that result with a formula to produce the prompt message from a label in cell C3:

+"{GET"&@IF(@CELL("type",D3) ="v","NUMBER","LABEL")&"/ "&C3&"?,REPLY}"

This formula will give you the {GETLABEL} prompt "Last Name?" if cell C3 contains the label **Last Name** and D3 contains a label. The location argument is REPLY. The same formula gives you the {GETNUMBER} prompt "Age?" if C3 contains the label **age** and D3 contains a value. This is very convenient when you have a series of labels for a column of mixed number and label data and you want data entry macro prompts for each.

The {GETNUMBER} rules for the *location* argument are the same as for {GETLABEL}. However, if the user enters a label in response to a {GETNUMBER} prompt the response in the location cell is ERR, produced by the @ERR function. This makes for a convenient method of trapping entry errors. If you follow a {GETNUMBER} command with an {IF} command you can direct the flow of the macro to an instruction in another cell if the user does not enter a number. For example, in

{GETNUMBER Age? ,ANSWER}
{IF @ISERR(ANSWER)}{BEEP}{BRANCH MESSAGE}

the macro flow goes to MESSAGE when the content of ANSWER is @ERR. Of course, MESSAGE could be a loop back to the {GETNUMBER} command but it could also be an error-message display routine. There is more on @ISERR and related functions later in this chapter.

The {LOOK} Command

The {LOOK} command is similar to {GET}, except that if a macro uses {LOOK} the user can type the entry ahead and the macro will still find it. This is because {LOOK} checks the keyboard buffer for data and places the first character from this buffer into the location defined in the command. The format of the {LOOK} command is {LOOK *location*}. The *location* argument refers to a cell used to store the character from the keyboard's typeahead buffer. If {LOOK} finds the buffer blank, it blanks the location cell. Whereas the {GET} instruction suspends macro execution while waiting for a response, {LOOK} does not. This makes {LOOK} suitable for use in a loop where you want to give the user some time to respond before the application is aborted.

The {MENUBRANCH} Command

As you saw earlier in this chapter, the {MENUBRANCH} command diverts macro flow to a set of cells into which you have placed the data required to build a custom menu. The format of the {MENUBRANCH} command is {MENUBRANCH *location*}, where *location* is the upper left cell of the area used for menu storage. Information for the customized menu must be organized according to certain rules.

The top row of the menu area must contain the words used for the menu items, entered one per cell, in contiguous columns. Each of these words should begin with a different character, just as in Quattro Pro 4's menus, if you want to be able to pick from the menu by pressing the first letter of an item as well as using the point and ENTER method. (If you use menu items with the same first letters, Quattro Pro 4 will pick the first of the similar items when you press the duplicated letter: from a menu consisting of Erase and Extract, pressing **E** will pick Erase). Menu-selection words can be up to 55 characters long, but remember that the longer the word, the wider the menu, and thus the more obtrusive it will be. You can have up to 256 items in a menu although you will only be able to see 13 different items in the menu box (the rest can be scrolled into view).

The second row of the menu area contains the expanded description for each menu choice that will display at the top of the screen when you highlight the menu selection. Because these are explanations they are likely to exceed the width of the column into which they are entered, particularly as they will occupy contiguous columns. Unsightly as this is, it will not affect macro performance.

The third row of the menu instructions contains the actual macro directions for each choice in the column with the menu item and description. These directions begin in the cell immediately under the description. They can extend down the column or branch to a subroutine. The subroutine approach makes for cleaner design, because macro instructions in contiguous columns can be hard to read, edit, and annotate.

The {MENUCALL} Command

The {MENUCALL} command works like {MENUBRANCH}, but whereas a macro using {MENUBRANCH} ends when the code for the selected option completes, {MENUCALL} returns control to the statement following {MENUCALL} in the main code for the macro, and execution begins again at that location. This has the effect of locking users into the menu system, returning them to a menu rather than dumping them when the action they chose from the menu is complete. The format of the {MENUCALL} command is {MENUCALL *location*}, where *location* is a cell address or block name that represents the upper left cell in the area for menu storage. The rules for the menu building are the same as those for {MENUBRANCH}.

The {WAIT} Command

The {WAIT} command is the "hold-up" command. With {WAIT} you can stay the execution of a macro until a stated time. The format of the command is {WAIT *time serial number*}, where *time serial number* is a decimal value that represents the serial number for the time of day when you want execution to resume. Suppose you want users to read a lengthy instruction on the screen. You need to pause the macro long enough for this information to be read, say 45 seconds. This can be accomplished by the following instruction:

{WAIT @NOW+@TIME(0,0,45)}

The wait value is computed by adding a time value to the value returned by @NOW. This results in a measured delay. The instruction adds the desired 45 seconds to the current time and waits until that time is reached before continuing execution. The mode indicator will say WAIT while Quattro Pro 4 is waiting.

Program-Flow Macros

Normally, a macro is read line by line, proceeding down a column from the cell that bears the macro name. However, you can redirect flow in many different ways, branching to other locations or calling subroutines, with the program-flow macro commands.

The {BRANCH} Command

The {BRANCH} command transfers the flow of a macro to a new location. The format of the {BRANCH} command is {BRANCH *location*}, where *location* is a cell address or block name that tells Quattro Pro 4 where the next instruction to be executed by the macro is stored. The {BRANCH} command is often combined with the {IF} command to change the flow of execution based on a test condition. The classic example of this combination is the loop controller, shown here in a macro called CENTER that turns a column of values into a centered label:

```
{EDIT}{HOME}^~{DOWN}~
{IF @CELLPOINTER("type")="b"}{QUIT}
{BRANCH CENTER}
```

After the edit is performed the macro moves the cell selector down one cell. The {IF} command tells Quattro Pro 4 to check the cell currently occupied by the cell selector and return the cell's type. If this is "b" for blank (as opposed to "v" for value or "l" for label) the macro will quit. If the cell is not blank the macro will branch, or loop, back to its beginning, the macro called CENTER.

Remember that {BRANCH} controls macro flow, not cell selector positioning. Do not confuse {BRANCH} with {GOTO}, because {GOTO} reposistions the cell selector without affecting the execution of the macro. {BRANCH} moves the macro's execution flow but does not move the cell selector.

The {QUIT} Command

The {QUIT} command, used to terminate a macro, has no argument. You simply include {QUIT} as the last line of the macro you want to terminate. Although it can be said that macros automatically stop when they get to a blank cell, this is not strictly true. If a macro has been called by {*subroutine*} or {MENUCALL}, Quattro Pro 4 returns to the calling point when it gets to a blank line. Placing a Quit option that uses {QUIT} in a {MENUCALL} menu thus provides the user with a way out of the menu. Placing a {QUIT} command at the end of a macro called by a subroutine ends both the subroutine macro and the one that called it. You will also find {QUIT} useful as a value at the end of an {IF} command. When the {IF} condition evaluates as True, the macro—including all subroutines—terminates.

The {RESTART} Command

The {RESTART} command cancels the execution of the current subroutine. This command also cancels all pointers or calls in the macro that reference the subroutine to prevent return. The {RESTART} command has no arguments. Placing this command anywhere within a called subroutine will immediately cancel the call, complete the routine, and continue executing from that point downward. In the process, any upward pointers to higher-level routines are cancelled.

The {RETURN} Command

The {RETURN} command is used to return from a subroutine to the calling routine. Used in conjunction with {MENUCALL} and {subroutine}, this command has the same effect on macro flow as a blank cell. This command has no arguments. When Quattro Pro 4 reads {RETURN} in a called subroutine it returns the flow of control back to the instruction beneath the one that called the subroutine. The difference between {RESTART} and {RETURN} is that the latter does not cancel upward pointers. The difference between {QUIT} and {RETURN} is that {RETURN} continues processing after returning to the call point, whereas {QUIT} actually ends the macro at the point where it is encountered.

The {subroutine} Command

This is the command that calls a specific macro subroutine. The format is {subroutine argument1,argument2,argumentN}. The subroutine is a macro name. The arguments, and there may be many of them, are values or strings to be passed to the subroutine. These arguments must have corresponding entries in a {DEFINE} statement.

The {subroutine} command is a great way to recycle common sections of macro code in a spreadsheet and to spread out macro sections for clarity. Remember that unless the macro called by the {subroutine} command ends in {QUIT}, program flow returns to the line below the one on which the {subroutine} command was placed.

The {BREAKOFF} and {BREAKON} Commands

The {BREAKOFF} command is used to disable the CTRL-BREAK key function, thereby preventing the interruption of a macro. The format of the command is simply {BREAKOFF} with no arguments. The {BREAKON} command reinstates the CTRL-BREAK key's function so that you can press CTRL-BREAK to interrupt a macro. The format of the command is {BREAKON} with no arguments.

Normally, CTRL-BREAK can be used to stop a macro. It will display ERROR as a mode indicator. When you press ESC, you can proceed to make changes in the worksheet from the READY mode. However, when you have designed an automated application and want to ensure its integrity by maintaining control throughout the use of the worksheet, you will want to disable the Break function by placing {BREAKOFF} in your macro. Be sure you have tested the macro before doing this; the only way to stop a macro that contains an infinite loop and {BREAKOFF} is by turning off the computer.

You may choose to disable the Break function during part of a macro and then restore its operation for a later section, such as printing or data entry. In any case, the Break function is automatically restored at the end of a macro.

The /X Macro Commands

In early versions of 1-2-3 the original concept of macros as a typing alternative was augmented by special macro commands that all began with /X. The earliest form of the macro-command language, these commands provided limited logic and program-flow control for macro execution. Still functional in 1-2-3 Release 2 and in Quattro Pro 4, each one now has a macro language equivalent. Refer to that equivalent for a full explanation of the /X commands. Unlike the macro language commands, the /X commands are preceded by a slash (/) and are not enclosed in braces. There is no space between the command and its arguments. The command is followed by a tilde (~) to actually enter the command.

The /XC Command

The /XC or "call" command corresponds to the {*subroutine*} command. The format for the /XC command is /XC*location*~ where location is the address or block name of a cell containing the subroutine that you are calling. After /XC executes the routine or when it encounters the /XR or

{RETURN} statement at the end of the routine, control will return to the macro line following the /XC instruction.

The /XG Command

The /XG command is the {BRANCH} command, directing the flow of a macro by branching to a new location containing the commands that will be entered next. The format of the /XG command is /XG*location~*, where *location* is the address containing the commands that you want executed next.

The /XI Command

The /XI command is the equivalent of the {IF} command. The format for the /XI command is /XI*condition~true*. The *condition* argument is a comparison of two values in cells or a formula. If the condition evaluates as True, the macro will execute the instructions on the same macro line as the /XI statement. If the condition is False, the next instructions executed will be on the macro line that follows the condition. The *true* argument is any valid macro instruction. For example, to tell a macro to beep if A1 is greater than 100 you would enter

/XIA1>100~{BEEP}

The /XL Command

The /XL command is equivalent to {GETLABEL}. It causes Quattro Pro 4 to wait for the operator to input a character string from the keyboard and then to store the entry in a specified location. The format for the /XL command is

/XL*prompt message~location*

The *prompt message* argument is a message of up to 39 characters that prompts the user for label input.

The /XM Command

This is the equivalent of the {MENUBRANCH} command, directing flow of the macro to a set of cells that form a custom menu. The rules for the custom menu are the same as for the {MENUBRANCH} command.

The /XN Command

The equivalent of the {GETNUMBER} command, /XN uses the format /XN*prompt message~location* to prompt the user for numeric input and enter it in the cell specified as *location*. If the user enters a label instead of a number the *location* cell will return ERR.

The /XQ Command

Used to terminate a macro, the /XQ command is the same as {QUIT} and is normally used at the end of a macro to ensure that it terminates correctly.

The /XR Command

The equivalent of the {RETURN} command, the /XR command returns the flow of a macro to the point at which it was called as a subroutine. There are no arguments to this command.

The Cells Commands

Quattro Pro 4 groups the following macro commands as cells commands because they let you manipulate values and strings stored in spreadsheet cells. You can use these commands to blank out a section of the spreadsheet or to store a value or a string in a cell. These are also the commands that you can use to recalculate the worksheet in row or column order.

The {BLANK} Command

A macro command alternative to the Block Erase menu option, {BLANK} erases a block of cells on the worksheet. It has the format {BLANK *location*} in which *location* is the address of a block of cells or a block name. Generally used to clean out a data entry area ready for new data, you will find {BLANK} effective when a macro has to reuse an area of the worksheet. Use a block name rather than the cell coordinates as the argument for better control and remember that {BLANK} does not reset cell formatting information; it just removes the contents.

The {CONTENTS} Command

The {CONTENTS} command copies the contents of one cell into another, converting to a label of specified format and width in the process. The correct syntax of the {CONTENTS} command is {CONTENTS *destination,source,width,format*}. The *destination* argument is the location where you wish the resulting label to be stored, stated as a cell address or a block name. The *source* argument is the cell address or block name of the value entry you want copied into *destination* as a label. The *width* and *format* arguments are optional. Thus, the command

{CONTENTS A1,B1}

would take the number 2001 from the fixed-format (0 decimal places) cell A1 and copy it into B1 as the left-aligned label 2001.

The *width* argument is only required if you want to control width or specify format. It determines the width of the resulting label, so omitting it lets Quattro Pro 4 use the width of the source location. The *format* argument provides control over the appearance of the value copied into the *destination*. Thus, the command

{CONTENTS A1,B1,12,34}

copies the same 2001 into B1 as $2,001.00 with three leading spaces. This is because 12 is the specified cell width and 34 is the code for currency format with two decimal places. The codes used for the different formats in the {CONTENTS} command are listed in Table 12-3.

TABLE

12-3

Width and Format Number Arguments for {CONTENT}

Number	Format
0...15	Fixed 0–15 places
16...31	Scientific, 0–15 places
32...47	Currency, 0–15 places
48...63	Percent, 0–15 places
64...79	Comma, 0–15 places
112	+/–
113	General
114	DD-MMM-YY (Dl)
115	DD-MMM (D2)
116	MMM-YY (D3)
117	Literal
118	Hidden
119	HH:MM:SS AM/PM (Tl)
120	HH:MM AM/PM (T2)
121	Full International Date (D4)
122	Partial International Date (DS)
123	Full International Time (T3)
124	Partial International Time (T4)
125	General

The {LET} Command

The {LET} command assigns a value to a location in the spreadsheet using the format {LET *location,value: type*}. This saves a macro from having to move the cell selector to a location to enter data. The *location* argument is the address or block name of the cell where you wish to store the value or label. (Specifying *location* as a multicell block means that the upper left cell in the block will be used.) The *value* is the data you want assigned to the *location*. Quattro Pro 4 will try to assign a numeric value but if it cannot it will assign a string. Use the optional *type* argument to control how the value is handled. Thus, the command

{LET A1,101}

places the number 101 in cell A1. The command

{LET A1,101:string}

places the left-aligned label 101 in cell A1. Of course, you can use cell references for the value argument. Note the use of a colon for the argument separator.

The {PUT} Command

Unlike {LET}, which accepts only a cell address, {PUT} enables you to place a value in a location by selecting a row and column offset within a block. The correct format for the {PUT} command is thus {PUT *location, column,row,value:type*}. The block of cells, identified by cell addresses or a block name, into which you want to place the data are stated in the *location* argument. The *column* argument is the column number of the cell within the block you want to use for the data (as in other Quattro Pro 4 commands, such as @VLOOKUP, the first column in the block is column 0). The *row* argument works the same way, with the first row being 0. Thus the command

{PUT A1..C5,0,0,20:string}

places the left-aligned label 20 in cell A1. The command

{PUT A1..C5,1,1,Help}

places the label Help in cell B2.

The {RECALC} Command

The {RECALC} command recalculates the formulas within a block you specify, proceeding rowwise within the block. The format for the

{RECALC} command is {RECALC *location,condition,iteration*}. The block to be recalculated is specified as *location*. The *condition* is an optional argument, specifying a condition that must be evaluated as True before the block is no longer recalculated. While the *condition* evaluates to False, Quattro Pro 4 will continue to recalculate the worksheet. Used in conjunction with *iteration*, which specifies a maximum number of iterations, the *condition* stops recalculation short of the maximum number of iterations if it evaluates to True.

The point of this command and the companion command {RECALCCOL} is to avoid unnecessary delays in processing data. When a worksheet gets large it is normal to make recalculation manual instead of automatic. New entries do not cause dependent data in the rest of the spreadsheet to be updated. Instead, this is done by returning to automatic calculation or pressing the Calc key (F9). Whereas this key recalculates the entire worksheet, the {RECALC} and {RECALCCOL} commands evaluate just a portion, which takes far less time. Use {RECALC} when the area you are recalculating is below and to the left of the cells referenced by the formulas in the area. Use {RECALCCOL} when the area you are recalculating is above and to the right of the cells referenced by the formulas in this area. Use these commands prior to printing a report to ensure that the reported data is correct and that there is no lengthy delay caused by updating the entire spreadsheet. (If the formula to be calculated is both above and to the left of cells with new values, you must use the Calc key.)

The {RECALCCOL} Command

The {RECALCCOL} command recalculates the formulas within the specified block, just like {RECALC}, except that it proceeds column by column. The format is {RECALCCOL *location,condition,iteration*} using the same argument definitions as {RECALC}.

The File I/O Macro Commands

The file I/O macro commands provide you with a means of manipulating data in a disk file, somewhat like the sequential file-handling capabilities you get in the BASIC programming language. In your macros, these commands enable you to read and write data in ASCII files. This is a fairly advanced activity and one that has the potential to corrupt valuable data files if not handled correctly, so the file control commands should be used with care.

Using I/O Commands

The I/O commands work with ASCII or text files. These are files like the ones created by the Quattro Pro 4 Print command when the Destination setting is File. Such files are sometimes used for exchanging information between programs that cannot read more sophisticated file formats, such as .WRl or .DBF.

A typical application of these commands would be when you want to write information, one line at a time, to a text file. The following macro code writes the contents of cell A21 to a file called INFO.DAT:

```
{OPEN "INFO.DAT",M}
{FILESIZE SIZE}
{SETPOS SIZE}
{WRITELN A21}
{CLOSE}
```

The macro opens the file to be modified, reads the size of the file in bytes into a cell called SIZE, and then positions the byte pointer at the end of the file. The byte pointer is like an invisible cursor within the disk file you open. When a file is first opened, the byte pointer is located at the first character of the file. Any reading from or writing to the file occurs at the location of the byte pointer. You can position the byte pointer with {SETPOS}.

Each of the file manipulation commands is described in the following sections.

The {CLOSE} Command

The {CLOSE} command closes a file that was opened with the {OPEN} macro command. It takes no arguments. This is one of several commands that enable macros to read from files on disk and write information to disk files.

The {FILESIZE} Command

The {FILESIZE} command has the syntax {FILESIZE *location*}. It records the size of an open file, stated as a number of bytes, in the cell specified as *location*, which can be a cell or range name.

The {GETPOS} Command

The {GETPOS} command has the syntax {GETPOS *location*}. It records (in the cell specified by the *location* argument) the byte pointer's current position. The position is read as an offset number; the first character of a file is 0, the second is 1, and so on.

The {OPEN} Command

The {OPEN} command has the syntax {OPEN *filename,access mode*}. The {OPEN} command opens a file named as *filename* for reading, writing, or both. The *access mode* argument is one of four characters:

W   Opens a new disk file to which you can write information. This is potentially dangerous, because there is nothing to stop you from overwriting an existing file. Be sure that the *filename* argument does not refer to a file that you want to preserve.

M   Opens an existing file so that you can modify it. This enables you to use the read and write commands. It, too, is dangerous; what you write to a file will overwrite existing data if the byte pointer is not positioned at the end of the file.

R   Opens a file so that you can read information from it. This is the safest form of file access, because it prevents writing to the file.

A   Opens a file and automatically positions the file pointer at the end of the file.

The {READ} Command

The {READ} command has the syntax {READ *byte count, location*}. The {READ} command copies the number of characters, specified by the *byte count* argument, from the file to the cell specified by the *location* argument. The command starts reading at the current position of the byte pointer.

The {READLN} Command

The {READLN} command has the syntax {READLN *location*}. This command copies a line of data from the file to the cell specified by the *location* argument. The command starts reading at the current position of the byte pointer and stops at the end of the current line.

The {SETPOS} Command

The {SETPOS} command has the syntax {SETPOS *file position*}. This command sets a new position for the byte pointer in the currently open file. If you read the file size and use this as the *file position* argument, you will locate the end of the file and be able to add data to it. Bear in mind that the first position is 0 (zero), the second is 1 (one), and so on.

The {WRITE} Command

The {WRITE} command has the syntax {WRITE *string*}. It copies characters into an open file at the byte pointer's current location. The *string* argument can be a single cell or a named single-cell range. The command does not add a line feed at the end of what is written.

The {WRITELN} Command

The {WRITELN} command has the syntax {WRITELN *string*}. The {WRITELN} command copies characters into an open file. The *string* argument can be a single cell or a named single-cell range. The command adds a line feed sequence at the end of the string of characters as it writes the string to the file. Thus, you can use a series of {WRITELN} statements to add successive lines of data to a file.

Utility Commands

A couple of commands make it easier for the macro writer to handle the chores of documentation and design. These enable you to insert comments and blank lines in your macros.

The {;} Command

When you want to place a comment in a macro you can do so with the {;} command. Entering {;**This line is a comment**} in a macro allows the comment to appear in the spreadsheet but not to affect the way the macro runs. The macro skips this line during execution. This is useful for documenting macros, particularly where space considerations prevent the use of comments to the right of the code cells.

The { } Command

To skip a cell completely during macro execution you can use { }, which lets a macro come as close as possible to containing a blank cell without stopping. This is sometimes useful when you want to have two macros arranged so that comparable commands are in adjacent cells but one macro is not as complex as the other, as in this example:

```
Enter               List
Enter data          Sort and print list
```

```
{ENTER}                {SORT_DATA}
{ }                    {PRINT_DATA}
{QUIT}                 {QUIT}
```

System Menu Building

The Quattro Pro 4 command language is not the only way you can develop a custom menu system with Quattro Pro 4. The entire Quattro Pro 4 menu structure is designed so that it can be redesigned. This means that you can make custom menus that are not specific to just one worksheet or macro library.

The .MU Files

The Quattro Pro 4 menu system is stored in a file called QUATTRO.MU. You can copy and modify this file. For example, you do not need to have the same set of items on the main menu bar as the program comes with. The file 123.MU, provided with Quattro Pro 4, contains a menu system that will be familiar to users of 1-2-3.

As you can see in Figure 12-11, which shows the Range menu displayed by the 123.MU menu system, the menu still has the look of the regular Quattro Pro 4 menu. If you have a mouse installed, the mouse palette will be displayed. Some items are named differently and the commands are grouped differently, however. For example, the Edit Erase command is found on the Range menu, shown in Figure 12-11. This command is functionally equivalent to the 1-2-3 Range Erase command. Note that commands that have no equivalent in 1-2-3, such as Output Style, are displayed with a small box. This display enables you to use the Quattro Pro 4 commands, even though you are working with a 1-2-3 menu.

To change from one menu system to another, you can use the Options Startup command and select Menu Tree. Menu files all have the extension .MU. You can select the .MU file you want by highlighting it and pressing ENTER. Your choice appears in the Menu Tree setting. As soon as you exit the Options menu, the new menu tree will be in place. If you are using

FIGURE
12-11

1-2-3 menu

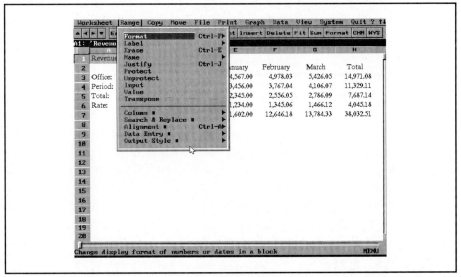

the Quattro Pro 4 menu tree, you can write your choice of menu system to the configuration file using the Update command on the Options menu. When you exit from Quattro Pro 4 and reload the program, the new menu system you selected will be in effect. To change the menu tree while you are using the 1-2-3 menus, select Worksheet Global Default Files Menu Tree. The Worksheet Global Default Update command will record your choice.

In addition to the 123.MU file that comes with Quattro Pro 4, you can create your own .MU file containing your personalized menu system. This is discussed in the following sections.

Customizing Menus

Quattro Pro 4 is written so that the actions it performs can be requested by several different methods, not simply by a specific set of keystrokes. This enables you to use menu equivalents in macros. The same design feature enables you to choose your own names for the program's actions and then access them from a menu that is arranged to suit the way you work. You define menu items and cut and paste menus by using the Edit Menus command from the Options Startup menu. (In some earlier versions of Quattro Pro this feature was referred to as the Menu Builder, and it is also sometimes called the menu editor.)

The Edit Menu Windows

To use the Edit Menus command, select the Options Startup command and pick Edit Menus. Quattro Pro 4 takes a moment to read the current menu file into memory, showing a bar graph of the task's progress. You then get a screen like the one shown in Figure 12-12. In the center of the screen, in the Menu Tree window, you see the top level of your current menu system. The one that is shown in Figure 12-12 is the default Quattro Pro 4 menu. The middle window is the current window, as shown by the cursor, which is highlighting the first menu item, File. The window above it is the Current Item window, which defines whatever item is highlighted in the Menu Tree window. Use the F6 key to move from one window to the next.

Using the Edit Menu feature

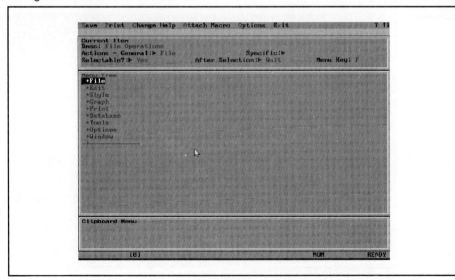

The Current Item window displays the six different fields of information by which Quattro Pro 4 defines each menu item. The Desc field stores the description of the menu item that appears at the bottom of the screen when you are using the menu tree. There are two forms of Action for each menu item: General and Specific. Items that lead to further menus have no Specific action. Most menu items can be selected and so carry the entry Yes in the Selectable field. However, some items are placed just for show, like the lines dividing the menus into parts, and these are not selectable. All items that can be selected have an action that they perform After Selection. In the case of the File item on the main menu, the After Selection setting is Quit, which is the case for all items that lead to further menus. You can select items on menus by a key letter. The Menu Key field stores this letter, which is *F* in the case of the File menu.

The Menu Tree window contains a highlight bar that you can move up and down to highlight different menu items. All items preceded by a plus sign have submenus, or child menus. When an item is highlighted, you can press the numeric plus key to show the corresponding child menu branching to the right. Thus, the Edit option on the top level shows the options on the Edit menu to the right, as seen in Figure 12-13. You can

The Edit Menu's child menus

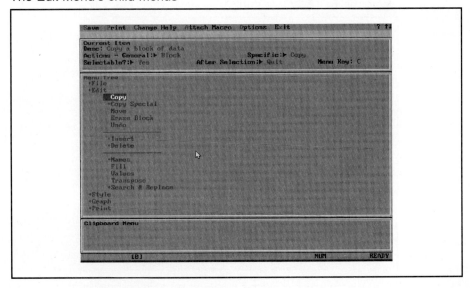

use the RIGHT ARROW key to move to this set of items and then DOWN ARROW to move down the list. In Figure 12-13 you can see that the Copy item has both a General action, Block, and a Specific action, Copy. Note that the lines on the menu are separate items. To shrink a set of submenus back under the parent item, press the minus sign (–) on the numeric keypad while the Menu Tree window is active and you are highlighting the parent item. Thus, to put the Edit menu items back under Edit, you highlight Edit and press minus.

The third window in the menu editor is the Clipboard Menu, which is a place to store items that have been cut from the menu structure. Using the middle and bottom window you can alter the placement of items on the menu tree by performing cut-and-paste operations, rearranging the menu items to suit your taste.

Moving a Menu Item

Suppose that you want to move the Insert Break command to the Print menu from the Style menu. You do this with a cut-and-paste operation. The first half of the cut-and-paste involves highlighting in the middle window the menu item you want to move, in this case Insert Break. Then you press the DELETE key to remove the highlighted item from the current menu to the bottom window, where it is stored, as you can see in Figure 12-14. The paste half of the operation involves first highlighting the item in the bottom window that you want to insert back into the tree. If you move only one item at a time, this item will already be highlighted, as seen in Figure 12-14. With the middle window active you move to the new location for the Insert Break item, above Quit in the Print menu. To do this you highlight Print, type the numeric +, and use the arrow keys to highlight Quit. Now you can press INSERT to insert the item from the Clipboard. You can see the results in Figure 12-15.

If you move a menu item that has child menus all of the child menus are moved with it. Once an item is pasted it disappears from the Clipboard Menu. Using this technique, you can rearrange items that are already defined. Items that have been cut are shown in the bottom window to remind you that they have been cut and need to be pasted or they will be lost when you save the new menu tree. Note that no menu can contain more than 16 items, including lines.

FIGURE 12-14

A menu item clipped

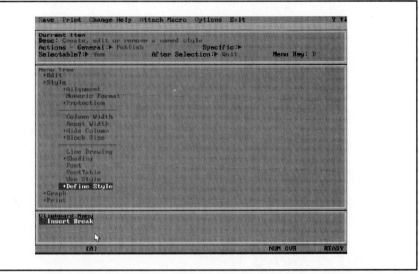

FIGURE 12-15

The Insert Break item pasted

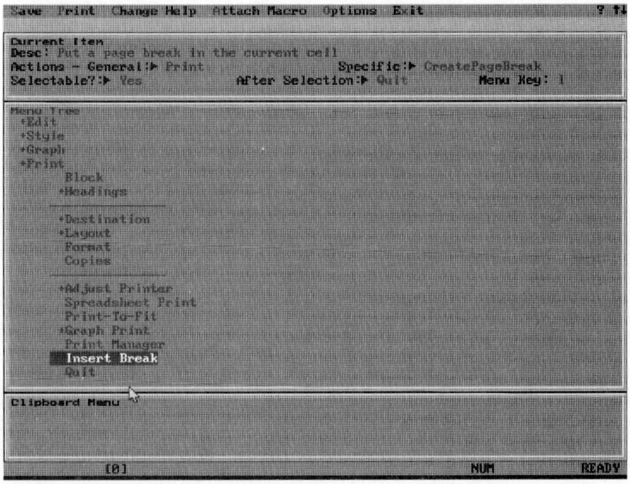

Defining Menu Items

When you are in the top window of the menu editor you can edit any of the items. By pressing the SPACEBAR while highlighting any entry except Desc and Menu Key, you get a menu of possible choices. For example, suppose that you want to add an item called Copy on the main menu, right after Tools. First, make the Menu Tree window active, and then place the highlight bar on Tools. Press ENTER and a space will appear. Now press F6 to move to the Current Item window to define this new item.

In the first field of the Current Item window, Desc, you could type **Copies a cell or block of cells**. After typing this entry, press ENTER. When you move the cursor to the General field, using the TAB key, you can press the SPACEBAR to see a list of actions, as shown in Figure 12-16. You want to pick Block. When you press TAB to move to the Specific field, the list that is displayed by pressing the SPACEBAR is more specific, showing a list of Block operations from which you can select Copy. Leave the Selectable field entry as Yes and move to After Selection. Pressing the SPACEBAR here lists three options entitled What to do next. The self-explanatory choices are Stay, Quit, and GoTo Parent. The Copy command

FIGURE 12-16   General action list

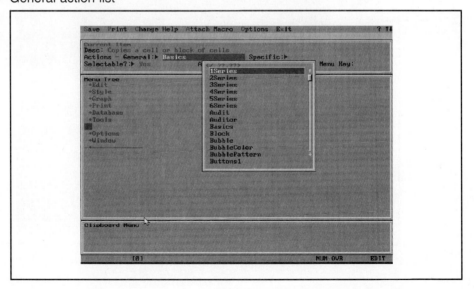

should Quit after being used. Select this and you can move to the next field and type **C** for the Menu Key.

The new menu item is almost completed, but it still lacks a name. In fact, as you enter **C** as the Menu Key, Quattro Pro 4 will remind you that the letter must refer to a named item on the menu. Press F6 to move to the Menu Tree window, type **Copy** in the empty slot, and press ENTER. The result is shown in Figure 12-17. Do not worry about the plus sign—this command does not get one, because it does not lead to a child menu. In the Current Item window Quattro Pro 4 has entered C for the Menu Key.

This is the basic procedure for defining new menu items. There is still a Copy option under Edit on this menu tree. Of course, if you simply want to move Copy from the Edit menu you can use the cut-and-paste procedure just described. Defining new menu items is useful when you want to add a specialized command in several places. You will also use this procedure when you are adding macros to menu trees, as described later in this chapter.

Defining Copy on the main menu

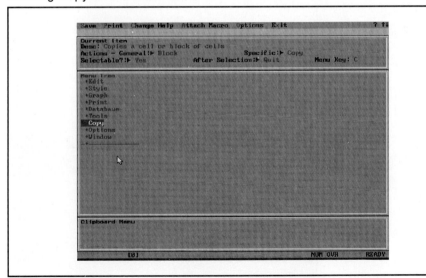

Saving Menus

When you have made your changes to the menu structure, type / for the menu editor menu and select Save. You will see a submenu requesting a name for your new menu system. When you type a name and press ENTER, Quattro Pro 4 will save the menu, which takes a little while. You are still left in the menu editor. Select Exit from the menu to return to the regular worksheet window.

When you are picking a name for a new or modified menu tree, avoid using one of the existing names from the list of .MU files unless you are sure you want to replace an existing menu file. Quattro Pro 4 will warn you before replacing an existing menu tree. You do not want to accidentally replace the QUATTRO.MU file with a faulty menu tree menu—one that does not include all of the options you need. If you damage the QUATTRO.MU file you must reinstall it from the original Quattro Pro 4 disks.

You activate the new menu system with the Options Startup Menu Tree command. As soon as you select your new menu file from the list and quit the menus, the new menu tree will be in place, as you can see in Figure 12-18.

For this reason, your menu designs should always include the Startup Menu Tree command as well as the Edit Menus command, even if they are disguised as something else to prevent novice users from getting to them. You will have a hard time changing back to the original menu tree

FIGURE 12-18

The new menu tree

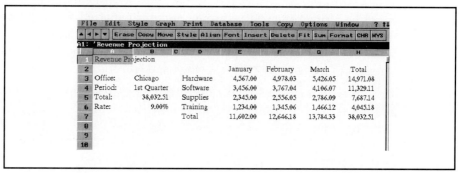

if you do not include these items. However, if you do not pick Update from the Options menu your choice of menu file will not be recorded. This means that you can call up a special simplified menu tree for a novice user, possibly using a macro. When the user is done, Quattro Pro 4 will revert to the original menu tree. If you do get stuck in a menu that has no Menu Tree option, you can get back to square one by recopying the QUATTRO.MU and RSC.RF files into your Quattro Pro 4 directory from the original program disk. Indeed, if you are going to do a lot of experimenting with menu designs, you might want to place a copy of your QUATTRO.MU and RSC.RF files in another directory in readiness for this eventuality. Note that the menu structure is stored in QUATTRO.MU and your choice of menu file is stored in RSC.RF, the Quattro Pro 4 configuration file.

Adding Macros to the Program Menu

With Quattro Pro 4 you can use the menu editor to add a menu item for running a macro to the program menu structure. The ability to call macros from the main menu system adds greatly to your ability to create customized menu-driven applications with Quattro Pro 4. Users can be prompted to enter and manipulate information by means of a set of specialized program and macro menus.

Figure 12-19 shows a customized program menu that includes the option Administer. This option was inserted into the menu tree with the menu editor, but the action it performs is not a normal program action. When Administer is selected, a macro called ADMIN is executed. There must be a macro with that name currently loaded, either in the current worksheet or in a macro library. If there is no ADMIN macro available when Administer is selected, nothing happens. The ADMIN macro was shown in Figure 12-8, where it was used to initiate a macro menu system.

To create a system menu item that executes a macro command you first select the Edit Menus option on the Options Startup menu. When the current menu is loaded you use the cursor keys to move around the Menu Tree window and locate the menu to which you want to add the macro command. Insert a new menu item by positioning your cursor on the menu item below which the new item is to appear. Press ENTER to insert a new line and type a menu name for the item then press ENTER. The name does not have to be the same as the macro's. Press F6 to get to

FIGURE
12-19

The Administer item on the menu

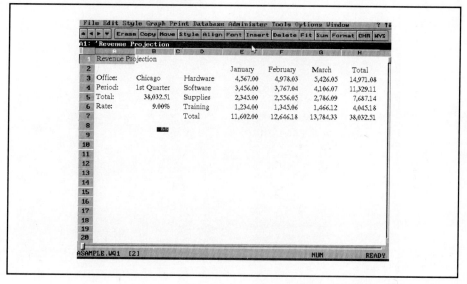

the Current Item pane of the menu editor screen. Enter a description of the menu item. In the General field enter **Name**. In the Specific action field enter **Attach**. Then type **/** for the menu editor menu and pick Attach Macro.

In the Attach Macro box, type the name of the macro as it is recorded in the worksheet, enclosed in curly braces. You can see this being done in Figure 12-20. Press ENTER to confirm the name. The box will disappear and the key letter will be selected.

Now that you have added the macro to the system menu you can save the new menu tree or exit the menu editing feature. By selecting the new tree with the Options Startup Menu Tree command and then picking Update to record this change, you can use the new menu in the current session and when you reload Quattro Pro 4. When you pick the macro item from the new menu, Quattro Pro 4 will look for a macro with the appropriate name in the current worksheet. If it does not find a macro with the correct name in the current worksheet, it will look for the macro in any open macro library worksheet. When the macro is found, Quattro Pro 4 will execute it. For example, you could have several different worksheets all containing a macro called ADMIN. The Administer item on the / menu would activate any one of them, depending on which

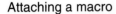

Attaching a macro

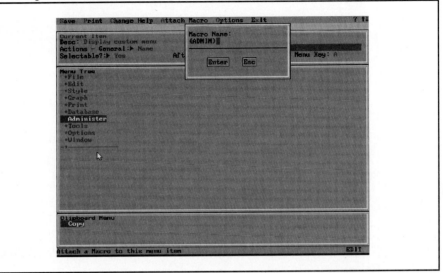

worksheet was loaded and current, even if they each contained different commands.

Edit Menu Options

There are several options that you can use when you are designing a menu system that affect how the menu will work. If you select Options from the menu editor menu, you can see these options listed, as shown in Figure 12-21. These options will be invoked whenever the menu structure you are designing is in use.

Files and Macros

The name of the autoload file that you want this set of menus to use can be specified. For example, you could enter **AUTO123.WK1** if you were using 1-2-3 style menus. Also, the default file extension can be

FIGURE
12-21

Menu Builder options

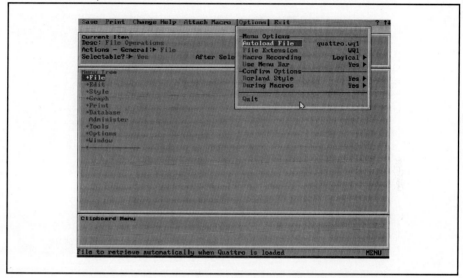

specified. The 123.MU file uses .WK1 in this setting. The Macro Recording option enables you to choose between Logical, the Borland-style menu equivalents, or Keystroke, the 1-2-3 style. Note that you can record macros in Logical style even if you are using a 1-2-3-style menu. This enables your macros to run under Quattro Pro 4 even when a different menu tree is in effect.

Use Menu Bar

The Use Menu Bar option enables you the turn on and off the menu bar across the top of the Quattro Pro 4 screen. When the option is set to No you will find that there is no menu on the screen until you type **/**, at which point the main menu pops up as a vertical list, as shown in Figure 12-22. In addition to Yes or No, you can use a third menu bar option: Compatible. This tells Quattro Pro 4 to use a pull-down menu but move the highlighting up and down the menu when you use the LEFT ARROW and RIGHT ARROW keys (in the normal menu bar these keys move you to the next menu, not the next menu item).

FIGURE
12-22

The pop-up vertical menu

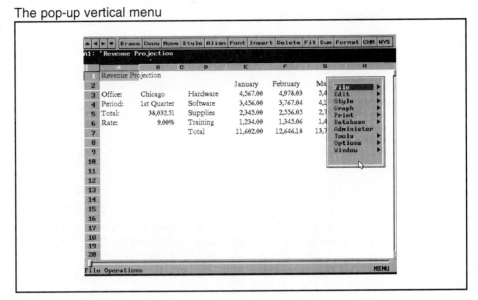

Confirm Options

Quattro Pro 4 normally displays a confirmation menu when you attempt an operation that will result in a loss of data, checking to see what actions you have performed and whether your work is saved. For example, you are prompted to confirm your choice when you are retrieving a file or resetting block names. You can set the Borland-style option to No to be compatible with 1-2-3.

The During Macros option is normally set to Yes to prompt for confirmation while macros are being run and recorded. To make macros compatible with 1-2-3, set this option to No. Remember that when you want to record macros compatible with 1-2-3, you change to the 123.MU menu tree, then set Macro Recording to Keystrokes, and finally alter the Confirm Options to No.

Remember

Although not shown on any menu, there is one more feature of menu operation that you can adjust in Quattro Pro 4. This is the Remember feature. When Remember is set to Yes, Quattro Pro 4 remembers the last item you picked from a particular menu. For example, when Remember is in effect and you pick the Edit Insert Columns command, the next time you activate the menu the Edit command will be highlighted. When you pick Edit, the Insert command will be highlighted. When you pick Insert, the Columns command will be highlighted. This means that you can type / and press ENTER ENTER ENTER to repeat the Edit Insert Columns command. This saves you a lot of time, particularly with commands like Style Numeric Format Percent. Instead of having to find Percent on the list of Numeric Formats, the Remember feature will take you there if that was the last format you picked.

Some tricks are useful when the Remember feature is in effect. Do not use the Quit option on a menu to leave the menu. Use CTRL-BREAK, which takes you directly back to the READY mode from just about any menu level. For example, when you pick Go from the Database Sort menu and you want to do more sorting after editing your list, exit the Sort menu with CTRL-BREAK. Then you can type / and press ENTER ENTER ENTER to repeat the Sort command. If you had used Quit to leave the Sort menu, that would be the remembered choice when you went back there. While some users prefer each menu selection to revert to the default top item, others enjoy the speed of repetition that the Remember feature provides.

To activate the Remember feature you must issue the following macro command in the spreadsheet area:

{/ Startup;Remember}

When you execute this command as part of a macro you will get a Yes/No option box. Select Yes and Quattro Pro 4 will now remember your menu choices for the rest of the current session. To activate Remember without using the option box use

{/ Startup;Remember}y~

Advanced Functions

A complete set of macro menus to enter, review, sort, and print data is a fairly involved undertaking. The elements that make up such a system were illustrated in the earlier examples in this chapter, some of which used a set of advanced Quattro Pro 4 @functions that can be very useful in more complex macros. Sometimes called the miscellaneous functions, these advanced functions enable you to perform such operations as data entry checks and macro control.

The @CELL Functions

The @CELLPOINTER, @CELL, and @CELLINDEX functions return information about a cell. The type of information produced by the function depends on the code specified in the function statement. The cell about which information is returned, in the case of @CELLPOINTER, is the cell that the selector currently occupies. In the case of @CELL, the cell is the one referred to by a cell reference or the one in the top left corner of a named block referred to by name in the function statement. For the @CELLINDEX function, the cell is the one referenced by the specified column and row of a defined block. The syntax is as follows:

@CELLPOINTER (*Code*)

@CELL (*Code,Cell*)

@CELLINDEX (*Code,Block,Col,Row*)

The *code* argument is a string that determines the information about the cell that the function references. There are nine of these codes, as shown in Table 12-4. With careful use of these codes, particularly when combined with the {IF} command and @IF function, you can extract valuable information about cells of the worksheet for use in macros. Remember that if you use a block name to refer to the cell required in the @CELL function, the cell addressed will be the one in the top left corner of the block. Because the cell used by the @CELLPOINTER function is the current cell, this function is useful for controlling looping macros. For example, the following macro, called ROUND, turns a column of formulas into results rounded to one decimal place:

```
{EDIT},1){HOME}@ROUND(
{CALC}{DOWN}
{IF @CELLPOINTER("type")="v"{Branch ROUND}
{Quit}
```

TABLE
12-4

Codes Allowed by the @CELLPOINTER and @CELL Functions

Code	Response
address	The absolute address of a cell
row	The row number of cell (from 1 to 8192)
col	The column number of the cell (from 1 to 256 corresponding to columns A through IV)
contents	The actual contents of the cell
type	The type of data in the cell: b if the cell is blank v if the cell contains a number or any formula l if the cell contains a label
prefix	The label-prefix character of the cell: ' if label is left-aligned ^ if label is centered " if label is right-aligned | if cell starts with that character \ if label is repeating
protect	The protected status of the cell: 0 if the cell is not protected 1 if the cell is protected
width	The width of the column containing the cell: (between 1 and 240)

TABLE
12-4
Cont.

Codes Allowed by the @CELLPOINTER and @CELL Functions

Code	Response
format	The current display format of the cell: Fn is Fixed (n=0–15) En is Exponential (n=0–15) Cn is Currency (n=0–15) + is +/– (bar graph format) G is General Pn is percent (n=0–15) D-D5 is Date 1=DD-MMM-YY 2=DD-MMM 3=MMMY 4=MM/DD/YY,DD/MM/YY, DD.MM.YY,YY-MM-DD 5=MM/DD,DD/MM,DD.MM,MM-DD D6-D9 is Time 6=HH:MM:SS AM/PM 7=HH:MM AM/PM 8=HH:MM:SS-24hr, HH.MM.SS-24hr, HH.MM.SS-24hr, HHhMMmSSs 9=HH:MM:-24hr, HH.MM-24hr, HH,MM,HHhMMm T is Show Formulas (Text) H is Hidden , is Commas, used to separate thousands

The first line of the macro edits a cell and places the @ROUND statements around the existing formula. The second line calculates the formula and then moves down to the next cell. The third line of the macro checks whether the next cell is a value and, if it is, the macro loops to the beginning. If the cell is a label or is blank, and therefore not a value, then the macro quits. Note that the response to the function as well as the code must be identified with quotes.

The @@ Function

Another function that responds with information about cells is the @@ function. The @@ function can play a valuable role in more complex macros, because it returns the contents of a cell that is referenced as a label in another cell. Thus, @@(A1) returns the answer 10 if A1 contains a reference to a cell that contains the number 10—either the label A1 or a label that is the name of a block, the top left cell of which contains 10.

The @COLS and @ROWS Functions

When you need to know how many columns or rows there are in a block of cells, you use the @COLS and @ROWS functions. Thus, @COLS(DATA) returns the response 7 if DATA is the name given to cells A1..G20. The response to @ROWS(DATA) would be 20.

The @N and @S Functions

Some spreadsheet programs cannot work with formulas that include cells containing labels or string values. The labels are not zero values and so can cause an ERR message to result from the formula. The @N function returns the numeric value of the cell or the top left cell of the block that it references. Thus, @N(DATA) returns the value 5 if the top left cell of DATA contains a 5 or a formula that results in 5. If the top left cell of DATA contains a label, the result will be 0. Because Quattro Pro 4 already considers labels to be zero values, there is not much need to use this function in a Quattro Pro 4 spreadsheet. However, the function is available to provide compatibility with other spreadsheet programs. The companion to @N is @S, which returns the string value of the cell it references. Thus, @S(DATA) will return Name if the top left cell of DATA contains the label Name or a string formula that results in Name. If the same cell contains 5, @S will return the empty label " ", which appears as an empty cell.

The Utility Functions

When you need to know the amount of regular and expanded memory available, you can use the Options Hardware command and read the screen. However, you can retrieve the same data into a spreadsheet cell with the @MEMAVAIL and @MEMEMSAVAIL functions. These functions are useful in macros when you need to check whether there is enough room for an operation to be performed or simply check that free memory is not getting too low. For example, the statement

{IF @MEMAVAIL/146389>.20}{/ Block;Copy}DATANEW

would cause the macro to execute the Copy command only if more than 20 percent of the total memory was free. The number 146389 is the total amount of memory, as you can read from the Options Hardware menu using @CURVALUE, described in a moment. Of course, if you have expanded memory installed, you will need to include that information in the equation (you can use @MEMAVAIL+@MEMEMSAVAIL). If you have no expanded memory in your system, the @MEMEMSAVAIL function responds with NA.

The @CURVALUE function has the very powerful ability to return the current value of any menu item that stores a value or setting. The menu item you want to read is defined by the arguments used in the @CURVALUE statement, which takes the form:

@CURVALUE("*general action*","*specific action*")

These arguments are the menu equivalents listed in the Quattro Pro 4 manual and by the SHIFT-F3 key, under / Commands. They are also found when you are using the menu editor. The items must be entered in quotes but capitalization is optional. For example, to read the current value of Normal Memory in the Options Hardware menu you use

@CURVALUE ("Basics","ShowMem")

The response to @CURVALUE is always a string, so it may need to be converted if it is to be used as a number or cell reference. Not all menu items have values that can be read, but the ability to read some, such as circular cell references, can be very useful in more sophisticated macros. To return the address of a cell occupied by a circular reference, you would use the command

@CURVALUE("Audit","ShowCirc")

True and False Tests

In some spreadsheet designs you may need to test whether a statement or condition is true or false. Quattro Pro 4 represents a true statement as 1 and a false statement as 0. Thus, +A1>99 results in 1 if A1 contains any number larger than 99, or 0 if A1 contains 99, a number less than 99 or a label (labels have a 0 value). The more likely place to find true/false tests is in an @IF statement, such as @IF(A1>99,1,0). Because this statement is somewhat difficult to read, you can use

@IF(A1>99,@TRUE,@FALSE)

The @TRUE and @FALSE functions return the responses 1 and 0, respectively, and require no arguments.

The @IS Functions

@@ISERR and @ISNA are true/false functions that give you the means to check whether a formula or cell entry results in either the ERR or NA response, respectively. These functions take the form @ISERR(*value*) and @ISNA(*value*), where *value* is a cell reference or a formula. The @ISERR function returns the response 1, meaning true, if *value* results in ERR, as is the case with @ISERR(1/0) or @ISERR(A1/A2), where A2 contains the value 0.

A typical application of the @ISERR function is shown in Figure 12-23, where a formula avoids the problem of dividing one column of numbers

FIGURE 12-23

An @ISERR formula

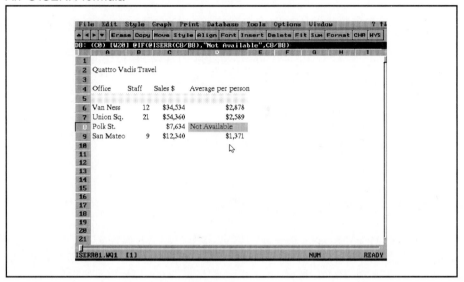

by another when some of the cells in the columns might be empty or contain zeroes. Thus, the division of total sales by the number of agents would result in an ERR message in cell D8 if the formula was simply C8/B8. The added @IF function uses @ISERR to turn the ERR result into the string of text "Not Available."

Another application of the @ISERR function is shown in Figure 12-24, where it is used in a data entry macro that completes the simple order form in the upper half of the screen. The {GETNUMBER} command places ERR in the destination cell if the user enters a label instead of the requested number. The macro code at B23 causes Quattro Pro 4 to beep and repeat the {GETNUMBER} command if the user accidentally enters a label.

Notice the other test in this macro in cell B25. The {IF} statement causes a beep and a repeat of the preceding {GETLABEL} prompt if the user enters a label less than A or greater than C. This statement restricts

FIGURE
12-24

Using @ISERR in data entry

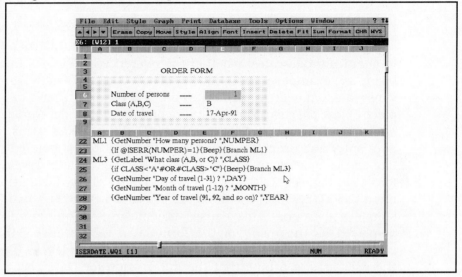

valid responses to the A, B, or C requested in the {GETLABEL} prompt. This line is an example of the # sign being used to join two conditions. The statement

CLASS<"A"#OR#CLASS>"C"

evaluates as true if the contents of the cell named CLASS are either less than A or greater than C. You can also use #AND# to join two conditions. In this way, both conditions must be met for the result to prove true. The operator #NOT# can be used to preface a condition to negate it.

The @ISNA function is used in the same manner as @ISERR, but is used less frequently. The value NA is less common than ERR, because few formulas give this result unless you design them that way. However, an example would be the following statement:

@ISNA (@MEMEMSAVAIL)

which returns 1 if your system has no expanded memory.

The statements @ISNUMBER(*value*) and @ISSTRING(*value*) are used in Quattro Pro 4 to test whether the referenced value is a number or a string. An example of these functions at work is shown in Figure 12-25, where a set of cells in column B is being used to receive data about a piece of lost baggage. The first piece of data, Passenger Name, has been entered in B5 and the Note in column C states "Okay." This method of data entry and prompting uses formulas next to the data entry cells to flag entries as they are made. You can see the formulas revealed in text format in Figure 12-26. Cell C5 evaluates to "Okay" because the statement @ISSTRING(B5) results in 1. In cell B6 there is a blank label, a simple apostrophe. This causes the message "Enter number" to be displayed as the result of the formula in C6 because @ISNUMBER produces 0 when it is applied to a cell containing a label. Of course, all the user sees is a note that the information for Date Lost must be a number rather than a label.

Data entry check

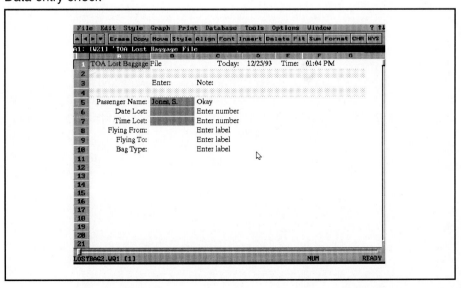

FIGURE 12-26 Data entry formulas

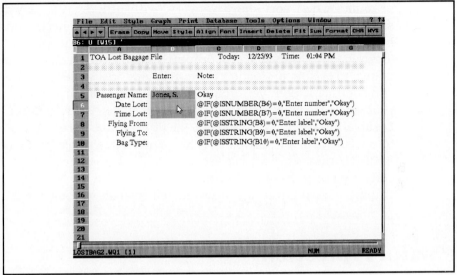

Note that the blank entry form should start with no entries in cell B6 or in cells B8 through B10. There should be blank labels in B6 and B7 to create the "Enter" prompts.

Protection and Input

The worksheets in Figures 12-24 and 12-25 are typical examples of a spreadsheet used for data entry. If there is much data to be entered, the person doing the entry may be accomplished at the keyboard but inexperienced with spreadsheet operation. To prevent accidental deletion or overwriting of important cells, you may want to take steps to protect your worksheet.

Complete Protection

To completely protect a worksheet, you use the Options Protection Enable command. This command prevents any cell of the worksheet from being changed. You use this feature in a number of situations. For example, when you share your PC with others, you may worry that someone will accidentally retrieve one of your worksheets and damage it before realizing they have the wrong file. Of course, password protection (described in Chapter 7) will prevent such file retrieval, but a less drastic step is to enable protection prior to saving the worksheet. The only way someone can alter your data is by turning off protection. Removing protection is done for the entire spreadsheet with Options Protection Disable. However, you can use Style Protection Unprotect to allow access to specific cells or groups of cells. When you enable protection for the entire worksheet, you will see the code PR in the cell descriptor of all cells, except those that have been unprotected by the Style Protection Unprotect command. Unprotected cells will show the code U.

Partial Protection

To turn on default protection and then remove it for specific blocks of cells is exactly what you need when turning over a spreadsheet to an inexperienced user. Quattro Pro 4 highlights the unprotected cells to make it easier to see which cells can accept data. The formulas and macros that run the worksheet are safe from damage while the data cells are clearly displayed. (If you try default protection and then block unprotect on your system and cannot see a different shading, try adjusting your monitor's contrast control and check the settings under Options Colors Spreadsheet.)

If you want to do more to restrict a user's access to a spreadsheet, you can use the Database Restrict Input command to define an area of the spreadsheet beyond which the cell selector cannot be moved. This area must coincide with a block of unprotected cells in an otherwise completely protected worksheet. When the Database Restrict Input command is issued, the top left cell of the Input Block is placed in the top left of the screen and the cell selector is placed in the first cell that is unprotected. At this point the cursor keys will not move the cell selector beyond the bounds of this block. However, pressing ESC will remove this movement restriction, so you should keep in mind that an input area will not keep prying eyes away from confidential areas of a spreadsheet.

Advanced Macro Notes

You can see that extensive use of the macro commands and advanced functions in Quattro Pro 4 can take you into areas that are not mere spreadsheet usage but applications development and programming—areas that are beyond the scope of this book. However, the macro-building methods that you have seen here contain the basic principles on which you can build complete customized systems. If you bear in mind some basic rules, you will be able to assemble sophisticated systems of commands as your confidence with macros increases.

One Step at a Time

When you have an idea for a complex macro or series of macros, try developing the ideas in a fresh worksheet with test data, rather than in the large worksheet in which they will eventually be applied. Testing helps ensure against accidental data loss as well as making the success of the macro logic easier to assess. Once you are comfortable with the basic structure, you can apply it to large sets of real data. You should also avoid making any single macro too large. This is particularly true in the case of menu macros. Just because the {MENUCALL} and {MENUBRANCH} commands require the menu options to be in consecutive columns does not mean that the entire macro for each menu option needs to be below the menu. You can use a {BRANCH} command as the first line of macro code for each menu item, directing flow from the menu macro to code for each item that is stored in a separate area of the worksheet. An example of this is shown in Figure 12-27.

One Line at a Time

One simple feature of Quattro Pro 4's macro environment is that you can execute a macro without naming it. All you need to do is simply point at it. To test the last 3 lines of a 10-line macro, you can use Tools Macro

Organization of menu with branches

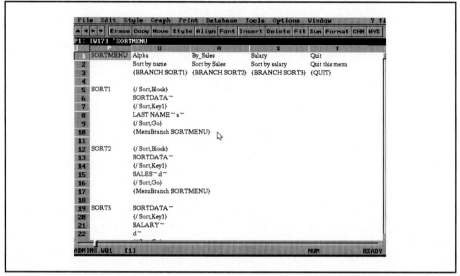

Execute, place your selector on the third to the last line of the macro, and press ENTER. This way there's no need to create temporary macro names just to test certain steps. If you assign the Shortcut CTRL-E to the Tools Macro Execute menu item you can execute macro code very quickly.

To check only one line of a macro, you can temporarily insert a blank row below the line you want to check to prevent the macro from continuing.

Debug

Do not forget the DEBUG command (SHIFT-F2), which will, at the very least, provide you with single-step macro execution. To see the macro execute in single-step mode, you repeatedly press the SPACEBAR. While you are executing a macro in DEBUG mode, you can type / to get the Macro Debugger menu shown in Figure 12-28. The Edit a cell option enables you to edit the cells of the macro and thus avoid errors that you

FIGURE
12-28

Macro Debugger menu

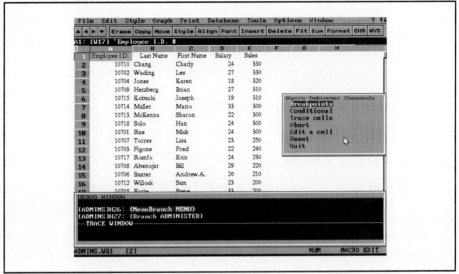

have noticed during execution. You select Quit from the Debugger menu to return to macro execution in DEBUG mode. If the macro appears fine during DEBUG playback, you can let it run to completion by pressing ENTER. To assist in problem solving when a macro is not running properly, you can use the tools provided on the Debugger menu.

Breakpoints

In addition to the single-step feature, you can set breakpoints to control macro execution. These are blocks or cells of macro code at which the macro should pause during execution. Breakpoints are an easier way of testing sections of larger macros than inserting blank cells after the last line you want to execute. By pressing ENTER during DEBUG playback, you can run the macro to the next breakpoint. As many as four breakpoints can be set from the Macro Debugger menu. If you want the breakpoint to be effective only on a repetition of the macro, you can set a pass count for the breakpoint. Use Reset from the Macro Debugger menu to clear the breakpoints.

Conditional

If you want a macro to run until a particular condition is met, you can use the Conditional option on the Macro Debugger menu to point to a cell in which you have entered a logical formula. An appropriate logical formula would be one that returns 1 for true and 0 for false. Thus, a cell containing the formula +A>99 could be used to make the macro playback pause if it caused A1 to exceed 99.

Trace Cells

If you are concerned with the macro's effect on particular cells of the spreadsheet, you can identify four trace cells that will be monitored in the Trace Window during macro execution in DEBUG mode. This method is very helpful for running a large macro that affects diverse areas of the worksheet.

Transcript Help

Bear in mind that Transcript will not be recording while you record a macro. When you are involved in critical operations, you may want to adjust the Transcript Failure Protection setting to reduce the number of keystrokes between saves from 100 to a smaller number. Use the Tools Macro Transcript command to display the Transcript log and then type / for the Transcript menu. Select Failure Protection and enter the number you want. Press ENTER and then ESC to clear the menu. A very small number, such as 5, will mean that Quattro Pro 4 slows down, saving to disk every five keystrokes. But a number like 25 is a good compromise between slow response and maximum recall in the event of a mistake or an equipment problem.

Full-Screen Effects

When you are managing a large number of macros, you may want to set up a menu from which to select groups of macros to be brought into the current worksheet. The menu in Figure 12-29 shows one method of

FIGURE
12-29

Macro choice menu

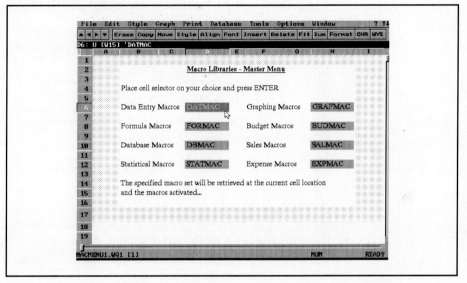

organizing a large number of choices. When the user has highlighted the desired file, ALT-M is pressed to initiate a Tools Combine of that file. The ALT-M macro, shown in Figure 12-30, copies the name to a cell called MACROSET, which forms part of the macro instructions.

The large menu design can be used with other macro choice techniques. In Figure 12-31 a large menu offers the user 14 options. Each number on the menu represents a different macro, which is chosen by typing the number of the desired option. A menu like this is effective as a first screen, activated by a Startup macro (\0). Figure 12-32 shows the code that uses this menu. After the cell selector is positioned by a pair of {GOTO} statements, the user is prompted by a {GETNUMBER} statement: "Enter the number of your choice:." The response is placed in the cell called TEST. The series of {IF} statements branch to the chosen macros—ENTER, REVIEW, and so on. This approach can be used in a number of different situations where the choices will not fit into a normal Quattro Pro 4 menu. (Remember that in a normal {MENUBRANCH} menu, Quattro Pro 4 allows 13 menu choices to be shown at once, and more can be incorporated into the menu, although the user will have to scroll down the list to see them.)

**FIGURE
12-30**

The ALT-M macro code

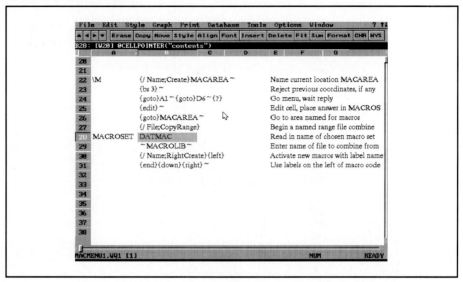

**FIGURE
12-31**

Large menu

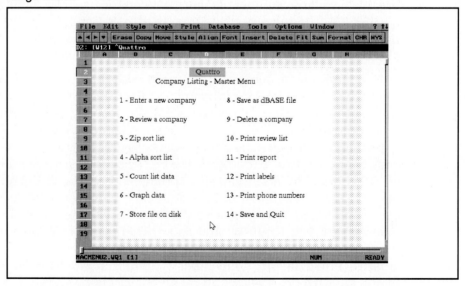

Code used to Evaluate menu selection

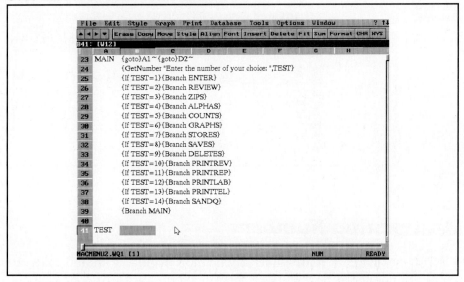

The slight pause while Quattro Pro 4 evaluates the {IF} statements in macros like this might become annoying. An alternative approach that provides faster response and far less code is shown in Figure 12-33.

The {DISPATCH} command is used to direct macro flow to the cell called WHERE. This cell contains a formula that reads the contents of the cell currently occupied by the cell selector. This macro employs a menu screen like that shown in Figure 12-34 to present the user with options that are actual subroutine names that can be highlighted. When the user presses ENTER, the contents of the currently highlighted cell are read into WHERE and thus used in the macro.

Notice the {?}, which is the pause for the user to move the cell selector and press ENTER. This command is followed by the code {edit}. This causes Quattro Pro 4 to update the @CELLPOINTER function in the WHERE cell. If this is omitted, WHERE may retain the cell selector's previous location and the macro will branch improperly.

**FIGURE
12-33**

Alternative evaluation method

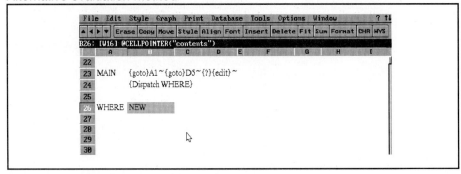

An Opening Number

When a novice user application begins, it should make the operator comfortable with the program. You can do this by careful use of the Startup macro (\0) and screen positioning. This is an excellent way to

**FIGURE
12-34**

Master menu made up of subroutines

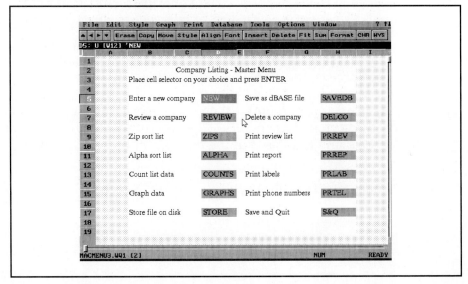

use the wide-screen menus shown in Figure 12-31. However, you can accentuate a regular Quattro Pro 4 macro menu to make an effective opening. In Figure 12-35 the user is shown the first menu and told how to use it. This was achieved by the {GOTO} command, first to the top left corner of the screen, and then to the highlighted label. The menu was then called. Note that Quattro Pro 4's menu positioning means some changes for those used to designing for 1-2-3's horizontal menu. Here the designer has positioned the message box accordingly.

While You Wait

Power users hate to wait, and one should assume the same for novice users. It is certainly prudent to let users know when they have initiated a procedure that takes time. The screen shown in Figure 12-36 is an example of this. The macro that performs the printing simply moves the cell selector to this screen before issuing the {/Print;Go} command. Similar screens are advisable when the user saves the file. You might

Opening menu

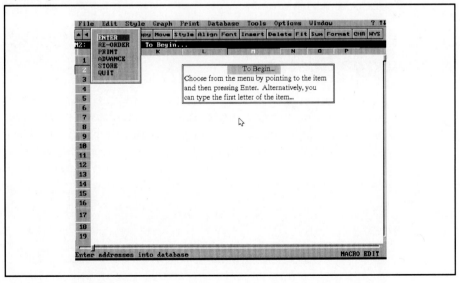

FIGURE

12-36

Print wait screen

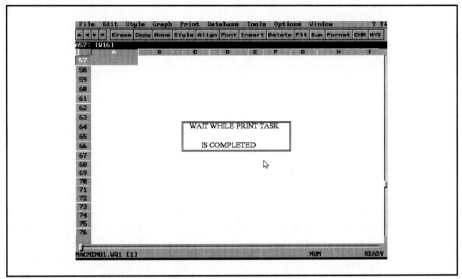

want to add an extra warning if the application is written for floppy-disk users, letting them know it is important not to remove the disk until the save process is complete.

A Message System

As an alternative to the previous techniques for displaying messages and menus, you can use text graphs. Graph message screens are not simply for use in presentations. By using the {GRAPHCHAR} command you can get user input while a graph is displayed and use this to branch to a series of macro instructions. For more on this technique and the design of graph buttons, turn to the next chapter.

CHAPTER

Special Features

*T*his chapter takes a closer look at some of the more interesting features of Quattro Pro 4. The chapter begins with a look at how Paradox and Quattro Pro 4 can work together to manage information. Then several aspects of presenting information are examined. Quattro Pro 4's ability to produce high-quality text charts is detailed. The Annotate feature is reviewed in depth, and you will see how to use clip art and simple drawing techniques to greatly enhance graphs that are then combined into a professional presentation. The creation of slide shows is covered, together with ideas for graph buttons with which you can put together self-paced presentations. By combining graph buttons with macros you can create visually effective custom menus that can form the basis of a tailor-made information system.

Working Together: Paradox and Quattro Pro 4

While Quattro Pro 4 has considerable power to organize and manage information, there are some applications that require the use of software with even more powerful database management capabilities. One such program is Paradox from Borland International, the makers of Quattro Pro 4. Paradox manages information in *tables,* which are column and row listings that look similar to Quattro Pro 4's databases.

About Paradox

Paradox has the ability to sort and search up to 2 billion records, and the size of the database that can be handled is limited only by disk space, not by the amount of RAM in your computer. Because it is a relational database manager, Paradox can work with several databases at once, based on links established between different fields. For example, your company's order desk may use a database that lists all customer orders, recording the customer name in a field called Customer. A separate database may be used by the credit department to keep track of customer addresses, contact names, and credit information, with the name of the customer recorded in a field called Name. Suppose you want a list of all orders over a certain size placed in a particular month together with the names and addresses of the customers who placed them. Paradox can create an answer table that pulls this information together based on query criteria and a link between the Customer field in the order database and the Name field in the accounting database. A third database could be involved, perhaps accounts receivable, to reduce the answer table to those companies that had paid for their orders. This answer table can either be treated as a temporary collection of information, or it can be saved, sorted, and queried as though it were a new database.

In addition to the ability to relate large collections of information, Paradox is particularly well-suited to network operations where numerous users are adding, editing, and searching records. Paradox can also relate to databases on larger sytems, such as minicomputers and mainframes, using Structured Query Language (often abbreviated as SQL and pronounced "sequel"). SQL is a standardized system for requesting information from a large database. Using SQL Link (a separate product), Paradox can gather information from SQL database systems. Where Quattro Pro 4 shines is in the analysis of data and the preparation of presentation-quality graphics and slide shows. As you might imagine, it is possible to establish a very close working relationship between Paradox and Quattro Pro 4, thereby using the best features of both programs. If you have access to both Paradox and Quattro Pro 4 on your computer, you can:

❏ Read Paradox database files directly into a Quattro Pro 4 spreadsheet, using File Retrieve, File Open, or Tools Combine.

❏ Extract specific records from a Paradox table into Quattro Pro 4 based on criteria, using Database Query Extract.

❏ Access Quattro Pro 4 from Paradox, and switch between the two programs with a single keystroke (you must have Paradox 3.5 or later to do this).

In the following sections you will read how to work with Paradox and Quattro Pro 4. It is assumed that you already have some knowledge of Paradox, but you will find all you need to know about the basic operation of Paradox in *Paradox Made Easy* from Borland/Osborne McGraw-Hill.

Reading Paradox Database Files

If the Paradox table you want to work on is not too large, you can read it directly into Quattro Pro 4. The simplest approach is to open the table from within Quattro Pro 4 using the File Retrieve command. The only limits to the size of table that Quattro Pro 4 can read are the amount of conventional and expanded RAM available and the limitations of the spreadsheet, that is, 256 fields or columns and 8191 records or rows.

Using File Retrieve

Simply select File Retrieve and then press ESC to edit the file specification for *.W?? to *.DB (Paradox tables have the extension DB). This enables you to show Paradox tables in the File Retrieve list, as seen in Figure 13-1. Alternatively, you can use the File Manager to list DB files and select from the list. When you open a DB file with Quattro Pro 4 the field names appear on row 1, and the records are listed on rows 2 and below, as shown in Figure 13-2. Numbers that were formatted in the Paradox table retain their formatting in the Quattro Pro 4 worksheet. In addition, you will find that the first data cell in each field has been named,

Paradox tables listed by File Retrieve

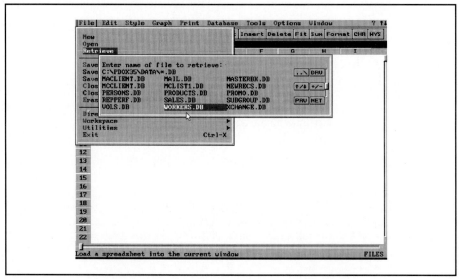

FIGURE
13-2

A Paradox table in Quattro Pro 4

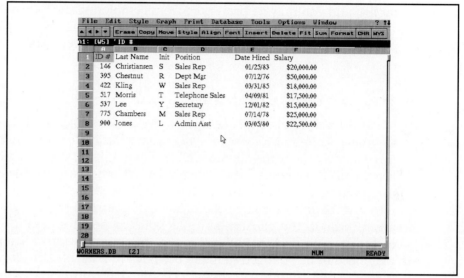

just as though the Database Query Assign Names command had been issued. Note that there are no Database Query settings in place in the file.

You can treat this worksheet just like a normal Quattro Pro 4 worksheet. You can edit, calculate, graph, query, and sort the data. However, you should be careful when using the File Save command to resave the file under its original name. When you issue the File Save command and the file has a .DB extension Quattro Pro 4 will save the file as a table, reading the closest text cell to A1 as the first field name and extrapolating a field and record structure from there. If you have added cell entries such as titles and calculations outside the table structure, then Quattro Pro 4 may have difficulty reading the worksheet back into a .DB file. In a situation like this you can use the Tools Xtract command to specify the exact cells you want Quattro Pro 4 to store as a Paradox table. When you use File Save or Tools Xtract and specify a .DB extension, Quattro Pro 4 presents a brief menu to allow you to review and change the file structure and confirm writing the .DB file.

For more on the Tools Xtract command, see Chapter 7. In some situations, using the original .DB filename may confuse Paradox, as happens when the table has special relationships with other Paradox tables, and you may be prevented from completing the command by the error message "Cannot save without destroying family files." In this case you can save the worksheet as a table under another name.

Using Tools Combine

An alternative to using File Open to read a Paradox table is to use Tools Combine. This enables you to read Paradox data into an existing Quattro Pro 4 worksheet at the current cell. For example, in Figure 13-3 you can see the user is about to complete the Tools Combine Copy File command by selecting a Paradox table called WORKERS.DB. This file will be read into cell B2 and as many cells below and columns to the right as there are records in the chosen table. As you can see from Figure 13-4, the incoming data does not alter the current column width settings, which may need to be changed to make the new data legible. Block names are not attached to the new data, but the date format is automatically assigned.

The Tools Combine command also enables you to import specific information from a Paradox table. This is done by choosing the Block

FIGURE
13-3

The Tools Combine Copy File command

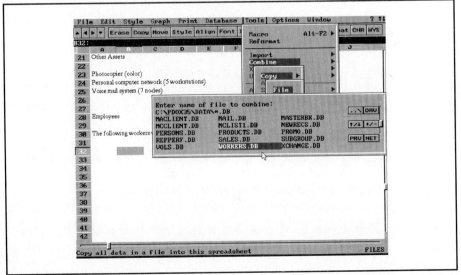

FIGURE
13-4

Paradox data combined into a worksheet

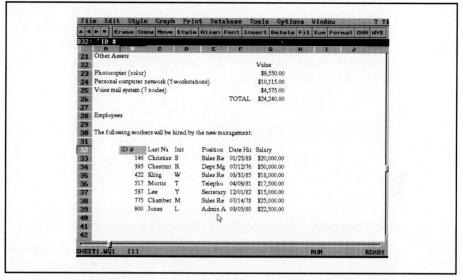

option instead of the File option. When you choose Tools Combine Copy Block, Quattro Pro 4 prompts for a block name or coordinates. You can describe the section of the Paradox table you want to import by using block coordinates. For example, the file WORKERS.DB is 6 columns wide and 8 rows long. Consequently it can be described as A1..F8. If you only want to read in a list of names, you can use Combine Copy Block and specify B1..C8. Obviously you have to know the structure of the Paradox table to make a selection like this, and you can only use a single contiguous group of cells per combine operation. You cannot specify two blocks at once, but you can perform two combine operations to bring in two separate parts of the table.

Extracting Specific Records from Paradox

Although the Tools Combine command allows a certain amount of discrimination when you read records from a Paradox table, the Database Query Extract command gives you complete control over the reading of Paradox records, using the same system of criteria that you saw in Chapter 5 in selecting records from a Quattro Pro 4 database. Suppose that in the workheet in Figure 13-5 you only want to read from WORK-ERS.DB the records of workers with salaries less than $20,000. Furthermore, you only want to read in the name, position, and salary fields. You set this up just as if you were performing a Database Query Extract on a Quattro Pro 4 database. You need to define the criteria table, as well as the database and output blocks.

The Output Block

First you enter the names of the fields that you want in the output. You can see this has been done in Figure 13-6 where the column widths have been adjusted to make the incoming data easier to read and the Database menu has been activated. Note that H31..H32 in Figure 13-6 represents the Criteria table described in a moment.

After selecting Query, you select Output Block to define the area that the incoming records will occupy. This must include the field names (matching capitalization is not necessary). In this case you might choose D31..G40, because you know there will only be a few names. If you are not sure of the number of records that will be read you can use just the field names as the output block, in this case D31..G31. However, if you

Worksheet to receive Paradox data

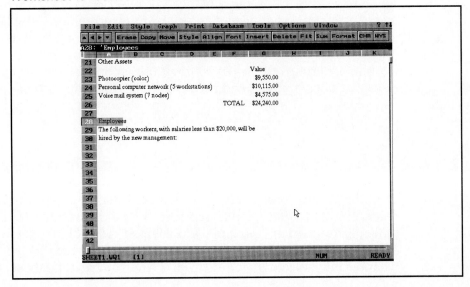

FIGURE 13-6 Prepared worksheet with output range

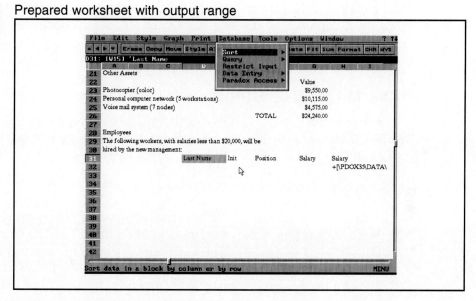

use this approach you should be sure that all cells below the field names are clear of data, because they could be overwritten by the incoming records.

The Criteria Table

There is one criterion in this case, a value in the salary field of less than 20,000. To create the criteria table you use an empty area of the worksheet and enter **Salary** as the field name. Below this you enter the criterion formula, which references the Paradox database as though it were another worksheet, as shown here:

Salary

+[C:\PDOX35\DATA\WORKERS.DB]SALARY<20000

When you enter this formula Quattro Pro 4 will read the file that you specify. This ensures that the file and field name are accurate. If they are not, you will be given an error message and the chance to alter the reference. If the reference is correct, Quattro Pro 4 may shorten it to just the file name, indicating that it already knows the correct drive and directory. You use Database Query Criteria Table to specify the two cells containing the field name and formula.

The Database Block

Now you can use the Database Query Block command to tell Quattro Pro 4 the name of the file you are querying. To do this you type the name of the file and then a "fake" cell reference, as in

[C:\PDOX35\DATA\WORKERS.DB]A1..A2

If Quattro Pro 4 can find the file you are referencing, it accepts this entry as the Database Query block setting, as in Figure 13-7. The coordinates A1..A2 are used by Quattro Pro 4 to register the fact that this is a set of records. You use A1..A2 regardless of the size and structure of the Paradox database you are extracting from.

FIGURE 13-7

Completed Database Query Extract settings

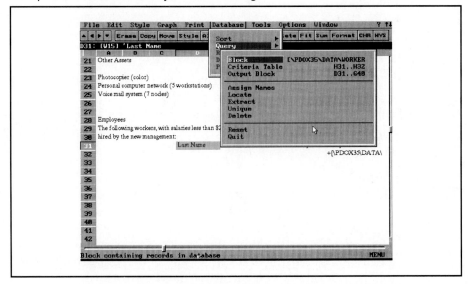

The Extract

In Figure 13-7 you can see the completed settings for the extract operation. All that remains is to issue the Extract or Unique command. You can see the results in Figure 13-8. This method of reading data from Paradox enables you to limit the information coming into Quattro Pro 4 to just those records and fields you need. For more on criteria, see Chapter 3.

Remember that the entries in the criteria table must reference the file and field name of the Paradox table. If you need to specify a range of records use the multiple field name approach. For example, to extract the records of all persons hired in 1988 and 1989 you would use the following as your criteria table:

Date Hired   Date Hired

+[WORKERS.DB]DATE HIRED<32874   +[WORKERS.DB]DATE HIRED>32142

The numbers 32874 and 32142 represent the dates 1/1/90 and 12/31/87, respectively.

FIGURE 13-8

Results of Database Query Extract

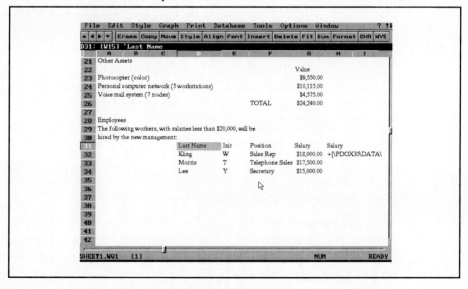

Accessing Quattro Pro 4 from Paradox

All of the techniques discussed for accessing Paradox data can be carried out without using the Paradox program itself and are useful for anyone who has to read .DB files with Quattro Pro 4. However, if you have both Quattro Pro 4 and Paradox on your system, you can switch between the two programs with a single keystroke (you must have Paradox 3.5 or later to do this). The Paradox Access command on the Quattro Pro 4 Database menu enables you to run Quattro Pro 4 from within Paradox, automatically load a Paradox table into a spreadsheet, work with the table in Quattro Pro 4, and then return to Paradox, without having to close either program. There are several advantages to Paradox-Quattro Pro 4 switching:

❑ By using the Paradox SQL Link you can bring SQL-hosted data (residing on mainframes, minicomputers, or OS/2 servers) into Quattro Pro 4 spreadsheets.

❑ By using Quattro Pro 4's presentation and publishing features you can graph, print, and present Paradox data, including that pulled from SQL sources, and even turn it into a slide show.

❑ By using Paradox's powerful Query by Example feature (QBE), you can easily select records instead of using a criteria table in Quattro Pro 4. The Answer table of selected data that Paradox creates, equivalent to the output block in Quattro Pro 4, can be automatically imported into Quattro Pro 4.

❑ By using the Paradox sort commands you can perform sorts on data before bringing it into Quattro Pro 4, thus avoiding the Database Sort command.

❑ By using macros in Quattro Pro 4 or scripts in Paradox you can automate many repetitive or time-consuming tasks.

Running Paradox Access

To use Paradox Access, you first load Paradox, then switch to Quattro Pro 4 by pressing CTRL-F10. To switch back to Paradox you press CTRL-F10 in Quattro Pro 4 or choose Go from the Database Paradox Access menu. To be able to perform this operation you need a fairly powerful system, the minimum specifications of which are

❏ *Paradox 3.5 or later* You will also need Paradox SQL Link if you want to access SQL data.

❏ *At least 2MB of RAM* Quattro Pro 4 needs 512K of RAM when run alone and 640K when installed for network use.

❏ *An 80286 processor* An 80386, 8036SX, or 80486 processor would be even better.

To work with very large spreadsheets in Quattro Pro 4, you might need additional expanded memory.

Before you use Paradox Access, there are several aspects of your system's configuration that should be checked. If the following steps for invoking Paradox Access do not work, refer to the section in Appendix B on Paradox Access. The best way to run Paradox Access is to run the PXACCESS batch file, which Quattro Pro 4 installed for you in the program directory. The file contains the following lines:

```
share
paradox -qpro -leaveK 512 -emK 0
```

As you can see, PXACCESS.BAT starts Paradox with a number of command line options. Most of the options concern how much memory Paradox uses. Usually the default settings in PXACCESS.BAT give optimum performance, but in some cases you might be able to improve performance by editing the file. Check the Paradox Access section in Appendix B for details.

After you run PXACCESS.BAT, Paradox starts and runs as usual. When you want to switch to Quattro Pro 4, press CTRL-F10; Paradox opens Quattro Pro 4 and passes control to it. If Paradox cannot open Quattro Pro 4, you will get the message "Can't load Quattro Pro." The first item to check is whether Quattro Pro 4 is on your DOS path in your AUTOEXEC.BAT file. If you do not start Paradox correctly (that is, by using the batch file or entering its contents directly), Paradox beeps when you press CTRL-F10. Exit Paradox and begin again by using the PXACCESS batch file. Note that pressing CTRL-F10 is the same as running a new Paradox Application Language (PAL) command called TOQPRO. (PAL is somewhat like the macro command language in Quattro Pro 4.) The TOQPRO command transfers control to Quattro Pro 4 and tells it the path to the user's private directory so that Quattro Pro 4 can find the file ANSWER.DB. This file is where Paradox stores the results of any queries. By enabling you to load ANSWER.DB directly into Quattro Pro 4 as you move from Paradox to the spreadsheet program, Paradox Access makes it very easy to query tables in Paradox and then analyze the results with Quattro Pro 4.

If you want to start Quattro Pro 4 whenever you run Paradox, create a Paradox startup script, INIT.SC, and keep it in the same directory as the Paradox system files. This file should contain the TOQPRO command. If this INIT.SC script exists, Paradox immediately transfers control to Quattro Pro 4 at startup. To automatically load a file when you first switch to Quattro Pro 4, use the qpro command-line option with an argument in the format shown here:

paradox -qpro [*filename macroname /options*]

The *filename* argument is the name and path of a spreadsheet, workspace, or .DB file that you want Quattro Pro 4 to open on startup. The name specified here automatically loads only when you transfer to Quattro Pro 4 for the first time. Subsequent transfers will load the file you specify with Quattro Pro 4's Paradox Access Load File command, as described in the next section.

The *macroname* argument is the name of a macro to run when Quattro Pro 4 opens the named file. The */options* argument refers to any of the regular Quattro Pro 4 command-line options, except for the /X option, which is disabled in Paradox Access. Note that the square brackets must be present.

Quattro Pro 4 and Paradox SQL Link

If you have SQL Link installed with Paradox, you can use Quattro Pro 4 to access data on a SQL database server. However, make sure that you have installed Paradox correctly for your SQL server, using the SQLINST program, as described in the SQL Link *User's Guide*. Bear in mind that switching to Quattro Pro 4 breaks your SQL connection and rolls back any uncommitted transactions. If you have changed the setting of Tools SQL Preferences AutoCommit to Off, be sure you save your changes before switching. See the SQL Link *User's Guide* for more about these commands. You should not attempt to load a SQL Link replica table into Quattro Pro 4 (you will get the error message "Cannot access SQL replica file" if you try).

Queries on SQL data can create huge Answer tables. If Quattro Pro 4 does not have enough memory to load the full Answer table, it warns you that there is not enough memory and loads as much as it can starting at the first record.

The Database Paradox Access Command

To control how Paradox Access works with Quattro Pro 4 you use the Paradox Access command from the Database menu in Quattro Pro 4. The Paradox Access menu consists of the following three options:

Go	This switches you to Paradox. If you have done some work in Paradox already, you return to the point where you left off. Your Quattro Pro 4 session closes but is not lost. If you switch back to Quattro Pro 4, you will be returned to where you were when you left.
Load File	This specifies the file that automatically loads when you switch to Quattro Pro 4. The file can be a spreadsheet or a Paradox table. The default setting is ANSWER.DB. Even though you can enter a path name here, Quattro Pro 4 knows to look in your private directory to find ANSWER.DB and any other Paradox temporary table, as well as in the current directory for all other tables and files. This command is appropriate only when Autoload is set to Yes.
Autoload	This specifies whether the file named with Load File is automatically brought into Quattro Pro 4 each time you switch from Paradox to Quattro Pro 4. The default is Yes.

If the file you specify with Load File is a spreadsheet with a startup macro assigned, the startup macro runs every time you switch from Paradox to Quattro Pro 4 (you assign a startup macro with Options Startup, Startup Macro). If you started Paradox with the command-line option -qpro [filename], as described previously, the file specified by filename autoloads instead of the file entered with the Load File command. This is true only for the first transfer to Quattro Pro 4. Subsequent transfers to Quattro Pro 4 automatically load the file specified with the Load File command. If Autoload is set to Yes, the Options Startup Autoload File command is ignored. Although you can change the settings of Load File and Autoload at any time, the Go command will work only when Quattro Pro 4 is run from within Paradox. (You must start Paradox with the -qpro option, as incorporated in the PXACCESS.BAT file, before switching to Quattro Pro 4.)

In addition to the commands on the Database Paradox Access menu, the Options Other Expanded Memory command also affects Paradox Access. For best use of memory, set this to Both. If your system is running on a network be sure the Options Other Paradox commands are set correctly. Bear in mind that if you make changes to these settings, you must exit Quattro Pro 4 and reload the program for the new settings to be active.

When you are done with your work in Quattro Pro 4, just press CTRL-F10 to return to Paradox. You don't have to close your spreadsheet files or choose File Exit. In fact, you can leave everything just as it is. If you later return to Quattro Pro 4 from Paradox, your workspace will be just as you left it. If there are unsaved changes in Quattro Pro 4 when you quit Paradox, you will be asked if you want to save these changes before quitting to DOS. If you want to include switching to Paradox in a macro, use {/ Paradox;SwitchGo}, which is equivalent to pressing CTRL-F10.

Paradox Tables

In Figure 13-9 you can see a Paradox database of flight information for Take Over Airlines. This information has been pulled, by SQL Link, from the mainframe computer that tracks every detail of TOA reservations and flights. You want to analyze the performance of TOA during 1992 and so have used SQL to pull selected pieces of data from the mainframe program. Each record in Paradox consists of a flight number, destination, and the number of passengers who travelled on the flight, broken down into three classes: First, Business, and Coach. Off the right of the screen there is also a Total field that shows the total number of passengers, plus a Revenue field, that shows the gross receipts from the flight. Suppose that you want to use Quatttro Pro 3 to analyze First Class traffic in the first quarter. You do not need details of flight numbers or revenue, just the flight destination, date, and the number of First Class passengers. Instead of dumping the entire database into Quattro Pro 4, you can first sift out the appropriate data with Paradox, using the Ask command.

FIGURE
13-9

Paradox table

```
Viewing Tvyear table: Record 1 of 627                          Main

TVYEAR   FLIGHT      DATE          DEST      FIRST   BUSINESS   COACH
     1      520     1/01/92    Rome            7        13        111   **
     2      420     1/02/92    London         19        31        199   **
     3      521     1/02/92    R-Base          8        17        141   **
     4      620     1/03/92    Tokyo          13        18         58   **
     5      820     1/03/92    Cairo           5         6         90   **
     6      421     1/04/92    L-Base         15        26        163   **
     7      720     1/04/92    Athens          5        11         89   **
     8      821     1/05/92    C-Base          4         5         77   **
     9      920     1/06/92    Paris          21        28        183   **
    10      621     1/06/92    T-Base         18        23         76   **
    11      921     1/07/92    P-Base         17        25        170   **
    12      721     1/07/92    A-Base          6        12         99   **
    13      520     1/08/92    Rome            6        12        104   **
    14      420     1/09/92    London         19        31        199   **
    15      521     1/09/92    R-Base          7        13        110   **
    16      620     1/10/92    Tokyo          14        19         62   **
    17      820     1/10/92    Cairo           6         7        103   **
    18      421     1/11/92    L-Base         19        31        143   **
    19      720     1/11/92    Athens          7        13        113   **
    20      821     1/12/92    C-Base          5         6         96   **
    21      920     1/13/92    Paris          20        27        174   **
    22      621     1/13/92    T-Base         13        18         57   **
```

Assuming that you have loaded Paradox with PXACCESS and have used the View command to select the desired table, you can use the Ask command to specify the information you need. First press F10 for the Paradox menu and then select Ask. You need to tell Paradox the table to be queried. Press ENTER to view a list of tables, and the table you are currently viewing is highlighted. Press ENTER to select it. You will see a list of the fields in the table with space to enter your criteria, as shown in Figure 13-10 where the criteria have been entered. In the DATE field you can see the following formula, used to specify records with a DATE entry in the first quarter:

>=1/1/92, <=3/31/92

Select the fields that you want in the resulting Answer table by pressing F6. This places a check mark in the field. You can now press F2 to execute the query. The resulting Answer table can be seen in Figure 13-11. If you now press CTRL-F10 to switch to Quattro Pro 4, this data will

FIGURE
13-10

Paradox criteria

```
√ [F6] to include a field in the ANSWER; [F5] to give an Example    Main  ─▼
┌────FLIGHT────┬───────DATE───────┬───────DEST───────┬────FIRST────┐
│              │√ >=1/1/92, <=3/31/92 │              │√            │
│              │                  │                  │             │
└──────────────┴──────────────────┴──────────────────┴─────────────┘

TUYEAR─FLIGHT───────DATE───────DEST────FIRST──BUSINESS──COACH──
   1      520    1/01/92    Rome         7      13       111   **
   2      420    1/02/92    London      19      31       199   **
   3      521    1/02/92    R-Base       8      17       141   **
   4      620    1/03/92    Tokyo       13      18        58   **
   5      820    1/03/92    Cairo        5       6        90   **
   6      421    1/04/92    L-Base      15      26       163   **
   7      720    1/04/92    Athens       5      11        89   **
   8      821    1/05/92    C-Base       4       5        77   **
   9      920    1/06/92    Paris       21      28       183   **
  10      621    1/06/92    T-Base      18      23        76   **
  11      921    1/07/92    P-Base      17      25       170   **
  12      721    1/07/92    A-Base       6      12        99   **
  13      520    1/08/92    Rome         6      12       104   **
  14      420    1/09/92    London      19      31       199   **
  15      521    1/09/92    R-Base       7      13       110   **
  16      620    1/10/92    Tokyo       14      19        62   **
```

FIGURE
13-11

Paradox Answer table

```
            Viewing Answer table: Record 1 of 156
        ANSWER──────DATE───────────DEST───────FIRST──
            1      1/01/92     Rome          7
            2      1/02/92     London       19
            3      1/02/92     R-Base        8
            4      1/03/92     Cairo         5
            5      1/03/92     Tokyo        13
            6      1/04/92     Athens        5
            7      1/04/92     L-Base       15
            8      1/05/92     C-Base        4
            9      1/06/92     Paris        21
           10      1/06/92     T-Base       18
           11      1/07/92     A-Base        6
           12      1/07/92     P-Base       17
           13      1/08/92     Rome          6
           14      1/09/92     London       19
           15      1/09/92     R-Base        7
           16      1/10/92     Cairo         6
           17      1/10/92     Tokyo        14
           18      1/11/92     Athens        7
           19      1/11/92     L-Base       19
           20      1/12/92     C-Base        5
           21      1/13/92     Paris        20
           22      1/13/92     T-Base       13
```

appear there, ready for you to work on, as shown in Figure 13-12. If you need to save the analysis you perform in the worksheet you can store it as a .WQ1 file using File Save As.

To understand how Paradox Access affects Answer tables, you need to be aware of the characteristics of Paradox temporary tables. There are 12 temporary tables, including Answer. You can use Paradox Access to open any temporary table in addition to any regular table to which you have rights. Table 13-1 lists the temporary tables and their contents. Remember that temporary tables are just that: Paradox deletes them when you exit. Paradox often overwrites temporary tables. For example, it generates a new Answer table whenever you make a new query. Simply switching back and forth between Paradox and Quattro Pro 4 does not, however, affect temporary tables. Temporary tables do not reside in the working directory. Unlike your working tables, they are written to your private directory. This means they will not appear in the file list when you choose File Open, for example, because that list shows your working directory, not your private directory. For more information on the contents of these temporary tables, refer to the Paradox *User's Guide.*

Paradox tells Quattro Pro 4 where your private directory is so it can open ANSWER.DB, STRUCT.DB, and the other necessary files. Both the

The results in Quattro Pro 4

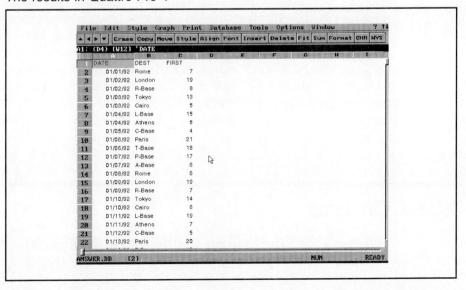

TABLE	Paradox Temporary Tables
13-1	

Name	Contents
Answer	Results of a query
Changed	Unchanged copy of changed records
Crosstab	Results of a crosstab operation
Deleted	Deleted records
Entry	New records for a table
Family	Records and forms for a table
Inserted	Inserted records
Keyviol	Records with duplicate key values
List	List of tables
Password	Auxiliary passwords
Problems	Unconverted records
Struct	Table definition

Autoload command and the regular File commands can open any of the temporary tables, but because all files in a private directory are locked, you cannot save these tables as is. You can, however, edit and save a temporary table in a different directory and under a different name by choosing File Save As. Because of the strict locking rules for private directories, make sure your Paradox working directory and private directory are different. If they are not, use the Custom Configuration Program in Paradox (Script Play Custom). Choose Defaults SetDirectory to permanently change the location of your Paradox working directory.

Word Charts

When the time comes to present the information you have organized with Quattro Pro 4 you will find it has capabilities that go far beyond those normally associated with a spreadsheet program. Later, this chapter explores the creative abilities of the Annotate and Slide Show commands. Quattro Pro 4 even improves on the basic spreadsheet ability to line up text in columns. This is appreciated by a wide range of users, from the secretary typing up a budget from a rough draft to the salesperson who has a sales presentation to make. Word processing programs often make heavy going of columns, requiring mastery of complex commands. A spreadsheet offers a simple way of typing up lists in column and row format, such as the one shown in Figure 13-13. Quattro Pro 4 has special features to dress up such information.

Quattro Pro 4 for Professional Text

The text in Figure 13-13 was simply typed into the worksheet. The figures in column W are summed in cell W33, but otherwise there is no calculation going on in this collection of information. To dress up text, perhaps to use it as part of a presentation, you can not only add lines and fonts (described in Chapter 3) but also bullet characters.

FIGURE 13-13

Basic list typed into worksheet

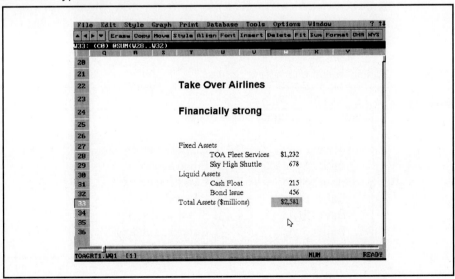

These are shown in Figure 13-14, which was printed directly from a spreadsheet. These bullet characters are graphic symbols that can be placed in spreadsheet cells. The bullets only print as images when you use Graphics Printer as the Print Destination for the Print Spreadsheet command.

You enter a bullet as a coded label that Quattro Pro 4 translates into an image during printing. For example, a style 1 bullet is created by the code

\bullet 1\

You *must* enter this preceded by a label prefix (', ", or ^); otherwise, Quattro Pro 4 will assume you are using the cell fill character (\). You can enter a bullet code into a cell on its own or you can combine it with other text. You can even use a bullet code in a string formula. For example, to combine the word "Present" with the number 5 bullet you can enter

'\bullet 5\ Present

Note that the apostrophe must be typed and that there is a space between the second backslash and the text that follows. This space is not mandatory, but without one the bullet would print too close to the text.

There are some minor inconveniences when you are using bullet codes. They do not look attractively formatted when you are working in character mode. However, when you switch to WYSIWYG mode you will see them.

Special bullet characters printed

Quattro Professional Bullet Styles:

Bullet Style	0	☐	Empty square
Bullet Style	1	■	Filled square
Bullet Style	2	☑	Checked square
Bullet Style	3	✓	Check mark
Bullet Style	4	☐	Shadow box
Bullet Style	5	☑	Checked shadow
Bullet Style	6	●	Filled circle

Bullets are hard to line up with text unless you give them their own column. You can then vary the printed location of the bullet within the column by using the left, right, and center label prefixes (', ", ^). In Figure 13-15 you can see the worksheet in Figure 13-13 printed with bullets. These were added in columns S and T. The bullets are all left-aligned except the one for Liquid Assets, which was centered in the column.

Adding Style

In earlier chapters you saw how the Style commands could be used to dress up text in Quattro Pro 4. You can use Style Line Drawing to add single, double, or thick lines that go over, under, or around labels and numbers. The Style Shading command can add several levels of gray to areas of your printouts. With the Style Font command you can vary the appearance of printed text, as shown in Figure 13-15. By combining these commands you can create impressive text charts and reports. For example, Figure 13-14 was printed from Quattro Pro 4 using the Style Line Drawing command with the thick line option to create the box around the text.

An alternative approach to creating text charts with Quattro Pro 4 is to use the Graph Annotate command. This provides more creative

FIGURE 13-15 Printed version of worksheet with bullets

Take Over Airlines

Financially strong

- Fixed Assets
  - ☑   TOA Fleet Services $1,232
  - ☑   Sky High Shuttle $678
- Liquid Assets
  - ☑   Cash Float $215
  - ☑   Bond Issue $456
- Total Assets ($millions) $2,581

freedom, including the ability to enliven charts with images from a clip art library.

The Power to Annotate

The Graph Annotate feature in Quattro Pro 4 enables you to create text charts and embellish graphs of spreadsheet data. In fact, Annotate is a full-featured drawing program capable of producing striking visual effects. A complete description of what can be done with Annotate could support a whole book, or at least several more chapters than will fit in this book. However, the following examples should give you an idea of what can be accomplished with this feature.

Exploring the Annotator

As you saw in Chapter 8, Annotate adds text and shapes to graphs created with the Graph command and displayed by Graph View, Graph Name Display, or the Graph key (F10). To access the Annotate feature you display a graph and then press the / key to bring up the Annotate screen. Alternatively, you can select Annotate from the Graph menu, which tells Quattro Pro 4 to display the current graph in the Annotate screen.

You do not have to add text or shapes to an existing graph. As you can see from Figure 13-16, the Annotate screen can be set up as a blank drawing board. To display it you should first make sure any existing graphs are named and saved, then use the Customize Series command on the Graph menu and select Reset followed by Graph to clear the current settings. You can now set the Graph Type to Text, which requires no series values to be established, and then select Annotate. Your screen should now look like the one in Figure 13-16.

The menu of icons across the top is called the Toolbox. The large blank rectangle is your canvas, where you will place text and shapes created with the Annotate tools. Each item you create is referred to as an *object*. The area on the right of the screen is called Properties. It enables you to change the appearance of the objects you create.

Annotate screen

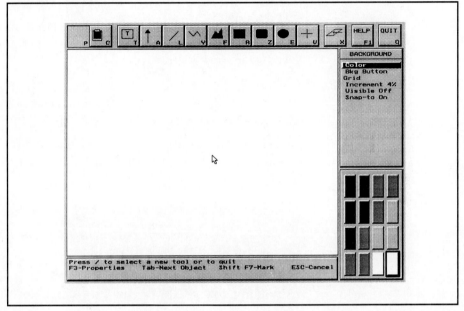

To activate the Toolbox menu you press the / key. You will see the outline of the boxes change. You can now press LEFT ARROW or RIGHT ARROW to highlight the tool you need, then press ENTER to activate it. This places a thick line around the tool. Alternatively, you can activate the menu and then type the letter that appears in the tool icon. Mouse users can simply click on the desired tool. The tools are described in Table 13-2.

As you highlight different tools in the Toolbox you will see the Properties area change. The top half of Properties lists attributes applicable to the type of object that the selected tool creates. The lower half shows the available choices. When you highlight a tool the name appears in the Properties area (except for the Clipboard), which reflects the name of the currently selected object. When the Pointer is selected the Background properties can be changed, including the color and the optional grid that may help you align objects.

The Toolbox menu is in several parts. The first two items are Pick and Clipboard. When the Pick option is active you can select items within the canvas area. To do this you place the mouse pointer over the item and click, or you draw a selection box around the object by dragging the

TABLE
13-2

Tools in the Annotate Feature

Tool	Function
P (Pointer)	Selects objects (you can also use TAB and SHIFT-TAB to select objects in turn)
C (Clipboard)	Copies and pastes objects within current graph to/from clip art files. Also used to move objects to top or bottom layer
T (Text)	Creates text and graph buttons (text will be boxed unless Box Type is set to None)
A (Arrow)	Draws straight line arrows at any angle
L (Line)	Draws straight lines at any angle
Y (Polyline)	Draws jointed lines or curves (by holding down SHIFT or enabling SCROLL LOCK)
F (Polygon)	Draws many-sided shapes or curved shapes (by holding down SHIFT or enabling SCROLL LOCK)
R (Rectangle)	Draws rectangular shapes with sharp corners
Z (Round Rectangle)	Draws rectangular shapes with rounded corners
E (Ellipse)	Draws circles and ovals
V (Line)	Draws straight vertical or horizontal lines
X (Link)	Links drawn objects to series within a graph so that they move with that part of the graph
F1 (Help)	Displays help information about Annotate
Q (Quit)	Quits back to full-screen display of graph (unless Annotate was accessed with the Annotate command from the Graph menu, in which case it quits back to the Graph menu with no graph display)

pointer across the screen. Keyboard users can select each object in turn by pressing TAB when the Pointer is active. The Clipboard holds the characters you copy and cut and also moves them to the top or bottom when there are overlapping items. The Cut To, Copy To, and Paste From commands enable you to export and import images in clip art files. These files have the extension .CLP, and a number of them are included with Quattro Pro 4. The next nine menu items are the drawing tools for such shapes as lines, arrows, polygons, filled polygons, rectangles, and circles. The last three menu items are Link, Help, and Quit. When you select Quit you are presented with the results of your annotation, drawn full screen. You can then press ESC to return to the worksheet, or / to return to the Annotator.

Drawing a Shape

Suppose you want to draw a free-form object, or a polygon. Press /, and then highlight the icon marked F and press ENTER (or type **F**). This places a cross on the screen, which is your pointer. To begin the shape, you move the pointer to the place on the screen where you want to begin, using the mouse or cursor keys. The specific actions of the cursor keys are listed in Table 13-3. To anchor the beginning point, click the mouse button or type a period (referred to as MouseDown and Dot, respectively, by the help section at the bottom of the Annotate screen). You can then move the pointer to begin drawing a line from the fixed point in the direction that you are moving the pointer. To fix the next point of the polygon you press ENTER again. You can press ESC to cancel the action or type / to change tools. When you have completed the polygon you press ENTER twice, and Quattro Pro 4 closes up the object's outline, as shown in Figure 13-17. If you want your polygon to include curves, you can hold down SHIFT while dragging the mouse pointer. This will produce free-form curves. When you release SHIFT the tool draws straight lines again. This also works with the Polyline tool. Alternatively, you can activate curves by pressing SCROLL LOCK once. The tools will draw curves until you press SCROLL LOCK again.

If you want to draw rectangular shapes, you should use the Background option called Snap-to. When you turn Snap-to on, the lines and shapes you draw will adhere to a fixed grid. You can see this grid if you turn on the Visible option in the Background tool. The coarseness of the grid can be adjusted. The default setting is 4%. A greater percentage will create a coarser grid.

FIGURE 13-17   Completed polygon

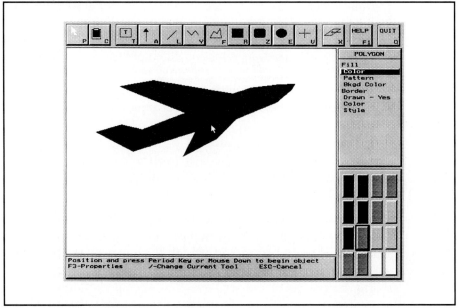

TABLE 13-3   Keys Used in Graph Annotate

Key	Function
ARROW keys	Move or resize a selected element or group of elements
TAB	Moves the pointer clockwise around the elements in the drawing area
SHIFT-TAB	Moves the pointer counterclockwise around the elements in the drawing area
SHIFT-F7	Selects elements in the drawing area; use in combination with TAB and SHIFT-TAB to select multiple elements
SHIFT	Used with a mouse, the SHIFT key held down as you click on elements in the drawing area selects multiple elements that are not connected

TABLE
13-3
Cont.

Keys Used in Graph Annotate

Key	Function
DELETE	Deletes a selected element or group of elements; if used with a mouse, point and press DELETE to delete one element
Period (.)	With an element or group of elements selected, the period anchors the selected area and allows you to resize it. The lower right-hand corner is the default corner, which will extend or contract the element as you press the ARROW keys or move the pointer with the mouse. To resize the area using a different corner, press the period repeatedly to cycle around the corners of the selected area
HOME, END	Moves the corners of a selected area diagonally
PAGE DOWN, PAGE UP	Moves the corners of a selected area diagonally
F2	With an element selected, enters MOVE mode so you can reposition the element; for a text element, enters text editing mode
CTRL-ENTER	In text editing mode, wraps inserted text to a new line
BACKSPACE	Used to erase characters and line breaks in text editing mode
Slash (/)	Activates the Toolbox
F3	Activates Properties
F10	Redraws the Graph Annotate screen
ESC	Returns to the drawing area from Properties or the Toolbox; with a selected element in RESIZE mode, switches to MOVE mode

Enhancing the Shape

Once an object has been drawn you can enhance it by changing its attributes. This is done by using Properties, the menu to the right of the main area that lists Fill, Border, and so on. Before you use Properties, you need to select the object you wish to change. You can do this by typing **/** to change tools and then selecting Pick, the first item on the left of the menu. Then point and click on the object with the mouse or press TAB to select the object. If there is more than one object on the canvas, pressing TAB selects each one in turn. A set of handles appears around a selected item, as you can see in Figure 13-18. These are used to move and size the object, following this process:

1. Any selected object has eight handles, one on each corner and four in between the corners. These are used to alter the size of objects.

2. A handle that is not on a corner can be dragged to increase/decrease the size of the object in one direction, inward or outward from that side.

3. A handle that is on a corner can be dragged to increase/decrease the vertical and/or horizontal size at the same time.

FIGURE 13-18

Selected item with handles

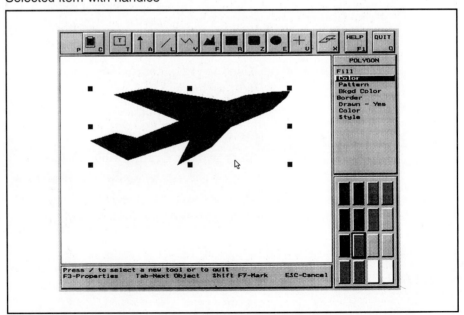

4. If you have difficulty selecting a small object with a mouse, press TAB or SHIFT-TAB to cycle the selection handles through all objects in turn.

5. If you drag a handle all the way across an object you will flip the object on one or more axes. This allows you to create matching objects. (For example to make two identical wings for a plane: create one wing, copy and paste, and drag one handle on the copy across the object so that it is the mirror image of the original.)

6. Adjusting the size of a boxed text object does not alter the text size, just the dimensions of the surrounding box. (Use the Font property to alter text size.)

7. If you have selected a group of objects they can be sized and otherwise adjusted as a single object by pressing F7. This gives the group eight handles, as just described.

To alter the attributes of an object, activate Properties by pressing F3. When you press F3 the box around Properties becomes a double line and you can highlight an item that you want to alter, such as the Pattern used to fill the polygon object. The items on the menu vary according to which object is selected. For example, when a polygon is selected the two main categories are Fill and Border. To change the filling of the shape you press DOWN ARROW to move the highlight to Pattern and then press ENTER (or click on it with the mouse). The palette in the lower half of Properties is activated and you can use the ARROW keys to move the highlighting to the attribute you want. The filling of the selected object will not change as you move from one pattern to another, but when you have highlighted the pattern you want, press ENTER or click the mouse, and the object is then filled with the chosen pattern, as shown in Figure 13-19. Note that the NO pattern means the shape will be given no filling. You can change the color as well as the pattern of the filling.

You can proceed in this fashion to alter the attributes of the object. You press ESC or click in the main section of the window to return to creating new objects. You can move the current object with the cursor-movement keys or by clicking with the mouse to select the object and then dragging it to a new location. You can choose a new tool from the menu to make a new object, such as lines, arrows, rectangles, rounded rectangles, or even text, as discussed next.

FIGURE
13-19
Filling with a pattern

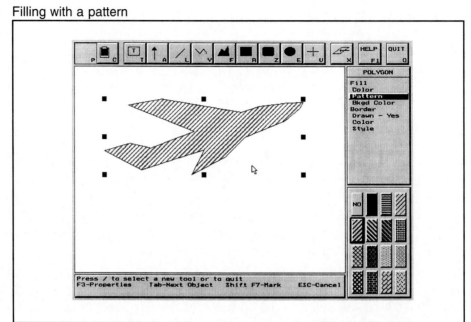

Adding Text

You could add the letters TOA to the plane in Figure 13-19. When you select the Text tool you can type text at a selected point on the screen. To create a second line of text you press CTRL-ENTER. You press ENTER to complete the text object. When you enter text, it is initially boxed in a rectangle. You can alter the attributes of this box, adding shading for example, or you can remove it. As you can see from Figure 13-20, you can alter the font of the text by using a selection process similar to that used when selecting fonts for your spreadsheet entries. When you have selected a font Quattro Pro 4 may take a moment to draw the necessary screen font for you. This only happens the first time you use a particular font.

To edit text that you have already created, you first select the text object and then press F2. This places an edit cursor after the last character of the text. You can use the UP ARROW and DOWN ARROW keys to move from line to line in the text. The LEFT ARROW and RIGHT ARROW keys move the edit cursor through the text.

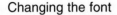

FIGURE
13-20

Changing the font

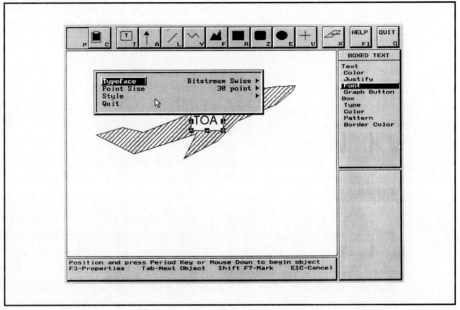

Using the Shape

When you want to see the drawing at full size you type **/** to activate the menu and pick Quit. This takes you to the full-screen graph view if you entered Annotate by typing / while viewing a graph. If you entered Annotate with the Graph Annotate command, Quit will return you to READY mode, and you can press F10 to view the graph. From here you can press ENTER to return to the worksheet. It is important to use the Graph Name Create command to save the work you do with Annotate.

There does not need to be any entry in the worksheet to support a text graph or drawing. However, you can use drawings effectively with worksheets that contain text and numbers. For example, you could enhance the presentation of facts about TOA by inserting the drawing into the worksheet. To do this you use the Insert command from the Graph menu. The procedure is the same as for inserting a numeric graph (described in Chapter 8). You select a named graph from the list provided and then indicate a block of cells for the graph to occupy.

WYSIWYG mode inserted graphs appear with impressive effects, as shown in Figure 13-21. Note that a circle and some clouds were added to the basic filled polygon to make the chart shown. The results of printing from this spreadsheet, including the inserted graph and the text with bullet characters, is shown in Figure 13-22. Remember that to print the inserted drawing and text together you must include both in the Print Block. Bear in mind that when you insert a drawn graph into a spreadsheet, the entire graphic is placed. You cannot place objects smaller than the full graph view screen. Although the Graph Insert command reduces the graph to fit the block of cells you define for it, the text in the spreadsheet will need to be placed outside of the insert block to be visible and printable. The graph can be inserted over text or numbers, but these will be hidden in the display and in any printout of that section of the worksheet.

Note that you must be using graphic display mode to see the graph in your worksheet. In character mode the inserted graph appears as a permanently highlighted blank block of cells. You may find that Quattro Pro 4's response time slows down when you are in graphics mode and have inserted one or more graphs into a worksheet. Furthermore, keeping track of cells that contain special formats, lines, and fonts can be cumbersome when you are engaged in writing formulas and setting up

Viewing the inserted graph

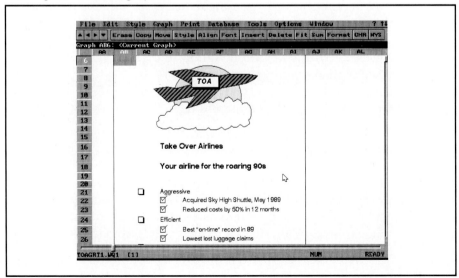

Printed results

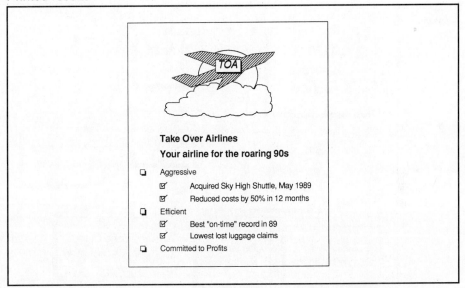

numerical analyses. For this reason you might want to consider placing highly formatted entries in a special worksheet and feeding data to that worksheet from a less intensely formatted worksheet, using linked cell reference formulas. This enables you to work quickly on one worksheet while providing correct numbers to the presentation worksheet.

You can use the Annotate feature for such projects as organization charts and flow diagrams. Figure 13-23 shows an example of an organization chart. All that you need for such a chart are a few lines and boxed text entries. The shadow attribute was selected for the boxes and the center attribute was chosen for the text with the Justify option. Although free-form drawing with Annotate is fun as well as practical, one of the primary uses of the feature is to enhance graphs, as seen in Chapter 8.

Power Slide Shows

The Graph Name Slide command in Quattro Pro 4 adds a new dimension to spreadsheet graphics, giving you the ability to develop

FIGURE 13-23 Organization chart printed from Quattro Pro 4

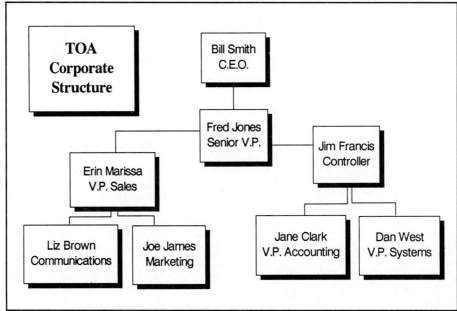

self-running presentations based on your Quattro Pro 4 graphs. A series of graphs are displayed one after another like a slide show. Quattro Pro 4 takes the information about each graph from a list of graphs. You can develop your own slide shows fairly easily or view one put together by another Quattro Pro 4 user.

Making a Slide Show

A slide show actually consists of two columns of information entered into the worksheet. The first column contains the graph names. The second column contains a list of numbers that indicate the length of time, in seconds, that each graph is to be displayed. In Figure 13-24 you can see a slide show arranged in columns A and B. The first slide, called INTRO, is identified in cell A13 and is to be displayed for ten seconds. The names you use in the first column are those assigned to your graphs with the Graph Name Create command. The graphs must be named in

FIGURE
13-24
Slide show instructions

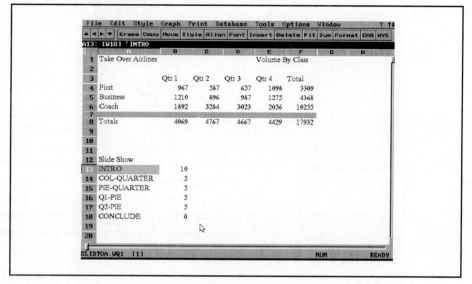

the current worksheet, although you can display graphs from the current worksheet that use data supplied by other worksheets.

When you issue the Graph Name Slide command you must identify the block of cells containing the slide show instructions. In Figure 13-24 the block is A13..B18. When you enter the coordinates the show begins. Each slide is displayed in turn, for the specified period of time. You can make the display self-paced by having the user press a key to advance to the next slide. You do this by entering **0** in the second column instead of a number of seconds. When Quattro Pro 4 encounters a graph name with 0 for the display time, such as the CONCLUDE graph in Figure 13-24, it waits until a key is pressed before going on to the next graph.

Suppose you have created a number of Quattro Pro 4 graphs that you want to use to highlight points in a sales presentation. Printed versions of the graphs form part of your handout. However, you would like to display the graphs during your speech for extra impact. You have a large-screen monitor connected to your PC so that the graphs can be seen properly, but you are nervous about having to type a series of instructions every time you want to move to a new graph. This is where the slide show feature comes in.

Instead of having to type a series of Graph Name Display commands and having to pick the correct graph name each time, you can use the slide show list to control your graphs. This avoids the F10 key and the constant need to return to the Graph menu. When a slide show is running you cannot tell that the program is actually a spreadsheet. If you need to break out of a slide show while it is running, perhaps to resume manual control of graphs, you can always press CTRL-BREAK. If Quattro Pro 4 encounters a graph name that does not exist in the current worksheet, it goes on to the next graph in the list. To provide complete control over a slide show and automate the process even further, you can use macro commands, as described in the next section. Before using a slide show in a live presentation, always do a dry run to make sure the graphs appear as you want them to. This will also ensure that all the fonts required by the graphs have been built; otherwise, the slide show will pause while fonts are built, which detracts from the professional appearance of the show.

Slide Show Macros

The ability to start a slide show with a macro and to make slide displays dependent on keystrokes gives you the ability to make some very sophisticated presentations with Quattro Pro 4. Slide shows are activated by the macro command

{/ Graph;NameSlide}

This is followed by the coordinates of the slide show instructions. Typically, you will use a block name for this to simplify matters. The following macro presents a slide show stored in the block named SALES as soon as the worksheet is retrieved:

\0 {/ Graph;NameSlide}SALES~

To make self-paced presentations you can use text graphs that contain instructions together with the \GRAPHCHAR\ command, which returns user input during graph display. Figure 13-25 shows an instruction graph that was created with the Annotate feature and named INTRO1. The following macro code is used to display it and handle user input:

```
SLIDES                    {/ Graph;NameUse}INTRO1~
                          {GRAPHCHAR RESPONSE}
                          {If RESPONSE="1"}{Branch VOLMAC}
                          {If RESPONSE="2"}{Branch REVMAC}
                          {Branch NEXT}
```

When the macro SLIDES is executed, the INTRO1 graph is displayed, and Quattro Pro 4 waits until the user presses a key. The {GRAPHCHAR} command places the user's response in a cell named RESPONSE and the {IF} statement evaluates the contents of this cell. If the user presses 1, the macro branches to code called VOLMAC. If the user presses 2, the macro branches to code called REVMAC. If the user presses any other key, the macro continues to the last line, branching to NEXT. The macro VOLMAC looks like this:

```
VOLMAC                    {/ Graph;NameSlide}VOLUME~
                          {Branch SLIDES}
```

The block named VOLUME contains the data for a slide show. The macro REVMAC is similar and looks like the following:

FIGURE 13-25

Graph giving instructions

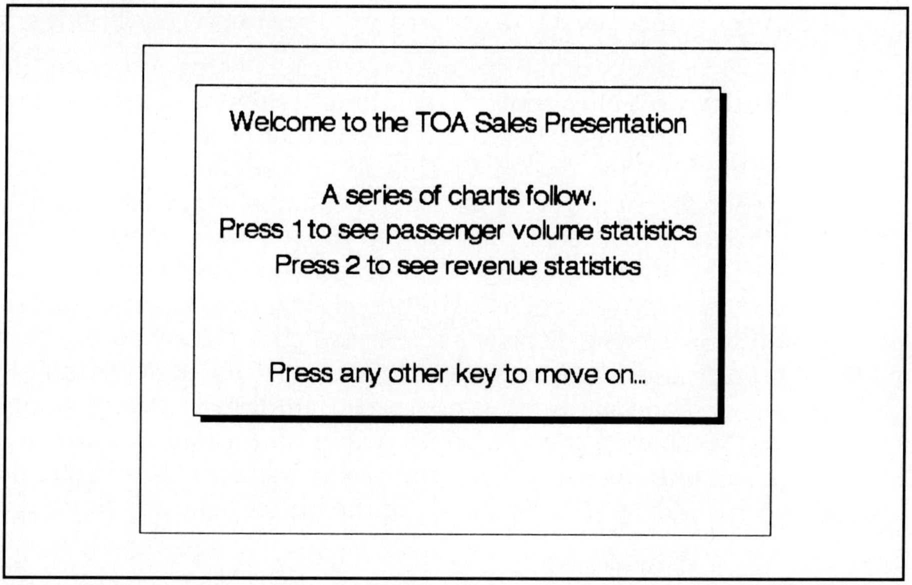

```
REVMAC              {/ Graph;NameSlide}REVENUE~
                    {Branch SLIDES}
```

There must be a cell named RESPONSE for the macro to work. The code loops the user back to the instruction screen until a key other than 1 or 2 is pressed. The {GRAPHCHAR} command is very useful for displaying graphs that act as menus. You can also use it with the {MESSAGE} command to get user response from a screen message. The {MESSAGE} command is discussed later in this chapter.

Graph Buttons

As you can see, the {/ Graph;NameUse} and {GRAPHCHAR} commands can be combined to create an interactive macro to display graphs, although the macro code required can get quite complex. The alternative method of displaying a series of slides, the Graph Name Slide command and its macro equivalent, is simpler, but it is strictly linear, only capable of displaying a series of graphs one after the other (you can press BACKSPACE during a slide show to go back one slide in the list, but this halts the slide show until another key is pressed). In Quattro Pro 4 the graph display system supports branching, enabling the user to choose what comes next. The feature that makes this possible is graph buttons. These can be used independently of the Graph Name Slide command.

You place a graph button on a graph using Annotate. Each graph button can "call" another named graph, causing it to be displayed. Graph buttons are simply boxed text objects that have the Graph Button option activated. When you have created and selected a boxed text object in Annotate you will see that Graph Button is one of the properties for that object. If you select Graph Button you are shown a list of named graphs for the current worksheet. The graph you select from the list is the one that is displayed when the button is activated. When a graph containing buttons is being displayed a user can click on any button to display the graph named by that button. You can see an example in Figure 13-26, where there are three buttons, each leading to a different graph. Typically you will have some text on the graph that explains to the user how the graph buttons work. Note that you do not have to activate the buttons with a mouse. The first letter of the button text can be used to activate

FIGURE
13-26

Graph of all classes with three buttons

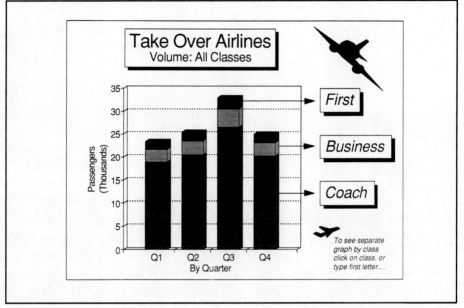

the button (for example, in Figure 13-26 you would type **F** for the graph of First Class volume).

This ability of graphs to call other graphs gives you tremendous flexibility when you develop presentations. If you are going to present a series of graphs/slides to an audience, the connections between graphs will make it much easier for you to navigate your way through the material and will give you the impressive ability to jump between connected graphs without having to cycle through a whole stack. If you are creating a presentation that users will view at their own pace, you can link related screens together in a way that gives the viewer an active rather than a passive role, making the experience more enjoyable and thus more memorable. Indeed, with Quattro Pro 4 you have "hypertext" capabilities that go far beyond a simple sequence of images. Hypertext is a way of presenting information that depends on multiple links between associated items, using lateral as well as linear connections.

Applying Graph Buttons

The key to a successful hypertext presentation using graph buttons is planning. The first step is to decide what graphs you need to make. Then you can use either pencil and paper, or a Quattro Pro 4 graph, to sketch a flow chart of the graphs, as shown in Figure 13-27. This will help you decide how many buttons each graph needs and which graphs each button will call. The flow chart does not have to be fancy, but it can be quite complicated. In Figure 13-27, which shows the buttons used in Figure 13-26, there are only four graphs involved: one for all classes combined and one for each of the three classes graphed separately. As you can see, even this simple arrangement requires a total of six graph buttons. (In the figure, each arrow represents one button.)

After you have decided on the flow of graphs, create and name each graph that is to be used by a graph button. This must be done before the buttons can be properly set up. However, you do not have to perfect each graph before you set up the buttons. (In fact, when you choose Graph Button from the Properties list for Boxed Text in the Annotate feature,

FIGURE 13-27

Flow chart for graph button

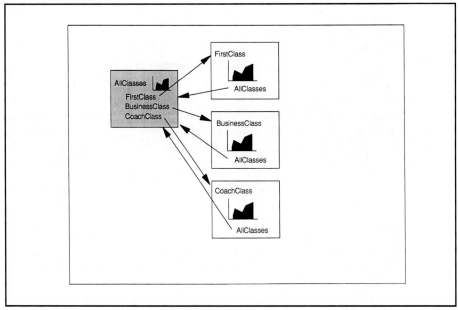

you can type in a graph name that does not yet exist, but you cannot use the button properly until a graph has been given that name.) Any graph can be safely worked on later *if* you remember to use the Name Create command after making changes.

When you have made the graphs you can place the buttons on them. Remember that a graph button is essentially a boxed text object. Also bear in mind that boxed text can be displayed without a box, turning it into free-floating text. You can make a graph button out of text you have already added to a graph by selecting the text and then choosing Graph Button from the Properties list (you cannot directly attach a graph button to standard chart text). You can also create a fresh piece of text to be used as a graph button, and you can even create "blank" buttons to be used with icons, such as the coffee cup on the "Pause the show" button in Figure 13-28. Note that the sculpted look of the buttons in Figure 13-28 was drawn in. You can also use the sculpted style for buttons that match those of Quattro Pro 4's WYSIWYG mode.

To create a blank button you select the text tool and choose None for the Box Type. Then, instead of typing characters, you press the SPACEBAR a number of times to create a shape of the size you want (select a large

FIGURE 13-28 Menu graph with "Pause the show" button

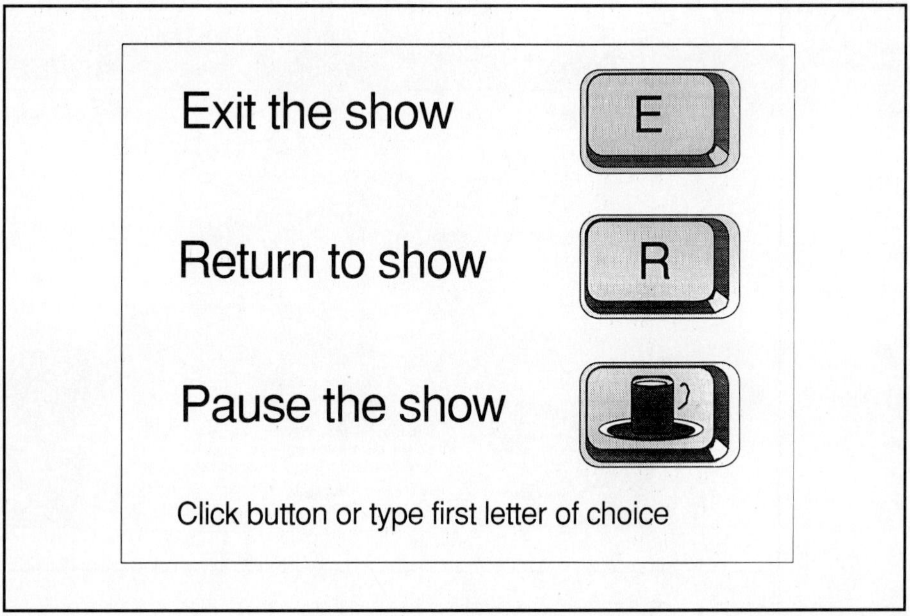

font size to give the box height). When you press ENTER you will have a clear rectangle that you can place over an icon. Choose Graph Button in the usual manner and enter the name of the graph that you want the button to call. This technique enables you to "hide" a graph button within a graph, so that, for example, each of the four bars in Figure 13-26 could lead to a pie chart of the appropriate quarter.

In Quattro Pro 4 you can also create a "default" button from the background of your graph. The Background properties include Bkg Button, so you can create a button that is effective whenever the user clicks on part of the graph that is not specifically designed as a button. This provides a form of error trapping in your slide shows.

The graph you see in Figure 13-28 is essentially a graphic menu. This gives you some idea of how you can place user controls into the series of graphs you are presenting. The series may be started by the Graph Name Display command. The first graph might look something like Figure 13-29, giving the user instructions. The graph in 13-26 would be selected by the Begin button. The graph in Figure 13-28 might be universally referred to as "Other" and referenced by buttons on many of the charts,

FIGURE 13-29

Opening graph with instructions

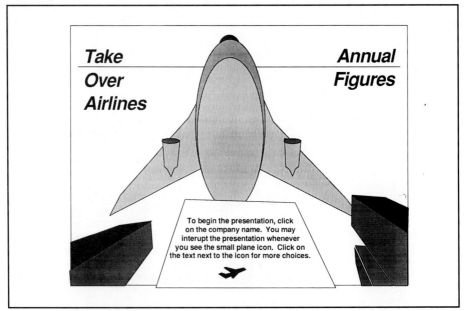

such as the one in Figure 13-30, which is the Business Class breakdown, displayed when the user clicks the Business button in Figure 13-26. Note the way the bars are filled with images of passengers. This type of histogram is created by using the Graph Customize Series menu to select Blank as the Fill Pattern for the series. The image is then drawn with Annotate. The drawing can be quite large when first created, then reduced in size to fit the columns before being duplicated using the Clipboard Copy and Paste commands.

Graph Button Strategies

As you can see, the ability to branch from one graph to another opens up a wealth of possibilities. The previous example can be set up without using the slide show command. The presentation simply begins when the first graph, Figure 13-29, is displayed. However, this type of presentation requires user input at every screen to trigger the next graph.

FIGURE 13-30

Graph of Business Class volume

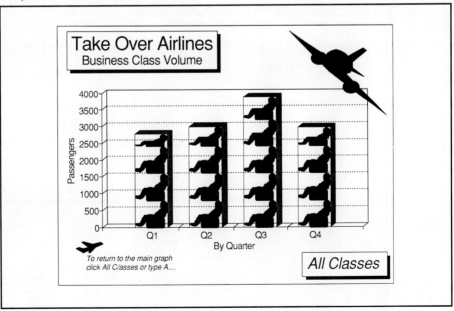

Another simple application of buttons is to include a button-equipped graph in a slide show. This enables the user to choose between several different sequences but also allows some graphs to be displayed automatically, on a timed basis, rather than having to wait for user input.

For example, suppose that you have graphs of volume figures and revenue figures for all classes of passenger and for each of the three classes. You create a beginning graph called OPENING, as shown in Figure 13-31, which gives the user a choice between volume and revenue figures. The slide show cells might appear as in Figure 13-32.

When the show begins the OPENING graph is displayed until the user selects one of the two buttons, leading either to TOTAL_REV or TOTAL_VOL. If the user selects Revenue, the TOTAL_REV appears, for a limited time, before leading to the next graph in the list, FIRST_REV. The BUSIN_REV and COACH_REV graphs then appear in timed sequence, followed by OPENING, which stays on screen until the user makes a selection. If the user selects Volume—either before or after viewing Revenue—then TOTAL_VOL appears, for a limited time, before leading to the next graph in the list, FIRST_VOL. The BUSIN_VOL and COACH_VOL

Opening graph with revenue/volume choice

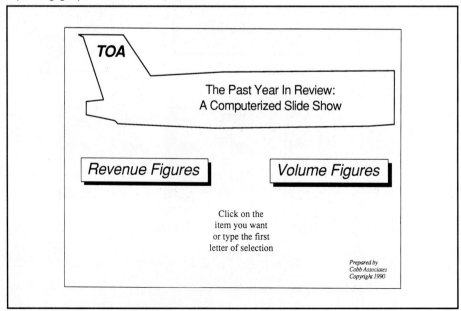

FIGURE
13-32

Slide show entries

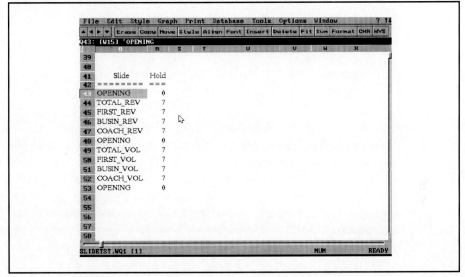

graphs then appear automatically, followed by OPENING, which stays on screen until the user makes a selection. Note that the OPENING graph is required in the middle of the sequence; otherwise, the flow would proceed from Revenue through all revenue *and* volume graphs, whereas the Volume option would only show volume graphs.

Further Slide Show Effects

Several new slide show features were added in Quattro Pro 4, notably visual and audio slide show transition effects that can be used in slide shows and with graph buttons. Normally, when one slide replaces another, the first slide disappears and the second one is drawn on screen. This transition gets the job done, but it is not very exciting. If a slide is complicated, the drawing process can be slow, and there is the possibility that the viewer's attention will wander. In Quattro Pro 4 you can use special visual slide transition effects to move from one slide to another while your presentation is holding and even heightening the viewer's attention.

There are the 24 transition effects in the following categories:

❑   Horizontal wipes (single and double edged)

❑   Vertical wipes (single and double edged)

❑   Spirals

❑   Dissolves

The full range of transition effects is listed in Table 13-4. Each has a range of speeds at which it can operate. You set up these visual effects by entering the appropriate number in a third column added to a slide show block. A fourth column is used to determine how long it will take for the effect to make the transition from one slide to the next, that is, the speed of the effect. In Figure 13-33 you can see two columns, Effect and Speed, added to the earlier slide show to control the transition effects (the fifth column, Sound, will be discussed in a moment).

This expanded table means that the OPENING screen appears spiralled in from the edges (effect 17), very quickly (Speed 0). On instruction from the user the slide TOTAL_REV is painted, spreading out from the center like an iris opening (effect 12), taking a few seconds to do so (speed

FIGURE 13-33

A slide show with visual and sound effects

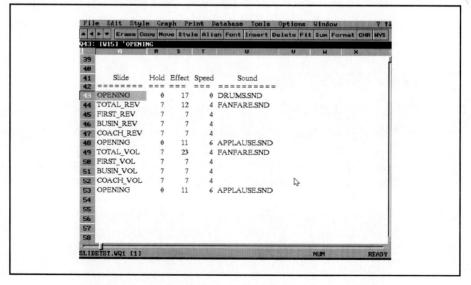

TABLE 13-4

Slide Show Transition Effects

Effect #	Speed Range	Description
1	0	Cut (instantaneous)
2	0	Switch to black, then new image
3	0–16	Wipe from right
4	0–16	Wipe from left
5	0–16	Wipe from bottom
6	0–16	Wipe from top
7	0–16	Barn door close (right/left to center)
8	0–16	Barn door open (center to right/left)
9	0–16	Barn door (top/bottom to center)
10	0–16	Barn door (center to top/bottom)
11	0–16	Iris close
12	0–16	Iris open
13	0–16	Scroll up
14	0–16	Scroll down
15	0–16	Vertical stripes right
16	0–16	Stripes right and then left
17	0–16	Spiral in
18	0–16	Dissolve, 2×1 rectangles
19	0–16	Dissolve, 2×2 squares
20	0–16	Dissolve, 4×4 squares
21	0–16	Dissolve, 8×8 squares
22	0–16	Dissolve, 16×16 squares
23	0–16	Dissolve, 32×32 squares
24	0–16	Dissolve, 64×64 squares

4). After 7 seconds' hold, FIRST_REV appears over the top of TOTAL_REV like a barn door closing (effect 7), also taking a few seconds (speed 4). The show progresses in this manner according to the parameters in the table. Entering 0 in the third column or leaving the cell blank indicates that a visual transition effect is not assigned to that slide.

Note that the speed measurement is relative to the hardware you are using and to the type of effect. For example, a speed of 4 for effect 12 results in about 4 seconds of transition time. A speed of 4 for effect 17 results in a 13-second transition. This is simply because some effects are more complex than others.

Transition effects also enable you to overlay one slide with another rather than simply replace it. Entering the transition effect number as a negative indicates that the transition effect will be used to overlay the current slide with the next slide. For example, if you enter **–19** in the third column of your slide show, the new slide is overlaid on the existing one using a slow dissolve. This opens up terrific possibilities for presentations. Suppose you have a text chart summarizing a series of points you want to make. The complete chart consists of a title line and three bulleted items. As you create the chart you name a copy at each stage, as follows:

❏   Title only—CHART0

❏   Title with first point—CHART1

❏   Title with first and second points—CHART2

❏   Title with all three points—CHART3

Your slide show can then present CHART0, the title. When you are ready to make your first point you transition to CHART1 as an overlay. Because the title in CHART1 is in exactly the same place as in CHART0, the title itself therefore does not appear to change. The effect gives the appearance of the first point being written onto the chart. The same happens when the second point is overlaid by a transition to CHART2, and so on.

Although slide transition effects are difficult to describe in print, they look very effective in a presentation. Figure 13-34 shows you how some of these effects operate, but the best way to get to know them is by experimentation.

Because the slide show transition effects place a heavy demand on video memory, Quattro Pro 4 displays them in EGA resolution even if you

FIGURE
13-34

Diagram of visual effects

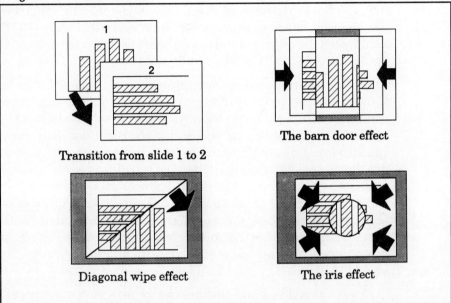

Transition from slide 1 to 2

The barn door effect

Diagonal wipe effect

The iris effect

have a VGA graphics adapter. This does not seriously impair the appearance of the slides. When you give the command to start a slide show, Quattro Pro 4 checks the slide show block to see whether it contains a third column. If it does, Quattro Pro 4 automatically switches your display to 640×350 EGA resolution, then returns it to the previous resolution when the slide show is over.

The finishing touch for Quattro Pro 4 presentations is sound effects. These can be incorporated in slide shows, graph buttons, and macros without additional equipment. The sound effects are digitized sound files stored on disk with the extension .SND. You can use sound effects in the following ways:

❏ Slide show (enter the sound file name in the fifth column of the slide show block, as shown in Figure 13-33).

❏ Graph button (after the visual effect speed, insert a semicolon and the file name).

❏ Macro (use the {PLAY *filename*} command).

Quattro Pro 4 assumes the sound file is in the program directory and the file name extension is .SND, unless you specify otherwise. You can see a sound effect column in the slide show in Figure 13-33. You can usually tell the nature of the sound effect from the file name. For example, file THANKYOU.SND is likely to be someone saying "Thank you."

Playing sounds makes extra demands on your PC hardware. If the sounds are distorted or fail to play, remove unnecessary items from your computer setup. Sounds might not work if your system is logged onto a network, if RAM-resident programs are running, or if you're running Quattro Pro 4 under Windows in Enhanced mode. These limitations are not that severe when compared to the terrific quality of sound the system provides, even through the small speaker on a normal PC (if you have facilities for an external speaker, the results are quite dramatic). For serious presentations you are likely to use a dedicated PC that will not need to run programs that interfere with the sound system. Quattro Pro 4 is shipped with several sound files, including FANFARE, THANKYOU, and APPLAUSE.

Transition effects and sounds can be attached to graph buttons even if the graphs containing the buttons are not part of a Quattro Pro 4 slide show. Quattro Pro 4 uses semicolons as delimiters to distinguish which type of effect is requested. To attach special effects to a graph button, use the following syntax:

Slide;Hold;Effect;Speed;Sound

where *Slide* is the name of the graph, *Hold* is the length of time it is to be displayed, *Effect* is the type of transition, *Speed* is the rate of transition, and *Sound* is the name of an .SND file. For example, you could attach OPENING;2;19;2;DRUMS to a graph button. When you click the button, a slow dissolve (effect 19) at speed 2 will fade into a graph called OPENING, which will display for 2 seconds. The transition will be accompanied by the DRUMS sound effect. If a graph button with special effects is used in a slide show, the number of seconds to display the next graph is ignored, but the visual and sound effects you specify on the button will be used. You can skip any item of the syntax by stacking semicolons with nothing between them (for this reason you should avoid semicolons within graph names).

If you use visual effects in graph buttons that are not in a slide show block, Quattro Pro 4 cannot automatically slip into 640×350 EGA resolution to display the effects. When using graph buttons that call various graphs or macros with effects, you should manually set Options Hardware Screen Resolution to 640×350 EGA before you begin the presentation.

By creating a macro to launch a presentation driven by graph buttons, you can automate the process of setting the screen resolution to 640×350 EGA before you begin your presentation. Simply begin the macro by changing screen resolution, then call the first graph of your presentation.

Graph Button Macros

Both the automated slide show technique and the user-prompted named-graph approach can be further enhanced with macros. You can use {/ Graph;SlideShow} to launch a slide show. From that point until the end of the show, the slide show feature takes control of user input. The only keys that are allowed are

CTRL-BREAK	Terminates the show and returns you to the worksheet
letters	The first character of any graph button text, which displays the slide attached to that button and branches to that part of the show
any other key	Ends the slide show if the last slide is displayed; otherwise it triggers the next sequence of slides
BACKSPACE	Freezes the current slide if on timed display; otherwise backs up one slide in the series

Note that you can use the right mouse button instead of BACKSPACE. If you prefer to exercise more direct control over the flow of charts and the handling of user input, you can start a button-driven presentation with {/ Graph;NameUse}. You can trigger the display of graphs with graph buttons, and even use graph buttons to run macro commands. Graph button macros give you almost unlimited power to control a series of events using the simplest of user interfaces: clicking a mouse.

A graph button macro can either be a named macro from the current worksheet or an open macro library, or it can be a separate piece of macro code up to 80 characters in length. You will recall that when you select

Graph Button from the Properties list you are prompted for a graph name. In fact, you can type a macro name instead or even a piece of macro code. For example, suppose you want to give viewers of a presentation the ability to print out a graph. You create a piece of boxed text on the graph that says Print. This will be the print button. You select Graph Button and enter {/ GraphPrint;Go} instead of a graph name. When the user clicks this button the currently displayed graph will be sent to the printer.

Note that graphs running in slide shows cannot use graph buttons for macros. When using a graph button to run a macro, Quattro Pro 4 returns to spreadsheet mode to execute the macro. Unless the macro specifically redisplays a graph, Quattro Pro 4 will not pass control back to graphics mode.

Of course, you will probably want to include a command that returns the user to the presentation after the print task. For example, this code displays the OPENING graph after the print task:

{/ GraphPrint;Go}{/ Graph;NameUse}OPENING~

If you want to provide the print feature on a lot of graphs you might want to set up a print macro in the worksheet like this:

```
GPRINT              {/ GraphPrint;Dest1sPtr}
                    {/ GraphPrint;Go}
```

This macro, called GPRINT, makes sure that the print destination is set to the graphics printer before beginning the print operation. To run this macro from a graph button you would enter {GPRINT} instead of a graph name. Note that named macros must be enclosed in braces for Quattro Pro 4 to recognize them when called from graph buttons.

A simple technique for returning the user to the current graph is to use a temporary name for the graph. For example, to have the GPRINT macro print the current graph and then redisplay it, you can use the following lines of code:

```
GPRINT              {/ Graph;NameCreate}CURRENT~
                    {/ GraphPrint;Dest1sPtr}
                    {/ GraphPrint;Go}
                    {/ Graph;NameUse}CURRENT~
```

This stores the currently displayed graph under the name CURRENT so that it can be recalled. It is still safely stored under its original name as well.

Graph button macros can be used to execute complex procedures beyond presentations. Indeed, with Quattro Pro 4 it is possible to use the macro ability of graph buttons to create mouse-operated, menu-driven information systems that even computer shy executives can use. In Figure 13-35 you can see what an executive information system might look like, dressed up in a graph menu. The Retrieve data button runs a macro that downloads current information from Paradox into the worksheet, based on parameters supplied by the user as the macro runs. The Analyze data button places the user in the spreadsheet area and carries out several calculations. The Chart data button displays a standard set of charts created from the data. Finally, the Home menu button takes the user to a screen where the current session can be saved, reports printed, and so on.

FIGURE
13-35

Information system menu

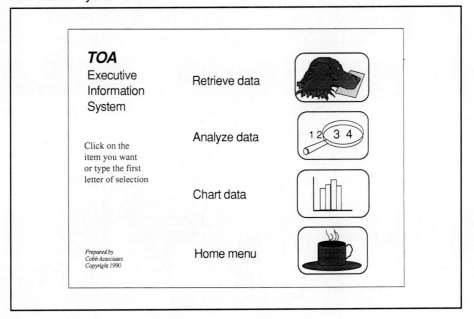

Another example can be seen in Figure 13-36. Here a map of the world, copied from the clip art file WORLDMAP.CLP, is used as the basis for accessing information about each of the airline's destinations. To insert the clip art that comes with Quattro Pro 4, you use the Paste From command on the Clipboard. To learn more about the clip art library, paste the 1-README.CLP file into a blank graph. To store your own creations as clip art to be used in other graphs simply select the object or group of objects and use the Copy To command on the Clipboard. You are then prompted for a name for the file. To move an object out of the current graph and into a file use Cut To instead of Copy To. In Figure 13-36 the world map was adjusted and the polar subcontinents were removed. Each city name added to the map then had a graph button macro attached to it, leading to details of that city.

Messages Without Pictures

Users with systems that do not have the graphics capability needed to make the most of annotated images and graph buttons may want to

FIGURE 13-36   A graphic menu with clip art

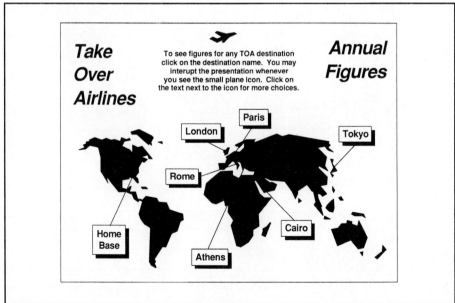

explore the {MESSAGE} command. This can be used to display boxed message text that appears over the top of your regular work area, as opposed to a graphic screen. Messages to users can be displayed during macro execution. The {MESSAGE} command can display the message text for a period of time or until a key is pressed. The {MESSAGE} command takes the form

{MESSAGE *Block,Left,Top,Time*}

where *Block* is the cell or cells occupied by the message text, *Left* and *Top* are the screen coordinates for the message box, and *Time* is the length of time for the message to be displayed. The block coordinates must be wide enough for the whole piece of text to be displayed. For example, in Figure 13-37 you can see a macro called MESS01. This can be called by another macro when a message needs to be displayed. The macro refers to a message block called MSGA. This is actually cells B62..G62. If you use a smaller block, the message will be truncated. This means that you cannot simply name MSGA with the Edit Names Labels command. To display the message called MSGB in Figure 13-37, you would have to name cells B64..F65 as MSGB.

FIGURE
13-37

Message macro

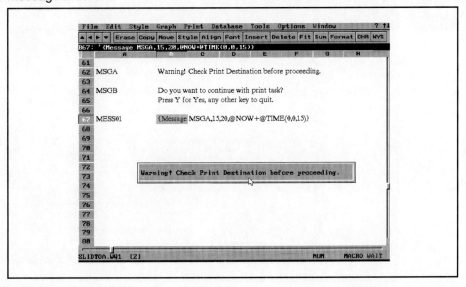

The macro MESS01 produces the results shown in Figure 13-37. The boxed message stays on the screen for 15 seconds, as defined by the formula @NOW+@TIME(0,0,15). The macro that calls this routine is suspended for that period of time, as indicated by the WAIT message in the lower right of the screen. If you enter 0 for the time, the macro pauses until the user presses a key, at which point the macro continues with whatever code is on the next line. The screen coordinates of the message displayed in Figure 13-37 are 15 characters from the left of the screen and 20 rows from the top, as defined by the *Left* and *Top* arguments. This locates the top left of the box.

By combining {MESSAGE} with the {GRAPGCHAR} command you can display messages and get user responses. Figure 13-38 shows a macro called MESS02, which displays the message shown in the figure, and waits for user response. When the user types **Y** the macro branches to CONTINUE, which in this case is a test macro of beeps. If the user presses any other key, the macro quits. Note that both lower- and uppercase Y are acceptable as a response. Also note the position of the message box, which is further across the screen and lower down than the one in Figure 13-37, as indicated by the screen coordinates of 25,15.

The {MESSAGE} and {GRAPHCHAR} commands make for convenient single-key user input routines. A series of {IF} statements can be used to

FIGURE
13-38

Message macro with question

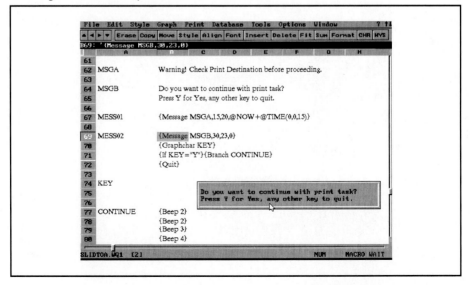

evaluate a whole range of inputs and branch to different macro routines, making this yet another means of providing a menu for users. The {MESSAGE} command can also be useful in presentation macros when the user needs to be returned to the worksheet during macro execution. A reassuring message can be displayed momentarily to assure the user that the graphics will reappear in a moment.

Presentation Tips

Given the power of Quattro Pro 4's graphic commands you may well decide to use this feature for preparing presentations. To ensure that your presentation is a success bear in mind the following design guidelines and presentation tips.

Keep It Simple

With Quattro Pro 4 you can produce excellent graphs as long as you follow the golden rule of graphics: Keep it simple. Use several separate graphs instead of placing too much on one graph. Remember that the key elements of a good graph are

❑ Unity

❑ Balance

❑ Contrast

❑ Meaning

If your graphs contain all four elements, they will be an effective means of communicating information. In the rush to add visual interest to everything that passes for information in today's office it is possible to end up with "chart junk." This is when someone goes too far in dressing up an otherwise clear and understandable chart. If you feel the urge to add drawings and clip art to a chart, step back after each addition and ask yourself whether they really add to the impact and clarity of the information being presented.

The Value of Text

In some situations there is no substitute for a number chart or data table. This is essentially a printed report with the numbers in the spreadsheet arranged in columns and rows with titles and totals. When you need to provide extensive detail as well as summary information, a spreadsheet printout is sometimes the best type of report to use. As you have seen in this chapter, there are several techniques that enable you to make charts with Quattro Pro 4 without using the graph commands. Particularly when it comes to word charts, Quattro Pro 4's publishing features help you to organize your words and print them out in attractive designs.

When you have the chance to use color in presenting information you should heed the words of Aristotle about painting: "The most brilliant colors, spread at random and without design, will give far less pleasure than the simplest outline of a figure." If you do not have a color display or printer you are not as limited in your presentation abilities as you may assume. Effective use of shading, fill patterns, and fonts can create stunning designs, which are usually cheaper to reproduce than color. Do not go to great lengths to produce charts in color unless there is a real need for them to be in color.

Slide Shows

When you have a lot of graphs to display you can use the slide show feature in Quattro Pro 4 to make presentations with your PC. How you actually mount the show depends on the facilities at your disposal. You may have a large monitor, an overhead adapter, or other wide-screen systems. Some of these systems have limited resolution and palettes. The first design consideration in such cases is to know what the final display method will be. Then you can choose your colors and fonts based on the way they look to the audience, not how they appear to you on your PC.

If you look at how television news programs use text and images you will see that they keep them simple to compensate for the fuzziness of TV images. If you have to use a fuzzy display system avoid putting text directly over images and choose bright colors. Text can be seen better as light on a darker background or when outlined in black to separate it from other images.

A good method of reinforcing your message and avoiding complete disaster when equipment fails during a presentation is to make printouts of all your slides and have them ready as handouts. These need not be in color, but having them closely match your slide show will increase the staying power of your message.

The Human Factor

Always remember that the key to a good presentation is not equipment or even handouts, it is the presenter. Computers and audio-visual equipment can be very effective, but without a good speaker they are a waste of money. A good speaker can get the message across even if the equipment fails, the handouts are late, and the room is cold and drafty. A good speaker will be warm, affable, and talk directly to the audience, making eye contact with as many people as possible. A lively and humorous approach is usually the most effective, particularly if the subject matter is essentially dry. A good speaker will enunciate clearly and adjust speed and volume to the specific audience, so that they feel this is a presentation made specially for them, not something you have done a dozen times already. Practice your presentation to friends and colleagues before going live, and when you are presenting to a real audience try for a relaxed demeanor. You will find that any time you step onto a platform you automatically create an impression of authority that can carry you through moments of hesitation.

Conclusion

This book has taken you from the basics of spreadsheet operation to the sophistication of graphics, macros, and even custom menus. You should not expect to retain everything you have seen on first reading. In many ways, the tremendous power of a program like Quattro Pro 4 is equivalent to that of an entire programming language, which students may take several semesters to study. You should not expect to learn or use all of Quattro Pro 4's capabilities right away. Unlike most programming languages, however, Quattro Pro 4 is easily applied to practical tasks almost immediately. You can also have fun with Quattro Pro 4, designing impressive graphs, charts, and drawings. Many examples of Quattro Pro 4 at work are given throughout the book, but the best way to become familiar with Quattro Pro 4 is to consider the tasks you perform in your own work and try to apply Quattro Pro 4 to them. By using Quattro Pro 4 you will get to know Quattro Pro 4, and you will become more productive and creative in the process.

APPENDIX

Installing Quattro Pro 4

*Q*uattro Pro 4 uses sophisticated programming techniques to make installation and startup a simple process despite the wide variety of hardware on which the program runs. Using the commands on the Options menu you can adjust most aspects of the way in which the program runs, as described in Chapter 6. However, to further integrate Quattro Pro 4 into your personal computer system, you may want to employ some of the techniques described in this appendix.

Basic Installation

Quattro Pro 4 arrives on a number of floppy disks that contain compressed files. You install Quattro Pro 4 by using the INSTALL program on the first disk (the one that has the serial number on it). Because the INSTALL program requires quite a large amount of memory, run it when you have booted up your PC and do not have any programs loaded.

To begin, place the first disk in your floppy disk drive. At the DOS prompt type **A:** and press ENTER (if you are using drive B, type **B:**). Now type **INSTALL** and press ENTER (if you are using a black-and-white monitor type **INSTALL /B**). Answer the questions the INSTALL program asks about the source drive and the hard disk directory you want to use. The necessary files from disk 1 will then be transferred to the hard disk, and the next disk will be requested. You will be asked which style of menus you want to use. The normal choice is QUATTRO.MU, the regular Quattro Pro 4 menus. This is highly recommended. Check Chapters 6 and 12 if you want to alter menus, and consult Appendix B if you want to operate Quattro Pro 4 in 1-2-3 mode.

When all of the files have been copied, Quattro Pro 4 will ask you to enter a company name and user name to identify your copy of the program. Also, you must enter the serial number from disk 1. Then you can choose a printer to use with Quattro Pro 4. Note that you can add other printers later using the Options Hardware command. To complete the installation, Quattro Pro 4 asks whether you want to create any fonts. Creating at least a basic set of fonts is a good idea, because this prevents too many Building font delays when you start using the program. However, you can build a group of fonts after you have installed Quattro Pro 4 by loading the worksheet called INSTALL.WQ1. This automatically operates a font-building macro for you. Note that the SC fonts do not require prebuilding.

When the installation is complete, place the original disks in a safe place. Load Quattro Pro 4 and check that the Options Startup Directory is set to the directory you want to use for your data files. Use Options Update to make the choice permanent. Alternatively, you can leave this setting blank and load Quattro Pro 4 from the data directory of your choice whenever you begin a session. To be able to do this, the Quattro Pro 4 directory must be in your PATH statement. For more on directories and paths see the next section.

Enhanced Installation

After you complete the initial installation process for Quattro Pro 4 using the INSTALL program on the first program disk, there are several steps you can take to make Quattro Pro 4 more convenient to use. Although not essential to the program's operation, these steps may be of interest to experienced users, particularly if they are setting up Quattro Pro 4 for less-experienced users.

Configuration File Enhancement

To efficiently use Quattro Pro 4 on your system you may need to fine tune the way the system, not just Quattro Pro 4, is configured. One file that greatly affects system performance is CONFIG.SYS. Remember that when your computer starts up, it looks to the floppy disk in drive A for DOS. If DOS is found on the disk in drive A, it is loaded into RAM. If not, the system looks to the hard disk, drive C, if you have one installed. If DOS is found on drive C, it is loaded into memory. One of the first pieces of information DOS looks for when it is loaded is the configuration file, CONFIG.SYS. This file contains information about how your system is configured.

If DOS does not find a CONFIG.SYS file it assumes certain default conditions. However, you will need to establish some settings with CONFIG.SYS when you run Quattro Pro 4. In fact, Quattro Pro 4's

INSTALL program can update the CONFIG.SYS file for you during initial installation. The two settings that affect Quattro Pro 4 involve two aspects of the way DOS manages information in RAM: buffers and files.

The number of buffers (temporary holding areas into which DOS can put information your programs use) is normally five. The number of open files that DOS can keep track of is normally 8. By increasing these settings with a CONFIG.SYS file, you can improve the speed with which DOS manipulates information in your system. A setting of 20 for buffers and 20 for files is often used. The settings are established by placing the following instructions in the CONFIG.SYS file:

BUFFERS = 20
FILES = 20

The instructions can be upper- or lowercase letters. They are placed one instruction per line. This may have been done to your system when you installed Quattro Pro 4; however, it is a good idea to check out the CONFIG.SYS file on your system.

You can check whether your system has a CONFIG.SYS file by typing the command DIR *.SYS at the DOS prompt while you are in the root directory of your hard disk or on the floppy disk with which you start your system. If you find a CONFIG.SYS file, you can examine its contents with the TYPE command, as in

TYPE CONFIG.SYS

If you plan to change the CONFIG.SYS file or create a new one, you should copy the original file to another file, such as CONFIG.OLD. You do this at the DOS prompt with the command

COPY CONFIG.SYS CONFIG.OLD

A new CONFIG.SYS file can then be created with the DOS COPY command. Type the following at the DOS prompt:

COPY CON CONFIG.SYS

After this press ENTER. The ENTER key gives you the first line for an instruction. Type the instruction, for example, **FILES = 20**, and then press ENTER for another line. After the last line of instruction, press F6 and then ENTER again. The file will be written to the disk. (Pressing F6 produces the CTRL-Z code, which DOS reads as meaning end-of-file.) This CONFIG.SYS file is a pure ASCII file. You could also create one with SideKick's Notepad, WordStar in the nondocument mode, and many other word processors that can save text in ASCII format.

Hard Disk Enhancement

The Quattro Pro 4 installation program places the program files in a hard disk subdirectory, typically called \QPRO. A hard disk directory system for a computer running Quattro Pro 4 and WordPerfect might look like the one shown in Figure A-1, drawn with Quattro Pro 4's Annotate feature. Note that the directory containing Quattro Pro 4 is called \QPRO. You may use other names, such as \Q3, or \QUATTRO. Substitute the name you are using for QPRO in the following examples.

Navigating Directories

For DOS to find either a program file or a data file, you must specify a path for it to follow. For example, the path to the worksheet file called PROJECT.WQ1 in the \SALES subdirectory of Quattro Pro 4 is \QPRO\SALES\. To identify files accurately on a hard disk, the path to the file becomes part of the file name. Thus, the full name of the PROJECT.WQ1 file is

C:\QPRO\SALES\PROJECT.WQ1

In order to navigate a hard disk with one or more subdirectories, you might want to change the uninformative C prompt, which tells you only that you are using drive C, to the C:\ prompt, which shows not only the current drive but also the path and the current subdirectory (in this case the root, or main directory). This more informative prompt will always tell you what subdirectory you are in. If you move into the Quattro Pro 4 subdirectory, the prompt will read

C:\QPRO>_

(If your hard disk is not drive C but drive D or E or any other valid letter, just substitute that letter for C in the instructions that follow.)

Hard disk directory system

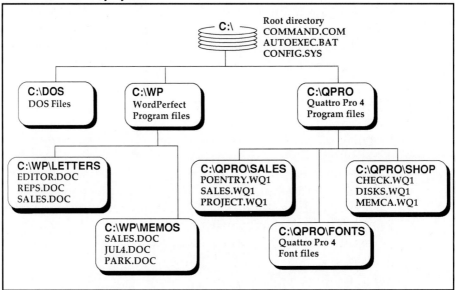

To change the prompt to a more informative version, type PROMPT PG at the C prompt. When you press ENTER you will see the drive letter, the path ($P) to whatever subdirectory you are in, and the greater-than sign ($G). Now change your location to a subdirectory such as the one for Quattro Pro 4. Type

CD \QPRO

and press ENTER. You will see your prompt change. To change your current location back to the root directory, type

CD\

and press ENTER.

Quattro Pro 4 data files should be kept in a separate directory from the program files. To create a subdirectory called \QWORK directly below the root directory, type

MD \QWORK

and press ENTER. To create a subdirectory called \MYWORK below the Quattro Pro 4 directory, type

MD \QPRO\MYWORK

and press ENTER. If you want to copy all the files from a disk in drive A into this new directory, you can move into the subdirectory by typing

CD \QPRO\MYWORK

pressing ENTER, and then entering

COPY A:*.*

Alternatively, you could type

COPY A:*.* C:\QPRO\MYWORK

from the root directory.

Using Batch Files

Unfortunately, DOS forgets the helpful PROMPT command when you turn off the system. To solve this problem, you use *batch files*, which are collections of instructions to DOS that are delivered in a group or batch. A batch file has the extension .BAT and is activated by typing the first part of the file name excluding the period and extension. For example, the file P.BAT might contain the following lines:

PROMPT PG
DIR/W

Typing P and pressing ENTER would tell DOS to change the prompt and then list the files in the current directory.

Every system can have a batch file called AUTOEXEC.BAT, which DOS looks for when the system starts up. For example, you might want to go straight to Quattro Pro 4 every time you turn on your computer. The following AUTOEXEC.BAT file on the hard disk would accomplish the following:

```
DATE
TIME
ECHO OFF
PROMPT $P$G
CD \QPRO
Q
```

To create this batch file, you copy the instructions from the keyboard directly into a file by typing

COPY CON AUTOEXEC.BAT

at the DOS prompt. Pressing ENTER gives you the first line for an instruction. Type the instruction (DATE), and press ENTER for another line. After the last line of instruction, press F6 and press ENTER again. The file will be written to the disk. This file is a pure ASCII file. Note that you can add items to the last line of this batch file that cause Quattro Pro 4 to load specific worksheets or configurations, as will be described shortly.

The PATH Statement

Consider what happens when you type the name of a program file at the DOS prompt and then press ENTER. First, DOS looks for a file in the current directory that has the name that you have entered, plus one of the valid program file extensions (.COM, .EXE, and .BAT). For example, if you enter Q, DOS looks in the current directory for a file called Q.COM, Q.EXE, or Q.BAT. If such a file is found in the current directory, DOS loads it. If such a file is not found in the current directory, DOS returns the rather unfriendly message "Bad command or file name," *unless* your system has a PATH setting in effect.

The PATH setting is created by the PATH command, which you issue at the DOS prompt. The PATH setting tells DOS which directories should be searched for a program file when it cannot be found in the current directory. For example, the following command tells DOS to look in the root directory of drive C and the \DOS subdirectory, as well as the current directory:

PATH = C:\;C:\DOS

Note that the two directory statements are separated by a semicolon. The following statement tells DOS to look in the same directories, plus the Quattro Pro 4 program directory:

PATH = C:\;C:\DOS;C:\QPRO

This means that you could enter Q while in a directory called QWORK and DOS would still load Quattro Pro 4 even though the program files are stored in a directory called \QPRO.

You can use the PATH command at the DOS prompt at any time. If you simply enter PATH, DOS tells you what the current setting is. If you enter PATH followed by the equal sign and one or more directory names, then those directories become the current path setting, superseding the previous setting. Typically, a PATH statement is incorporated in the AUTOEXEC.BAT file to set the various paths required for the programs you normally run. You may want to add your Quattro Pro 4 program directory to the PATH statement in your AUTOEXEC.BAT file to enable you to start Quattro Pro 4 from anywhere on your hard disk.

If you have not used the Directory command from the Options Startup menu to record a preference for a data directory, Quattro Pro 4 will assume that you want to list files in the directory that was current when you entered Q to start the program. This means that if you are in the \QWORK directory when you enter Q and you have \QPRO in your current path, Quattro Pro 4 will list files in \QWORK when you use the File Retrieve or File Open commands. This gives you the flexibility to load Quattro Pro 4 from different data areas depending on the files you are going to use. You can always issue the File Directory command to specify a different temporary data directory.

If you use the Directory command from the Options Startup menu and then use the Options Update command, Quattro Pro 4 will present the same data directory regardless of where you load the program from. To remove a directory preference so that Quattro Pro 4 will use the directory that was current when the program was loaded as the data directory, you do the following:

1. Select Directory from the Options Startup menu.
2. Press ESC to clear the current setting.
3. Press ENTER, select Quit, and then select Update.

A Batch File Menu System

If you have a hard disk, you can easily move among different programs stored on the hard disk by using a series of small batch files and a message file. This section shows how this is done.

Message Files

A message file is simply an ASCII file that contains text you want DOS to display. If you use the TYPE command together with the name of an ASCII file, DOS reads the text from the file to the screen. By preceding this command with the CLS command, which clears the screen in DOS, you can achieve a display such as this:

Main Menu

===

1 Run Quattro Pro 4

2 Run WordPerfect

3 Use Backit program

Type the number of your choice and press ENTER.

You can display this message any time you return to DOS from another program by writing a batch file called Z.BAT, shown here:

```
ECHO OFF
CD \
CLS
TYPE MENU.MSG
```

This changes the directory back to the root (CD \), clears the screen (CLS), and types the message ("TYPE MENU.MSG").

If you write a batch file called 1.BAT that starts Quattro Pro 4, you can load Quattro Pro 4 simply by pressing 1 and ENTER. The 1.BAT file might look like this:

```
ECHO OFF
CD\QPRO
Q
Z
```

If the 1.BAT file that starts Quattro Pro 4 also runs the Z.BAT file after Quattro Pro 4, you have created a loop from the menu to Quattro Pro 4 and back. You could set up other batch files such as 2.BAT and 3.BAT to load other programs such as WordPerfect (2.BAT) and Backit (3.BAT).

You may want to place these batch files in a special subdirectory. Most systems have a subdirectory called \DOS, which is to used store the DOS files. If you place your batch files in a subdirectory make sure that your AUTOEXEC.BAT file uses the PATH command to let DOS know where to look for a batch file if it does not find it in the current directory. If you place the Z.BAT file in the \DOS subdirectory and then include this subdirectory in the PATH command in your AU-TOEXEC.BAT file, as in

PATH = C:\;C:\DOS;C:\QPRO

DOS will always be able to find Z.BAT. Thus, you will always be able to return to the root directory and the menu from anywhere on the disk by pressing **Z** and then ENTER at the DOS prompt. You can easily adapt this system to your own needs by substituting the commands for other software programs and expanding the list.

Improving Menus

Programs on your PC have the ability to display line and corner characters that can be used to create boxes. Some word processing programs, like WordPerfect and DisplayWrite, can perform an operation called Cursor Draw, in which boxes made of lines are easily drawn around text. If saved as ASCII files, these boxes can be displayed with the TYPE command. The boxes help make attractive menus. Figure A-2 shows an example of an enhanced menu.

FIGURE
A-2

Enhanced batch file menu

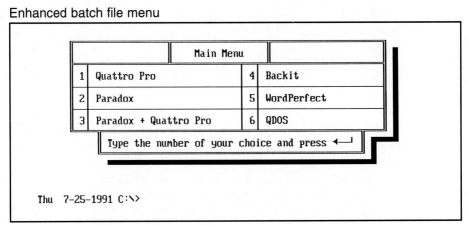

Alternative Menus

A command to load Quattro Pro 4 can be given with an accompanying worksheet name, so that as soon as the program is loaded, the worksheet is retrieved from disk. For example, if you enter the following at the DOS prompt in the Quattro Pro 4 directory

Q SALES

then Quattro Pro 4 will load, followed by the worksheet SALES.WQ1, if there is a worksheet called SALES in the default directory with the default extension. This ability can be used in batch files to load Quattro Pro 4 in several different ways. You can set up a menu like this to offer a choice between different Quattro Pro 4 configurations:

Quattro Pro 4 Menu

==

1 Run Quattro Pro 4 for Pricing

2 Run Quattro Pro 4 for Budget Analysis

3 Run Quattro Pro 4 with no file

The file 1.BAT used to activate this menu contains the instruction

Q PRICING.WQ1

so that Quattro Pro 4 loads the pricing worksheet as soon as the program loads. The 2.BAT file loads Q BUDGET.WQ1 and so on. You could use a variation of these instructions to load Quattro Pro 4 for different users. Bear in mind that the file you call needs to be available to Quattro Pro 4. To help ensure this, you can use a more specific request such as

Q C:\DATA\SALES.WQ1

You can set up this menu system in your QPRO directory. To use this system, the batch file called from the Main Menu to load Quattro Pro 4 contains the command ECHO OFF, followed by

```
CD \QPRO
CLS
TYPE Q.MEN
```

The file Q.MEN is the menu of Quattro Pro 4 choices.

Parameter Passing

Another useful technique in batch file construction is to add a parameter to the file. This can then be replaced by a value that you provide when you use the batch file. This is similar to the technique Quattro Pro 4 uses when loading. When you enter Q followed by a file name to load Quattro Pro 4 you are passing a parameter, in this case, the file name. If you create a batch file called 3.BAT that looks like this

```
ECHO OFF
CLS
Q %1
Z
```

you can load Quattro Pro 4 with a worksheet by entering

3 *filename*

The %1 entry in the batch file is parameter 1. The nice feature of parameters is that they are optional. Thus, you can enter **3** on its own just to load Quattro Pro 4, or **3** followed by a space and a file name to load Quattro Pro 4 and a file.

Managing Shortcuts and .RF Files

You may want to use batch files to manipulate Quattro Pro 4 configuration files. Quattro Pro 4 uses a special configuration or resource file to store basic definitions that specify the way the program is to be run. The file where the default settings are stored when you use the Options Update command or assign Shortcuts is called RSC.RF. You can create additional configuration files that all contain different sets of defaults. To create a file other than RSC.RF, first copy the current RSC.RF to a new file. For example, use the command

COPY RSC.RF MY.RF

Now load Quattro Pro 4 with the command

Q /dMY.RF

at the DOS prompt. Using **/d** and the .RF file name loads the .RF file that you specify, meaning in this case that changes made to the configuration will be stored in MY.RF. Now make the changes you want to the Shortcuts and program options. Use the Options Update command to make sure that the current default settings are stored in the configuration files. The next time you load Quattro Pro 4 you can either use the program defaults by typing **Q** to start the program, or you can use your own defaults by loading with the command

Q /dMY.RF

You can specify both a resource file and a worksheet on the command line, as in

Q /dMY.RF PIE

to load your .RF file plus the worksheet PIE.WQ1.

By using batch file language with a parameter you can establish a batch file to run Quattro Pro 4 that looks like this:

```
ECHO OFF
CLS
Q /d%1.rf %2
```

If you call this file QP.BAT, you can load Quattro Pro 4 with a special .RF file and a worksheet called PIE by simply entering

QP MY PIE

By incorporating batch file code like this into a menu system you can provide users with a choice between default settings. For example, for those who like to use Quattro Pro 4 in 1-2-3 emulation mode you can set up a configuration file to run Quattro Pro 4 in 1-2-3 mode, as discussed in Appendix B.

About Memory

To get the most out of Quattro Pro 4 on your personal computer you need to understand how your system uses memory. For those who are already familiar with the terms *RAM, expanded memory,* and *extended memory,* the important point to note about Quattro Pro 4 is that it prefers expanded memory. You can alter the way Quattro Pro 4 works with RAM by using the Options Other Expanded Memory command, described later in this section.

Types of Memory

There are two types of memory in a PC: read only memory (ROM) and random access memory (RAM). Although some people refer to disks as a third type of memory, it is easier to think of disks as storage rather than memory. ROM holds instructions, permanently burned into the chips, that your computer uses immediately after the power is turned on, even before a disk is read. RAM is where all of the instructions for the programs that the computer is to execute are held prior to being carried out. RAM is also where data is held before it is stored onto disk. When you turn off your computer you wipe out the contents of RAM.

In a typical personal computer session with a typical piece of application software, such as Quattro Pro 4, memory works like this:

1. You turn on the computer. Almost immediately instructions are read from ROM. This includes the testing of memory that gives the numeric display in the top left of the screen, as well as the BIOS (Basic Input/Output System) instructions that lay the ground rules for the exchange of information between different parts of the system, such as the keyboard, display, and disks.

2. The ROM instructions tell the computer to look to the drive(s) to find software on disk. When the computer finds a disk with DOS on it, DOS is read into memory. DOS actually consists of several parts, the two most important being the hidden system files and the command processor, COMMAND.COM. Then, after COM-MAND.COM is loaded, DOS looks for two special files that tell it about the computer, CONFIG.SYS and AUTOEXEC.BAT. The CONFIG.SYS file is a list of settings for DOS to use, plus instructions about any special equipment that is part of the hardware configuration. The AUTOEXEC.BAT file is a list of instructions about what DOS should do first, like set the date and time and display a menu of programs.

3. As manager of the flow and storage of information, DOS then enables you to issue an instruction that loads an application, such as Quattro Pro 4 (this is known as an *application program*, as opposed to an operating system program or utility program, because it applies your system to a useful task). When you issue the command, Quattro Pro 4 is read from disk into RAM. DOS remains in RAM as well.

4. As you use the application you enter some numbers or text from the keyboard. This is held in RAM.

5. You issue the program's save instruction, and a copy of the spreadsheet in RAM is stored on disk but remains on screen as well for further editing.

6. When you are done editing you resave the file, replacing the old version on disk with the new one, and then exit Quattro Pro 4, which removes both text and the program from RAM.

Memory Size

The preceding story is simple enough *if* you have enough RAM to hold both DOS and Quattro Pro 4. How much is enough and how much have you got? Like file storage space on disk, RAM is measured in bytes and kilobytes. You can tell how much RAM is in your computer by using the CHKDSK command from the DOS prompt. To do this you type CHKDSK and press ENTER. The results will look something like this:

```
Volume TOWER 386 created Jun 16, 1990 8:23a
33449984 bytes total disk space
569344 bytes in 57 hidden files
69632 bytes in 26 directories
26648576 bytes in 1139 user files
2048 bytes in bad sectors
6160384 bytes available on disk
655360 bytes total memory
 146496 bytes free
```

Most of the information is about the current disk and the files on it, but the last two lines are about memory. The memory referred to is "normal" RAM. To run Quattro Pro 4 a computer needs at least 512K of normal RAM. With 512K of RAM in your PC, Quattro Pro 4 will be able to handle modest spreadsheets. Your capacity to handle larger worksheets increases when you have 640K of RAM.

Depending on market conditions, RAM can be a fairly inexpensive commodity, and it is definitely worth upgrading to at least 640K. The benefits in speed and capacity will be reflected in your use of other programs as well as Quattro Pro 4. Due to the different types of information that make up spreadsheets, including values, calculations, and formatting, it is not really possible to give an upper limit to the size of spreadsheet Quattro Pro 4 can handle with 640K of RAM. Suffice it to say that Quattro Pro 4 can work better with more memory. The question is how to add more memory to your system in such a way that Quattro Pro 4 can recognize it.

As you have learned, if you type CHKDSK at the DOS prompt and press ENTER you will see a report on memory. This indicates the total amount of memory recognized by DOS, plus what is left after accounting for the space occupied by such information as the COMMAND.COM file. When the IBM PC was first introduced it came with 65,536 bytes or 64K of RAM. This was considered a lot of RAM at the time. Because the power users back then had 64K machines, the designers of DOS figured that ten times that much would be sufficient "user RAM" for DOS and any future applications; hence the figure of 640K, which is the maximum amount of user RAM that DOS can recognize. Although this sounded like a reasonable limit at the time, users kept demanding more features from software, and each new wave of programs required more RAM. New functions have been added to DOS, which used to occupy less than 30K but now requires about 80K. In addition to DOS and regular application programs, a new breed of software, called TSRs or terminate-and-stay-resident programs, gained popularity and consumed RAM. A TSR program, such as the original Borland SideKick, is loaded into memory after DOS but before application software and stays there as you unload one application and then load another. This way, a TSR program can offer the same features, such as a Notepad or Clipboard, within whatever application you are using.

There is also pressure on memory space from users' thirst for more exotic hardware. The designers of the original PC and DOS could not anticipate every type of storage system, communications equipment, and hardware interface that was to be developed for PCs. Equipment like removable hard disks, FAX boards, and MIDI interfaces simply did not exist then. However, DOS was designed so that someone who designed a new piece of equipment could also write a piece of software that told the PC how to relate to that equipment. This specialized software is called a *device driver,* and many products for the PC come with a device driver. The problem with device drivers is that they are loaded into memory when the computer starts up, right after COMMAND.COM. You cannot use such equipment as Bernoulli boxes without these drivers occupying space in memory.

So, this is how the 640K limit of DOS came to be such a squeeze: bigger and better applications and versions of DOS, plus TSR software and specialized equipment. Add to this the growing need to network computers together, which requires memory resident network software, and you have the situation known as RAM-CRAM: not enough memory to do all the things you want to do.

Memory Architecture

You might wonder why DOS has not been altered to recognize more than 640K of RAM. The answer lies in the original design of the PC and what many users have seen as the necessity to keep each new wave of PC designs compatible with the last. The problem begins with *addresses*. In order for a computer to keep track of the data it handles it needs to know where the data is. The location of each byte that is going to be processed needs to be defined. This is done by assigning a unique address to every byte. Think of a delivery person attempting to make deliveries: If every customer has a unique address the job of locating them is made much easier. In a computer each piece of data that is processed has to pass through memory. Every address in memory has to be coded in binary code. If you have eight digits, or bytes, to work with you can come up with 256 unique addresses. With 16 bits you can create 65,536 unique addresses.

The 8088 chip, the central processing unit that was at the heart of the first PCs, had the capacity to use 20 bits for addressing. This was a function of the physical design of the chip. This results in a maximum potential number of addresses of 1,048,576. This is exactly 1 megabyte of addresses or addressable memory. The 8088 chip can thus be said to have a 1 megabyte address space. However, not all of this space can be used by programs that you load from disk. Some of the area needs to be reserved for information passing through memory from and to displays. There also needs to be room to address the BIOS, which controls how the pieces of hardware communicate with each other. To allow for these factors IBM engineers preallocated 640K for programs and 384K for system overhead. Remember that this 640K is the limit of user RAM. In addition to this user RAM, there is the memory area occupied by ROM.

The total amount of ROM and RAM that a PC can work with is limited by the type of chip that is running the system. The chip must move data and program code in and out of memory. The Intel 8088 and 8086 chips can address up to 1024K, or 1 megabyte, of memory. This space is made up of the 640K of RAM, plus 128K reserved for use by video boards, plus 256K reserved for the system ROM (640K + 128K + 256K = 1024K = 1MB). Therefore, beyond the 640K of user RAM the rest of the PC's 1MB total address space is reserved for system operations, a 384K range of memory locations where the CPU finds data or instructions for its own use. The space from 640K to 768K is for video buffers, the data used to draw and redraw the screen display. Optional or installable ROM modules, such as those used by hard disk controllers and enhanced graphics boards, fit between 768K and 896K. The computer's own built-in ROM that starts the computer is addressed from 896K to 1024K.

The 8088/8086 processors can thus see a total memory space no bigger than 1024K, of which no more than 640K can be RAM. Even if you have more than 640K worth of RAM chips, DOS will not recognize it. However, the address area above 640K is rarely full. An 80-column, 25-line text display uses 4K of video memory. The Monochrome Display Adapter occupies just the area from 704K to 708K. Only the most colorful EGA and VGA modes fill or exceed the 128K assigned to video. Also, only IBM's PS/2 models, not PCs or ATs, use all the address space above 896K for system ROM. Having vacant space in high memory can come in handy. With a 64K gap amidst the video buffers and BIOS routines, the use of EMS, expanded memory, is possible. EMS is described in a moment.

Although the early 8088 chip stops at 1MB of RAM, the 80286 chip introduced in the PC AT can address 16MB. The 80386 chip can address as much as four gigabytes (4096MB). RAM above the 1MB boundary is fairly simple to deal with compared with the busy addresses below it. Known as *extended memory,* this upper area of RAM is simply additional space for 80286 or 80386 systems running OS/2, Xenix, or some 80386-specific software. Unfortunately, an 80286 or 80386 using DOS runs in something called *real mode,* which has the same 1MB address limit as the 8088. This was designed into the chip for backward compatibility with earlier computers. The 8088-based PCs were around so long that hardware designers built their peripherals to take advantage of the addresses above 640K. Altering the limit would affect your ability to use many popular hard disk controllers, video boards, and so on.

There is an alternative mode that can be addressed by operating systems other than DOS. This is called the *protected mode,* and it can use large extended memory spaces. Some DOS programs, such as Paradox 3.5 and some utilities, can work with extended memory. For example, many PC ATs come with 384K of actual RAM memory installed beyond 640K, but DOS normally cannot use it. An AT with 1MB of built-in RAM gives the same CHKDSK report of available memory as one with 640K. Some 1MB systems use the extra memory as *shadow RAM,* loading a copy (or shadow) of slow video and BIOS ROM code into RAM for quicker performance. Shadow RAM makes screen displays more responsive, especially for graphics, but will not stop ordinary DOS programs from displaying "Out of memory" messages.

EMS Architecture

In contrast to the simple linear addressing of extended RAM, expanded memory relies on a technical trick known as *paging,* or *bank-switching.* This takes a "window" within the region visible to the processor (the 8088's 1MB address space) and swaps different areas, or pages, of expanded memory in and out of that space as needed. What happens is that an unused 64K section of the memory between 640K and 1024K is used as the address for a larger area, like a mail drop that is one stop on the postal route but that has boxes for lots of customers. The CPU is fooled into operating within this virtual space on data whose real, or physical, address may be many megabytes away.

Simple bank-switching is nothing new, but the Expanded Memory Specification (EMS) is a sophisticated scheme. It involves hardware and software working together—the extra RAM and memory-mapping hardware on an EMS board, combined with a software driver added to your CONFIG.SYS file. This driver, the expanded memory manager (EMM), lets DOS and your applications recognize the paged memory. Given at least 64K of contiguous, vacant address space above 784K (one of the unused gaps), EMS creates a page frame holding at least four 16K pages. The memory manager can map any 16K segment, anywhere within expanded RAM, into any of these pages, fielding CPU requests while preventing collisions among multiple programs and among data areas.

The original Expanded Memory Specification, EMS 3.2, supported 8MB of expanded memory, mostly as work space for spreadsheets and other data files. AST and other firms modified that standard to create the Enhanced Expanded Memory Specification (EEMS), which can swap more pages, including some below the 640K line as well as in the page frame above it. This helps environments such as DESQView shuffle programs in and out of conventional memory. Now EMS 4.0 has surpassed the EEMS standard. With EMS 4.0 you get support for up to 32MB at 8MB per expansion slot. This is swapped into pages almost anywhere below 1MB, and it has many more functions and routines for executing program code as well as handling data.

Understanding the difference between expanded and extended memory can take some effort, but there is a simple rule to follow when you install RAM in your system for use with Quattro Pro 4: Configure as much memory as possible as expanded. Quattro Pro 4 can make use of expanded memory but not extended. Many memory boards can be configured as either extended or expanded. Even if you have an extended memory board you may find software that allows the extended memory to be treated as expanded.

The Memory Crunch

Now that you know why memory is organized the way it is in a PC, you can evaluate some techniques for getting around the limits imposed by this state of affairs. After you take steps to maximize the amount of memory in your system and configure as much of it as expanded memory as you can, you may still run into memory problems, typically when you have loaded Quattro Pro 4 and then built a very large worksheet. Quattro Pro 4's VROOMM feature enables you to keep building very large worksheets by reducing the amount of memory used by the program itself. The Virtual Real-time Object-Oriented Memory Manager is a technology designed by Borland to allow software to perform more efficiently under the 640K limitations of DOS. Programs written to run under VROOMM are composed of small modules that can be quickly loaded into memory as needed, allowing more room for data in memory. However, at some point the amount of disk access that this process requires will slow you down. Moving from one cell to the next will require a disk read, and this is the point at which you really need more memory.

You could also run into a memory problem trying to load Quattro Pro 4 after you have just installed and loaded a new piece of memory-resident software such as a network program. Try some of the following techniques to cope with the memory crunch.

Slimming Your CONFIG.SYS File

Computer systems that have been around for a while can accumulate a lot of unnecessary additions. You may have noticed this in the case of disk files—dozens of files that have been on a hard disk for ages, but nobody is sure why. A similar thing can happen to your CONFIG.SYS file. Some applications add information to CONFIG.SYS when they are installed, and some hardware requires that lines be added to CONFIG.SYS. If the application or hardware falls into disuse it can be removed, but the additions to CONFIG.SYS may remain. Devices loaded in CONFIG.SYS can take up precious memory, so you should remove ones you no longer need. Make sure you know why the items in your CONFIG.SYS file are there.

Mapping Out Your Memory

A valuable tool for checking what you have in memory and where it is located is a utility program called a *memory mapper*. There are several of these available from bulletin boards, such as IBMNET on CompuServe. Some of these programs are free once you have downloaded them; others are shareware, which you pay for later if you decide to use them. If you are doing extensive work with memory—for example, configuring several different machines—a program of this kind is very helpful.

Hardware/Software Solutions

Because 80386 and 80486 systems have the capacity to address larger memory areas and have better memory-management functions built into their hardware, you can use software solutions to achieve results on an 80386 or 80486 that require hardware solutions on earlier systems. An example of this is 386MAX from Qualitas. With 386MAX you can treat extended memory as expanded, access high DOS memory, and perform other tricks. Using programs of this nature requires you to coordinate several aspects of your computer system: video display, hard disk controllers, and network interface card. There are a lot of optional commands with 386MAX that enable you to alter the way it runs in order to avoid conflict with other programs. In some situations problems with high memory will require extensive analysis to resolve conflicts. For example, there are some VGA cards, such as the FastWrite VGA from Video7, that use up an area of memory often used by memory-swapping routines. If you load the VGA BIOS into RAM as described in the VGA utilities manual, you can get around this conflict, but you will need to coordinate memory addresses with your memory expansion software.

Another memory management product is QEMM-386, from Quarterdeck Office Systems, makers of DESQView, a multitasking windows environment for DOS-based machines. While you can run DESQView on just about any PC, on 386-based machines DESQView is most commonly used in conjunction with QEMM-386, Quarterdeck's 386 Expanded Memory Manager. QEMM-386 has two major functions. First, like 386MAX, it can transform extended memory into expanded memory (LIM EMS 4.0 and EEMS 3.2), which can then be accessed by programs designed to take advantage of expanded memory, as well as by DESQView, which can use it to create virtual DOS environments for simultaneous operation of multiple programs. Second, it can map RAM into the unused addresses between 640K and 1MB and allow a user to load TSR modules into it, thus making more conventional RAM available to applications.

Expanded Memory Use Within Quattro Pro 4

The extra work of shuffling data through the DOS memory window into expanded RAM means that EMS RAM responds less quickly than RAM below 640K. For this reason Quattro Pro 4 enables you to make some trade-offs when you are using expanded memory. The Options Other Expanded Memory command provides these options:

Both

Spreadsheet Data

Format

None

The Both option allows EMS to be used for all types of worksheet information, permitting the largest possible models. The Spreadsheet Data option is the default setting, which limits EMS use to just formulas and labels, giving faster response than Both. The Format option is the fastest operation you can get while still making some use of EMS. The None option shuts off EMS so that your worksheet responds faster, although it cannot grow as large as when one of the other three options is used. Try changing your selection in this area when you need to increase worksheet capacity or program response times.

APPENDIX

Networks, Paradox, and Other Programs

*Q*uattro Pro 4 has exceptional capabilities when it comes to its compatibility with other programs. This appendix explains how to set up Quattro Pro 4 to work on a network. This appendix contains tips for combining Quattro Pro 4 on the same system as Paradox and for exchanging files with other programs, such as 1-2-3.

Quattro Pro 4 and Networks

Quattro Pro 4 operates well in network environments. Users can share program files and fonts. User screen and menu preference files can be stored locally. Each user's default setting files can be stored in the same directory as private data files.

Network Installation

Installing Quattro Pro 4 for use on a network gives you the advantages of shared data access and reduced file storage requirements. By storing program files, including fonts, on a central file server equipped with a large hard disk, network users without hard disks can still make full use of Quattro Pro 4. Expensive peripherals, such as laser printers and tape backup units, can be attached to the server, so that many users can benefit from them. Bear in mind that you must purchase a copy of Quattro Pro 4 for every network user of the program (except those using the network at different times). Instead of buying the full Quattro Pro 4 package for each user you can buy the Quattro Pro LAN pack, which allows you to add one concurrent user to the network (because each copy of Quattro Pro 4 has its own unique serial number that is registered on the network, the program will recognize if more users attempt to run Quattro Pro 4 on the network than there are serial numbers).

Installing Quattro Pro 4 for network use is not particularly difficult although you should be familiar with DOS directories and commands, and with the workings of the network operating system. Quattro Pro 4 can be used with Novell Advanced NetWare version 2.0A or later, 3Com 3Plus version 1.0 or later, and any network fully compatible with either of these systems. You should use DOS 3.1 or higher. If you are using NetWare 286 2.15 or later, or NetWare 386 3.1 or later, there are several network tasks that you can perform from within Quattro Pro 4. These are described in a moment.

In Figure B-1 you can see the type of file server directory structure recommended to run Quattro Pro 4 on a network. There are three basic requirements:

System file directory — For the main program files (use \QPRO, with the subdirectory \FONTS for shared font files)

Shared data directory — For shared spreadsheet files (use \QPRODATA)

Private directories — For each Quattro Pro 4 user to store their own defaults and private data files (use subdirectories of a single directory called \QPROPRIV)

You can vary the names of private directories to match your needs, but you will find installation easier if you do not stray too far from this model.

You can see that in addition to the directories for program files, you will also create private directories for each user, beneath the directory \QPROPRIV. Each user's private directory will contain that person's Quattro Pro 4 private data files and program defaults (screen colors, hardware settings, and so on). Although it is possible for two users to

FIGURE B-1

File server directory structure

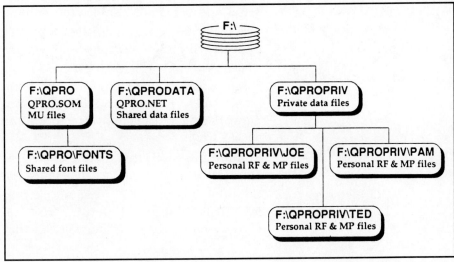

share a private directory this is not recommended, because they could overwrite each other's defaults. The arrangement in Figure B-1 has \QPROPRIV as a subdirectory of the root, with each user's directory beneath it. Each user should have full read/write/create rights to his or her private directory. If you prefer, you can place each user's private directory on their local hard disk, on their home directory on the network, or on a floppy disk. (The best location for a user's private directory depends on the speed of his or her local hard disk and that of the network server. When a lot of users are accessing files on the network at the same time, it may be faster to retrieve files from the local hard disk unless it is an older, slower model.)

In addition to the INSTALL.EXE program that is used in regular installations, network installation makes use of the following files:

QPUPDATE.EXE	Lets you enter the serial numbers for all other copies of Quattro Pro 4 that you want to run on the network. Use QPUPDATE if you need to add additional Quattro Pro 4 network users or to remove a serial number from the network.
QPRO.SOM	Contains all of the serial numbers you've pledged for network use; it contains the path to the QPRO.NET file.
QPRO.NET	Controls the user count, so that the number of concurrent users cannot exceed the total number of serial numbers dedicated to run on the network.
MPMAKE.EXE	Creates personal menu preference (.MP) files, which indicate run time settings and whichever menu tree(s) each user will work with.
.MU files	Let users work with Quattro Pro 4 via alternate menu trees. These menu files will reside on the network server in a shared directory, so all users can access them.
.MP files	Contain the user's menu preferences. Users should store .MP files on local hard disks to save disk space.
.RF files	Contain Quattro Pro 4 default settings; the file RSC.RF is shipped with Quattro Pro 4, but each user can customize their .RF file however they want.

The following steps cover the basic procedure for installing Quattro Pro 4 on your network:

1. Create a shared network directory to contain the Quattro Pro 4 program files (\QPRO). The INSTALL program will need to copy files into \QPRO, so it should not be made read-only until after installation.

2. Create a shared network directory for data files (\QPRODATA). This will hold shared spreadsheet files; users who need these files should have read/write/create rights to \QPRODATA. (If you need additional shared data directories at any time, you will find it convenient to create them now.)

3. Install the Quattro Pro 4 software in the \QPRO directory. Using the disks from a single-user Quattro Pro 4 package, run the INSTALL program as described in Appendix A. You will enter company name and the serial number from the label on Disk 1.

4. When asked if you are going to use a network, respond Yes. When asked for the location of QPRO.NET specify the full DOS path to the shared data directory \QPRODATA. (Although INSTALL can create QPRO.NET in whatever server directory you specify, the shared data directory is recommended because Quattro Pro 4 needs read/write access to this file.)

5. If you want to build fonts for your users ahead of time, choose Final and pick the desired set of fonts from the list (bear in mind that this step will take several minutes).

6. When you are prompted for other hardware and default information, answer according to the computer you are actually installing onto. These defaults can be customized later on for each user's computer.

7. When INSTALL returns you to DOS, switch to the \QPRO directory and enter QPUPDATE. Then, enter the serial numbers of all copies of Quattro Pro 4 you want to dedicate to network (concurrent) use.

8. Establish a private directory beneath \QPROPRIV for each Quattro Pro 4 network user. Its preferable to place private directories beneath \QPROPRIV; wherever they are, make sure users have read/write/create access to their directories.

9. For each user, create an .MP file for his or her menu preference. Network users have the usual choice of menu trees: QUATTRO.MU,

the normal Quattro Pro 4 menu tree; 123.MU, the 123-compatible menu tree; and Q1.MU, the old Quattro 1 menu tree, *not* the Quattro Pro 1 menu tree. From an administrative perspective it will be easier to support users if they all use the same menu tree. Store each user's .MP files in his or her private directory. Do not store .MP files in the QPRO directory. To create each .MP file, from the \QPRO directory use the following syntax:

MPMAKE *QQQ.MU DIRECTORY* \

where *QQQ.MU* is the name of the menu file the user wants to use and *DIRECTORY* is where to write the .MP file containing this information (this directory must be in the user's PATH statement). For example, here is the command to create an .MP file for the regular Quattro Pro 4 menu tree and place this .MP file in Pam's private directory:

MPMAKE F:\QPRO\QUATTRO.MU F:\QPROPRIV\PAM\

10. Create a default (.RF) file in each user's private directory. To do this you first copy the RSC.RF file from \QPRO into each private directory. Afterward, you must delete the RSC.RF file from the \QPRO directory (if you do not, Quattro Pro 4 will read the .RF file in \QPRO instead of the RF file in the user's private directory).

11. Now you can make the \QPRO directory read-only to prevent anyone messing with the program files which no longer needed changing. If your network software cannot make the QPRO directory read-only while keeping the FONTS subdirectory read-write, you should use the DOS ATTRIB command to make the program files read-only (for example, ATTRIB +R *.*). Users should only be able to open files and search in this directory, not change files.

12. Modify each user's CONFIG.SYS file where necessary. The CONFIG.SYS file in the root directory of each user's computer should contain the following statement:

FILES=20

For more on the FILES parameter, see Appendix A.

13. Add the SHARE command to each user's AUTOEXEC file or network log-in script.

14. Add (or change) the PATH statement in each user's AUTOEXEC.BAT or other network log-on file to include paths to his or her private directory and to \QPRO. You must add the PATH statement after the log-in commands, and the path to \QPRO must appear after the path to the private directory. For example, the last lines of AU-TOEXEC.BAT might look like this:

F:LOGIN ADMIN\PAM
PATH F:\QPROPRIV\PAM;F:\QPRO

The first line, F:LOGIN ADMIN\PAM, logs Pam onto the Admin network. After the log-in statement, the PATH statement defines the paths to the Quattro Pro 4 directories.

You can now restart each computer to put the revised CONFIG.SYS and AUTOEXEC.BAT files into effect. Start Quattro Pro 4 at each computer to ensure the installation is working correctly. Quattro Pro 4 automatically detects each computer's hardware setup, so all users should be able to run Quattro Pro 4 regardless of monitor type.

While in the program, you can change default settings (see the next section), or exit and let users make their own changes. Now everyone is ready to use Quattro Pro 4. If you entered six serial numbers during this process, you should be able to start Quattro Pro 4 on six workstations concurrently. Make sure each user has a copy of the documentation and knows the location of the Quattro Pro 4 directories.

Bear in mind that if users want to switch from one menu tree to another, they must have separate .MP files for each. Also, you must set up a path to each user's private directory and the QPRO directory. Quattro Pro 4 must know where the QPRO directory is in order to read the program files, and it must know where the QPROPRIV directory is in order to read and write each user's Quattro Pro 4 defaults.

Network Upgrades from Quattro Pro Version 1

If you have been running an earlier version of Quattro Pro 4 from your network server, you already have directories containing the previous program files, defaults, fonts, and data files. You will need to make substantial changes to upgrade to Quattro Pro 4. You must upgrade all copies of Quattro Pro version 1 to version 3 because version 3 monitors user count on a network, and requires version 3 serial numbers to do so.

You must delete the Quattro Pro version 1 program files before installing the version 3 program files. To do this without erasing spreadsheet data files, go into the existing Quattro Pro program directory and check for any spreadsheet, graph, or personal files. You can use the DOS DIR command to list all files with the extension .W??. This will catch all .WQ1 and .WQ! files, but if users have assigned other file extensions to their data files, check for these as well. Copy any data files you find to a data directory, such as \QPRODATA. Because version 1 fonts may not be compatible with version 3, which features improved font files, delete existing font files. After verifying that all data files are safely stored in a separate directory, you should delete all files in the existing Quattro Pro program directory.

Now move to the \RESOURCE subdirectory, which the Network Administrator's Guide in version 1 recommended creating. It should contain the .MU files from version 1. These files are not compatible with version 3, so delete them and remove the \RESOURCE directory. Now switch to the \QPRORES directory, which the Network Administrator's Guide in version 1 recommended creating. Delete the contents of this directory, which are .RF files, and then delete the directory. All that should remain is the Quattro Pro program directory (which should be empty), the \QPRODATA directory (with its shared data files), and the \QPROPRIV directory (with its subdirectories containing private data files). You can now proceed with the regular installation steps given earlier.

Network Printing

If you encounter extraneous blank pages before and after printing to a network printer, go to the Options Hardware Printers menu and choose

Device Parallel 1 or Parallel 2. Do not use the logical device options LPT1 or LPT2. The Parallel 1 device is equivalent to LPT1, and Parallel 2 is equivalent to LPT2. If your network printers are installed using LPT3, LPT4, or LPT5, you must redefine these options for LPT1 or LPT2 and use Parallel 1 or Parallel 2 Device options within Quattro Pro 4. See Appendix C for advice on using the Quattro Pro 4 Print Manager on a network.

Paradox Access

Before you use Paradox Access, the feature that enables you to switch between Paradox and Quattro Pro 4 with the CTRL-F10 key, there are several configuration items you will need to check and several that you can alter to improve performance.

Configuration

The FILES setting in CONFIG.SYS must read at least FILES=40. If you start Quattro Pro 4 and get an error message stating that there are not enough file handles available, you must increase this number. (Remember that you need to reboot your computer for this setting to take effect; see Appendix A for more on CONFIG.SYS.)

You also need to run the SHARE command from the DOS prompt for Paradox and Quattro Pro 4 to work together. The SHARE command loads a memory-resident module that allows file sharing and locking. Add this command to your AUTOEXEC.BAT file to avoid running SHARE each time you want to run Paradox Access. If SHARE is already loaded, DOS gives you the message "SHARE already installed." You must also make sure that the directory containing Quattro Pro 4 is in your current PATH. You may want to add the directory to the PATH command in your AUTOEXEC.BAT file.

You should not have Quattro Pro 4 and Paradox program files stored in the same directory. There is no problem keeping both .DB and .WQ1 data files in the same area, but because of the strict locking rules in Paradox for private directories, make sure that your Paradox working directory and private directory are different. (If you are already using

Paradox on a network without any difficulty then it is likely that your working and private directories have already been set correctly.)

To alter the Paradox working directory choose Defaults SetDirectory after running the Paradox Custom Configuration Program (this is a special script file, called CUSTOM.SCR, supplied with the Paradox program; to run it you choose Script from the main Paradox menu, then select Run and enter **Custom**). Choose Ok to permanently change the location of your Paradox working directory. Quattro Pro 4 respects all Paradox locks. For more information on locking and private directories, see your Paradox documentation.

When running Quattro Pro 4 from within Paradox, you must run Paradox in protected mode. You can set this as a default using the Paradox Custom Configuration Program. If you are using Paradox on a stand-alone system—that is, not as a network server—you still need to follow some network configuration procedures. First run the Paradox NUPDATE.EXE program, configure the network type to OTHER, and specify a path for the PARADOX.NET file. On a stand-alone system this file can be placed anywhere on your hard disk where both Paradox and Quattro Pro 4 can find it.

Next run Quattro Pro 4 and choose Paradox Access from the Options Other menu. Choose OTHER for the network type and specify the same path you used in NUPDATE.EXE for the PARADOX.NET file. Press ESC until you return to the main Options menu, then choose Update to save this configuration to disk. Exit Quattro Pro 4 and load Paradox with PXACCESS. You should now be able to retrieve Paradox .DB files while running Quattro Pro 4 from within Paradox. In Figure B-2 you can see a suggested file and directory layout for running Quattro Pro 4 and Paradox on a non-networked system.

Loading Up

The best way to start Paradox with Quattro Pro 4 access is to use PXACCESS.BAT, which comes with Quattro Pro 4. The PXACCESS.BAT batch file contains these lines:

SHARE

PARADOX -qpro -leaveK 512 -emK 0

In most cases, you will not need to change the contents of the PXACCESS batch file. However, if you want to include command-line options for Quattro Pro 4 you can edit them into PXACCESS.BAT. For example, to load the file SALES.WQ1 with Quattro Pro 4 you would enter

PARADOX -qpro [SALES] -leaveK 512 -emK 0

Alternatively, you can place a batch file parameter in the command line which can then accept different files, as in

PARADOX -qpro [%1] -leaveK 512 -emK 0

which enables you to enter the command **PXACCESS SALES** to load the SALES worksheet.

FIGURE
B-2

File and directory layout

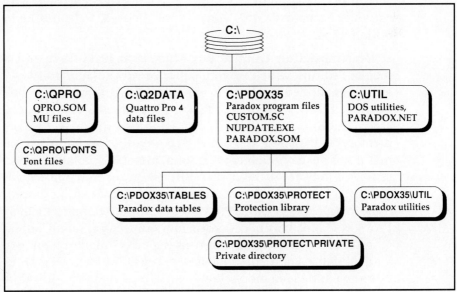

If your computer has more than 2MB of extended memory, you might want to edit PXACCESS.BAT to alter some parameters and improve performance. The first line of PXACCESS.BAT loads the SHARE module, and the next line starts Paradox with the command-line options necessary for using Paradox Access. The -qpro command sets up Paradox for use with Quattro Pro 4. You must use this option when you use Paradox Access. The leaveK 512 statement prevents Paradox from using 512K of extended memory, reserving it for a memory manager program to convert to expanded memory. Once it is converted, Quattro Pro 4 can use it, as long as the -emK 0 option is included. This option prevents Paradox from using any expanded (EMS) memory, so that Quattro Pro 4 can use it.

You might want to alter these settings to make more memory available for Quattro Pro 4. With an 80386 or higher class of computer, you probably have a memory manager device driver like QEMM-386 from Quarterdeck Office Systems. Such programs convert the onboard extended memory (which Paradox prefers) to expanded (which Quattro Pro 4 prefers). In this case, set leaveK to about 1MB less than the total and keep -emK set to 0. With an 80286 AT-class computer, you may or may not have expanded memory installed through an expansion card (like the Intel AboveBoard or the AST Rampage card). If you have an expanded memory card, you can set -leaveK to 0 and keep the -emK option as is.

Remember that Quattro Pro 4 needs at least 384K of conventional memory to run, which is what -qpro provides. Quattro Pro 4 also needs all the expanded memory it can get, which is what the other options provide. When you are using Paradox Access, the Quattro Pro 4 /X command-line option (which lets Quattro Pro 4 use 512K of extended memory) is disabled. If Quattro Pro 4 cannot run at all, your computer might not have enough conventional memory available. In that case, try removing any RAM resident (TSR) programs you have loaded. If your computer has no expanded memory available (either because there is none installed or because Paradox is using all the extra memory), Quattro Pro 4 will still be able to run, but only using small spreadsheets. If Quattro Pro 4 shows signs of running out of memory, such as failing to load all entries of a spreadsheet, increase the -leaveK setting to free up more expanded memory. For best use of memory, in addition to the commands on the Database Paradox Access menu, set the Options Other Expanded Memory option in Quattro Pro 4 to Both.

Relating to Other Spreadsheets

Quattro Pro 4 is similar in some respects to other electronic spreadsheet programs such as Lotus 1-2-3 and Microsoft Excel. The actual arrangement of data in Quattro Pro 4, Excel, and 1-2-3 is very similar, because all three programs use indexed columns and rows for managing data. However, there are considerable differences in terminology. The arrangement of indexed columns and rows in an electronic spreadsheet produces a collection of boxes, or *cells*. A cell is named or indexed by the column and row forming the cell. Thus, column B, row 3 is named cell B3. When a contiguous group of cells must be acted on collectively, it is called a *block* in Quattro Pro 4. In 1-2-3 a group of cells is called a *range*. Excel uses that term as well but generally refers to *selected cells* rather than ranges. Commands that affect a group of cells are handled differently by the three programs. Excel and Quattro Pro 4 gather many block-related commands into an Edit menu. Formatting of grouped cells is handled by the Style commands in Quattro Pro 4, and the Format commands in Excel. In 1-2-3 there is a main menu item called Range that covers most commands affecting a group of cells, both formatting and editing. However, two editing commands for ranges, Copy and Move, are presented on the main menu.

When a command affects the entire spreadsheet, 1-2-3 refers to it as *global.* In 1-2-3 the Global commands are a subset of Worksheet commands. Even the program defaults are handled by the /Worksheet Global menu. Quattro Pro 4 refers to commands that affect the whole spreadsheet as *options,* as does Excel. Quattro Pro 4 distinguishes between default settings made for a particular worksheet and those written to the configuration file permanent settings. This is done with the Options Update command. The global commands in 1-2-3 and their equivalent default settings in Quattro Pro 4 are as follows:

1-2-3 Global Commands	Quattro Pro 4 Settings
/Worksheet Global Column-Width	Options Formats Global Width
/Worksheet Global Format	Options Formats Numeric Format
/Worksheet Global Recalc	Options Recalculation
/Worksheet Global Protection	Options Protection

Interfacing

Both Quattro Pro 4 and Excel enable you to use a mouse to select cells and issue commands. Excel does this through the Windows operating environment whereas mouse support is an integral part of Quattro Pro 4. Both Quattro Pro 4 and Excel allow you to select cells before issuing commands that affect those cells, whereas 1-2-3 requires you to issue a command and then select the cells. In fact, Quattro Pro 4 can operate in both modes. Although all three programs use menu bars across the top of the screen, the 1-2-3 menu bar is only present when you press the / key. In Quattro Pro 4 and Excel the main menu bar normally remains on screen and you then pull down vertical menus of additional commands.

Both Quattro Pro 4 and Excel enable you to add or subtract items from the menu system, including macros. In Quattro Pro 4 this is done with the Options Startup Edit Menus command. This command also enables you to alter the style of menu between the normal pull-down style and pop-up menus that only appear when the menu is activated. You can adjust the width of Quattro Pro 4 menus to either display settings or hide them. You can even tell Quattro Pro 4 to remember the last item you picked from the menu, allowing rapid repetition of commands.

File Sharing

To use a 1-2-3 worksheet in Quattro Pro 4, all you need to do is select it from the list of worksheet files. Quattro Pro 4 automatically translates the file into a Quattro Pro 4 worksheet. When importing a 1-2-3 file that contains linking, the link references are converted to Quattro Pro 4 syntax. Spreadsheet formatting done with the Allways add-in is also translated if the .ALL file is present. Format files with the .FMT and .FM3 extensions, created by WYSIWYG, are also recognized.

To save a Quattro Pro 4 worksheet file with 2.2 linking, simply give the file a .WQ1 extension. If you keep the .WK1 extension when you save the file, Quattro Pro 4 asks you how you want to handle the file saving. You have three options: No, Yes, and Use 2.2 Syntax. The No option aborts the Save and you are warned that the file has been removed from the disk. The Yes option saves the file, but converts all links to their end result. The third option, Use 2.2 Syntax, saves the file and preserves 2.2 syntax, but only for single cell references.

For Quattro Pro 4 to use macros in a 1-2-3 worksheet you can either set up Quattro Pro 4 with the 1-2-3 menu, as described in the next section, or you can set the Key Reader option on the Quattro Pro 4 Tools Macro menu to Yes. To share files with users of Excel you can also use the .WK1 format, which can be read by both Excel and Quattro Pro 4. For a complete list of file formats that can be read and written by Quattro Pro 4, see Table B-1.

Obviously, there are some situations in which Quattro Pro 4 cannot directly store your worksheet as a .WK1 file. When you use a Quattro Pro 4 feature that has no equivalent in 1-2-3, that feature is lost when the file is saved in 1-2-3 format. This affects those @functions that Quattro Pro 4 supports but 1-2-3 does not. When you save a file containing such functions, Quattro Pro 4 will warn you that it is about to convert an unknown function to a value and you are given a chance to cancel the file save operation and use a Quattro Pro 4 format instead. Table B-2 shows a list of Quattro Pro 4 @functions that should not be used in a worksheet you are saving in 1-2-3 format. When you are exchanging files between Quattro Pro 4 and 1-2-3 you will need to pay particular attention to macros. See the following section on sharing macros for more details.

Note that when you are reading a worksheet from 1-2-3 Release 3 or later (.WK3) and the file contains multiple worksheets, Quattro Pro 4 will ask whether you want to save each sheet as a separate file. If you choose Yes, the files are named by using the first six characters of the original name plus a letter sequence beginning with 0A. This means that sheet A in REVEXPEN.WK3 would become REVEXP0A.WQ1.The lettering continues with sheet B as 0B and so on to 0Z, then AA to AF, up to a maximum of 32 sheets. Quattro Pro 4 will convert #D formulas in .WK3 files into the equivalent Quattro Pro 4 formulas, so that @SUM(A:B3..B:G7) in REVEXPEN.WK3 becomes @SUM(B3..G7+@SUM ([REVEXP0B]B2..G7) in REVEXP0A.WQ1.

Quattro Pro 4 and 1-2-3

The differences between Quattro Pro 4 and 1-2-3 can be minimized for the user by implementing the emulation features that Quattro Pro 4

TABLE B-1

File Formats Read/Written by Quattro Pro 4

.WK3	Lotus 1-2-3, Release 3.0, 3.1, and 3.1+
.WKS	Lotus 1-2-3, Release 1A
.WK1	Lotus 1-2-3, Release 2.01, 2.2, and 2.3
.WKE	Lotus 1-2-3, Educational Version
.WRK	Lotus Symphony, Release 1.2
.WR1	Lotus Symphony, Release 2
.WKQ	Earlier versions of Quattro
.WQ1	Quattro Pro (all versions)
.WKP	Surpass
.WK$	SQZ (Lotus 1-2-3, Release 1A)
.WK!	SQZ (Lotus 1-2-3, Release 21)
.WR$	SQZ (Lotus Symphony, Release 1.2)
.WR!	SQZ (Lotus Symphony, Release 2)
.WKZ	SQZ (Earlier versions of Quattro)
.WQ!	SQZ (Quattro Pro all versions)
.DB	Paradox
.DB2	dBASE II
.DBF	dBASE III, III PLUS, and IV
.RXD	Reflex (early versions)
.R2D	Reflex (Version 2)

Note: Not all programs that import or export .DIF files use exactly the same file format. Quattro Pro 4 supports the .DIF file format developed by Software Arts Products Corporation and used by VisiCalc. Files in other versions of .DIF may not be readable by Quattro Pro 4 and some programs may not read .DIF files from Quattro Pro 4.

provides. You may want to do this either to run 1-2-3 macros or to minimize retraining employees who already know how to use 1-2-3. In the long run you will probably find that users of 1-2-3 adjust quite

TABLE B-2   Quattro Pro 4 @ Functions to Avoid When Exporting to 1-2-3

@CELLINDEX	@HEXTONUM	@PAYMT
@CURVALUE	@IPAYMNT	@PPAYMT
@DEGREES	@IRATE	@PVAL
@DSTDS	@MEMAVAIL	@RADIANS
@DVARS	@MEMEMSAVAIL	@STDS
@FILEEXISTS	@NPER	@SUMPRODUCT
@FVAL	@NUMTOHEX	@VARS

happily to the Quattro Pro 4 menu system without using the 1-2-3 emulation features. However, if you do wish to make Quattro Pro 4 emulate 1-2-3, for example to run 1-2-3 macros, you should follow the steps given next.

The 1-2-3 Menu

Quattro Pro 4 provides a menu tree that will be familiar to users of 1-2-3. Found in the file 123.MU, this menu set appears much like the Quattro Pro 4 menus, but options have names to match the 1-2-3 menu system and the commands are grouped differently. The Quattro Pro 4 Edit Erase command, for example, is found on the 1-2-3 Range menu, as the Range Erase command.

The 1-2-3 menu can be selected for use with Quattro Pro 4 during the installation process. If you did not select the 1-2-3 menu tree during installation you can switch to the 1-2-3 menu tree after loading Quattro Pro 4 with the regular menus. If you would like to switch menu trees during a session, you can use the Options Startup command. You can also use this command if you selected the 1-2-3 menu system during installation and would like to try the regular Quattro Pro 4 menu. When you select Options Startup you will see from the menu the name of the current menu file. Normally, this is QUATTRO.MU, the regular Quattro Pro 4 menu tree. Select Menu Tree from the Startup menu and you will see a list of currently available menu files, including 123.MU. When you highlight 123.MU and press ENTER, you will be returned to READY mode, and the 1-2-3 menu will be visible across the top of the screen.

The 1-2-3 menu in Quattro Pro 4 remains on screen at all times, like the regular Quattro Pro 4 menu. However, you still have to press **/** to activate it. When the 1-2-3 menu is activated, the word "Worksheet" is highlighted, just as in 1-2-3, and you can select items by either the first letter method or the highlight and ENTER method. Take a moment to explore the 1-2-3 menu tree. Some commands look slightly different. For example, the System command in 1-2-3 itself takes you immediately to DOS, whereas in Quattro Pro 4's 1-2-3 emulation mode the System command requires that you make a further menu selection before reaching DOS. You will also notice that the 1-2-3 menu tree has some items that are not found in 1-2-3 itself. These items are marked by small boxes next to their names in the menu list.

To make your menu tree file selection permanent you need to use the Options Update command. Under the 1-2-3 menu tree this command is Worksheet Global Default Update. When you select Update, Quattro Pro 4 writes your choice of menu system to the configuration file. When you exit from Quattro Pro 4 and reload the program, the new menu system you selected will be in effect.

Comfort Features

If you are using Quattro Pro 4 in 1-2-3 mode you will probably want to make Quattro Pro 4 save files in a 1-2-3 file format. If you install 1-2-3 emulation, the default file extension is automatically changed to .WK1. You can alter this extension, for example to the SQZ version of the 1-2-3 format, by using the Worksheet Global Default Files command in the 1-2-3 menus, or Options Startup from the Quattro Pro 4 menu tree.

Borland designed Quattro Pro 4 so that it does not prompt you to save data before it executes the Erase or Exit command if you have already saved the data. However, because erasing block and graph names can waste hours of work, Quattro Pro 4 always prompts before completing an Edit Names Reset or a Graph Names Reset command. If you are familiar with 1-2-3, you will know that this approach to name resetting and file saving is different from that used by Lotus. If you are comfortable with the Lotus-style confirmation prompts, you can use them. To make the change while using the Quattro Pro 4 menu tree, use the Options Startup Edit Menus command and select Options. Select Borland Style and change the setting to No. Use the Worksheet Global Default Files Edit Menus command in the 1-2-3 menu tree to switch to Lotus-style save and reset prompts. Select Options, then Borland Style, and change the setting to No. This is done automatically when you switch to 1-2-3 menus.

You will notice that while you are using the Edit Menus command there is another Confirm Options setting on the Options menu called During Macros. Setting this option to Yes preserves the Borland style of confirmation during the recording and execution of macros. Changing this option to No helps you to successfully share macros with 1-2-3. This option is automatically set to No when you invoke the 1-2-3 menus.

Sharing Macros

There are major differences between 1-2-3 and Quattro Pro 4 in the area of macros. When making macros in Quattro Pro 4 you do not have to use lists of actual keystrokes when replicating menu choices. For example, suppose that you want to print the cells you have named TOTAL. In 1-2-3 the macro code would be

/PPRTOTALAG

This is compact, but far from obvious to decipher. If you happened to use /PFRTOTALAG by mistake, the macro could have unpleasant effects. In the menu equivalent approach used by Quattro Pro 4 the macro would look like this:

{/ Print;Block}TOTAL~
{/ Print;Align}{/ Print;Go\

This is very easy to read and debug. Because Quattro Pro 4 records macros for you, it takes no longer to create than the 1-2-3 version. The style of macro recording normally used by Quattro Pro 4 language is called Logical. The 1-2-3 style is called Keystroke.

When it comes to sharing macros, Quattro Pro 4 offers two ways to run macros made with 1-2-3. You can load Quattro Pro 4's 1-2-3 menu tree to run your 1-2-3 macro. Alternatively, you can set the Key Reader option on the Tools Macro menu to Yes. Quattro Pro 4 can record macros that 1-2-3 can run, but only if you record them with the 1-2-3 menu tree in place and the Keystroke style of macro recording in effect, instead of the usual Logical or menu equivalent style. The style of macro recording is set by the Worksheet Macro Macro Recording command in the 1-2-3 menu tree. This is automatically set to Keystroke when you invoke the 1-2-3 style menus. In the regular Quattro Pro 4 menu tree, the command is Tools Macro Macro Recording. Of course, for your macros to be compatible with 1-2-3 you cannot use any of the menu items or macro commands unique to Quattro Pro 4. These are listed in Table B-3.

Note that Quattro Pro 4 macros recorded with the Logical style will run regardless of the menu tree that is in place. This means that you can be using the 1-2-3 style menu and still run a Quattro Pro 4 macro developed under the normal Quattro Pro 4 menu. Because Quattro Pro 4 enables you to run macros from libraries, this feature gives users of the 1-2-3 menu tree access to macros developed by regular Quattro Pro 4 users. To make a macro library, first open the worksheet containing your collected macros. Use the Macro Library command and set the option to Yes, then save the file. As long as the file is open you can use macros that are in it, even if the library file is not the current worksheet.

Added Features

Several features found in Quattro Pro 4 are not found in 1-2-3. These features have been incorporated into Quattro Pro 4's 1-2-3 menu system where appropriate. They include the Worksheet Macro command and such Graph commands as Area and Rotated Bar. Note that saving graphs in worksheets with the .WK1 or .WKS format removes color information about the graph. Use the regular .WQ1 format to retain color settings.

There are some Quattro Pro 4 features that are not part of the menu system that 1-2-3 users need to know about. These include the use of the DELETE key for deleting the contents of a cell (the equivalent of /Range Erase ENTER in 1-2-3) and the Undo key (ALT-F5). The CTRL-D date entry method, the rest of the Shortcuts feature, and the ability to assign menu

TABLE
B-3

Menu Items and Macro Commands to Avoid When Exporting Macros to 1-2-3

Menu Items		
Edit	Search & Replace	
File	New	
File	Open	
File	Workspace	
File	!SQZ!	
File	Update Links	
Print	All Final Quality options	
Graph	Instant Graph	
View	All options	

Macro Commands		
{;}	{GRAPHCHAR}	{NUMON}
{BACKTAB}	{INSOFF}	{PASTE}
{CAPOFF}	{INSON}	{READDIR}
{CAPON}	{MACROS}	{SCROLLOFF}
{CHOOSE}	{MARKALL}	{SCROLLON}
{CLEAR}	{MARK}	{STEPOFF}
{COPY}	{MESSAGE}	{STEPON}
{CR}	{MOVE}	{STEP}
{DATE}	{NAME}	{TAB}
{DELEOL}	{NEXTWIN}	{UNDO}
{FUNCTIONS}	{NUMOFF}	{ZOOM}

items to CTRL keys should also be pointed out to 1-2-3 users switching to Quattro Pro 4. The use of the Record feature and Transcript for macro making is part of Quattro Pro 4 that experienced 1-2-3 users will want to explore. The function keys are largely used in the same way in Quattro Pro 4 and 1-2-3. Exceptions in Quattro Pro 4 are the following:

❑ ALT-F2 for macro options

❑ F3 to activate the menu (in addition to /)

❑ ALT-F3 to list @functions

❑ SHIFT-F3 to list macro commands

❑ ALT-F5 to undo your last action

❑ ALT-F6 to zoom a window

Also note the use of the plus key on the numeric keypad to expand menus, and the use of the minus key to contract them. Expanding menus shows the current settings of items when they exist. Contracting menus makes them less obtrusive. These keys make for more flexible and informative uses of menus than in 1-2-3, where many of the current settings cannot be seen from the menu.

APPENDIX

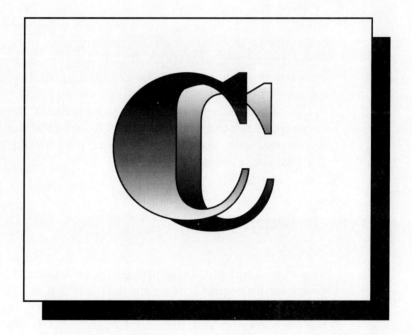

Support and Print Manager

*T*echnology as powerful as that used by today's personal computers is not always easy to understand and is bound to give rise to questions. This appendix provides some suggestions for when you run into problems using Quattro Pro 4, along with some tips on using the Print Manager program that enables you to print "in the background."

Getting Support

When you are facing a problem using Quattro Pro 4, one of the first steps to take is a break. Give yourself a few minutes away from the computer to relax; you can then return to the problem in a better, and often clearer, frame of mind. If that does not help, trying asking fellow workers for their suggestions. Describing the problem to someone else can often help you see the solution. Be sure to check relevant sections in the manual. Check the spelling and syntax of any formula, functions, or macro commands you are using. Refer to the index of this book for the relevant subject. If you still do not have an acceptable answer, consider the following sources of support.

Written Support

Do not underestimate the venerable process of putting the problem into words and putting those words on paper. This process can sometimes solve the problem as you think it through. If you still need help, send the problem, together with any printouts, screen prints, plus the software version and the serial number from the front of the original program disk to the following address:

Borland International, Inc.
1800 Green Hills Road
P.O. Box 660001
Scotts Valley, CA 95066-0001
1-408-438-5300

Although this is not the fastest way of finding support, it is sometimes the best way, particularly if you feel you need to present printed data from the program.

On-Line Support

If you have a modem and communications software, you should consider subscribing to CompuServe, the on-line information bank. Here you will find the Borland Applications Forum (accessed with GO BORAPP from the CompuServe prompt). The Forum contains answers to many common questions, a few of which are included at the end of this appendix. The Forum also has many useful Quattro Pro 4 worksheet files that you can copy, and a message and discussion system for exchanging views and news with other Quattro Pro 4 users. Many computer stores and bookstores sell sign-up packages for CompuServe, or you can write to

CompuServe Information Service, Inc.
P.O. Box 20212
Columbus, OH 43220

Note that CompuServe is available via a local phone call in many countries, so although it is operated from somewhere in the United States, it is a valuable support system for users around the world.

Registration

If you have just bought Quattro Pro 4, be sure to fill out and return the user registration card in the front of the manual. Registering your software protects your investment in it and ensures that you will hear of upgrades and related product announcements. For information about the latest version of the program, plus complementary products as they become available, write to Borland at the address just provided.

Print Manager and BPS

Quattro Pro 4 comes with a sophisticated program called the Borland Print Spooler, or BPS for short. This feature enables you to perform "background printing." Normally you select Spreadsheet Print and then wait until all of the print information has been accepted by the printer before regaining control of Quattro Pro 4 and carrying on with your work. With BPS installed you regain control of Quattro Pro 4 much sooner. This is because BPS Manager writes the information onto your hard disk instead of sending it to the printer. Then, while you return to work with Quattro Pro 4, the Print Manager feeds the information to the printer.

Using BPS

You load BPS before you Quattro Pro 4. At the DOS prompt you move to the Quattro Pro 4 program directory, then enter **BPS**. Then you load Quattro Pro 4. You can include this step in a batch file used to load Quattro Pro 4, as described in Appendix A. Once Quattro Pro 4 is loaded make sure that background printing is enabled by checking the Options Hardware Printers menu. The Background option should be set to Yes (in itself this command does not load or unload BPS, it merely enables or disables it). Beyond this, you need do nothing else in order to enjoy the benefits of BPS. Simply select Spreadsheet Print and the spooler will take care of the print job. However, you can use the Print Manager command on the Print menu to control printing with BPS, as described in a moment.

The files that BPS uses to process print jobs have the file name QPPRNX.SPL, where *X* is the job number. You might wonder what happens if you quit Quattro Pro 4 or turn off your machine before all print jobs have been processed. Because BPS is a smart piece of software, printing will automatically be resumed when you reload BPS and Quattro Pro 4. To prevent printing from resuming delete all of the .SPL files. If you exit Quattro Pro 4 and want to free up the RAM used by BPS, enter **BPS U** at the DOS prompt.

You can adjust the speed at which BPS sends information to your printer by loading with a command line parameter. Enter **BPS Sx** where x is the rate at which data is sent to the printer. The value of x can be from 0 to 9, with 0 being the slowest and 3 being the default. You can also enter **BPS Cx** where x is one of the following numbers signifying hardware handshaking: 0 for None, 1 for Xon/Xoff, 2 for DTR then CTS/DSR, 3 for CTS only. The default setting is DTR the CTS/DSR.

Print Manager Commands

The Print Manager command on the Print menu opens a special type of window with its own menu. The window lists the following information about print jobs that are being processed with BPS:

Seq	Job sequence, the order in which items will be printed
File Name	The .SPL spool file used for the print job
Status	The state of the print job, where Active means currently printing, Ready means prepared to print, and Held means suspended
Port	The port on your computer that is being used
File Size	The size, in bytes, of the print job
Copies	The number of copies that will be printed, as set by the Print Copies command

The information in the window will be updated as printing proceeds. You can use the Job menu in the Print Manager window to affect printing of a specific job. To select a print job from the list use the mouse, the arrow keys, the Select key (SHIFT-F7), or the Select All key (ALT-F7). To cancel printing select the job from the list and then use Job Delete. To pause a print job, that is stop it being sent to the printer without deleting it, use Job Hold. To allow a previously paused print job to go ahead, use Job Release.

The Window menu in the Print Manager window enables you to adjust the display, with Zoom, Tile, Stack, Move/Size, and Pick commands that match those in Window menu for File Manager and the regular work area. The File menu in Print Manager is used to put away the current window (Close) or all windows (Close All). The Queue menu in the Print Manager allows you to switch between viewing the background printing queue and a network printing queue, as described in a moment.

Network Printing

You may be printing to a printer that is on a network. If the Options Hardware Printers command was used to set the Device to Network Queue, you can still use BPS. The Print Manager window can display the status of the queue if you use the Queue Network command on the Print Manager menu. In addition, you can set the Options Network Queue Monitor option to Yes in order to display the status of network print jobs at the bottom of the Quattro Pro 4 screen. A message will appear such as

```
2jobs|4ahead|Actv
```

This particular message indicates that two jobs are being processed by BPS and there are four jobs ahead of them in the network print queue. The following message appears when the BPS jobs have been processed:

```
0jobs|complete
```

The rate at which this message is updated is determined by the Refresh Interval on the Options Network menu. The default setting is every 30 seconds. Choose Yes for the Banner setting on the same menu to send a print banner ahead of your print job. This is a page that identifies the print job and the person who sent it to the network printer, which is handy when many people are sharing the same printer. The User Name option on the Options Network menu allows you to register a User Name that will appear on the banner.

Index

Osborne McGraw-Hill

Computer Books

(800) 227-0900

Bookmarker Design — Lance Ravella

Tear off for Bookmark

You're important to us...

We'd like to know what you're interested in, what kinds of books you're looking for, and what you thought about this book in particular.

Please fill out the attached card and mail it in. We'll do our best to keep you informed about Osborne's newest books and special offers.

▶ **YES, Send Me a FREE Color Catalog of all Osborne computer books**
To Receive Catalog, Fill in Last 4 Digits of ISBN Number from Back of Book (see below bar code) 0-07-881 _ _ _ – _

Name: _____ Title: _____

Company: _____

Address: _____

City: _____ State: _____ Zip: _____

I'M PARTICULARLY INTERESTED IN THE FOLLOWING *(Check all that apply)*

I use this software
- □ WordPerfect
- □ Microsoft Word
- □ WordStar
- □ Lotus 1-2-3
- □ Quattro
- □ Others _____

I use this operating system
- □ DOS
- □ Windows
- □ UNIX
- □ Macintosh
- □ Others _____

I rate this book:
- □ Excellent □ Good □ Poor

I program in
- □ C or C++
- □ Pascal
- □ BASIC
- □ Others _____

I chose this book because
- □ Recognized author's name
- □ Osborne/McGraw-Hill's reputation
- □ Read book review
- □ Read Osborne catalog
- □ Saw advertisement in store
- □ Found/recommended in library
- □ Required textbook
- □ Price
- □ Other _____

Comments _____

Topics I would like to see covered in future books by Osborne/McGraw-Hill include:

_____

IMPORTANT REMINDER
To get your FREE catalog, write in the last 4 digits of the ISBN number printed on the back cover (see below bar code) 0-07-881 _ _ _ – _

Osborne McGraw-Hill

Computer
Books

(800) 227-0900